Soviet Strategic Deception

Soviet Strategic Deception

Edited by
Brian D. Dailey
Patrick J. Parker
Naval Postgraduate School

Lexington Books
D.C. Heath and Company/Lexington, Massachusetts/Toronto

Hoover Institution Press

The chapters contained in this manuscript are the proceedings from a conference on *Soviet Strategic Deception* held at the Naval Postgraduate School September 26–28, 1985. The opinions expressed in these chapters are those of the authors and they do not necessarily represent the views of the Department of Navy, Department of Defense, or any other Government organization.

Library of Congress Cataloging-in-Publication Data

Soviet strategic deception.

Includes index.
1. Soviet Union—Military policy. 2. Strategy. 3. Deception. I. Dailey, Brian D.
II. Parker, Patrick J.
UA770.S6678 1987   355'.0335'47   86-45799
ISBN 0-669-13208-X (alk. paper)

Copyright © 1987 by D.C. Heath and Company

All rights reserved. No part of this publication may be reproduced or transmitted in any form or by any means, electronic or mechanical, including photocopy, recording, or any information storage or retrieval system, without permission in writing from the publisher.

Published simultaneously in Canada
Printed in the United States of America
Casebound International Standard Book Number: 0-669-13208-X
Library of Congress Catalog Card Number 86-45799

The paper used in this publication meets the minimum requirements of American National Standard for Information and Sciences—Permanence of Paper for Printed Library Materials, ANSI Z39.48-1984.™

88 89 90 91 8 7 6 5 4 3

Contents

Figures and Tables ix

Foreword xi
Andrew W. Marshall

Acknowledgments xiii

Introduction xv
Brian D. Dailey and *Patrick J. Parker*

Part I   Soviet Organizational Structure for Deception and Active Measures   1

1. Soviet Deception: The Organizational and Operational Tradition   3
   John J. Dziak

2. Soviet Organization and Doctrine for Strategic Deception   21
   Richards J. Heuer, Jr.

3. Themes of Soviet Strategic Deception and Disinformation   55
   John Lenczowski

4. Soviet Active Measures and Democratic Culture   77
   Arnold Beichman

Part II   Language, Ideology, and Diplomacy   91

5. On Soviet Linguistics: Expropriating Utopia   93
   Robert Bathurst

6. Ideology and Deception   119
   Robert Conquest

7. **Deception in the Political-Military Arena   133**
   Uri Ra'anan

8. **"A Mask to Cover Shady Deeds": Soviet Diplomatic Deception, 1917–1939   147**
   Kerry M. Kartchner

Part III   Arms Control and Verification   171

9. **Soviet Deception and Arms Control   173**
   William R. Graham

10. **Soviet *Maskirovka* and Arms Control Verification   185**
    William R. Harris

11. **Deception, Perceptions Management, and Self-Deception in Arms Control: An Examination of the ABM Treaty   225**
    Brian D. Dailey

12. **Soviet Deception at MBFR: A Case Study   261**
    Richard F. Staar

Part IV   The Soviet Military and *Maskirovka*   273

13. **The Role of Deception in Soviet Military Planning   275**
    Notra Trulock III

14. ***Reflexive Control* in Soviet Military Planning   293**
    Clifford Reid

15. **Postwar Soviet Strategic Economic Deception   313**
    Steven Rosefielde

16. **Chemical and Biological Warfare: The Covert Dimension   325**
    Joseph D. Douglass, Jr.

Part V   Regional Deception   341

17. **The Soviet Campaign against INF in West Germany   343**
    David S. Yost

18. Seizing Power: Deception in the Nicaraguan Revolution   375
    David Blair

19. Anticipating the Next Arab-Israeli Round: Soviet Deception
    in Syria   399
    Avigdor Haselkorn

Part VI   Deception and Strategic Planning   429

20. Impact of Deception on U.S. Nuclear Strategy   431
    Leon Sloss

21. Surprise Nuclear Attack   449
    William R. Van Cleave

22. Space, Intelligence, and Deception   467
    Angelo M. Codevilla

23. Deception and the Formulation of National Intelligence
    Estimates   487
    Thomas P. Rona

Part VII   Conclusion   509

24. Soviet Strategic Deception and U.S. Vulnerability: A Net
    Assessment   511
    Patrick J. Parker

Glossary   519

Index   525

About the Contributors   535

About the Editors   539

Figures and Tables

Figures

2–1. Soviet Organization for Active Measures 26

19–1. Coverage Profile of Soviet Integrated Air Defense System Deployed in Syria 410

21–1. Warheads 462

21–2. EMT 463

23–1. Engagement Hierarchy 488

23–2. NIE's Domains of Interest 491

23–3. Time Congruence 492

23–4. Two-Sided Information Flow Logic 497

23–5. One Element of the Decision Model 502

Tables

I–1. Overview of Soviet Deception xviii

10–1. Presidential Reports to the Congress on Soviet Noncompliance with Arms Control Obligations—Strategic Nuclear Arms Agreements 210

10–2. Presidential Reports to the Congress on Soviet Noncompliance with Arms Control Obligations—Restraints on Nuclear Weapons Testing 212

10–3. Presidential Reports to the Congress on Soviet Noncompliance with Arms Control Obligations—Other Soviet Arms Control Commitments 213

10–4. Arms Control Commitments Regarding Which the Soviet Union Is in Apparent Compliance 214

10–5. Presidential Reports to Congress Regarding Selective Restoration of Soviet Compliance   215

11–1. Evolutionary Testing of SAM Interceptors and Radars against Reentry Vehicles   234

11–2. Netting of Various SAM and ABM Radars   235

11–3. Soviet Strategic SAM Characteristics and Numbers   236

11–4. ABM Treaty Radar Violation Issues   237

11–5. Ballistic Missile Early Warning, Target-Tracking, and Battle Management Radars   239

11–6. ABM Systems and Related Activities   240

11–7. Development of Directed Energy Weapons and Other Advanced ABM Technologies   241

11–8. Development of ASAT Capabilities   242

11–9. Developments in Civil Defense   243

12–1. Disparity between Forces of Eastern and Western Direct Participants in the Reduction Area, 1 January 1981   263

15–1. Real Soviet Defense Expenditures, 1960–1985   315

15–2. U.S. and Soviet Defense Procurement, 1976–1984   317

19–1. Introduction Sequence of Major Components of Advanced Air Defense System into Syria   406

21–1. Assumed January 1986 Force   460

21–2. Post-Attack Forces—Generated Alert   460

21–3. Post-Attack Forces—Surprise Attack   461

Foreword

Andrew W. Marshall
Director of Net Assessment
Office of the Secretary of Defense

This is an important and interesting book—important because it deals with an important subject area and interesting because of the wide range of subjects it covers and insights that it contains. It is focused on the Soviet preparations for and use of deception. Mainly it deals with the peacetime uses of deception. There are also some papers that focus on the military operational uses.

The book deals with a topic that is uncongenial to many people and not a major focus of attention. People understand in a general way that deception is practiced by some states, but awareness of the extent of the preparations for substantial, concerted, long-term efforts at deception in the case of the Soviet Union is more limited. Our own political and social practices do not incline us to look for deception as much as would be the case in people coming from other societies. Even in our military, which has often done well in the use of deception in wartime, our military doctrine and concepts of operations do not emphasize deception as a major aspect of the art of war, although some of the Services are more active in operational techniques than others.

There is another reason why focusing attention on Soviet efforts at deception is uncongenial. If you really believe that they are involved in substantial efforts at deception, the difficulties in analyzing the data we obtain on all aspects of Soviet society become extraordinarily difficult. If part of the data that we have is falsified or fudged in some way, what methods of analysis do we apply in order to reach valid conclusions? Almost all areas of analysis first try to convince themselves that the data and observations we have have not been tampered with.

The origins of this book go back to 1972 when Pat Parker and I participated in a number of meetings, attended by scholars, government officials and others who shared a common concern about Soviet capabilities and interest in deception. Subsequently, when Mr. Parker left his position as Deputy Assistant Secretary of Defense (Intelligence), he continued to have a serious interest in information, misinformation and deception in international relations, negotiations and war. Ten years ago he organized a small interdisciplinary research group, focused on deception, from the faculty and visiting scholars at the Naval Postgraduate School. This group has made an important contribution by advancing our understanding of this important aspect of the art of war and of the competition between states. This book is the latest product of their efforts. It is a natural and important outgrowth of a continuing effort to understand the political use of military power in general and Soviet efforts in particular. The political use of military power to deter unfriendly or hostile acts and to coerce and intimidate others plays a central role in Soviet strategy, as does the management of external perceptions of the size and quality of their forces and the will to use force.

This book by Professors Parker and Dailey lays out in a careful and detailed way much of what we know about this important aspect of Soviet behavior. It goes beyond documenting the general cultural aspects of Soviet deception. It details the size and scope of the Soviet organization for deception and those active measures undertaken to see that key western opinion makers and people of influence believe what the Russians want them to; it provides some important new theoretical insights into the twin roles of language and ideology in Soviet deceptive behavior; and it provides analysis of Soviet deceptive behavior in arms control, the development of Soviet forces and politics.

It also addresses these same issues in the context of the nuclear balance, nuclear war and surprise. It should become an essential part of the background of all who seek to understand and deal with the Soviet Union.

Acknowledgments

As with any conference, as well as the book that results from it, there is a seemingly endless list of individuals that deserve an expression of appreciation and thanks. Space does not allow, however, a complete acknowledgment of all the organizations and individuals that contributed to making this conference and book possible. To those who are not listed below, we would like to express our sincere appreciation.

We would, however, like to acknowledge in particular the contribution of the following. With respect to the conference on Soviet strategic deception which was the genesis of this book, the editors would like to express their appreciation to the conference coordinator, Kerry M. Kartchner, as well as department staff members of the Naval Postgraduate School and Student volunteers without whose help the conference would not have been as stimulating and rewarding. Those that deserve particular thanks are Annette DuCoeur, Irene Dixon, Albertine Potter, Carol Wilkins, Mark Clark, LCDR. Dave Kohler, USN, Lt. Steve Harris, USN, and Lt. Sam Tangredi, USN. We would also like to take this opportunity to express our appreciation to the Hoover Institution on War, Revolution, and Peace for providing the grant that, in part, made this conference possible.

Organizing and editing the fruits of this conference was a particularly onerous and challenging task. It is, therefore, with a sense of indebtedness that we acknowledge the tireless and dedicated efforts of Eric Thoemmes in helping to prepare this manuscript. Finally, our typist Phyllis McClelland also deserves an expression of gratitude as well as Brienda Maanao and our secretary Janet Quenga for their invaluable assistance during the final push to complete this work.

Introduction

Brian D. Dailey
Patrick J. Parker

Since 1978, a group of faculty at the Naval Postgraduate School has been conducting multidisciplinary research in deception and perceptions management. An early product of that effort was *Strategic Military Deception* by Donald Daniel and Katherine Herbig.[1] Initial research focused on methodology and the history of deception in military campaigns. This work provided improved understanding of the roles of deception and self-deception in international relations, negotiations, crisis management, and war.

On the twenty-sixth through the twenty-eighth of September 1985, the Naval Postgraduate School sponsored a conference that focused exclusively on Soviet strategic deception. The lessons learned from earlier efforts in deception, perceptions management, and self-deception formed the basis for this examination of Soviet behavior. The objective of the conference was to bring together eminent and knowledgeable scholars and professionals in national security affairs, Soviet studies, and intelligence, to study systematically historical and contemporary Soviet uses of deception and perceptions management. The effort was comprehensive. It addressed and analyzed such critical issues as the historical and contemporary organizational and doctrinal structure of Soviet strategic deception and active measures; semantic misperceptions or complexities stemming from dissimilarities in the English and Russian language and the Marxist-Leninist lexicon; examples of past and present Soviet diplomatic and political active measures, disinformation, and perceptions management, as well as military deception or *maskirovka*; case studies of Soviet and Soviet-sponsored regional deception; and problems of national security planning when Soviet deception is present.

The subject is important for American national security. The roles that deception, perceptions management, and self-deception play in furthering the political and military objectives of the Soviet Union needs to be kept in mind by policy makers and analysts responsible for United States national security. In an era of intercontinental missiles and nuclear weapons, it is essential that the Western world comprehend the decisive importance of deception and surprise in military strategy and planning, particularly with respect to totalitarian regimes such as the Soviet Union, where secrecy and internal discipline provide a much greater opportunity to employ deception than is possible in the West.

At the same time, it is crucial to realize that deception is not used only in war. The studies in this book demonstrate that the Soviet Union employs deception and perceptions management regularly in its day-to-day foreign policy and military planning.

The success of Soviet perceptions management efforts, however, relies to a large extent on the exploitation of tendencies toward self-deception seemingly inherent in the Western democracies. One example entails conveying to the Western audiences sentiments consonant with their beliefs, so as to influence the formulation of policies and perceptions in areas of concern to the Kremlin. Consequently, an essential dimension in the preparation of this book has been the exploration of the role played by self-deception in support of Soviet deception objectives.

Thus, Soviet *strategic deception* as used in this volume is a political and/or military strategy that conceals its true goals. Included within it are the propaganda, active measures, and policy statements by the national leadership that implement this strategy; the concealment of intentions or misrepresentation of information to gain advantages through arms control negotiations; and finally, those measures that act to limit or preclude Western knowledge of strategic (mainly nuclear) military weapons, installations, or activities. By this definition, strategic deception is pervasive in Soviet foreign and military policy.

While strategic deception as defined above was the basis on which these chapters were organized, one of the more academic but instructive and interesting lessons learned at the conference (and not immediately apparent from reading the papers themselves) centered on the use of the term, *strategic deception*. Among some members of the United States intelligence community, for example, *deception* was generally used to describe a more limited set of activities. A distinction was made between broad *perceptions management* activities aimed primarily at Western policy makers and the public and, on the other hand, disinformation passed through controlled intelligence channels (double agents or technical intelligence collection systems) for the purpose of deceiving United States intelligence analysts. (Even within the intelligence community, however, it was admitted that there is no consensus on whether the term *deception* properly applies to only one of these activities or to both, and it was generally recognized that the lines between them are not sharp.)

Some members of the United States intelligence community made a further distinction between efforts at denial and those intended to deceive. *Denial* was referred to as security measures, such as camouflage or encryption for the purpose of denying information to United States national technical means of intelligence collection. Obviously, there is a close relationship between denial and deception; the ability to conceal the truth is a prerequisite to successful deception. *Denial*, however, may also be undertaken for its own sake as a basic military security measure.

Disagreements on the prevalence and significance of Soviet deception are, in part, attributable to the lack of consensus on how best to define *deception*. Those who adhered to the broader definition saw deception as pervasive and as an essential key to understanding Soviet policy and for determining the appropriate American responses. Those who thought of deception in a narrower context—as disinformation passed through controlled intelligence channels to deceive intelligence analysts—argued that there exists little, and in some cases no, successful Soviet deception. The assertion, however, that little or no successful Soviet deception exists is unfounded and perplexing since numerous cases of successful Soviet deception during past periods of American national security planning are well known and many examples can be found in this book. Amrom Katz has adeptly put this issue in perspective with the pithy comment: "we have never found anything that the Soviets have successfully hidden."

The issue, though, is not which usage is correct. We must recognize that *deception* is a term with multiple meanings, all of them legitimate. The problem lies in agreement concerning how best to draw these sometimes conflicting meanings under a general rubric and the analytical implications of one usage as compared with another.

The disagreement that often accompanies discussion of the definitional problem stems from the political and emotional connotations associated with the term *deception*. *Deception* is a pejorative term in the West. If Soviet deception is pervasive, it implies that the Soviet Union is nefarious; that arms control agreements reflect Soviet duplicity; and that United States intelligence agencies have become channels for Soviet disinformation. All of these views were expressed during the conference.

Admittedly, a problem with using the broadest definition of the term *deception* is that it becomes all-encompassing and bears on all aspects of Soviet behavior. Concepts that apply to a wide range of activities and phenomena soon lose their usefulness because they lack precision and thus cease to serve the purpose for which they were intended. Conversely, the narrowest view of deception comes close to defining the problem out of existence.

Thus an essential step in examining this problem (as is the case with any new field of inquiry) is the development of a taxonomy suitable for the systematic analysis of types of deception. One can communicate and draw inferences about deception when the type of deception is precisely specified.

Table I–1 presents one possible taxonomy. Other classifications are possible and may be equally useful. The one used here emphasizes two broad categories of deception: perceptions management and intelligence deception. Each type is further classified according to the channel or means employed.

Perceptions management refers to that complex of activities directed mainly (but not exclusively) at policy and opinion makers and the public. The channels

Table I–1
Overview of Soviet Deception[2]

	Perception Management		Intelligence Deception
Target:	Decision makers, opinion makers, public, and to some extent, intelligence analysts	Target:	Intelligence analysts
Channels:	Public and private statements by Soviet leaders, negotiators	Channels:	Controlled human sources
	Articles in authoritative Soviet journals		Photographic intelligence
			Communications intercept
	Information made available to foreign journalists and diplomats in Moscow		Telemetry intercept
			Other sensors
	Overt propaganda, front groups, conferences, exchanges, visitors		
	Covert press placement		
	Forgeries		
	Agents of influence		
Objective:	Influence the opinions and policies of foreign countries by manipulating their perceptions of Soviet activities and objectives. This can be both tactical and strategic in nature.	Objective:	Mislead or distort the analysts' opinions and products relating primarily to military affairs, but also to political and economic affairs.

include self-serving or deceptive statements by Soviet leaders or arms control negotiators, covert placement of articles in newspapers, forgeries, and agents of influence. Intelligence deception is directed specifically at intelligence services through controlled human or technical collection channels.

The analytical importance of this distinction goes far beyond the usual difference in targets. Soviet perceptions management in peacetime is pervasive; *confirmed* instances of current intelligence deception in peacetime may be more unusual.

History and past research in this area has shown, however, that, in wartime, intelligence deception *may* be more common than perceptions management. But, as this book illustrates, Soviet perceptions management is already extensive in peacetime, and it should not be assumed that it will not play an important role in wartime. For example, it could have an important influence on the West's view of Soviet wartime goals and postwar behavior during war termination negotiations. It should thus be stated that while secrecy is crucial to the success of intelligence deception, perceptions management commonly retains its effectiveness even though the means and channels for dissemination are well known.

Moreover, in peacetime it is also important to note that deception and perceptions management do not necessarily operate separately. For example, we know the Soviets employ intelligence deception and denial with respect to the quantity and characteristics of their weapon systems. It is only the extent and success of this intelligence deception that is uncertain. Yet, of what we can identify of past and present Soviet deception efforts we notice that they also employ perceptions management in denying the existence or threatening characteristics of those systems to policy makers and the public writ large. The former is related to what we have called *intelligence deception*, while the latter is a case of *perceptions management*. The distinction, then, between these two types of deception determines the questions concerning Soviet practices.

Furthermore, one may also inquire whether *perceptions management* influences American intelligence analysts and their products. In other words, it is not the existence of *perceptions management* that is in question, but its impact on policy making and intelligence products. The question that must be put forth is whether United States intelligence, or some other element of the government, can or should play a more active role in combating the impact of Soviet *perceptions management* on foreign governments, United States policy makers, Western public opinion as well as intelligence analysts.

For *intelligence deception*, the key questions concern the extent *and* success of its impact on intelligence products. For example, what is the extent of Soviet passive cover, denial, and deception efforts on technical intelligence collection systems? How can we improve ways to guard against the active manipulation of information fed through these systems? Does it bias the intelligence product? For what purpose and with what success is it implemented? It is these and other questions that are addressed in this book.

In sum, *deception* constitutes an umbrella concept that has several meanings and covers many different forms of activity. Objective analysis and accurate communication will be facilitated to the extent that we can avoid the general term *deception* and refer instead to the more specific forms of activity that fall under this general heading. We must take care to use terminology that clearly identifies the type of deception being discussed.

To help facilitate a more careful and systematic approach to the general subject of deception, this book is organized into six parts each containing three or four chapters that comprise the specific area of study. Part I examines the Soviet organizational structure for deception and active measures; part II is devoted to the question of perceptions management and the roles played by language, ideology, and diplomacy in enhancing its effect; the use of intelligence deception and perceptions management in arms control and verification constitutes part III; Soviet *maskirovka* or military deception is covered in part IV; part V focuses on deception issues relating to Soviet and Soviet surrogate states and intelligence services in vital regional areas of the world; and finally, the thrust of part VI is the possible effect and implications of Soviet deception on United States strategic planning.

Notes

1. Donald C. Daniel and Katherine L. Herbig, *Strategic Military Deception* (New York: Pergamon Press, 1982).
2. We are indebted to Richards J. Heuer, Jr., for his substantial contribution to this taxonomy and for his thoughts on the definition and usage of the term *Deception*.

Part I
Soviet Organizational Structure for Deception and Active Measures

1
Soviet Deception: The Organizational and Operational Tradition

John J. Dziak

The Context

What has come to be known as Soviet active measures, deception, disinformation, and *maskirovka* may be mistakenly perceived as a phenomenon dating from the post-Khrushchev, or at most, the post-Stalin phases of Soviet history. It is worth noting, however, that such actions derive from a lengthy organizational milieu and operational tradition. The Russian language and Soviet operational practice provide a rich and highly developed vocabulary dating back to tsarist antecedents and up through almost seven decades of the Soviet party-state.

Strategic deception, whether military or political, has been an integral feature of the Slavic tradition.[1] Mongol methods of warfare masterfully deflected enemy attention toward false threats, a lesson absorbed by their Muscovite vassals and, in turn, their tsarist successors. The mirage quality of Russian political deception is captured by Potemkin's notorious "villages," noted by Ronald Hingley as "the prime emblem of Russian *pokazukha* (bull) and *ochkovtiratel'stvo* (eyewash)."[2]

Active measures, disinformation, and *maskirovka* are only the latest iteration of a stylized Russian and Soviet lexicon of operational vocabulary used in the integrated implementation of varied direct action initiatives. These include among others:

Provocation—*provokatsiya*

Penetration—*proniknovenniye*

The views expressed or implied in this paper are solely those of the author and do not necessarily represent the views of the Defense Intelligence Agency or Department of Defense.

Fabrication—*fabrikatsiya*

Diversion—*diversiya*

Agent of Influence—*agent po vliyaniyu/agent vliyaniye*

Disinformation—*dezinformatsiya*

Combination—*kombinatsiya*

While the first six words evoke recognizable images, the last term is indicative of the Soviet fixation with complex operational initiatives analogous to intricate chess moves. *Combination* is an insider's term for relating, linking, or combining operational undertakings in different times and places to enhance overall operational results; yet this does not even begin to scratch the surface. The art of *vran'yo* (fibbing, nonsense, rot—see Hingley) or the supreme art of the outrageous falsehood (*naglaya lozh*) could, by themselves, constitute the subject of a separate study, as could target receptivity or self-deception.

Operationally, the Soviets did not find it necessary to centralize strategic political or military deception in highly bureaucratized party-state-security matrixes until the Khrushchev period (approximately 1959). Given the nature of the Lenin-Dzerzhinskiy era and then the unique style of Stalin's leadership, a large centralized deception bureaucracy was not necessary. Only after Stalin's death, which brought about an evolution of political leadership, did large-scale and continuous bureaucratic centralization emerge.

This does not mean that centrally controlled deception operations did not occur before the late 1950's. Indeed they did, but under the auspices of senior party and state security leaders, beginning with Lenin and Dzerzhinskiy and then Stalin himself. Operations apparently were conceived and executed through coordination among such seniors with operational oversight, first within state security and later within Stalin's personal secretariat or chancellery—also known as the Secret Department (*sekretnyy otdel*) and later as the Special Sector (*osobyy sektor*).

Dzerzhinskiy, a Pole, brought a number of conationals into the CHEKA (including some he personally converted when they were captured during the Russo-Polish war) who figured critically in early Soviet deception operations. Other key individuals included Artur K. Artuzov (also known as "Fraucci" and "Renucci"), chief of CHEKA/OGPU counterintelligence, who directed the *Sindikat* and Trust deception operations; and Yakov S. Agranov, a senior Chekist, who later was closely linked with Stalin's secretariat and was First Deputy Chairman of the NKVD under Yagoda. Both Artuzov and Agranov were executed in 1937.

Information on identifiable deception components within Soviet security and intelligence apparently first appeared in the West in the mid-1920's in French and English sources. A former tsarist intelligence officer, Colonel A.

Rezanov, wrote that two organizations (one in the Intelligence Directorate of the Red Army and the other subordinate to the Executive Committee of the Communist International) were responsible for the circulation of spurious information and the forgery of political documents.[3]

Concurrently, the *Whitehall Gazette and St. James Review* identified the Foreign Department of the GPU as bearing the responsibility for disinformation. Two bureaus of this department, a press section and a document section respectively, "spread false news in the foreign press," and falsified "all kinds of documents of a financial, governmental, and political nature."[4] The journal further added that still another

> . . . special foreign section [of the Foreign Department of the GPU] was kept busy . . . issuing false banknotes of foreign countries in order to change them for good ones and use these later in the respective countries for Soviet propaganda.[5]

It also identified one of the Trilliser brothers as responsible for "the so-called 'disinformation' of foreign countries against which the Soviet policy is now working with the idea of worldwide social revolution."[6] However, most sources mention only Mikhail Abramovich Trilliser, who headed the Foreign Department of the CHEKA/GPU/OGPU and later transferred to the Comintern. He was executed in 1937 or 1938. The above-mentioned article may be referring to the same individual; Trilliser is known to have used at least one pseudonym, M.A. Moskvin.[7]

A Russian language newspaper from Riga, in 1927, connected a "Disinformation Bureau" to Soviet intelligence, but incorrectly fused the GPU and military intelligence into one parent body.[8] That both the GPU and the Red Army Staff had been running sophisticated deception games is concluded by George Leggett, one of the foremost authorities on the CHEKA, making it probable that the sources of the Riga information confused the two services, wittingly or otherwise.[9]

Little information has surfaced about the role of the People's Commissariat of Foreign Affairs in early deception operations, although it has been shown that, as early as 1921–22, it circulated spurious documents.[10] Similarly, the Comintern, a subservient Soviet creation carefully linked to the CHEKA, likewise performed its part in Soviet deception operations.[11]

Thus, while the data on organizational focal points within the USSR for early strategic deception is somewhat confusing and fragmentary, the operations show that many things were indeed going on and that some very senior party and security personnel were deeply involved. Focusing precisely on such senior leadership involvement, a style of operation had emerged and was carried on through the Stalin years. A personalized centralization characterized this operational style. Despite the new institutional forms ushered in by Khrushchev (to be discussed later), the involvement of senior Soviet leaders in broad-gauged strategic deception is the norm. It should come as no surprise, therefore, that the latest Party General Secretary should be projecting the image of a benign, Western-type manager presiding over a pluralistic polity. Gorbachev is scripting himself and the USSR as something other than the persistent, changeless reality both truly represent. Lenin is alleged to have instructed Dzerzhinskiy to "tell them what they want to hear" in constructing the Trust legend against the emigration and Western governments. Whether or not that particular guidance was apocryphal, Gorbachev has assimilated the spirit of the tradition that Lenin and Dzerzhinskiy initiated.

The operations that follow are illustrative of that tradition. While technology may affect procedural mechanisms, especially in the realm of strategic military deception, or *maskirovka*, the persistence of operational style and objectives continues unabated. In a counterintelligence state—which is what the amalgam of the party-police-military complex truly represents—deception, dissembling, penetration, provocation, and notional constructs are the stuff of reality.

The "Lockhart Plot"

Recall the Lockhart Plot of August 1918, in which the British diplomatic agent R.H. Bruce Lockhart is claimed to have been central (along with Sidney Reilly) in a plot to overthrow the Bolshevik government.[12] In actuality, there were two plots: that of Felix Dzerzhinskiy, which very ably entrapped Lockhart, and Reilly's audacious plot, which the CHEKA handily smashed.[13] The two were quite effectively meshed together in a matrix of *kombinatsiya* provocation, penetration, fabrication inter alia. In retrospect, Lockhart and Reilly played at conspiracy and apparently were the unwitting tools of Dzerzhinskiy who called the events of August 1918 into existence and terminated them when his objectives had been reached.[14]

The Trust Legend, 1921–27[15]

The Trust (*Trest*) may be viewed as the premier and prototypical strategic deception and provocation operation in the Soviet repertoire. However, it was only one of 40-50 "legends" initiated and run by the secret police during the inter-war period. The Trust involved the creation of a notional opposition organization within the USSR by state security (successively named CHEKA, GPU, OGPU) and was targeted against the anti-Soviet emigration in the West and Western intelligence services. It also comprised counterintelligence operations against opponents within the USSR, who were induced into surfacing themselves through Trust provocations.

Planning began in 1921, and the operation was orchestrated by state security until fall 1927. In addition to disinformation and provocation, the Trust simultaneously employed other techniques mentioned earlier: penetration, diversion, fabrication, agents of influence, and combination.

The official title given by state security to this bogus operation was the Monarchist Association of Central Russia (MOTsR). Its cover title was the Moscow Municipal Credit Association (hence the Trust) operating under New Economic Policy (NEP) dispensation. The direction of the Trust was provided by the highest echelons of state security.

Through the Trust, the Soviets were able to identify, expose, and neutralize opponents within the USSR. Many were allowed to operate for several years, not knowing that their activities were completely controlled by state security. It became possible, through Trust channels, for the secret police to prevent the establishment of a genuine anti-Communist underground in the USSR. Outside the Soviet Union, state security was able to penetrate the White paramilitary groups, who were then used to funnel disinformation to unsuspecting Western intelligence services and governments.

It was through Trust channels that Boris Savinkov, the prominent anti-Soviet revolutionary, and Sidney Reilly, connected with British intelligence, were lured back into the USSR and eliminated (Savinkov in spring/summer 1924, Reilly in August/September 1925). Another well-known emigre, V.V. Shulgin, undertook a lengthy "underground" trip (September 1925 to April 1926) through European Russia, handled all of the time by Trust (OGPU) operatives. His manuscript account of the trip, *Three Capitals*, was read and approved by the Trust leadership and published in Berlin in 1927—the year the Trust was folded by the OGPU. Its disinforming message focused on how communism was fading in Russia, how the Soviet leaders were really nationalists/monarchists of a new stripe, and why any direct action by the West, military or otherwise, would be undesirable.

Strikingly similar themes were advanced by the "returnism" (*vozvrashchentsvo*), and "change of landmarks" (*smenovekhovtsvo*) movements among certain emigre circles in the diaspora of the early 1920's. The latter tendency, the *Smena vekh* movement, had its own newspaper, *Nakanune* (*On the Eve*), in Berlin and journals in Riga, Helsinki, Sofia, and Harbin. Also, several *Smena vekh* journals were allowed by the Soviet government to appear in Russia, Lenin having acknowledged that the movement was "very useful" in garnering non-Bolshevik support for his regime while allowing him to keep an eye on such "candid enemies."[16] *Nakanune* faithfully reflected the Soviet party line and was of immense value to Moscow as an emigre instrument of conversion to the Soviet cause. It was backed by Soviet subsidies until it was closed in June 1924. The Soviets allowed *Smena vekh* inside the USSR to continue for another year and a half before they suppressed it.[17] Like the Trust, when it had served its purpose it was handily terminated.

The Poles were among the first to suspect the Trust. In 1926, Marshal Pilsudski determined that the Trust was funneling spurious intelligence to its customers. Suspicions in several other quarters that the Trust was a notional creation of the OGPU had also surfaced, probably causing the OGPU to conclude that it no longer served Soviet purposes. In 1927, Moscow closed down operation. The ensuing expose was shattering to the emigres.

In the Soviet view, the Trust legend and operation was a monumental success. It disorganized the Russian emigration, spread mistrust among the various emigre groups, deglamorized them as experts on Soviet affairs, and compromised them in the eyes of Western intelligence services. For Western intelligence services, exposure of the Trust brought the tragic realization that they had been duped and that several years worth of spurious intelligence salted their files. Finally, the Trust operation fostered the feeling in many circles in the West that, while no internal resistance to the new order in Moscow was possible, the new regime was tempering its actions and was amenable to doing business with Western governments and commercial enterprises. Indeed, the disinformation fostered through the Trust reinforced the initiatives of the New Economic Policy, which was also overseen by Dzerzhinskiy in his dual capacity as Chief of State Security and Chief of the Supreme Economic Council. From this perspective, the NEP itself served a deception purpose in that it helped to refinance Soviet industry at Western political and economic expense.

The Trust legend probably still serves as a paradigm for Soviet deception purposes. Several different versions originating with, or influenced by, the Soviets have appeared over the years, none of which presents the truth.[18] A recrudescence of a Trust-type provocation occurred as late as 1977 against the NTS (*Narodnyi Trudovoi Soyuz*) or People's Labor Alliance.[19] It entailed almost carbon copy elements of the Trust legend—underground cells in the USSR, secure means of communications, and so forth.

The Tukhachevskiy Affair, 1937

In 1937, as part of the purges known as the "Great Terror," Stalin savaged the officer corps of the Red Army following the "discovery" of a massive "conspiracy" involving senior Soviet officers in league with the German high command. Some knowledgeable former insiders and observers contend that there had been stillborn moves against Stalin by certain senior officers, such as Marshal Mikhail Tukhachevskiy, to put a stop to Stalin's terror.[20] However, Stalin did not publish a shred of proof to support his charges of treason. It is known that documents were fabricated by Hitler's SD (*Sicherheitsdienst*/Security Service) Chief, Reinhard Heydich, purporting to show treasonous collusion between Tukhachevskiy and the German military. They were passed by the unwitting President Benes of Czechoslovakia to an apparently fully-witted Stalin and his

NKVD henchman, Yezhov. Indeed, prior to the SD fabrications, the NKVD itself also had attempted to plant materials in Prague to compromise senior Soviet officers. In this almost unique fabrication/disinformation/combination operation, two allegedly enemy totalitarian powers collaborated in smashing one power's senior military leadership, along with roughly half of its officer corps.

The War Years, 1941–1945

Harbin, 1941

A case that merits further examination as a possible major example of Soviet strategic political manipulation is that involving the German Consulate in Harbin, Manchukuo, from approximately March to May 1941. The German Consul, Dr. August Ponschab, regularly forwarded to Berlin "intercepted" Soviet diplomatic traffic to Soviet missions in the Far East. David Kahn suggests that this series of intercepts was something of an exception to the established record of security of Soviet diplomatic channels.[21]

Another author noted that the material seemed "designed for interception," including Soviet understanding of German interests in the Balkans, the need to maintain the Russo-German Treaty necessary for the destruction of the British Empire, and the maintenance of normal trade relations with Germany, should the latter start a conflict in the Balkans, even if the Danube were closed as a result. One message specifically eschewed Soviet opposition to the German attack on Greece so as to ensure pressure on English forces in Africa.[22] Moscow seemed bent on using this channel to manipulate German perceptions at the expense of other countries, but little beyond what is cited here has been seriously probed by researchers.

The Abwehr, *[Military Intelligence and Counterintelligence]*
"Foreign Armies East," and the German High Command

In a Seventh Army interrogation report, dated 24 June 1945, General Major Reinhard Gehlen, formerly Chief of Foreign Armies East Department (OKH), talked freely of Soviet deception and propaganda efforts. While crediting the Soviets with effective deception through manipulation of the foreign press and through the careful use of POWs, he makes a negative declaration about Soviet "radio deception," but offers no supporting evidence:

> No major radio deception scheme has ever been attempted by the Russians, who realize that such a scheme is easily detected if it is not accompanied by thoroughly planned deceptive measures and in all other fields. Tactical radio deception has been employed, but was of only limited importance.[23]

The MAX Case, 1941–45[24]

One of the important deception operations run by Soviet State Security during World War II is the MAX case. This involved a phoney agent network allegedly working in the USSR, which supplied the German *Abwehr* wireless transmissions via Sofia to Berlin from July 1941 to February 1945. Two of the principals in the case, Anton V. Turkul and Ira Lang, were former White officers who were suspected of having been recruited by the NKVD. The reputed MAX was one Fritz Kauder, alias Klatt, a Viennese Jew with connections to both Turkul and the *Abwehr*. The MAX reports dealt with Soviet military matters, strategic and tactical, and were accepted at face value by Gehlen, the *Abwehr*, and the German General Staff, despite suspicions voiced by others. NKVD Chief Beria is believed to have personally controlled the Moscow end of the operation. Several thousand MAX messages were transmitted to Berlin. The Germans were frequently confronted at critical junctures with more Soviet forces than they had estimated, while the Soviets are reported to have sacrificed considerable numbers of troops to validate the MAX reports. Following the war, U.S. military intelligence discovered the network and determined that Anton Turkul and Ira Lang were Soviet agents and was convinced that Kauder, too, was run by the Soviets.[25].

In his memoirs, Gehlen gives no indication that he was aware that MAX was a notional source directed by the NKVD.[26] One of his tendencies—and of the German High Command—was to rely on MAX because it confirmed German estimates of Soviet strategic intentions, itself an indication of Soviet penetration of the Germans.

Was MAX really that good? Probably so, according to Anthony Blunt (as reported by Chapman Pincher) who had served the Soviets while in MI-5. In this account, Blunt admitted that he passed the deciphered MAX traffic intercepted by the British to his Soviet controller, but was told that Moscow was fully aware of what was going on. From that point, Blunt assumed that the MAX affair was a major Soviet deception operation whose costs in Soviet manpower underscored its strategic utility.[27]

Operation Scherhorn[28]

One of the more bizarre military deception episodes reported on the Eastern Front during World War II was Operation Scherhorn, an elaborate creation of the Soviets centered on a notional group of 2,500 trapped German troops led by *Oberstleutnant* (Lieutenant Colonel) Heinrich Scherhorn. On 19 August 1944, the German High Command received a message from an alleged network in

Moscow about Scherhorn and his unit being trapped behind Soviet lines at the Beresino River. From that date until Scherhorn's last message on 4 April 1945, the German SS (*Schutzstaffel*) and High Command expended considerable effort, men, material, and aircraft in vain attempts to rescue the trapped unit. In addition to sending numerous radios and radio operators, the Germans reportedly even sent in two SS groups, which never returned. Otto Skorzeny was alerted to create a special air task force to mount a rescue, but that was in March 1945, when the Reich was near collapse. Despite doubts by some German officers, radio messages from Scherhorn and certain of the inserted radio operators kept hopes high that Scherhorn and his men were still operating. Hitler promoted Scherhorn to *Oberst* (Colonel), awarded him the *Ritterkreuz* (Knight's Cross), and promoted all of the officers whose names had been mentioned in messages.

In reality, the group never existed. There had been a 1,500-man German Battle Group defending the Beresino River during the Belorussian offensive in the summer of 1944, but the group was smashed, and the Soviets took Scherhorn and 200 survivors as prisoners. Colonel Scherhorn did, indeed, send messages to the OKW, but under Soviet duress. Thus, from 19 August 1944 to 4 April 1945, the Soviets ran a most audacious deception operation against a credulous German High Command. Valuable German time, energy, men, and materiel were directed at the chimera, and evidently the Soviets enjoyed the game.

The Win Operation, 1947–52[29]

In an episode reminiscent of the Trust, both the Soviets and the Polish security service (the UB) succeeded in penetrating a remnant of the World War II Polish Home Army called *Wolnosc i Niepodleglosc*, (WiN)—Freedom and Independence. After concerted and brutal drives by the Soviets and their UB subordinates in 1946–1947, WiN Outside (General Anders and his London group) and U.S. and British intelligence concluded that WiN Inside had been wiped out. Then a controlled UB contact convinced WiN Outside (and the British and Americans) that the Polish underground group was still viable and merited Western support. The support was given, but by that time, WiN Inside was a complete Soviet-UB creature. Its internal purpose was to surface those Polish anti-Communists still capable of organizing and running resistance cells and, at the same time, demonstrate to the Poles that Soviet rule was there to stay. Externally, the Soviets sought to control channels of information to the United States and Britain so as to manipulate and check their anti-Soviet initiatives as well as to pass on spurious intelligence.

It was almost a literal replay of the Trust provocation, even to the extent of using U.S. funds to support the operation. In late December 1952, the Soviets and Poles broke the story with a radio broadcast that stunned the Americans and

British, the exiled Polish government in London, and the Polish populace. All of them reacted in a manner similar to that following the Trust expose. Why Stalin chose that time to wrap it up is unclear and rather odd, since from their shocked reactions, it appears that the principal victims were unsuspecting. It may have had something to do with the impending developments in Moscow leading up to Stalin's death in March 1953. Whatever the motives for the termination, the WiN operation was a signal Soviet success. The scope of compromise was such that no major Western covert action initiatives aimed at tapping Polish unrest were again attempted.

Similar Soviet operations in the Baltic and Ukraine finally put an end to the active guerrilla movements in those regions.[30] Smaller-scale deception and manipulation accompanied the denouement of these groups. U.S. and British covert operations against Albania in the late 1940's and early 1950's were compromised by Kim Philby, a British MI-6 official in Moscow's service.[31]

A Watershed Year—1959: The Reorientation of State Security

Up through the immediate post-Stalin period, operations such as these were conducted by state security or the Comintern (among others), with a changing composition of oversight at the political level, such as Stalin's "secret department," or Stalin himself. The organizational trace varied with the changing fortunes of Stalin's minions and the institutional shakeups characteristic of Stalin's reign. There were, indeed, deception operations, active measures, and so forth, but the institutional stability undergirding present actions was not clearly evident.

Stability came with a vengeance with the consolidation of Khrushchev's grip on the party leadership in the late 1950's. First, General Serov was dropped as KGB chief in December 1958 and replaced by a career party man, Alexander Shelepin. The head of the Leningrad KGB, N.R. Mironov, became Chief of the Central Committee's powerful Administrative Organs Department. With Khrushchev's full concurrence, Shelepin created Department D within the KGB's First Chief Directorate, and assigned it to Colonel Agayants, a man of no small reputation for his successful work in the KGB's Paris residency several years earlier (1947–55).

Agayants generally was believed to be the guiding spirit behind a spate of spurious books originating in France, some probably authored by Gregoriy Bessedovskiy, a former Soviet diplomat who had defected in Paris in 1929.[32] Bessedovskiy has been suspected of literary enterprises ranging from fabrication for profit to outright disinformation on Moscow's behalf. The books at issue included such titles as *My Career at Soviet Headquarters*, *The Soviet Marshals Address You*, and *My Uncle Joe*—all by invented authors. While making light of one of the most vicious epochs of Soviet history, the themes of the books tended to cast Stalin's Russia in benign hues and at the same time stress its military strengths—echoes harking back to the Trust. This period of Agayants's career is seen by some as the early laboratory for his later efforts as Chief of Department D.

At the same time, the International Department of the Central Committee, under the veteran Comintern operative Boris Ponomarev, was growing in importance. Thus, in a few swift moves, a stable institutional network was emplaced that exists to this day with few modifications.

Under Khrushchev's overall direction, Shelepin guided state security in a conscious return to the traditions of Dzerzhinskiy and his GPU. Under Stalin, the KGB had degenerated to the repressive instrument of a one-man cult. Under Dzerzhinskiy and Lenin, the GPU was the true action arm of the party, implementing policy in subtle and effective ways a la the Trust. Shelepin directed that the new role of the KGB should focus on positive, creative political activity under the proper direction of the party leadership.[33] Disinformation and other forms of active measures were to occupy critical roles in this redirection under the guidance of Agayants' Department D, Ponomarev's International Department, and Mironov's Administrative Organs Department.

To execute the new focus properly, in May 1959, Shelepin called a major conference of senior KGB officers, the Ministers of Defense and Internal Affairs, and senior Central Committee members. In all, over 2,000 were reported in attendance.[34] The following were among the tasks that Shelepin placed before the conference:

> The main "enemies" of the Soviet Union were the United States, Britain, France, West Germany, Japan, and all countries of NATO and other Western-supported military alliances.
>
> The security and intelligence services of the whole bloc were to be mobilized to influence international relations in directions required by the new long-range policy, and, in effect, to destabilize the "main enemies" and weaken the alliances among them.
>
> The efforts of the KGB in the Soviet intelligentsia were to be redirected outwardly, against foreigners with a view to enlisting their help in the achievement of policy objectives.
>
> The newly established disinformation department was to work closely with all other relevant departments in the party and government apparatus throughout the country. To this end, all ministries of the Soviet Union, and all first secretaries of republican and provincial party organizations, were to be acquainted with the new political tasks of the KGB to enable them to give support and help when needed.

Joint political operations were to be undertaken with the security and intelligence services of all Communist countries.[35]

The contemporary period of Soviet active measures and strategic deception was thus ushered in. By the time Agayants (head of Department D) died, he was a KGB general. By 1970–71, his creation had been elevated from a department (*otdel*) to a service (*sluzhba*), known today as Service A. In the Soviet operational tradition, such changes connote much more than mere bureaucratic honorifics; undoubtedly the elevations were in keeping with performance and importance of function.

The organizational layout for coordinated deception operations gradually took shape with the party and the KGB leading a condominium of players throughout the party and state bureaucracies. Ponomarev's International Department seemed to become something of a Politburo "general staff," providing the overarching initiative and guidance for the KGB and others to follow. Similar developments occurred in Eastern Europe in view of the coordination requirements called for in Shelepin's conference.

It should be stressed that Golitsyn was not the only source talking about long-term deception planning and operations. The themes and specifics from the 1959 conference were reflected in the data and insights brought out later by defectors from other Communist countries, especially from Czechoslovakia. General Jan Sejna (Assistant Secretary to the Czech Defense Council, Chief of Staff to the Czech Ministry of Defense, member of Parliament and member of the Czech Communist Party Central Committee) is one of the most senior, well-placed officials to defect from the Soviet bloc. His unusual access was the basis for his detailed exposition of the early 1960's Soviet Strategic Plan, which he insists set out Moscow's long-term objectives.[36] According to Sejna, direction for strategic deception was included in the Strategic Plan for the USSR and for each of the Warsaw Pact countries.[37] Specific military deception actions would be part of the military operational plan for each Warsaw Pact country and each action must be approved by the Commander of the Warsaw Pact Forces, a Soviet officer.[38]

Another Czech, Ladislav Bittman, had been an intelligence officer whose service included that of Deputy Chief of Department D of the Czech intelligence service from 1964 to 1966. Bittman spoke of the work of his service on long-term deception plans covering a period of five to seven years, which were required to follow basic guidelines articulated by Moscow. This was to ensure that satellite deception planning was synchronous with Moscow's own long-range plan.[39] In addition to oversight on these matters by local KGB advisors, Bittman observed that General Agayants himself periodically checked in person on Bittman's organization and was the approving authority for Czech deception operations and even phases of operations.[40] According to Bittman, Agayants was a dedicated, stern professional, almost ascetic in his commitment to Soviet objectives.⁴¹ Shelepin and Khrushchev had picked the right man to help return the KGB to the style and spirit of Dzerzhinskiy.

The Military Question

Up to this point, little has been offered on questions addressing the organizational configuration of Soviet military deception or *maskirovka*. Unlike the KGB and the party, the Soviet military has left a relatively scant and contradictory trail on the workings of its deception component(s).

It may indeed be that sensitive Soviet military elements have the best operational security in the system, and surpass the KGB in protecting state secrets. For example, whereas the shield-and-sword of the KGB graces dust jackets of Western books, it is not even known whether the GRU has a logo.

It is known that during World War II, Soviet military deception operations were centralized in the extreme, with miniscule numbers of aware officers being determined by Stalin himself. Control worked down from the State Defense Committee (GKO), through STAVKA and the General Staff, to the given front(s).

The most assertive voice on the subject of late is Viktor Suvorov, the pseudonym of a former Soviet military intelligence officer who defected in 1978. In 1982, Suvorov first publicly identified a Chief Directorate of Strategic Deception in the General Staff.⁴² He claimed that it was then commanded by General N.V. Ogarkov and that it was even more powerful than either the First (Operations) or Second (GRU) Chief Directorates.

In a more recent work, Suvorov states that this Directorate was formed in 1968 because of the inadequacies of a decentralized military deception structure (commanders and chiefs of staff) to deal with nuclear weapons and satellites.⁴³ GUSM, or *Glavnoe Upravleniye Stratigicheskoy Maskirovki* (Chief Directorate of Strategic *Maskirovka*), was created to rectify this deficiency and was tasked with the following:

Collection and processing of information on hostile satellites; prediction of their orbits.

Defensive and deceptive measures for state and military targets against satellite reconnaissance.

Control of the Soviet press concerning state secrets and implementation of disinformation for the Soviet foreign press.

Use of deception in international negotiations.

Protection of state secrets within the military and defense industry; dissemination of false information.

Collection of information and assessment of the enemy's knowledge and knowledge gaps on the USSR.

Generation of false information to confuse the enemy.

Coordination of all Soviet military activities to assure the achievement of surprise.[44]

Suvorov claims that, in addition to passive defenses against enemy reconnaissance such as radio and radar switch-offs at predesignated times during satellite orbits, GUSM commands special radio-electronic deception units that transmit deceptive signals.

No doubt Suvorov's claims will be challenged and debated heavily, as have some of his earlier published interpretations, however, the broad outlines and missions of what he does posit are not that far removed from what we know of Soviet military deception in World War II. Whether the GUSM is a separate Directorate or lodged in the GRU or Operations Directorate may be a Talmudic tangent. The missions Suvorov ascribes to it make eminent sense in light of what is known about Soviet military practice.

Despite Suvorov's information, the command and control relationship between the military, the KGB, and the party in the conduct of strategic military deception is still unclear. In the foregoing cases, a high degree of centralization within the party and senior state security echelons characterized strategic political deception operations. World War II strategic military deception pointed to a centralization under State Committee of Defense (GKO)/STAVKA auspices, with Stalin at the helm. If the World War II analogue still holds for the 1980's, then some decision entity could be expected at the Defense Council/Supreme High Command (VGK) levels, with the KGB exercising some degree of security monitorship over the full range of strategic military deception programs. The latter function would be in keeping with the established military security and communications security functions of the KGB's Third and Eighth Directorates, respectively.[45]

Whither the Tradition?

Much ado has been made in the West over the last several Soviet leadership changes, beginning with Brezhnev's death in 1982. An underlying assumption that has characterized received Western opinion was that the man (that is, the new leader) somehow transcended the system. The foolishness of the musings over Andropov's private liberality yielded somewhat before the wooden void of Chernenko. However, it reemerged in torrents of gushiness at the chic swath the dashing Gorbachev couple cut across the Western media. Such shallow trendiness aside, a persistent refusal to assimilate the nature and structure of the Soviet party-state seems to dog Western opinion and governing elites. A concurrent disregard, even contempt, for the relevance and meaning of the traditions and history of the Soviet system complements this screening-out process.

Arguments over what is, or is not deception, the definitions of deception, and the feasibility of deception in an era of high-tech intelligence collectors, have reached intensity levels reminiscent of medieval theological disputes. What too many disputants forget is that deception is an integral feature of the Soviet system—an attribute of the counterintelligence state of which the USSR is the most salient example. Sun Tzu, in his timeless wisdom, saw all warfare as based on deception. Were the sage walking the earth in the late twentieth century, he might be moved to declare that deception energizes the counterintelligence state.

From the very beginning, the Soviet Communist Party predicated its survival on an ability to outmaneuver its *Okhrana* antagonists in a mutual penetration-counterpenetration struggle in which subterfuge and stratagem were operational givens. At the same time, Lenin and his Bolshevik colleagues waged their own counterintelligence war against their ideological enemies on the non-Bolshevik left.

With the victory of October 1917 came a role reversal; Lenin's new party-state took on the *Okhrana's* former duties, vesting these in Dzerzhinskiy's CHEKA. But the CHEKA's extra-legal mandate was far broader than any the *Okhrana* enjoyed; difference in degree made for difference in kind. While the *Okhrana* perpetrated its own share of bizarre provocations, nothing in its repertoire could match the scope and audacity of the Lockhart plot or the Trust and other concurrent legends.

The party, then, was not merely a "have not" political entity that suddenly acceded to power and then sublimated its revolutionary energies to enjoy the fruits of political legitimacy. A conspiracy before 1917, for all practical purposes it remained a conspiracy even after solidifying its position following the civil war. Only in that context do the elaborate internal and external deception games, fostered from the start of the regime, make any sense.

In that light, the reorientation by Khrushchev and Shelepin of the KGB in 1959 takes on a new dimension. Returning to the traditions of Lenin and Dzerzhinskiy meant something more than the reaffirmation of party primacy following the depredation of Stalin's unitary reign. It meant returning to the Leninist counterintelligence culture *sans* Stalin. How else to explain the lionization of the KGB, commencing in the 1960's, which trumpeted the exploits of its early star operations and officers?

It was under Andropov and Brezhnev that Khrushchev's and Shelepin's reorientation was carried out. Both Gorbachev and Chebrikov are products of that critical, formative period. Can a diminution of the Soviet organizational and operational traditions be expected under the new leadership? I would propose that that would be a systemic impossibility.

Notes

1. For an incisive study of this theme, see Wlodzimierz Baczkowski, *Toward an Understanding of Russia: A Study in Policy and Strategy* (Jerusalem: Liphshutz Press, 1947). See also Ronald Hingley, *The Russian Mind* (New York: Charles Scribner's Sons, 1977), ch. 3. This author is indebted to Raymond G. Rocca and Natalie Grant for their assistance and encouragement. Their earlier research on this subject and their extensive personal libraries were indispensable to the preparation of this chapter.
2. Hingley, *The Russian Mind*, p. 94.
3. Colonel A. Rezanov, *Le Travail Secret des Agents Bolchevistes* (*The Secret Work of Bolshevik Agents*) (Paris: Editions Bossard, 1926), pp. 67, 81–82.
4. "The Embassies and Foreign Affairs," *The Whitehall Gazette and St. James Review* (May 1926), p. 8.
5. Ibid., p. 9.
6. Ibid., p. 8.
7. George Leggett, *The CHEKA: Lenin's Political Police* (New York: Oxford University Press, 1981), p. 458. Branko Lazitch with Milorad Drachkovitch, *Biographical Dictionary of the Comintern* (Stanford, Calif: Hoover Institution Press, 1973), p. 412.
8. *Segodnya* (*Today*-Riga), 27 October 1927, 2–4 November 1927. See also Natalie Grant, "A Thermidorian Amalgam," *The Russian Review* 22 (July 1963), pp. 253–273.
9. George Leggett chronicled this data in his seminal work, *The CHEKA*, p. 296. The source of the Riga information, Eduard Opperput (also known as Selyaninov and Staunitz, among other names), was a star figure in the Trust operation and has been the subject of intense controversy since those events.
10. Natalie Grant, *Dezinformatsiya* (Disinformation), unpublished manuscript, Lovettsville, Virginia: 1974. (Used with permission.)
11. While the fiction of Comintern independence of Moscow is no longer seriously debated, it is still worth noting that Felix Dzerzhinskiy, the first head of Soviet State Security, represented the Polish Communist Party at the Fourth Comintern Congress in late 1922, *after having represented the Russian Communist Party at the first three Comintern congresses*.
12. R.H. Bruce Lockhart, *British Agent* (New York: G.P. Putnam's Sons, 1933); Sidney Reilly and Mrs. Pepita Reilly, *Britain's Master Spy: The Adventures of Sidney Reilly* (New York: Harper and Brothers, 1933); Michael Kettle, *Sidney Reilly: The True Story* (London: Corgi Books, 1983), ch. 3. Both Lockhart and Reilly have been the subjects of Soviet invective and invention. On the Western side, equally troublesome myth and legend, unencumbered by reliable documentation, surround both men—especially Reilly.
13. Richard K. Debo, "Lockhart Plot or Dzerzhinskiy Plot?" *Journal of Modern History*, vol. 43, No. 3, (September 1971): pp. 413–439.
14. Ibid., p. 349.
15. This account of the Trust draws principally from the following sources: Geoffrey Bailey, *The Conspirators* (New York: Harper and Brothers, 1960), pp. 1–86; S. Voytsekhovskiy, *Trest: Vospominaniya i dokumentiy* (*Trust: Reminiscences and Documents*) (London, Ontario, Canada: Zarya Publishers, 1974); G. Struve, V. Shulgin, S. Voytsekhovskiy, "New About the Trust," *Novyy Zhurnal* [*New Journal*] (1975): no. 125, pp.

194–214; S. Voytsekhovskiy, "Conversation with Opperput," *Vozrozhdeniye* No. 16 (July-August 1951), pp. 129–137; Richard Wraga, "The Trust," *Vozrozhdeniye (Renaissance)* No. 7 (January-February 1950), pp. 123–133; Vladimir Burtsev, "Police Provocation in Russia," *The Slavonic Review*, Vol. VI (December 1927), pp. 311–320; Basil Shulgin, "How I Was Hoodwinked by the Bolsheviks," *The Slavonic Review* (March 1928), pp. 505–519.

16. V.I. Lenin, *Selected Works*. vol. 3 (Moscow: Foreign Languages Publishing House, 1961), pp. 744–746. From Lenin's 27 March 1922 report to the 11th RKP(b) Party Congress.

17. Robert C. Williams, " 'Changing Landmarks' in Russian Berlin, 1922–1924," *Slavic Review* Vol. XXVII (December 1968), pp. 581–593.

18. See especially Lev. V. Nikulin, *Mertvaya zyb'* [*The Dead Swell*] (Moscow: Voyenizdat, 1965). A changed version appeared a year later published by *Sovetskiy Pisatel* [*Soviet Writer*]. French and German editions appeared in 1969; an English translation was issued by the Department of Commerce (JPRS 55686) in 1972. A Western work on the Trust case and other Soviet operations, and charged in Congressional testimony as having originated in Moscow is Michael Sayers and Albert E. Kahn, *The Great Conspiracy: The Secret War Against Soviet Russia* (Boston: Little, Brown and Co., 1946). On the charge of Soviet origin, U.S., Congress, Senate, Committee on the Judiciary, *Institute of Pacific Relations, Part 13. Testimony of Igor Bogolepov*, 82nd Cong., 2d sess., 1952 (Washington, DC: GPO), pp. 4513–4514.

19. "The Failure of One KGB Operation," *Novoye Russkoye Slovo* [*New Russian Word*] (16 January 1983).

20. Bailey, pp. 133–224; U.S., Congress, Senate, Committee of the Judiciary, *The Legacy of Alexander Orlov* (Washington, DC: GPO, 1973), pp. 119–121, 141–150.

21. David Kahn, *The Code Breakers* (New York: Macmillan Co., 1967), pp. 1083, fn. 650.

22. James E. McCherry, *Stalin, Hitler and Europe 2* (New York: World Publishing Co., 1970), pp. 229, 296. The Ponschab telegrams concerned include: N.A. 105-104/113116-7, 113138, 113257, 113283, 113293, 113323, 113331, 113383, 113409, 113417, 113424, 113431, 113432, 113434, 113435, 113437, 113438, 113441, 113445, 113451, 113465, 113463, 113469, 113471.

23. Reference number SAIC/R/2, 24 June 1945; RG 238. Records of the National Archives Collection of WWII War Crimes, Entry 160, SAID/R/2, folder 87 (Box 18).

24. See David Kahn, *Hitler's Spies* (New York: Macmillan, 1978), pp. 312–317, 335, 368–369; Reinhard Gehlen, *The Service* (New York: World Publishing, 1972), pp. 57–58. The most incisive summary ot the "MAX" case is found in David L. Thomas, "The Legend of Agent 'MAX'," *Foreign Intelligence Literary Scene*, Vol. V, No. 1 (January 1986), pp. 1–2, 5.

25. CSDIC Special Interrogation Report No. 1716, 9 August 1945, "Notes on *Gruppe I Luft*"; and CSDIC Special Interrogation Report No. 1727, 16 September 1945, "Notes on *Adwehr* I, Appendix I".

26. Gehlen, Ibid.

27. Chapman Pincher, *Their Trade Is Treachery* (London: Sidgwick and Jackson, 1981), pp. 104–107.

28. See Dieter Sevin, "Operation Scherhorn," *Military Review* Vol. 46 (March

1966), pp. 35–43. Sevin's account of this operation is the only one this writer has been able to surface in Western literature. However, various Soviet writings hail similar operations on the Eastern Front. See, for instance, N. F. Yudin, *Pervaya Partizanskaya* [*The First Partisan Division*] (Moscow: Izdatel'stvo Moskovskiy Rabochiy, 1983); S. Z. Ostryakov, *Voyennye Chekisty* [*Military Chekists*] (Moscow: Voyenizdat, 1979); and A. Fyodorov, *The Underground R. C. Carries On*, 2 vols (Moscow: Foreign Languages Publishing House, 1949).

29. Harry Rositzke, *The CIA's Secret Operations* (New York: Reader's Digest Press, 1977), pp. 169–172; and Thomas Powers, *The Man Who Kept the Secrets* (New York: Alfred A. Knopf, 1979), pp. 41–43.

30. K. V. Tawcas, *Guerrilla Warfare on the Amber Coast* (New York: Voyager Press, 1962).

31. Nicholas Bethell, *Betrayed* (New York: Times Books, 1985); Kim Philby, *My Silent War* (New York: Ballantine Books, 1983). Philby discusses the Anglo-American Albanian venture, but says nothing of his treacherous role in compromising it.

32. Grant, *Dezinformatsiya*, chap. 9; and Gordon Brook-Shepherd, *The Storm Petrels* (New York: Ballantine Books, 1982), chap. 5.

33. Anatoliy Golitsyn, *New Lies for Old* (New York: Dodd, Mead and Co., 1984), p. 48.

34. Golitsyn was *not* the only source for this conference. It had been reported in *Pravda*, 18 May 1959; and by V. Minyailo, "The Conference of the State Security Organs, *Bulletin: Institute for the Study of the USSR* (September 1959), pp. 21–23. Golitsyn was the first to present the details and fully explain the ramifications.

35. Golitsyn, p. 49.

36. Jan Sejna, *We Will Bury You* (London: Sidgwick and Jackson, 1982).

37. Discussions with General Sejna, 1978–1980. [Used with permission.]

38. Ibid.

39. Ladislav Bittman, *The Deception Game* (New York: Ballantine Books, 1981), p. 86.

40. Ibid., pp. 153–155, 112–113.

41. Discussions with L. Bittman, 1984. [Used with permission.]

42. Viktor Suvorov, *Inside the Soviet Army* (London: Hamish Hamilton, 1982), pp. 102–105.

43. Viktor Suvorov, "GUSM: The Soviet Service of Strategic Deception," *International Defense Review*, no. 8 (1985), p. 1236.

44. Ibid.

45. John Barron, *KGB Today: The Hidden Hand* (New York: Reader's Digest press, 1983), pp. 451–452.

2
Soviet Organization and Doctrine for Strategic Deception

Richards J. Heuer, Jr.

What almost certainly ranks as the largest, most complex, most sophisticated, and most successful military deception operation in history was conducted by Great Britain with the United States—not by the Soviet Union. It was the cover and deception plan for the Normandy landings and related operations in World War II.[1] The Soviets also conducted deception operations during the war, but these did not approach the scale or level of sophistication of the Allied effort.[2]

This is noted at the outset for its shock value, for so many people assume the Soviets are the pros at deception while the West is like a babe in the woods. This assumption is true in some ways, but like most generalizations about deception, it conceals important distinctions. In examining Soviet deception, it is advisable to start by putting preconceptions on hold.

This chapter presents an overview of Soviet organization and doctrine for deception. Before we move directly to that subject, it will be useful to discuss what is meant by deception, to evaluate the state of available knowledge about Soviet deception, and to identify sources of information.

Deception is used as an umbrella concept that covers many different forms of activity: management of perceptions through overt and covert propaganda, exploitation of agents of influence, disinformation through double agents, camouflage and concealment, display of dummies and decoys, and manipulation of data made available to an adversary's technical sensors.

Within the Soviet Union, activities that Westerners may regard as strategic deception fall within the scope of three quite distinct programs, each of which is conducted by different organizations: active measures, counterintelligence, and *maskirovka*. Active measures is the Soviet term for a form of political action aimed at foreign public opinion, political elites, and decision makers. Counterintelligence endeavors to neutralize the activity of foreign intelligence and security services. *Maskirovka* encompasses camouflage, cover, and deception by the military. Each of these programs is discussed in a major section of this chapter.

The West has a long record of experience with Soviet intelligence. Since the inception of the Soviet intelligence services, they have suffered from a constant stream of defectors and penetrations. During the past 30 years or so, over 100 (perhaps closer to 150) Soviet or East European intelligence officers have either defected to the West or been recruited as agents in place by Western intelligence services.[3] Roughly one-third of these were Soviets. Some of the Eastern European intelligence services follow the Soviet model so closely that information on these services can, by analogy, also contribute to the understanding of the Soviet services. These knowledgeable sources have identified many thousands of Soviet and East European intelligence operations. The information they have provided on organization and doctrine is detailed, covers most facets of the KGB and GRU[4] (especially their foreign operations), and displays a remarkable continuity over time.

It is an interesting paradox that the KGB and GRU, those most secret institutions of the secretive Soviet state, are among the best known Soviet organizations to the West. There have probably been more and better sources of information on Soviet intelligence than on any other element of the Soviet government. This is because the KGB and GRU personnel serve and travel abroad, where they have the opportunity to establish and maintain contact with Western intelligence, and they have a better opportunity than most Soviet officials to learn about and become disillusioned with the inner workings of the Soviet system. Moreover, since Soviet intelligence officers already know the techniques of clandestine operations, they sometimes have the confidence to turn these techniques against their own service.

In evaluating the state of Western knowledge of Soviet deception, however, several distinctions are important. First, Soviet intelligence is only one part of the overall Soviet apparatus for deception. Soviet deception starts at the Politburo. Central Committee departments play a major role, as do various military units subordinate to the Ministry of Defense. Much less information is available in the West about these other organizations than about Soviet intelligence.

Another key distinction is between intelligence organization and methods, on one hand, and specific intelligence operations, on the other. Soviet intelligence organization, goals, and methods are well-understood. Knowledge of specific clandestine operations is severely limited by compartmentation procedures and the need-to-know principle that are normal within all intelligence services, but especially effective in Communist countries. Obviously, most current Soviet intelligence operations remain undetected; others have been detected only after very serious damage has been done.

Finally, it is important to recognize the difference between individual intelligence operations and operational programs. While current Soviet intelligence operations may be undetected, one can presume that they are, in most cases, a continuation of operational programs that have been well known for some time. Western knowledge of organization and methods and of the many thousands of individual operations that have been identified over the years is probably a valid guide to the generic types of activity one should expect.

Anyone who writes about ostensibly secret matters and expects to be taken seriously should identify his sources of information. I was a CIA officer for twenty-eight years prior to retiring from government service in 1979. More recently, I reviewed the open literature on Soviet deception, drawing on past experience to separate the wheat from the chaff. Through the State Department, I wrote to several former Soviet officials now living in the West to request a meeting or information. In the summer of 1985, I met with Stanislav Levchenko, a former KGB major who defected in Tokyo in 1979, after serving as the active measures officer in the KGB Tokyo residency. My discussion with Levchenko provided useful clarification and expansion of previously published information from him.[5] I also received unpublished written material from other former Soviet officials.

Despite the availability of considerable information, Soviet deception remains a controversial subject. Knowledgeable persons both inside and outside the U.S. government have honest differences of opinion on subjects discussed in this chapter. In compliance with security regulations to which I am subject as a former CIA officer, this manuscript was reviewed by the CIA prior to publication. The purpose of the prepublication review was exclusively to prevent inadvertent disclosure of classified information. The review does not constitute CIA authentication of factual material, nor does it imply CIA endorsement of the views expressed herein.

Active Measures

The Soviet term active measures (*aktivnyye meropriyatiya*) describes a wide variety of deceptive techniques to promote Soviet foreign policy goals and undermine those who oppose Soviet actions. Within the KGB, the term distinguishes operations intended to influence opinions or policies in foreign countries from more classic espionage or counterintelligence operations. Active measures undertaken by the KGB include agents of influence, disinformation, forgeries, and covert press placement.

Active measures are not exclusively an intelligence activity, and in this sense it differs from the similar American concept of covert action. The International Department (ID), and International Information Department (IID) of the Communist Party Central Committee also play major roles in implementing active measures through foreign political agitation and propaganda activities and through covert manipulation of international front groups.

According to Levchenko, the former KGB officer who specialized in this activity, the term active measures is not widely known or used in the Soviet Union. Rather, it is a professional expression used only by the KGB and Central Committee officials who are informed of or participate in this activity. Appearance of the term in a UN document prepared by the Soviet UN delegation was probably a security slip by a KGB officer under UN cover.[6]

There are many differences between active measures and the American concept of covert action. One is the Soviet ability to mesh overt and covert influence activities through centralized coordination of party, government, and ostensibly private organizations dealing with foreigners. Despite interagency coordination mechanisms, the United States is far too pluralistic to achieve full coordination among all the overt and covert means of exercising influence abroad. Other major differences are in scope, intensity, and importance attributed to active measures and covert action and in immunity from legal and political constraints. Agents of influence, who are a most important part of active measures, are developed and exploited far less systematically by American intelligence, perhaps because this activity does not fit neatly into the sharp organizational separation between overt and covert activities that distinguishes the American intelligence system. Paramilitary activities are sometimes considered part of covert action, but are not normally part of active measures.[7]

Active measures exemplifies the terminological confusion encountered in translating Soviet concepts relating to deception. One of the Russian terms commonly translated into English as deception is disinformation (*dezinformatsiya*). Soviet usage of this term has changed; what used to be the Disinformation Department of the KGB was renamed the Active Measures Department, with no discernible change in its functions. Now, disinformation appears to be one form of active measures dealing with dissemination of false or misleading information. Whether all disinformation is (in American terms) deception depends upon whether one uses a broad or narrow meaning of deception. Forgeries, for example, which the Soviets regard as disinformation, are viewed by many in the U.S. intelligence community as propaganda rather than deception. Many persons in the intelligence community think of deception only as an activity directed against the intelligence community, while persons outside the intelligence community tend to regard it as a much broader problem. Clearly, there is much ambiguity in the terms used to equate Soviet action with American concepts of deception.

This study includes two important activities under active measures that are not generally considered in Western discussions of Soviet active measures. One is deceptive statements by Soviet leaders, such as Khrushchev's statements that led to perception of a "missile gap" in the late 1950's. The other is Soviet manipulation of information received and reported by Western diplomats and journalists in Moscow. Whether their inclusion as active measures accords with current Soviet usage is not clear, but these are certainly important elements of the Soviet effort to manipulate Western perceptions of the USSR.

A CIA study lists the long-term, strategic objectives of Soviet active measures as:

> To influence both world and American public opinion against U.S. military, economic, and political programs which are perceived as threatening Soviet objectives.
>
> To demonstrate that the United States is an aggressive, colonialist, and imperialist power.
>
> To isolate the United States from its allies and friends, and discredit those that cooperate with it.
>
> To demonstrate that the policies and goals of the United States are incompatible with the ambitions of the undeveloped world.
>
> To discredit and weaken U.S. intelligence efforts (particularly those of the CIA), and to expose U.S. Intelligence personnel.
>
> To create a favorable environment for the execution of Soviet foreign policy.
>
> To undermine the political resolve of the United States and other Western states to protect their interests from Soviet encroachments.[8]

Voluminous examples of active measures are described in the open literature and are not repeated here.[9] Our focus is on the Soviet organizations that plan or implement active measures. Figure 2–1 is an organizational chart, and the principal organizations are described in subsequent paragraphs. Evaluative comments discuss the impact of Soviet active measures on U.S. intelligence analysis.

Politburo

In all countries, major deception operations must be approved at the top leadership level. In the USSR, however, the Politburo role is not limited to approving deception plans implemented by others. Rather, official statements by Politburo members themselves play an important part in achieving Soviet deception goals.

De Mowbray, for example, described the wartime role of Stalin and Molotov in deceiving Britain about Soviet postwar intentions in Eastern Europe.[10] Khrushchev's key role in creating the fictional missile gap in the late 1950's is well-documented.[11] Mihalka has collected the false or misleading statements by civilian and military leaders concerning the Soviet ABM, mobile missiles, heavy missiles, and missile accuracy.[12] Additional examples of top Soviet leadership involvement in deception abound in other chapters of this book.

If the Soviets needed feedback from inside the U.S. intelligence community

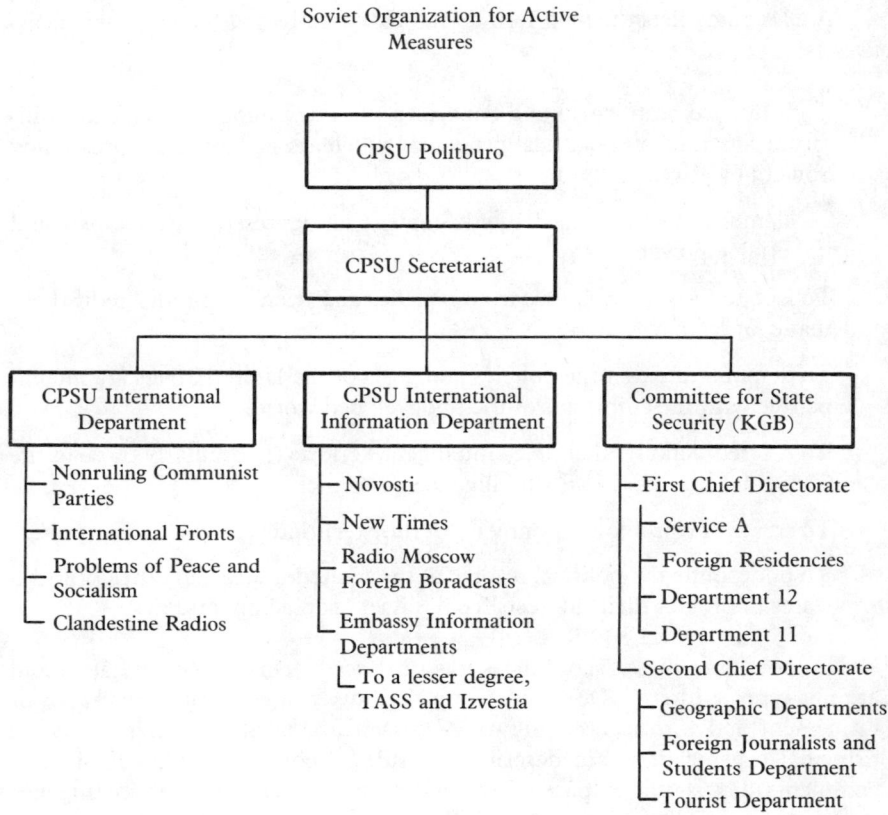

Figure 2–1. Soviet Organization for Active Measures

to appreciate fully the effectiveness of such deception, they reportedly received it in 1960. Lieutenant Colonel William Whalen, a U.S. Army intelligence officer assigned to the Joint Chiefs of Staff, had become a KGB agent. Whalen had access to national intelligence estimates on Soviet strategic forces, and evidently passed these documents to the Soviets. According to Marchetti and Marks,[13] the estimate on Soviet ICBM development quoted public statements by Khrushchev and other Soviet leaders. The estimate accepted these statements as indicators of Soviet progress in development and deployment of intercontinental missiles.

Even in the West, deception is recognized as a necessary and important activity under some circumstances, especially in wartime. It is, however, relegated to a game of wits between intelligence specialists or military commanders, so that diplomats and top civilian leaders may keep their hands clean. By contrast, in the Soviet Union as in most non-Western societies, deception is an integral part of national policy and strategy; the top leaders are the principal players. It is in this context that the Soviets really are the pros, and we are, indeed, babes in the woods.

International Department (ID)

The ID of the Communist Party of the Soviet Union (CPSU) is the most senior element in the Soviet bureaucracy dealing with foreign affairs.[14] It reports directly to the Politburo and Secretariat. It coordinates and reviews inputs on foreign policy by the Ministry of Foreign Affairs, KGB, Ministry of Defense, and the foreign policy research institutes under the Academy of Sciences, such as the Institute of the USA and Canada, and the Institute of World Economics and International Relations. In the sense that it provides tasking and coordinates the activities of the entire foreign policy establishment, the ID fulfills a function somewhat analogous to our National Security Council (NSC). It prepares decision options for the politburo and supervises implementation of these decisions by the appropriate government offices. The ID provides direction to the KGB on active measures themes, but it does not control how these themes are implemented through the KGB's clandestine assets.

In addition to its coordinating role, the ID also has direct operational functions that make it the lineal successor to the Comintern. It maintains the official liaison with the so-called nonruling Communist Parties throughout the world. It provides guidance and, as needed, funding to these parties. In those countries where the Communist Party is in power, the ID maintains liaison with its counterpart ID in that party.

The ID directs, administers, funds, and coordinates the many international front organizations for political action and propaganda: the World Peace Council, Afro-Asian People's Solidarity Organization, World Federation of Trade Unions, World Federation of Democratic Youth, and so forth. Covert Soviet control over these international organizations is exercised by the International Social Organizations Sector of the ID, through the Soviet affiliate of the front to Soviet representatives or agents at the front's international headquarters.

The ID also directs publication of the monthly journal *Problems of Peace and Socialism*, known in its English language version as *World Marxist Review*. This is the official, overt mechanism for communicating Soviet views, and in a sense, issues instructions and the party line to foreign parties and front groups.

Attached to the ID is a full-time "Consultants Group" made up of academics from the social science research institutes who "conduct in-depth research, carry out long-range studies, and help draft major doctrinal statements."[15] The research institutes themselves are also tasked regularly to conduct studies for the ID and to disseminate Soviet views that the ID wishes known in the West.

International Information Department (IID)

The IID of the CPSU is responsible for improving the effectiveness of Soviet propaganda abroad and for improved treatment of foreign affairs news in the Soviet domestic media.[16] Its chief is Leonard Zamyatin, former director of the Soviet news agency TASS, and a full member of the Central Committee. Zamyatin often serves as official spokesman for Soviet policy, but that policy is determined or coordinated by the ID rather than by the IID. According to Levchenko, the IID is considerably less important than the ID. It is the ID that sets propaganda lines and determines programming policy, and the IID simply implements these policy directions.

Organizations whose dissemination of information abroad come under the supervision of the IID include the press agencies *Novosti* and *TASS*, the periodical *New Times* (which is printed in ten languages), Radio Moscow, and all the regional radios broadcasting abroad. Foreign news coverage in the domestic press also comes under the IID's purview, although *Pravda*, as the official organ of the Communist Party, enjoys an independence not available to other publications.

This centralized direction of all media dealing with foreign affairs obviously ensures the capability to insert themes or specific articles as required, and this department does play an important role in the overt aspects of active measures campaigns.

KGB Service A

The third pillar of Soviet active measures is Service A of the KGB's First Chief Directorate.[17] It, too, takes guidance from the ID, which determines overall propaganda and disinformation themes and coordinates Service A's covert operations with the more overt activities of the ID itself and the IID.

Service A is the current designator for the component that began in 1959 as Department D (for Disinformation). It was subsequently redesignated Department A (for Active Measures) and then, in 1970, upgraded in bureaucratic status to Service A. Although its operations are quite varied, a former Czech intelligence officer who specialized in covert active measures classified this activity into three broad categories: disinformation, propaganda, and influence.[18]

Influence. Influence operations insinuate Soviet views into leadership groups, often in a nonattributable manner. The agent of influence may be a well-placed, controlled agent, a "trusted contact" who consciously serves Soviet interests on some matters while retaining his integrity on others, or an unwitting contact who is manipulated to take actions that advance Soviet interests on specific issues of common concern. The KGB enlists a person who tends to agree with the Soviet position on at least one significant issue (such as opposition to some element of U.S. policy) and then seeks ways to motivate and help that person to become a successful advocate on that issue within his or her own circle of influence. The KGB offers a variety of tangible and intangible rewards, often exploiting a person's ego and desire to influence policy rather than greed.

One usually successful ploy with persons visiting Moscow is to arrange a private meeting with "a very senior advisor to the Central Committee," who is actually an officer of Service A. The potential agent of influence is briefed on the "real" Soviet position, and asked to serve as a private channel of communication between the Soviet leadership and the person's own government, party, or organization.[19] A different type of influence operation is covert financial support to parties, political candidates, or organizations that support positions advantageous to the Soviet Union.

Covert Propaganda. Articles supporting approved disinformation themes are placed in the Western and Third World press. The activity is covert since there is no attribution of Soviet origin. The newspapers and magazines are often conservative or moderate publications; insertion of material in left-wing publications can usually be handled openly by the *Novosti* office or through Communist Party or front group contacts. The insertion is sometimes made through controlled agents; it may also be done, however, by "trusted contacts" developed on the basis of common interest on some limited issue, or anonymously by mail. Once a story appears in one area, a variety of methods are employed to ensure it is replayed in other countries.

Disinformation. Forgeries are the best known form of disinformation. Sometimes they are complete fabrications. More commonly, however, they are modified versions of actual U.S. government documents. The doctored portions are designed to incite enmity toward the United States. Another common disinformation technique uses witting or unwitting agents of influence to disseminate false stories that serve Soviet interests.

Levchenko estimates that Service A has about 200 officers in Moscow.[20] Unlike most other KGB First Chief Directorate components, Service A is basically a staff unit that does not send its officers abroad. Rather, it works through the overseas officers of other components, especially the geographic division officers responsible for political intelligence. When Levchenko was stationed in Japan as a political intelligence officer for Department 7 (Japan, Indonesia, the Philippines, Thailand, Singapore), he was assigned for a time the function of residency coordinator for active measures. He had been taught at the KGB training academy that agents who can influence the policy or national decisions of their country are more valuable than those who steal secrets.

As the active measures coordinator in Tokyo, Levchenko received all guidance from the Center in Moscow concerning active measures goals and themes and then assessed which of the residency assets offered the best means to achieve these goals or spread these themes. He then worked with the KGB officers responsible for handling those assets to help them implement the active measures. Levchenko estimates that he received from three to five messages per day from the Center on some aspect of active measures.[21]

In addition to the Service A officers at KGB headquarters, Levchenko reports that there were about fifty Service A officers under cover in the *Novosti* headquarters in Moscow. He believes these officers were responsible for preparing and directing the placement of disinformation articles in the foreign press and for the fabrication of books for distribution abroad.[22]

Novosti is the news service that provides feature articles about the Soviet Union to foreign media. Its activities have expanded greatly since a 1973 report that *Novosti*:

> exchanges information with 101 international and national agencies, 120 publishing firms, more than 100 radio and television companies, and more than 7,000 of the world's largest newspapers and magazines. It maintains bureaus and correspondents in 80 countries. [*Novosti*] claims an annual transmission to foreign media of 60,000 literary pieces, and more than two million photographic prints.[23]

Several other First Chief Directorate headquarters components also play important roles in active measures. Department 12 is an operational unit similar to a geographic division, except that its officers are in field work in Moscow.[24] Department 12 directs hundreds[25] of KGB officers under cover in various organizations in the Soviet Union that deal with foreigners. Their mission is to assess, influence, and if possible, recruit as agents foreign journalists, professors, scientists, and government officials with whom they and the organizations they represent come into regular contact.

The many KGB officers under cover in the Institute of the USA and Canada and the Institute of World Economics and International Relations report to Department 12. In the Institute of the USA and Canada, about one-third of the staff members are KGB personnel. They are especially well-placed to play important roles in active measures, particularly influence operations, under the direction of Service A.[26] In the words of one student of this phenomenon, the personnel of these institutes:

> have become the Soviet Union's main resource for learning about Western intellectual prejudices and spreading disinformation that plays on these prejudices. The exposure given to them in the United States is so great as to give the Soviet Union an effective voice in the U.S. domestic political process. . . . [They] participate as speakers at nuclear freeze rallies, make regular appearances on American television, attend academic conferences, serve as visiting

fellows at U.S. university centers, sit on the editorial boards of U.S. academic journals, and contribute frequent op-ed articles for U.S. newspapers.[27]

In the Academy of Sciences, the First Deputy Chief of the International Department is one of many KGB officers reporting to Department 12. All approvals of foreign scientists traveling to the Soviet Union and of Soviet scientists traveling abroad are processed through this department. That information would be of obvious interest to Service A for planning its extensive active measures campaign against the Strategic Defense Initiative (SDI). Levchenko believes Service A probably formed a special section to concentrate on the SDI issue.[28]

Department 11 of the First Chief Directorate handles liaison with the East European intelligence services, each of which has its own equivalent of Service A. Most of these components were formed by KGB request in 1963 or 1964. The Czech and East German services are especially active in this field. Through Department 11, Service A coordinates the activities of its counterparts in the other services.[29]

KGB Second Chief Directorate

The Second Chief Directorate, which is much larger than the First, is responsible for internal security and the recruitment of agents among foreigners stationed in or visiting the Soviet Union. It has about six departments working against foreign diplomatic personnel stationed in the USSR, departments to cover foreign journalists and students living in the Soviet Union and a department for foreign tourists, as well as a variety of other units.[30]

It is the foreign diplomats and journalists stationed in Moscow who are most interesting from the standpoint of Soviet deception. The Second Chief Directorate views its mission as being aware of, if not controlling, all contacts between foreign diplomats or journalists and Soviet citizens. A large percentage of the Soviet contacts of diplomats and journalists in Moscow report to the KGB. The Second Chief Directorate has very effective control over the entire environment in which foreigners live, work, and move socially in Moscow.[31]

The KGB controls rather well what information and impressions foreign diplomats and journalists receive, both officially, from the government, and unofficially, through personal contacts. In this way, it can, when desired, manipulate what the embassies and journalists report back to their home countries.

The KGB system is not perfect by any means, but when one considers how many of our impressions of what is happening in the Soviet Union are ultimately based on embassy or journalistic reporting, there certainly is cause for serious concern. This aspect of active measures has received insufficient attention, as neither diplomats nor journalists are prone to question the validity of their own reporting. While some may acknowledge that they could be targets for influence operations, most regard themselves as too sophisticated to be manipulated by the KGB.

Evaluation

Soviet efforts to manipulate Western perceptions through active measures are pervasive and widely recognized. The open questions about Soviet active measures concern their impact, not their existence nor methods.

Western journalists writing about Soviet active measures generally focus on the most visible elements: forgeries and placement of articles in the international press designed to exacerbate mistrust of the United States or to blame all the world's ills on American imperialism.[32] These active measures present problems for American policy, but they are well-known and manageable problems. Exclusive focus on these obvious aspects of active measures diverts attention from other, more serious but less apparent concerns: deceptive statements by Soviet leaders, manipulation of agents of influence, and control of information available to Western embassies and journalists in Moscow.

In chapter 17 of this book, David Yost's study of the Soviet active measures campaign to block modernization of intermediate-range nuclear forces in Europe provides a path-breaking analysis of the impact of this Soviet campaign on West Germany. The campaign did not block deployment of the Pershing missiles, but it may have effectively constrained future strategic policy options in NATO. Soviet active measures are effective to the extent that they mobilize existing opinion, influence the terms of political debate, provide significant ammunition used in that debate, or deposit an ideological residue that eases the path for subsequent Soviet perception manipulation operations.

The charge that nuclear freeze advocates and other opponents of a strong strategic defense posture are victims of Soviet propaganda probably misses the point. The channel of influence actually may be in the opposite direction. The Soviets may modify their public positions (but not their true policy) to fit what will have the greatest impact on Western policy debates. Lenin's dictum on disinformation was to "tell them what they want to believe," and most serious students of deception have recognized that feedback on the target's attitudes and reactions is a vital element of successful deception.[33] Feedback permits a deceiver to adapt to changing circumstances and to tailor the deception to the target's prejudices.

Starting with the "peace" program initiated at the Soviet Party Congress in 1971, the Soviets have gradually modified their publicly expressed military doctrine on the use of nuclear weapons. The provocative nuclear war-fighting doctrine of the 1950's and 1960's has given way to a benign public image of Soviet nuclear strategy. Soviet leaders have flatly denied strategic superiority as a goal, publicly proclaimed no first use of nuclear weapons, stated that victory cannot be a meaningful goal in a nuclear war, and disavowed previous emphasis on nuclear preemption. Such public statements are at variance with the continuity in nuclear doctrine evident in Soviet research, development, and deployment of strategic systems, and in the pattern of Soviet military exercises.[34] Several analysts of Soviet affairs have suggested that since the early 1970's, Soviet public pronouncements on strategic military doctrine represents a deliberate disinformation campaign to mislead Western opinion.[35] A good case can be made that the Soviets modified their public position (but not their actual doctrine) in response to Western policy debates in order to strengthen the hand of those who oppose a strong Western defense posture.

A key question, which has not been systematically addressed, is the extent to which Soviet active measures influence U.S. intelligence analysts and their analytical product. The impact of disinformation on intelligence analysis may be either direct or indirect. If disinformation is included in the data base of evidence used by analysts, it may have a direct impact on their conclusions. If not directly relevant to the question at issue, the disinformation may have an indirect impact by influencing an analyst's assessment of Soviet intentions or capabilities, or what drives Soviet policy. Such broad preconceptions influence how analysts interpret ambiguous evidence on a wide range of lesser issues, or how they judge the credibility or relevance of evidence.

In fact, public statements by Soviet leaders form an important part of the data base used by analysts and scholars. It was true in the 1950's when Khrushchev's statements on Soviet ICBM capabilities deceived U.S. analysts, and it is true today with Soviet leaders' statements on arms control policy, doctrine governing the use of strategic weapons, and a host of other issues. To the extent that such public statements are taken at face value, when they are in fact deceptive, analysts may make erroneous judgments. Articles in specialized Soviet military and scientific journals also form an important part of the data base used by analysts. They, too, are commonly taken at face value.

Soviet economic statistics are used despite recognition of their unreliability. Their lack of reliability is probably not the result of deliberate deception, but because the Soviet system of centralized planning creates so many internal incentives for doctoring production statistics. To information-dependent intelligence analysts, however, potentially unreliable information is generally preferable to no information at all.

Embassy and journalistic reporting from Moscow also becomes part of the analyst's data base. Such reporting is easy to manipulate. One of the more egregious disinformation campaigns in Moscow was the program to depict Yuri Andropov as a "liberal reformer" after his selection as Secretary General of the CPSU.[36] Even senior Soviet officials were

> amazed . . . at how quickly and easily so many in the West, especially students of Soviet affairs, appeared to fall under the spell of the KGB's disinformation campaign.[37]

Levchenko feels certain that any information given by any ostensibly well-informed Soviet to a foreign journalist or diplomat about the personal background or political attitudes of Politburo members is manipulated for disinformation purposes. He also believes that such operations are controlled by the International Department, or directly by the Secretariat, rather than by the KGB.[38]

The principal impact of active measures on intelligence analysis comes from the Soviet ability to provide centralized control over and direction of so many different channels of information that people normally use to form impressions of what is going on in the Soviet Union. It comes from a comprehensive, multichannel approach to implementing a political strategy that starts at the top with deceptive (or, at best, self-serving) statements by the leadership. These themes are then reinforced through a broad range of overt and covert activities to create a false impression of Soviet goals and the strategy for achieving those goals.

When an analyst studying a non-Communist country receives fifteen items of information and they all seem to point to the same conclusion, it is possible to have reasonable confidence in that conclusion. If each of these fifteen items comes through independent channels, they provide valid confirmation of each other.

With the Soviet Union there is far less certainty, since deception is always a strong possibility. When Brezhnev says the Soviets no longer think victory is a meaningful goal in a nuclear war, and the Soviet military attache in New Delhi says the same thing to his American counterpart, the Soviet military press writes about it, and several other sources repeat it, that does not necessarily mean it is true. It may simply mean this theme has been orchestrated from a central location.

An article by Stephen de Mowbray, "Soviet Deception and the Onset of the Cold War," is an excellent case history that illustrates this problem. De Mowbray examined British government documents to determine the basis for the government's optimistic judgment, in 1943, about the postwar policies that would be pursued by the Soviets. He concludes:

> Information from one Communist source was accepted as independent confirmation of information from another Communist source. . . . The lesson of the

period from 1943 to 1945 is that we should reassess the extent to which our knowledge of, and opinions about, the Communist world are derived from sources controlled or inspired by the Communist authorities themselves.[39]

That lesson is not limited to the period 1943 to 1945. It is the principal lesson to be learned from an understanding of the Soviet active measures program.

Counterintelligence

A second major Soviet program related to deception is counterintelligence. Counterintelligence aims to neutralize the efforts of foreign intelligence and security services. Double agents and provocateurs are among the standard methods used. In most cases, they serve tactical counterintelligence objectives such as the identification of hostile intelligence personnel, methods, and information requirements. Double agents and false defectors may also be used to pass disinformation to foreign intelligence services and thus serve broad, strategic deception goals.

Counterintelligence outside the Soviet Union is the responsibility of Directorate K of the KGB's First Chief Directorate.[40] In addition to its work against foreign intelligence and security services, this unit is also responsible for the security of all Soviet citizens abroad. This includes Soviet officials stationed abroad in diplomatic, trade, journalistic, and other posts, as well as merchant seamen, Aeroflot crews, and Soviet delegations traveling abroad. Directorate K also maintains the physical security of Soviet installations in foreign countries. KGB defectors observed that these other duties sometimes provide a rationalization for lack of action toward its most important, but also most risky and difficult, goal: recruitment of foreign intelligence and security officers as Soviet agents.

Inside the Soviet Union, counterintelligence operations against foreign embassies and consulates are handled by the appropriate geographic department of the KGB Second Chief Directorate. The First Department, for example, works against American diplomats in Moscow. Work against the many other foreign embassies in Moscow is divided among about six geographic departments.[41]

As with Directorate K, the geographic departments of the Second Chief Directorate have other tasks. Counterintelligence is one element of a multifaceted attack against all foreign diplomatic offices. The geographic departments seek to recruit embassy personnel as agents, collect intelligence from the embassy through audiosurveillance or clandestine entry to photograph documents, identify all Soviet nationals who have dealings with the embassy or its personnel, identify intelligence activities conducted from the embassy or by embassy personnel, and, as previously noted, feed disinformation as part of the active measures program.[42]

All double agent operations are run by the KGB, usually either Directorate K or the Second Chief Directorate. The GRU is not authorized to run double agents. If the GRU learns that one of its agents has been doubled against it, direction of the case is supposed to be turned over to the KGB. GRU sources have advised that, in practice, if the KGB is not already aware of the problem, the GRU may terminate the operation rather than inform the KGB.

In examining the role of double agents in deception during peacetime, it is useful to distinguish three categories of double agents based on their level of access to valuable, documentary intelligence. The three categories are the non-Soviet agent, the Soviet national who does not have regular access to highly classified documents, and the well-placed Soviet official who does have regular access to sensitive, classified documents.

Non-Soviet Double Agents

Most Western intelligence agents working against the Soviet Union are not Soviet nationals. They are Western or Third World nationals, who, for one reason or another, have dealings with the Soviets. Their principal task is to report on the Soviets they meet in an effort to identify likely recruitment targets, but some of them may also elicit information or make observations of positive intelligence interest.[43] When such an agent is doubled by the KGB, the Soviets can achieve standard counterintelligence goals, such as identification of Western intelligence personnel and methods and the tying up of limited Western intelligence facilities in fruitless activities.

The KGB may also use a non-Soviet double agent as a channel for disinformation. It is likely to be tactical counterintelligence disinformation, such as misleading information on the functions or vulnerabilities of Soviet officials, or it may be a political line to support an active measures campaign. It is unlikely to be a carefully crafted deception to mislead intelligence analysts about strategic weapons systems, since the KGB must recognize that such a deception would have little chance of success. The non-Soviet source simply does not have plausible access to valuable, classified information from the Soviet Union. If a non-Soviet source obtained such a windfall from a Soviet contact, the credibility of the information and the source certainly would be subjected to extremely close scrutiny.

Soviet Double Agents—Limited Access

The KGB occasionally permits, and in some cases will provoke, Western intelligence services to recruit Soviet nationals who do not have regular access to highly classified information. In the early 1950's, for example, the KGB permitted the CIA to recruit a Soviet national working in Vienna as an official of the Soviet Petroleum Administration supervising oil production in the Russian-occupied zone of Austria. Journalists, low level trade officials, and many scientists are examples of other categories of Soviets who do not have regular access to classified documents, who work or travel abroad, and whom the KGB might run as double agents.

This category of double agent has several advantages from the viewpoint of a KGB officer planning a deception operation. Through such an agent, the KGB can seek to determine how Western intelligence services communicate with agents inside the Soviet Union; this must be an important KGB counterintelligence goal. As a Soviet national with a variety of personal contacts, such an agent could develop a plausible explanation for obtaining whatever information the KGB may want passed to the adversary. Since the agent's job does not give regular access to highly classified documents, the credibility of the source may be maintained without giving away a large volume of valid, sensitive information. Thus, the KGB can hope to achieve an important counterintelligence goal, while maintaining a deception channel at a reasonable cost.

Soviet nationals involved in any form of organized opposition to the regime are especially attractive to the KGB as double agent candidates. It is standard practice for counterintelligence services to take the initiative in organizing underground or dissident groups under their own control. This is the counterintelligence equivalent of a police "sting" operation.

Through a handful of controlled agents, the security service forms an opposition group, attracts other legitimate regime opponents to join the group, then seeks support and assistance from one or more foreign intelligence services.

The KGB and its predecessors enjoyed immense success with this type of deception. The classic example of the genre was the Trust operation, which ran from 1921 to 1927. This counterintelligence operation was run to neutralize, deceive, and then discredit the principal opposition to the Communist regime. In connection with the New Economic Policy also launched in 1921, the Trust pushed the line that an anti-Soviet monarchist movement was well-established in Soviet Russia, that Communist ideology had failed, that the Soviet regime was changing, and, that hostility by the European powers would be counterproductive, since it would unite the people behind the government and thereby slow the inevitable evolutionary process. Once the Soviet regime stabilized, both the Trust and the New Economic Policy were terminated.

Inside the Soviet Union, a series of public trials intimidated the remaining opposition. Outside the Soviet Union, Trust supporters were blackmailed into cooperating with Soviet intelligence, tried in absentia, kidnapped, and held up to public ridicule for their naivete.[44]

The Trust was one of the most successful operations in the history of intelligence, but the operational doctrine and tactics were by no means a Soviet invention. Similar operations were conducted in England under Cromwell and in France at the time of Napoleon.[45]

Under KGB direction, the Polish security service conducted a similar operation against the CIA and British intelligence in the early 1950's. It organized an underground "army" known by the acronym WiN (Freedom and Independence), and received arms, radios, and money from the West. In December 1952, the Polish government's deliberate exposure of WiN as a deception led to the end of Western intelligence efforts to organize active internal opposition to Communist regimes in Eastern Europe.[46]

Learning from these and other experiences, for many years the CIA has followed the practice of avoiding clandestine contact with members of organized dissident groups in the USSR. This is because known dissidents do not have current access to valuable classified information, and exposure of CIA contacts with dissidents would compromise the legitimacy of their opposition.

The CIA is alleged to have made an exception to this policy in 1975. The Soviets claim the CIA accepted the services of a volunteer, Sanya Lipavsky, a Jewish neurosurgeon who had previously treated Soviets assigned to nuclear submarine bases in Murmansk. Lipavsky was deeply involved in dissident activities. He shared a room with Anatoly Scharansky, a spokesman for the human rights movement in the USSR. Two years later, Lipavsky published an account of his alleged CIA activities in the government newspaper *Izvestia*. Scharansky and other dissidents were arrested and charged as CIA agents. The case became the basis for an active measures campaign to embarrass President Carter, who had publicly supported the Soviet human rights movement.[47] If the Soviet claims are true and the CIA actually was lured into contact with Lipavsky, then the KGB again used a common counterintelligence deception ploy to neutralize opposition.

Soviet Double Agents—Well-Placed Officials

The principal controversy about Soviet use of double agents for deception, and one of the main disputes about Soviet deception in general, concerns Soviet officials in sensitive positions with access to highly classified documentary information. Does the KGB use such officials as double agents or false defectors? How much valuable, classified documentary information is the KGB willing to sacrifice to establish the bona fides and credibility of a double agent? Is it possible that the CIA's best Soviet agents actually have been KGB plants deceiving the U.S. government?[48]

The main case at issue has been Yuri Nosenko, a KGB Second Chief Directorate officer who was a CIA agent in-place for two years before he defected in Switzerland in 1964. After debriefing by the CIA, Nosenko originally was judged to be a KGB plant dispatched to the West on a twofold mission: to divert the investigation of important KGB agents partially identified by a previous KGB defector (including an alleged penetration of the CIA) and to deny KGB involvement with Lee Harvey Oswald, a former U.S. Marine who had defected to the USSR, returned to the United States, and who had assassinated President

Kennedy just several months before. There were many implausible elements and contradictions in Nosenko's story, and the circumstantial evidence against him appeared to be very strong.[49]

The Nosenko case became the centerpiece of a "master plot" theory with wide ramifications. Some believed that the KGB planned the Nosenko defection and monitored its results with the aid of a high-level penetration of the CIA comparable to Soviet agents Kim Philby in British Intelligence and Heinz Felfe in the West German Federal Intelligence Service (BND).[50] Those who believed in the existence of such a well placed penetration assumed that virtually all CIA operations against the USSR were actually under KGB control, or at least known to the KGB. Especially suspect were several other well-placed penetrations of Soviet intelligence who seemed to support the information provided by Nosenko.[51]

This enormously complex case (one of the many analyses contained almost 900 pages)[52] eventually was subjected to a comprehensive reevaluation with the finding that Nosenko was not under Soviet control.[53] The atmosphere of suspicion created by the master plot theory and the feeling of helplessness from thinking that operations against the Soviet Union may be fruitless until the penetration is identified caused serious damage to CIA operations against the USSR.[54] Several published accounts of the Nosenko case suggest that the original assessment of Nosenko as a KGB plant was correct and that the subsequent reevaluation was the product of bureaucratic expediency and wishful thinking.[55]

Although the Nosenko case still elicits disagreement among those who were professionally involved in this controversy, many former believers in the theory of a KGB master deception plot have genuinely modified their views. The theory logically led to certain predictions. When these predictions failed to materialize, doubts about the theory grew.

The predictions and actual results were as follows: Since Nosenko was "known" to be under KGB control and the purpose of the Soviet operation was also known, it was felt that a hostile interrogation would succeed in breaking him and gaining a confession. It did not. Similarly, it was believed that a hostile interrogation would break a confessed KGB illegal who had been arrested in South Africa. That, too, was unsuccessful. A proper counterintelligence analysis and security investigation should identify a KGB penetration of CIA Soviet operations who was being built up or protected through this KGB deception. No such penetration was discovered despite a very extensive investigation.

Since the KGB would want to limit the cost of the information it was giving away, it was judged that investigation of leads to seemingly well-placed KGB agents would show these agents had recently lost their access or for some other reason were expendable to the KGB. In fact, investigation showed some agents still in place and producing valuable information for the KGB. Similarly, there were tantalizing leads to Soviet agents who could not be fully identified by

Nosenko. It was believed that investigation of these leads would lead to a dead end, so the KGB had really sacrificed nothing. In fact, investigation of these leads did identify valuable KGB agents. [56]

As the years passed, and other Soviet sources originally thought to be under KGB control (or at least known to the KGB) continued to pass large quantities of extremely valuable information, the theory of a grand deception collapsed of its own weight. It was also determined that Nosenko had personal motives for concealing and exaggerating information about his personal background and his knowledge of KGB operations.

The question remains, however, how much valuable information the KGB will give away to establish a credible deception channel? If the stakes are high enough, they may sacrifice whatever is required to do the job. As far as I have been able to determine, however, postwar experience provides little evidence of KGB willingness to give up much at all.

To the best recollection of several former counterintelligence specialists, none of the Soviet or East European intelligence officer defectors or in-place sources ever identified any case of a well-placed Soviet or East European official with regular access to secret documents who was permitted by his own government to copy those documents and pass them to Western intelligence. Similarly, the many intelligence officer defectors and in-place sources are not known to have reported any case of a defector who was sent to the West for the main purpose of passing deceptive intelligence. Phoney defectors certainly have been sent out and passed through the debriefing process, but the positive intelligence they provided was incidental to Soviet or East European objectives and was probably valid.

It cannot be said that these things have never happened or that they could not happen in the future. Nonetheless, the known record seems clear. The absence of reports of such operations is significant, but not conclusive. It is not conclusive because compartmentation within the KGB is effective in limiting knowledge of such operations. It is significant because there have been enough well-placed sources that such activity probably would have been reported if it were a common practice.

Evaluation

Although the KGB makes extensive use of double agents and provocateurs, these operations seem to be run to achieve tactical counterintelligence goals, rather than for strategic deception. The targets are Western intelligence operations officers, rather than intelligence analysts, and the operations do not involve regular passage of classified documents to Western intelligence.

Post-World War II cases in which Western intelligence received significant positive intelligence through agents subsequently determined to have been under the control of the KGB (or any of the East European services) are distinguished by their rarity. One such case was in the early 1950's, when an agent controlled by Heinz Felfe produced a sample of Czech uranium ore—much sought after at the time.[57] Felfe was a West German intelligence officer, later identified and arrested as a KGB agent.

The Berlin tunnel operation is often cited in discussions of how much information the KGB is willing to sacrifice to achieve its goals. In 1955, the CIA and British Intelligence collaborated in an operation to dig a tunnel under the border between West and East Berlin to tap Soviet communications lines.[58] From its inception, the operation was compromised by George Blake, a KGB penetration of British Intelligence who participated in its planning. Nevertheless, the KGB permitted taps to be installed and to produce voluminous intelligence data for eleven months before the KGB "found" the taps and terminated the operation.

It should be noted, however, that the conception and implementation of the Berlin tunnel operation was far more spectacular than the intelligence it produced, which was voluminous but largely limited to routine order-of-battle information and operational data on personnel. Further, it appears that the CIA was able to read the clear text of enciphered messages sent over these lines and that this was not revealed to the British. If true, this aspect of the operation was probably not compromised by Blake.[59] From the KGB point of view, Western intelligence apparently was permitted to monitor unclassified telephone and telegraph communications to protect the security of a valuable penetration of British Intelligence. This is not a precedent for KGB initiative in releasing highly classified documents to support a deception operation.

The Soviet passion for secrecy seems to inhibit KGB release of highly classified information to Western intelligence in order to establish the credibility of a deception channel. If there is one thing that is more important to the Soviets than deceiving the enemy, it is protecting their own security.[60] Any credible channel for strategic deception on key issues of national policy is also a major breach in the wall of secrecy. Information of lesser value will be sacrificed, but this commonly serves the counterintelligence objectives of Directorate K rather than strategic deception goals.

Cooperation between Directorate K and Service A on deception operations is subject to strains that arise from the nature of the missions and the backgrounds of the personnel of these two KGB units. Directorate K officers tend to have less education and training than do the average First Chief Directorate officers. Many of them previously served in the Second Chief Directorate, where they acquired the mentality of internal repression. Their security responsibilities in embassies abroad include recruiting colleagues as informants to report on one another. As a group, Directorate K officers are distrusted and often disliked by other KGB First Chief Directorate personnel.

In contrast, Service A is staffed with the best educated officers in the KGB. Personnel are chosen on the basis of creativity, writing and analytical ability, and substantive expertise on countries or issues of intelligence interest.[61] According to Levchenko, Service A has so little confidence in the ability of Directorate K officers that it tries to avoid using them in active measures work.[62]

Personality differences may be exacerbated by differences in operational mission. The counterintelligence officer emphasizes security above all else. Many active measures officers are engaged in inherently low security activities that often become known. The Directorate K officer may fear his agent would be compromised if he were used to disseminate disinformation themes provided by Service A. Such differences probably do circumscribe the range of cooperation between these two KGB components and limit the extent to which counterintelligence assets are exploited for deception on strategic issues.

Maskirovka

In the military field, the Russian term that equates most closely to deception is *maskirovka*. It is broader than the Western concept of deception, as it encompasses routine camouflage, cover, and the denial of information as well as deception.[63] *Maskirovka* has often been translated as camouflage. For the Soviets, *maskirovka* is strictly a military concept, not a specialized intelligence term. It is not used by the KGB, and in turn the military does not use the term active measures. Thus, the Soviets do not appear to have a single concept of deception.

Soviet military doctrine defines *maskirovka* as an operational function, not a staff function. This means that it is planned and directed by the military commander, not by a staff component such as the GRU. The GRU plays no central role in *maskirovka*, although it does provide intelligence support to the commanders and ensures the security of its own personnel, installations, and intelligence collection operations.

As a standard element of military art, there is considerable writing about *maskirovka* in the open Soviet military press. Their doctrine identifies four broad categories of *maskirovka*:

1. Camouflage (*skrytiye*): Any natural or technical means used for purposes of concealment.
2. Simulation (*imitatsiya*): Decoys, dummies, fake weapons effects, any action to change the identifying characteristics of weapons, installations, or force groupings.
3. Feints and demonstrations (*demonstrativnye deystviye* or *manevry*): Military movements or combat actions to disguise true intentions or to cause the enemy to take a desired action.

4. Disinformation (*dezinformatsiya*): Dissemination of false or misleading information by technical means of communication, the media, agents, or false documents.[64]

The *Soviet Military Encyclopedia* article on *maskirovka* identifies three levels on which this activity is conducted:

1. Strategic *maskirovka* is implemented by a decision of the Supreme High Command (VGK) for preserving the secrecy of preparation for strategic operations and campaigns, and for disorienting [*dezorientatsiya*] the enemy with respect to the real intentions of the [Soviet] Armed Forces.
2. Operational *maskirovka* is effected upon decision of a front [army] or fleet [flotilla] commander, and is directed at ensuring the secrecy of preparations for operations.
3. Tactical *maskirovka* is conducted in major units [*soyedinyeniye*], units, and subunits, and in individual installations with the goal of concealing preparations for combat, or an installation presence [configuration].[65]

Stalin downplayed the initial success of the German surprise attack on the Soviet Union in World War II. Although the USSR was almost destroyed by the German blitzkrieg, Stalin asserted that the lesson for Russia was that surprise could not determine the outcome of war. Stalin's emphasis on the "permanently operating factors" in determining the outcome of military conflict led him to minimize the importance of "transitory factors" such as surprise and deception.

During the early war years, the Soviets learned bitter lessons as a result of inadequate *maskirovka*. As the war continued, they gradually came to excel in the use of tactical and operational *maskirovka*, especially camouflage, security of troop movements to conceal offensive preparations, and extensive use of dummy tanks and aircraft as decoys. These changes were initiated by the military leadership, not by Stalin. It was not until after Stalin's death that surprise and deception regained their place as central themes in Soviet military doctrine.[66]

In the postwar period, the *maskirovka* component of one of the USSR's most important strategic initiatives, emplacement of offensive missiles in Cuba in 1962, was wholly inadequate. The cover and deception plan for sea and ground transport of the missiles showed appropriate concern for security, but no effort at all was made to conceal the missile site construction from aerial reconnaissance, despite Soviet knowledge of U-2 overflights. Construction of SAM, MRBM, and IRBM launch sites and nuclear warhead storage bunkers followed the same tell-tale pattern as in the Soviet Union. The Soviets did not begin to camouflage these sites until after they had already been publicly identified.[67] This failure of *maskirovka* contributed to early detection and U.S. counteraction before the missiles were operational.

During the decade of the 1970's, the Soviet Union had ample cause to review and reevaluate its *maskirovka* program. Extensive engagement in arms control negotiations created strong additional incentives to conceal information and to deceive the West about deployment of specific weapons, research and development of new weapons systems, and numbers of troops in Eastern Europe. Moreover, arms control negotiations inevitably revealed to the USSR the surprising extent of U.S. knowledge of their weapons systems. A series of Soviet espionage successes (the Boyce/Lee, Prime, and Kampiles cases) confirmed to the Soviets the origin of U.S. knowledge and compromised operational details of U.S. systems for photoreconnaissance, communications intercept, and monitoring missile telemetry.[68]

Soviet concern about these developments is evident from the military press,[69] although the extent to which this concern may have prompted changes in Soviet organization or doctrine for *maskirovka* is not yet known with certainty. It takes several years for such information to filter from the Soviet Union and still longer until it becomes available to Western scholars outside the government.

The most recent information comes from a former Soviet military officer who writes under the pseudonym of Viktor Suvorov. Unfortunately, Suvorov's writings do not differentiate the many stories he heard from what he knows by direct personal experience. His information on strategic *maskirovka* is a useful personal statement of what Suvorov (and presumably other Soviet Army officers) heard and believe to be true, but its ultimate source and reliability are uncertain. Suvorov's information needs to be evaluated accordingly.

Suvorov reports that in 1969, strategic *maskirovka* was centralized in a Chief Directorate of Strategic *Maskirovka* under the General Staff.[70] Its first head was General N.V. Ogarkov, who later was promoted to Marshal and became Chief of the General Staff. This unit tracks Western intelligence-gathering satellites and prepares short- and long-term forecasts of the exact times these intelligence collectors will pass over various areas in which Soviet forces are located. Instructions are sent to all units advising them of the type of intelligence collector (photoreconnaissance, signals intelligence, and so forth), and the exact time it will overfly their area. Orders are issued to cease radio transmissions, turn off radars, and keep equipment under cover during specified time periods. Although Suvorov does not mention it, the same warning system would have to cover factories and shipyards engaged in military production, as well as many scientific research institutes.

Again according to Suvorov, each military division has radio transmitters and radars that are turned on to provide deceptive signals when the reconnaissance satellites are overhead. Similarly, certain aircraft flights, rocket tests, troop movements, and other military activities are planned to take place as the satellites pass within range to detect them, with the aim of emphasizing one aspect of activity while concealing others.

To maintain control over information that becomes available to the West,

Suvorov believes the *maskirovka* unit "supervises" all military parades and any military exercises where foreigners are present and that it "runs" all military newspapers and journals such as *Red Star, Soviet Union, Standard Bearer*, and *Equipment and Armament*. That it "supervises" parades and "runs" the military press is almost certainly an overstatement. It is reasonable to believe, however, that it performs functions in the military sphere comparable to the active measures function of the International Department and International Information Department in the political sphere. In other words, this unit may set disinformation themes and write specific articles for the military press; it may coordinate plans for parades or military exercises having foreign observers, and in so doing, it may arrange to show modified or dummy equipment or veto plans for showing off new equipment.

Exploitation of parades for deception is well known. At the 1955 Air Force Day ceremonies, for example, the Soviets mobilized every one of the new Bison jet bombers that had been produced as of that date and flew many of them by the reviewing stand twice. At that time, U.S. intelligence reportedly was so dependent on such information that this led to an upward revision of national intelligence estimates of Soviet heavy bomber strength and to claims of a "bomber gap" that preceded a so-called "missile gap." Taken at face value, the flyover indicated Soviet heavy bomber strength at four times the number of modern B-52 bombers then available to the U.S. Strategic Air Command.[71]

According to Suvorov, other activities that come under the purview of the strategic *maskirovka* unit are relations with foreign military attaches stationed in the Soviet Union; all military construction; and non-military construction including factories, pipelines, or railways.

To the traditional Soviet use of camouflage, simulation, and feints as elements of *maskirovka*, Suvorov's description adds an increased emphasis on disinformation through false radio signals, radar emissions, and articles in the military press. Two points are of particular interest. One concerns how the Soviets exploit their knowledge of U.S. reconnaissance satellite capabilities and orbits. Suvorov believes the program includes the extensive showing of what they want to be seen, as well as the hiding of what they want to conceal. That sort of active deception through false signals and dummy equipment or installations is difficult to do effectively, given modern reconnaissance resources and analytical methods. It is unfortunate that Suvorov could not provide more details.[72]

A second point of interest is the reported use of Soviet military journals as channels for deceiving Western intelligence. A Czech intelligence active measures specialist who defected in 1968, Ladislav Bittman, also reported a large Czechoslovak military disinformation project that used the media as a channel for military disinformation.[73] This is significant, as some intelligence analysts assume that specialized journals intended for an internal audience are reliable sources of information. They argue that Soviet requirements for accurate internal communication preclude extensive use of these publications as channels for deceiving the West, because the cost of deceiving their own military or scientific personnel would be too high. Given the Soviet emphasis on internal as well as external propaganda, plus the circulation of classified journals for those with a need-to-know, this view seems open to question.

Evaluation

As previously noted, the Soviets distinguish between strategic, operational, and tactical *maskirovka* according to the level of organization that initiates the action. By Soviet definition, camouflage and concealment to reduce effectiveness of U.S. satellite reconnaissance is clearly strategic *maskirovka*, but some Western analysts regard this as a security measure rather than as deception per se. In most cases, camouflage and concealment are defensive, intended to protect security and to deny intelligence to the enemy. They are intended to hide, not to show; to keep the enemy ignorant of the truth, not to actively create a false impression that prompts the enemy to take action harmful to his own interests.

The role of camouflage and concealment in deception is illuminated by Michael Handel's distinction between two approaches to deception, passive and active:

> Passive deception is primarily based on secrecy and camouflage, on hiding and concealing one's intentions and/or capabilities from the adversary. Some experts view passive deception as inferior. . . . While measures of secrecy do not have the same aura of romance and intellectual excitement as that associated with active deception, they frequently can be as effective as any more elaborate type of deception operation. *Moreover, active types of deception are dependent on the success of passive deception*. What is even more important, passive deception can tremendously complicate and therefore increase the costs of intelligence work.
>
> In contrast to passive deception, active deception normally involves a calculated policy of disclosing half-truths supported by appropriate "proof" signals or other material evidence. This information must be picked up by the intelligence network of the deceived. The deceived must "discover" the evidence himself; he must work hard for it to be more convinced of its authenticity and importance.[74]

British deception operations during World War II are the quintessential example of active deception. The known history of Soviet military deception in World War II is one of passive deception, with the possible exception of the Manchurian Campaign in 1945.[75] One can only speculate on what evidence of more active deception might still be locked in Soviet archives. A potentially important example of deception through double agents is the Max-Moritz case (also known as the Klatt case) described briefly by John Dziak in chapter 1.

Unfortunately, not enough information is available on how the Soviets exploited this channel to deceive the Abwehr and the German General Staff.

When Barton Whaley compared the concepts of surprise and deception in the national security doctrines of nine major countries, he concluded that Soviet doctrine on surprise and deception "still lags that in, at least, the British and Israeli armies."[76] He noted that the Russians " . . . continue to be obsessed with the false notion that 'negative security' is the crucial factor in surprise."[77] Whaley's view is supported by Ziemke's study of Soviet deception during World War II, which shows it to be unimaginative, but nonetheless effective. The largest Soviet deception on the Eastern Front was Operation *Bagration*, the Belorussian offensive in the spring of 1944. In this operation, the Soviets prepared two offensives, concealed one while allowing the Germans to observe the other, and then attacked from the concealed positions.[78]

Today the Soviets have the organization and incentive to engage in strategic military deception operations, both passive and active. It is noteworthy that there is no consensus on whether, or to what extent, U.S. intelligence analysis of Soviet strategic forces has been skewed by Soviet deception. Sometimes U.S. intelligence estimates have been wrong, but the extent to which they were wrong because of Soviet deception is open to question. This question has generated much heat and some seemingly persuasive arguments, but there has been little hard evidence available in the public domain to resolve it.[79]

Conclusion

Organizational structure is important because of the bureaucratic imperative—that organizations formed and trained for certain tasks will seek to perform them. The Soviet Union has the organization, doctrine, and historical experience to conduct an extensive program of deception to support national goals. In an era of strategic competition, with prospects for arms control determined in large part by the ability to verify compliance with agreed limitations, the Soviet propensity for deception is a serious concern.

The Russian language has no direct analogue to the Western concept of deception. The Russian words most commonly translated as deception (*dezinformatsiya* and *maskirovka*) are very imperfect equivalents. Similarly, the American concepts of covert action and propaganda do not have a one-to-one correspondence with their Soviet counterparts. Using Western concepts to reason about Soviet activities often causes faulty inferences. This chapter has, therefore, stayed with Russian terminology and striven to understand deception from a Soviet perspective.

The USSR has three quite separate and distinct programs relating to deception: active measures, counterintelligence, and *maskirovka*. While there is central direction on key issues of national strategy, these different forms of deception are implemented by different organizations, often motivated by different goals, conditioned by different circumstances, face different obstacles to effective implementation, and follow different historical traditions. Because of this diversity, many generalizations about Soviet deception are likely to be misleading. In forming expectations and evaluating fears about Soviet deception, it is important to specify at all times exactly what kind of deception is under discussion. Failure to do so has been a major source of confusion in analyzing Soviet deception.

Notes

1. One of the more comprehensive studies is Charles G. Cruickshank, *Deception in World War II* (Oxford and New York: Oxford University Press, 1979).

2. For example, see Earl F. Ziemke, "Stalingrad and Belorussia: Soviet Deception in World War II," in Donald C. Daniel and Katherine L. Herbig, eds., *Strategic Military Deception* (New York: Permagon Press, 1982).

3. A recent bibliography on Soviet intelligence lists works by, or about, thirty Soviet and seven East European intelligence officer defectors or in-place sources. Raymond G. Rocca and John J. Dziak, *Bibliography on Soviet Intelligence and Security Services* (Boulder, Colo.: Westview Press, 1985). Many other intelligence officer defectors who have not written books are discussed in the burgeoning open literature on intelligence. See George C. Constantinides, *Intelligence and Espionage: An Analytical Bibliography* (Boulder, Colo.: Westview Press, 1983); Walter Pforzheimer, ed., *Bibliography of Intelligence Literature*, 8th ed. (Washington DC: Defense Intelligence College, 1985); and *Scholar's Guide to Intelligence Literature: Bibliography of the Russell J. Bowen Collection in the Joseph Mark Lauinger Library, Georgetown University* (Frederick, Md.: University Publications of America, 1983).

4. The Soviet Union has two foreign intelligence services. The KGB (*Komitet Gosudarstvennoy Bezopasnosti*), or Committee for State Security, is the civilian service. The GRU (*Glavnoye Razvedyvatelnoye Upravleniye*), or Main Intelligence Directorate of the General Staff, is the military service.

5. Principal sources for information provided by Levchenko are U.S. Congress, House Permanent Select Committee on Intelligence, *Soviet Active Measures*, 97th Cong., 2d sess. (Washington, DC: Government Printing Office, 1982); John Barron, *KGB Today: The Hidden Hand* (New York: Reader's Digest Press, 1983); and Richard H. Shultz and Roy Godson, *Dezinformatsia: Active Measures in Soviet Strategy* (Washington, D.C.: Pergamon-Brassey's, 1984).

6. Personal discussions with Levchenko. The reference to active measures was in a Soviet report submitted to the United Nations on actions to implement UN resolutions on apartheid. UN General Assembly, "Measures Taken by Member States and Intergovernmental Organizations in the Light of United Nations Resolutions on Apartheid," A/CONF 107/5, 5 May 1981. The pertinent text reads:

In accordance with United Nations decisions, efforts are underway in the Soviet Union to mobilize world opinion in the fight to eliminate colonialism, racism, and apartheid in southern Africa. Active measures in this direction are being carried out by Soviet social organizations, including the All-Union Central Council of Trade Unions, the Soviet Afro-Asian Countries Solidarity Committee, the Soviet Committee for the Defence of Peace, the Committee of Soviet Women, the Committee of Youth Organizations of the USSR, and the Union of Red Cross and Red Crescent Societies.

7. Personal discussions with Levchenko. Any military operation can be an active measure, however, if it is undertaken for the purpose of influencing political attitudes; for example, the Kuriles operation reported by Levchenko in his 1982 testimony before the U.S. House Select Committee on Intelligence.

8. U.S. Congress, *Soviet Active Measures*, p. 33.

9. The most extensive treatments are U.S. Congress, *Soviet Active Measures*; Schultz and Godson, *Dezinformatsia*; Barron, *KGB Today*, ch. 6; John Barron, *KGB: The Secret Work of Soviet Secret Agents* (New York: Reader's Digest Press, 1974), ch. 8; Ladislav Bittman, *The Deception Game* (Syracuse, N.Y.: Syracuse University Research Corp., 1972); U.S. Congress, House Permanent Select Committee on Intelligence, *Soviet Covert Action: The Forgery Offensive*, 96th Cong., 2d sess. (Washington, D.C.: Government Printing Office, 1980); Clive Rose, *Campaigns Against Western Defence* (London: Macmillan, 1985).

10. Stephen de Mowbray, "Soviet Deception and the Onset of the Cold War," *Encounter* (July–August 1984), pp. 16–24.

11. Arnold Horelick and Myron R. Rush, *Strategic Power and Soviet Foreign Policy* (Chicago: University of Chicago Press, 1966).

12. Michael Mihalka, "Soviet Strategic Deception 1955–1981," in John Gooch and Amos Perlmutter, eds., *Military Deception and Strategic Surprise* (London: Frank Cass Co., 1982). Mihalka's valuable study was also published under the same title in *Journal of Strategic Studies* (5 March 1982).

13. Victor Marchetti and John D. Marks, *The CIA and the Cult of Intelligence* (New York: Dell Books, 1974), pp. 212–214. See also, John Prados, *The Soviet Estimate: U.S. Intelligence Analysis and Russian Military Strength* (New York: Dial Press, 1982).

14. Principal sources of information on the International Department are Robert W. Kitrinos, "International Department of the CPSU," *Problems of Communism*, Vol. XXXIII (September–October 1984), pp. 47–75; Leonard Shapiro, "The International Department of the CPSU: Key to Soviet Policy," *International Journal*, Vol. XXXII (Winter 1976–77); Shultz and Godson, *Dezinformatsia*; and U.S., Congress, *Soviet Active Measures*, p. 35, plus personal discussion with Levchenko.

15. Kitrinos, "International Department," p. 52.

16. Principal sources of information on the International Information Department are Schultz and Godson, *Dezinformatsia*, pp. 25–31; U.S. Congress, *Soviet Active Measures*, p. 35, and personal discussion with Levchenko.

17. Principal sources of information on Service A are those listed in note 9, plus discussion with Levchenko.

18. Bittman, *The Deception Game*, p. 20.

19. U.S. Congress, *Soviet Covert Action*, p. 83.

20. U.S. Congress, *Soviet Active Measures*, p. 10.

21. Ibid., p. 143.
22. Personal discussion with Levchenko. For information on fabrication of books, see Bernard Gwertzman, "Fake Books as International Weapons," *New York Times*, 11 Jan. 1976, p. 20-E.
23. *External Information and Cultural Relations Programs of the Union of Soviet Socialist Republics* (Washington, D.C.: USIA Office of Research Assessment, 1973), pp. 36–37.
24. Barron, *KGB Today*, pp. 26–27.
25. Levchenko has no direct knowledge of the number. In personal discussion, he estimated at least 300, but possibly as many as 1,000.
26. Personal discussion with Levchenko. Information on percentage of KGB personnel is from Barron, *KGB Today*, p. 221. Also see Arkady Shevchenko, *Breaking with Moscow* (New York: Alfred A. Knopf, 1985), pp. 208–211. Shevchenko identifies Georgi Arbatov, director of the Institute of the USA and Canada, as a protege of former KGB Chief Yuri Andropov.
27. William C. Green, "Soviet Disinformation and Strategic Deception Concerning Its Nuclear Weapons Policy," Report no. 4, Contract no. N-62271-82-M2200, for the Naval Postgraduate School, February 1984, pp. 30–32.
28. Personal discussion.
29. Barron, *KGB Today*, p. 382.
30. Ibid., pp. 113–117.
31. Ibid., ch. 6. Regarding manipulation of Western journalists in Moscow, see David Satter, "Moscow Feeds a Lap-Dog Foreign Press," *Wall Street Journal*, 22 October 1985; and Andrew Nagorski, *Reluctant Farewell* (New York: Holt, Rinehart and Winston, 1985).
32. For example, Elizabeth Pond, "Disinformation: Planting False Information to Influence Public Opinion," *Christian Science Monitor*, four installments, 26 February to 1 March 1985; Michael Getler, "Soviet Disinformation Tactics Get Bolder, State Department Says," *Washington Post*, 17 December 1983; "The Soviets' Dirty Tricks Squad," *Newsweek*, 23 November 1981.
33. Daniel and Herbig, *Strategic Military Deception*, pp. 20–21.
34. Dan L. Strode and Rebecca V. Strode, "Diplomacy and Defense in Soviet National Security Policy," *International Security* 8 (Fall 1983), pp. 92–94.
35. John J. Dziak, *Soviet Perceptions of Military Power: The Interaction of Theory and Practice* (New York: Crane, Russak, 1981), pp. 66–67; Joseph D. Douglass, Jr., "Soviet Disinformation," *Strategic Review* 9 (Winter 1981), pp. 16–26; William F. Scott, "Continuity and Change in Soviet Military Organizations and Concepts," *Air Force Magazine* 65 (March 1982), pp. 47–48; and Green, "Soviet Disinformation Concerning Nuclear Weapons Policy."
36. Michael Voslensky, *Nomenklatura: The Soviet Ruling Class* (New York: Doubleday, 1984), pp. 378–381.
37. Shevchenko, *Breaking with Moscow*, p. 183.
38. Personal discussion.
39. De Mowbray, "Soviet Deception", p. 24
40. Barron, *KGB Today*, pp. 378–379.
41. Barron, *KGB: Secret Work*, pp. 113–115.

42. Ibid., ch. 6.

43. Harry Rositzke, *The CIA's Secret Operations: Espionage, Counterespionage and Covert Action* (New York: Reader's Digest Press, 1977).

44. Geoffrey Bailey, *The Conspirators* (New York: Harper and Brothers, 1960).

45. Richard Wilmer Rowan, *The Story of Secret Service* (New York: Literary Guild of America, 1937); D.L. Hobman, *Cromwell's Master Spy: A Study of John Thurloe* (London: Chapman and Hall, 1961); and G. Lenotre, *Two Royalist Spies of the French Revolution* (n.p., 1924), especially pages 101–124 and 162. I am grateful to George Constantinides for calling these references to my attention.

46. Thomas Powers, *The Man Who Kept the Secrets: Richard Helms and the CIA* (New York: Alfred A. Knopf, 1979), p. 41; and Rositzke, *The CIA's Secret Operations*.

47. Edward Jay Epstein, "The War Within the CIA," *Commentary* (August 1978), pp. 38–39.

48. Even Colonel Oleg Penkovskiy, one of the most productive Soviet sources the CIA has ever had, has not been immune from suggestions that he was a Soviet plant. See Joseph D. Douglass, Jr., "Soviet Strategic Deception," *Defense Science* 2002, 3 (August 1984): pp. 87–99.

49. David Martin, *Wilderness of Mirrors* (New York: Harper & Row, 1980), ch. 7.

50. When Philby first came under suspicion as a Soviet agent, he was the British Intelligence liaison officer in Washington in 1951. He subsequently sought asylum in Moscow. Felfe was arrested as a KGB agent in 1961. Philby and Felfe had both held positions as chiefs of counterintelligence operations against the Soviet Union—while they were working as KGB agents! One of the better books on the Philby case is Andrew Boyle, *The Climate of Treason: Five Who Spied for Russia* (London: Hutchinson, 1979). For a self-serving account of the Felfe case by the former chief of the BND, see Reinhard Gehlen, *The Service* (New York: World Publishing, 1972), pp. 245–251.

51. Martin, *Wilderness*, ch. 9.

52. Ibid., p. 173.

53. Ibid., pp. 175–176.

54. Ibid. On pp. 190–191, Martin states that the CIA's Soviet operations were "totally incapacitated," but Constantinides, *Intelligence and Espionage Bibliography*, p. 318, observed that Martin's account is considerably overstated on this point.

55. Henry Hurt, "Is This American a Soviet Spy?" *Reader's Digest*, Vol. 119 (October 1981), pp. 83–93. Also, three works by Edward Jay Epstein: "Disinformation: Or Why the CIA Cannot Verify an Arms Control Agreement," *Commentary*, Vol. 74 (July 1982), pp. 21–28; *Legend: The Secret World of Lee Harvey Oswald* (New York: Reader's Digest Press, 1978); and "The War Within the CIA."

56. Martin, *Wilderness*, ch. 7.

57. Epstein, "Disinformation," p. 26. For a discussion of a sensitive document passed to Polish intelligence through the Trust in 1926, see Bailey, *The Conspirators*, pp. 57–58.

58. Martin, *Wilderness*, pp. 74–89.

59. Ibid., pp. 100–102.

60. Stalin was reportedly especially strict on this point. Anatoliy Golitsyn recounts one case where Stalin fired a KGB officer for authorizing a Soviet agent to support his cover story by making public statements critical of the Soviet Union and a second case in

which Stalin refused to authorize passage of disinformation which created an impression of political instability in Poland. A. Golitsyn, *New Lies for Old* (New York: Dodd, Mead, 1984), pp. 21–22, and 42. Golitsyn's political analysis is controversial and properly so, but his factual reporting from personal knowledge of KGB activities was valuable and accurate.

61. Barron, *KGB Today*, pp. 379–380.

62. Personal discussion.

63. For a discussion of Soviet usage, see James T. Reitz, *Lexicon of Selected Soviet Terms Relating to Maskirovka (Deception)* (Washington, DC: Defense Intelligence Agency, DDB-2460-3-83, October 1983).

64. Based on Reitz, *Lexicon*; and Jennie A. Stevens and Henry S. Marsh, "Surprise and Deception in Soviet Military Thought," pt. 2, *Military Review*, (July 1982): p. 28.

65. Reitz, *Lexicon*, p. 5, condensing an article in *Soviet Military Encyclopedia*, vol. 5 (Moscow: Military Publishing House, 1978), pp. 175–176.

66. For a discussion of Soviet doctrine and World War II *maskirovka* experience, see Ziemke, "Soviet Deception in World War II;" Stevens and Marsh, "Surprise and Deception;" John Despres, Litita Dzirkals, and Barton Whaley, *Timely Lessons of History: The Manchurian Model for Soviet Strategy*, Report R-1825-25-NA (Santa Monica, Calif: Rand Corp., July 1976); Roger Beaumont, "*Maskirovka*: Soviet Camouflage, Concealment, and Deception," Stratech Studies SS82-1 (College Station, Tex.: Texas A&M University, Center for Strategic Technology, November 1982); John M. Caravelli, "The Role of Surprise and Preemption in Soviet Military Strategy," *International Security Review*, 6(Summer 1981), pp. 209–263; Jiri Valenta, "Soviet Use of Surprise and Deception," *Survival*, 24(March–April 1982); and Walter Kerr, *The Secret of Stalingrad* (New York: Doubleday, 1978).

67. Graham T. Allison, *Essence of Decision: Explaining the Cuban Missile Crisis* (Boston: Little, Brown, 1971), pp. 106–112.

68. For an account of the Boyce/Lee case and the compromise of satellite reconnaissance systems, see Robert Lindsey, *The Falcon and the Snowman* (New York: Pocket Books, 1980). For the Kampiles case, which compromised the technical manual for the KH-11 satellite photography system, see Andrew Tully, *Inside the FBI* (New York: McGraw-Hill, 1980); James Ott, "Espionage Trial Highlights CIA Problems," *Aviation Week and Space Technology* (27 November 1978):, pp. 22–27; or Henry Hurt, "CIA in Crisis: The Kampiles Case," *Reader's Digest*, 114(June 1979): pp. 65–72. For an account of damage done by Geoffrey Prime, who compromised U.S. and British communications intercept operations, see James Bamford, *The Puzzle Palace* (New York: Penguin Books, 1983), pp. 479–481 and 502–532 (only in the Penguin edition); or *New York Times*, 25 October 1982.

69. Beaumont, "*Maskirovka*," p. 1. notes a substantial increase in military press interest in *maskirovka* starting in the early 1970's. Stevens and Marsh, "Surprise and Deception," p. 33, cite a 1979 Soviet article that discusses with gravity a pervasive "lethargy" toward *maskirovka* in the Soviet Forces. Their reference is to an article by Colonel Iu. Malisov, "*Maskirovka—delo vazhoe,*" *Voennyi Vestnik* (1979) no. 12.

70. Victor Suvorov, *Inside the Soviet Army* (New York: Berkeley Books, 1984), pp. 123–130. Also by Suvorov, "GUSM: The Soviet Service of Strategic Deception," *International Defense Review*, Vol. 18 (August 1985).

71. Prados, *Soviet Estimate*, p. 43.

72. One of the more obvious problems from the Soviet point of view is the inability to know if a deceptive message is really received by U.S. intelligence. Reconnaissance satellites actually monitor only a fraction of what they are theoretically in a position to monitor. That which is monitored may not be processed in a manner that brings the deceptive message to immediate attention. Prados, *Soviet Estimate*, pp. 178–179, for example, notes that masses of unprocessed tapes were stored in boxcars at NSA. Under these circumstances, it is difficult for the Soviets to be certain a deceptive message has actually gotten through and had the desired impact.

73. Bittman, *Deception Game*, p. 21.

74. Michael I. Handel, "Intelligence and Deception," *Journal of Strategic Studies* 5 (March 1982): pp. 133–134. This valuable article was also published in Gooch and Perlmutter, *Military Deception and Strategic Surprise*.

75. Despres, Dzirkals, and Whaley, *Manchurian Model*.

76. Barton Whaley, *Strategem: Deception and Surprise in War* (Cambridge: MIT Center for International Studies, 1969), mimeographed, p. 70.

77. Ibid., p. 73.

78. Ziemke, "Soviet Deception in World War II," pp. 257–271.

79. The most extensive retrospective analysis of U.S. intelligence estimates of Soviet strategic forces is Prados, *Soviet Estimate*. While noting several instances of Soviet deception, Prados concludes that most estimative errors were caused by uncertainties inherent in the task. Also see Lawrence Freedman, *U.S. Intelligence and the Soviet Strategic Threat* (Boulder, Colo.: Westview Press, 1978), especially ch. 4. For a very critical view that attributes estimative errors to Soviet deception, see Epstein, "Disinformation." For a discussion of psychological pitfalls in conducting intelligence analysis and identifying deception, see Richards J. Heuer, Jr., "Cognitive Factors in Deception and Counterdeception," in Daniel and Herbig, *Strategic Military Deception*.

3
Themes of Soviet Strategic Deception and Disinformation

John Lenczowski

In C.S. Lewis' *Screwtape Letters*, Screwtape, an experienced devil, instructs his young understudy that a key task of a devil is to convince his "patients" that he does not exist:

> My dear Wormwood, I wonder you should ask me whether it is essential to keep the patient in ignorance of your own existence. That question, at least for the present phase of the struggle, has been answered for us by the High Command. Our policy, for the moment, is to conceal ourselves. Of course, this has not always been so. We are really faced with a cruel dilemma. When the humans disbelieve in our existence we lose all the pleasing results of direct terrorism, and we make no magicians. On the other hand, when they believe in us, we cannot make them materialists and sceptics.

Such deception is central to the effectiveness of the evil spirit in exercising his influence. Although some people will serve as his full-fledged and willing collaborators, that is, "magicians," most people will collaborate only if they are unwitting accomplices, if there is no external appearance of evil in their behavior, if they can rationalize their behavior as contributing ostensibly to some greater good, if they can be convinced that there will be no harmful consequences, or if they can be convinced that what they are doing may actually be good or otherwise socially acceptable behavior. In each circumstance, however, the appearance of evil must be modified or concealed in some way for the evil behavior to take place.

Screwtape's lesson is not without merit as a paradigm for the study of Soviet foreign policy. The devil's "cruel dilemma" is the communist's as well. On the one hand, the communist needs to make himself known in order to recruit fully collaborating "magicians." On the other hand, because a large part of Soviet-communist foreign policy is designed to effect political transformations of foreign countries against the wishes of their peoples and existing governments, the concealment of such policies is essential if they are to be effective. (This observation is based on the historical fact that the full majority of a free electorate has never elected a Communist Party into power, with the exception of tiny San Marino.) Such concealment is the conceptual origin of Soviet strategic deception.

Soviet deception efforts can be broadly placed into two categories: strategic and tactical. Tactical deception concerns questions of military and economic capabilities and political tactics; whereas strategic deception principally involves the question of political-strategic intentions. Tactical deception includes such things as the Soviet practice of *maskirovka*, the concealment and deception techniques having to do with Soviet military capabilities, and the doctoring of production and consumption statistics for the purpose of deceiving the world about Soviet economic capabilities and levels of military spending. Strategic deception, however, involves painting a picture of the entire political climate in which the Soviet Union operates among its allies and its adversaries. It involves the manipulation of concepts that describe the nature of the Soviet system and its leadership, its ambitions, its fears, its constraints. On a tactical level, it involves the manipulation of words that define the conceptual framework through which the Soviet Union is perceived. Its principal goal is to convince the non-Communist world that Soviet global intentions are other than what they are in reality.

The Basic Psychological Technique: Exploitation of Existing Tendencies of Thought

Soviet strategic deception succeeds not so much because of the ability of Soviet propagandists and agents of influence to deceive us, as because of our tendencies to deceive ourselves. Thus, the best Soviet strategic deception efforts are geared toward exploiting existing Western tendencies of thought. Principal among these is our tendency to engage in mirror-image perceptions, that is, where we tend to attribute to the Soviets such behavior as we would attribute to ourselves, to look upon the Soviet political system as similar to ours, to see the Soviet leaders as having motivations similar to our own, and to imagine that the Soviets have the same concepts of peace, common human decency, fair play, and national interest.

Soviet strategic deception also attempts to take advantage of our inclination to engage in wishful thinking or psychological denial. This manifests itself principally in our reluctance to admit the possibility of certain ugly realities. It may take the form of an unguarded optimism about the nature of the international situation or the Soviet threat. (In the context of our contemporary culture, for example, it has become a social *faux pas* to adopt an unduly pessimistic assessment about the nature of the Soviet threat to American vital national interests. And, it is equally bad form to use such taboo expressions as the word "communism" to describe political realities in the Soviet Union.) Solzhenitsyn calls this general category of behavior "the desire not to know." Ambassador Jeane Kirkpatrick calls it "the will to disbelieve the horrible."

We need only look at certain historical examples to bear out this analysis. We had the evidence that the Jews were being sent to their deaths in Nazi Germany and few were prepared to believe it. It was something that was either too ugly to look at or that we could not believe was possible. We behaved similarly when over two million people were sent to their deaths in Cambodia. Today the Soviets take advantage of such psychological inclinations by exploiting a number of themes that encourage us to believe that they are not so much of a threat to us as in fact they are.

The Central Deception:
The Soviet Union Is No Longer Communist

The principal theme of Soviet strategic deception is to convince the West that the Soviet Union is not communist any more. There are two basic objectives that underlie this theme. The first is to encourage us to believe that Soviet global objectives are no longer, of necessity, unlimited, as defined by the very nature of the communist system. Instead, the Soviets would like us to believe that they are a traditional, imperial, great power. As such, their objectives would not necessarily have to be unlimited by virtue of the requirements of their domestic political system. If we could be convinced of this, then it would follow that we would view the USSR as much less of a threat to our national security. First of all, we would no longer consider that the political transformation of the United States into a communist system must be one of the necessary goals of Soviet foreign policy. Secondly, it would follow that a spheres-of-influence policy would be possible between the United States and the Soviet Union. Finally, if we can begin to believe that Soviet goals are limited, then we may be more inclined to view appeasement as a legitimate diplomatic tool in our relations with the USSR. Appeasement, after all, is a legitimate policy option—particularly when the price we must pay to buy off another power is not unacceptably high. But this can be possible only when it can satisfy a limited appetite. Otherwise, if attempted in situations where the power in question has unlimited objectives—as was apparently the case with Naziism—appeasement can only whet that appetite and be perceived as a sign of weakness.

The second objective behind the theme that the Soviets are no longer communists, is to confuse us as to what constitutes the true source of U.S.-Soviet tensions. Much of Soviet propaganda, for example, promotes the idea that the "arms race" is the principal source of suspicion and tension between the two sides. If we accept this notion, then we can come to accept the possibility that our own behavior—our own efforts to defend ourselves—actually contributes to those tensions. And once we accept this, we put ourselves in the position of searching for things we can do unilaterally to reduce those tensions.

What then is the true source of tensions? As George Kennan once explained, a communist power hates America not because of what we do, but because of who we are. The very existence of America as a democracy represents a threat to the security of the Soviet regime. So long as our democracy survives, it will remain a living example of the viability of a system based on several essential ideas: government by the consent of the governed; a recognition of the fallibility of human nature and the consequent necessity of placing limits on those in power; and the idea that all men are created equal and are endowed by the Creator with unconditional rights. These ideas themselves are a major threat to the Soviet internal security system: to the Communist Party, they represent a potential ideological infection that could form the basis of internal resistance to its rule.

Insofar as we are committed to remaining a democracy and defending our sovereignty, we also represent an obstacle to the further advance and ultimate worldwide victory of communism. If Soviet communism ever meets such resistance, it risks suffering further major challenges to its internal security system. That system depends greatly on the continued success of communist expansion abroad. As Vladimir Bukovsky has explained, every time the Soviet regime conducts an aggressive action abroad, it is sending a message to its own people. That message says "Attention, people of the USSR! We can shoot down Korean airliners, invade Afghanistan, and send our Cuban proxies to Angola, yet not even the greatest imperialist power on earth can resist us. The imperialists have nuclear weapons and navies that can sail the seas, and they still cannot stop us. How, therefore, can you people, who are imprisoned behind the Berlin Wall, even contemplate resisting us?" So, if communism fails to advance in America or among America's allies, this may prove the predictions (or "laws") of Marxist-Leninist theory to be incorrect, and thus challenge the basis of the regime's legitimacy. Furthermore, if the U.S. and its allies successfully resist communism, thus halting or reversing the allegedly "inexorable forces of history," then the message is conveyed to peoples within the Soviet empire that, contrary to what the Communist Party would have them believe, resistance against the regime is indeed possible.

Thus, the Soviet regime judges its own historical progress in the world by measuring the political alignment of the world's different countries. Ultimately this measurement is achieved by determining which countries consider the Soviet regime to be a legitimate one. The very fact that we are a democracy means that we can never truly recognize the Soviet government as legitimate. It is this fact and its consequent threats to the internal security of the Soviet system that are the true sources of tensions between the United States and the Soviet Union. Therefore, so long as the Soviets remain communists, and so long as the United

States remains a democracy, there is nothing that we can do short of renouncing democracy and recognizing the Soviet government's legitimacy that could actually reduce the principal source of tensions between the two system.

Disinformation Themes

"The Ideology Is Dead"

Since the Soviets never directly come out and say that they are no longer communists, they have a number of other more subtle means of imparting this fundamental disinformation theme. One of the principal means is to get us to believe that the ideology is dead and therefore no longer politically operational in the USSR. Westerners are encouraged to entertain this assumption in a number of ways. Friendly Soviet trade representatives will make jokes about the ideological orthodoxy to American businessmen over canapes at industrial trade fair receptions. Western journalists in Moscow, who have neither learned Russian nor studied Soviet communism, will be told by the "unofficial sources" supplied to them by the International Information Department (upon whom they excessively rely for information to fill their dispatches) that the new Soviet leadership is more "pragmatic," and less doctrinaire when it comes to trying to solve many of the most intractable problems of the country. We are then showered with press reports that nobody in the USSR believes the ideology anymore. Ambassador Anatoly Dobrynin or visitors from the USA Institute in Moscow will conduct "remarkably frank" discussions with an earnest eye to overcoming mutual problems with American congressmen, lobbyists, or other habituees of the Washington diplomatic circuit. With these kinds of reinforcements, it becomes increasingly easy to view the ideology as simply a ritual atavism or antiquated relic that may be used for little more than to supply a veneer of tradition for the regime. It also becomes easy—especially for people who fancy themselves as pragmatic problem solvers—to wonder how anybody in the Soviet Union could possibly believe in the ideology when its predictions have so manifestly not materialized and when Soviet society appears to be such a failure.

This last perception, of course, is very much a function of the mirror-image tendency to apply Western standards of political-economic success and failure to a political system that arguably sets its purposes, defines its success, and establishes its priorities by entirely different standards. The perception that the ideology must be dead because it has failed is also a function of another type of mirror-image thinking, namely, the inclination to think that it is necessary to believe in an ideology for it to be politically operational. While this may be true in the United States, it is not necessarily at all the case in the Soviet Union.

What has been decreasingly understood in the West over the past two decades is that communist ideology is operational in the Soviet Union whether people fully believe in it or not. There are several reasons why this is so that deserve to be reviewed in this context. They all revolve around the central fact of political life of the Soviet regime—namely, that it does not rule by the people's consent. Because it is an illegitimate government by modern democratic standards, the regime must entertain the suspicion that, if the peoples of the USSR were free to choose their governors, they might not choose the Communist Party. This means that the Party has an internal security problem, the scale of which can be judged only by the scale of the measures imposed to address it: The Party-state's monopoly of information and communications; the vast domestic propaganda and political socialization apparatus; the control of the entire educational system, textbooks, literature, radio, television, newspapers, telephones, films, theater, music, and art; the use of the military as a vehicle of political socialization; the various specialized organs of agitprop such as the Znaniye Society; the KGB; the MVD's domestic militia; the Gulag Archipelago; the psychiatric "clinics;" the system of block committees; the system of border controls and customs; the pervasive jamming of foreign broadcasts; the internal passport system; the laws against unauthorized contact with foreigners; the exploitation of differences among Soviet nationalities for domestic security purposes; the Party-state's monopoly over employment, promotion, and job transfer combined with the parasitism laws; the persecution and control of religion; and so on. To make this internal security system work as well as it does, the Communist Party considers the ideology as an indispensable element, to be used in both the psychological and physical dimensions of that system.

The first use of the ideology in the psychological sphere is to supply legitimacy to the Party-state. Given its illegitimacy, the Party feels compelled to convince the people that there is a rational, practical, or moral reason why it deserves to be in power. The Marxist-Leninist ideology is the only vehicle that can be used for this purpose; hence it cannot be abandoned. That the question of legitimacy is one of the burning political issues facing the Kremlin can be understood only by extricating oneself from the American democratic political culture, wherein the legitimacy of our government has long been taken for granted.

While the ideology provides a legitimacy in theory to the Communist Party, that theory can only serve its purpose if it continues to be convincing. Because of the failure of the theory's predictions to materialize in the domestic sphere, the Party must find some other way to demonstrate that the theory itself is a legitimate one. The solution to this problem is found in the external sphere. So long as communism continues to advance around the world, the Party can plausibly claim that this is the result of an inevitable, law-governed, historical process. Then it can declare that it deserves to be in power because it is riding the crest of that wave of history that cannot be stopped. The global advances of communism thus supply credibility to the Party's claim to legitimacy. But legitimacy in its theoretical aspect cannot by itself assist the maintenance of internal security in the psychological dimension. What is needed in addition is the message to the peoples of the Soviet Union, as explained above, that the "inevitable" process of global communization spearheaded by the CPSU cannot be resisted either abroad or at home. This is the message that is designed to produce the attitude of fatalistic defeatism that can psychologically incline a people to be resigned to accepting the Communist Party in power.

The Party also makes use of the ideology in the "physical" sphere of internal security. The ideology is used to establish conformity in the society to discourage independent behavior, which could represent a challenge to the regime. The ideology, then, sets the standard against which deviation is measured and by which the self-discipline necessary for advancement within the Party is measured. It becomes the vehicle for determining friends and enemies of the regime, both domestically and externallly. When juxtaposed against the manifold instruments of coercion maintained by the regime, it contributes to what indeed may be the most efficient internal security system ever devised in history.

Under these circumstances, even the most highly placed members of the Soviet leadership must behave according to the ideology whether they believe in it fully or not. While the Party as a whole has it within its power to make doctrinal modifications, attempts by individuals to make such modification in theory or practice risk inviting charges of deviationism. That even the highest leaders are not immune from sanctions derived from such charges can be attested to by the ouster of Nikita Khrushchev whose excessively individualistic pattern of decision making was branded by his subordinates in the collective leadership as "opportunism" of various varieties that threatened the cohesion of the Party and the foundations of its control.

All this analysis is not to suggest that the character of belief in the ideology is utterly irrelevant or that the system could survive with absolutely no one believing any part of it. The question of the character of such belief or nonbelief is too complex to be covered in this context. Suffice it to say, however, that while many if not most Communist Party members may not believe in all the rosy predictions of the Marxian future, it is this writer's contention that most accept, and live by, a large portion of the basic philosophical and materialist premises of Marxism-Leninism. It is this fact that explains how "ideas have consequences" in the Soviet Union and how the consequence of those philosophical premises is the oppressive nature of its political system.

"Hawks and Doves in the Kremlin"

A second related disinformation theme, informally promoted by Soviet diplomats, scholars, trade officials, and others is the whole idea that there are such categories as "hawks and doves" in the Kremlin, or alternatively, Stalinists and moderates, ideologues and pragmatists, proponents and opponents of detente, hardliners and softliners, and so on. If the West can be convinced to accept the idea that such categories exist, then it follows that the Stalinist, hardline, hawkish, ideologues must be the communists, and, by implication, the moderate, pragmatic, softline doves must not really be communist anymore. After all, isn't there a faction in the Kremlin that must recognize the dangers of war in the nuclear age, and is willing to reach some kind of permanent peace with the West?

The idea that surely such a faction must exist derives, once again, from a mirror-image perception that there must be people in the Soviet leadership who are as rational as we are about problems of nuclear war. We, for example, do not seek actively to bring about the downfall of the Soviet regime. We recognize that any effort to present the Soviets with an aggressive threat to their regime might risk a major confrontation and possibly war. If there are Soviets who share the reciprocal prudent and rational view, then they could not possibly harbor such an aggressive design as the communization of the United States—surely the active effort to achieve such a goal would risk nuclear war. The conclusion of this logic, of course, is that there must be doves in the Soviet Union who are not truly communists.

If we can be brought to believe that Soviet politics represent a competition between polarized factions whose cleavages are so great that they make a considerable amount of difference for East-West relations, then we may well conclude that we should try to make a deal with the "doves," because it would be much more difficult to make a deal with putative "hawks." Similarly, we would have to support the "doves" in power because, should they be ousted by the "hawks," relations between the United States and the Soviet Union would get much worse.

To accept the idea that there are "hawks" and "doves" in Moscow, the division between whom makes a strategic difference, is to fail to understand the mechanisms of conformity built into the Communist Party control system. That system establishes discrete terms of political discourse that delineate certain definite parameters which cannot be exceeded without risking the Party's sanctions. While there may be disagreements within the Kremlin that may occasionally be manifested in the pages of the Soviet press, these invariably are not of a strategic nature. What may appear in the press to be disagreement between members of apparently differing groups within the USSR often represents nothing more than differences in emphasis based on the differing bureaucratic functions and foci of the authors. The genuine disagreements are almost always over differing assessments of the correlation of forces and correspondingly different tactical recommendations and never over system goals or general strategy.[1] As a matter of consistent policy, the Soviet press does not present debates on its pages: there is no juxtaposition of one article in favor versus another against. There are times, however, when the appearance of a debate may be orchestrated by the propaganda authorities: nothing could be easier than to insert an article in *Pravda* with one point of view and another article in *Kommunist* with an opposing view, with the purpose of providing "evidence" of factional struggle within the Kremlin for Western Sovietologists, whose fine-toothed combing of the Soviet press invariably unearths such "nuggets." Given the nature of deception, of course, it can never be possible to prove such an orchestration. However, to dismiss the possibility (or even the probability, under certain circumstances), given the totally controlled character of the Soviet media, the potential ease of such orchestration, and the testimony of numerous defectors who participated in this system is to indulge either in wishful thinking or in false mirror-imaging.

If we can be convinced that there are hawks and doves in the Kremlin, then we will have taken a big step toward believing that the Soviet Union is a great power like any other. As such, its foreign policy would not be principally a proactive policy as it would have to be if it were communist; instead, it would be a reactive policy, which would be more susceptible to external influences. Once we start thinking along these lines, we are well along the road toward applying to the Soviet Union the same stimulus-response model that we are accustomed to applying to any circumstance of international politics. This model, of course, postulates that all that is necessary to change the behavior of another actor in the international arena is to apply the appropriate stimulus and await the reward of a beneficial response. Needless to say, this model is not capable of coping with situations in which the actor may not be susceptible to external stimuli in such a way that could change the fundamental motivating engine of that actor's international behavior. Yet, if we cling to this model in spite of the facts, we put ourselves again in the position of having to search for things we can do unilaterally to improve relations with the USSR.

"The Individual, and Not the Party, Counts in the USSR"

A variation on the hawk-dove theme is the idea that individuals make a significant difference in the Soviet Union—specifically that the accession to power of a new individual can make a strategic difference in the foreign policy of the USSR. Every time we approach a succession in the Party leadership we are regaled with stories about the personality, tastes, and other personal predilections of the individual in question. Western journalists are encouraged by their Soviet hosts to look for every possible clue in the character of the new potential General Secretary, much in the same way that commentators attempt to divine the character of presidential candidates in the United States. The fundamental assumption here, of course, it that a new Soviet leader could bring about the same kind of vast changes in policy that a new president can in the American political system. We are thus encouraged in yet another way to believe that the Soviets are basically just like us and the Soviet political system is no longer communist.

This analysis, of course, is not to suggest that the individual makes no difference in the Soviet system. The question, once again, is whether the difference he may make is tactical or strategic. Until we have further evidence, we must proceed on the basis of historical experience—that is, that a new individual is not likely to change the basic goals and elements of Soviet strategy. In other words, an individual is unlikely to make the USSR cease to be communist.

"The Soviet Union Has Changed"

Another disinformation theme that contributes to the central deception is that the Soviet Union either has changed or is in the process of changing in a fundamental way. Playing upon our tendencies to engage in mirror-image perceptions and wishful analysis, this form of deception was realized early on by Lenin after he had been forced by circumstances to conduct some real changes in Soviet policy. When the exigencies of economic collapse impelled him to institute market reforms in the Soviet economy in the early 1920's, many in the West began to believe that the Soviet Union had come to its senses and was now willing to join the Western community of civilized nations. Seeing this manifest willingness to extrapolate on limited evidence and to derive wishful conclusions, Lenin saw an opportunity to take advantage of a classic example of the Western capacity for self-deception. He won all the financing, managerial expertise, and Western technology that he needed for the moment, yet continued to implement his communist program as he saw fit.

The wishful thinkers in the West again gave the most benevolent interpretation when faced with evidence that Stalin was restoring Russian nationalism, rehabilitating historic Russian figures, and permitting some freedom for the Church. Similarly, the de-Stalinization program under Khrushchev convinced many people in the West that the Soviet system was changing in a fundamental way and that it could no longer be called a totalitarian state. Although the vast numbers of political murders drastically declined after Stalin, none of the political structures and processes that had originally permitted those murders to take place changed at all. Again, when Western observers were confronted with the "Let a Hundred Flowers Bloom" campaign in China and the Democracy Wall, all too many of them were convinced that China was also changing in a fundamental way, indeed renouncing communism. In each case, the Soviets and the Chinese encouraged such thinking, and in each case the wishful thinkers were wrong. After a time, many recognized as much. Nevertheless, the immediate purpose of the communist strategic deception was realized: it succeeded in encouraging debate and disunity on policy making in the West.

"Soviet Military Doctrine Is Defense-Oriented"

Yet another set of disinformation themes contributing to this central Soviet deception falls under the rubric of military doctrine. Among these themes is the idea that the Soviet military is fundamentally deterrence-oriented and defense-oriented. Here Soviet doctrine is set forth in a way that would make it appear that Soviet strategy is essentially a retaliatory one and that Soviet military acquisitions are principally designed in reaction to those made by the West. Of course, not all Soviet military doctrine is presented this way. There are, as one can plainly see, clear-cut differences of opinion that appear within the pages of the Soviet press. However, all too often, Western analysts are inclined to view these as a debate between the different schools of thought or factions within the Soviet politico-military establishment, and rarely is it intimated that some of these doctrinal presentations could be composed primarily for foreign consumption and perhaps even for purposes of strategic deception. For what purpose, other than deception, did N.N. Azovtsev (or his editors or political superiors) completely reverse the message of a key sentence in the new edition of his book *V.I. Lenin and Soviet Military Science?*[2] As William C. Green discovered, the 1971 edition of Azovtsev's book states: "Our military doctrine has an *offensive* character." (p. 285, emphasis added.) However, in the 1981 edition, on the same page in an otherwise similar context, the sentence reads: "Our military doctrine, as already pointed out above, has a *defensive* character, with the goal of the protection of the gains of socialism."[3] (p. 290, emphasis added.)

"The Soviets Have a Self-Interest in Mutual Arms Control"

Related to this is the whole theory that the Soviets have a self-interest in arms control—that is, in limiting *their own* arms production. This theory is buttressed by two critical ideas that Soviet propaganda encourages us to entertain. One of these is the idea that the Soviets would prefer to spend their money on domestic, economic purposes, rather than on military purposes. This, of course, is the mirror-image of the situation in the United States. The problem with this proposition is that there is simply no evidence whatsoever to demonstrate that domestic economic goals have ever held a higher priority than the buildup of the Soviets' means of coercion.

Despite the tremendous volume of Soviet propaganda boasting of economic achievements on the one hand, and more recently, emphasizing the necessity of reforms to spur domestic production on the other, the purposes of the Soviet Party-state are just not the same as those of the American republic. Whereas increasing the standard of living for the greatest number is arguably one of our society's principal purposes, the same cannot be said of the Soviet Union. Furthermore, given the pattern of Soviet strategic deployments, there is no evidence to demonstrate that arms control has ever been used by the Soviets to divert resources from the military to the domestic economy. To the contrary, the weight of historical evidence shows that the Soviets have been willing to spend whatever they deem necessary, no matter what privations their people may suffer, to achieve their military-strategic goals.

It is plausible that the Soviets would not want to permit a full-blown arms race to bring about the collapse of the very industrial infrastructure that sustains military production in the first place. But that is not the same as saying that they would prefer to spend their money on the domestic economy. It is merely to point out that they do not want to see their military production capabilities destroyed by what, in effect, would be a major crisis in their system.

This gives rise to a second idea that buttresses the theme that the Soviets, especially in recent years, have had an interest in limiting their arms production through arms control agreements. This idea is that the Soviet economic system, and perhaps even the political system, is facing a tremendous crisis—one brought on by the strains of the arms race, which has allegedly pushed the Soviet economy to its limits. Although the Soviet economy may be facing some strains, there is a risk in applying too many mirror-image criteria to this analysis as well. Measured by standards of success and failure that we set for ourselves in the West, the Soviet economy may indeed be facing a crisis. But measured by the standards that they have set for themselves, especially judging by the priorities by which they choose to dispose of their resources, it is not clear that the Soviet economic system is facing any crisis at all. In fact, the case can be made that until the Soviets face: a crisis in their means of acquiring and adapting Western technologies; a crisis in their instruments of power and coercion—their military power, their secret police, and the internal cohesion of the Communist Party; a crisis in their means of maintaining ideological and political conformity and mass mobilization; and a crisis in their underground economy, which is the single vehicle for ensuring the survival of the population and compensating for the inefficiency of the planned economy; then there is some doubt as to how much we can say that the Soviet system is facing such a crisis that would render them desperately in need of the respite that an arms control agreement could accord them. Although tactical methods of economic and statistical disinformation may be involved here, the main deception may lie in the effort to convince the West that the Soviet system is not governed by priorities dictated principally by communism, but rather by priorities that are very much the mirror-image of those which we establish for ourselves in the West.

"The U.S. Is Not under Attack": The Indirect Approach

For a long time, the Soviets have been attempting to convince the United States and the West that we are not under low-intensity attack and that we are not the targets of communist political ambitions. There are two forms that this kind of deception has taken: an indirect approach and a direct approach. The indirect approach has emphasized the Soviet attempt to avoid any decisive confrontation with the main enemy in the imperialist camp. In the earlier years, this was done not only for the purpose of deception but also for the purpose of avoiding the risk of losing everything in such a confrontation. One tactic in this indirect approach is the use of localized conflict and a strategy of attrition: it is better to attack the principal center of imperialism by nibbling gradually around the edges of the Free World than by engaging in a major conflict. The use of proxies is another technique here. If it is Cubans, Bulgarians, or East Germans who are conducting the dirty work, then it is easy to convince enough people in the West that neither the Soviets nor the international communist movement have anything to do with it. Communist front organizations, of course, are yet another way of accomplishing this same objective. Although many people do recognize that front organizations are organized explicitly for the purposes of serving Soviet foreign policy objectives, enough people are misled by these organizations so that the Soviets can claim some success in sowing disunity within the ranks of the West.

"The U.S. Is Not under Attack": The Direct Approach

The effort to convince us that we are not under attack also takes the form of a much more direct approach. The peace movements in the West as well as Soviet peace propaganda work tirelessly to convince us that the Soviet objective is "peace" or "peaceful coexistence," as we understand those terms in the West. In fact, as the Soviets understand these expressions, peace is synonymous with communism, and peaceful coexistence is merely another form of class struggle, where all forms of struggle are permissible except all-out war. The Soviet policy of detente serves these purposes in a very direct way as well. An intrinsic part of this strategy is the effort to convince the Western business community that peace, as we understand it, can be made more possible by increasing the links between the two societies. If Western businessmen can buy the theory of "peace through trade," then by implication, they are convinced that the Soviets are not really communists and that, therefore, the communization of the West is no longer a Soviet goal. The very conduct of negotiations can also be seen to be a part of this kind of direct strategic deception. By merely sitting at the negotiating table, Soviet interlocutors encourage us to believe that *political* compromise is possible and to accept the idea that the Soviets have an identical interest in peace, stability, and world order.

"International Communism No Longer Exists"

Related to the idea that the Soviet Union is no longer communist is the persistent theme that the international communist movement no longer exists and that, therefore, the expression we have now expunged from our vocabulary, namely "international communism," should properly be considered archaic.

The Soviets long ago recognized that it is not in their interest to encourage the West to be conscious of an international communist threat to its bourgeois existence. Hence, they disbanded the Comintern and later, the Cominform. The same functions served by these organizations are carried out today by the International Department of the CPSU Central Committee. But the Soviets know that the International Department is effectively invisible to the West in comparison to its predecessors, with most of its political operations concealed from public view. If the international communist movement does not even have an organization that people can see, then how could it exist? The whole phenomenon of polycentrism, of course, supplies considerable fuel to this general analysis and, to be sure, the Sino-Soviet split, the Tito-Soviet split, and Albanian separatism have demonstrated that international communism is not a monolithic phenomenon. But there is a considerable difference between saying that it is not monolithic and saying, or assuming, that it no longer exists. How else can one explain the presence in Nicaragua in recent years, of Czechs, North Koreans, Bulgarians, Vietnamese, East Germans, Cubans, communist elements of the PLO, as well as of Soviets? Under the circumstances, it should not be beyond the realm of possibility that the Soviets could attempt to use what differences may exist even within the Warsaw Pact, such as Romania's independence on certain foreign policy issues, for purposes of encouraging us to believe that international communism no longer exists, even within the Soviet bloc.

Exculpatory Themes:
"The U.S. Military Threat"
and "Soviet Insecurity"

Another set of disinformation themes serves not only the purpose of strategic deception but also the political purpose of exculpating Soviet behavior. One of these themes is designed particularly to justify the Soviet military buildup. This is the theme that the United States poses a military threat to the USSR. Once again exploiting our mirror-image perceptions, the Soviets encourage us to put ourselves in their shoes: "If you had nuclear missiles pointed at you, wouldn't you have reasonable cause to be afraid?" Since the U.S. has such missiles pointed at the Soviets, it follows that they must have a legitimate cause to be afraid, and that the very existence of these missiles is prima facie evidence of a hostile American intention.

What is assiduously obscured in Soviet propaganda is the fact that the Soviet leadership for years has realized that the United States poses no offensive military geopolitical threat to the USSR whatsoever. They know that even during the most intensive periods of American anticommunism, periods that witnessed the American nuclear monopoly and military superiority, the United States maintained a consistent policy of avoiding any action that could possibly risk a military confrontation with the Soviet Union. They know that now, during the period of rough nuclear parity and in the wake of Vietnam when we have been even less anticommunist than we were in the 1950's, there is even less of a political constituency in favor of taking any hostile, offensive action against them. Instead of hearing, unequivocally, that Soviet leaders know these things, we hear a chorus of other themes that are designed to bolster the idea that they face a *military* threat which they can legitimately fear.

We often hear from Western commentators the theme about Soviet "paranoia." Paranoia can be either an irrational fear or a rational fear. Given that there is no military threat that the Soviets can fear rationally, the paranoia theme is something that amounts to nothing more than an insanity plea—in other words, an effort to excuse the behavior of an antagonist on the grounds that he could not perceive reality properly. While the Soviets are not necessarily the originators of this theme, they do encourage its repetition in the West. Constant reference to the "capitalist encirclement" helped fuel this perception of Soviet "paranoia" for many years. More recently, Soviet actions such as the shoot-down of the Korean airliner and the Kremlin's defense of the crime as a legitimate act of self-defense encourage Westerners to believe that such extreme Soviet touchiness about even the most innocent mistaken instrusions could only stem from paranoia.

Similarly, we hear Westerners repeat the argument about "traditional Russian insecurity" as if the Soviets, on the basis of a few experiences of external invasion, somehow have greater reason to feel insecure than any number of their neighbors. Again, while the Soviets may not necessarily have invented this expression, they do encourage its repetition by constantly reminding everyone, from scholars to tourists, of the times Russia and later the USSR were invaded, while scrupulously neglecting to mention the vastly larger number of times that they themselves were the aggressors. (In *Survival Is Not Enough*, Richard Pipes cites a study produced in 1898 by the Russian General Staff that recounts the history of Russian military engagements over the previous two centuries. Of the thirty-eight campaigns, the editor proudly observes that thirty-six of these were offensive, while only two were defensive.)[4]

Into the same category we can also place the constantly repeated theme about the "traditional Russian penchant for secrecy," a theme that is also designed to complement the Soviets' alleged paranoia and, therefore, to excuse their conduct when it comes to such things as the verification of international agreements. While the regimes of the tsars may indeed have necessitated secrecy, it is difficult to assert with confidence that this secrecy could be distinguished from that employed by either rulers or subjects in any other authoritarian, despotic, or militarily active regime throughout history in which secrecy served to protect insecure rulers, opposition movements, military operations, or national security. The Soviets, of course, have made secrecy an integral element of their apparatus of repression and their military buildup. Nevertheless, their travelling officials and propagandists encourage their Western interlocutors to believe that this is virtually a genetic characteristic born of the habits of old Russia. Although each of these themes has its own separate tactical utility, each works to bolster the fundamental strategic deception, namely, that Soviet objectives, motivations, and behavior may be explained by phenomena that are distinct from communism, phenomena that derive from national, historical, and cultural propensities.

Themes to Keep the United States on the Defensive

Some disinformation themes are designed for the specific purpose of keeping the United States on the defensive. Principal among these is the Soviet attempt to define the boundaries of the battleground in the struggle between the two political systems. Although the expressions are not often used currently, the Soviets have divided the world into the "peace zone," the communist world, and the "war zone," those countries in which capitalism and imperialism (the source of war) continue to prevail. Proceeding from this division, Soviet propaganda encourages the West to believe that anything that occurs within the peace zone is something off-limits for international concern, whereas anything that occurs in the war zone is something that should be the focus of such concern. A scrimmage line, therefore, has been drawn, and it is impermissible for the West to cross it. The inviolability of that line is bolstered by the constant threat that war would break out should that line be breached. One must commend the Soviets for the remarkable success that this psychological conditioning operation has enjoyed over the years. In 1956 this deception had already succeeded in convincing the United States against giving any material support to the Hungarian Freedom Fighters lest World War III break out.

The whole idea that the USSR is not only strong and ruthless but unbeatable is designed specifically to complement this delineation of the international battleground. By creating a climate of fear and intimidation, the West is encouraged to remain solely on the defensive, while the Soviets and the international communist movement choose the time, place, and venue of offensive action. Whether intended for such purposes or not, the way the Soviets handled the aftermath of the shoot-down of the KAL 007 demonstrated their ability to take advantage of such a situation for deceptive purposes. By embracing the shoot-down as a legitimate act of state policy and threatening to do it again if similar circumstances arose, the Soviets served their enduring purpose of convincing the world that the USSR makes good its threats. If we can become convinced of this, then it follows that we should be all the more restrained in any behavior that could conceivably be interpreted as the smallest step across the inviolable scrimmage line.

Themes to Keep the U.S. from Taking the Offensive

A final set of disinformation themes designed to serve the broader purposes of Soviet strategic deception consists of those that have the ancillary purpose of preventing the United States and the West from taking the offensive. First among these is the notion that the USSR has no domestic vulnerabilities. From this we are supposed to infer that there is no need to exploit any vulnerabilities. Primarily, we are encouraged to believe that there is no domestic opposition to the Soviet government and that the peoples of the Soviet Union have willingly resigned themselves to Soviet rule. Essential to this general disinformation theme is the continuous effort to conceal the existence of millions of people within the USSR whose relatives and friends have been victims of the regime over the years. This, of course, principally consists of deception by omission rather than commission. Just as the Soviet media never report on such domestic disasters as airplane crashes, neither do they mention the occurrence of strikes, demonstrations, riots, or other forms of civil unrest within the country, which are much more widespread than is commonly believed in the West.

Structural/Institutional Deceptions

In addition to themes that are disseminated by the Soviet propaganda apparatus and implanted in the Western press and academic literature through other means, the Soviets have constructed a panoply of various institutional entities that serve the broader purposes of strategic deception. Their main purpose is to encourage Westerners to accept Soviet ersatz reality as genuine reality. Once again the goal is to convince us that the Soviet state is a state like any other and not a communist state with unique objectives that are irreconcilably opposed to the very existence of democracy in the world. The key to the success of each of these deceptions is semantic manipulation and distortion. These structural/institutional deceptions are too numerous to spell out individually, but suffice it to mention a few. For example, the Soviets have a "constitution." The purpose of this, of course, is to convince the West that the Soviet Union is governed by the rule of law, just as we are in the United States. Even American presidents have cited the Soviet constitution as evidence that certain rights and freedoms are guaranteed in that country.

The Soviets also conduct "elections." These have very high "voter" turnouts, which are designed to impress the world with the broad base of social support enjoyed by the regime. Rarely are we reminded that in these "elections" there is no choice on the ballot for the "voters" except for the Communist Party candidate and that the high voter turnouts are nothing more than ritual exercises in coercive mass mobilization. The people being elected serve in such capacities as members of the Supreme Soviet, a "parliamentary" body that engages in interparliamentary exchanges with American congressmen. The very existence of this Supreme Soviet and its bogus parliamentarians is designed to encourage us to believe that these parliamentarians actually represent real constituencies.

The Soviets have the institution that they call the *kolkhoz*—the "collective farm." The impression one is supposed to get is that this is a cooperative enterprise on the part of a number of individual farmers, whose combined efforts are designed to produce greater efficiencies, economies of scale, and so forth. The reality, of course, is that these are farms directed by an external bureaucracy that operate under a system of repression. The farmers work when they are told to do so and not according to their own judgments about the time to sow and the time to harvest. They are told what to plant and what not to plant, and they receive only such fruits of their labor as the state will authorize them. A more accurate term to describe these people would be *serfs*. And what they call *kolkhozy* or *sovkhozy* (the state farms) would more accurately be called *plantations* for want of a better term. So long as more accurate words are not used to describe such phenomena, Soviet semantic manipulation will continue to encourage us to believe that ersatz Soviet reality is genuine reality.

The Soviets publish things that they call "newspapers" and the articles written in these so-called newspapers are written by people they call "journalists." The United States government gives journalistic credentials to these writers who appear at news conferences at the State Department and White House. Sometimes they participate in journalistic exchanges. In fact, these people are nothing more than paid propagandists who are hired to present current realities entirely within the context of the Marxist-Leninist world view and to serve the foreign policy interests of the USSR.

The Soviet government has a division called the "Ministry of Foreign Affairs." This ministry establishes embassies in foreign countries, that are manned by diplomats, who negotiate with Western governments various agreements, which are part of the broader framework of "bourgeois" international law by which the Soviet government abides from time to time. While the Soviet Foreign Ministry indeed performs these functions, the impression the West is supposed to get is that this ministry is just like the U.S. State Department or the foreign ministry of any other normal state—that is, the principal institution making foreign policy and conducting foreign relations.

What is obscured by this institutional deception, however, is that the USSR has other foreign affairs institutions whose role in policy making is considerably more important than that of the Foreign Ministry. One is the Central Committee's International Department, whose job is to further the interests of the Party-state and international communism, regardless of the strictures of bourgeois international law and to work to transform that body of law into communist international law: that is, a new law based on the principles of proletarian internationalism. The policy conducted by this department works deliberately at cross-purposes with that conducted by the Foreign Ministry. Whereas the latter ostensibly accepts the legitimacy of bourgeois states, the former works toward the overthrow of those states. Another institution is the Central Committee's Department for Liaison with Communist and Workers' Parties of Socialist Countries, which is the principal policymaking institution in charge of relations with other Communist Party-states. Since, according to the principles of proletarian internationalism, relations with fraternal parties are more important than state-to-state relations, the kind of foreign relations conducted by this department represents the ideal model of the relations desired by the Kremlin. Finally, in contrast to the usual practices in Western foreign ministries, which have their own control over personnel policies and most diplomatic assignments, all personnel appointments to key foreign policy posts in Moscow and to foreign diplomatic posts abroad are controlled by the Central Committee's Party Organs Department. What is obscured, in other words, is that the Communist Party's institutions are the leading foreign policy agencies and that the foreign policy of the USSR is a bifurcated one with one part deceptive conventional diplomacy and the other part the foreign policy of international communism.

The Soviets have organizations that they call "trade unions," the members of which they call "trade unionists." Sometimes these people try to come to the United States to meet with "fellow" trade unionists. However, there is at least one organization in our country that understands this form of structural/institutional deception and which takes it seriously—that is the AFL-CIO. The AFL-CIO recognizes that when such a trade unionist comes from the Soviet Union, he is not, in fact, a genuine trade unionist representing the interests of the working people, but is rather a Soviet agent of influence disguised as a trade unionist who is trying to come to this country for other political purposes.

The Soviets permit the continued existence of the Russian Orthodox Church. They like to emphasize, vocally and often, that there is freedom of religion in the USSR. In fact, in 1917 there were 77,000 churches in Russia alone. Today, in the entire Soviet Union there are only some 7,000 churches. Nevertheless, whenever somebody such as the evangelist Billy Graham shows up in Moscow to pursue his ministry, the Soviets trot out a couple of well-trained metropolitans who strive to give the visitor the impression that religion is free and prospering within the Soviet Union. Somehow we rarely hear about the fact that many of these "prelates" have either been coopted by the KGB or, in fact, are KGB agents who have received seminary training and who have entered the Church to ensure that it does not acquire a momentum of its own or deviate in any substantial way from what is expected of it by the Soviet regime.

A brief survey of such structural/institutional deceptions should not go without mention of the vast apparatus known as Soviet "tourlandia." This is the modern-day series of Potemkin villages that have been set up by the regime to impress all foreign visitors in the Soviet Union. This part of the Soviet Union, which comprises about 1 percent of the land area of the country (the other 99 percent being off-limits to foreign visitors), receives the lion's share of the state's resources to give the impression that the Soviet Union is a more modern and prosperous country than in fact it is. Visitors and tour groups are given the benefit of an Intourist guide, who invariably is a direct agent or cooptee of the KGB. This guide ensures that visitors see only what the regime wants them to see and that individuals do not stray too far from their tour group. While it is possible, with some effort, to see things that the regime would prefer to keep from the view of the Western public, the average visitor will encounter certain simple, yet generally effective, obstructions. It is difficult, for example, to take a day train from Moscow to Leningrad, because the regime prefers that travellers not see the nineteenth century living conditions in the Soviet countryside. The only train usually available for this journey leaves at midnight and arrives at 8:30 the next morning. Some tours of the Soviet Union include a visit to the Soviet War Memorial at *Khatyn*. This memorial to the Soviet war dead was constructed specifically to confuse visitors about what happened at *Khatyn* where 10,000 to 15,000 Polish officers were massacred during World War II by the red Army and shoved into mass graves. Visitors are encouraged to lay wreaths at numerous war memorials and are constantly reminded that the Soviets lost millions of people during World War II and, because of this, never want to see war again. These same visitors never get to see the graves of Soviet soldiers who lost their lives in Afghanistan.

Conclusion

It is the combination of the various disinformation themes, tactical policies, and institutional/structural deceptions that makes up the overall Soviet effort at strategic deception. Taken together, they are aimed principally at influencing the entire intellectual-analytical climate in which the USSR is perceived by the West. In addition to taking advantage of our tendencies to engage in mirror-imaging and wishful thinking, we must not forget that Soviet strategic deception exploits yet another related Western tendency of thought—our frequent inability to discipline ourselves mentally in such a way as Alain Besancon counsels us to do when analyzing the USSR—namely to force ourselves to believe the unbelievable. This may be especially difficult when the popular culture and contemporary etiquette (which is surely much more important than truth) consider a focus on communism and particularly on its more unbelievable features a subject of humor and ridicule: It is to see a "bogeyman—a communist—under every bed." As Screwtape observes, under such circumstances, deception is all the easier to achieve:

I do not think you will have much difficulty in keeping the patient in the dark. The fact that "devils" are predominantly comic figures in the modern imagination will help you. If any faint suspicion of your existence begins to arise in his mind, suggest to him a picture of something in red tights, and persuade him that since he cannot believe in that (it is an old text book method of confusing them) he therefore cannot believe in you.

Since we are so unaccustomed to believing the unbelievable, lest we risk being branded as analytical extremists, the Soviets know that Danton's strategic advice is particularly applicable here: *"De l'audace, et encore l'audace, et toujours l'audace!"* Hence the enduring success of the technique of the "big lie"—not only does it disturb the comfortable parameters of our perceptual frame of reference but it also works to desensitize us to the significance of deceptions—such as front organizations—that we have long taken for granted. Only when we grasp the nature of our perceptual vulnerabilities and realize that the intent of Soviet deception is to translate those vulnerabilities into politico-military-strategic vulnerability, will we begin to understand that Soviet strategic deception itself is a form of low-intensity aggression against the United States and the forces of freedom in the world today.

Notes

1. For a more extensive analysis of how disagreements within the Party are principally on matters of peripheral political significance, see John Lenczowski, *Soviet Perceptions of U.S. Foreign Policy* (Ithaca, N.Y.: Cornell University Press, 1982), ch. 7 and conclusion.
2. N.N. Azovtsev, *V.I. Lenin i Sovetskaia voennaia nauka* (Moscow: Nauka, 1971 and 1981).
3. William C. Green, *U.S. Interpretations of Soviet Publications on the Nuclear Weapons Policy of the USSR 1950–1980*, Ph.D. dissertation, University of Southern California, 1986, ch. 5: "1975–1980 Polarization and Politicization." See also ch. 7: "Soviet Disinformation and Strategic Deception Concerning Its Nuclear Weapons Policy."
4. Richard Pipes, *Survival Is Not Enough* (New York: Simon and Schuster, 1984), p. 38.

4
Soviet Active Measures and Democratic Culture

Arnold Beichman

> The United States of America has long shown itself to be the most magnanimous, the most generous country in the world. Whenever there is a flood, an earthquake, a fire, a natural disaster, disease, who is the first to help? The United States.
> And what do we hear in reply? Reproaches, curses, "Yankee Go Home." American cultural centers are burned, and the representatives of the Third World jump on tables to vote against the United States.
> —Alexander Solzhenitsyn

> The distinctive mark of our century is the humility with which democratic civilization agrees to disappear and works to legitimize the victory of its mortal enemy.
> —Jean-Francois Revel[1]

Introduction

How is it possible that anti-American feeling, both at home and abroad, remains high despite the fact that the United States, by any standards, has encouraged more of that rare virtue—plain, simple decency—than any other society in memory? How is it possible that anti-American feeling remains high in the face of almost seven decades of Soviet history—decades of barbarism, savagery, and inhumanity, of an esurient imperialism that has destroyed whole nations?

Let us begin by acknowledging that this anomaly is a solid fact. For example, the UN has not, in any of its resolutions, condemned the Soviet Union *by name* for its invasion of Afghanistan, much less for its destruction of the Chechen ethnic group, the starvation of millions of Ukrainians, and the persecution of Jews, Christians, and Moslems. These undeniable facts simply are not a part of international discourse. On the other hand, fourteen UN resolutions denounced the United States by name in 1982, and sixteen in 1983.[2]

No one argues directly that the United States has perpetrated such crimes. The United States does not have forced labor camps; it lives under a rule of law; racism is ebbing; it does not shoot down unarmed passenger planes; it permits free worship, and generally its government hesitates to interfere with the Bill of Rights; it holds free elections with tedious regularity on village, county, state, local, and national levels; its media is undoubtedly the freest, most irresponsible, and most untouchable in the world; it has given far more money than any other world power to the UN and its ancillary agencies for four decades. As a country, it is embarrassed at not yet having reached utopian perfection. Immigration today is all in the direction of the industrial democracies, especially to the United States. (A special issue of *Time* recently revealed that an amazing two-thirds of all immigration in the world consists of people entering the United States.) People who live in socialist countries do what they can—swim, walk, crawl, fly, sail—to escape from Socialist repression, no matter the risks to life and limb. Yet the United States seems to be the international polecat.

No matter. Hundreds of thousands around the world sit in or march, or even bomb, to emphasize to the world just how detestable is the United States. The USSR, on the other hand, is predictably forgiven because it has not incorporated into its political system any humanitarian standards to violate, except on the meaningless parchment of the Helsinki Agreement. In fact, as far as the left-liberal culture is concerned, its acolytes never hold grudges—against the USSR, that is. Such an anomalous, even unnatural, state of things does not just happen. It can only be brought about by carefully shielding the prejudices of certain "bourgeois leftists" from reality and, of course, by carefully crafted "active measures," both overt and covert.

This chapter argues that Soviet active measures (AM) work best in cultural circles that are already in tune with the Soviet propaganda line—that is, with people who have already disposed themselves to think well of socialism and ill of the United States, and who are accessible to the influence of Soviet officials. The most prominent of these are "regulars" such as Georgi Arbatov, the peripatetic director of the Soviet Institute for the Study of the USA and Canada, and Vladimir Posner, a frequent guest on U.S. television news programs. The overt part of Soviet AM also includes visits and appearances by Soviet delegations of diverse specialists. These overt measures serve a key purpose. Anytime a Soviet spokesman or delegation is treated as a legitimate interlocutor in a give-and-take, the impression is necessarily conveyed to the participants and to the audience that the Soviets stand on at least the same moral plane as others. From that position of moral equivalence, the Soviets can, and do, wage their psychological attacks. In some instances, Westerners eager to make the Soviet foreign policy line acceptable argue that because things are improving in the Soviet Union while they are deteriorating in the United States, that the Soviet Union has actually reached a higher ethical plane than the United States now occupies. For example, Richard J. Barnet, cofounder of the radical left Institute for Policy Studies, says that America is suffering from

> A decline in official respect for human rights [while] ironically, one area of the

world that can point to some improvement . . . is the Soviet Union, which . . . is far from the giant concentration camp that Stalin made it.[3]

Another example of moral equivalence, a rhetorical technique that has become so usual, so normal that it is hardly noticed anymore, is a paragraph from a review by Professor William Taubman, a political scientist at Amherst, of a book by Raymond L. Garthoff:

> He [Garthoff] is also right that America was hardly a patsy in the 1970s. In addition to trying (in Mr. Kissinger's word) to "expel" Russia from the Middle East, Washington aligned itself with Moscow's arch rival, China, helped topple President Salvador Allende of Chile, conspired against the Communists in Portugal and frustrated Soviet designs elsewhere—all the while proclaiming, more sanctimoniously than the Russians, that detente's rules of mutual restraint must be obeyed.[4]

Here is moral equivalence with a vengeance. In order to be even handed, the professor feels compelled to imply that there is not much difference between the two societies. But he cannot help charging that his country behaves "more sanctimoniously than the Russians" and is, therefore, worse than the USSR.

Moral equivalence as a tool for predisposing free people to accept the totalitarian message is neither new nor of Soviet invention. The *New Yorker*, some years ago, began one of its casuals by stating that a document which describes the Russian methods of forced labor and exile had been obtained by the British government and that it was about to be submitted to the United Nations. The *New Yorker* then pointed to what it called the growth of " . . . a group of American political prisoners who are being marched steadily, imperceptibly, toward the queer Siberia of our temperate zone."[5]

It certainly was an imperceptible march. All of this is to say that Soviet active measures do not aim at brute force conversions of dyed-in-the-wool democrats so much as at the mobilization of minds already predisposed. That mobilization, in turn, affects the bulk of Western societies—but slowly and indirectly.

AMs work best among those who are eager to accept Soviet fabrications. When these fabrications are not forthcoming, they themselves produce hazy images of American Siberias. For example, the direct targets of Soviet active measures do not bother themselves to ask whether or not a Soviet-inspired story that the CIA assassinated Mrs. Gandhi is true. It is enough for them that the story, regardless of its truth, weakens the United States and tends to destroy trust between the United States and its allies or neutral countries. Who cares who killed Mrs. Gandhi? So long as the person predisposed to believe the message understands its virtuous intention—the overthrow of U.S. power—he will then spread it to a wider public. That receptive public will get the core of the message: the United States is bad. It does not matter if doctored conversations between

President Reagan and other democratic world leaders (manufactured by splicing different sentences of their public speeches) show up on European television and radio shows and are recognized as such. If the forged words show that President Reagan is going to start a nuclear war, there will be no cognitive dissonance—that is, no inconsistency between attitude and behavior among large sectors of opinion for whom such sentiments have become the conventional wisdom. In such circles, exposure of a story's untruth or fraudulence does not diminish its purveyor's standing. That standing rests on the purveyors' intentions—on their alignment against U.S. imperialism and for progress. One might say that the Soviet approach to AM is reflected in the old Italian maxim: *Se non e vero, e ben trovato* (If it is not true, it should be).

In emphasizing the importance of intention, I am dissenting from Professors Shultz and Godson, who argue that the objective of disinformation is to manipulate target groups to believe in the veracity of the message.[6] In fact, the reason that false messages have been so impervious to the truth, purveyed by U.S. films, literature, Voice of America broadcasts, translated films on TV, and so forth, is that the identity and the intention of the message sender proves more important to the recipient than its substance or veracity.

The Problem

The Soviet Union has been able to capitalize on this tendency to value intention above truth because of its unique historical achievement, the rise of a whole class of people whose rule of life is the slogan, *pas d'ennemis a gauche*, "no enemies on the left," as well as the availability of Western "High Culture" * to Soviet active measures. The "no enemies on the left" syndrome was well expressed by Jean Paul Sartre:

> Russia is not comparable to other countries. It is only permissible to judge it when one has accepted its undertaking, and then only in the name of that undertaking.[7]

This rule of life bans criticism of the Soviet Union as "red-baiting" and automatically places all Soviet actions beyond suspicion. The Soviet Union shoots down a 747 passenger plane, killing 269 people. Much of the world's press naturally focuses on possible U.S. wrongdoing and even complicity in the affair. Suspicion becomes accusation and, in turn, becomes an indictment of the United States through a process that never confronts the question of whether and under what circumstances the USSR or any other nation would be justified

---

* "High Culture" is represented by a self-styled political-literary avant garde in a democratic society. High Culture seeks a dominant, indeed a monopoly, role in determining societal values so that they will run counter to prevailing values.

in shooting down an unarmed passenger plane. Such a question would be too embarrassing for the USSR and for those inclined to enhance the Soviet image at the expense of the United States.

But how can anyone deal with any question while consciously neglecting its very core? The answer is to absorb into one's very habits and bones the slogan: "no enemies on the left." Acceptance of that slogan makes a defense of communism such as Jean Paul Sartre's, "To keep hope alive one must, in spite of all mistakes, horrors, and crimes, recognize the obvious superiority of the socialist camp."[8]

Thus, "to keep hope alive," which is defined as the highest good, anything that might be anti-Communist must be unacceptable. And when those who cherish that hope must refer to anti-Communists, say, in reference to anti-Castro Cubans, the words must often be prefaced by a pejorative adverb, such as *rabidly* anti-Communist. By the light of that hope, of course, no one can ever be rabidly anti-Fascist or rabidly anti-apartheid or rabidly pro-Sandinista. Indeed that hope sanctifies all excesses perpetrated on its behalf and condemns as excessive anything at all done against it. One would never have suggested in defense of facist "mistakes, horrors, and crimes" the cloying excuse that you cannot make an omelette without breaking eggs, so effectively used to excuse Communism's murder of millions in the 1930's.[9]

"No enemies on the left" guarantees that the arrival on the international stage of a new Soviet *vozhd* (leader) will be accorded a friendly welcome in the Western media and among Western foreign policy establishmentarians. We need but recall the good cheer that greeted Yuri Andropov's alleged passion for scotch and cheap American novels in the *New York Times* and the *Washington Post* within days of his accession. Similar treatment was accorded the arrival of Mikhail Gorbachev, although instead Gorbachev was praised as someone with whom the West could do business. In addition, the very same people who find President Reagan's wife obscenely well dressed, find in Raisa Gorbachev's gold lamé slippers and expensive clothes good omens for world peace and even more reasons for being flexible in making concessions to the Soviet Union.

"No enemies on the left" means that the Soviet Union's daily labors for the overthrow of so-called imperialist systems because of the laws of Marxism-Leninism must be accepted as progressive or at least inevitable, while President Reagan's "crusade for freedom" speech must be greeted with catcalls about strident rhetoric endangering world peace. "Soviets Paint Reagan as the New Hitler," read a headline in the *Wall Street Journal* (12 September 1984), while *Pravda* was running caricatures of President Reagan as Hitler. Had an official State Department organ or the Voice of America referred to a Soviet executive as the new Hitler, there would have been a deafening uproar in the establishment media and excoriation of President Reagan for endangering the peace.

The Soviet Union can hold monster parades in Red Square on May first or on the anniversary of the Bolshevik Revolution to show off its latest missiles, its latest artillery, its massed troops, its tank corps, its fighter jets overhead. The Soviet leadership looks on benignly at all that military power and waves collectively at banners imprinted with slogans calling for victory over "imperialism" and for "crushing" a variety of enemies. Were President Reagan to hold a similar march before the White House with similar demonstrations of hardware, slogans, and massed troops jackbooting it along Pennsylvania Avenue, it would not be forgiven him.

The night of President Reagan's reelection and for days thereafter, the stock-in-trade of commentators was to assure their audiences that Reagan's landslide victory (forty-nine out of fifty states) in no way implied a mandate to the Republican victor from the U.S. electorate to do the things for which he had campaigned all his life. On 11 March 1985 (the day that Mikhail Gorbachev was announced as Chernenko's successor), no one in the media questioned that Gorbachev had every right in the world to take his country wherever he could manage to take it. But the world did see and hear interviews with all kinds of friendly Soviet propagandists praising Gorbachev as the "New Soviet Man." Offering no evidence whatever, Seweryn Bialer exploded the startling revelation that Gorbachev was a man "open to new ideas."[10] What those "new ideas" might be we were not told. The impression was clear: whither this dictator leads, so many in the Western press were willing to follow. But these very same people would emphatically resist Ronald Reagan moving in the direction approved by forty-nine out of fifty states in a free election.

Another aspect of U.S. political culture that makes life so easy for Soviet AM is that the derelictions of U.S. democracy are a running news story day and night, broadcast after broadcast. No Soviet story ever gets an on-the-scene followup with the same thoroughness as does U.S. activity (or inactivity) in Central America. There may be a number of writers, such as William Shawcross, who are trying to run down the story of the Soviet aggression against Afghanistan, but when and if they get that story, will it receive the same attention that Shawcross received with his report on Southeast Asia and his tendentious assault on Henry Kissinger? Said Meg Greenfield:

> A Martian reading about [the world according to journalism] might in fact suppose America to be composed entirely of abused minorities living in squalid and sadistically run state mental hospitals, except for a small elite of venal businessmen and country commissioners who are profiting from the unfortunates' misery.[11]

This sort of thing has consequences. For example, at a recent American Political Science Association convention a professor discoursed on the superiority of Soviet trade unions to U.S. trade unions. Now, it is not remarkable that someone should take such an outrageous position. What is remarkable is that the non-Stalinoid members of the panel, all distinguished political scientists, plus the audience, listened stolidly without a murmur. Had another speaker suggested, say, that trade unions in South Africa were superior to those of the United States (by the way, at least South African unions actually exist while Soviet unions do not), he would undoubtedly have been booed off the platform as an intolerable racist. But it has simply come to be out of the question, that is, in bad taste, to object to anything Soviet. The vast majority of those who follow this custom could not justify doing so, they merely follow it.

Why the Problem?

How has it happened that a responsible sector of U.S. public opinion demands a higher standard of behavior from the U.S. government than it does from the Soviet Union? Why are serious and probable charges against the Soviets, even when admitted, regarded as minor peccadilloes, venial sins, while President Reagan's speech to the British Parliament in June 1982 is still regarded as a mortal sin? Is it all due to Soviet active measures? We can begin to answer these questions by noting where the problem does *not* exist—that is, among the U.S. workers. For example, to this day there have been no exchanges of trade union delegations between the AFL-CIO and the Soviet or Bloc trade union organizations, despite enormous pressures on the U.S. labor body to do so. There is assuredly a harmony of view between the AFL-CIO leadership and the rank-and-file membership. The laborers' resistance to Soviet active measures is all the more remarkable given the amount of effort that the Soviet Communist Party has dedicated to making the working class into a transmission belt for Soviet foreign policy. One of the most instructive case histories of Soviet AM against the labor movement is the historic relationship between the British Trades Union Congress and the Soviet All-Union Central Council of Trade Unions.[12] There is an extensive scholarly literature that deals with Soviet AM against trade unionism, an integral part of Soviet national security policy, and transitional strategy.[13]

For the Kremlin, labor is a target area because Soviet leaders believe that:

1. The international labor movement has become so important in world affairs that it can play a role in shifting the balance of forces in a pro-Soviet direction.
2. The socialist world is gaining strength while the capitalist world, unable to solve its socioeconomic problems, grows weaker.
3. Détente is a form of class struggle and a method of weakening capitalist states by intensification of ideological struggle.

Although the Soviet Union is no longer as confident as it was in the post–World War II era about successful exploitation of international trade unionism, it still maintains a powerful transmission belt in the World Federation of Trade Unions (as competition for the International Confederation of Free

Trade Unions). There can be no understating the significance that international trade unionism plays in Soviet AM strategy. But while U.S. workers cannot seem to forget the basic facts about Communism, a large sector of the intellectual classes are imbued by a leftist mystique that is impervious to facts.

This difference between strata—the average man and his intellectual betters—is recognized by Soviet AM managers. For example, Alexander R. Alexiev, a Rand scholar, has noted that the Soviet campaign against intermediate-range nuclear forces (INF) had a two-tiered strategy: a "campaign from above" and a "campaign from below." (This distinction was noted in the 1930s, when the Comintern sought a "united front from below," that is, with the working class, rank-and-file union membership and also sought a "united front from above," that is, with union officials.) In the INF campaign, a full-scale Soviet "peace" offensive and the "campaign from above" were directed at European establishment and decision-making elites with the aim of overturning the deployment decision. The "campaign from below," through concerted "active measures," sought

> To exploit European and especially West German popular fears, anti-Americanism, and misgivings about nuclear arms to create sufficient mass opposition to prevent deployment.[14]

Few have noted that, although the "campaign from above" scored success after success and piled up endorsement after endorsement, the "campaign from below" failed miserably. Despite the talk of mass anti-Americanism, the parties favoring deployment of American missiles and closer relations with the United States won elections in every European country affected by the INF plan. Thus, when the U.S. government tried to counteract the Soviet Union's campaign against INF by trying to negotiate with the left wing of Europe's Social Democrats, it played directly into the Soviet Union's strength, because among the most trusted and true allies of Soviet Communism today is a large part of the Social Democratic left. Its spokesmen such as, inter alia, Willy Brandt; the late Olaf Palme of Sweden; the British Trades Union Congress; President Mitterand's aides, Jack Lang and Regis Debray; Australia and New Zealand left-liberalism; the Michael Harrington wing of social democracy in the United States; and the Canadian New Democratic Party specialize, at best, in anti-anticommunism; at worst, it flacks for any so-called new nuclear arms initiative from the Kremlin or, for that matter, from any other Soviet proposal on any subject whatsoever.[15]

The Essence of Soviet Active Measures

The essence of Soviet active measures is simply to calumniate the United States of America. Lenin in his fashion understood something that Tacitus has described:

> [W]hile men quickly turn from a historian who curries favor, they listen with ready ears to calumny and spite; for flattery is subject to the shameful charge of servility; but malignity makes a false show of independence.[16]

The United States became the Soviet Union's chief target for two reasons: it is the primary obstacle to Communism in the world, and it is the primary focus of the resentment of the world's intellectuals, would-be intellectuals, and members of the High Culture. One key to this resentment is the inevitable discrepancy between democratic ideals in theory and those ideals in practice—that is, the difference between *le pays legal* and *le pays reel*. Propaganda that points to such discrepant politicocultural behavior can create the kind of guilt, especially among the intellectual classes, that arises from unfulfilled utopianism.[17] Such discrepant behavior has a *tu quoque* advantage for Soviet propaganda targetted to domestic opinion, namely to demonstrate the many "failures" of U.S. democracy. And since the first target of Soviet AM are the Soviet peoples,[18] reports of such "failures" are particularly useful in controlling internal public opinion when the AM managers deal with the problem of human rights violations in the USSR and Eastern Europe. Whatever is necessary to weaken the *glavni vrag* (Russian for "main enemy") can be adopted without regard to what the Soviets call "bourgeois morality." What is the weakness of the non-Communist world? The "quality of life" discrepancy between the industrial democracies, headed by the United States, and the emerging Third World. Therefore, the weapon to be fired is anti-Americanism, defined by Leonard Schapiro as

> The cement by which the Communist movement is held together, now that the unity of doctrine and disciplined allegiance to Moscow have been eroded as a consequence of the Sino-Soviet split.[19]

Marxism has a special value to Soviet AM. It supplies the essential rationale for anti-Americanism, which, Lewis Feuer points out "early became a Marxist theme, for America offered a social alternative that threatened to reduce Marxist modes of thought and feeling to irrelevancies and absurdities."[20]

Professor Hook has written that

> The disillusioned fellow-travelling American intellectuals have bequeathed anti-Americanism rather than pro-Communism to the contemporary generation of disaffected intellectuals. This anti-Americanism is manifest on every issue in which there is a conflict between the Soviet Union or one of its proxies and the American national interests, whether in Central America, Africa or Western Europe.[21]

I would amplify Professor Hook's astringent comments and argue that, without latter-day Marxism, which has become an ideological anti-Americanism, Soviet AM would have little chance of success among left-liberal intellectuals. To a Marxist, a capitalist democracy is antihistorical, antiprogressive and, therefore, doomed by the impersonal workings of history. When a Marxist state such as the USSR commits some atrocious act, the Marxist intellectual can shrug it off by saying what happens far away is no concern of his brand of Marxism. And he can still march with the Soviet-inspired battalions, whether it be for Nicaragua or the environment.

Conclusion

A theoretical model of the "Soviet Marxist Concept of Propaganda" (or "propaganda-as-science" in the Soviet sense) created by Professor Paul Kecskemeti may be helpful in understanding the basis of present-day Soviet AM:

1. Revolutionary Marxism makes no sharp conceptual distinction between instrumental (that is, promotional, propagandistic) and informative (that is, factual, theoretical) communications.
2. The basic presuppositions of all thought systems, are designed to promote either the cause of the exploiter or that of the exploited.[22]
3. Since theory and practice are inseparable, the distinction between truth and falsehood applies to thought-action complexes identified either with the cause of exploiter or exploited not to "factual-theoretical discourse," as in the Western norm system.
4. Since Leninism rejects relativism in favor of "absolute truth," revolutionary propaganda of the working class and its vanguard *is* truth. Everything else is reactionary propaganda.
5. The principle of unity of thought and action means that theory must be applied to concrete issues. No matter how the principle is applied by the Party leadership, its assessment of a given situation and its concomitant application is always correct because the Party is the embodiment of not only absolute but also scientific truth. An error in assessment and application to a concrete issue only means that the Party learns from its mistakes. In other words, whatever the circumstance and outcome, the Party's possession of "absolute truth" is presented in terms either of infallibility or flexibility.
6. Because Soviet AM targets differ in educational background, there is necessarily one approach for ordinary people, "agitation," as distinguished from propaganda proper. Agitation (of internal and external public opinion) seeks to stimulate mass action by hitting a salient feature of a given situation (that is, outrageous, iniquitous, threatening) whereas propaganda would provide a better-educated audience with "a comprehensive conceptual

framework for dealing with social and political reality "scientifically" in all its aspects."[23]

On the basis of both the model and Bolshevik history, one can be certain that the pressures on non-Soviet elites to adapt themselves to Soviet foreign policy aspirations will expand during the next few years to a greater degree than in the past. As U.S. rearmament and U.S. research and development continue at their present high level, the intensity of Soviet AM can be expected to spread to new areas of the world hitherto relatively untouched, such as the archipelagic island states in the South Pacific. Despite all the above, we do not now have enough data to understand adequately how Soviet active measures work in our democratic society. The following measures would be helpful in acquiring such knowledge:

1. The Senate and House committees on intelligence oversight ought to undertake, jointly or separately, as thorough a public investigation of KGB activities as is consistent with considerations of national security. Such a study has been called for by Senator Malcolm Wallop (Republican, Wyoming).[24] In 1982, a Senate panel held hearings on Soviet active measures, but they were limited in their scope and of relatively short duration. While the KGB has been written about extensively (although not to the degree that the CIA has been written about), by and large, such activity has been undertaken by writers and some scholars with little, if any, access to classified materials. A congressional committee could have a positive effect on such classification with a view to increasing public knowledge through useful documentation.

2. The media must more and more be supplied with properly documented materials presented by reliable scholars, witnesses, and defectors about Soviet AM. If American investigative reporters applied their considerable skills to following the tracks of Soviet disinformation to its sources, we would see a quick expansion of what is now a small body of knowledge about Soviet or surrogate intelligence activities.

3. The U.S. government should give greater encouragement (largely by releasing as much intelligence data as possible) to scholars and organizations such as the Consortium for the Study of Intelligence that research and provide the public with solid understanding of intelligence matters—inter alia, Soviet AM. Giving increased currency to the harsh realities of intelligence and active measures within the academic community would help to challenge the Marxist ethos that has spread and continues to spread in American universities. No more useful ally, witting and unwitting, to Soviet AM is to be found in America than the metastasizing influence of Marxist academics in our universities.[25]

Notes

1. Jean-Francois Revel, *Comment les Démocraties Finissent* (Paris: Bernard Grasset, 1983), p. 14.
2. The United States Ambassador to the UN, General Vernon Walters said, in August 1985, that the so-called nonaligned nations vote "86.2 percent of the time with the Soviet Union." *Washington Times*, 21 August 1985, p. 3–A.
3. *New York Times Magazine*, 26 April 1981, p. 106. For a full expression of this concept, see Jeane J. Kirkpatrick, "Doctrine of Moral Equivalence," U.S. State Department, Current Policy No. 580, 9 April 1984.
4. *New York Times Book Review* (30 June 1985), p. 7. Review of the book by Raymond L. Garthoff, *American-Soviet Relations from Nixon to Reagan*, (Washington, D.C.: Brookings Institution, 1985). Another example of moral equivalence that always works out against the United States. In Britain, the BBC *Today* program, on the morning after the expulsion of three Soviet diplomats for spying, asked a Foreign Office minister whether the action was consistent with the Thatcher government's "professed desire to improve Anglo-Soviet relations." As Peregrin Worsthorne wrote in the London *Spectator*, (27 April 1985), p. 7:

> Surely, any normal person might feel that the act inconsistent with wanting to improve Anglo-Soviet relations was the original act of spying, rather than the British Government's reaction to this provocation. But when the Soviet Union is involved, common sense seems to give way to sycophancy to a degree that has to be heard to be believed.

5. *New Yorker* (6 August 1949). Permission was requested from the *New Yorker* to use the full text of this piece. Permission was denied. *The New Yorker* stated that "we have been in contact with the author's estate and are very sorry to have to tell you that the material is not available for the use you suggest." Consequently we have paraphrased the quote to the extent possible and used only enough of the quote to stay within the legal limits of "Fair Use" copyright law (the editors). An even earlier example of this pernicious moral approach was the statement, shortly after the end of World War II, by former U.S. Ambassador to the Soviet Union Joseph Davies. He said that "Russia in self-defense has every moral right to seek atomic-bomb information through military espionage if excluded from such information by her former fighting allies." *New York Times* (19 February 1946), p. 10. This statement was published coincident with the 1946 Canadian atomic spy scandal, for which, see *Report of the Royal Commission* (Ottawa: Controller of Stationery, 1946). Also, "Testimony of Former Russian Code Clerk Relating to the Internal Security of the United States," *Senate Internal Security Subcommittee* (11 January 1955). The reports on the Igor Gouzenko affair are one of the best case histories of Soviet AM.
6. Richard H. Schultz and Roy Godson, *Dezinformatsia: Active Measures in Soviet Strategy*, (Washington, D.C.: Pergamon-Brassey's, 1984).
7. Jean-Paul Sartre, "Merleau-Ponty," in *Situations* (London: Hamish Hamilton, 1965), p. 266. In fairness, one should point out that the slogan is of minor importance to people not on the left. In 1981, Soviet Bloc debts to Western banks and governments were more than $80 billion. When General Jaruzelski imposed martial law on Poland, a leading New York bank executive, Thomas Theobald of Citibank, commented: "Who knows what political system works? All we ask is: Can they pay their bills?" Quoted in John W. Coffey, "Profit Is Not Enough," *This World* 11(Spring 1985): p. 110. Also see, Joseph

Finder, *The Red Carpet* (Cambridge: Harvard University Press, 1984). This is a study of wealthy pro-peace American influentials such as Averell Harriman, David Rockefeller, Armand Hammer, and others who give full faith and credit to the Soviet regime. Also, Paige Bryan, Scott Sullivan, Steve Pastore, "Capitalists and Commissars," *Policy Review* 22(Fall 1982): pp. 19–54. The article points out that under the Kissinger-Ford-Carter-Vance rubric of détente and interdependence, a massive foreign aid program of government credits and guarantees to the Soviet Bloc far exceeded U.S. credits to Western Europe even under the Marshall Plan and even after allowing for inflation.

   8. Quoted in Francois Bondy, "Jean-Paul Sartre," *The New Left*, ed. Maurice Cranston (New York: Library Press, 1971), p. 52. H.G. Wells, visiting Russia after the Revolution, wrote: "Apart from individual atrocities, it did on the whole kill for a reason and to an end." Quoted in George Watson, *Politics and Literature in Modern Britain* (Totowa, N.J.: Rowman and Littlefield, 1977), p. 49. An even more ghastly sentiment was expressed by G.D.H. Cole: "Much better to be ruled by Stalin than by a pack of half-witted and half-hearted Social Democrats." Ibid., p. 67.

   9. The omelette metaphor is attributed to Beatrice Webb. When an eyewitness told her about Stalin's starvation of the peasants in the Ukraine she replied, "I know, but you can't make an omelette without breaking eggs." Watson, *Politics and Literature in Modern Britain*, p. 52.

   10. Seweryn Bialer, "Gorbachev's Tightening Grip on Power," *New York Times*, Op Ed Page, 14 July 1985. The exact quote: "Mr. Reagan will find Mr. Gorbachev a young and energetic man, open to new ideas and firmly in charge of his country's foreign and security policy."

   11. Meg Greenfield, "Why We're Still Muckraking," *Newsweek*, 25 March 1985, p. 94.

   12. For a fascinating examination of this relationship, see Daniel F. Calhoun, Jr., *The United Front: The TUC and the Russians, 1923–1928* (New York: Cambridge University Press, 1976). Also, see the essay-review of the Calhoun book, Arnold Beichman, in *Labor History* 19(Spring 1978): pp. 312–318. Soviet AM can sometimes become the cause of internal Soviet debate as in the TUC-AUCCTU relationship.

   13. There are actually few studies of organized labor's role as an instrument of Soviet national security policy. See Roy Godson, *The Kremlin and Labor: A Study in National Security Policy* (New York: Crane, Russak, 1977); Joseph R. Starobin, *American Communism in Crisis, 1943–1957* (Berkeley: University of California Press, 1975); Alfred Fernbach, *Soviet Coexistence Strategy* (Washington, D.C.: Public Affairs Press, 1960); Daniel Bell, "The Background and Development of Marxian Socialism in the United States," in *Socialism and American Life*, Donald Drew Egbert and Stow Persons, eds., (Princeton, N.J.: Princeton University Press, 1952). The writings of Professors John P. Windmuller and Philip Taft on international trade unionism and the Soviet Union would be indispensable to such a study.

   14. Alexander R. Alexiev, "The Soviet Campaign Against INF: Strategy, Tactics, Means," N-2280-AF (Santa Monica, Calif.: Rand Corporation, February 1985) p. 5.

   15. Nick Eberstadt has discussed the frequently striking differences between the general public and elite political cultures on foreign policy, in this case the discrepancy between the two groupings over U.S. foreign aid policies. In "The Perversion of Foreign Aid," *Commentary*, 79(June 1985): p. 19, he writes:

> This cleavage between the public and opinion-makers is highly significant. At different times in American history the general public has come to an understanding about the world before its leaders. . . . The American people seem to recognize an important fact about world affairs that continues to elude their leaders—namely, that the American government's efforts to bring relief, prosperity, and security to impoverished peoples in other countries have gone seriously wrong.

Regarding Social Democracy and the Moscow relationship, see David Gress, "Whatever Happened to Willy Brandt?" *Commentary*, 76(July 1983): p. 94.

16. *The Histories of Tacitus*, Book I, 1, (Loeb Classics), p. 3.

17. In Ithiel de Sola Pool and Wilbur Schramm, eds. *Handbook of Communication*, (Chicago: Rand McNally, 1973), p. 844, Paul Kecskemeti defines propaganda as "streams of instrumentally manipulated communications from a remote source that seek to establish resonance with an audience's predisposition for the purpose of persuading it to a new view that the propagandist prefers."

Among the devices used by the propagandist is "channel sharing": introducing his message into channels that already carry attractive material to which the audience voluntarily turns.

18. At a cost of $300 to $500 million a year, the USSR and the Bloc try to jam Western news and feature radio broadcasts. Arnold Beichman, "The Story of Radio Free Europe," *National Review*, 36(2 November 1984): p. 29.

19. Leonard Schapiro, statement, before Subcommittee on National Security and International Operations (16 April 1970), 91st Congress (Washington, D.C.: U.S. Government Printing Office, 1970), p. 34. Professor Schapiro in the same statement described détente as "an illusion current among some of the Western powers."

20. Lewis Feuer, *Marx and the Intellectuals* (New York: Anchor Press, 1969), pp. 4–5.

21. Sidney Hook, "Communism and the American Intellectuals: From the Thirties to the Eighties," *Free Inquiry* (Fall 1981), p. 15.

22. That dichotomous, either-or concept is, of course, pure Leninism (V.I. Lenin, *What Is To Be Done?* (New York: International Publishers, 1969), p. 40:

> Since there can be no talk of an independent ideology formulated by the working masses themselves in the process of their movement, the *only* choice is—either bourgeois or socialist ideology. There is no middle course (for mankind has not created a "third ideology").

23. Kecskemeti in Pool and Schramm, *Handbook*, pp. 849ff. The model may be better understood in the context of a literary interpretation of Soviet rationality. In "The USSR at the Moment of Brezhnev's Death," *National Review* 15(Winter 1981): pp. 93–101, Solzhenitsyn has written that

> We would understand nothing about Communism if we tried to comprehend it on the principles of normal human reason. The driving force of Communism, as it was devised by Marx, is political power, power at any cost and without regard to human losses or a people's physical deterioration.

24. *Washington Times*, "Wallop Issues Call for Probe of KGB," 20 July 1985, p. 6. Considering the surrogate intelligence agencies like those of Eastern Europe and Cuba, Wallop described the KGB as "a multinational corporation of espionage and active measures." The Senator, in 1985, had completed eight years as a member of the Senate Select Committee on Intelligence, during which, as a quasi-subcommittee of one, he supervised CIA budgetmaking.

25. See Arnold Beichman, "Is Higher Education in the Dark Ages?" *New York Times Magazine*, 6 November 1985, p. 46 and passim.

Part II
Language, Ideology, and Diplomacy

5
On Soviet Linguistics: Expropriating Utopia

Robert Bathurst

> In the beginning was the Word.
> —John 1:1

When we read the following bizarre statements of General Secretary Gorbachev for the instruction of the French prior to his 1985 visit to Paris, we know that we are in a world where words have a different relationship to reality than the one to which we are accustomed. It is the world described in the language of Sovietspeak. Gorbachev said:

> Historical experience has convinced us that Russia's peoples made the right choice in 1917 when they made the Revolution and did away with exploitation and social and national oppression. . . . All of this is discussed widely and openly in our society, on a democratic basis. . . . And, of course, we devote paramount attention to seeing to it that the norms of social justice, the democratic rights of citizens and Soviet laws are strictly observed.[1]

One could easily dismiss such assertions as egregious lying or tedious propaganda, but that would be to miss the point. Gorbachev is speaking in a language that has a special relationship to its own "reality," its own vocabulary, and its own grammar. It is Sovietspeak—a language largely formulated by Lenin and enriched by Stalin, who forced the entire Soviet empire to practice it. It is now an international language, the lingua franca of the Leninist socialist movement with even an Ethiopian dialect.

Secretary of State Shultz, conferring with Gorbachev, and later President Reagan, when speaking to the Soviet people, assured them that "we do not threaten your nation and never will."[2] Their words could be translated into Russian, but not into Sovietspeak. If the President and Secretary of State did not understand that the United States does not have to *do* anything to threaten the USSR, that it is enough just to *be*, and we are a threat, then they are among a distinguished group of political leaders, beginning with Franklin D. Roosevelt, who did not understand the Soviet language.

What is remarkable about this language is that it is not, for the most part, a deception. Its grammar is coherent and consistent. The problem is that many in the West, even after the experience of seven decades, have not learned to translate it. Therefore, what passes for deception is really self-deception.

The grammar we are discussing has at least five voices: (1) for speaking to foreigners (as Gorbachev did above); (2) for speaking to other elite Leninists; (3) for speaking to the Soviet and other captive peoples; (4) for speaking to free people; and (5) for speaking to the Third World. For example, when we read the following about the late, pallid, Soviet leader Leonid Brezhnev, we know that it is in the second voice—that of the Soviet elite ritually speaking to itself:

> The most eminent politician of the modern world, by whose example we must educate ourselves to work in a Leninist way, to think in a Leninist way, and to live in a Leninist way.[3]

This eulogy of Brezhnev—a Soviet creation who tried but did not become a Leninist icon, although by the end of his life he had acquired sixty medals (fourteen more than the World War II hero and military leader, Marshal Zhukov's forty-six)—was made by the present Foreign Minister, E. Shevarnadze, in an address that he termed a "business-like" appraisal of the general secretary. When Shevarnadze talks to Western leaders in what we would call a business-like way, two languages are obviously functioning.

In discussing the Soviet grammar, it is useful to understand the problem of form and content. There is often a mistaken supposition that the same words in our two languages, such as "peace," connect in the same way and operate in a similar context. The most simple example is the use of "good" and "bad." In Sovietspeak, "rich" is always "bad" and "poor" is always "good." That is because the words are understood in an economic, not a moral, context. This is particularly true in comparing the Soviet and American military establishments in which there are similar vocabularies: strategy, operations, victory, military science, and so forth. These words, in their national context, have quite different meanings and will be discussed later.

"Democracy" as used by Gorbachev is another oxymoron. What he means is "dictatorship of the proletariat," a term that Lenin formulated and used interchangeably with *democracy*. Indeed, by 1922, Lenin had so identified his will with what he considered the sensible will of the people, that he ruled by a process that was to become institutionalized as interpreting the state as an extension of his thought. By that time, when he spoke of the bourgeoisie and the privileged, he was always turning the words upside down, for it was the Communists in power who were the privileged, and their collaborators who were to succeed as the new bourgeoisie. The originals had become outcasts, deprived of identity.

The apparatus of the Soviet state is another example of the different form. A modern country has a constitution, newspapers, congresses, a foreign ministry, literature, art, and science. The Soviet Union adopts the same forms, but the content is different. The newspaper is a government propaganda organ; the constitution, like the Helsinki Accords on human rights, has not been in effect for one day; the congresses do not debate, and they make no choices; *Glavlit* censors writers, and the Writers' Union is not a union; the Academy of Sciences is not an academy, but an arm of the political control of scientists; and so forth.

The Grammar of Sovietspeak

There are two curious aspects of the verb in the new Soviet grammar. First there are its tenses: the future and the past are the primary tenses because the Soviet verb cannot very well relate to the present. In an official sense, the present does not quite exist. Life is becoming; the past, history, is the changeable property of the Party. To speak of the conditions of the present has often been a crime—a slander on the Soviet state, the future workers' paradise. Accurate knowledge of the present is often a state secret; the past has become part of the changeable mythology; the radiant future is all that is real. Mention that there was starvation in the 1930's—even Khrushchev referred to cannibalism in the Ukraine—is again censored. For example, a doctor of history, a member of the Academy of Sciences, describes the cause of the death of several million people:

> At the same time, the numerical size of certain major nationalities declined between 1926 and 1939. The low growth rate among Ukranians [due to the genocidal policies of the Moscow government] was due to a decline in the natural increase connected with the 1932 crop failure in the Ukraine.[4]

"Decline in the natural increase" is, of course, Sovietspeak for unleashing terror in the countryside, confiscating grain, and withholding aid from inside and outside of the Soviet Union. (Leninist Ethiopia had a precedent for dealing with famine during a period of the consolidation of power.) Until recent years, the death of some of the heroes who disappeared was attributed to the "excesses of the cult of personality," but even that explanation is no longer being used. Thus, it will be impossible for those now being educated to know anything about the Stalin purges except through hearsay.

The Soviet seizure of history, of the past, of the right to determine who may remain in history and who is to be abolished, deprives the Soviet citizen of logical references. He may understand that he lives in a fictional world, but he has trouble distinguishing its dimensions. The Molotov-Ribbentrop Pact was described in *Pravda*, 24 August 1939, as a "pacific act" that would contribute without a doubt to "a lessening of the atmosphere of tension in the international sphere." Rather than learning that it led to the partition of Poland, the occupation of the Baltic states and other territorial aggrandizements that made World War II possible, the Soviet citizen now hears that he is surrounded by the same imperialist enemies who unleashed "an uncompromising class clash between the first country of victorious socialism and the strike detachment of internationalist imperialist reaction, fascist Germany . . ."[5]

Why Soviet troops marched into Poland and the Baltic states is not a mystery either.

> To save the population of these oblasts from Fascist occupation, by an order of the Soviet government, September 17, 1939, the Red Army crossed the border of White Russia, thus uniting its brother in the East within the framework of the Ukranian and White Russian Socialist Republics. But there remained a serious threat of German-Fascist aggression against the peoples of Latvia, Lithuania, and Estonia.[6]

Finland would be next, but without such an easy solution.

Another function of history in Sovietspeak is to reinforce the conception of isolation in a hostile world. The most terrible event in the memory of the Soviet people is World War II. Soviet history has, in many ways, rewritten that war as one without Soviet defeats, fought alone against great odds with the unstable support of conniving and evil allies. A recent publication, solemnly introduced by a respected historian who is a director of an institute of the Academy of Sciences, explained the Yalta Conference as follows:

> History has put on the record in clear-cut terms the political moves made by our partners both before the war and during it. Great Britain and the USA were deliberately and purposefully taking an active part in preparing the Second World War in the hope that it would be spearheaded against the East, against the Soviet Union and that after the land of socialism was defeated they would be in a position to harvest golden fruits once their imperialist competitor—Nazi Germany—had been brought to his knees.[7]

A second aspect of the verb in Sovietspeak is that it is heavily militarized. This was, undoubtedly, the influence of Lenin who often expressed himself in militant terms. "We must accompany our steps towards peace with all of the pressure of our military preparedness," Lenin typically wrote. (That sentence is a short course in modern Soviet strategy.)

Beginning with him, decrees, slogans, and analyses were and are all heavily dependent on military concepts: "attack" a problem, "mobilize" the masses, "liquidate" the opposition, "open a front," etc. Workers and intellectuals also are "recruited" into Sovietspeak. They are "shock workers," (*udarniki*), a "vanguard," "cadres." The militarized vocabulary engulfs all of life. Art has been called "a powerful weapon" in class warfare. Musicians are admonished to "march at the front;" accountants, must observe "Bolshevik vigilance;" in psychoneurology, once it was permitted, workers "opened an offensive."

The current usage differs very little from the language of the Bolsheviks. Here is an admonishment at the twenty-fifth CPSU in 1976:

> In the keen ideological struggle which our party is waging, an important part is played by our musical art. The ideological struggle is also taking place on the musical front. We must strive for the ideological, artistic purity of popular music, resolutely defending this field of our musical life from the penetration of philistine sentiments and bad artistic taste.[8]

Verbs also have moods in Sovietspeak. Slogans, for example, employ the imperative. The people are always admonished on the anniversary of the Revolution to accomplish herculean tasks: "Workers of the World, Unite!" is, of course, a sacred antique; "Hail Proletarian, Socialist Internationalism!" emphasizes the current foreign policy without giving obvious direction; "Brotherly Greetings Communist and Workers' Parties" is rather like the commercialized sentiments on Christmas cards. Another perennial admonition is to "Put the decisions of the __th Party Congress into Life!." There are calls for international action that tell the Soviets of the terrifying world around them: "Demand the end of aggressive U.S. acts against Nicaragua;" "Get the Israeli troops out of captured Arab lands;" "Stop Imperialist interference in the affairs of Arab Countries!" and so on.

To many observers, such slogans seem harmless enough. After all, what can anyone do about them? But if they are understood in the context of the mythical world that the Soviets have created, then their function is clear: they are the frightening reminders of the surrounding enemy who can unleash violence, famine, and war at any moment. Circled by a bewitched forest, the average Soviet citizen, like a child, is not allowed to go out of the circle of light.

Capturing Reality

Creating a fictional world on such a scale cannot be done, as Lenin realized, without violence. The men who spoke for utopia learned how to use slogans for that purpose. In the first two decades after the revolution there was so much terror, hunger, and death that even World War II was greeted with relief. The slogans—"All Power to the Soviets," "All Land to the Peasants," "Expropriate the Expropriators," "Liquidate the Kulaks as a Class"—were followed at various times by civil war, chaos, and starvation throughout the country. After such an experience, the Soviet citizen does not read slogans with the same bored puzzlement that the West read them. Bored he may be, but he understands their latent power.

The slogans became weapons for controlling the masses. For example, the slogan "Exterminate the Kulaks as a Class" established that there were Kulaks, that they were evil, and that history no longer needed them. But in a village where after years of war, revolution, and starvation, everyone was very poor, there were few distinctions between classes of peasants. Who were the poor peasants, the middle, and the rich? Still, action was demanded. Quotas were assigned. So many Kulaks had to be found in each village and they were to be liquidated. Fathers, mothers, and their children were loaded onto barges, which were then sunk in midstream as one expression of the new consciousness. In one of the more bizarre episodes in history, through the power of the word, largely fictional class distinctions were created; a whole family's life depended on whether it had one, but not two, cows.

One of the major assaults in Sovietspeak was on the noun. Renaming things, creating new people, and liquidating others, helped to wipe out the past and suspend the individual in the mythical socialist dark forest. To isolate the people from their history, towns, cities, boulevards, parks, palaces, and historic monuments disappeared and were born again as tributes to the conquerors of the Red October.

Ceremonies and traditions were transformed. There was a Red Easter, a Red Baptism. Christmas became the new year. Churches and cathedrals became museums of athiesm. Heroes of the past were created or refurbished—such as Aleksandr Nevsky and Ivan the Terrible, or eliminated—such as Trotsky and Bukharin. Marriage and family were assaulted. Only love of the party was recognized.

That was what was happening to Russian culture; the cultures of the subject peoples in the Soviet empire were being treated even more brutally. The eternal friendship of peoples was being declared, while the national literatures, histories, languages, and leaders were being exterminated.

Fortunately, the period when girls were named Industria, Kommuna, Oktyabrina, and boys named Red Flag, Spartacus, or Vladlen did not last beyond the 1930's. Nevertheless, the need for a disguise forced the creation of many aliases, for instance, for Jews who did not fit the parameters of the new classless society.

The Grammar of Construction

One of the first fruits of the new Leninist regime was to confiscate the proper noun, to seize identities, to eliminate, in effect, the personae. As the dead Marx gave no notion of how a workers' state was to be run, and as he did not instruct

Communist Party members through visions and dreams, as the dead Lenin was to do, his conception for ruling a totally materialistic and scientific state had to be interpreted by the Bolsheviks. To establish their authority, they called themselves the vanguard of the proletariat—in effect they put on a mask. (Their qualifications to speak for the workers were dubious, indeed, considering that very few of them had worked in factories.)

That they proceeded to deprive the great majority of the population of an identity was plausible. They were playing to history, not to an electorate. For them, people existed to be used in the dialectical process. Whole classes disappeared—those who got in the way of the historical process, the inefficient workers, petty bureaucrats, or unresponsive functionaries.

Given Lenin's vast oeuvre with its many changes of tactics and strategies, it is easy to read him selectively. But there was a consistently violent pattern of his thought not often discerned by those who awaited the founding of utopia, those who projected their humanistic and progressive ideals, and those passionately antagonistic to the old Russia. As did many idealists who come to power, behind his vast schemes he lost (if he ever had it) the sense of the individual man. More often than not, his solution to obstacles in the path of realizing his schemes was to shoot the offender or to liquidate the opposition. Probably quite unnecessarily, he advised Stalin to have a telephone operator shot who had given him a bad connection—a solution he also advised for prostitutes who distracted soldiers at the front.[9] Even when he did not directly order or advise such atrocities, he acquiesced in their adoption. Peasants who did not adequately clear the snow could be shot to teach a lesson—a plan also adopted to solve the problem of foresters who did not fulfill their quotas of firewood.[10]

While totally absorbed in creating the workers' state, he manipulated the trade unions but apparently did not listen to them.[11] His method of bringing legality and order to the Russian empire was, very often, by means of "terroristic purging, summary trial, and death by shooting."[12] As a leader with a marshal's mentality and an autocrat's authority, Lenin inevitably attracts a most curious cultural comparison with the Prussianized tsars before him. Even in 1922, only a year and a half before his death (by then he was living in a palace and being driven in a Rolls-Royce), in a last appearance before a Party Congress, Lenin used a military analogy to explain the methods of dealing with the New Economic Policy if the retreat became a rout:

> When a real army is in retreat, machineguns are kept ready, and when an orderly retreat degenerates into a disorderly one, the command to fire is given, and quite rightly, too. . . . The slightest breach of discipline must be punished severely, sternly, ruthlessly.[13]

To be a member of the working class was to be among the chosen, but that good fortune still did not give a laborer a voice. Instead, he was to be transformed, eventually, into the iconic new Soviet man with privileges, but no rights, and to be forced to speak in the Soviet language of unreality, or to be silent. The identity of the Soviet laborer was defined by his work—by what he produced. Without that, he was outside of time and thought. As Platonov, the brilliant novelist of that period, characterized the language of the new mythology:

> "Just what are you, girl? What did your papa and mama do?"
> "I am no one," said the girl.
> "How can you be no one? Some kind of principle of the female sex obliged you by giving birth to you under Soviet rule."
> "But I didn't want to be born myself. I was afraid that my mother would be a bourgeois."
> "So how did you organize yourself then?"
> "When [Lenin and Budonny] weren't there, and only the bourgeois people lived, then I was not born, because I didn't want to be. And when Lenin appeared, then I came."[14]

While later, after World War II, whole nationalities—the Tatars, Volga Germans, Balts, Jews, and many others—became as Platonov put it, "a good class by death," the process of eliminating groups of people because of their "class"—a term as inherently imprecise as "town and country" in modern America—began immediately after the Revolution. As there were very few workers in the Russian empire, the administrative problems the Bolsheviks undertook were, indeed, difficult.

In determining which squads could march into the Communist paradise or which proper nouns could become part of history, the utopian leaders began the process of eliminating not just the rich, the noble, the anti-Bolshevik, the spies, saboteurs, and criminals, who were in every corridor and factory it seemed, but also, selectively, the farmers, engineers, shopkeepers, intelligentsia, and eventually many of the peasants. As these people were not chosen, their often cruel fate—a social process frequently instituted by ideological leaderships—seemed a matter of indifference to the new humanists.

It is one of those puzzles of history that although Lenin disliked and distrusted intellectuals, large numbers of them have always been very attracted to him and his teachings. In any case, they were repressed and decimated like the rest. The process was accomplished both by physical liquidation and incarceration and by denial of a ration card, which in the early 1920's and 1930's, was tantamount to a death sentence for many. The war against workers in the fields of pediatrics, genetics, psychology, botany, cybernetics, sociology, and of some branches of physics was launched. The seizure of science by the party has become institutionalized. The key word enabling the party to intervene in the control of science is "Lenin." It operates very like references to the *Bible* as an authority in fundamentalist Christianity. For example, it is claimed that Lenin's essay, "Materialism and Empirocriticism," . . . "provides a general method for analyzing the development of science whatever its stage."[15]

Writers who survived found themselves living in pre-Gutenberg times, as Anna Akhmatova called it, in which their works could not be printed. The very name of "writer" was being confiscated by the party. The writer was to be reborn as a hum-drum socialist worker on the ideological front, an "engineer of the human soul."

That the Bolshevik leaders had so little regard for the dignity and worth of the individual was probably inevitable. The ideology taught them that man was a working machine or nothing, that the soul was a surplus product, and that "happiness results from an indifference to life," in Platonov's words. The focus was not on the man, but on his class and his work, and the work was often judged by men of limited taste and experience.

The Bolshevik leaders had long led hunted lives in the underground. Many of them had criminal records, and nearly all of them had learned the use of violence without hesitation. They changed their identities with ease, and when they were catapulted (to their enormous astonishment) to power, they inevitably continued to use the methods that had been crowned by such unexpected success. It is interesting that many of them kept the pseudonyms of the underground, which subsequently revealed something of their hidden natures. Stalin, man of steel, disguised his non-Russianness; Molotov, the hammer, distracted attention from his aristocratic origin; Trotsky, Radek, and many others took names that hid their bourgeois, Jewish origin.

Since these powerful men themselves lived a kind of masquerade, it is not surprising that they saw traitors and saboteurs behind many honest faces. By the 1920's, and later in 1930's to 1950's, it would be revealed that almost no one was who he appeared to be. Dedicated Communists turned out to be spies; doctors were murders; workers were saboteurs. To live in the Soviet Union was to live in a world possessed by devils, it seemed.

The Threshold of Deception

How could the Bolsheviks have succeeded in holding power when they angered every class, including the workers, and nearly every nation? This is probably the most important question the twentieth century will want to ask of history. The answer seems to be that Lenin and his men, using the vocabulary of utopia, stole reality, substituted a myth, and managed to force or seduce countless millions to live in it. This success is not without parallels. The process was similar to that of fundamentalist religions, Hitler's Germany, and of Khomeini's Iran.

Considering the empire that he founded, it is not surprising that Lenin understood what God meant: "In the beginning was the Word."

> People [Lenin wrote] for the most part (99 percent of the bourgeoisie, 98 percent of the liquidators, about 60–70 percent of the Bolsheviks) don't know how to *think*, they only *learn words by heart*. They've learnt the word "underground." Firmly. They know it by heart. But *how* to change *its forms* in a new situation, how to learn and think *anew* for this purpose, this we do not understand.[16]

This statement was not just an expression of cynicism, depression, or disgust, but the assertion of Lenin's fundamental concept for a philosophy that has gained a political base on every continent but Australia.

The only weapons that Lenin and his cohorts had when they arrived at Petrograd's Finland Station were words and the utopian expectations not only of the peasants and workers but also of much of the intelligentsia of the whole world. Words were the basic ingredients for the construction of one of the most powerful political systems the world has seen since Roman times.

Much energy in the study of the Soviet Union, as this book testifies, is devoted to the documentation of Soviet deception. Whether it is an illegal antimissile radar, a forged document, or false infant mortality statistics, we spend vast amounts of time surprising ourselves with new evidence of Soviet misrepresentation and deceit. But the deception that succeeded is the one that occurred voluntarily in the mind. As Gregory Bateson said, knowledge "at any given moment will be a function of the thresholds of our available means of perception."[17] Since knowledge is based upon the perception of differences, and since differences are observed through cultural screens that alert us to some information (and conversely screen out other information), we are the powerful prisoners of our preconceptions or thresholds.

The problem of cultural misperception is not, of course, an exclusively American characteristic. It is shared by the Soviets as well. When President Carter was alarmed and furious, adopting the role of the punishing parent, by the Soviet Union's execution of leaders of the Afghan government and imposition of a new set of more obedient puppets in a way perfectly consistent with the behavior of colonial powers, the Soviets were astonished as well. After the massive notification in *Pravda* of their international policy (which had already been demonstrated in Hungary and Czechoslovakia) how could the President of the United States be surprised?

A dramatic and fascinating example of the role of thresholds in limiting information—and surely very interesting for those who think that there is a military mentality that is always a party of war—was the curriculum of the Naval War College at Newport, Rhode Island, from 1972 until about 1975. In 1970, the Soviet Navy staged the largest naval exercise the world had ever seen, with operations taking place primarily in the North Atlantic and Mediterranean, but—ominously it would seem—also in all of the oceans of the world. One of the operations that should have fascinated the U.S. Navy was a demonstration meant to show that the Soviets had solved the problem of sinking aircraft carriers. Those were the years when, in the Soviet Union, there was the largest naval building program that had ever taken place anywhere in peacetime, and the ships that were being built promised a great change in the missions of the Soviet Navy from defense to adventures in international waters.

In spite of all of this factual evidence of new, aggressive naval policies, the Naval War College abandoned teaching about the operations of the Soviet Navy, Soviet military strategy, and the political ideas of Marx and Lenin. The explanation was that the Cold War was over, and the United States and Soviet Union had agreed to detente. It is obvious that the cleverest Soviet deception can be less effective than our own process of misperception and self-deception.[18]

Lenin, in his brilliance, realized that to hold power he had to operate within two contexts—two forms: one for the masses would be the context of an advanced, democratic state with all of the normal attributes such as newspapers and constitutions; the other form would be secret, authoritarian, ad hoc, arbitrary, and pragmatic. To the watching world, he could respond in terms of a familiar context, while the secret one, which exercised the power, was denied and hidden from view. It was a formula for political schizophrenia, but it succeeded in expanding the power of the party and confusing and weakening external opposition. The problem that this dual-structured system created was one of its authority and legitimacy. In times of famine, war, purges, and terror, who could speak for the people? Lenin answered that by claiming to be the spokesman for labor, for Marx, for socialism, and for the future—the dictator of the proletariat. As the spokesman for utopia, he created a dictatorship.

After Lenin's death, the problem recurred. Who would legitimize the Soviet government? Like Lenin, his successors had not worked in factories, so how could they be the conscience of the proletariat? The answer was to create a mythical world having many of the characteristics of a religion with its own trinity, its own socialist creed, its own hierarchy of saints, its immortal God-man (Lenin), and its heaven (the Soviet Union).

It is difficult for twentieth century man to understand the implications of the Lenin mausoleum on Red Square; nevertheless, in 1924, seven years after the Revolution, the Bolshevik leaders consciously set about developing a cult out of the uncorrupted body of the leader of materialism.[19] The Politburo assembled atop the Lenin Mausoleum on solemn occasions and from that rostrum, periodically threatened the world with its military celebrations. It derived its authority from that marble podium similar to that which the Roman Church derived from St. Peter's rock. The Politburo stands over Lenin's body and speaks for Lenin, as Gorbachev did, as if he were alive. That is the institutionalization of myth.

There is a Soviet language of authority which avoids the problems of legitimacy, of facts, and of proof. Gorbachev used it when he said "Historical experience has convinced us." Other manifestations are: "as everybody knows," "as has frequently been said," "history proves," "scientific materialism demonstrates," and most frequently of all, invocations of Lenin, Leninists, and Leninism.

The structuring of the Soviet language is the story of the gradual detachment of religion, history, literature, politics, the family, and the national spirit from their roots in the Russian soil and transferring them to the new culture. It was as if these Bolsheviks, who had communicated with each other in an Aesopian language for years, had become the prisoners of their own deception and come to live in the world of the illusions which they imposed upon reality. In any case, once they founded their new religion on the "living" body of Lenin—who "spoke" to the Twenty-second Party Congress through a medium—and demanded that the world accept that they were building a workers' paradise, there was no turning back from mythology. Myth had become the new reality. Consequently, the political process began by destroying the Russian imagination.

Thirty years ago, speaking of this new language, Gerhart Niemeyer wrote:

> It is difficult for Westerners to grasp the rationale of Soviet conduct, but it is next to impossible for Communists to grasp the purpose of Western policy however explicit it may be in words and deeds. The Communist mind has so defined its world that it shares neither truth nor logic nor morality with the rest of mankind.[20]

Niemeyer was, of course, thinking of Sovietspeak, that language used by the secret governmental structure whose voice is that of the utopian myth. Thus, it is true that we do not share "truth nor logic nor morality" in the context of Sovietspeak, but in the other context, that of the nonsecret governmental structure, the one without power, there are similarities. The voices of these two contexts are infinitely confusing. Some of the power and success of the Soviet Union is derived from manipulating them. (There is usually no confusion about the two contexts in Moscow, although sometimes one of the structures leads the other into something of a trap such as the Helsinki Accords on human rights, or the decision to allow the Jews to emigrate—both decisions having shattered the myth of the workers' paradise in ways difficult to repair.)

Correcting the Grammar

One problem for the Western mind is dealing with the fact that the system is not self-correcting. A frequent Soviet answer to most social and economic problems is to find out who is to blame, but the inherent weaknesses in the system are not acknowledged. The solution to creating the ideal society Lenin introduced—simply eliminate by violence or other means whatever does not fit; close the borders and force those who stay inside to learn Sovietspeak—is the one more or less still applied. Andropov and Gorbachev both call for greater efficiency and honesty, and they accompany that admonition with the execution of speculators and grafters. But the fundamental system is not challenged.

This design for establishing the state began with Lenin. When he and his men seized power, they had already laid the foundation of the new Soviet language. This was first dramatically demonstrated at the very contentious Second Party Congress in 1903, when Lenin adopted the name of Bolshevik (majority) for his group, although it did not represent the majority of democratic socialists. He somehow managed to get the opposition to assume the self-defeating name Menshevik (party of the minority).

However tiresome the Menshevik and other opposition parties may have been, they seldom deserved the slanders that Lenin applied for political effect and used without regard for the truth. He referred to Mensheviks as monarchists; to Socialist Revolutionaries as petty-bourgeoise, criminals, bandits, or murderers. One of Lenin's favorite whipping boys was the respected German Marxist, Karl Kautsky. He earned Lenin's hatred for expressing dismay at Lenin's violence. The way in which Lenin responded is a cameo representation of the Soviet way of dealing with reality, a method that reappeared in the purges of the 1930's and 1950's, and that has branded Soviet society today. Calling Kautsky a "perfect example of reactionary philistine stupidity," Lenin attacked him for "bewailing the culture of violence."[21] Instead of answering his accusations, Lenin recommended branding him a traitor and letting it go at that.

When the Bolsheviks set up their state, they made many guarantees of freedom of the press, secrecy of the ballot, freedom of religion, the right of assembly, elections, and all of the norms of advanced societies. These declarations, seldom observed, were repeatedly embodied in constitutions of the RSFSR in 1920, again in the constitution of the USSR for 1923, the Stalin constitution of 1936, and the Brezhnev constitution of 1977.

Stalin's constitution was particularly interesting because it was such a macabre artifact of utopia. It was hailed by the Soviet press as a great watershed in human development, "a document which proved that the dream, past and present, of millions of honest people in the capitalist countries, this dream is already realized in the Soviet Union." This occurred at the height of the purges, when thousands of innocent people were going to their deaths in the camps without the suggestion of any legal protection of any kind.

One of the first acts of the new government was to impose censorship, although freedom of the press had been promised. The Bolsheviks had fulminated against the Kerensky government for wanting to institute the death penalty for desertion at the front. In power, Lenin used executions on a wide scale, and when there was opposition, argued that there could not be revolutions without them. Nationalities were promised their independence; therefore, some of them innocently supported the Bolsheviks who, when they had the power, sent the Red Army to subdue independent movements. Equality was promised while inequality was institutionalized. Whole families were deprived of their rights, among them the right to life, and were given neither ration cards for food, jobs, nor education for their children. A special word was created for them as a class: *lishentsy* (the deprived ones). Legal protection was promised, but hostages were shot without evidence and without trial for no better reason than that they might prove to be troublesome in the future. "We are on the way to creating a civilization which will be to capitalism what Beethoven's 'Heroic Symphony' is to the 'Waltz of the Dogs,' " said Nicholas Bukharin as his government was preparing the extermination of the Kulaks as a class.[22]

The Grand Illusion

One of America's most sensitive and brilliant literary critics, a man trained for delicate discrimination, Edmund Wilson, wrote in the 1930's, during the worst years of purge and famine, that he felt himself to be in a "moral sanctuary where the light never ceased to shine." The quarrelsome music critic, playwright, and political activist, George Bernard Shaw, wrote during the Soviet famine "that he had never been better fed, and that when he returned to England he would be leaving the land of hope for the land of despair."[23] Although "many political pilgrims," including Edmund Wilson, were awakened to the realities later, the fact of their extraordinary misperception and self-deception cannot be dismissed. Like the Naval War College, Franklin Roosevelt, President Carter before Afghanistan, and many others, they apparently created a Soviet Union out of their expectations. In most cases, they were responding to the context supplied by the Soviet government, the democratic, utopian facade, which masked the secret structure of the party apparatus. They cooperated, as any child does with his bedtime stories, in the willing suspension of disbelief. They acquiesced to the fairy tale.

The political pilgrimages continue with less enthusiasm, perhaps, but with some illusions. Although not so easily convinced that the Soviet Union is the land of the radiant future for all mankind, prominent figures still serve to demonstrate to Soviet people that there are very limited alternatives to Soviet power. In 1985, Billy Graham expressed himself more cautiously about the "measure of religious freedom" in that land of militant state atheism than he had on his 1982 visit to the Soviet Union. But he supported the mythical world, using Sovietspeak in reporting his trip. (Many Soviet believers will doubt that he can be trusted.) The following are not the words of one fighting for the religious freedom guaranteed by the Soviet constitution, but of someone cautiously protecting his relationship to Caesar.

> Many churches are open and active; and it is my understanding that they usually are allowed to carry out their work on church premises as long as they

abide by the government's requirements for religious organizations. At the same time, [the evangelist felt constrained to add in the pure language of Sovietspeak] the Soviet Union does not allow churches to be a rallying point for what it considers anti-Soviet activities.[24]

Izvestia had already reported his trip in such a way as to make him sound like a fellow traveler:

> Christians, Moslems, Jews, and Buddhists freely profess their faiths in the Soviet Union. Billy Graham said that he had cordial meetings in Orthodox churches and Baptist houses of prayer.[25]

The process of detaching the Soviet people from their normal reality, destroying their familiar institutions, and forcing them to live in the Soviet mythology engulfed classes, structures the government, all phases of learning, research and art, and ultimately the family. The effective political tool Lenin used and taught his followers, that of creating factions and then setting them against each other, was eventually applied to friends and relatives. Children of twelve were declared to be subject to the criminal law in 1935 and could be tried and executed by firing squad. Fathers were made responsible for the loyalty of their families; and all members of a family, regardless of relationship, were subject to reporting on each other. A model, Pavlik Morozov, a boy who denounced his father, was lionized in all the schools and papers. This was on the eve of the Stalin constitution, that "great watershed in human development." Ultimately, the family was silenced; the party intruded into the household; the individual had only the world of his unshared imagination for his own.

The Soviet's theft of the humanitarian dreams of Karl Marx, and use of those utopian goals to create a totalitarian state, were foretold by Dostoevsky in the "Grand Inquisitor" chapter of *The Brothers Karamazov*. There the church was shown to have perverted Christ's teachings and taken away the freedom that the people did not have the strength to sustain. In return, it gave them (as the Soviet government claims to do) security. Marx promised much more, of course, even beyond a narrowly materialistic society. If he returned to Red Square on May Day, he would be astonished that anyone could see a connection between his writings and the Lenin altar, the rumbling tanks and rockets, goose-stepping troops, and diamond-studded cravats of the admirals and marshals.

The Past Tense of Marx

Perhaps excuses can be made for the un-Marxist excesses at the beginning of the Soviet state. After all, Marx required a newly postfeudal state such as Russia to mature into a capitalist society before there could be any attempts to create utopia. We have already demonstrated that there was little of the humanitarian dream in Lenin, but the intentional abandonment of Marxist philosophy can be almost precisely dated. It was in 1931. Stalin declared war on the idea of the equality of wages. In effect, he abandoned the idea of a classless society. That was, he said, a petty bourgeoisie idea. Although there had long been different stores for the elite, and different prices for the hierarchy of leaders and administrators, the idea of the equality of wages had been maintained as the most basic Marxist idea. It has not been reinstituted.

The distorted language of Marxism was retained, of course, and absorbed into Sovietspeak, although references to Marxist ideals became as empty as descriptions of the happy present ("people are becoming gayer," Stalin proclaimed during the purges) and the radiant future.

A large amount of Sovietspeak utilizes a now debased and perverted Marxism. When people are said to enjoy democracy, it is qualified as a "socialist" democracy. That means, of course, that they "participate" in the dictatorship of the proletariat. Freedoms are "socialist" freedoms. The "classless" society is run by the "workers." Since only the state has the right to define socialism, and the workers do not have the right to question the state, there is little hope for a liberated Marx.

The detachment of the state from reality has proceeded so far that poets have become the psychiatrists of that pre-Freudian, pre-Gutenberg world. As all other commentators were silenced, only poets could tell people about reality, about their lives, or the journey of the spirit. (Of course poets who wrote about such things were silenced.) The theme of many were the questions: Who am I? What is the life I should have lived? Who are the people I should have met? One of the greatest poets, Anna Akhmatova, summed up Soviet reality in a language defying the world of Sovietspeak:

> I drink to our ruined house,
> to the dolor of my life,
> to our loneliness together;
> and to you I raise my glass,
> to lying lips that have betrayed us,
> to dead-cold, pitiless eyes,
> and to the hard realities:
> that the world is brutal and coarse,
> that God in fact has not saved us.[26]

Using a similar voice in 1985, an ordinary worker complained in a letter to the Central Committee of the brutality of life. He did not employ Sovietspeak, but the strangely moving, rarely heard, authentic voice of Russia. He lamented that 40 years after the war, Soviets still had ration cards, people had to stand in line in the cold all day for bread and milk in some places, in many villages there were not even telephones to call for medical help, while in Moscow there were many clinics that ordinary people could not use. But his main complaint showed the basic schizophrenia of Soviet life, that the Communist Party has even stolen the worker's identity. The common man, he said, belonged:

> . . . to that working class which your Party defines as the leading force and the vanguard of the Soviet society. All of the newspapers, all of the magazines, the radio and the television repeat that daily. But if, in a private conversation, a worker among us says such things, people will look at him with astonishment. Can he be normal? Isn't he an idiot? . . . Do you know why so many are silent? They are afraid. Why?[27]

Seldom do the Soviets display their theft of reality and the dominance of the secret context as clearly as in the Public Health Instruction "On Emergency Confinement of Mentally Ill Persons Who Represent a Social Danger."[28] Here we are given an example of the party adopting a "scientific" disguise to achieve its purposes, even to the extent of denying the validity of the data of the senses.

According to the instruction, those in the Soviet Union who oppose the collective by:

> . . . showing aggressive behavior towards certain persons, organizations and institutions . . . may be committed to a psychiatric hospital without his consent or the consent of his relatives, guardians or others.[29]

Giving helpful suggestions for recognizing such psychopaths, the document states quite astonishingly: "The symptoms of illness . . . may be accompanied by outwardly correct behavior and dissimulation."[30] This appearance of "seeming normality" is defined as deception. As a psychiatrist in the trial of a dissident stated: "The absence of the symptoms of an illness cannot prove the absence of the illness itself. . . . The presence of this form of schizophrenia does not presuppose changes in personality noticeable to others." To whom, then, one wonders.

Managing Utopia

Evolution and reform cannot be part of a structure in which the past is abolished to justify the present, and in which important factual information is secret. A vision of the mythical future is then substituted for the current reality, and the people are required to acknowledge the future as contemporary. There is much about life in the Soviet Union that duplicates the story of the emperor's new clothes. Thus in Gorbachev's statement, when he speaks of a democratic process in the present tense, the subtext for Soviet citizens is in the future tense. This is called socialist realism.

A way of dealing with calamities such as starvation, the abysmal failure of collective agriculture, or the failure to prepare (in spite of countless warnings) for the German invasion of 1941 is simply to deny the data of the senses. In dealing with the civil war unleashed by the horrors of collectivization, for example, in 1930 Stalin wrote a macabre article, "Dizzy With Success," announcing the basic popularity of the idea and designating those who were to blame for some "minor" excesses. (Stalin's article will surely rank with Nero's fiddling as one of the most cynical acts of human history.) That typified an important method for dealing with failure in the Soviet system. The correction frequently consists in eliminating from society those elements or classes that do not fit the plan, rather than making the plan fit the people.

In Sovietspeak, there are standard enemies to be used for a variety of occasions, such as the CIA, saboteurs, capitalists, spies, etc., and specialized enemies who are associated with particular campaigns (often cyclically repeated). In Sovietspeak, the vocabulary of enemies is used very much in the same way as the names of participants in a witches' coven in medieval times and North European fairy tales. They lurk in odd places, such as streetcars in Tashkent, parks of rest and recreation, and in the bushes around remote missile sites. According to the state poet, Evgeniy Evtushenko, they even lurk along railroad tracks waiting to poke sticks into the wheels of trains. (CIA's training programs have become very innovative, apparently.) Evtushenko's poem ("they jammed sticks/in the wheels of the 1st locomotive") repeats a theme used in the 1930's.[31] Why were the trains running badly? Because "the class enemy, the white guard, the kulaks, have always the possibility of infiltrating the trains and occupying modest and discreet posts such as oiler."[32] (Perhaps it was because of these foreign and class enemies sticking objects into the wheels of trains that caused Brezhnev, in a curious and lengthy aside at the Twenty-fifth Party Congress, to thank the organs of state security for "reliably protecting Soviet society from the subversive activities of all sorts of foreign anti-Soviet centers and other hostile elements."[33])

This constant fear of foreign infiltration (in truth a fear of another reality) was probably the reason for the rather strange and vague decree of the Presidium of the Supreme Soviet, 25 May 1984, which established greater control over foreign visitors and also deterred Soviet citizens from meeting them. The decree established a fine for providing foreign visitors with housing, transport, or other services that "broke the rules for the presence of foreigners." This decree was adopted, even after the Articles of the Criminal Code had been intensified to make it a crime to have materials in any form that were anti-Soviet or to conduct activities that are anti-Soviet with funds received from foreign organizations.

These measures are more evidence of a creeping re-Stalinization that occurred after Brezhnev became the General Secretary in 1964—an intensified fight against reality. With the modern means of communication, the flood of tourists, and the increasing numbers of Soviets participating in foreign brigades, it is difficult for Soviet leaders to maintain their enchanted forest peopled with CIA hobgoblins, bourgeois witches, and capitalist sorcerers.

The Thresholds of Illusion

A question useful to ask is how can such a very large segment of the population allow itself to participate in this self-deception? The implications for our diplomatic relations and strategic policy are enormous. If the Naval War College does not respond to new designs of aggressive ships for long voyages, and our Armed Forces continue to assume in their plans that if the Soviet Forces attack, they will do so at times and places of our own choosing, then it is obvious that many are creating a Soviet Union to suit an American preconception.

Whether or not God was accurately quoted, that in the beginning was the Word, the author understood, with Lenin, a most fundamental idea: that we construct reality in our minds, and that we create it out of words. Wittgenstein said that "our relation to reality is accomplished in the activity of thinking. . . . Language is the vehicle of thinking."[34] In forming conceptions, it is easy to forget that objective reality occurs inside, not outside, the mind. As Gregory Bateson noted, it is not a trivial observation:

> . . . that very few persons, at least in occidental culture, doubt the objectivity of such sense data as pain or their visual images of the external world. Our civilization is deeply based on this illusion.[35]

Objects are our creations, and what we make of them is subjective. At the time they visited the Soviet Union, Wilson, Laski, Graham, and others did not transcend the subjective thresholds of their means of perception.

Language, of course, is always a partial deception, for we are dealing in words as symbols, which convey only a fraction of the thing they stand for. Deception then proceeds through words and thresholds, through choosing those images that suit the structures or contexts of meaning our brains have prepared for us.

Lenin and his successors have been very successful in understanding this use of language to manipulate men's minds. The danger for them is that when reality breaks into the mythical world they have created, the whole structure tends to shatter. The invasions of Afghanistan, Hungary, and Czechoslovakia did that for many. The human rights issue, aided by Solzhenitsyn's heroic work, is shattering the image for others. We can be enchanted by the charm and innocence of the story of Sleeping Beauty and happily participate in that perfect land. But if it is suggested that the prince's kiss awakening her to maturity is not really a kiss but a copulation, and that perhaps in the context of the story he is a child abuser, then a threshold has been breached. We are back in our world; the structure of the story is laid bare and its content is understood in a new context.

That our preconceptions can distort the significance of concrete facts is undeniable, and, like the Sleeping Beauty, we lie within the thresholds of our enchanted world. The intelligence community, surely suspicious and experienced enough to have escaped over its own thresholds, nevertheless "disregarded the massive evidence available to it concerning the size, scope, and purpose of the Soviet Union's program for building strategic weapons."[36] This shows the power of preconceptions in limiting reality.

One of the results of the Esalen Experiments in Soviet-American Understanding, an attempt to locate cultural thresholds,[37] was that educated Americans are much more prone to complete a mental framework with what they expect to learn than are a similarly educated group from the central Soviet-Russian culture. In four different experiments testing 40 Americans and 30 ex-Soviets, the Americans invariably made major unfounded assumptions about missing information in order to complete a logical mental construct. They created the enemy, and when he did not behave according to their script in mock negotiations, they invariably became frustrated and hostile, quickly escalating to violence. The experience was reminiscent of President Carter's bewilderment, in 1977, at the:

> . . . unfriendly rhetoric coming out of Moscow . . . the public statements that the Soviets make attacking me personally or our own nation's good faith are both erroneous and ill-advised. But what their reasons for it might be, I do not know.[38]

He had filled the gaps in his knowledge of the Soviet Union with his own expectations, and when those were frustrated, he turned to anger. This is the danger of not understanding Sovietspeak.

A characteristic of Soviet-American relations has been the difficulty in acknowledging the international evidence of announced Soviet strategic concepts such as the Brezhnev Doctrine. In that manner we can enjoy the luxury of not having to take action. After 60 years of Soviet propaganda, President Carter's not understanding that as the leader of the free world he was, in Soviet preconceptions, an implacable enemy, no matter how nice his intentions, illustrates Bateson's point about the thresholds of perception.

The Strategy of Sovietspeak

The most fundamental idea in Soviet mythology—that Bolshevik power was born to remake the world, not to preserve it—appears to be outside of our own strategic grammar. Actually, our incomprehension simply shows the functioning of the two cultural contexts of thought. We deal in balances and stability; the Soviets deal in the dialectics of struggle and change. We operate tactically almost totally in the present; the Soviets operate, strategically, primarily in a future and, unlike us, without a timetable. We attach great value to human life and the "dignity of man;" the Soviets attach value to the working class and to the radiant future. We understand space as divided by national borders; the Soviets understand space as occupied by classes and an international-minded, no matter how bewildered, proletariat.

The Soviet strategic vocabulary is far more clear, more consistent, and more coherent than that of the United States because it is based on one ideology and spoken, more or less, with one voice. It is necessary to know Sovietspeak to translate it and to understand that it does not pertain to a reality we share. The world it visualizes is one in a necessary transition toward a specific political structure. In Sovietspeak, the obstacles to communism have a moral obligation to disappear. Our use of the words strategy and tactics are quite different, partly because of the different structures or contexts of thought. For example, as the Soviets necessarily have a long-range strategic concept and we do not, many of the moves their military forces make are part of a strategic picture. They are playing chess while we are playing checkers. An offensive position at the mouth of the Red Sea or a fishing agreement in Western Samoa are part of a strategic pattern that we, typically, interpret tactically.

Even our analysis of Soviet strategy tends to be fractured into segments. We analyze militarily in terms of army, navy and air force strategies. Therefore, we study the strategies of the Soviet armed forces in those categories. But in Sovietspeak, there cannot be a navy strategy or an army strategy, except as part of an overall strategy.

Soviet strategy also is developed on many levels, but is coordinated by a central (Politburo) direction. Nationally, we develop strategy and analyze it almost entirely militarily. Therefore we are very slow to see a relationship, called the correlation of forces, which takes into account many factors such as the economy, technology, morale, stability, loyalty, political control, and so forth. In our system, the complex problem tends to be divided into separate administrative bits politically, militarily, and academically. The problem of the whole becomes obscured. For example, it is easy to avoid the total implications of why the Soviets would have sent a very old submarine with nuclear weapons to spy on Sweden, a country whose support they had hoped to enlist for a nuclear-free zone. In analyzing such a problem, it is helpful to remember the two voices of Sovietspeak, the two contexts of decisions: the secret and the governmental.

Sovietspeak uses another term, inspired by Marx, that causes confusion— "scientific." When it is used in a Russian, not a Soviet, context it means more or less what we understand in the West. When it is used in Sovietspeak, it is another deception for seizing reality, for pretending to speak with authority. When it is used in a military context, it should be understood according to the audience being addressed.

There is a military science that does use the term "scientific" to eliminate subjective judgments. That study makes use of all available scientific means. (In fact, military analysts in the Soviet Union consider their scientific approach so superior to our own that they refer to our very individualized approach as antiquated, subjective, and inspired by mysticism.)

When the Soviets analyze problems using their notion of military science, they are primarily working on a professional level. It is sometimes thought that they are arguing for war, when in fact they are discussing how to win a battle, end a war victoriously, or gain a military advantage under modern conditions. Morality, which relates to a non-Marxist grammar in Sovietspeak, is not part of military science. Instead, enormous emphasis is placed on the psychological aspect of war because the battle is also fought for the control of men's minds. This is very different from U.S. strategy, which considers psychology only tactically, usually superficially, and which concerns itself more with targets than people.

The other use of "military science" is directed not toward the professional officers of the general staff, but toward the rank and file and foreigners. It is Sovietspeak, a language that Marshal Ogarkov writes perfectly:

> On the historical plane, the theoretical and practical activity of the leader of the world proletariat, V.I. Lenin, and his creative development of K. Marx's teaching under new historical conditions serve as a classic example of a society's development, including the vitally important problem of wars and peace.[39]

By the time the American language of deterrence gets translated into Sovietspeak, the leaders of the United States can, indeed, appear to be "pathological" warmongers as they are frequently described in the Soviet press. When translated, "deterrence" becomes any of a number of words of aggression including containment, intimidation, and restraint. The problem becomes compounded. In Sovietspeak, the legitimate business of the state is the pursuit of its internationalist mission—to destroy the capitalist/colonial system—and when the United States interferes, by that act it is committing aggression.

When the United States discovered that it was impossible to affect the situation in Angola or Ethiopia with nuclear weapons, it surely understood that there were many meanings for the word "parity." Words out of context are always meaningless, and it is useful to understand parity in its Soviet usage. There it means that the U.S. has agreed to Soviet superiority in numbers of certain weapons, and has agreed not to consider relative numbers of others. We are at the point of standing Clausewitz on his head; politics, as we now play it, is the continuation of war by other means. (In Sovietspeak, parity [*ravnovesiya*] is a complex word which we do not translate well because it has too many implications—such as correlation of forces—that are not in the structure of American thought.)

Finally, we have trouble understanding that in Sovietspeak there are no borders. There is no country where the Soviet grammar is not operative. It is an international language, the Esperanto of totalitarianism, the language of the Leninist empire. Sovietspeak makes constant reference to the internationalist duty of the armed forces. Internationalism is the opposite of our strategy of containment because it implies an active, aggressive role in rolling back capitalism by a greatly expanded multinational brigade made up of Leninist (Sovietspeak would say "progressive," an oxymoron, certainly) forces. In the words of Marshal Ogarkov, that is the program for

> . . . the Soviet Armed Forces whose sacred duty, together with their combat allies in the Warsaw Pact, the armies of the other socialist community countries, is to reliably defend the gains of socialism and peace on earth.[40]

As Eugenia Ginzberg, the dedicated Communist victim and ultimate heroine of the Stalinist purges, said of her experience in the 1930's: "What is the point of looking ahead when you are playing chess with an orangutang?" What she had not understood was that she had believed the language of utopia and had been seduced by the radiant future of communism. She did not notice the difference between the form and content of Sovietspeak.

We can only have a limited perception of parts of the world we live in and have to guess about the whole around us. But after seven decades, there are enough experiences to know that we are not playing chess with an orangutang. It is unfortunate that for many people and many countries it has required a significantly disturbing event to breach the threshold of preconceptions—often a war, terror, or other violence—to awaken us to the universe created by the word. Fortunately, although a language builds a thick wall around the mind, it is not like geography or climate. It can be shattered, and as the Esalen Experiments showed, sometimes quickly.

Notes

1. M.S. Gorbachev, "Address on French Television," *Pravda*, 2 October 1985, quoted from *The Current Digest of the Soviet Press* 37 (30 Oct 1985).

2. George Skelton, *New York Times* correspondent quoted in *Los Angeles Times*, 27 September 1985.

3. E.A. Shevardnadze, *Record of the 25th CPSU Congress, 1976*.

4. V.I. Kozlov, *Istoria SSSR*, no. 4, (July-August 1983) abstracted in *The Current Digest of the Soviet Press* 35, p. 12.

5. The phrase "strike detachment of imperialism" became the set formulation to describe the relationship between Nazi Germany and the Western democracies. The thesis is even more insidiously advertised in the propaganda posters available for schools and institutions in which American and other Western business, political, and military representatives are often presented as satanic figures ambiguously wearing Nazi and U.S.

insignia. For a standard treatment of the political causes of World War II, see, for example, D.F. Ustinov, "Defending Peace," *Pravda*, 22 June 1981, p. 2.

6. *Kommunist vooruzhenykh sil*, May 1979, p. 84.

7. Alexander Yakovlev, *The Yalta Conference, Lessons of History* (Moscow: Novosti Press Publishing House, 1945), p. 6

8. T.N. Khrennikov, 1st Secretary of the Composers' Union, in Shevardnadze, Record of the 25th CPSU. I am indebted to Dr. David Powell of the Harvard Russian Research Center for bringing my attention to this example of applied aesthetics.

9. Cited in Adam Ulam, *The Bolsheviks* (New York: Macmillan, 1965), p. 422. It is curious that the Soviets who do not hesitate to write history, omitting embarrassing facts of even a minor nature, republish Lenin's works with all of the damning evidence of his antihumanistic instructions to shoot, kill, imprison, or liquidate those who annoyed him. Soviet censors have discovered what Lenin already knew, that the expectation of utopia is a powerful screen against reality.

10. See Robert Payne, *The Life and Death of Lenin* (New York: Simon and Schuster, 1984) for a description of Lenin's consistent use of violence, especially pp. 480–518.

11. V.I. Lenin, "Left-Wing Communism, an Infantile Disorder," *Selected Works*, vol. 10 (New York: International Publishers, 1943), pp. 95–96.

12. V.I. Lenin, "The Food Tax," *Selected Works*, vol. 9, p. 192.

13. V.I. Lenin, "Speech to the 11th Congress of the R. C. P. (B)," *Collected Works*, vol. 33 (Moscow: Progress Publishers, 1966), p. 282.

14. Andrei Platonov, *The Foundation Pit*, trans. by Thomas P. Whitney in *Collected Works* (Ann Arbor, Mich: Ardis, 1978), p. 69.

15. I. Kikoin, "Leninist Approach to Analyzing Developments in Physics," *Moscow Kommunist*, no. 9, (June 1984), p. 77.

16. V.I. Lenin, *Collected Works*, vol. 35, p. 131.

17. Gregory Bateson, *Mind and Nature* (New York: Bantam Books, 1980), p. 34.

18. See Edward Hall's books, especially *Beyond Culture*, for valuable and accessible insights into the ways in which culture channels perception.

19. See Nina Tumarkin's brilliant study of the conscious decisions of the Bolshevik leaders to convert Lenin's body into an icon to mislead the people, *Lenin Lives!* (Cambridge: Harvard University Press, 1983).

20. Gerhart Niemeyer, *An Inquiry into Soviet Mentality* (New York: Praeger, 1956), p. 70.

21. Throughout Lenin's later works, there are many diatribes against the respected Communist, Kautsky. He became a dark figure in Lenin's pantheon of devils ready for use in ritual damnations. See V.I. Lenin, "The Military Programme of the Proletarian Revolution," *Selected Words*, vol. 1, p. 784.

22. Nicholas Bukharin, *Put' k sotsializmy v Rossii* (New York: Omikron Books, 1967), p. 375. Cited by M. Geller, "*Langue Russe et Langue Sovietique*," *Le Monde*, 5 (July 1979). When I read Michael Heller's article seven years ago, I was very impressed with his argument, and have been very much influenced by the work that he and Alexander Nekrich have done in the field of Soviet history and the use of language. See note 23.

23. Mikhail Geller and Aleksandr Nekrich, *Utopiya u vlasti* I, (Frankfurt: Polyglotts-Druck GmbH, 1982), p. 271. For a full treatment of the extraordinary fascination of the West with the dream of a Soviet utopia, see Paul Hollander, *Political Pilgrims* (New York: Oxford University Press, 1981).

24. Billy Graham, "Special Report of the Soviet Union Trip," October 1984.
25. *Izvestiya*, 25 September 1984, p. 5.
26. Anna Akhmatova, "The Last Toast," *Poems of Akhmatova*, trans. by Stanley Kunitz with Max Hayward (Boston: Little, Brown, 1973), p. 81.
27. Oleg Alifanov, "*Je suis un ouvrier tout a fait ordinaire* . . .," *Le Monde*, (22 August 1985), p. 5.
28. Alexander Podrabinek, *Punitive Medicine*, (Ann Arbor, Mich: Karoma, 1980), p. 195.
29. Ibid.
30. Ibid., p. 196.
31. Evgeniy Evtushenko, quoted in *Time*, (23 September 1983): p. 41.
32. Geller and Nekrich, *Utopiya*, p. 243.
33. Ibid.
34. Gerd Brand, *The Essential Wittgenstein*, trans. by Robert E. Innis (New York: Basic Books, 1979), p. 53. Wittgenstein also argued that "what I am thinking is reality itself."
35. Bateson, *Mind and Nature*.
36. Daniel O. Graham, "Analysis and Estimates," in Roy Godson, ed., *Intelligence Requirements for the 1980's: Elements of Intelligence*, (Washington, D.C.: National Strategy Information Center, Inc., 1979), p. 23.
37. See the *Esalen Catalogue*, January-June 1985, pp. 5–7.
38. President Carter's news conference, 13 July 1977, *New York Times*, 14 July 1977, p. A–10.
39. N. Ogarkov, "On the 40th Anniversary of the Great Victory: Unfading Glory of Soviet Arms," *Kommunist vooruzhennykh sil*, no. 21, November 1984.
40. Ibid.

6
Ideology and Deception

Robert Conquest

The Soviet approach to strategic deception is, naturally, rooted in basic Soviet attitudes and beliefs. More generally, we cannot understand the Soviet leadership and its activities unless we are clear about their central motivation.

Ideology, properly speaking, is the whole body of doctrine we call Marxism-Leninism, or rather a particular interpretation of that body of doctrine, for, of course, it is interpreted rather differently by various non-Soviet Communist parties and regimes. Soviet-style Marxism-Leninism is the whole justification for the despotic one-party state, and for its extension on a global scale. For the regime is founded solely on the argument that it possesses the only correct interpretation of the laws of history; and that these provide for a "class struggle" everywhere. In this struggle the "proletariat," represented by the Communist Party of the Soviet Union or parties accepting its authority, should and will triumph, thus bringing into being the perfect society.

On the other hand, ideology, the overt system of belief they adhere to, is only the conscious and formulated aspect of their motivations. We have to seek out, in addition, the way in which their political psychology has been determined by their party's history and their own life experience.

I.

From the 1820's, Russian revolutionaries spoke not of democracy or liberty, but of dictatorship to establish Utopia. Even among the revolutionary sects, Lenin's Bolsheviks were noted for their extreme centralization, extreme ruthlessness, and extreme narrowness of mind. In 1912, the Bolsheviks numbered fewer than 10,000 members; five years later they were in power. A very thin slice of the political spectrum had imposed its rule by force. A strange, and by most standards highly aberrant, political psychology had triumphed. Even before the

Russian Revolution, Rosa Luxemburg, future leader of the German Communists, had noted how the idea of the infallible Bolshevik Central Committee was no more than a mirror image of Tsarist autocracy, aggravated by the Leninists' "Tartar-Mongolian savagery." It is true that there has always been an alternative tradition in Russia and that from about 1860 a Europeanized civic attitude had grown up, with courts, juries, eventually a fairly free press, and a Duma; but this development was crushed between the millstones of traditionalist and revolutionary messianic despotism, and the fruit of two generations of precarious civic development was destroyed. This may be seen as the main achievement of the October Revolution.

Under traditional Russian despotism, with all of its gloomy and tyrannical features, there was never the lack of restraint arising from the "moral nihilism" which the late Professor Hugh Seton Watson, doyen of British Sovietologists, sees as the central characteristic of both Nazism and Leninism.

The Leninist Party may be historically regarded as one of the millenarian sects which have often appeared over the centuries. As Norman Cohn points out in his famous study of apocalyptic movements in medieval and postmedieval Europe, *The Pursuit of the Millenium*, modern revolutions picture the coming society much as their predecessors did,

> as a state of total community, a society wholly free from inner conflicts. [And each in turn has] claimed to be charged with the unique mission of bringing history to its preordained consummation.

Cohn notes with special point:

> And what followed then was the formation of a group of a peculiar kind, a true prototype of a modern totalitarian party: a restlessly dynamic and utterly ruthless group which obsessed by the apocalyptic fantasy and filled with the conviction of its own infallibility, set itself infinitely above the rest of humanity and recognised no claims save that of its own supposed mission.[1]

In a sense, the particular content of a closed ideology is of less importance than the mere fact that, in principle, it justifies total rule by total revelation.

II.

The Soviet leaders are men whose attachment to Leninist attitudes is part of their whole personality, rather than a matter of "opinions" they hold, in the sense of accepting a view they might be argued out of by logic or evidence. They cannot see the world in terms other than those of their own past. As I have said elsewhere, Gorbachev need not be envisaged as kneeling down and reciting the *Theses on Feuerbach* every night. He has enough ideology to get along, and the rest is soaked into his bones.

To think in terms of "doctrine" is thus to give only a partial picture of the sort of process involved. The Marxist-Leninist language used by the ruling party is not merely some sort of formula. It is the only way in which the leaders are able to represent to themselves the phenomena with which they deal. "Each language cuts out its own segment of reality. We live our life as we speak it." This fairly typical comment by a prominent student of language (George Steiner) is certainly applicable to the use in politics, from birth onward, of a particular political dialect. Soviet leaders, it seems clear, are simply unable to think in other categories.

In one sense, some of the younger men may not "believe" in Marxism as such (or so it is sometimes suggested), but they believe in struggle, denunciation, the totalitarian machine; and Marxism is the established password in the corridors of power which gives access to all these. No one need believe in a password, but it may be indispensable.

Adherence to ideology above all demonstrates political loyalty—a very essential pragmatic function—so they continue at least to profess Marxism. It is hard to know what people really believe. As Lenin said, no one has yet invented a "sincerometer." Moreover, it is very easy to believe, or assent to, something which justifies one's own power and position, as is common historical experience and which is, of course, the essence of Marx's "false consciousness."

Djilas notes that the rule of the Soviet leaders continues to be

> anchored in ideology, as the divine right of kings was in Christianity; and therefore their imperialism, too, has to be ideological or else it commands no legitimacy.

He adds that this is the reason why Western hopes that the Kremlin may be pressed or humored into a truly comprehensive detente is based on a misunderstanding, since

> no Soviet leader can do that without abdicating his title to leadership and jeopardizing the justification of Soviet rule.

Djilas sums up:

> Ideology in the Soviet Union is both dead, and very much alive! Dead at the level of faith; alive as an indispensible rationale of policy.[2]

III.

We have various definite examples of the way in which ideology, at one level or another, affects Soviet policy. There are even a few occasions in which we can see the Soviet leadership, in confidential rather than propaganda situations, deploying ideological criteria. For example, we have accounts of long and serious sermons from their ideological representatives and others to representatives of foreign Communist parties, even to the degree of insisting on a Marxist formulation that might be politically disadvantageous to the party concerned. For example, the 1972 confidential Soviet advice to the Syrian Communist Party, later leaked to the Egyptian press, was a long and considered set-piece, in the preparation of which Soviet ideologists and political experts, including Suslov and Ponomarev, had made separate studies. It laid down Marxist criteria highly offensive to much of the Arab world, in particular asserting that Marxism-Leninism makes clear that there is no such thing as an Arab nation, so that even though the denial of the existence of the Arab nation was politically harmful, to assert its existence in the program of the Syrian Communist Party was not correct. (The Soviet spokesmen went on to urge that, not Arab unity, but the establishment of socialism piecemeal in various Arab countries was the "principal target.")

We can see, too, how considerations of ideological struggle influence the Soviet leadership in the demands put by them to the Czechoslovak Politburo at Cierna-nad-Tiszu in 1968. Of the five demands, four were for the removal of specific individuals from party positions, or for the suppressing of specific active groups. The fifth demand, however, was for a guarantee that the Social-Democratic Party should not be legalized. This was the sole point of long-term political principle involved; its significance should be obvious. Again, the confidential documents which fell into American hands in Grenada, are a rich and revealing source on the ideological attitudes required of Soviet, and Soviet sponsored, Communists.

Of course there are broader examples: apart from the mere power-mania of the apparatus, the sole rationale of the disastrous collective farm system of agriculture can be thought of as ideological. The imposition of a Soviet-style agrarian policy in Ethiopia, too, with the resulting ruin of the rural economy, reflects orthodox Moscow-Marxist attitudes.

Most important in the heritage of Leninism (rather than Marxism) is the idea of *partiinost*, the special blend of commitment engendered by the "party of the new type" itself. And beyond that, they have the Leninist conception of revolutionary tactics—in effect to make any maneuver or concession so long as the fundamental commitment to the eventual total victory of the party is not compromised.

And the essential content of the ideology is the basic Marxist theory of the class struggle leading to socialism, but with the effective substitution of the party for the working class—so that half-crazed Ethiopian Army officers, or spoiled rich youths in Cuba or Nicaragua, ideologically represent the world proletariat as much as do the pampered bureaucrats in Moscow. Nor can a hint emerge that proletarian rule is merely a codeword for party dictatorship.

IV.

As against ideology in any broad sense, the central principles with which the teaching of the Communist Party and their own experience have equipped the present Soviet leadership may, for our purposes, be defined under five headings.

First, it is a way of seeing the world which is in the very strictest sense dogmatic; that is, it accepts the idea that a final world philosophy, political philosophy, and theory of society have been devised, and that the nature of the perfect human order which will prevail throughout the future is known and can be realized by theoretically prescribed methods. That is, it is a closed system of thought, and one which, being "true" in contrast to the falsehood of all others, implies a closed society. As a result, in Solzhenitsyn's words, "the primitive refusal to compromise is elevated into a theoretical principle and is regarded as the pinnacle of orthodoxy."[3]

Second, this way of thinking implies that the political leaders and political considerations generally are on a higher and more comprehensive plane than all other elements in society and are empowered to make the final decision in all fields.

Third, it is based on a view of history and of the world in general that sees struggles and clashes as the only essential mode of political or any other action (on Lenin's principle *kto-kogo?*/who-whom? that is, everything is a struggle in which there is a winner and a loser). And long practice in putting this principle into operation has generated an attitude so deeply ingrained as to be almost automatic.

Fourth, the dogma's claim is universal, applicable to the whole world. All other political orders—even "Communist" ones which deviate in any significant way from that of the USSR (for example, Dubcek's Czechoslovakia or Mao's China)—are in principle illegitimate and should be destroyed when tactically convenient, just as deviant political or other views within the USSR are subject in principle to total suppression.

Fifth, the interests of the party are the only moral principle, and no considerations of truth or humanity are relevant. Such are the foundations, both theoretical and instinctual, of Soviet policy.

V.

Alexander Solzhenitsyn said of the Communists, in his Nobel Speech, that "anyone who proclaims violence as his method is inexorably bound to choose the lie as his principle." Boris Pasternak, in the Epilogue to Doctor Zhivago, described the essence of the Stalin regime as the "inhuman power of the lie." Admitting no external or immanent source of ethics and accepting the transcendental nature of the party's own task, Leninism has no moral criteria beyond the interests of the party. As Lenin himself put it:

> We deny all morality that is beyond men, beyond class; we say that it is a deception . . . a fraud and a stultification of the minds of the workers and peasants in the interests of the landowners and capitalists.[4]

As to his own and his party's actions, he concluded

> Our morality is completely subordinated to the class struggle of the proletariat . . . everything that is done in the proletarian cause is honest.[5]

The methods to be used in forwarding the Communist leadership's ends thus derive naturally, as we have noted, from the absolute nature of their attitude. In effect, nothing is excluded, particularly force and fraud. In practice, and well before the Revolution, the party's reliance on these became habitual. No political system is free from a measure of both, but the completeness of the Communist commitment is of a different order, being unhampered even by theoretical restraints. Nor is this some political antiquarianism; Lenin's teaching on this as on other matters, is massively and routinely inculcated into the party membership in the USSR and is obvious in the conduct of the leadership, both internally and externally.

On deception, in a classical dictum Lenin remarked in his *Left-Wing Communism: An Infantile Disorder*:

> It is necessary . . . if need be, to resort to all sorts of devices, maneuvers, and illegal methods, to evasion and subterfuge, in order to penetrate the trade unions, to remain in them, and to carry on Communist work in them at all costs.[6]

And, of course, this attitude was not confined to trade union matters.

Such pronouncements are for the open instruction of Communists, printed regularly to this day. When it comes to particular orders not designed for publication, we get such things as Lenin's note to Sklyanski:

> under the guise of "Greens" (and we shall pin it on them later) we shall go forward for 10–20 *versts* and hang kulaks, priests and landowners. Bounty: 100,000 rubles for each man hanged.[7]

The "Greens" were non-Communist peasant guerrillas.

The prerevolutionary history of the party is full not only of fund-raising bank robberies but also of schemes to obtain money based on fraudulent marriages to heiresses and the diversion of others' resources into the party treasury. Later Lenin attacked the Italian Socialist leader Serrati in terms that struck the then Secretary of the Comintern, Angelica Balabanoff, as both gross and dishonest. Zinoviev was sent to explain things to her: "We have fought and slandered him because of his great merits. It would not have been possible to alienate the masses [from him] without resorting to these means."[8]

Again, there can be few political organizations that have seen incidents such as the following, in which a dead and respected leader is publicly revealed in falsification by his supposedly devoted adherent. At the Fifteenth Party Congress, Kamenev defended himself against a charge of having sent Bolshevik greetings to the Grand Duke Michael, in February 1917, by pointing out that Lenin had denied this. Stalin answered matter-of-factly that Lenin had merely lied in the Party's interest.

These are a few individual examples from what is thought of as the most "idealistic" period of the party's history. But later, and on a vaster scale, we can note that the central political events of the late 1930's, when the regime took its present form, were the vast public fantasies and forgeries of the Moscow Trials. Moreover nowadays no story, true or false, is available from official sources about that crucial period.

It is even the case that some of those then shot have been rehabilitated while others have not; but of course, the "confessions" were equally damning in all cases and involved the accused in a single complex conspiracy. One of the crimes alleged—an attempt on the life of Molotov—has long since been denounced as a falsification, but not a word has been said to restore the names of those shot for organizing it. What are we to think about the standards, the attitude to truth and terror, of a ruling group which for years seems to have found such a state of affairs natural and acceptable? From this point of view, it remains an oligarchy founded not simply on lies, but on stupid and universally discredited lies.

VI.

Soviet rewriting of encyclopedias constitutes a classical showpiece of this attitude. Many will remember the occasion when, after the fall of Beria, the subscribers to the *Large Soviet Encyclopedia* were sent a fresh set of pages on the Bering Sea and on an obscure eighteenth century courtier named Bergholz, with instructions to remove certain unspecified but numbered pages with razor blade or scissors and paste these in instead. There are many other examples, as when Malenkov lost the premiership and the next edition of the *Encyclopedic Dictionary* only differed from its predecessor in making up space with the insertion of information about a minor fortress, an engineer who had invented a six-wheel bogie, and a hitherto neglected strawberry called *malengr*. An even more remarkable example is to be found in the volume of the *Small Soviet Encyclopedia* which was rolling off the presses in June 1941. In some copies, evidently the earlier part of the printing, Franklin Roosevelt appears as an agent of Wall Street and an instigator of imperialist war. In other copies, he becomes a representative of the people and an opponent of Fascist aggression. When a new edition of the most used Russian dictionary came out in Khrushchev's time, it had a single detectable change from the previous one: *khrushch*, a type of beetle, had hitherto been described as "deleterious to agriculture;" this phrase was now omitted.

The most striking illustration of this attitude to truth is, indeed, to be found in the manipulation of photographs. The most famous case is the classic picture of Lenin addressing a crowd in which two faces originally visible, Trotsky's and Kamenev's, have, for the past fifty years, been eliminated. There are pictures of delegates to the Party Congresses in which, for later versions, previously existing faces have been blurred into other people's greatcoats. There is, too, a celebrated picture of Stalin in exile with a group of other revolutionaries. In the earlier version, Kamenev is on his left; in the later, he has become a tree. The tradition continues. The Soviet authorities have twice published successive versions of pictures of cosmonauts in which the second version, in each case, shows one of the cosmonauts transformed into a doorpost or airplane wall. We do not know why.

There is a photograph story which is stranger still and even more astonishingly illustrative of the Soviet mentality. In the mid-1960's, some of those shot in the Bukharin trial of 1938 were rehabilitated. The question arose of rehabilitating Faisulla Khodzhayev, the Uzbek Communist leader, who had been one of the victims. Meanwhile, a local party history printed a photograph taken in the 1920's. As originally published, it had shown Khodzhayev sitting in the front row. But republishing it presented problems. He had not yet been formally rehabilitated, but those in the party media were clearly aware that the procedures were afoot. Thus, to blank him out altogether in favor of a potted palm would show political short-sightedness, while to put him in would impermissibly anticipate official action. It is hard for us to envisage the debate that must have taken place at quite important levels, harder still to imagine the committee agreeing, when a solution had been found, that it was a splendid idea. For the decision was to print the photograph with one small change: the concealment of the greater part of Khodzhayev's face behind a large beard which had not appeared in the original. (We happen to know that he never wore a beard.)

It is the strangeness of the falsifications, the extravagant mania of the party notion of the relation between power and truth, which makes such details worth recounting. More essential, though, is the refusal to admit that crimes on an enormous scale have been committed. An entirely false account of the Katyn massacre is still maintained. Historic restitution is still denied to the victims of Kolyma. Suppression of the truth of the events of the Stalin period makes the present leaders not only his inheritors, but also his accomplices.

It is not only a matter of falsified history, of false information in the Soviet press, of faked statistics, and so on. In fact, not only these, but everything official in the USSR is founded on falsehood. The Soviet Constitution is a work of fiction with its fine guarantees of civic freedom. Fictitious institutions abound: The Supreme Soviet as an elected and legislative body, the trade unions, the autonomous republics and provinces. The idea that the USSR is, or ever was, a workers' state is itself fictional.

To inflict all this upon their captive population, the party deploys a huge apparatus of propaganda, and an equally huge machinery of suppression, *Glavit*, with its 70,000 censors. *Glavit's* list of banned subjects includes: the earnings of government officials, any reference to food shortages, reference to the existence of censorship, or any reference to rising living standards in non-Communist countries. There is a long list of "unpersons." Indeed, one notes that in the new *Encyclopedia of the Civil War*, there is no article about Trotsky, the victorious War Commisar, although there is still a piece on Trotskyism, wholly devoted to its divergence from Leninism on such issues as the trade unions.

VII.

The way in which deceit (and petty, shameless, obvious deceit at that) penetrates every cranny of Soviet society may be seen at an individual level in, for example, Galina Vishnevskaya's new autobiography, *Galina*. She recounts, among several such experiences, how the Scala Opera Company came to Moscow and, its soprano falling ill, approached the Ministry of Culture to ask for Vishevskaya's services. The cultural official replied that she was not in Moscow. The Italian replied that he was having dinner with her in her Moscow flat that very evening. The official then said that, be that as it might, she did not sing "Tosca." The Scala man pointed out that she had actually sung it with his company only the previous year. The official then said that he would let the other know his answer shortly, and soon afterwards telephoned him at his hotel to say that Vishnevskaya had refused to play in "Tosca." The Italian went to dinner with her and found that she had never been consulted. When he expressed astonishment, she explained "This is the Soviet Union."[9]

Another striking example is to be found in Vladimir Voinovich's book, *The Ivankiad*, which recounts the efforts of the cultural bureaucrat Sergei Ivanko to obtain an illegally large apartment in the Writer's Union block, at the expense of genuine writers with large families.[10] As an appendix, Voinovich prints a letter from Elena Chukovskaya, granddaughter of the famous writer Kornei Chukovsky, whose famous miscellany of short or personal pieces by Russia's leading novelists, poets, dramatists, and others over fifty years had already gone to press when Ivanko intervened and, after having held it up for a year, told her that the roof had fallen in at the printers and the plates had been destroyed. She went round to the printing works, a solid ferro-concrete building, and found no such accident was known there. Ivanko (who last year appeared on television sponsoring the returned, or kidnapped, defector Bitov) has lately, as deputy head of the *Novosti* agency, been a stalwart spokesman for the new insistence on clean government.

On the world scale, Communist propaganda has, of course, always contained a large element of conscious falsification. A characteristic example can be found in Arthur Koestler's autobiography *Arrow in the Blue*, where he describes his work at the Comintern's Western European office in Paris during the Spanish War. His superiors called his output too weak, and insisted on stories that they felt would really rouse public feeling—complete inventions about how the Francoites poured gasoline over their prisoners and burned them alive, or ran over them with tanks.

VIII.

If we look at their conduct in foreign affairs, the Soviet leaders have a special need for massive deception in the present international situation. For the USSR officially launched an "offensive against the positions of imperialism" in 1965, when this expression began to appear regularly in the Soviet press. The first use of this phrase seems to have been by Brezhnev in an address to the Congress of the Rumanian Communist Party on 20 July 1965, when he noted that "some years ago" the Communist Parties had already concluded that the relation of forces had shifted in their favor, and that, in the meantime, this had reached such a stage that "the progressive forces are now on the offensive." The call for this "offensive" was formalized in the Manifesto of the Communist Parties in November (*Pravda*, 28 Nov. 1965). As to the scope of this offensive, in June 1968 the then Foreign Minister Gromyko flatly asserted in his speech to the Supreme Soviet that

> The Soviet Union is a great power situated on two continents, Europe and Asia, but the range of our country's international interests is not determined by its geographical position alone. . . . During any acute situation, however far away it appears from our country, the Soviet Union's reaction is to be expected in all capitals of the world.

Though, of course, equivalent Western reactions to events in Poland and Afghanistan are illegitimate.

The USSR and the whole Soviet bloc were and are economically far weaker than the United States and the West. Moreover, the Soviet economy was also— and permanently—years behind in technology. On any analysis, but especially a Marxist one, the case was hopeless. The Kremlin decision was for steps to be taken to ensure that the West be persuaded, by every possible means of misdirection, not to translate its economic and technological superiority into military power, nor to maintain its political will.

Much is done by political maneuvers of various types, or by speeches and gestures—even of "solemn" (such is the wording) acceptance by the Soviet Union of the Helsinki Accords, which guarantee improvement in the free movement of people and ideas.

Something of the Soviet attitude to solemn international undertakings might indeed have been noted in connection, for example, with their seizure and continued occupation of the Baltic States, still not recognized by the West. We do well to recall that in 1920, the Soviet government signed a treaty with each of the three states renouncing "all rights of sovereignty forever." Later, nonaggression pacts were signed between the USSR and the three states, and a convention defining aggression was also signed in 1933, which stipulated that "no political, military, or other considerations shall serve as an excuse or justification for aggression." Six years later, the Russians and Nazis made the first moves against the Baltic States which, under the Secret Additional Protocol and Secret Supplementary Protocol of the Nazi-Soviet Pact, were to fall within the "sphere of influence" of the USSR. By the end of October 1939, the Soviet government had forced the three Baltic States to sign Mutual Assistance Pacts with them, granting naval and military bases on their territory. These pacts still guaranteed the independence of the three states and promised that it would "not in any way affect their state organization, economic and social systems, military measures, and in general, the principle of nonintervention in internal affairs." Six months later, after ultimatums, Soviet troops occupied the three countries, and they were annexed to the USSR.

The principles under which the USSR occupies the Baltic States contrary to solemn treaty obligations are central to the Kremlin's whole attitude to treaties, and we need not be surprised at recent breaches of arms agreements. We will not here consider the various techniques and methods used, which are dealt with elsewhere in this book. But, in fact, in one sense the whole of Soviet foreign policy is definable in terms of a deployment of force and fraud.

IX.

The points made here are clearly of the utmost importance to all foreign policy decisions made in the West. There is a school of thought, or at least of speech, which continually asserts that the Soviet order has changed in an absolutely essential fashion; that it is no longer the vehicle of an irreconcilable Leninist dogma. If this were true, it would be of great importance. To accept it as true, if it is not true, would mean that we were basing foreign policy on a major fallacy.

One would think that those who believe that such a change has taken place would offer evidence of some sort that this has indeed occurred.

Such evidence might include showing that the state and party institutions, which are the vehicle of the Leninist dictatorship, have changed; here we are on safe ground—no change whatever has taken place. Then, it might be shown that there was a tendency to pluralism in the thought of new Soviet rulers, and hence to tolerance of other ideas; no sign of such a change has appeared either in the conduct of the Soviet rulers toward unorthodox ideas within the Soviet Union, or in their attitudes to political and other views they regard as heretical or wrong in the outside world. Again, a tendency to reconciliation with other orders might be expected to manifest itself in the acceptance of a lower level of armament than that now in place and the avoidance of a "forward" foreign policy in various parts of the world. This, too, does not sound like a very reliable description of what is actually going on. Finally, of course, if such major change had indeed taken place, we would expect to find some decline in falsification—some tolerance of truth.

What we get, instead, is a situation in which less truth is admitted, for example, about the Soviet past than was the case twenty years ago. To take one example, the Soviet Embassy in Ottawa recently put out an account of the 1933 famine in the Ukraine which is best described as a pack of lies. And perhaps we might reflect on the fact that the present Head of the Soviet State was caught lying to the United Nations during the Cuban Missile Crisis of 1963.

Nor should we expect any better from the new generation of leaders, who are just as much a product of Stalin's party as their predecessors. So we are faced with a power group which rules its own citizens by an enormous network of falsification, and which conducts itself in international affairs with the aid of every conceivable misrepresentation it finds useful. The attitudes behind this conduct derive from the Leninist principle that the interests of the party justify any action whatever and, in particular, deception.

The Soviet leaders are men selected for their suitability to the Leninist attitude. Their life experience has been entirely in Leninist terms. Political cultures and political psychologies have great intrinsic momentum, and there is no sign of any serious change in theirs.

Moreover, as we have said, in addition to their mind-set and general motivations and principles, they have the added incentive to a special effort in the sphere of falsifications on the world scale in the fact that, lacking the economic and technological power to outmatch the West, they can only achieve their ends by massive deception of the Western publics and governments.

Notes

1. Norman Cohn, *The Pursuit of the Millenium* (Oxford: Oxford University Press, 1970).
2. Milovan Djilas, *Encounter*, (December 1979).
3. Alexander Solzhenitsyn, *Lecture* (London, 1973), p. 52.
4. V.I. Lenin, *Collected Works* Vol. 41, 5th ed. (Russian), p. 310.
5. Ibid.
6. Ibid.
7. Lenin quoted in *The Trotsky Papers 1917–1922*, Vol. 2, (The Hague, 1964), pp. 278–279.
8. Angelica Balabanoff, *Impressions of Lenin* (Ann Arbor, 1964): pp. xi, 88.
9. Galina Vishnevskaya, *Galina* (New York, NY: Harcourt, Brace, Javonivich, 1985), p. 436.
10. Vladimir Voinovich, *The Ivankiad* (New York, NY: Farrar, Straus, and Giroux, 1977).

7
Deception in the Political-Military Arena

Uri Ra'anan

The topic of this chapter, like all attempts to address the issue of deception, is beset by definitional problems. There is no need to be dogmatic on this matter; nevertheless, some fundamental distinctions have to be drawn. The most important of these concerns the difference between strategic and tactical deception. The latter is practiced widely, both in diplomacy and in armed conflict, although even within those parameters, there are questions of degree that, in many instances, begin to have qualitative aspects. In other words, deception employed habitually and as an integral part of the conduct of international relations, albeit of a tactical kind, has to be distinguished from occasional resort to subterfuge.

For the purposes of this chapter, *strategic deception* implies the deliberate and sustained disguise of fundamental objectives in the international arena, regardless of whether these targets are to be attained by military, political-psychological, or various other nonconventional (or even traditional) means. A rather dramatic, if somewhat primitive, example of such deception was provided by the Nazis. One of their party songs contained the illuminating verse: "*heute gehört uns Deutschland, und morgen die ganze Welt,*" which, for foreign consumption, was changed to read: "*heute hört uns Deutschland, und morgen die ganze Welt.*" The simple elimination of the prefix *ge* changed the meaning from "today Germany belongs to us, and tomorrow the whole world," to "today Germany hears us, and tomorrow the whole world."

However, even the example quoted points to a basic problem in perpetrating such subterfuge—namely, one has to be able to keep the domestic and foreign audiences in watertight compartments, so that the message addressed to one does not "leak" somehow to the other. This is not a simple task, particularly in an age of instant electronic communication with diligent monitoring of the spoken and written word emanating from the various portions of the globe. It might even be a nearly impossible job, unless aided by what the poet Wordsworth coined "the willing suspension of disbelief." That is, the party to be deceived must collaborate wholeheartedly in the effort to mislead it by abandoning the healthy skepticism with which transparent explanations would be treated under normal circumstances. The prospective victim must become blind and deaf, to all intents and purposes, vis-à-vis any material emerging from the other side that would throw doubt upon comforting illusions harbored about an adversary's goals.

Two illuminating examples of such a tendency come from the history of the Nazi state. In one case, the opposition to Hitler dispatched emissaries to London who pleaded with the Chamberlain government to remain steadfast in supporting Czechoslovakia against the Führer's claims, in which case German officers would remove him from power. The apostles of appeasement refused to take seriously the warnings concerning Nazi goals that these brave Germans risked their lives to convey. In the margins of the minutes of the conversations held in London, a member of the Chamberlain government scribbled something along the lines of: "We should refuse to lend an ear to the allegations of these men who are, after all, traitors to their fatherland."

In "Slow Pearl Harbors and the Pleasures of Deception," Roberta Wohlstetter points to the 1936 Anglo-German Naval Agreement, which was violated almost immediately by the Germans, who took it for granted, however, that their transgressions would be noted in London. It never occurred to them that the British Admiralty would be at pains to explain away these violations as being unavoidable for purely technical reasons. As Dr. Wohlstetter explains:

> This had something to do with the discomfort of acknowledging the truth. It was difficult, first of all, . . . to take action against the violations. . . . Not to be deceived was uncomfortable. Self-deception, if not actually pleasurable, at least helps to avoid such discomforts.[1]

This syndrome appears to have persisted over many decades, at least where open societies are concerned. It has led to a corollary, namely, willful blindness to material the other side intends for consumption by its own populace and, particularly, its own elite. Thus, Neville Chamberlain's ambassador to Berlin, Sir Neville Henderson, averted his eyes from the strategic goals outlined so blatantly in *Mein Kampf*, and reiterated almost daily in the *Völkischer Beobachter*, substituting instead what "Herr Hitler himself" might have whispered at some reception for the diplomatic corps. It occurs rarely to Western observers that the aims presented to its own followers by the regime of a closed society may constitute a far more meaningful commitment than any comforting words breathed to a foreign emissary. Few misnomers are more misleading than the assertion that a statement may be intended "only" for "internal consumption."

The question may be raised why such regimes should risk any potential unmasking by leaving in place a major discrepancy between messages aimed at an internal—as opposed to a foreign audience. Why not simply deceive both? The answer has a great deal to do with the very essence of such leaderships. The common factor linking many of the societies in question is the absence of a *legitimate* modality of transfer of power. In the vast majority of instances, the leadership has come to power by violence. However, to ensure a smooth succession means appointing an heir apparent while the previous leader is still in place, thus endangering a "setting sun," by confronting it with a "rising sun," to which power inevitably will gravitate. Consequently, it is not in the interest of Numero Uno to establish a transfer of power mechanism, which, implemented in a reasonably consistent and fair manner and hallowed eventually by time, would confer legitimacy upon the regime as a whole.

In the absence of such a modality, power is grabbed by the contender who is strongest and most ruthless—sometimes by covert means and frequently by open use of force. In the Soviet case, it may suffice to recall that Malenkov was deprived of the first secretaryship of the CPSU, in March of 1953, by means that still remain mysterious; that, while visiting Finland, Khrushchev was ousted by a majority of the Politburo (then called the Presidium), but overturned that majority with the aid of the Red Army upon his return, only to be removed in another coup seven years later (1964) and kept under house arrest for the remainder of his life. No one really knows how (or by whom) Brezhnev, Andropov, Chernenko, or Gorbachev were "chosen"—public declarations notwithstanding.

In the face of such realities, something else has to serve as a legitimating factor in place of a nonarbitrary and time-hallowed transfer of power mechanism. That role can be assumed only by ideology. Confronted by usually bloody usurpations of power replacing individuals or even whole dynasties, the Byzantine precursors of Russian rulers used religion (that is, orthodox Christianity) to explain why a new emperor (however bloodstained his hands might be) deserved to be on the throne, unlike his predecessors. The reason usually given was "The Mandate of Heaven;" that is, he was implementing the will of the deity; whereas the last ruler had been a heretic or schismatic in propagating a deviant view of the Trinity (or some other essential element of the creed).

In the Soviet case, the ideology under the label of Marxism-Leninism (actually an oxymoron for the purist) plays a similar role. In this case, the implementation of the "Mandate of History," serves to legitimize the leader who can defame his adversaries as being deviationists (capitulationists or adventurists), thus indicating that he alone is pursuing the orthodox path. Ex post facto, this can make him appear to be the only deserving heir of his predecessors, regardless of the manner in which he may have seized power. Under such circumstances, one must spell out repeatedly the basics of the official ideology (including ultimate objectives) for the domestic audience, since legitimation is essential primarily to ensure the power base at home.

There is another factor that makes it unfeasible to "hide" these concepts and aims in internal propaganda for the sake of continued deception of adversaries abroad. This derives from the fact that universal laws of power render closed societies notoriously incapable of producing a truly monolithic apparatus; instead they develop competing factions that use ideological arguments in an effort to delegitimize one another.

The truth is that the political process cannot be outlawed in a closed society by mere fiat or ukase. Rather than ceasing to exist, political conflict and rivalries simply are driven into less open channels—as compared, for instance, with the legitimized existence of competing political parties in pluralistic societies. In theory, and in accordance with CPSU statutes, even factions within the single party are supposed to be nonexistent; that is, they are illegal. In practice, such entities are created constantly, and, if only by denouncing them, as in the case of the 1957 "Anti-Party Group," Soviet publications implicitly recognize their presence.

The organization of factions comes into play, inter alia, when the Number One in the leadership dies, is seriously ill, or is otherwise out of action. In such instances, would-be heirs feel that the time has come to engage in the contest for succession. However, that is by no means the only occasion in which factional deployment comes into effect. The Number One himself has every reason for surreptitiously encouraging rivalry and competition among personalities and institutions just below the apex of leadership. This provides the simplest way of keeping potential contenders busy with one another, thus preventing the formation of potentially dangerous power monopolies, particularly in the crucial security and defense agencies. Consequently, the current leader may intentionally duplicate (or overlap) bureaucratic functions (and delimitations) in such sectors as a method that is likely to precipitate antagonism and strife among potential contestants for his "crown." This phenomenon has surfaced in closed societies, time and again, regardless of a particular polity's precise location in the ideological spectrum.

The inevitable result of this process is the appearance of mutually antagonistic (and kaleidoscopically changing) coalitions of personalities, concerned less with issues than with jealousies and conflicts among individuals. Rival leaders and factions attempt to bolster their respective positions by creating "armies" of retainers, strongly reminiscent of the feudal age. In effect, this means that persons close to the apex of power do their best to ensure the appointment of reliable friends and clients to key positions just below their own level; in turn, these appointees try to emplace their own dependents lower down in the hierarchy, and so on. The result is a strikingly feudal chain of overlord and client relationships, with the former providing protection and benefices and the latter owing loyalty, service, and support in return. Alliances between individual "lords" have been known to be cemented even by bonds of intermarriage—in truly feudal fashion.

Thus, personal ties provide the basis of most Soviet elite alignments. However, on frequent occasions, these factions have been known to exploit substantive issues as ammunition against one another (even if, fundamentally, they do not tend to be issue-oriented). After all, their primary aim is to have serious rivals "unmasked" as schismatics, deviationists, or heretics. Issues, therefore, may be exploited usefully as a means of demonstrating that the line advocated by a competing faction simply is incompatible with established ideology.

There is a second consideration that relates even more directly to tactics. During a period of intensified factional strife, it becomes particularly urgent to encourage supporters, demoralize the followers of adversaries, and attract waverers and neutrals into one's own camp. The simplest method of rallying support is to raise one's banners high on the battlefield, precisely like medieval warlords, indicating that one has the upper hand and providing a symbol around which supporters and dependents can gather. Under Soviet conditions, a similar function can be performed with more modern means by groups able to ensure access to the media. In other words, whether pictorially or verbally, each competing faction must be able to demonstrate that it possesses sufficient influence to have the media display its respective hierarchial symbols. In many cases, this may amount to portraying significant changes in the order of protocol by means of such signals as: seating arrangements, number of references in print to a particular name, prominence in receiving important guests, or in signing major documents. More subtly, however, conflicting groups may seize upon a topical issue and attempt to "score brownie points" against one another by stressing differences in approach, often by means of special emphasis, additions or omissions in the wording of a slogan relating to the question concerned, and other forms of semantic manipulation.

As posited earlier, the intent of the exercise usually is to demonstrate that "our" posture is ideologically orthodox and that "they" are suspect of heresy (if not worse).[2] These factors explain why it would be difficult for Soviet leaders to enhance deception operations abroad by delivering to the domestic audience(s) a message clearly at odds with the ideology and its professed objectives. To do so would make life too easy for (factional) adversaries on the prowl, providing them with useful ammunition against anyone who could be labeled with some credibility as a deviationist, schismatic, heretic, and so forth.

The question remains whether it would not be possible for the CPSU leadership at least to exercise less candor in unclassified publications, so as to avoid statements undermining deception ploys in the international arena. It appears that discussions have taken place during the last decade in the Soviet Union and other Communist countries on whether such a change would not be desirable—at least rumors to this effect have reached the West. However, it seems that, on each of these occasions, the decision was reached to continue current practice, since the regime needs to maintain its line of communications with the *"nomenklatura."* Moreover, such a channel is required also to reach a broader elite (numbering hundreds of thousands) even if that represents only a minuscule proportion of the population as a whole. Once it becomes necessary to convey directives to an audience of this size, classification is no longer a viable modality; one simply cannot whisper to over a half million individuals. Since the regime is concerned, above all, to reach the elite with *operational* directives, no feasible alternative has emerged to the utilization of esoteric communication, relying upon Aesopian allusions, and upon a jargon by which every nuance of policy change can be expressed through the employment of slightly different terminology.

Against these advantages of continuing the practice of many decades, no serious collateral damage has been discerned as far as the effect on foreign audiences is concerned. The Soviet leadership found that policy makers and analysts, particularly in the West (for reasons touched upon earlier), tend to avert their eyes from strategic goals outlined rather bluntly in publications of closed societies, or, if any attention at all is paid to such statements, they are dismissed frequently as being meant "only" for "internal consumption." Moreover, the size and quality of the Western Sovietological community has shrunk alarmingly during recent decades. For many years it was staffed by former party members, emigrés, and defectors, trained by their own experiences to read and extrapolate the operational meaning of Soviet publications, with political instincts honed by "life itself."

By the 1960's and 1970's, biology had wreaked havoc upon this community, many of whose finest members succumbed to illness and old age. Their place was taken by a new generation, born and educated in the West, untutored politically by experience. In many cases, their political instincts had atrophied to some extent, causing them to gravitate toward safe topics, particularly if quantification could be substituted for political analysis. Consequently, there was less willingness and/or ability to resort to "content analysis" of Soviet publications. Indeed, increasing doubt was cast upon the utility of that exercise. These factors added to the impunity with which the regime in the USSR and other closed societies could continue to give directives to its own elite, that, if interpreted accurately, would contradict deception ploys in the international arena. To underline this aspect still further, few instances can be found in which the conclusions reached by the relatively small number of Sovietologists left in the field had any significant impact on Western policy decisions.

For these reasons, Soviet material in the public domain continues (with relative candor) to provide indicators of the concepts and objectives of Soviet international strategy. Frequently these are at variance with Soviet deception operations implemented abroad, either directly or through various surrogates, including "fronts." At least, Soviet publications express policy intentions with allusions to appropriate historical episodes or by attribution to other sources of views actually espoused by the Soviet leadership. Occasionally this can produce rather amusing results. For instance, the veteran (former) leader of the Soviet Navy, Admiral S.G. Gorshkov, in describing the Battle of the Atlantic, states with almost poignant regret that German

> submarines did not receive support from the other forces, and above all from the Air Force, which would have been able both to carry out reconnaissance for the submarines, and to destroy ASW forces, as well as to operate against the enemy's [sic] economy by attacking his ports and targets in the shipbuilding industry, not to mention attacks against ships at sea.[3]

He waxes almost lyrical in his admiration of the achievements of German U-boats despite the handicaps he mentions; of course, the use of the term "the enemy" is priceless under the circumstances, since this adversary happened to be an ally of the USSR at the time. Needless to say, Admiral Gorshkov is preoccupied with improving upon the performance of German submarine warfare in a putative conflict with the West, and this preoccupation produced the Freudian slip in question.

In any case, proper attention to, and interpretation of, Soviet material in the public domain leaves very little excuse for Westerners to fall victim to Soviet deception ploys—but for the willingness, even eagerness, of Western societies to be deceived, because of (in Dr. Wohlstetter's words) "the discomfort of acknowledging the truth. . . . Self-deception, if not actually pleasurable, at least helps to avoid such discomforts."[4]

As stated at the outset, the analysis presented here deals primarily with strategic deception, according to the definition presented earlier. This refers above all to attempts to conceal or minimize the fundamental asymmetry between the posture of open and closed societies—and particularly the USSR. Soviet leaders do not differentiate sharply between military and civilian aspects of strategic doctrine, their approach having much more in common with (German) classical "grand strategy" than with circumscribed Western definitions of military doctrine. In Soviet thought, *war* and *peace* are not mutually exclusive antitheses, as they might be perceived in Western minds. In some aspects, the Leninist world view is beholden to social Darwinism as much as were ideologies at the other extreme of the political spectrum. Like Engels, Lenin viewed conflict as the norm of social and political organisms no less than of nature itself. In that context, war and peace constitute no more than hash marks between which the course of permanent conflict meanders.

Despite all the caveats required by the exigencies of a thermonuclear age, Soviet doctrine continues to favor "war-waging" and "war-winning" scenarios, rather than mere "deterrence" and "war-avoidance." To be sure, when dealing with conflict in the current international arena, Soviet literature frequently places emphasis upon "ideological struggle." However, Russian publications leave little doubt that this term is not intended to confine confrontation to the etherial realm of the contest of ideas. Rather, it emerges that such struggle encompasses a veritable gamut of means—conventional and unconventional, overt and covert—through which one system is to attain irreversible hegemony over its adversary, if not eliminating that antagonist entirely.

Thus, Soviet statements emphasize that the USSR will not allow opponents to implement even primarily defensive countermeasures—subsumed conveniently under the heading of "export of counterrevolution." Judging from the examples provided, this category covers Western efforts to ward off the overthrow or defeat of friendly governments. Consequently the status quo is accepted as viable only with regard to the possessions of one of the parties, but remains entirely fluid where the territories and spheres of its adversaries are concerned. To date, the ideological struggle against export of counterrevolution has embraced:

1. Soviet organization, training, arming, and logistical infrastructure for surrogate forces operating in remote regions, including Cubans, East Germans, and others;
2. Similar support for the expanding terrorist international, leaving in abeyance whether or not this implies full Soviet control; and
3. Increasingly direct intervention of Soviet armed forces, (for example, in Afghanistan).

In few, if any, of these instances has the role of the USSR been reactive—that is, it has not been compelled to respond to any military initiatives by the adversary jeopardizing the territorial integrity of the Soviet Union itself. Rather, these have been cases either of Soviet offensives resulting from opportunism (particularly in the Third World), or of Soviet attempts to resolve primarily political problems that have threatened (that is, questioned) the entrenched power monopoly of a Communist Party or of a pro-Soviet regime—with regard to prestige or legitimacy much more than in mainly military terms.

The USSR's rejection of the role of a mere "reactor" reflects an essential ingredient of Soviet doctrine, namely, that it is imperative to seize and to maintain the initiative in military and political arenas alike. This element is linked integrally to two other components of the doctrine—specifically, the penchant for the "offensive," and for "surprise and deception." These are characteristics with profound implications not only for Soviet strategy but also for tactics. It is hardly necessary to define the role these factors can assume in a thermonuclear age. Strategically, "the offensive" wedded to "surprise and deception" may be translated into "first strike" without undue effort of the imagination.

It should not be deduced from these propositions, however, that the Soviet leadership necessarily is committed to short war scenarios. To be sure, Soviet literature stresses that the side enjoying the initiative and resorting to the offensive, with maximal exploitation of surprise and deception, may be able to achieve major, probably decisive, advantages at the initial stages of a global conflagration. This does not mean, however, that, under all circumstances, conflict termination will be achieved rapidly. On the contrary, the Soviet leadership remains convinced of the (typically Continental) view that final victory requires seizure and occupation of enemy soil.

Despite the technological revolution of our age, certain general principles continue to dominate Soviet concepts. Lenin's notebook with comments on Clausewitz has been published. It reveals not only his penchant for Clausewitzian terminology that permeated so much of his work, but his fundamental agreement with the proposition that warfare essentially is an extension of politics. The concept that war qualitatively is not to be viewed as on a plane higher than related forms of political, diplomatic, civil, economic, or social conflict is expressed in Soviet literature from Lenin's time onward. There has been no tendency to review the tenet that conflict is endemic, that it will continue from time to time to take the form of international warfare, and that there are no compromises—only the victors and the defeated. In other words, the USSR subscribes to a dynamic, not a static, view of history. For that matter, the literature continues to posit that ideological struggle is bound to end in the annihilation of one system by the other, as a result not merely of verbal, but of extremely physical conflicts.

As one might expect, Soviet doctrine does not neglect the possibility that the penumbra of military power may prove sufficiently potent for the purpose of achieving political hegemony, precisely because Soviet war-fighting scenarios seem increasingly credible; consequently, actual resort to military might—at least as far as its most devastating strategic manifestation is concerned—may not prove necessary. It is in this sense that one should, perhaps, interpret the remaining echoes of Khrushchev's contribution to the issue of the "inevitability of war" (which he questioned). If the *threat* of force will suffice, then, indeed, use of force may not be essential. In his "Navies in War and in Peace," *Morskoy Sbornik*, Admiral S.G. Gorshkov stated that the purpose of deployment of vast military power was

> to vividly demonstrate the economic and military power of a country beyond its borders. . . . to show readiness for decisive actions, so as to support friendly states . . . to surprise probable enemies with the perfection of the equipment being exhibited, to affect their morale, to intimidate them right up to the outbreak of war, and to suggest to them in advance the hopelessness of fighting. . . . In many cases [this] has permitted the achievement of political goals without resorting to military operations.[5]

Nevertheless, the literature of recent years is replete with war-fighting assumptions (moderated by very few caveats), apparently as the most realistic point of departure for the work of Soviet planners and decision makers. On the other hand, Western war-avoidance theories are usually mentioned with contempt.

The Soviet leadership obviously does not feel it is feasible to eschew war altogether as an instrument of policy. A major doctrinal reason is that Moscow continues to posit a sharp distinction between "just wars" and "unjust wars" and, in this context, goes on to denounce sharply Western pacifists who oppose all wars, regardless of their class content. Soviet doctrine maintains flatly that, by their very nature, wars waged by "socialist countries" against "imperialists" are just with regard to the former, and unjust as far as the latter are concerned, regardless of how the conflict originated or who initiated it. The same concept applies to "wars of national liberation" and to civil wars between the proletariat and the bourgeoisie. Since at least the latter two cases are regarded as endemic, because of the dynamic assumptions of Historical and Dialectical Materialism, and because, in these instances, "the export of counterrevolution" by the "imperialists" is taken for granted, the high probability of a U.S.-Soviet military confrontation is implicit.

Moreover, Soviet doctrine assumes that military conflict between the superpowers, regardless of how and where it starts, most probably will escalate to the nuclear level, so that the respective strategic nuclear forces may be expected to come into play. There are, to be sure, exceptions to this proposition, but they refer only to wars between bourgeois states and to such local wars as may be viewed by the superpowers as being of marginal importance, so that they may be contained. However, even the latter case is not free of Soviet caveats, since the concept of "wars of national liberation" applies not merely to guerrilla actions against established governments, but even to military operations between sovereign states, whenever the USSR sees fit to promote one of them to honorary membership in the National Liberation Movement. Very obviously, therefore, Soviet doctrine (as stated so lucidly and candidly in the relevant portions of Soviet literature) diverges to a very significant extent from the way in which it is perceived by many Westerners, who prefer to make assumptions based on their own world view rather than on careful examination of documentation published in the Soviet Union—and analyzed in the context of Soviet operations and other "hard data."

In this framework, Soviet propaganda (as well as disinformation and other active measures) makes the most not only of such willful blindness, but also of the Western tendency to resort to mirror images, when dealing with other societies. This reflects ignorance of fundamental asymmetries. The Western elite is steeped in a *Weltanschauung* which, at one and the same time, is more narrowly practical and more generously optimistic (or perhaps naive) than that of the Soviet leadership. It postulates a neatly rational "cost-benefit" model of human affairs that grades gain and loss on a rather different scale than the

Kremlin does. The contemporary version of the Judeo-Christian ethic does, of course, acknowledge the reality of competition, both between individuals and larger social entities, including states. It assumes, however, that this particular form of contest is tightly constrained by sophisticated self-interest, causing each party to weigh rationally the possible benefits of winning against the potentially high costs in terms of absolute values as the West sees them (such as human life and human welfare), both in the material and spiritual sense. Thus, the "reasonable" man, who has been the ultimate ideal of Western society since the Age of Enlightenment, will always tend to compromise—to seek a deal in which a fair balance may be struck between the various costs and benefits.

It is almost inconceivable to most Western thinkers and statesmen that there may be societies and leaders who do not necessarily follow or even comprehend this model. Hence, the peculiar difficulties encountered in negotiations between representatives of open and closed societies, in which the former usually will assume that the objective is "compromise," while the latter will take it for granted that the aim of diplomacy is to achieve "by other means" what, perhaps, cannot be gained by force alone—namely, victory of one sort or another. (In this context, our political approach is strangely at variance with our sports ethic in which the National Football and Hockey Leagues have followed baseball rules in outlawing ties, as far as possible, and in assuming that no amount of attrition, time, and energy should be spared in the pursuit of victory.)

Consequently, Westerners tend to take it for granted that Soviet moves are purely reactive and defensive (when the very essence of the Leninist approach to the dialectic demands that one seize and maintain the initiative), and, moreover, that the Soviet leadership views itself as "encircled" because of the many invasions that Russia is said to have suffered throughout history (with many of the conflicts of the past being viewed strangely as one-way streets), so that, understandably, it tends to be paranoid.

Under these circumstances, it requires no vast effort on the part of the USSR to engage in strategic deception, simply exploiting such predispositions on the part of Westerners, which render the creation and feeding of "fronts" (of various types) a relatively straightforward proposition. For the reasons given, this can be accomplished despite the glaring discrepancies between the image projected abroad and the very candid concepts contained in Soviet open literature with its clear operational connotations.

However, it is also true that the Soviet resort to *tactical* deception has become an habitual device in the conduct of international relations to an extent that significantly exceeds the more sporadic and fortuitous instances that can be found in the diplomatic histories of open societies in the contemporary world. Outstanding examples, in terms of the duplicity and fatal consequences involved, include the Hungarian Revolution of 1956, which provided at least two of these instances. One involved the famous 30 October *Pravda* statement seemingly accepting changes in Hungary as a fait accompli and concomitant "negotiations on the withdrawal of Soviet troops." Although some interpretations of these steps still hold that they may have represented a moment of irresolution within the Soviet leadership, in the light of subsequent events it seems far more likely that this was a deception maneuver intended to lull the Hungarian resistance, while gaining the necessary time for the redeployment of Soviet forces required to subdue Hungary by force. There is, of course, no doubt whatever concerning the subsequent development when leaders of the Hungarian forces (particularly Pal Maleter) were invited to Soviet military headquarters purportedly to conclude arrangements for the evacuation of Soviet units from Hungary, but, following their arrival, were seized and subsequently shot—a very effective way of decapitating Hungarian resistance.

A third instance concerned the immunity from persecution promised to Imré Nagy (and to his Yugoslav "hosts"), as a way of extricating him from the Yugoslav embassy where he had taken refuge. As history tells us, he no sooner emerged than he was seized, transported to Romania, and subsequently executed. Even without counting the *Pravda* statement, therefore, Hungary 1956 offers two well-authenticated cases of major tactical deception.

Another comes from the prehistory of the Cuban Missile Crisis. As will be remembered, President Kennedy (already in possession of the aerial photographs showing the infrastructure for the deployment of the Soviet missiles on Cuban soil and the arrival of some of these weapons) met with Gromyko, who went out of his way, without batting an eyelid, to deny any untoward Soviet activities on the island. It is not clear whether he did so in the hope of gaining additional time for full deployment, in the belief that the United States was merely "fishing" but not certain of the facts, or under the impression that the United States would be happy to be fobbed off with a lie providing an alibi for not doing anything—particularly with congressional elections pending. The latter is possible in view of the generally accepted belief that Khrushchev felt he had "taken the measure" of the young President during their Vienna meeting and found him wanting in terms of resolution.

There are instances that straddle the thin dividing line between cases of tactical deception and disinformation. They involve an old ploy known as the "strawman gambit." This calls for the setting up of a straw-man target and knocking it down at a time when one lacks the power to deal with a real antagonist. By defeating the strawman, one can impress everyone with one's "power," thus gaining time to gather real strength and adding to one's credibility in the meantime.

In 1957, Moscow informed a startled world that Turkey and Iraq, supported by Britain and the United States, allegedly were plotting to invade Syria. Before proceeding with this move, the Soviet Union had made quite sure, of course, that there was no such plot. If there had been, the disinformation ploy would have been counterproductive. Having unmasked the "plot," the Soviet Union then proceeded to "deter" it, orchestrating its warnings and threats with sinister moves in the Transcaucasian military district. Of course, the "invasion" never took place, and the Soviet Union claimed and received credit in the Middle East for having been vigilant and powerful enough to "rescue" Syria.

This whole scenario of fabricated threats was dug up again in April-May of 1967. The disinformation experts were not unduly worried about repeating themselves. They had learned from the Kaznacheyev affair that they could be "burned" and unmasked without necessarily having to jettison the compromised persons, newspapers, and stories, for the simple reason that few persons in the West pay attention to such revelations, and fewer still remember for any time what they read.[6]

In 1967, the Egyptians (who had come to rely heavily on Soviet intelligence concerning Israel since there were no Arab diplomatic representatives in that country) were informed by Moscow (via a parliamentary delegation headed by Sadat) that the Israelis had mobilized thirteen brigades, allegedly to attack Syria, and that the only way in which Syria could be saved was through a countermobilization of the Egyptians in the Sinai Desert, thereby creating a second front. This would deter Israel from invading Syria. The Egyptians appear to have believed their Soviet friends and acted accordingly. From the subsequent trial of the Egyptian Minister of War, Badran (for losing the June War), it is known that—when it was too late, and the Egyptians had already mobilized—he ascended the Golan Heights to see the Israeli troop concentrations against Syria and found that the Soviet allegations had been "a mere hallucination."

Of course, the KGB thought that it had come up with a foolproof plan. The Egyptians would mobilize, the nonexistent invasion plot would fail to materialize, the Soviet Union would gain credit from having unmasked it and, together with President Nassar, for having "deterred" it. Most importantly, the U.S. Sixth Fleet would have been totally circumvented as if it did not exist at all. It would have been unable to intervene, since, as Moscow believed, there was not going to be any armed conflict.

The Soviet plan was very clever and should have been utterly safe for the simple reason that Moscow assumed that the UN Emergency Force (UNEF) would stay exactly where it was—at least as far as the vital Straits of Tiran were concerned. There were excellent reasons for this assumption, since Soviet representatives knew perfectly well that the files of the UN Secretary General contained the so-called Hammarskjöld memorandum, which detailed the procedures that Hammarskjöld had told the Egyptians would be employed if Cairo were to demand the unilateral withdrawal of UNEF. The issue was to be brought before the countries contributing troops to UNEF (among which a deadlock was likely), then before the General Assembly (where a two-thirds majority was required), and finally, perhaps, before the Security Council. Months would pass and, Moscow assumed, by that time the crisis would have passed. The Soviet leaders had reason to believe that a weak Secretary General simply would act according to the memorandum. They did not expect (nor did anyone else) that he would withdraw the UNEF overnight from the vital Straits of Tiran, thereby presenting Russia's Egyptian friends with an irresistable temptation that would land them in a catastrophic war. Thus, the Soviet Union, making the one mistake of overlooking human frailty, was left facing the dilemma of either intervening directly to rescue its clients and, thus perhaps, confronting the United States, or seeing its credibility go down the drain. After Egypt declared a blockade of the Straits of Tiran, the purges that took place in Moscow late in May of 1967 were due to this bungled intelligence operation.

This example is characteristic of the mix of components—tactical and strategical, concealment, and disinformation—involved in many Soviet deception moves. What is important to remember is that they must be viewed in their *operational* context. To be sure, as in the last case described, they have been known to backfire. However crucial many of these ploys may have been at particular instants of history, they do not compare in longer-term significance to the ongoing strategic deception described and explained in considerable detail throughout most of this chapter.

A detailed description of the skewed image of Soviet doctrine conveyed through various fronts has not been discussed inasmuch as it is dealt with in other chapters.

Notes

1. Roberta Wohlstetter, "Slow Pearl Harbors and the Pleasures of Deception," in Robert L. Pfaltzgraff, Jr.; Uri Ra'anan; and Warren H. Milberg, eds., *Intelligence Policy and National Security*, (London: Macmillan, 1981), p. 25.
2. Uri Ra'anan, "Soviet Decision-Making and International Relations," *Problems of Communism*, 30 (November-December 1980), pp. 44–45.
3. Admiral S.G. Gorshkov, "Navies in War and in Peace," *Morskoy Sbornik*, no. 12 (1972).
4. Wohlstetter, "Slow Pearl Harbors," p. 25.
5. Gorshkov, "Navies."
6. The counsellor at the Soviet Embassy in Rangoon, who had been in charge of disinformation throughout Southeast Asia, defected and revealed the organs and institutions that had been set up, particularly in India, to serve as his tools; although this was widely publicized, soon thereafter Western media were citing items from these same organs as bona fide information.

8
"A Mask to Cover Shady Deeds": Soviet Diplomatic Deception, 1917–1939

Kerry M. Kartchner

> A diplomat's words *must* contradict his deeds—otherwise, what sort of diplomat is he? Words are one thing—deeds something entirely different. Fine words are a mask to cover shady deeds. A sincere diplomat is like dry water or wooden iron.
>
> —Stalin, 1913

Introduction

The Russian Revolution of 1917 bore with it the seeds of a diplomatic revolution as well, one that made diplomacy an instrument, not for promoting and servicing an international system of diverse nation-states, but for pursuing war against that system. Soviet diplomacy in the 1920's and 1930's was in this sense a charade. It assumed the appearance of normalcy and tradition, but harbored the forces of revolution, hostility, and anti-status quo.[1]

Even Tsarist diplomacy, while characteristically "conspiratorial and manipulative,"[2] sought to realize traditional Russian objectives within the context of the balance of power system. Deception, to the extent that it was to be found, was largely confined to tactical intrigues for bargaining leverage. In contrast, Soviet diplomatic practice of the 1920's and 1930's constituted a systematic effort to disguise the fundamental character of Lenin's grand scheme, deflect objections to its Marxist-Leninist context, and serve as a "legal" cover for agents of espionage, subversion, and diplomatic war on the West.

One of the first acts of the newly empowered Bolshevik government was to abolish the foreign ministry—and with it the vestiges of Tsarist diplomacy. "When the Bolsheviks seized power in October 1917, they confidently expected that the world revolution would quickly sweep away the capitalist states and, with them, the need for the devious arts of bourgeois diplomacy."[3] However, in the words of Vernon Aspaturian: "The failure of world revolution to exfoliate according to expectations and the *de facto* survival of the Soviet state in a hostile world forced the Bolsheviks to reappraise diplomacy as a means of conducting foreign relations with capitalist powers during the period of coexistence."[4]

To this end, Lenin and his coconspirators aspired to "an honest, popular, truly democratic foreign policy," one that would abolish "secret diplomacy and its intrigues, codes, and lies."[5] And yet, if such practices as using diplomatic negotiations, public posturing for foreign audiences, dissemination of propaganda via diplomatic missions, and manipulation of other instruments of foreign policy, to mask, disguise, or obscure the true ends of a state's national objectives can be called "diplomatic deception", then the Soviets must be considered early masters among twentieth century governments of "intrigues, codes, and lies" for ostensibly traditional diplomatic ends.[6]

Particularly hypocritical is the Soviet repudiation of secret diplomacy. Within months of the establishment of the new Bolshevik regime, secret military protocols had been signed with Germany at Brest-Litovsk, and other secret agreements were to follow on 30 Jan. and 7 May 1920.[7] Obviously, some characteristics of "bourgeois diplomacy" would still be useful to the fledgling Bolshevik party and its embattled country.

In the following pages, I will attempt to characterize Soviet diplomatic deception during the 1920's and 1930's; suggest its social, historical and political basis; identify its objectives; and illustrate some of its manifestations. Some observations on the role of Western self-deception will be followed by concluding remarks.

It is not difficult to trace the bases or origins of Soviet diplomatic deception, nor is it difficult to establish significant reasons that compelled the Bolsheviks to resort to "bourgeois" (that is, petty and desperate) forms of diplomacy. These sources include primarily the writings of Lenin,[8] but more generally they encompass Marxist-Leninist ideology, domestic Bolshevik political ethics (or operational codes), and the material inferiority of the Soviet state.

Marxist-Leninist ideology was an important rationalization for Soviet diplomatic deception. It provided the overall strategic objective of the Soviet state, identified the enemy and his characteristics, and prescribed the means necessary to thwart that enemy and advance the cause of socialist revolution. Most important, it endowed the Bolshevik leaders with a basic moral hierarchy. Nathan Leites has suggested that, for the Bolsheviks, "The fundamental law is to do all that enhances the power of the Party, the great and only instrument in the realization of communism, the great and only goal."[9] Writing later, Leites offered this simplified characterization of Bolshevik morality and its justification of the resort to any means for a "supreme end:" Another way to reduce the moral dimension is to recognize no more than two moral statements: one specifying the supreme end, the other requiring that any other aspect of the world be treated only as a means useful for—or as an obstacle to—the attainment of this end.[10]

And what was this "supreme end"? From the beginning Soviet policy (foreign and domestic) had one aim—worldwide socialist revolution, led by the Bolshevik party.[11] The greatest threat to the survival of the Bolshevik regime and its status as the vanguard of international socialist revolution was Western recognition of (1) its true character and inimical ambitions; and, perhaps even more important, (2) its exhausted condition. This, then, was the fundamental rationale for Soviet diplomatic deception in the inter-war period—to convince the West not to resist the stated aims of Marxist-Leninist ideology while the Soviet state lay depleted and weakened from nearly seven years of world and civil war.

Understanding the Bolshevik attitude toward agreements also sheds light on Soviet diplomatic deception. Treaties, memoranda of understanding, aides-memoire, are all the standard fare of traditional diplomacy—the currency of efforts to resolve disagreements by negotiated settlement. The Bolsheviks had an entirely different attitude toward the instrumentality of agreements with the 'class enemy,' one that underscores the justification, even requirement, for resort to deception through diplomacy. Leites has formulated three insightful characterizations of this Bolshevik attitude toward 'deals:'

> "(1) Any agreements between the Party and outside groups must be regarded as aiding the future liquidation of these groups and as barriers against the liquidation of the Party by them. . . . Therefore there is no essential difference between coming to an ostensibly amicable arrangement with an outside group or using violence against it; they are both tactics in an overall strategy of attack.
>
> "(2) When an attempt by the enemy, or by the Party, to advance by violent means has failed, the conditions for an effective agreement between the Party and the enemy come into existence.
>
> "(3) The Party must always expect outside groups to violate agreements."[12]

In these characterizations can be seen a visceral belief that the class enemy himself resorts to deception for his own ends and therefore must be confronted with whatever means and ends necessary, including matching deception with deception. As one author notes: "duplicity in dealing with the class enemy is deeply rooted in Soviet doctrine and practice." [13]

What the Bolsheviks practiced in diplomatic intercourse with other nations was no different in character (or motivation) from that which marked their dealings among themselves, or with contending extra- or intra-party factions. On this note, Professor Aspaturian observes that "The diplomacy of individual states rarely rises above the ethical standards of conduct which characterize their internal political practices and struggles, which in turn are largely shaped by their social, political, and economic structures that their diplomacy is designed to preserve or promote as the occasion demands or the opportunities invite." [14]

In the 1920's and 1930's, the Bolshevik state was inferior in nearly every traditional index of national power. It had little to bargain with for international recognition and was at a disadvantage in dealing with the "class enemy" on conventional terms. So, naturally, unconventional terms had to be resorted to. Soviet Russia was substantially inferior in material terms to those nations it most depended on for economic, military, and diplomatic assistance, acquiescence, neutrality, or nonaggression. Deception was deemed necessary by Bolshevik leaders to deter incentives for attack, secure advantageous terms in trade agreements, and to stabilize its internal situation free from external interference.

Other important sources of Soviet diplomatic deception may be conceived as follows:

1. A totalitarian form of government which provides an internal organizational environment conducive to the formulation and implementation of tactical and strategic deception on all fronts, including diplomacy;
2. Russian/Soviet cultural and historical precedents;
3. Leadership commitment to tactical compromises portrayed as strategic concessions;
4. An organizational structure which provided the resources, capabilities, and plans for implementing deception;
5. Willing and receptive audiences susceptible to deception and its self-inflicted variants; and,
6. A diplomatic style (confrontational and intransigent) that facilitated tactical deception, and thus promoted deception at the strategic level.

The motives for Soviet diplomatic deception are thus readily identified. In attempting a better understanding of the objectives of Soviet diplomatic deception, it may be useful to list the types and varieties of activities here understood as "diplomatic deception." These include:

Concealing actual purposes or objectives not directly related to the subject of particular negotiations;

Diplomatic surprise (for example, the Treaty of Rapallo, 16 April 1922);

Deliberate dishonesty in negotiations for the sake of gaining some tactical advantage;

Making an agreement with the intention of abrogating it (for example, the Treaty of Brest-Litovsk, 3 March 1918);

Misleading a third party concerning negotiations with another party (for example, the British at Genoa, April 1922 and again in August 1939 with the Molotov-Ribbentrop Pact);

Other motives for Soviet diplomatic deception probably included:

Compensating for traditional Soviet weaknesses in negotiations vis-à-vis the West;

Reaching certain propaganda targets for which other means were unsuitable or ineffective;

Exploiting antagonisms among the "imperialist powers" in the West;

Disguising, obscuring, misrepresenting, or hiding internal crises that may reveal indications of Soviet weakness, and so forth;

Exaggerating, or fabricating some Western weakness or crisis in order to show the superiority of the Soviet system or enhance relative Soviet prestige and standing in the international community;

Many of the above deceptive activities and motives are more accurately characterized as tactical in nature. For the purposes of this chapter, those that are properly strategic in nature can be broken down into two areas (or objectives)—corresponding to what certain Soviet scholars have termed "simulation" and "dissimulation" as defined by the following passage: "Diplomacy always has at its disposal two obedient slaves: *simulation* and *dissimulation*. Simulate what is *not*, but that which *is* dissimulate."[15]

Soviet diplomacy of the 1920's and 1930's involved strong elements of both simulation and dissimulation which can be represented as follows:

simulation: diplomacy used to promote an alternative view of the Soviet Union as something other than an implacable ideological foe; and,

dissimulation: diplomacy used as a cover for espionage, subversion, and other acts one would expect of an implacable ideological foe.

Diplomacy as Simulation

From the point of view of simulation, (here taken to mean the use of diplomacy to promote an alternative view of the Soviet Union—one that downplays or dismisses its ideological hostility toward the West), the principal task of Soviet diplomacy has been strategic deception almost from the beginning—to obscure the differences between the democracies and communism, to promote the illusion of a Soviet state with which one "could do business," and to disguise Soviet hostility toward opposing social systems. John Lenczowski aptly captured this rationale for Soviet diplomatic deception in an earlier chapter of this book. He states that "because a large part of Soviet-Communist foreign policy is designed to effect political transformations of foreign countries against the wishes of their peoples and existing governments, the concealment of such policies is essential if they are to be effective." Early on this took the form of promoting the notion that the Soviet state had recognized the impracticality or inadvisability of its own ideological campaign for world revolution and had adopted more traditional national interests.

This is what Joseph Whelan terms "the shift toward traditional diplomacy." It is one of the most important aspects of Soviet diplomatic deception in the 1920's and 1930's. Whelan succinctly identifies five factors precipitating this shift, paraphrased as follows:[16]

1. Defeat at Brest-Litovsk;
2. Disillusionment with the failure of revolution abroad;
3. Fear generated by the unexpected recovery and consolidation of the bourgeois governments in Europe after 1918;
4. The isolation of a Soviet Russia weakened by war, revolution, and civil war, making it vulnerable to what was perceived as capitalist encirclement; and,
5. An awareness of economic interdependence as a necessity for Russian recovery.

It may be argued that the Soviet assumption of traditional modes of diplomacy was not in itself deceptive—that Soviet Russia did, in fact, concede the necessity of engaging countries of the West on their terms; that Chicherin, the new Foreign Commissar (who was delegated the responsibility of adapting Soviet diplomatic practice to these traditional modes of diplomacy) was no less sincere or forthright about his objectives than were his Western counterparts. Certainly there was cause for Lenin's "change of course" in 1921.[17] What can clearly be identified as deception, however, are the long-term objectives to which this "shift toward traditional diplomacy" was subordinated. This shift did not signal a fundamental Soviet "change of heart" toward the West, although that is precisely the impression to be conveyed. Therein lies the deception. When its tactical objectives were satisfied, and when this shift no longer was effective in achieving them, the Soviet Union showed no hesitation in dropping the pretense of peaceful coexistence and returning to a hostile posture toward the West, one more superficially compatible with its Marxist-Leninist commitment to world revolution.

Speaking specifically of the early 1920's, Anatoliy Golitsyn characterized this shift as intended to project

> an image of evolution away from an ideological toward a conventional, national system. The intention is that the nations of the noncommunist world, accepting the alleged disunity and evolution of the communist world as genuine, will fail

to respond effectively to communist offensive strategy and, in their confusion, will be induced to make practical miscalculations and mistakes in their dealings with the communist world.[18]

There are several important episodes, or aspects, of Soviet diplomacy that demonstrate a form of cover, or mask, for an inherent hostility toward the norms of the international system of capitalist states. They are Bolshevik objectives and tactics at Brest-Litovsk during the winter of 1917–1918; the early 1920's "change of course" toward relaxation of "War Communism" at home and "calculated ideological moderation" abroad; disassociation of the Soviet government from links to the Comintern; concealing military cooperation with Germany; and semantical homage to Western ideals and political values. These are treated in turn in the following pages.

Brest-Litovsk

The Soviet-German agreement at Brest-Litovsk is important to this discussion of Soviet diplomatic deception for several reasons even though it predates the shift in the 1920's toward the traditional diplomacy discussed previously. It is because it predates this shift that it is so important, for Brest-Litovsk revealed the earliest Bolshevik attitude toward diplomacy. In many ways the Soviet-German agreement reached at Brest-Litovsk set precedents in terms of the Soviet approach to diplomacy, negotiating style, and (non)compliance with bilateral agreements. Despite its lessons for East-West diplomacy, it is rarely referred to in contemporary analyses of Soviet diplomacy, foreign policy, or treaty compliance standards. Yet, Brest-Litovsk is one of the best examples of the Soviet use of tactical deceit in negotiations and of diplomacy as an instrument for misleading an adversary about the nature and intentions of one's national policy.

Brest-Litovsk was "conceived from the outset as a revolutionary weapon." As Trotsky explains:

> We are conducting these negotiations . . . so as to accelerate the rising of the working masses against the imperialist cliques. We are ready to support this uprising with all the forces at our command. . . . We do not doubt for a moment that, in consequence of the present war, the workingmen of Europe will repeat the fight of the Russian proletariat, a month sooner or later, on more powerful economic foundations and in a more perfect political form. . . . Our whole policy is built on the expectation of this revolution. The peace-program, as submitted to us, can be fully accomplished only by overthrowing the capitalist governments.[19]

Further evidence of this open declaration of revolutionary intention is provided by the following passage from Louis Fischer, *The Soviets in World Affairs*, wherein he quotes Trotsky:

> Almost in the very hour of the opening of the Brest-Litovsk peace conference . . . Trotsky announced in Petrograd that "yesterday a freight car full of propaganda for peace and socialism was dispatched to Germany." "Although we are negotiating peace with Germany," declared the Foreign Commissar, "we continue to speak our usual revolutionary tongue."[20]

The significance of Brest-Litovsk is further underscored in the following passage:

> Trotsky's performance at Brest-Litovsk dramatized the new Bolshevik approach to diplomacy and in many ways set the mold for the future. This approach was a radical departure from both the old and the new as it was then taking shape; it was, as Nicolson said, 'something else.' It ignored the premises and values, the style and the ethics of traditional European diplomacy and declared its own based on a uniquely designed revolutionary Marxist-Leninist ideology. It set for itself revolution as a primary goal and linked this ultimate purpose to a radical negotiating style. In brief, it made diplomacy an instrument of revolution, and negotiations one more weapon in the arsenal of the class struggle.[21]

An aspect of Soviet diplomatic deception mentioned earlier regards Soviet intentions of noncompliance once an agreement or a set of negotiations no longer serves their interests. Here again, Brest-Litovsk provides the earliest example. Soon after its ratification, Lenin boasted of "thirty or forty" violations.[22]

Calculated Ideological Moderation

Soviet diplomatic deception in the inter-war period was most active and effective during times of ostensible detente and peaceful coexistence.

This was true during the early 1920's when the Soviet Union adopted the New Economic Policy (NEP) and assumed a posture of "calculated ideological moderation" (to use Anatoliy Golitsyn's phrase), and again during the early 1930's, when the Soviet government sought collective security against the fascist threat in the West and the Japanese imperialist drive in the East.

The NEP was only one manifestation of the overall "change of course" mentioned earlier and was marked by conciliation on several fronts. Elements of this new stance included an apparent moderation in communist ideology, avoidance of references to violence as a communist method, exaggeration of the degree of capitalist restoration in Russia, the use of traditional businesslike styles in diplomatic negotiations, concessions for recognition and trade, the theme that "one can do business with Soviet Russia," and an emphasis on peaceful coexistence (in particular, Lenin's disarmament "volte face" of 1922).[23] The Soviets

> intended that the NEP would not only bring about economic recovery, but would also serve to prevent internal revolt, expand foreign trade, attract foreign capital and expertise, gain diplomatic recognition from noncommunist countries, prevent major conflict with the Western powers, help to exploit the contradictions in and between the capitalist countries, neutralize the emigre movement, and help promote revolution through the communist movement.[24]

Certain tactics characteristic of this period have been delineated elsewhere, and I include them here as examples of the uses of diplomatic deception:[25]

1. "[U]nderstate the actual strength and aggressiveness of communism" and emphasize real and artificial weaknesses in the system in order to avoid alarming temporary allies;
2. Cast policy readjustments as necessitated by failures;
3. Downplay ideological differences between communist and noncommunist systems;
4. Appear practical rather than dogmatic, demonstrate apparent ideological permissiveness;
5. Exaggerate areas of common interests between communist and democratic systems; and,
6. Obscure and conceal long-range Communist objectives.

Denial of Links to the Comintern

Another important aspect of Soviet diplomacy as an instrument for obscuring its ideological hostility toward the West involves denial of Soviet government and party links to the Comintern. The Comintern was a Communist instrument of direct "agitation"—aimed at accelerating the overthrow of established governments and facilitating the progress of the proletariat revolution. It was necessary for the Soviet government to disassociate itself from this organization to support the notion of "calculated ideological moderation" which in turn supported the mendacity of Soviet-Western moral equivalence.

This is substantiated by a memo allegedly written by Lenin to Chicherin in 1922 which reveals not only the substance of Soviet deception but also a certain callousness toward Soviet sympathizers in the West:

> Following my direct observations during my years of immigration, I must conclude that what one calls the cultivated circles of Western Europe and America are totally incapable of comprehending either the present situation or the real correlation of forces.

These circles must be considered deaf-mutes. The revolution never develops in a straight line or by uninterrupted exchange; revolution consists of a series of accelerations, sudden brakes, attacks, truces, and periods of relative calm, during which the power of the revolution reinforces itself and prepares itself for final victory. . . . given the long length of time required for the growth of a world socialist revolution, we must resort to special maneuvers that can accelerate the ultimate victory over capitalist countries.

A. Announce, with a view to reassuring the deaf-mutes, the fictitious separation of our government and government organs, on the one hand, and the Politburo —especially the Comintern—on the other. The Comintern must be clearly categorized as an independent political group whose presence is merely tolerated within our borders. The deaf-mutes will believe this.

B. Express our hope to establish immediate diplomatic relations with all capitalist countries on the basis of total non-interference in their internal affairs. The deaf-mutes will believe us again. They will even be delighted and will throw their doors wide open. Through these doors will enter the emissaries of the Comintern and our secret service under the cover of diplomatic, cultural, and trade representatives. To tell the truth is a petty bourgeois habit, whereas to lie is justified by our objectives.

The capitalists of the whole world and their governments will close their eyes on the kind of activities I have described and will become blind as well as deaf-mutes.

They will extend loans which will provide us with the equipment and technology we lack and will thus help rebuild our military industry which we need to launch subsequent victorious attacks against our suppliers. In other words, the capitalist nations will always work to prepare their own suicide.[26]

It was necessary for the Comintern to carry out the deception of appearing autonomous from the Soviet government because the Comintern was the explicit Bolshevik instrument for implementing the program of world communism.

When confronted with an apparent coincidence, Litvinov and Stalin feigned ignorance of a July 1935 meeting of the Comintern in Moscow, for which it was rumored that "resolutions and directives had already been prepared in final form." (The implication being, of course, that Stalin himself had previously approved or otherwise oversaw the drafting of these resolutions and directives.)[27]

Concealing Military Cooperation with Germany

Concealment of its military ties with Germany was another dimension (albeit indirect) of Soviet diplomatic deception. This cooperation was again indicative of inimical Soviet objectives vis-à-vis the international system and its disregard for both the accepted norms of international behavior and for the sanctity of multilateral agreements (Soviet military aid to Germany helped circumvent Treaty of Versailles restrictions on German rearmament).

In early 1922, the Soviets were invited by Western powers to attend the Genoa Conference as a gesture of goodwill. It was a signal that certain Western nations were prepared to bring them into a "community of nations." While at Genoa, the Soviets signed a separate treaty with Germany (Rapallo), causing a great deal of consternation among the Western delegations and playing Western foreign policies off against each other. The element of deception here is twofold. First, the Soviet Union deceived the West regarding its imminent gesture toward Germany. Second, the Soviet Union deceived the West concerning the military dimensions of Soviet-German relations.[28]

E.H. Carr relates this episode as follows:

> The Rapallo Treaty was represented to the British Ambassador as a sudden and unpremeditated act; nothing, he was told, with an accuracy so precise as to border on falsehood, had been "initialled" in Berlin before the departure of the delegation for Genoa. A few days later he was "formally and deliberately assured that the subject of military preparations had never been mentioned between the Germans and the Russians."[29]

For the purposes of this chapter, this relationship serves to illustrate the following points. First, this process of clear deception was not primarily diplomatic in character and thus would seem to fall outside the scope of this inquiry. Yet, Soviet diplomacy was charged with disguising Soviet-German military cooperation as commercial cooperation. This episode indicates that, in certain situations, Soviet diplomatic deception served as cover for deception not directly related to diplomatic intercourse.

Professing Western Political Ideals

The Soviets, in their efforts to deflect overreaction to the more explicitly hostile elements of their ideology and self-proclaimed program of world revolution, espoused, at various times and in various forms, the very Western political ideals they were accused of subverting. Soviet use of terms similar to Western terminology but with different connotations, as well as certain other language ambiguities, compounded this deception. This tactic included feigned espousal of traditional Western democratic ideals such as noninterference in the internal affairs of other nations (provisions to this effect were inserted in nearly all treaties and agreements of friendship, non-aggression, and neutrality signed by the Soviets in the 1920's), the honoring of debts, "democracy," freedom of religion,[30] free elections, and even certain human rights.

In the 1930's, the Soviets adopted many of these same themes and techniques and once again employed diplomacy as but one method among a plethora of national instruments to perpetuate falsehoods and misconceptions regarding the Soviet Union's internal weaknesses and external ambitions. The results can be tabulated as follows:

The success with which the Soviet Union was able to convince other important countries that it had evolved into a responsible member of the international society of states is demonstrated by admission into the League of Nations in 1933;

Treaties of alliance were concluded with France, Czechoslovakia, and others;

The Comintern shifted its emphasis from violent revolutionary agitation to advocacy of the "popular front" strategy, or alliances with other socialist, radical, and liberal groups;

At the League of Nations, Litvinov preached the doctrine of the indivisibility of peace (linking Western security with the survival of a stable Soviet regime) as a component of the Soviet "collective security" gambit; and,

The Soviet Union portrayed itself as the champion of peace and the status quo, where before it had agitated for the destruction and overthrow of the world capitalist system.

Diplomacy as Dissimulation

For the purposes of this chapter, "dissimulation" is taken as referring to the use of diplomacy as cover for "illegal" espionage activities. The use of diplomacy as a convenient cover for intelligence, subversion, and monitoring was an important aspect of Soviet diplomatic deception in the 1920's and 1930's. As with other symptoms noted earlier, it is reflective of the Bolsheviks' low regard for both the traditional character of diplomacy and the integrity and national sovereignty of those nations and the state-system with which they dealt.

The Use of Embassies and Diplomatic Posts as Cover for Espionage

All our [diplomatic] missions are equipped with agents of the Tcheka, of the Komintern, and of the military spy system called the resident agents. Their heads bear nominal titles: the president of the Tcheka would be the second secretary, the representative of the Komintern would be known as head of the Intelligence Department, the attache at the legation would be in reality chief of the military spy system.

This representative [that is, the attache] is in no way subject to the Minister or Ambassador. His work is "autonomous." He receives money directly from Moscow, through the diplomatic post; he has his own code, undecipherable by the embassy, his own staff, entered on the Embassy records as Embassy typists, record-keepers, and clerks. In order that the utmost secrecy may be preserved, this staff is paid by the Embassy, which renders an account to Moscow. And only at Moscow are the amounts disbursed to these functionaries regularly authorized by the books of the War Department, the Komintern, and the Tcheka respectively.[31]

This is how a former Soviet "diplomat" (who first learned of this deception while acting head of the Ukrainian Commissariat for Foreign Affairs—itself perpetuating a fraud by sustaining a facade of independence from Moscow) reported the exploitation of his diplomatic mission for "illegal" activities. Diplomatic immunity served a convenient purpose other than spying on the host country—it also allowed easy monitoring of the diplomatic staff (whose exposure to corrupting influences in the West always cast shadows on their ideological loyalty to the Soviet state and Communist Party). Bessedovsky continues:

> The representative of the Tcheka also has secret agents among the embassy officials in order to keep himself informed of what goes on among them, the people they associate with, and the means at their disposal. In fact he has external agents who are answerable only to the representative of the Tcheka and the military spy system; none of the professional diplomats, not even the Ambassador himself, has the right of surveillance over these external agents, nor may he know their names.[32]

Protecting the integrity of these agents' cover naturally took priority over diplomatic duties, thus further supporting the notion that diplomacy took a back seat to deception and revolution:

> When a clash occurs between diplomats and the agents around them, the diplomats are as a rule considered to be in the wrong; so that it doesn't do to have enemies among these people.[33]

Apparently, the deception was carried so far as to involve codewords to be used when referring to these agents:

> All correspondence must be discreet. The Central Committee of the Communist Party must be called "the competent authority," the Komintern and its agencies "our friends," the Tcheka "our immediate neighbors," the military spy system "our remote neighbors," for their position in Moscow is further from the Commissariat for Foreign Affairs than that of the Tcheka.[34]

Bessedovsky further substantiates these claims by noting that the Ukrainian embassy in Poland was dominated by TCHEKA agents, as was the Soviet embassy in Paris.

It should be noted, however, that others are skeptical about the extent of this diplomatic deception. Teddy J. Uldricks, for example, argues that:

> The role of Soviet diplomatic missions in espionage operations has . . . been greatly exaggerated. The small amount of reliable evidence available on this subject suggests that the Narkomindel's embassies occasionally provided cover for members of the Soviet intelligence network, but that this practice was soon restricted. . . . By 1927 the diplomatic and intelligence services had been decisively separated from each other.[35]

Uldricks later notes in a footnote that "after Litvinov lost control of the NKVD in 1937 the situation changed and NKVD agents were once again given license to expand their covert operations, using diplomatic posts as cover."[36]

Uldricks does, however, allow that "most embassies included a sizable contingent of *Tcheka* (later GPU) officers, but their principal duties involved monitoring the political loyalty of the mission staff and combating anti-Soviet intrigues among Russian emigre circles"—thus supporting the notion that diplomacy was in some cases a subservient instrument employed for deceptive ends.[37]

The Funding of Subversion

Diplomacy as a cover for revolutionary activities is readily documentable. A decree of the Council of People's Commissars, issued 13 Dec. 1917, directed that two million rubles be placed "at the disposal of the foreign representatives of the Commissariat of Foreign Affairs for the needs of the Revolutionary Internationalist Movement."[38] Furthermore, revolutionaries of many nationalities were given highly responsible posts in the Soviet hierarchy.[39]

John Reed relates this account:

> Upstairs functions disjointedly the Bureau of the Press, with an army of translators, under the erratic direction of Comrad Radek, of Austria and other places—a violent young Jew. Next door is the newly founded Department of International Propaganda, presided over by Boris Reinstein, American citizen and incorrigible mainstay of the Socialist Labor Party of the U.S.A.—an excessively mild-mannered little man who burns with a steady revolutionary ardor. Under him are formed committees of the various peoples—German, Hungarian, Rumanian, South-Slavic, English-speaking—engaged in propagating the ideas of the Russian Revolution abroad.
>
> Every week the "diplomatic couriers" of the People's Commissariat leave Smolny for the capitals of Europe, with trunk-loads of this material, bent on stirring up revolution.[40]

The Role of Western Self-Deception

The key to any successful deception is endowing it with some element of truth. The essence of self-deception is in insisting upon seeing and believing what one wants to believe, despite evidence to the contrary, and therefore the key to exploiting self-deception is playing upon what the opponent wishes to believe. In each of the previously cited episodes, both the citizens and leaders of Western nations in the 1920's and 1930's were able to rationalize their accommodation of the Soviet Union by exaggerating evidence of genuine change in the Soviet system. It was these deliberately cultivated misperceptions about the nature of the Soviet system and its (in)compatibilities with democracy that led to important successes for Soviet diplomacy in the 1920's and 1930's.

Two aspects of self-deception warrant brief comment here. First, the West insisted, once again, upon interpreting an essentially tactical maneuver as presaging radical and fundamental changes in Soviet policy. By adopting Western diplomatic customs and practices, the Soviets promoted this interpretation. Louis Fischer notes that "Moscow's behavior fed the high hopes which the Western nations set on Genoa. For when the Communist delegates appeared in Berlin and later in the Italian seaport wearing top-hats and cut-aways, the bourgeois world said, 'These outward forms have a deep and symbolic meaning. They herald a change in conviction'."[41]

Second, the Soviets also successfully promoted the false appearance of separate branches of government. The implication was that economic branches of the Soviet government were less driven by ideological considerations (and more by pragmatic considerations) than were the other branches of the Soviet government. "The Communists encouraged and the West accepted the fiction that despite the Soviet monopoly of foreign trade, the Soviet economic branches of the government were less official than the political."[42] In the negotiations leading to the trade agreement signed with Great Britain on 16 March 1921, these presumably "less official" departments were more reliable, and less repugnant, to the British government than were the ideological motivations eminating from the Kremlin.

Although Lenin's New Economic Policy of 1921 was motivated by genuine military and political imperatives, Soviet leaders never claimed it would be a permanent change. In fact, Lenin often referred to the necessity for "tactical retreats" and "breathing spaces." Nevertheless, important leaders in the West were anxious to herald these tactical maneuvers as harbingers of fundamental and long-term changes in the nature of the Soviet regime, particularly with regard to the ideological hostility of that regime toward opposing social systems.

David Lloyd George, British Prime Minister from 1916 to 1922, was a key proponent of disregarding Soviet Communist ideology and of treating Russia in conventional terms—that is, as driven by traditional national interests rather than as ideological myths. He vigorously promoted the idea that "settlement of the Russian problem is essential to the reconstruction of the world."[43] He anticipated arguments that gained intellectual currency in the 1960's by stating that "It is a small world and nations are very dependent on each other. We are dependent on Russia, and Russia is dependent on us."[44]

These attitudes directly culminated in the Anglo-Soviet Trade Agreement, signed 16 March 1921, effectively granting de facto British recognition to the Bolshevik regime. The importance the Soviets attached to this recognition should not be underestimated. It was perhaps more important than the substance of the trade agreement itself. Similar commercial agreements with other countries soon followed. Lenin's tactical shift yielded immediate benefits in terms of Soviet prestige, trade credits, and Bolshevik standing at home. British de jure recognition followed in 1924.

The conviction that Russia must be brought into the "community of nations" extended to issues of disarmament and Soviet membership in the League of Nations. David Lloyd George declared on 15 June 1926: "You will never know peace in Europe or peace in the world until Russia is included in the fraternity of nations. I know it is not a popular thing to say, but unpopular things are not always untrue, and popular things are not always true."[45]

Soon afterwords, Viscount Grey, another prominent British politician, echoed these same sentiments:

> Unless you get Russia into the League of Nations, bonafide, in favour of disarmament she will always be an obstacle in the way of disarmament. So far as the constitution of the Government is concerned, whether it is a despotism or whatever it is, I would treat it as we have always done other Governments, whose constitutions we did not approve.[46]

In no way did these efforts result in a lessening of Bolshevik devotion to the ultimate goal of world socialist revolution. They did, however, have two significant ramifications. First, they substantiated the appearance of a Russian nation guided by purely Russian geopolitical interests. After all, the domestic aspects of the NEP were helping restore the standard of living among the Russian people (or at least keeping it stable). In its foreign policy manifestations, the NEP paralleled traditional Tsarist efforts to avoid international isolation. Second, the trade and recognition concessions granted by West European nations to Soviet Russia nurtured the growth of the Communist Party, securing its control of the Soviet state and providing it with the assets (foreign credits and diplomatic status) it needed to carry on its covert war against the democracies.

A similar stance was assumed by the West European nations in the early 1930's and was rationalized by reference to the devastating effects of the first Five Year Plan and Stalin's forced collectivization of agriculture. The series of domestic crises that ensued were, once again, said to force "practical" considerations of national interest upon the Soviet leadership, and, once again, the West saw an opportunity to draw the Soviets into a responsible relationship with the rest of the civilized world. Soviet membership in the League of Nations and U.S. recognition followed.

Western dealings with the Comintern provide substantiation for the point that the West was predisposed to dismiss the Soviet Union as a threat and to accept the preferred Soviet deception of being politically, morally, and socially like other states. The Comintern was an obvious and direct instrument of Soviet foreign policy. Its activities belied Soviet pledges of noninterference in the internal affairs of other countries.[47] This masquerade was tolerated, in part, because "in Europe of the 1920's Communism could no longer be considered a serious threat."[48]

U.S. Recognition of the Soviet Union

Soviet obligations to the British in connection with the Anglo-Soviet Trade Agreement of 1921 (particularly non-interference in the internal affairs of the other party) were either violated covertly by Soviet officials posing as trade representatives or were circumvented by the operations of the Comintern. Almost a decade later, the United States was destined to learn the lessons of the British experience on its own. Succumbing to the chimera of large, untapped Soviet markets and raw material bonanzas, many in the United States believed they saw in de jure recognition of the Soviet Union an economic remedy for the lingering recession of 1929. Conceding recognition first, in exchange for Soviet pledges to negotiate in good faith a final resolution to the issue of Tsarist debts and for protection for American citizens in Russia, the United States placed a great deal of trust in five factors:[49]

1. the surface aura of respectability that Russia had studiously cultivated in the years preceding the agreement;
2. Soviet Russia's soft-pedaling of revolutionary activity;
3. the evidence of increasing Soviet "desire(s) to be accepted as a member of the world community" (An adjunct to this was the view that Russia was content with the policy of "Socialism in one country");
4. the overconfidence and exaggerated optimism of Franklin Delano Roosevelt (an individual case of self-deception); and,
5. the hope that expansion of commercial trade would contribute to reduction of unemployment.

The promised resolution of outstanding issues never materialized.[50]

When the newly elected British Labour government formally extended recognition to the Soviet Union on 2 February 1924 (less than two weeks after Lenin's death), the Soviets said they had been recognized by those who wished to "strangle" them, that it was not Russia who had changed but the "imperialist" powers of the West (foreshadowing contemporary Soviet claims that the "correlation of forces" has "forced" moderation on Western military and foreign policies), and that recognition brought with it a tremendous increase in the international prestige of the Soviet Union.[51] According to Soviet commentaries, British recognition meant that "in the future we will be even better able than before to use, in the interests of the toilers of our own Union and the world in general, the antagonisms among the imperialist powers."[52]

Soviet reactions to U.S. recognition were in a similar vein, proclaiming that this "new foreign policy success of the U.S.S.R. is an indication of the strength of its position in the struggle for peace." Recognition had been sought and obtained, not due to any commitment to maintain the international system, but as leverage in the Soviet Union's campaign for "collective security," by which it meant a collective capitalist contribution to the protection of socialist development in Russia. A *Pravda* editorial on U.S. recognition was careful to note that: "A new stage in the competition of the two systems has been completed. The Soviet Union has become a major force by its economic and political strength, which even the most important capitalist powers cannot help but take into consideration."[53]

Conclusion

In times of internal crisis or external threat, the Soviet Union has found it convenient to promote an alleged desire for detente and peaceful coexistence partly through diplomatic means. In the early 1920's, an internal crisis necessitated resort to a diplomatic ruse, the New Economic Policy, intended to "calm the fears of the adversaries of international communism by understating real communist strength and to confound the policies of those adversaries by masking the realities of communist policy."[54] The payoff was handsome. By making the West believe the New Economic Policy to be a genuine change of course in Soviet character, the Soviet Union benefitted from American, British and German aid.

In the 1930's, an external crisis provoked another episode of apparent ideological moderation. Japan had invaded Manchuria and was threatening the Soviet far east while Germany was militarizing in the west. The Soviet Union embarked on a foreign policy designed to mitigate its isolationism. It joined the League of Nations. It made promises to the United States which earned it de jure recognition and then reneged on these promises.

The West has been consistently all-too-willing to accept Soviet professions of ideological repentance, as it were, and to ascribe purely national interest motives to Soviet behavior, thus contributing to the success of Soviet diplomatic deception through self-deception. The target of Soviet diplomatic deception was the intellectual elite, the diplomats and politicians, as well as the media of Western nations, particularly France and Britain—the so-called "high culture" of Western society.

And yet there were those in the West not entirely blind to the reality of Soviet diplomatic deception. William C. Bullitt, America's first ambassador to the Soviet Union, was acutely aware of the Soviet penchant for secrecy and espionage. In a memorandum to the U.S. Secretary of State dated 20 April 1936, Bullitt warns that Soviet Russia

> will not, in good faith, enter into any international agreements which have as their object improvement of the general economic condition of the world. It will, on the contrary, try to produce as much chaos as possible in the economies of capitalist countries in the hope that misery may beget communist revolution. . . . We should not cherish for a moment the illusion that it is possible to establish really friendly relations with the Soviet Government or with any communist party or communist individual.[55]

On U.S. recognition of the Soviet Union in 1933, Robert Paul Browder has written:

> On the American side, misconceptions and naivete paved the way for future disillusionment [placing] an undue amount of faith in Russian promises. . . . The experiences of other nations should have convinced Washington that Russia was not prepared to abandon her basic principles of conduct in more than token fashion, even to gain recognition from the United States.[56]

In summary, important incentives for diplomatic deception on the part of the Soviet Union were present during the inter-war period. These included relative weakness vis-à-vis adversaries and rivals; important potential diplomatic gains at low cost; ideological and historical rationalizations; and a willing, receptive, and well-defined target audience. Furthermore, the apparatus for deliberate efforts aimed at deception were also present. These involved primarily the Comintern and departments within the Narkomindel for the dissemination of propaganda and disinformation. Finally, the Soviet Union availed itself of a diplomatic style that fostered skill at tactical deception in negotiations.

In the end, periods of ideological moderation and "openings" to the West proved illusory. In August 1939, the Soviet Union signed a pact of nonaggression with Nazi Germany, representing perhaps the nadir of its ideological prostration, and sealed the fate of the world of the 1930's by clearing the way for global war and revival of open hostility toward the West. War on Finland resulted in the Soviet Union being expelled from the League of Nations, but this action was symbolic and foreshadowed the imminent demise of the League itself. David Lloyd George's "community of nations" foundered on the illusions of Soviet reform fostered in the speeches of Litvinov and Chicherin and the West paid for its myopia on the battlefields of World War II.

Notes

1. Vernon V. Aspaturian, "Diplomacy in the Mirror of Soviet Scholarship," in John Keep and Liliana Brisby, eds., *Contemporary History in the Soviet Mirror*, (New York: Praeger, 1964), p. 269.
2. Frederick C. Barghoorn, "Propaganda: Tsarist and Soviet," in Ivo J. Lederer, ed., *Russian Foreign Policy: Essays in Historical Perspective*, (New Haven, Conn.: Yale University Press, 1962), p. 281.
3. Teddy J. Uldricks, *Diplomacy and Ideology: The Origins of Soviet Foreign Relations, 1917–1930*, (Beverly Hills, Calif.: Sage Publications, 1979), p. 7. Vernon V. Aspaturian ("Dialectics," p. 248) reports that:

> According to Trotsky, when the Bolsheviks met to organize their first government and the question of foreign relations was raised, Lenin exclaimed: 'What, are we going to have foreign relations?' And upon his own appointment as the first Foreign Commissar, Trotsky announced: 'I will issue a few revolutionary proclamations and then close up shop.'

4. Aspaturian, "Diplomacy," pp. 248–249.
5. Leon Trotsky, "Statement by Trotsky on the Publication of the Secret Treaties," in Jane Degras, ed., *Soviet Documents on Foreign Policy*, (London: Oxford University Press, 1951), Vol. I, pp. 8–9.
6. Although deceptive aspects of Soviet diplomatic practice are often alluded to in the literature on Soviet diplomacy, there is a notable lack of reference to Soviet diplomatic deception per se. Some noteworthy exceptions are two articles by Vernon D. Aspaturian, one of which has been cited earlier (see Note # 1), and the other is "Dialectics and Duplicity in Soviet Diplomacy." *Journal of International Affairs*, 17, 1 (1963): 42–60; both of which share much of the same material, but to which I owe a considerable debt in the preparation of this chapter.

As to explaining this dirth of scholarly treatment of Soviet diplomatic deception I would venture to offer the following observations only because it relates to themes developed in this chapter. There are, in my view, two possible reasons why diplomatic historians have failed to substantially treat Soviet diplomacy as deception. First, there is the problem of defining diplomatic deception. What is deceptive may be regarded as a matter of perspective or as a question of intention. Intentions are clearly difficult to establish, especially for those scholars dedicated to mere historical elaboration, and may often represent the product of judgment calls the diplomatic historian would prefer left to the reader or policy analyst.

Second, diplomatic deception, by definition, contradicts the very basis and rationale of traditional diplomatic practice—that is, to promote relaxation of tensions through building trust and reliance on negotiated settlements. Diplomacy that is deceptive implies a callous, even malicious, disregard for the objectives of diplomacy as established in Western practice. It betrays a fundamental hostility toward the abstract goals of fostering improved interstate relations. Its ends can only be the promotion of some national interest at the expense of another nation's interests. In this sense, diplomatic deception is characteristic of a zero-sum view of world politics. Diplomatic historians, with understandable scholarly caution, may be reluctant to label diplomacy, no matter what its ideological or moral basis, as duplicitous.

7. See Jan F. Triska and Robert M. Slusser, *The Theory, Law, and Policy of Soviet Treaties*, (Stanford, Calif.: Stanford University Press, 1962), pp. 372–374.

8. Vernon V. Aspaturian has dealt with Leninist diplomatic precepts in "Soviet Conceptions of Diplomacy," in V.V. Aspaturian, ed., *Process and Power in Soviet Foreign Policy*, (Boston: Little, Brown, 1971), pp. 350–400.

9. Nathan Leites, *The Operational Code of the Politburo*, (New York: McGraw-Hill, 1951), p. 7.

10. Nathan Leites, *A Study of Bolshevism*, (Glencoe, Ill.: The Free Press, 1953), p. 99.

11. See Elliot R. Goodman, *The Soviet Design for a World State*, (New York: Columbia University Press, 1957), especially chapter II, "The World State as an Explicit Soviet Goal," pp. 25–49.

12. Leites, *The Operational Code*, pp. 88–90.

13. Aspaturian, "Dialectics and Duplicity in Soviet Diplomacy," p. 43.

14. Ibid., p. 46.

15. This quote is cited in Aspaturian, "Diplomacy," p. 257.

16. U.S. House of Representatives, Committee on Foreign Affairs, "Soviet Diplomacy and Negotiating Behavior: Emerging New Context for U.S. Diplomacy," 96th Congress, 1st Session, House Doc. No. 96–238, p. 50.

17. See, inter alia, Branko Lazitch and Milorad M. Drachkovitch, op.cit., chapter 12, "1921—The Change of Course," in *Lenin and the Comintern*, (Stanford, Calif.: Hoover Institution, 1972), pp. 528–569; Lennard D. Gerson, comp., *Lenin and the Twentieth Century: A Bertram D. Wolfe Retrospective*, (Stanford: Hoover Institution, 1984), chapter 9, "1921: Lenin's Change of Course," pp. 131–169; and Walter C. Clemens, Jr., "Lenin on Disarmament," *Slavic Review*, 23, 3 (Sept. 1964): 504–525.

18. Anatoliy Golitsyn, *New Lies for Old: The Communist Strategy of Deception and Disinformation*, (New York: Dodd, Mead, 1984), p. 10.

19. Lazitch and Drachkovitch, *Lenin*, p. 31.

20. Louis Fischer, *The Soviets in World Affairs*, Vol. 1, (Princeton: Princeton University Press, 1951), p. 32. Fischer is citing the preface to Trotsky's pamphlet, "What Is a Peace Program?", Petrograd, February 1918, pp. 2–4.

21. U.S. House, "Soviet Diplomacy and Negotiating Behavior", p. 49.

22. Adam B. Ulam, *Expansion and Coexistence: Soviet Foreign Policy, 1917–1973*, 2nd ed., (New York: Praeger, 1974), p. 85.

23. On the reversal in Lenin's opposition to disarmament, see Clemens, op. cit. "Lenin on Disarmament."

24. Golitsyn, *New Lies*, p. 12.

25. Ibid., p. 11.

26. This memo has appeared in at least three English versions. The one given is from the *Washington Times*, 19 March 1986, p. D1. A somewhat different translation can be found in Lazitch and Drachkovitch, *Lenin*, vol. I, pp. 549–550. Lazitch and Drachkovitch cite as their source *Novye Zhurnal*, (New York, 1961), no. 65, pp. 146–47; they note that the text of the memo was also printed verbatim in *Bulletin of the Institute for the Study of the USSR*, (Munich, May 1962). Several reasons for accepting the memo's authenticity are given by Lazitch and Drachkovitch as well (see p. 550fn). The third English language version appeared in the *Congressional Record*–Appendix, 21 November

1966, p. A5929, and is accompanied by a lengthy discussion of its history and significance.

27. U.S. Department of State, *Foreign Relations of the United States: Soviet Union 1933–39*, (Washington, D.C.: U.S. Government Printing Office, 1952), p. 221.

28. For treatments of Soviet-German relations, including the deception dimensions, see: Raymond James Sontag and James Stuart Beddie, eds., *Nazi-Soviet Relations: 1939–1941*, (New York: Didier, 1948); J.H. Morgan, *Assize of Arms: The Disarmament of Germany and Her Rearmament: 1919–1939*, (New York: Oxford University Press, 1946); and E.H. Carr, *German-Soviet Relations Between the Two World Wars, 1919–1939*, (New York: Harper & Row, 1951).

29. Ibid, pp. 65–66.

30. On Soviet professions of freedom of religion, see the Decree of 23 Jan. 1918, article 3, cited in Litvinov correspondence to Roosevelt, U.S. Department of State, *Foreign Relations*, op. cit., pp. 30–32.

31. Grigory Bessedovsky, *Revelations of a Soviet Diplomat*, trans. by Matthew Norgate, (Williams and Norgate, 1931), reprinted (Westport, Conn.: Hyperion, 1977), pp. 12–13.

32. Ibid., p. 13.

33. Ibid.

34. Ibid., pp. 13–14.

35. Uldricks, *Diplomacy and Ideology*, p. 162.

36. Ibid., p. 168, fn.82.

37. Ibid., p. 162.

38. Lazitch and Drachkovitch, *Lenin*, p. 32.

39. Ibid.

40. John Reed, *Liberator*, (June 1918), no. 4, pp. 27–28; cited in Lazitch and Drachkovitch, *Lenin*, p. 32.

41. Fischer, *The Soviets in World Affairs*, p. 321.

42. Xenia Joukoff Eudin and Harold H. Fisher, *Soviet Russia and the West, 1920–1927: A Documentary Survey*, (Stanford, Calif.: Stanford University Press, 1957), pp. 20–21.

43. W.P. Coates and Zelda K. Coates, *A History of Anglo-Soviet Relations*, (London: Lawrence & Wishart, 1945), p. 3.

44. Ibid., p. 53.

45. Ibid., p. 233.

46. Ibid.

47. Ulam, *Expansion and Coexistence*, p. 130.

48. Ibid., p. 132.

49. Robert Paul Browder, *The Origins of Soviet-American Diplomacy*, (Princeton: Princeton University Press, 1953), pp. 217–219.

50. For correspondence relating to the U.S. recognition of the USSR, see U.S. Department of State, *Foreign Relations*, pp. 1–63; also see ibid., pp. 166–192 for documents and materials on the "failure of negotiations to implement the agreements of November 1933."

51. F.A. Rotshtein, "Kakaia polza ot priznaniia," *Pravda*, No. 59, March 12, 1924, p. 1. Translated and reprinted in Eudin and Fisher, *Soviet Russia and the West*, pp. 325–336.

52. Ibid., p. 235.

53. "Krupneishaia pobeda sovetskoi politiki mira," *Pravda*, No. 318, 19 November 1933, p. 1; cited in Xenia Joukoff Eudin and Robert M. Slusser, *Soviet Foreign Policy, 1928–1934: Documents and Materials*, Vol. II (University Park, Penn.: The Pennsylvania State University Press, 1967), p. 550.

54. Golitsyn, *New Lies*, p. 13.

55. U.S. Department of States, *Foreign Relations*, pp. 292–294.

56. Browder, *Origins*, p. 216.

Part III
Arms Control and Verification

9
Soviet Deception and Arms Control

William R. Graham

Introduction

Concealment and deception in arms control strongly supports the Soviet doctrine that surprise has great military and political value. The *Soviet Military Encyclopedia* explains that surprise is achieved

> . . . by leading the enemy into error concerning one's own intentions; by keeping secret the concept of the battle, and by concealment of the preparations for actions.[1]

The encyclopedia further explains that strategic surprise can be accomplished

> . . . by the unexpected use of new means of armed combat which have a strategic effect, of new methods of strategic actions, by a skillful choice of the direction of the main attack, by *disinformation*, and by other means.[2] (emphasis added)

A KGB training manual describes strategic disinformation as follows:

> Strategic disinformation is directed at misleading the enemy concerning the basic questions of the state policy, the military-economic status, and the scientific technical achievements of the Soviet Union.[3]

Arms control provides the Soviets with an accepted, legitimate arena in which to practice illegitimate concealment, deception, and disinformation in coordination with other strategic objectives.

During his nineteenth century travels in Russia, the Marquis de Custine described the Russian perception of foreigners:

Every traveler is indiscrete, so it is necessary, as politely as possible, to keep track of the always too inquisitive foreigner lest he see things as they are—which would be the greatest of inconveniences.[4]

In addition to its being entertaining, it is enlightening to read this travel record. It indicates that the Soviet penchant for secrecy and deception is not a recent aberration, but rather has been a clear theme throughout Russian history.

Russia was schooled in the Byzantine tradition (when it was a part of that ancient empire), and its tradition of secretiveness and deception has only grown with time. Byzantium stressed the use of extraordinary artiface when dealing with foreigners and showed visitors only what they wished them to see. Some Byzantine tricks showed a genuine talent for the practical applications of magic created through the use of ingenious settings, mechanisms, and displays. Charles Roetter, a student of diplomacy, reflected: "Let us not forget that the pulleys and sham parades helped the Byzantine Empire to survive for over eleven centuries"[5]—far longer than the more western Roman Empire survived.

This chapter deals with present and future Soviet deceptive activities in the area of arms control. The meaning of deception in the arms control context is described and related to Soviet arms control commitments. Soviet deception is shown to exist on a wide range of scales, from global and comprehensive to specific and in detail. With the use of a conceptual framework for deceptive processes, the opportunities and hazards for deception in arms control are considered. The conclusion is reached that arms control provides a field of substantial opportunity and potential payoff for Soviet deceptive activities.

If the United States is to deter Soviet deception and deny them the benefit of its practice, this nation must first avoid complementing Soviet deceptive practices by falling prey to self-deception based on wishful thinking and unrealistic aspirations for arms control. The United States must also continue to develop a systematic, consistent, long-range approach requiring Soviet compliance with existing arms control commitments and must publicly disseminate Soviet deception (and other activities) that violate the letter and intent of Soviet arms control commitments.

Arms Control Treaty Commitments

In three separate arms control treaties negotiated between the United States the Soviet Union in the last fifteen years (the ABM Treaty, the SALT I Interim Agreement, and the SALT II Treaty), the Soviet Union has specifically committed itself not to interfere with the national technical means of verification of the other party and not to use deliberate concealment measures that impede verification by national technical means. At a minimum, deceptive activities designed to defeat U.S. national technical means for verifying Soviet compliance violate the intent and purpose of these treaty provisions, in specific contravention to the norms of international law as codified in the 1969 Vienna Convention on the Law of Treaties.[6] Furthermore, the prohibition of actions that defeat the object and purpose of international commitments necessarily extends beyond the treaties cited that contain explicit antiobstruction language and provide a general framework for the prohibition of deception, concealment, and related activities regarding some twenty-six documentary arms control agreements and numerous unilateral arms control commitments made (or reaffirmed) by the Soviet Union since World War II.

While damaging to U.S. national security and to future prospects for arms control, specific obstruction of national technical means of verification is not the only area of arms control where deception has a damaging effect. Larger scale deception activities can have an even greater, though more subtle, effect upon U.S. perceptions of Soviet activities.

What Is Deception?

Deception is a rather general term that can cover a great deal of territory. It would be beneficial to have a more specific structure than yet developed for the general concept of deception. Unfortunately, there is little agreement on what the specific structure should be. At the most circumscribed end of the definitional spectrum, deception is held to occur only when the United States has been successfully misled by the Soviets. When the United States uncovers a fiction created to mislead it, the uncovering itself is taken as proof that there was no deception, because the United States was not deceived. It is held that deception only occurs when the United States is unaware that it is being misled. The logic of this approach to deception has been summarized epigrammatically: "We have never found anything that the Soviets have successfully hidden."[7]

When strictly followed, this approach leads to the logical impossibility of knowing that a deception exists. While this observation is tautologically trivial, a more substantive variant argues that any apparent deception uncovered by the United States must not have been a serious attempt, since the United States was able to see through it. This argument (at its roots also largely tautological) can be used as a broad-spectrum refutation of the seriousness of Soviet deception attempts, blurring the distinctions between the unsuccessful deception and no deception.

At the opposite end of the definitional spectrum, a macroscopic view of Soviet deception should include Soviet actions

> . . . taking advantage of our tendency to engage in wishful thinking, to view the Soviets as just like us—decent, freedom-loving, and democratic. As the Soviets try to confuse adversaries about their global ambitions, Moscow's

assertion that it is sincerely interested in detente or arms control is part of its deception or disinformation program.[8]

This more global view of deception is by far the more relevant point of departure for a discussion of Soviet deception and arms control. Those who can be persuaded that arms control transcends being an instrument of national security and diplomacy are candidates for accepting inequitable agreements in the pursuit of arms control as a goal unto itself, rather than a means to achieve U.S. goals of freedom, security, and peace.

The following historical notes describe such an arms control bias and its effect between World Wars I and II:

> At the close of the Second World War in complete good faith we occupied ourselves with programs for the nuclear disarmament of the victorious alliance—the United States, the United Kingdom, France, and the USSR. How adversely this preoccupation with weapons, continued since that time, eroded the relations between the members of that alliance no man can yet assess. But we can say that the disarmament movement after the First World War did produce disastrous results. One of the brilliant apostles of disarmament after World War I was the man who is now America's most respected political analyst, Mr. Walter Lippmann. In a book written in 1943, he explained why he had been wrong in crusading for disarmament. I ask you to ponder Mr. Lippmann's words and decide for yourselves whether or not they are relevant to the problem we have faced ever since the end of World War II.[9]
>
> In the interval between the two great wars, the United States sought to promote peace by denouncing war, even by "outlawing" it, and by disarming itself, Great Britain and France. . . . The disinterested and idealistic theory of disarmament was that if everyone had less capacity to wage war, there would be a smaller likelihood of war. Big warships meant big wars. Smaller warships meant smaller wars. No warships might eventually mean no wars. . . . On the theory that disarmament could promote peace, laborious negotiations and elaborate diplomacy and splendid international conferences were promoted in Washington, Geneva, and London. . . . It soon transpired that though the premise of these conferences was that smaller armaments would banish war, the working premise of all the governments was that each of the former allies was now the rival, and therefore the potential enemy, of all others. The disarmament movement was, as the event has shown, tragically successful in disarming the nations that believed in disarmament. The net effect was to dissolve the alliance among the victors of the First World War, and to reduce them to almost disastrous impotence.[10]

Truth and Fiction

The practical art of deception seldom is able to use pure fabrication uncontaminated by substantial amounts of reality. Reality is difficult to eliminate, but, fortunately for the deceiver (and unfortunately for the deceived), it does not have to be eliminated. It must only be selectively suppressed, so that the deception maintains its plausibility against the background of the residual truth available. Deception is thus a truth-versus-fiction problem. In areas where the Soviets wish to deceive they can minimize the truth-to-fiction ratio, and selectively leave only those parts of the truth that support (or at least do not damage) the desired fiction. This can be undertaken by two complementary actions: selectively suppressing the truth and elaborating the fiction.

Selectively suppressing the truth depends heavily upon concealing information from the United States and denying the United States insight into much of what is actually taking place. Substantiating fiction then involves inserting erroneous information into the data that flows from the Soviet Union to the United States.

A legendary figure of British technical intelligence, Reginald B. Jones, described a simple but useful model for discussing intelligence collection and analysis processes.[11] His conceptualization of the external influences that bear upon intelligence provide a further framework in which to consider deceptive measures. Jones visualizes each intelligence issue as connected to the world through a series of discreet information channels. The integration and comparison of relevant information from a wide variety of channels provides both the accumulated substance and the means to cross-check the information and verify the conclusions drawn. To conduct a successful deception, as Dr. Jones has done upon several occasions, the selective suppression of accurate information channels is first necessary so that the erroneous information provided through other channels becomes plausible and consistent.[12] Thus, it follows that the creation of a successful fiction will be closely associated with concealment and other data denial activity and, in fact, all such activities are necessary and complementary aspects of deception.

With the use of Jones' framework, the role of deception in the arms control process becomes immediately obvious. While the arms control process adds new channels of information to the intelligence process, many of these channels can be manipulated by the Soviets to provide erroneous information to replace accurate information that is being suppressed.

Deception Opportunities and Hazards

There are both deceptive opportunities and hazards for the Soviet Union in the arms control environment. Soviet deception opportunities are well-served by common American assumptions about arms control. These assumptions include:

That the Soviets always negotiate sincerely and in good faith;

That the Soviets would not risk losing the benefits of arms control by violating their arms control commitments;

That the United States view of the mutuality of arms control benefit is necessarily fundamental to Soviet motives; and

That a mirror-image of U.S. arms control attitudes and considerations is a reliable model for predicting Soviet arms control behavior.

Unfortunately, none of these assumptions is consistent with the record of Soviet arms control practices, but they are reinforced by Soviet propaganda. They constitute the largest scale of Soviet arms control deception. Of course, by far the most successful forms of deception are those that the party being deceived strongly wishes to believe.[13]

The increase in arms control diplomacy over the last fifteen years predictably has been paralleled by an increase in Soviet concealment and deception activities. While suppressing information concerning their military buildup, the Soviets focused deceptive information on the United States: during the preparations for arms control negotiations (where many of the terms of reference are defined),[14] during the negotiations,[15] after agreements have been reached (by influencing public opinion),[16] and, in the Standing Consultative Commission and other diplomatic channels, after agreements have been put into effect. The arms control process also provides the Soviets with leverage on the United States by giving them forum for manipulating the perceptions of citizens of other Western governments. The combined effects of these influences has been largely to keep the United States occupied in responding to whatever narrow set of arms control issues and concepts the Soviets seem willing to discuss. As a result, the United States moves less aggressively than it might otherwise into U.S.–initiated arms control issues and approaches.

Arms control also creates new potential hazards for Soviet deception activities. For example, arms control occasionally generates new commitments for the Soviets to consider; however, the Soviets have shown themselves to be willing to violate many of their arms control commitments.[17] Theoretically, more reliable information channels are made available to the United States. However, these channels are often rendered worthless by Soviet data denial practices, such as concealment, encryption, or by the transmittal of deceptive information, such as the strategic data base associated with SALT II, which made no mention of the mobile Soviet strategic SS-16 missile deployed at Plesetsk in all probability. Arms control agreements have committed the Soviets not to interfere with our national technical means of verification; however,

> Soviet denial activities significantly increased over the last quarter century and today are challenging U.S. verification capabilities despite improvements in U.S. verification technology. Deliberate Soviet efforts to counter U.S. national

technical means of verification strongly indicate a Soviet intention to persevere in circumventing and violating agreements.[18]

Future Arms Control Compliance Practices

Past Soviet noncompliance practices were too systematic to have been the result of ad hoc activities and random errors. Since there has been little change in Soviet arms control approaches for more than a decade, future Soviet practices are likely to continue to follow past policies and actions. In recent history, the Soviets have shown a willingness to circumvent and violate both unilateral commitments and documentary agreements. They have used data denial, and, it is alleged, "dummy" system mockups to provide at least a veneer and (on occasion) a deep cover for such actions.[19] They even prepared to violate their arms control commitments while they were negotiating, signing, and ratifying those commitments by, for example, deceiving the United States and other signatories of their actual intentions to pursue offensive biological and toxic weapon development.[20] They have also shown a willingness to provide false and deceptive information during negotiations, such as the troop strength data they provided in MBFR (Mutual Balanced force Reduction) negotiations, the absence of the required data on the SS-16 force size, and deceptive representation of the SS-17 and SS-19 ICBMs as "light" ICBMs.[21] There is no present indication that the Soviets will cease to engage in such deceptive practices in their arms control diplomacy, negotiations, and programs.

It is likely that deceptive Soviet negotiating practices, violations, circumventions of commitments, and other prohibitive activities will continue as long as the overall military and political benefit accruing to the Soviet Union outweighs any potential disadvantage. The Soviets also will continue to accuse the United States of violating arms control commitments. Since the Soviets know the accusations are untrue, they will be largely deceptive, issued in response to U.S. charges.

Deception Opportunities in Future Soviet Programs

The Soviets have a great deal of continuity in their military programs. Therefore, useful predictions can be made concerning three principal Soviet program areas involved with arms control: the strategic nuclear offensive, the strategic defensive, and nonnuclear programs.

In the strategic offensive area, the Soviets responded to U.S. charges that the SS-25 was a prohibited new type of ICBM by asserting that the missile was only an upgrade of the older SS-13 missile.[22] When taken together with the nearly total use of telemetry encryption to block access to necessary arms control verification data, this approach strongly suggests that most future Soviet missiles will be advertised as modernizations of existing missiles and that the true missile characteristics will continue to be obscured by Soviet concealment practices and other measures.

The Soviets may have deployed the maximum number of overt deployed missiles that they find useful. Their future missile problems, if any, are likely to lie in the areas of survivability, strategic reserve forces, and reliable post-first-strike capabilities. In a tightly closed and controlled society, these problems can be solved by the covert and deceptive deployment of missiles. Such practices will be made easier by overt deployment of some missiles in a mobile mode, such as that now underway (or anticipated) with the Soviet SS-16, SS-24, and SS-25 ICBMs and the deployed SS-20 IRBM. Overt deployment would provide the justification for mobile missile facilities, tests, and operations, while the covert component of the mobile force could remain hidden from Western intelligence and hence from Western perceptions, but ready to be deployed on short notice.

Submarine activities may also become more concealed if the reported development of Soviet submarine tunnels proceeds.[23] Deception may occur in relation to the total number of submarines and their deployment. Offensive aircraft is another area of concern, and one should look for aerial refueling capabilities, dispersion of bases, and aircraft production rates among other areas that could have deceptive activities associated with them.

Strategic Defensive Activities

In the area of strategic defenses, Soviet air defense systems will continue to become more technologically sophisticated and will continue to evolve into ABM-capable components. Concurrent testing of air defense and ballistic missile systems will continue to be a distinct possibility, although the Soviets will state that their surface-to-air antiaircraft missile systems and their antiballistic missile systems are separate and distinct.

In the area of antisubmarine warfare, the Soviets may attempt to use deception by associating some types of activities (particularly nonacoustic antisubmarine warfare) with other purposes.[24] Despite the bias held by some in the United States that Soviet antisubmarine warfare currently is ineffective and likely to remain so, deception in this area may be augmented.

The Soviets will continue to pursue ASAT capabilities, but may deceptively attempt to associate these capabilities with other types of space activities, including their man-in-space programs.[25]

Nonnuclear Programs

The Soviets may pursue the development of chemical and biological warheads for both tactical and strategic missiles, as well as the development of offensive biological weapons (under the deceptive guise of developing biotechnology and producing pharmaceuticals). Chemical weapon production can be masked as other chemical processes, such as the production of pesticides. Testing activities in all of these areas may prove difficult to identify—particularly in view of the Soviets' extensive use of concealment.

Conclusions

For some decades, the arms control process has provided a field of substantial opportunity and payoff for Soviet deceptive activities. Arms control can be both a producer and a consumer of fictional information as well as of fact. The United States has a strong desire to live in a world in which the Soviet Union: (1) has abandoned national ambitions and conflict with arms, (2) has foresworn the use and threat of force, (3) and is as anxious to disarm itself as it is to disarm others. This can act as a powerful source of motivation for believing what the Soviets wish the West to believe concerning the benignity of their intentions and activities.

Soviet deceptive activities are not harmless efforts designed to smooth diplomatic relations, but rather, are fundamental threats to the security of the Western nations. In a society such as the United States, where national priorities and directions are frequently chosen only after the formation of a broad consensus, deception can be reflected in misinformed and unwise choices for national policies. The deceptive process is insidious, with all levels of the government and the citizenry being potentially susceptible—particularly when the deception takes advantage of the self-deceptive reinforcement that accompanies any inherent desire to believe the fiction created.

For the United States to overcome Soviet deception in arms control, it is essential that an accurate picture be developed of Soviet behavior regarding their own freely accepted arms control constraints. The Reagan administration has taken the first giant step in this direction by releasing to the public and to Congress—for the first time—information that has been laboriously obtained over the last twenty-five years concerning specific Soviet activities prohibited by arms control commitments. In view of the strong desire by elements of political, diplomatic, and arms control lobbies to keep the information from the public view, it is both remarkable and laudable that this information has been released.

If Soviet deception is to be deterred, it is also essential for the United States to continue to develop a systematic, thoughtful approach to Soviet arms control compliance. One of the fundamental elements of that approach must be a long-term official policy of public disclosure of deceptive practices and other Soviet activities that defeat both the letter and the intent of arms control commitments. Official disclosure and dissemination must not only be U.S. practice, but must be an integral part of a long-range, comprehensive U.S. compliance policy that is carried out in a consistent, determined, and persuasive manner to overcome the effects of Soviet propaganda abroad and wishful thinking at home.

Notes

1. M.M. Kir'Yan, "Surprise," *Soviet Military Encyclopedia* 2(Moscow: 1976), trans. by Harriet Fast Scott, as discussed by Joseph D. Douglass, Jr., in "Soviet Disinformation," *Strategic Review* (Winter 1981): pp. 16–25.

2. Kir'Yan, "Surprise."

3. Deputy Director for Operations, CIA, *Soviet Covert Action and Propaganda*, 16 February 1980. Reprinted with editing as *Soviet Covert Action (The Forgery Offensive)* (Washington, D.C.: U.S. Government Printing Office, 1980).

4. Marquis de Custine, in Phyllis Pen Kohler, ed. and trans. *Journey for Our Time*, (New York: Pellegrini and Cudahy, 1951), p. 190.

5. Charles Roetter, *The Diplomatic Art* (Philadelphia: Macrae Smith, 1963), p. 27.

6. William R. Harris, "Breakers of Arms Control Obligations and Their Implications," in *Arms Control: Myth vs Reality* (Stanford, Calif: Hoover Institution Press, 1984), pp. 139–140.

7. Amrom Katz, "Verification and SALT: The State of the Art and the Art of the State," *Critical Issues*, (The Heritage Foundation, 1979), p. 11.

8. John Lenczowski, National Security Council Director of European and Soviet Affairs, quoted in *Washington Times*, 17 May 1984, p. 6–A.

9. David G. Lilienthal, *Change, Hope, and the Bomb* (Princeton, N.J.: Princeton University Press), p. 57.

10. Walter Lippmann, *U.S. Foreign Policy* (Boston: Little, Brown, 1943), p. 54–55.

11. Reginald V. Jones, "Intelligence and Deception," in Robert L. Pfaltzgraff, Jr., ed., *Intelligence Policy and National Security*, (Hamden, Conn.: Archon Books, 1981), pp. 4, 19.

12. Reginald V. Jones, *The Wizard War* (New York: Coward, McCann & Geoghegan, 1978). See, for example, ch. 25, "Jay," describing the successful deception of German intelligence concerning a new British radio navigation system in spite of the fact that the Germans had obtained a key element of the system; and ch. 37, "Full Stretch," describing the manner in which German intelligence was so deceived about British ten centrimetric radar detection of U-boats that they invented and implemented two clever countermeasures to nonexistent British detection systems.

13. William R. Van Cleave, "The Arms Control Record: Successes and Failures," in Richard F. Staar, ed., *Arms Control: Myth vs Reality* (Stanford, Calif: Hoover Institu-

tion Press, 1984), pp. 4–11. This presents a cogent history of U.S. arms control illusions that gained considerable popularity in the United States during the SALT era.

14. See, for example, the Shultz and Gromyko communique from Geneva, 10 January 1985. In this joint communique, the United States agreed to Soviet requests that future arms control negotiations be cast in terms that include "space arms"—a vague concept that is subject to a wide range of definitions that have substantially different policy and arms control implications. The communique further states that

> . . . the objective of the negotiations will be to work out effective agreements aimed at preventing an arms race in space and terminating it on earth, . . .

thus reaffirming the principles that: (1) the United States and the Soviets are engaged in an arms race, a concept that legitimizes the enormous Soviet military buildup as merely a response to U.S. actions; (2) the extensive Soviet antisatellite (ASAT) program has had no effect on the military balance (since there is now no "arms race in space"); and (3) that space armaments are distinct and separable from armaments "on earth." Each of these principles is a deceptive fallacy that may return to haunt the U.S. administration in future negotiations with Congress, the Allies, and the Soviets.

15. See, for example "What Holds Back Progress at the Geneva Talks," (advertisement placed in the *New York Times*, 13 August 1985, by the Information Department of the USSR Embassy in Washington, D.C.; and *Star Wars: Delusions and Dangers* (USSR: Progress Publishers, 1985).

16. William J. Eaton, "Soviets Urge U.S. to Affirm ABM Treaty," *Los Angeles Times*, 6 July 1985, p. 1.

17. The President's Report to Congress on Soviet Noncompliance with Arms Control Agreements," The White House, Office of the Press Secretary, 23 January 1984; The General Advisory Committee (GAC) on Arms Control and Disarmament, "A Quarter Century of Soviet Compliance Practices Under Arms Control Commitments: 1958–1983," unclassified summary, Washington, D.C., October 1984; "The President's Unclassified Report to the Congress on Soviet Noncompliance with Arms Control Agreements," The White House, Office of the Press Secretary, 1 February 1985.

18. GAC on Arms Control and Disarmament, "Soviet Compliance Practices," p. 14.

19. Q. Crommelin, Jr. and D.S. Sullivan, *Soviet Military Supremacy* (Los Angeles: Defense and Strategic Studies Program, University of Southern California, 1985), p. 141.

20. GAC, "Soviet Compliance Practices," p. 6.

21. Ibid., p. 8.

22. Ibid., p. 11.

23. *Soviet Military Power 1983* (Washington, D.C.: U.S. Government Printing Office, March 1983), p. 17.

24. K.G. Moore, "Antisubmarine Warfare," in M. McGwire and J. McDonnell, eds., *Soviet Naval Influence: Domestic and Foreign Dimensions* (New York: Praeger, 1977), p. 185–200.

25. *Aviation Week and Space Technology*, 2 Aug. 1982, p. 19.

10
Soviet *Maskirovka* and Arms Control Verification

William R. Harris

Prologue: A Fable on Disarmament

Once upon a time all the animals in the zoo decided that they would disarm, and they arranged to have a conference to arrange the matter. So the rhinoceros said when he opened the proceedings that the use of teeth was barbarous and horrible and ought to be strictly prohibited by general consent. Horns, which were mainly defensive weapons, would, of course, have to be allowed. The buffalo, the stag, and the porcupine and even the little hedgehog all said they would vote with the rhino, but the lion and the tiger took a different view. They defended with teeth and even claws, which they described as honourable weapons of immemorial antiquity. The panther, the leopard, the puma and the whole tribe of small cats all supported the lion and the tiger. Then the bear spoke. He proposed that both teeth and horns should be banned and never again used for fighting by any animal. It would be quite enough if animals were allowed to give each other a good hug when they quarreled. No one could object to that. It was so fraternal, and it would be a great step toward peace. However, all the others were very offended with the bear, and the turkey fell into a perfect panic. The discussion got so hot and angry, and all those animals began thinking so much about horns and teeth and hugging when they argued about peaceful intentions that had brought them together that they began to look at one another in a very nasty way. Luckily the keepers were able to calm them down and persuade them to go back to their cages, and they began to feel quite friendly with one another again.[1]

—Winston S. Churchill

Verification and *Maskirovka*: Arms Control without Safe Shelter

In Winston Churchill's disarmament fable, the animals who "began to look at one another in a very nasty way" returned from their negotiations to the safety of their cages. From this vantage point, free from fear of inequitable disarmament, they "began to feel quite friendly with one another again."

Why has the arms control process caused so many to wish there were a safe shelter *from* arms control? Why has the arms control process occasioned such friction among nations? Why have certain nations, in our time most notably the Soviet Union, entered into arms control treaties while initiating defense programs (such as the Soviet biological weapons program) that will necessarily violate those treaties?

Part of the dissatisfaction with U.S.-Soviet arms control arrangements results from the success, not the failure, of our verification capabilities. *Verification* is the process of demonstrating an assertion, whether an assertion of fact, of the extent of compliance with a duty of law, or some other hypothesis. One of the problems with arms control today, more acute now than between World Wars I and II, is the ability to verify, with all too high confidence, patterns of material breaches of arms control commitments.

When verification of Soviet noncompliance has resulted in requests for cessation of those breaches of duty that may be reversed, and illicit acts continue, verification becomes the messenger of worse than bad news. The bad news is that there is insufficient mutuality of interest for the breaching party to comply with a shared obligation before learning of a capacity to verify noncompliance. The news that is worse is the knowledge that the breaching party, knowing that the injured party (or parties) has verified noncompliance, is not deterred from continued or expanding already-detected violations.

It is small consolation that the Soviet Union has apparently ceased, on a selective basis, forbidden activities after deriving from them useful experimental and operational benefits. For example, the Soviet Strategic Rocket Forces probably deployed the mobile SS-16 ICBM system at Plesetsk before and after the signing of SALT II; the SS-16's at Plesetsk are reported to have been removed only after a follow-on SS-25 mobile missile had been readied for nationwide deployment. Similarly, lethal chemical weapons used by the Soviets (or Soviet-allied forces in Kampuchea, Laos, and Afghanistan) provided experimental and evaluative opportunities before the apparent cessation of Soviet-sponsored use in 1983.[2]

Why then should *maskirovka* (defined as the art of masking by means of denial and deception activities) be of special concern? For despite extensive and nationwide Soviet *maskirovka* activities, the U.S. government has recurringly verified significant noncompliance with Soviet arms control commitments. If the United States has been able to verify breaches of arms control duties, despite *maskirovka*, why should Soviet *maskirovka* be of concern?

First, *maskirovka* programs that are at least partially observed place the observer on notice that there may be successful masking by some combination of deliberate concealment measures and coherent deception measures. Unless one is confident that one understands the full ramifications of *maskirovka* activities, the capabilities or intentions that remain shielded by the mask must be contemplated.

Second, *maskirovka* programs are restricted by various arms control commitments—in particular, the SALT I Interim Agreement, the ABM Treaty of 1972, and the SALT II Treaty of 1979. Deliberate concealment measures that impede verification are illegal. Their continuation after notice that they impede verification is itself a material breach of treaty obligations.

Third, *maskirovka* programs, both those that are legal and those that are mounted in disregard of arms control duties, degrade the reliability of strategic assessments. These assessments are an important element in avoiding or containing crises. Whether or not there are legal restraints on deliberate programs to deny or deceive foreign intelligence services, greater Soviet self-restraint in the practice of *maskirovka* is essential to the maintenance of international peace and security. Nation states are simply too prone to conflict, too incapacitated in attempting to avert conflict, too vulnerable to surprise, and too aware of the value of surprise to discourage its recurring exercise. *Maskirovka* that is unrestrained is but prelude to war.

The relationship between arms control verification and *maskirovka* that is most disturbing is not that *maskirovka* impedes verification, but that verification induces *maskirovka*. Once two or more nations are committed to negotiate restrictions on armaments that may affect their defense posture, they are committed to allow other nations to affect their own conduct in a sector vital to their survival as nation states. An arms control commitment that restricts national freedom of action encourages manipulation of the perceptions of treaty partners: (1) to attain a beneficial agreement and (2) to protect vital interests during the course of, or after, the lapsing of that agreement. Whenever arms control negotiations are underway, or arms control agreements are in effect, whether as political commitments or legally binding treaties, *maskirovka* serves a *raison d'état* —a vital state interest; but so does national restraint in the design and scope of *maskirovka* activities. This restraint appears to be lacking in the Soviet Union, which has expanded its deliberate concealment and deception activities relating to strategic forces in disregard of the SALT obligations in effect since 1972.

When agreements to reduce war risks provide a mutuality of benefits (as with accident avoidance, hotline agreements, and military exercise data exchanges), verification of compliance is beneficial, but not essential. It is helpful to confirm compliance with an agreement conceived to be in mutual interest, and useful to learn when an agreement is not self-enforcing. Soviet disregard of a duty to provide advance notice of military exercises when the mutual interest in avoiding accidents is preempted by Soviet interest in coercing the government of Poland (in 1981, to crush internal dissent) is a reminder of the limits of "confidence building" measures, even though the Soviet Union returned in 1984–86 to a posture of minimal compliance with the notification duties of the Helsinki Final Act.

When arms control is not based on a mutuality of interests, but is based on a reciprocity of bargained interests or the illusion of reciprocal compromise arms control begets verification, which begets *maskirovka*, which destroys arms control. When negotiators of arms control treaties make agreements that are in the mutual interest of all parties (as with certain coordinating measures to avoid accidental war), the existence of the agreement does not particularly strengthen incentives to engage in *maskirovka*. But when negotiators of arms control agreements use those agreements as the wallpaper that covers unpatchable gaps, such as incompatible strategic objectives, then those agreements encourage what contract lawyers sometimes term "fraud in the inducement," as well as "fraud in the execution" of contracted obligations.

Arms control is not a sheltered port—a safe haven from *maskirovka*. Arms control beckons deception planners to rescue vital security interests from guilt-ridden scientists, lawyers, diplomats, and others whose aspirations jeopardize national or bureaucratic interests.

Before we turn to Soviet denial and deception practices relating to arms control, it is important to keep clearly in view the expected relationships between the functions of verification and the arms control regime that verification supports—for deception in the arms control process must fulfill, in an illusory sense, the functions of verification, and those functions have varied over time.

What Functions Does Verification Serve?

If arms control begets *maskirovka*, why not do away with the verification process as a means of diminishing incentives to deceive arms control partners? Even if there were no attempt to verify compliance with arms control obligations, incentives would remain to deceive potential treaty parties about national security objectives and advantages sought in strategic competition. The verification process merely channels the targeting of *maskirovka* activities—in part because intelligence that is utilized as part of the process of arms control verification carries a perceived importance that other information may not. The mere fact that compliance or noncompliance with a solemn legal obligation is being verified adds to the weight of the evidence derived, and adds to the utility of *maskirovka* that conceals or delays understanding the significance of arms control noncompliance.

Why not do away with verification of arms control commitments altogether, for what one learns frequently exacerbates tensions and renews political conflict? In responding to Soviet proposals for disarmament without concurrent measures of independent verification, the French representative to the UN Disarmament Commission in 1956, Jules Moch, explained that disarmament without verification

> regards as solved the very problem which is crying for solution; it assumes that confidence exists, whereas the problem is to create confidence. If each Power could rely on the others for the verifications of the undertakings they had signed, the undertakings themselves would be superfluous, and the security of all would depend on the good faith of each. But so long as that good faith is not clearly apparent, security can be created only from the certainty, confirmed by "controle,"[3] that the undertakings of each have been duly carried out.[4]

It is imprudent to engage in arms control without verification, but verification is no longer the watchword of those who distrust Soviet intentions. Many of those who insist upon reciprocity of benefits in the arms control process have obtained sufficient knowledge through the verification process to become more interested in responsive and anticipatory action to preserve international security from the arms control process itself.

With its ritualistic exchanges in the Standing Consultative Commission (SCC) and elsewhere, the verification process remains of primary interest to "conciliationists"—those who would reconcile conflicting interests at virtually any price and preferably with a maximum of delay. Among the conciliationists, a vocal minority of apologists for Soviet misconduct cling to the uncertainties of verification as justification for inaction, even when many of those uncertainties only result from Soviet failure to reveal their conduct more fully, through some combination of data disclosure and physical access.

If arms control is the opiate of the intelligentsia, then verification of arms control commitments is the opiate of the "apologentsia" (a term coined by Dr. Manfred Eimer, Assistant Director of the U.S. Arms Control and Disarmament Agency). For those who have not labored in the trenches of arms control verifications, the apologentsia are apologists among the intelligentsia. If negotiators have agreed, despite irreconcilable differences, then the verification process is the safety belt that the apologentsia snap on as they proceed along the inconsistent highways of policy. When calamities occur, the verification process may aid in translating wanton disregard of others' rights into mere "accidents." For those who would avert sanctions or self-help measures by any means, verification can be a perpetual process of seeking greater certainty, clarification, compensatory reinterpretation, protection from public disclosure, or any other excuse to protect the conciliating process from the harsh realities of conflicting national interest. The apologentsia would ask us to verify in perpetuity, long after cheating has been verified, as a palliative for the failure to take responsive actions.

Verification accomplishes different objectives for different audiences. For some it is symbolic, but not necessary; for others, it is proof of the perfidy of the misconduct of an adversary; for still others, it is an excuse for inaction, even when all who have examined the full range of verification data have found Soviet noncompliance across a broad spectrum of activities and of the type that can only increase the risk of war.

The differing functions of verification for these different audiences affect incentives to use or limit deception and denial activities. However, the market for Soviet *maskirovka* is also affected by the structure of the regime for arms control verification. The procedures of verification are different today from what they were in the aftermath of World War I, and these differences are worth keeping in mind when considering the significance of Soviet deception activities in the era of SALT and beyond.

Evolving Regimes for Arms Control Verification

A "regime of verification" includes the capabilities to collect and analyze pertinent information, the legal rights of the observer and observed parties, and the customary verification practices in effect. These characteristics of the verification regime affect incentives for, and modes for, conducting *maskirovka* activities.

In this century, at least six verification regimes are pertinent to an understanding of the relationships between deception and *maskirovka*:

1. The Versailles Verification regime: dictated verification and control.
2. Verification by data exchange in the 1930's.
3. Verification by limited inspection: concepts without agreement, 1946–1961.
4. Verification by national technical means: the Woods Hole assumptions.
5. Verification by national technical means supplemented by data exchanges and verification presumptions.
6. Verification by national technical means with systematic countermeasures impeding verification.

The Versailles Verification Regime:
Dictated Verification and Control

The regime of verification in effect in Germany after World War I is instructive because it reflects the limited value of on-site inspection even with the ceding of elements of sovereignty by a defeated nation. Under the 1919 Treaty of Versailles, Germany assumed the obligation to allow inspections by nationals of foreign powers, seemingly without territorial or quota limitations. Article 205 of the Versailles Treaty provided that the Inter-Allied Control Commissions

> shall be entitled as often as they think desirable to proceed to any point whatever in German territory, or to send subcommissions, or to authorize one or more of their members to go, to any such point.[5]

Because it established rights of recurring, on-site inspection, this verification regime focused German countermeasures around the Inter-Allied Commissions of Control and their district offices. How did a regime of virtually unlimited on-site inspection work? Not as well as might be supposed. Documentation furnished by the host government frequently was falsified. When British and French inspectors found discrepancies between nationally furnished and locally available information, they adapted by depending more and more upon surprise inspections. The German government responded by establishing its own liaison offices to countercontrol the Control Commission at the local level and by discouraging candor on the part of those interviewed. The controllers worked under diplomatic conventions of secrecy and rationalized their failure to publicize German breaches of the treaty, in part by the need to protect their methods of verification, although mainly these were known to the host government. As a result, the German nationalist press, understandably hostile to the demilitarization requirements of the Versailles Treaty, dominated public perceptions in the 1920's, until the control commissions were withdrawn in January 1927.

It was the German government that boasted of the hundreds of inspections it had tolerated, not the Allied inspectors, who knew how little they had learned and how little of what they had learned was shared with the publics of Europe. The senior British representative to the Inter-Allied Control Commission, Brigadier General J.H. Morgan explained:

> It requires two parties to make a visit a success—one to call, the other to receive; one to ask, the other to reply. . . . The number of visits of inspection we have made, and have had to make, is proof not of how much we have been told, but of how little.[6]

It was not the system of verification, but the German failure to meet a reparations payment that caused France to occupy the Ruhr in 1923—an action that caused friction among the Allies. The senior British officer had to resign from the Inter-Allied Control Commission in 1924 to set forth in public the story of Germany's covert rearmament.[7]

A British diplomatic note ensued, in June 1925, advising Germany that breaches of the Versailles Treaty were a "serious menace to the peace of Europe."[8] Shortly thereafter, the British government participated in the Locarno Pact of 1925, which demilitarized the Rhineland, until German reoccupation in 1936, and which led to German entry into the League of Nations (notwithstanding evidence of German noncompliance with the demilitarization duties of Versailles). Despite continuing German evasion of disarmament provisions and at least partial evidence of noncompliance derived from on-site inspections, the resulting intelligence did not spur British politicians to take remedial action. Without British support, French politicians, who were prepared to act, lacked the means to compel compliance. Other nations left the problem of noncompliance to the British and French-dominated Inter-Allied Commissions of Control. Without advance warning, the Soviet Union made a separate peace at Rapallo in return for German recognition of the revolutionary government.

After the Locarno Pact, it became "bad form" to complain about German noncompliance, at least until Hitler's rise to power in 1933 and exploitation of covert rearmament initiatives that had previously occurred. The British and French viewed Germany as more effectively disarmed than was the case, and, although specific Allied Control officers knew otherwise, the verification system failed to get the necessary information into the mainstream of public opinion.

Verification by Data Exchange in the 1930's

Three naval agreements of the 1930's typify a regime of verification based upon exchange of data between treaty parties, without on-site verification:

> Article 10 of the London Naval Treaty of 1930 provided for exchange of data on ship construction and ship armaments.
>
> The Anglo-German Naval Agreement of 1935 (articles 11 and 12) provided for data exchanges, with the proviso that the data exchanged would remain confidential until published by the supplying party (per article 11, paragraph 3).
>
> The Anglo-German Naval Agreement of 1937 also provided for data exchanges.

One of the inducements for the Anglo-German Naval Agreement of 1935 was the prospect, relayed by Admiral Raeder of the German Navy, that after an agreement had been signed, Germany would disclose its past and proposed shipbuilding program. The June 1935 Agreement and associated discussions led British Admiralty intelligence in 1935–36 to exaggerate both German shipbuilding capabilities, and the restraining impact of the 1935 Naval Agreement upon the number and tonnage of the German fleet. German intelligence (the *Abwehr*) passed exaggerated reports of German submarine construction and bogus deployments in the Atlantic, together with a notional concept that the submarine fleet was intended primarily for defense of the Baltic Sea. Concurrently, mandated German disclosures of data on the tonnage of the battleships *Bismarck* and *Tirpitz* involved false underreporting of tonnage and armaments.[9]

The naval data exchanges within the naval arms control framework of the 1930's produced data that was neither reliable nor of particular pertinence in assessing the role of naval threats in the ensuing war. More important, the false sense of reassurance from the 1935 Naval Agreement and associated data exchanges led to a complacency within British naval intelligence that was not paralleled in British estimates of the German army or air force strength and intentions.

> . . . as the German rearmament effort emerged from secrecy, much effort was spent on the British side in the pursuit of arms limitation agreements with the Germans as a substitute for the failure of the Geneva conference [on disarmament]. With the exception of the Anglo-German Naval Agreement, regarded as a model by few outside the circle of the Admiralty, these pursuits were sterile.
> . . . The assertions of various German officials, from the Führer downward, signaling the limits on rearmament, fitted easily into the already established image of German military power.[10]

The overt warnings associated with German withdrawal from the World Disarmament Conference and the League of Nations in 1933, renunciation of the Versailles Treaty in 1934, and occupation of the Rhineland in 1936 were of greater value, but these diplomatic warnings were insufficient to build early and sustainable public support for rearmament programs. If the provisions for data exchange in arms control agreements appeared to offer some safeguard for these treaties, they perhaps contributed to the illusion that the appeasement policies in effect were successfully averting war, without the need to strengthen deterrent capabilities.

Verification by Limited Inspection:
Concepts without Agreement, 1946–1961

After World War II, the Baruch-Lilienthal Plan for control of atomic energy called for a system of international inspection and supervision of atomic energy facilities. The Soviets rejected this. In the ensuing fifteen years, most disarmament proposals or related war-avoidance measures gained Soviet acquiesence only if they contained restrictions on rights of inspection. The first actual agreement to incorporate rights of limited inspection involved an exchange of military observers in occupied Germany, beginning in 1946. This arrangement led to a more formal undertaking: the so-called Huebner-Malinin Agreement of April 1947. This agreement is the basis for the Military Liaison Missions in Germany—an arrangement now viewed as a "confidence building measure."[11]

Both Molotov's disarmament plan of 10 May 1955 and the regional demilitarization plan of the Polish Foreign Minister Rapacki in 1957 called for aerial and ground inspection. These safeguards would only take effect after initial disarmament measures. One year later, the United Nations Peacekeeping Force in Lebanon established a border surveillance system, manned by UN personnel, with limited inspection capabilities. Each of these proposals, or actions, involved rights of limited on-site inspection.

The concept of on-site inspection without limitation gained acceptance in the Antarctic Treaty of 1959, but this accomplishment should be construed in relation to the impracticality of basing significant military forces in the region. Reliance upon on-site inspection and international "control" in disarmament is once again found in the September 1961 U.S.-Soviet agreement on principles for disarmament negotiations, but no agreement resulted.

Perhaps the most enduring element of a verification regime based on limited rights of inspection is the "safeguard" system of the Vienna-based International Atomic Energy Agency, founded in 1957. Through bilateral and multilateral agreements (some relating to compliance with the Nonproliferation Treaty of 1968), nation states and regional organizations (such as EURATOM—the European Atomic Energy Community) may allow international inspection of declared facilities (excluding undeclared facilities under national control). The safeguarding of atomic energy facilities allows nations seeking to demonstrate their compliance with antiproliferation safeguards to do so, while allowing nations committed to covert nuclear weapons programs to proceed with minimal inconvenience. With this notable exception, arms control initiatives have tended to avoid relying upon on-site inspection as the foundation for treaty verification.

Verification by National Technical Means:
The Woods Hole Assumptions

In the summer of 1962, the newly established U.S. Arms Control and Disarmament Agency convened its first major summer study on what appeared to be the major barrier to disarmament agreements: verification and response to arms control noncompliance. Soviet objections to robust on-site inspection systems even led to a Soviet proposal for a "troika" control system in which the host state could effectively block verification of noncompliance.

As prospects for an on-site inspection regime dimmed, the technological capabilities of nationally controlled verification systems appeared to brighten. As early as 1948, Colonel Richard Philbrick proposed that space satellites might render arms control more feasible. In 1954, another Air Force colonel, Richard S. Leghorn, drafted a concept for Governor Harold Stassen for aerial inspection of disarmament, proposed in revised form by President Eisenhower in the "open skies" speech of 1955.[12] Merton E. Davies of the Rand Corporation gave explicit consideration to "space observation" satellites in an experts' paper for the Geneva Conference on Surprise Attack in 1958.

The 1962 Woods Hole Summer Study (which this author attended as the most junior of the professional staff) addressed the following questions:

What criteria should be used in determining the information needed for verification?

How may the disarmament agreement be designed so as to minimize the incentives for violation?

Can it contain incentives for compliance?

What functions are seen for inspection in a disarmament agreement?

How is the ability to detect violations related to the ability to deter violations?

What does the willingness or unwillingness of a nation to accept certain kinds and degrees of inspection indicate about its intentions?

How should inspection be related to intelligence collection activities?

How does the intended response to violations affect the kind of information required?

What verification techniques require the minimum cost, manpower, and amount of access?

Are aerial overflights necessary to effective verification?

What evidence of compliance might an inspected country voluntarily provide? How can this voluntary self-disclosure be used to reduce the need for inspection?

Under what circumstance is the use of international bodies desirable?

Under what conditions is inspection of each side by the other side more desirable?

What range of unilateral or collective security actions is appropriate in the event that specific actions of noncompliance are discovered? How should the type of sanction depend upon the type of violation?

Under what circumstances is abrogation of the agreement an appropriate response? How may these circumstances be limited and distinguished from those in which abrogation is neither necessary nor desirable?[13]

Two key assumptions incorporated into the Woods Hole Summer Study report were (1) Verification acts as a deterrent to evasion only to the extent that a potential violator is concerned with the risks of exposure, and (2) national self-interest, rather than the fear of detection, will remain the principal inducement to compliance. Key findings of the Woods Hole Summary Report related to inspection and verification are:

Inspection as a Method of Verification:

1. A policy of insistence on inspection only when needed to satisfy verification requirements enhances the possibilities for achieving arms control and disarmament.
2. The pursuit of other gains from inspection must be weighed against specific arms control objectives.
3. There are significant arms control measures which can be verified with little or no inspection.

The Relation of Verification to Responses:

1. Verification conditions response. . . . If a government wants to terminate or to take other responsive action in respect to an arms control agreement, it must be able to persuade both its own public and those of its closest allies of the basis for this decision.
2. Verification must facilitate the decision on response.
3. Obstruction of verification may itself require response.
4. Verification should inhibit over-response as well as a lack of response. If militarily significant violations are discovered or are suspected to exist, responses which redress the military balance may be required. However, if the response is not to upset the balance or unnecessarily endanger other aspects of the arms control agreement, it is in the interest of all parties that the verification system give a clear picture of the military environment and of the apparent violation.[14]

The Woods Hole Summer study established a working group on "minimum access" methods of verification. This group, aided by consultants such as Amrom H. Katz, an expert on aerial and space reconnaissance, led an intellectual revolt from inspection-dependent agreements and rendered respectable agreements that would be verified by what came to be known as *national technical means (NTM)*.

The Woods Hole study participants were realistic in assuming that verification is a deterrent only to the extent that a potential violator is concerned with risks of exposure. It is important that the participants concluded that it is a function of verification to provide information upon which to base and justify responsive action. Both U.S. intelligence agencies and arms control advocates in the 1970's have retreated from this important standard. The rhetoric of verification has all too often asked whether the means of verification are adequate for detection, without asking whether these means are also adequate to determine and justify responses in the event of noncompliance.

Surely verification is inadequate if it merely ascertains the facts of compliance or noncompliance without providing the informational foundation by which to identify and evaluate alternative responses. Five public presidential reports in 1984–85 on the facts and legal status of Soviet acts regarding breach of arms control commitments appear an inadequate foundation by which to develop a U.S. compliance policy or strategy, but this should come as no surprise. Even without the uncertainties abetted by Soviet *maskirovka* programs, it should be obvious that the illumination of the legal periphery of arms control agreements is insufficient to effectuate a strategy responsive to a pattern of sustained arms control violations.

The Woods Hole study assertion that it is in the interests of all parties that the verification system give a clear picture of the military environment and of the "apparent violation," appears to be premised on the dubious assumption that violations are likely to be inadvertent. In the 1920's and 1930's, violations generally were intentional, as were efforts to conceal them. The historical record was at odds with this Woods Hole assumption, even in 1962. The last quarter-century of Soviet arms control behavior indicates both that most violations are not inadvertent and that violators recurringly lack incentive to provide the clearest picture possible of the violation in its military environment.

For example, the Soviets expanded a covert, offensive biological weapons capability during the period between signing, in 1972, and ratifying, in 1975, the Biological Weapons Convention. They expanded their program and its facilities thereafter. Not only did the Soviets avert on-site inspection within the treaty test, but after the Sverdlovsk incident, in April 1979 (when pulmonary anthrax infected civilians in the environs of that city), the Soviets refused to allow a site visit by a United Nations investigating team. Moreover, as indicated in the GAC report of 1983 (publicly summarized in 1984), the Soviets probably initiated certain violations in order to understand the limits of U.S. verification capabilities better (as with maintenance of excess SS-7 ICBM launchers in 1976–77). It is no longer realistic to maintain that it is in the interests of all parties that the verification system give a clear picture. The expanding Soviet program of countermeasures to verification by NTM is a powerful indicator that the Soviets have no intention of providing a clear picture of their arms control misconduct.

In one important respect, the Woods Hole study underrepresented U.S. verification capabilities: it concluded that development and production of chemical and biological weapons seem virtually uninspectable, but, since most uses could be rapidly detected, the summary report recommended an agreement restricting or outlawing their use—but not their development or production. However, all five reports transmitted by the President to the Congress on Soviet noncompliance during the 1984–85 period, have found violations—not probable violations—of the Biological and Toxin Weapons Convention of 1972. Verification may have taken more time than desired, but verification was possible.

Depending on "national technical means" of verification made feasible the arms control agreements from the Limited Test Ban Treaty of 1963 to the present. The Cuban Missile Crisis, which followed the Woods Hole Summer Study by only a couple of months, was an important transitional event. Not only did the threat of thermonuclear war appear closer than many had thought but also Fidel Castro blocked the on-site inspection procedures established in connection with the removal of Soviet offensive weapons. The United States depended on "national technical means" of verification because there simply was no other choice.

The Limited Test Ban Treaty of 1963 (which banned atmospheric nuclear testing), the Outer Space Treaty of 1967, and the SALT I agreements of 1972 all depended upon NTM. None provided for on-site inspection. This regime of verification strengthened incentives for Soviet *maskirovka* programs that could defeat, or at least delay, verification and diffuse or dilute countermeasures to Soviet material breaches.

Verification by National Technical Means Supplemented by Data Exchanges and Verification Presumptions

The Threshold Test Ban Treaty of 1974 (TTBT), together with its 1976 Protocol, provided for potential calibration of nuclear test sites. On-site calibration of nuclear test sites did not occur before "likely" Soviet testing above the 150 kiloton yield limit had led to reexamination of the verifiability of this treaty as initially negotiated.[15]

The TTBT at least stands for the proposition that some on-site facilitation of NTM may be required for reliable verification of arms control commitments. The SALT II Treaty paralleled the uninspiring precedents of the Anglo-German naval treaties of the 1930's by including provisions for treaty-specified exchanges of data. These provisions yielded material omissions and misrepresentations by Germany in the 1930's and by the Soviet Union since 1979.

Given the falsification of the Warsaw Pact data base in Mutual Balanced Force Reduction (MBFR) talks in the 1970's[16] and nondisclosure of Soviet SS-16 mobile ICBM's at Plesetsk (a "probable violation" of SALT II according to each of the five Presidential reports of 1984–85 on Soviet noncompliance), data base exchanges with the Soviet Union in the Brezhnev era appear no more reliable than were those with Germany in the Nazi era.

SALT II also has certain presumptions relating to the timing of deployments and the counting of regulated systems. Unfortunately, the rules on when to count a deployed system (that is, when removed from the final assembly area before deployment) only strengthen the case that the Soviets have been breaching their contracted duties.

U.S. negotiators of the SALT II Treaty can be credited with trying to complement national technical means of verification by also providing for data base disclosures, counting rules, and requirements for functionally related-observable-differences (known both as "frods" and "frauds" within the verification community). This was a vision of a regime for arms control verification that might have been; but this has not been the reality of arms control verification since SALT I. As the report by the President's General Advisory Committee on Arms Control and Disarmament observed in 1984, the Soviets have violated the prohibition against "deliberate concealment measures impeding verification" of the ABM Treaty, the SALT I Interim Agreement, and the SALT II Treaty. Hence the regime for verification of the arms control commitments since 1972 is not one to be inferred merely by reading treaty language and wishing that obligations stated are obligations fulfilled.

Verification by National Technical Means with Systematic Countermeasures Impeding Verification

The Soviets came to understand that the security measures of the 1950's were inadequate to cope with synoptic overhead reconnaissance in the 1960's. In August 1961, an Alsop brothers' column in the *Washington Post* indicated that U.S. intelligence had acquired a capability to estimate deployments of Soviet ICBMs with significantly reduced uncertainty. Even before Deputy Secretary of Defense Gilpatric confirmed, in October 1961, that minimal Soviet ICBM deployments were known to the United States, Soviet military counterintelligence reportedly issued strengthened regulations. Soviet defector Aleksei Myagov's memoirs note that Soviet Military Counterintelligence Regulation number 00270 of 8 September 1961 established as a duty of counterintelligence departments:

> To prepare and carry out, together with State Security and Ministry of Defense organs, special measures for disinformation of the enemy, for recording and for camouflaging especially important military objectives.[17]

Press reports suggest that the Soviet Union initiated a satellite warning system in 1966—that is, before SALT I—hence a "current practice" at the time of SALT I's inception in May 1972.[18] In 1968, the same year that the National Security Council adopted the principle that it would utilize national technical means to verify the proposed SALT I agreement,[19] then-General N.V. Ogarkov reportedly took charge of a newly established Principal Directorate for Strategic Deception (GUSM) within the Soviet General Staff.[20] Thus, by the inception of the SALT I Interim Agreement and the ABM Treaty, the Soviets had in place a set of national countermeasures to U.S. verification by NTM. Hence, the critically erroneous assumption of the 1962 Woods Hole Summer Study was the implicit expectation that the Soviet system of internal secrecy would remain benignly neutral to foreign verification by NTM. If there had been merely a cultural aversion to on-site inspection or to some perceived challenge to party authority by an international inspectorate, then there would have been no necessity for the Soviet government to block nonintrusive remote observation. But the Soviet system of countermeasures was not mindless. The Defense Ministry component of this system was directed by a general who rose to become the principal military officer assigned to the Soviet's SALT I delegation. Thereafter, Marshal Ogarkov became the Chief of the General Staff.

Even national technical means of verification are not immune to a systematic program of countermeasures. This systematic attack upon the means of national verification that made arms control a reality in the 1970's was simply not contemplated by the Woods Hole study participants of 1962—Nobel laureates and all.

Soviet *Maskirovka* and the Arms Control Process

Public Soviet writings on *maskirovka* variously defined as strategic, operational, and tactical masking by means of denial and deception,[21] tend to emphasize its operational role in military combat, not its relation to arms control verification.[22] The practice of Soviet *maskirovka* in the arms control arena emphasizes the attention of Soviet politicians to the political opportunities in masking Soviet strategies to obtain advantage, despite arms control limits.[23]

Maskirovka Preceding Negotiations

Perhaps one of the more important lessons from SALT I is that *maskirovka* is likely to impact the verification process at the outset of negotiations—not after an agreement is signed. Arms control provides opportunities for what economists sometimes call "gains in trade." These may be real, and these may be illusory. The arms control process may be directed, like iron filings to a magnet, to sectors where divergences of strategic concept and outright misestimates combine to satisfy both parties, largely because the sides have fundamentally incompatible estimates of the situation. An efficient market will induce arms control negotiators to incorporate commitments that leave each side in a better apparent position than it would be without the commitment. The "hidden hand" of the market will all too often make deals among adversaries that stand or fall on the basis of incompatible perceptions.

Such was the situation *before* SALT I negotiations began in earnest in 1968.

As this author has noted before, there is evidence that the Soviets biased technical indicators of ICBM missile accuracy and missions before the onset of SALT I negotiations. The Soviets may have estimated that, by the close of the 1966–70 Five Year Plan, they would have a capability for a substantially lethal preemptive attack upon the Minuteman II and Titan silos then housing most of the U.S. ICBM force.[24]

In contrast, U.S. defense posture statements indicate that it was not until the mid-1970's that senior U.S. defense planners projected a *future* "window of vulnerability" for U.S. land-based ICBMs. A Soviet deception program that apparently preceded the SALT I negotiations naturally attracted both U.S. and Soviet negotiators to this sector. On the U.S. side, the test of the SS-9 with three reentry vehicles (from August 1968) encouraged U.S. negotiators to seek a numerical limit on "heavy" ICBMs, such as the SS-9, that were projected to be capable of destroying Minuteman III launcher silos (but not necessarily command and control silos).

If the Soviets sought to maintain a capability for preemptive destruction of most U.S. land-based forces in war, the ABM Treaty and the 1972 Interim Agreement, taken together, would maintain U.S. confidence in undefended, fixed-site ICBM launchers while failing to restrain the replacement of "light" SS-11 ICBMs with SS-19 and SS-17 ICBMs. These ICBMs could extend performance of a Soviet counterforce mission into the era of the more survivable Minuteman III silo, despite SALT I limits. Press reports indicate the possibility that deception activities *preceded* negotiations and provided mutual perceptions of "gains-in-trade" through the signing of the Biological Warfare and Toxin Weapons Convention of 1972.[25]

If the Soviets estimated that the United States had a lead in biological weapons (BW) research, the Biological Weapons Convention (agreed by both sides to be inadequately verifiable) was a potential vehicle to eliminate U.S. offensive BW capabilities, while allowing the Soviets to develop a covert, albeit illegal, weapons stockpile. This offensive weapons capability would provide Soviet forces antipersonnel and area denial options that NATO nations (limited by the BW Convention) and China (not a Convention signatory) would be unlikely to match.

If U.S. politicians, facing opposition to ongoing research programs in Utah and elsewhere, were convinced that there was no practical future for U.S. biological weapons, the 1972 Convention could be viewed as precluding Soviet acquisition of practical BW weapons, assuming that all parties were to comply with the treaty. Five presidential reports to the Congress (in 1984–85) indicate with high confidence that the Soviets have maintained an offensive and illegal biological weapons capability. Each of the five reports finds a Soviet "violation"—not a "probable violation"—of this Convention, from 1972 to the present.

The point is that, where starkly different perceptions of relative advantage precede arms control negotiations, arms control commitments may follow—especially if both sides appear to be "winners." So, *maskirovka* may not initially be directed toward the means of verifying compliance; rather, the path of least resistance to arms control is to make agreements built upon misperceptions. Merely because the spotlight of verification discloses evidence of deception is not to conclude that deception resulted from the arms control process. Arms control commitments have a tendency to gravitate toward sectors of incompatible perceptions, just as flies are attracted to flypaper.

This curious relationship between preexisting misperceptions, arms control commitment, and verification makes the verification process all the more difficult. When the Soviets were assuring U.S. negotiators that the replacement for the SS-11 ICBM would be more like the SS-11 than the SS-9, this was comforting to U.S. negotiators in part because of the failure to perceive at least one strategic mission of the SS-11, an attack on the older Minuteman II ICBM silos. If reliable verification requires unlearning a past understanding of history, it does not take a large dose of new *maskirovka* to remain uncomprehending of why an adversary-partner is at least as pleased by an arms control commitment that appears particularly advantageous to the West.

Maskirovka during Negotiations

The negotiating process may well induce further deception. The literature previously cited treats assertions that during the negotiations, the Soviets misrepresented the volume of the SS-19 ICBM, the testing and probable deployment of the SS-16 mobile ICBM, the range of the SS-N-8 SLBM, the rate of construction and deployment plans for SLBM forces, and the commitment of the Soviet Union to dismantle an offensive biological warfare capability. Thus, there is evidence of deception during negotiations, and this too complicates post-agreement verification of compliance.

Verification as an Aid to *Maskirovka*

The debate about verification before signing and ratifying an arms control treaty, and during the debate about the significance of detected noncompliance, must be of considerable and recurring value in perfecting Soviet *maskirovka* efforts. This is a cost of a democratic society that must be borne, and it is a cost that is widely recognized. There is a less-well understood relationship between arms control verification and deception. This involves the predictability of intelligence tasking and policy interest in arms control verification, and the opportunities of this predictability for the perfection of *maskirovka* programs.

... To meet political needs, even Soviet actions like the dismantling of obsolete missile launch facilities under agreed procedures must be watched more closely than national security needs would dictate.[26]

Hence, in 1976–77, before the October 1977 expiration of SALT I, when it was uncertain there would be a new agreement, the Soviets maintained excess SS-7 ICBM launchers in numbers that were noticeable, but adjudged not be of high military significance in themselves. The October 1984 report of the President's General Advisory Committee on Arms Control and Disarmament finds this violation of the SALT I Protocol and agreed dismantling procedures "probably not inadvertent, but rather [the retention of excess launchers] was part of a deliberate Soviet effort to challenge U.S. arms control verification capabilities."[27]

Soviet experiments with telemetry encryption, when coupled with U.S. press accounts and formal exchanges on the matter, must have aided Soviet *maskirovka* efforts in the sector of weapons testing. Similarly, the extensive public review of methods to estimate the yields of underground Soviet nuclear tests during the Threshold Test Ban ratification hearings of 1977 must have enlightened Soviet readers.

Equality of Apparent Guilt: Verification of Compliance in Aid of Future *Maskirovka*

From time to time, a Soviet arms control commitment constrains the actualization of existing or modified defense plans. Under such circumstances, it is not unusual for the Soviets to make a preemptive charge of possible U.S. misconduct in a similar sector of activity. Here, the verification process is utilized so that, under the principle of "equal noise, equal wrong" or the principle of "the first to complain has clean hands," the Soviets have been able to lay a foundation for campaigns to limit responses to later-detected Soviet violations.

The Vance report on SALT I compliance, issued in February 1978, contains several instances of implausible Soviet charges that occur in apparent proximity to the likely period of Soviet decisions to disregard arms control limits. In early 1975, the Soviets complained about the possible failure of the United States to dismantle Atlas and Titan I ICBMs. These were deactivated in 1966, and silo headworks had been sealed. It was not long after this preemptive but groundless complaint that the Soviets retained illegal SS-7 launchers in active status, according to the GAC Report.

This was almost certainly part of a deliberate Soviet effort to challenge U.S. arms control verification capabilities. During this same period, the Soviets were removing SS-9 and SS-11 ICBMs from silos that were converted to house heavier

SS-19 and SS-17 missiles. Where did the SS-9's and SS-11's go? These are not known to have been dismantled in the decade 1976–1985. By preemptively expressing concern about U.S. ICBM dismantling that was indisputably apparent and by experimenting, through apparent violations, with means to perfect *maskirovka* programs, the Soviets effectively blunted the U.S. response to any strategic reserve missile force that the Soviets retained. The verification process has recurringly aided Soviet *maskirovka* efforts—perhaps more effectively than Soviet *maskirovka* efforts aided in countering U.S. verification, for despite Soviet *maskirovka*, the United States has verified a broad scope and substantial number of Soviet arms control violations. But, what can be done about how and where the Soviets have learned to hide their arms control violations more successfully? Where the Soviets have acted as if they were the wronged party, who among the apologentsia will disbelieve them? Who among the conciliationists will support sanctions or self-help measures when there are "arguments on both sides?"

Soviet Maskirovka *as a Threat to International Peace*

The pervasiveness of Soviet denial and deception activities by nationally authorized entities has resulted in complementary nationwide systems of *maskirovka* within a society that is unsurpassed in raw military power. If the weak require secrecy and perhaps a touch of deception, that is understandable, but when a superpower requires a nationwide system of *maskirovka*, that system can only be a threat to international peace. *Maskirovka* can create more mistrust than arms control can dispel—even if there were a degree of compliance that is lacking on the Soviet side.

Even if there were no obligation under arms control treaties to refrain from deliberate concealment measures that impede verification by national technical means, the scope of Soviet *maskirovka* activities would be irresponsible.

> For some inexplicable reason, there seems to be a widely held belief that monitoring capabilities that are not sufficient for arms control are somehow sufficient to guide "unconstrained" defense planning. . . . In terms of potential military risk, a given set of monitoring capabilities that cannot provide early detection in the contest of verifying arms control agreements also cannot provide early detection in the context of revising and modernizing U.S. military force posture.[28]

The Soviet style of arms control necessitates an increase in distrust. *Maskirovka* expands the fear of the unknown. Failures of *maskirovka* confirm that the Soviets do cheat and that they do not merely nibble at the edges, but defeat the central purpose of arms control agreements if it suits the purposes of their leadership. Soviet requests for clarification of what parameters are needed for verification cannot be taken at face value—for in the past, the Soviets have exploited the arms control verification process to make it harder to depend upon verification in the future. With or without arms control, the new Soviet leadership under Gorbachev must come to grips with the irresponsibility of nationwide *maskirovka* programs if they are continued at current levels of effort. Otherwise, the nations of the globe must assume the worst and prepare to face a greater than expected Soviet challenge.

U.S. Failure to Deter the Illegal Expansion of Soviet Maskirovka *Programs*

How well has the United States coped with the growth of Soviet denial and deception programs after the restriction of "current practices" in May 1972. From a deterrence perspective, the United States has done abysmally. President Carter asserted that if the Soviets expanded deliberate concealment measures, the United States would consider abrogating the SALT II treaty.

> . . . Deliberate concealment measures are themselves a violation, and if detected could be grounds for abrogating the [SALT II] treaty, even if we are not certain what activity is being concealed.[29]

Despite President Carter's tough stance on deliberate concealment measures, three NSC-sponsored reports (transmitted by President Reagan to the Congress between January 1984 and June 1985) failed to go beyond the narrow concern regarding encryption of missile test data. Not one of the first three Reagan administration reports (prepared under the auspices of the NSC on 23 January 1984, 1 February 1985, and 10 June 1985) publicly addressed the adverse consequences of an expanding Soviet *maskirovka* program for arms control verification, for framing appropriate responses to violations, or for the alleviation of international tensions. In contrast, the report by the independent but presidentially appointed General Advisory Committee on Arms Control and Disarmament (GAC) found no arms control violation of more profound and continuing significance than the illegal Soviet system of deliberate concealment measures in violation of the SALT I Interim Agreement, the SALT II Treaty, and the ABM Treaty.

Deliberate concealment measures that are elements of a nationwide Soviet program to deny intelligence information to adversaries have a profound effect upon the role of arms control in inducing distrust among nations. This is so, even if the intent of counter-reconnaissance initiatives is to protect national security and not to foil arms control initiatives. What is legally pertinent is not the intent of a deliberate concealment program, but whether the elements of that program do, in fact, impede another party's verification of the treaty provisions. That is why there were explicit provisions in the previous treaties—to proscribe the scope of legitimate defense security programs when they impeded treaty verification. A duty to facilitate treaty verification supersedes a duty to protect national security information.

Despite an unprecedented level of Soviet concealment activity and despite President Carter's warning in 1979, when President Reagan finally announced the end of U.S. commitment to the widely violated SALT II Treaty in May 1986, the House of Representatives passed a resolution urging continuing SALT II compliance. And by a vote of 225 to 199, the House voted in August 1986 against suspending U.S. compliance in event of Soviet violations. So much for deterrence of an expanding Soviet program of deliberate concealment measures. Since past arms control efforts tended to induce further Soviet deception, how much credence should be given to whatever measures of facilitated verification the Soviets are willing to allow? The United States and its allies must depend upon self-help, upon ingenuity in collection and analysis of information, and not upon professions of Soviet goodwill or forebearance.[30]

A precondition of Soviet self-restraint with regard to nationwide *maskirovka* programs is for the United States to recognize—first within the executive branch and then within the Congress and the attentive public—that nationwide Soviet *maskirovka* activities constitute more than a material breach of past arms control commitments. Without an abatement in Soviet counter-reconnaissance efforts, it is unrealistic to premise U.S. arms control policies on an assumption that intelligence capabilities will be adequate to verify the state of compliance, to identify appropriate responses to violations and evasions, and to justify those responses to the Congress and the public.

This second step (admitting that the adequacy of U.S. verification depends in significant ways upon the conduct of the Soviet Union) is particularly difficult for a government that takes pride in its intelligence technology, and its abilities to apply esoteric analytic techniques to treaty verification. If the verification standards of the Woods Hole study of 1962 are utilized—as they should be—then it is necessary to find that verification is adequate to aid in the implementation of appropriate responses before concluding that verification is adequate at all. The adequacy of verification depends in greater measure upon the ability of intelligence to inform decisions on responsive measures than upon the ability to report whether a treaty partner has transgressed the boundary between permitted and illicit activities.

Through the summer of 1985, it appeared that (excepting the GAC report's objections to deliberate Soviet concealment activities) even the Reagan administration was resigned to an ever-expanding program of Soviet concealment activities. Consequently, the subsequent willingness of the Reagan administration to challenge, in public, Soviet efforts to mask the association of ballistic missile launchers and ballistic missiles has a greater significance than the actual charge itself. For the first time since January 1984, in December 1985, the Reagan administration expanded the scope of its publicly expressed concerns regarding Soviet *maskirovka* programs:

> *Issue*: This report examines for the first time the issue of whether the Soviets have concealed the association between an ICBM and its launcher during testing, in violation of their obligation not to use deliberate concealment measures which impede verification.
>
> *Finding*: The U.S. Government judges Soviet activities related to the SS-25 to be a violation of the Soviet Union's political commitment to abide by the SALT II Treaty provision prohibiting concealment of the association between a missile and its launcher during testing.[31]

U.S. Verification of Soviet Noncompliance despite Soviet *Maskirovka* Programs

Despite the expanding scope of Soviet *maskirovka* programs, the United States' system of arms control verification demonstrated a remarkable capacity to verify broad scope and some detail regarding Soviet noncompliance with arms control obligations. As Amrom Katz reminds us, in *Verification: The State of the Art and the Art of the State*, since the United States does not know what it has not found, and since patterns of illegal acts relating to quantitative and qualitative limits have been found, it is only prudent to assume that there are other Soviet violations of significance that are not yet detected. There is reason to expect that the arms control breaches detected are not all that exist. This is particularly so because the Soviets know that a system of deliberate concealment activities has been observed with a scope and design that they know the United States considers to be illegal. It would only be worthwhile to incur this distrust and adverse public reaction if there were other fruits of illegal Soviet conduct ripening outside our field of view.

Accordingly, the United States must have diminished confidence in its understanding of the state of Soviet compliance with those arms control commitments, which the Soviets appear to be meeting without any material breach. The Soviets appear to be in compliance with various commitments to reduce risks of accidental conflict or to contain the spread of technology of weapons to new nations or geographic spheres. But because of the illegal Soviet *maskirovka* programs—themselves a warning of undetected illegalities—there must be diminished confidence in evidence of apparent Soviet compliance than in evidence of apparent noncompliance. This is an expectable consequence of Soviet deception and denial programs, of the scope and increasing intensity since strategic arms control agreements became a reality in the 1970's.

Notwithstanding uncertainties of a factual and legal nature, a broad consensus has developed within the verification community—those of diverging political and philosophical persuasion who have to grapple with the evidence of recurring Soviet noncompliance.

The Soviet Record of Noncompliance with Arms Control Commitments, 1958–85

Tables 10–1 through 10–5 compare the declassified findings on Soviet noncompliance with arms control commitments in effect after World War II, for each of five reports submitted to the President and reported by the President to the Congress, over the two-year period 1983 to 1985. The first report, the GAC report, was submitted to the President on 2 December 1983, but only released to the Congress in a declassified version on 10 October 1984. Four subsequent reports that the President transmitted to the Congress treat subsets of the issues evaluated in the GAC report and in some instances, consider subsequently raised compliance issues. Generally, the different groups that have utilized extensive intelligence information, as well as diplomatic and legal information, have come to remarkably similar conclusions. They have disagreed on both the degree of confidence and the state of legal duties. This is natural and healthy, but the five reports here summarized indicate a growing consensus on the general scope of those Soviet activities that breach contracted obligations.

Despite extraordinary Soviet deception and denial activities and despite false charges of U.S. violations, those who have looked back without fear, those tasked with assessing the state of arms control compliance, reached strikingly similar conclusions. As the public becomes more aware of what has been learned, the preconditions for effective response will be in place. However, it remains necessary to analyze alternative responsive options, from both an intelligence and a policy perspective, so that the result is not self-defeating.

Table 10–1 treats strategic nuclear arms agreements. Table 10–2 treats restraints on nuclear weapons testing. Table 10–3 treats breaches of other Soviet arms control commitments, and table 10–4 lists commitments with which the Soviets appear to have complied.

Evaluating Impacts of U.S. Compliance Initiatives upon Limited Restoration of Soviet Compliance

Soviet *maskirovka* activities do not cease merely because concealed activities have been detected, assessed, and publicly reported as violations by treaty partners. It has become a customary Soviet practice to deny the fact of the activity challenged, rather than to defend its legal status. Hence, the Soviets deny the transfer or use of lethal chemical munitions, deny the possession of biological weapons, deny the deployment of SS-16 missiles at Plesetsk, and deny they have tested or deployed two new-type ICBMs, the SS-24 and SS-25.

If it is infeasible to conceal a regulated system from observation, the Soviets tend to delay discussion of illegal deployments until foreign detection is assured. Thereafter, the Soviets simply misclassify the impermissible system as a permissible system and stick to their story no matter how absurd it may seem.

For example, after the Soviets completed construction of the aircraft carrier *Kiev*, they timed its illegal passage through the Turkish straits to coincide with the fortieth anniversary of the signing of the Montreux Convention, the very treaty that bans passage of aircraft carriers through those straits. The Soviets classified the vessel as an "antisubmarine cruiser" and, concurrently in July 1976, published a legal misanalysis of the Convention's terms purporting to show that the ban on passage of aircraft carriers did not apply to the Soviet Union.[32] More recently, the Soviets characterized the large radar near Krasnoyarsk as a "space tracker," despite features nearly identical with those of the Pechora-class radars that are only permitted on the periphery and facing outward. The Soviets did not acknowledge the Krasnoyarsk radar until queried about it. Since 1983, they have denied its illegality relative to the ABM Treaty, offered to freeze its construction if the United States froze modernization, at an earlier stage, of two early warning radars permitted by the ABM Treaty,[33] but continued its construction.

Soviet diplomatic deception, even *after* successful detection and assessment of illegal acts, presents yet another verification challenge. Since the Soviets will not admit their illegal conduct even after it has been detected, it is difficult for the Soviets to take credit for cessation of arms control violations. This places a burden on the arms control verification system to detect—insofar as possible—the cessation of Soviet arms control violations of an ongoing nature.

The December 1985 Presidential report on Soviet noncompliance identifies four areas of apparent cessation of previously ongoing Soviet arms control violations. Table 10–5 summarizes these findings and those in earlier reports.

To what extent do changes in Soviet compliance practices relate to defense program needs, or to U.S. policies, and to compliance initiatives in particular? If the United States failed to induce a restoration of Soviet compliance with the ABM Treaty, the Biological Weapons Convention, and various other obligations, what is the prognosis for future arms control agreements? Soviet *maskirovka* activities delay acknowledgment of restored Soviet compliance, the significance of changes in behavior related to arms control duties, and the significance of violations that are so important to the Soviets that they continue, notwithstanding U.S. compliance initiatives.

Table 10–1
Presidential Reports to the Congress on Soviet Noncompliance with Arms Control Obligations—Strategic Nuclear Arms Agreements

Obligation	Issue/Report	GAC Report 12/02/83[a]	President 1/23/84[b]	President 2/01/85[c]	President 6/10/85[d]	President 12/23/85[c]
1972 ABM Treaty	Deployment of large Krasnoyarsk radar, neither on periphery nor oriented outward, 1981 to present	Violation	Almost certainly a violation	Violation	Violation	Violation; no corrective action has been taken
	Testing and deployment of mobile FLAT TWIN ABM radar in 1975, and continuing development 1975 to present	Violation	—	—	—	Apparent testing and development of ABM components
	Concurrent testing of ABM and SAM components	Violation	—	Potential violation	—	
		—	—	Highly probable violations	—	and highly probable concurrent testing; SA-X-12 may have some ABM capabilities
	Deliberate concealment measures	Violations	—	—	—	—
	ABM and ABM-related actions in preparation for defense of the national territory.	—	—	Potential violation	Serious cause for concern	May be preparing ABM defense
	Rapid reload of ABM launchers	—	—	Classified report	—	Serious cause for concern
1972 Salt I Interim Agreement	Deployment of large throwweight SS-19 and SS-17 ICBMs despite limit on heavy ICBM launchers, 1972 to present	Circumvention defeating object and purpose	—	—	—	—
	Deliberate concealment measures	Violations	—	—	—	—
Protocol limiting launchers of modern ballistic missiles	Deployment of "DELTA" modern SLBM launchers exceeding SALT I Protocol limit, 1976–1977; dismantling of older launchers	Violations (probably deliberate)	—	Currently in compliance (political)	Compliance with the letter of the agreement	—
Dismantling Procedures effective 3 July 1974	YANKEE SLBM submarine conversion into elongated cruise missile carrier	—	—	Not a violation but threat to U.S. and Allies' security	Not a violation but threat to U.S. and Allies' security	—
	Mobile missile base (SS-25) at dismantled SS-7 ICBM sites	—	—	Future violation	—	Violation; use of SS-7 facilities for SS-25 ICBMs

Table 10–1 (continued)

Obligation	Issue/Report	GAC Report 12/02/83[a]	President 1/23/84[b]	President 2/01/85[c]	President 6/10/85[d]	President 12/23/85[e]
1979 SALT II Treaty (unratified) (duty not to defeat object and purpose)	Flight testing or deployment of second new type ICBM (SS-X-25)	Probable violation	Probable violation (political)	Violation (political)	Irreversible violation	Clear and irreversible violation
	Anti-MIRV limit on RV-to-throwweight ratio (SS-X-25)	Violation	Violation (political)	Violation (political)	Serious concerns unresolved	Violation (political)
	Encryption impeding verification	Violation	Violation (legal, 79–81) (political, 82–)	Violation (legal, 79–81) (political, 82–)	Violation	Violation (legal, 79–81) (political, 82–)
	Deliberate concealment:					
	Plesetsk test center	Violation	—	—	—	—
	Association of missiles and launchers during testing	—	—	—	—	Violation (political)
	Deployment of the SS-16 mobile ICBM at Plesetsk	Probable violation	Probable violation (legal, 79–81) (political, 82–)	Probable violation (legal, 79–81) (political, 82–)	Probable violation	Probable deployment Probable removal in 1985
	Falsification of SALT II database, 1979–	Probable violation	—	—	—	—
	Backfire bomber production above 30 per year	—	—	—	—	More than 30/yr before 1984; less than 30/yr since 1984
	Exceeding strategic nuclear delivery vehicle ceiling	—	—	—	—	Violation (political) deploying more than 2504 SNDVs

[a] Unclassified summary report of the President's General Advisory Committee on Arms Control and Disarmament, 10/10/84.
[b] Report of the President on Soviet Noncompliance, per FY84 Arms Control Act, 1/23/84.
[c] Report of the President on Soviet Noncompliance per FY85 Defense Authorization Act, 2/01/85.
[d] Report of the President, Building an Interim Framework for Mutual Restraint, 6/10/85.
[e] Report of the President on Soviet Noncompliance, per PL99–145, 12/23/85.

Table 10-2
Presidential Reports to the Congress on Soviet Noncompliance with Arms Control Obligations—Restraints on Nuclear Weapons Testing

Obligation	Issue/Report	GAC Report 12/02/83[a]	President 1/23/84[b]	President 2/01/85[c]	President 6/10/85[d]	President 12/23/85[e]
Nuclear Test Moratorium, 1958–61 (Unilateral Soviet commitments)	Resumption of atmospheric testing, 1961–62, during negotiation of treaty banning atmospheric tests	Breach of unilateral commitment	—	—	—	—
1963 Limited Test Ban Treaty	Venting radioactive debris outside the Soviet Union, when available and reasonable precautions could have contained debris, 1965 to present	Numerous violations	—	Numerous violations	Violations	—
1974 Threshold Test Ban Treaty and 1976 Protocol (unratified) (effective March 31, 1976)	Underground nuclear testing with yields in excess of 150 kt limit	Suspicion of repeated violations	Likely violation	Likely violation	Likely violation	Likely violation

[a] Unclassified summary report of the President's General Advisory Committee on Arms Control and Disarmament, 10/10/84.
[b] Report of the President on Soviet Noncompliance, per FY84 Arms Control Act, 1/23/84.
[c] Report of the President on Soviet Noncompliance per FY85 Defense Authorization Act, 2/01/85.
[d] Report of the President, Building an Interim Framework for Mutual Restraint, 6/10/85.
[e] Report of the President on Soviet Noncompliance, per PL99-145, 12/23/85.

Maskirovka and Arms Control Verification • 213

Table 10-3
Presidential Reports to the Congress on Soviet Noncompliance with Arms Control Obligations—Other Soviet Arms Control Commitments

Obligation	Issue/Report	GAC Report 12/02/83[a]	President 1/23/84[b]	President 2/01/85[c]	President 6/10/85[d]	President 12/23/85[e]
Offensive Weapons in Cuba, 1962 (Unilateral)	Deployment of offensive weapons (MRBM and IRBM missiles; medium bombers) in Cuba, September–October, 1962	Breach of unilateral commitment	—	—	—	—
Offensive Weapons in Cuba - (Reciprocal unilateral commitment) - 1970	Deploying and tending Soviet nuclear missile-carrying submarines in Cuban territorial waters, 1970–1974	Breach of unilateral commitments	—	—	—	—
Biological Weapons Convention, 1972	Retention of facilities, continued biological munitions production, storage transfer and use; maintaining an offensive biological warfare program and capability; 1972 to present	Violations	Violations	Violations	Significant violations	Violations; expanded BW and toxin facilities since 1972
Geneva Protocol of 1925 (Chemical and Toxin Weapons)	Transfer of chemical and toxin weapons to Vietnam, with subsequent use, 1975–83, and Soviet use in Afghanistan, 1980–82, against nationals of Protocol nonparties	Circumventions defeating object and purpose	Violations (codification of customary international law)	Violations (codification of customary international law) - not continued '84	Significant violations	Violations; no evidence of lethal attacks in 1985
Montreux Convention of 1936 and Law of the Sea Convention of 1982	Transit of aircraft carriers through the Turkish Straits; Black Sea construction necessitates future violations.	Violations	—	—	—	—
Helsinki Final Act of 1975	Failure to provide 21-day notice and specified data before exercises involving more than 25,000 troops, 1981 and 1983	Violations 1981 and 1983	Violation (political) 1981	Violation (political) improved notice—1983	Violation of terms	Violation 1981; minimal notice provided in 1984–1985
Conventional Weapons Convention, 1981	Use of booby-trap mines and incendiary weapons against civilians in Afghanistan, 1981–1982, before entry-into-force of Protocols in December 1983	Violations (codification of customary international law)	—	—	—	—
SS-20 Mobile IRBM Deployment Moratorium, March 1982–November 1983 (Unilateral)	Completion of construction of mobile IRBM launcher bases, despite pledges of March and May 1982	Breach of unilateral commitment	—	—	—	—

[a] Unclassified summary report of the President's General Advisory Committee on Arms Control and Disarmament, 10/10/84.
[b] Report of the President on Soviet Noncompliance, per FY84 Arms Control Act, 1/23/84.
[c] Report of the President on Soviet Noncompliance per FY85 Defense Authorization Act, 2/01/85.
[d] Report of the President, Building an Interim Framework for Mutual Restraint, 6/10/85.
[e] Report of the President on Soviet Noncompliance, per PL99–145, 12/23/85.

**Table 10-4
Arms Control Commitments Regarding Which the Soviet Union Is in Apparent Compliance**

Accident Avoidance Measures

U.S.-USSR Direct Communications Link Agreement of 1963, amended in 1971 and 1984.
U.S.-USSR Accidents Agreement of 1971 (one violation, judged to be inadvertent)
France-USSR Accidents Agreement of 1976
United Kingdom-USSR Accidents Agreement of 1976

Nonproliferation of Nuclear Weapons

Nonproliferation Treaty of 1968
IAEA Guidelines for Nuclear Transfers, INFCIRC/209 of 1974
IAEA Guidelines for Nuclear Transfers, INFCIRC/254 of 1978
Treaty of Tlatelolco (Latin American Nuclear Free Zone), Protocol II, USSR ratification 1979
Convention on the Physical Protection of Nuclear Material, USSR ratification 1983

Other Agreements

Antarctic Treaty of 1959
Outer Space Treaty of 1967
Seabed Treaty of 1971
Convention on Environmental Modification of 1977

Sources: Report of the General Advisory Committee on Arms Control and Disarmament, 10 October 1984; Reports of the President to the Congress on Soviet Noncompliance, 23 January 1984, 1 February 1985, and 23 December 1985.

The Will to Respond Despite Soviet *Maskirovka*

An earlier interest in sanctions and collective security measures dwindled in the period after Mussolini had secured victory in Ethiopia, and after Germany had remilitarized the Rhineland. But after turning away from measures of collective security, what was left but war? If the United States is to persist in the arms control arena, it must recurringly reevaluate options to strengthen incentives for arms control compliance, and it must be prepared to respond to arms control breaches that make a difference.

The Standing Consultative Commission as an Inadvertent Instrument of *Maskirovka*

The Standing Consultative Commission (SCC), established under article 13 of the ABM Treaty, must be understood as an important instrumentality to resolve inadvertent treaty violations and concurrently as a counterintelligence resource of Soviet *maskirovka* planners. Which use of the SCC is the more important will depend largely upon the nature of the problems confronting the treaty parties. Since most Soviet violations, or evasions defeating the purpose of arms control commitments, appear to be intentional, the SCC has contributed more exten-

Table 10-5
Presidential Reports to Congress Regarding Selective Restoration of Soviet Compliance

Obligation	Issue Report	GAC Report 12/02/83	Interagency 1/23/84	Interagency 2/01/85	President 6/10/85	Interagency 12/23/85
SALT I PROTOCOL	Excess modern SLBM launchers	1976–1977 probably deliberate violations	—	Currently in compliance	In compliance	—
SALT II TREATY	SS-16 mobile ICBMs at Plesetsk	Probable violation	Probable violation	Probable violation	Probable violation	Probable removal of SS-16 equipment
	Backfire Bomber Production	—	—	Not publicly reported	—	Evidence of decrease to under 30/yr in 1984–85.
GENEVA PROTOCOL OF 1925	Transfer and use of lethal chemicals	Circumventions defeating object and purpose	Violations	Violations not continued in 1984	Significant violations	No unambiguous evidence of lethal attacks in 1985
HELSINKI FINAL ACT	21-day advance notice of military exercises	Violations in 1981 and 1983	Violation in 1981	Violation in 1981; improved notice in 1983	Violation	Improved notice in 1983; minimal compliance in 1984–85

Sources: GAC Report, 10 October 1984; President's reports to the Congress on Soviet Noncompliance, 23 January 1984, 1 February 1985, 10 June 1985, and 23 December 1985.

sively to Soviet strategies for regulatory avoidance than to resolution of genuine compliance disputes.

An article co-authored by former ambassador (to the SCC) Sidney Graybeal and Michael Krepon, is indicative of the difficulty for SCC participants to acknowledge the role of that body in facilitating Soviet treaty evasions.[34] During Ambassador Graybeal's SCC tour (1973–77), one of the more important functions of the SCC was to establish criteria for the dismantling of strategic forces to comply with SALT limits. Both during the drafting of the dismantling procedures and after their signing, on 3 July 1974, the Soviets were busily experimenting with prototype forces for a covert strategic reserve force and with experimental masking procedures to test against U.S. verification capabilities. Building on legal concealment practices that were current in May 1972, the Soviets expanded concealment and deception activities between the signing of SALT I and the agreement on dismantling criteria in July 1974.

After several variants of Soviet masking programs failing to gain credit for "dismantling" strategic forces that would remain as part of a strategic reserve force, the Soviets purposefully left in operational status older ICBM facilities, knowing that U.S. verification resources would focus on a violation of the SALT I Protocol limits resulting from Soviet unwillingness to delay sea trials for newly constructed Delta submarines. By keeping the older SS7 ICBMs in operational status, the Soviets were able to maintain coverage of strategic targets while awaiting more modern missile deployments. Moreover, the Soviets were able to test the limits of U.S. verification of ICBM missile and launcher deployments of the Strategic Rocket Forces. For a number of weeks after 1 June 1976, the Soviets were in technical compliance with the SALT I Protocol and drew attention to their planned compliance by June 1st of that year, but the Soviets had excess ICBM launchers before June 1976 and from later in that year to the expiration of SALT I in October 1977, as noted in the GAC report.[35]

The military significance of several dozen illicit Soviet ICBM launchers is probably far less substantial than were the consequences of Soviet experiments with U.S. verification systems (aided by feedback through the SCC) for the successful concealment of SS-9 and SS-11 ICBMs and launching systems after their withdrawal from declared silo launchers during the 1976–80 Five Year Plan. To point to the all-too-brief Soviet compliance with the SALT I Protocol limit of 740 modern ballistic missile launchers (June 1976) as an example of the SCC success in resolving compliance issues is nothing short of a travesty. The "success story" of June 1976, reported by the Department of State in February 1978, is sandwiched between two periods during which the Soviets violated the 740 modern ballistic missile launcher limits.[36] More important, the price of this ephemeral success was to aid the Soviets in perfecting a system to mask deployment of any SS-9's and SS-11's retained after their removal from declared silos, as they were replaced by SS-17, SS-18, and SS-19 missiles in the late 1970's. Although the full story of what the Soviets accomplished with their illegal *maskirovka* experiments relating to SALT I may not yet be known, enough of the pattern of Soviet misconduct is known for there to be confidence that a substantial cost was paid with regard to Soviet strategic reserve forces that have not been declared in SALT II, and that have not been verified to be dismantled.

The Standing Consultative Commission has been no more effective with regard to concurrent testing of Soviet air defense systems and components and components of ballistic missile and ABM systems. The Soviets never stopped testing to comply with the ABM Treaty. It took the United States more than two years to complain. The Soviets paused in their testing about seventeen days after the U.S. complaint in the SCC during February 1975.[37] Not only did concurrent testing resume, but worse—the concurrent testing sufficed for the Soviets to deploy thousands of strategic surface-to-air-missiles (SAMs) that have at least some ability to destroy incoming ICBMs. Two Soviet officials have admitted as much, in June 1983 and October 1985.[38] Those Soviet admissions are of particular significance because of the number of strategic SAMs and radars deployed (about 12,000 and 10,000 respectively) and because of the siting of the large radar near Krasnoyarsk near the center of a large ellipse comprising strategic SAM sites (as illustrated in the publication *Soviet Strategic Defense Programs*).[39]

The SCC reduced the costs of Soviet arms control violations that are within its jurisdiction both by providing feedback to defeat verification and by adopting rules that have the effect of burying charges of violations. The agreed SCC rules do not provide for public plenary sessions at which the failure of a noncomplying party to remedy reversible violations can be made visible to the attentive public. At present, it requires agreement by both commissioners to have a public session of the SCC, and this has not been in Soviet interests. The SCC has assisted the Soviets in rendering *maskirovka* programs more effective. It has failed to implement effective safeguards for older strategic offensive forces that have disappeared without confirmation of their dismantling. It has failed to halt the concurrent testing of strategic air defense and ballistic missile defense systems, with a resulting Soviet evasion of ABM treaty duties and the deployment of strategic SAMs that threaten ICBMs. It has failed to restrict Soviet *maskirovka* activities, such as the encryption of missile test data that began one year after the creation of the SCC. It has deflected the energies that might be channeled into effective responses to Soviet noncompliance across a broad front.

Intelligence Requirements to Respond to the Challenge of Persistent Soviet Violations and Evasions

Now that the Cabinet papers of the British government are available to historians, it is becoming clear that intelligence assessments reinforced the appeasement policies that preceded the onset of World War II:

Undeniably, this [appeasement] policy was influenced by the pessimism that flowed from intelligence circles. The near and medium-term military balance was presumed to be perilous, a perception that was instrumental in convincing the cabinet to avoid the dangers of any attempt at deterrence, above all during the Munich crisis. An Anglo-German confrontation was thereby postponed, yet the German Armed Forces of September 1938, in terms of war readiness and overall mobilized strength, were a much inferior foe compared to the military machine that performed so impressively in the campaigns of 1940. The label *blindness* seems appropriate to the way in which the intelligence authorities failed to provide a balanced reading of German strengths and weaknesses under the cumulative worst-case assessments.[40]

How can the United States do better in the present and future? The will to act decisively is needed, but first there must be assessments that encourage wise actions. At the outset, evidence of arms control noncompliance threatens cherished beliefs regarding the role of arms regulation in the avoidance of war. Hence, many wish to disregard the evidence of persistent treaty violations and other acts that defeat arms control objectives.

Others may consider that it is too late for remedial action. A period of ten years and six months separated the signing of SALT I and the tasking by President Reagan of a comprehensive review of Soviet arms control compliance, in November 1982. The passage of time without remedial action can have the effect of producing assessments that induce appeasement policies echoing those of the 1930's.

A contemporary illustration of the effect of timidity of response upon incentives for acquiescence in treaty violations is found in the Congressional debate on the FY 1987 Defense Authorization Act. The majority of the House of Representatives voted to mandate U.S. SALT II compliance without allowing presidential response to ongoing Soviet violations. Prior inaction now justifies outright appeasement, because the Soviets might outbuild us.

Verification requires some courage in evaluating and reporting findings of arms control noncompliance. It requires even more courage in assessing responsive options. Among the apologentsia are some with such vivid imaginations that, if left to their own devices, they would endlessly delay taking effective response. This is a course the nation cannot tolerate.

Those with conflicts of interest based on an attachment to negotiations in which some statesmen participated and those who fear self-help measures outside the conciliationist framework may continue in their apologies and obfuscations for a time to come. They may still assert that bees deliver mycotoxins (some with traces of man-made synthetic chemicals) with particular attention to anti-Communist areas in war zones, or that the Krasnoyarsk radar might be a space tracker, and if not, we should build one too instead of impairing the hallowed "process" of arms control conciliation. However, the foundation for a more prudent course in the minefield of arms control is nearly in place.

Yet, it remains imprudent to assume that perseverance in responding to material breaches is the only course of conduct. It should not be assumed that a safeguards program for any retained or future arms control commitments will obtain an institutional home within the executive branch and budgetary approvals within the Congress.

It is worth remembering that after the disclosures about German rearmament in the 1920's, the spirit of Locarno led to a burial of noncompliance concerns until Hitler came to power and exploited the covert rearmament initiatives before him. And in October 1933, when those around Hitler talked of possible sanctions, Hitler remarked: "a pretty crew they are! They'll never act! They'll just protest. And they will always be too late."[41]

It should not be forgotten that the formalism and ritual of diplomatic demarche are a comfort to those who lack the fortitude to act. When pressed, many today are so committed to a conciliationist pathway that they would not know where to set their mark upon a different course.

Those involved in the verification process cannot rest on their laurels merely because they have described those acts that are in compliance and those that are not. The verification process extends to the analysis of options for response and other initiatives to strengthen international security. Without care, merely withdrawing from an agreement or imposing mildly distasteful sanctions may only encourage further misconduct.

Ineffective sanctions led Mussolini (in Ethiopia in 1935) and Brezhnev (in Afghanistan in 1980) to the use of lethal chemical weapons—despite the Geneva Protocol—so as to achieve victory before sanctions exacted high costs. Therefore, sanctions that are ineffective can induce further arms control breaches.

As the April 1985 edition of the Defense Department's *Soviet Military Power* observes:

> Our verification capabilities have not deterred the Soviet Union from violating arms control agreements. Moreover, if the Soviets are not made to account for their actions, it is unlikely that they will be deterred from more serious violations. We must approach arms control today more carefully than we have in the past.[42]

The capacity to report publicly on Soviet noncompliance issues is an act of presidential courage. So was the President's announcement of May 27, 1986 calling an end to SALT II. These responses are supported by patriots in the Congress who, like the back-benchers of the British Parliament in the 1930's, resisted appeasement in their own day.

Verification has been successful so far as it has gone, but it has not gone half the way to providing the assessments that national and allied leaders require in perilous times. Intelligence has retreated from the objectives of the Woods Hole Summer Study of 1962—an intellectual watershed in thinking about the verification process. The Woods Hole report recommended that verification support the development and assessment of appropriate responses to noncompliance. This is a necessary but insufficient condition for effective response. It is not Soviet *maskirovka*, but our own lack of will that is the principal barrier to achieving a national policy to strengthen incentives for arms control compliance.

Two observers of the interwar period, 1919–39, shed light on the psychological condition that may afflict us. Eugene Rostow wrote of an "illness of spirit" that prevented the mind from registering what the eyes had seen. R.B. McCallum, an Oxford don who published a book in 1944, *Public Opinion and the Last Peace*, observed that, in the 1930's, as perhaps today, democracies had

> . . . refused the initiative. We preferred not to commit ourselves to cross the stiles when we "came to them;" to treat situations on their own merits, to evade the consequences of a cut and dried "logical" policy; in a word, we were guilty of all those miserable substitutes for thought which are dignified by the name of Anglo-Saxon empiricism.[43]

Brigadier General John H. Morgan derived similar insights while observing Germany's covert rearmament in the 1920's and the resulting disbelief and inaction in London. He remarked for our benefit:

> . . . A certain anxious consciousness at times an almost morbid introspection . . . disarmed us. As we profess standards which [our adversaries] do not, we feel a compulsion to observe them from which they are wholly emancipated. We were therefore pressed by them, and will be again, to behave with a consideration which they would not extend to us. . . . We nurture doubts about our own honesty of purpose, we interrogate our consciences. . . . Our weakness lies in our doubts as to our honesty of purpose, our strength in their lack of foundation.[44]

Maskirovka and arms control verification appear to be a contradiction, but they are companions when arms control does not rest on common interests, and they are inseparable when an expansionist power has chosen a course in disregard of law. Verification must do more than ascertain whether conduct is, or is not, permissible. It must help to understand why hopes are unfulfilled, how national security is jeopardized, and what alternative courses of action are likely to serve the cause of international security.

What can be done to improve prospects for compliance with those arms control obligations that remain and those that may commence in the future? What initiatives are essential to cope with treaty violations and evasions that are beyond remedy, and those breaches that ought to be anticipated in the light of past Soviet misconduct? In what ways should the menu of arms control objectives be restructured or narrowed, and what alternatives to arms control should be pursued to minimize war risks that remain untouched by, or exacerbated by, the arms control process to date? In key respects, the verification system has overcome the obstacles of Soviet *maskirovka*. The challenge ahead is no less difficult.

Notes

1. Winston S. Churchill, *Arms and the Covenant* (London: George G. Harrap, 1936), p. 17.

2. See the *Report of the President on Soviet Noncompliance*, 23 December 1985, and prior compliance reports by the presidentially appointed General Advisory Committee on Arms Control and Disarmament of 2 December 1983 (with public summary on 10 October 1984); *The President's Reports to the Congress* dated 23 January 1984, 1 February 1985, and 10 June 1985, each released by the Office of the Press Secretary, The White House. Their findings are summarized in tables 10–1 through 10–5.

3. The French concept of *controle* involves verification and checking by an independent authority.

4. U.S. Department of State, *Documents on Disarmament, 1945–1959*, vol. I, Doc. 170 (Washington, DC: Government Printing Office, 1961).

5. T.N. Dupuy and G.M. Hammerman, *A Documentary History of Arms Control and Disarmament* (New York: R.R. Bowker, 1973), p. 94.

6. J.H. Morgan, *Assize of Arms: The Disarmament of Germany and Her Rearmament (1919–1939)* (New York and London: Oxford University Press, 1946), p. 338. See also the history by Paul Roques, *Controle Militaire Interalie en Allemagne, Septembre 1919–Janvier 1927 [Inter-Allied Military Control in Germany, September 1919–January 1927]* (Paris: Berger-Levrault, 1927), especially ch. 3.

7. J.H. Morgan, "The Disarmament of Germany and After," *Quarterly Review*, (October 1924).

8. Note of 25 June 1925, Cmd. 2429, p. 3.

9. Wesley K. Wark, *The Ultimate Enemy: British Intelligence and Nazi Germany, 1933–1939* (Ithaca, N.Y. and London: Cornell University Press, 1985), pp. 130–154, 248.

10. Ibid., p. 229.

11. Generals Clay and Sokolovsky agreed upon an exchange of military observes by the oral agreement of 15 August 1946. The deputies of the U.S. and Soviet military governors in Germany entered into a written agreement on 5 April 1947. See Jean Edward Smith, *The Defense of Berlin* (Baltimore, M.: Johns Hopkins University Press, 1963), p. 217.

12. *Documents on Disarmament*, vol. I, pp. 56–59.

13. Institute for Defense Analyses-U.S. Arms Control and Disarmament Agency, "Summer Study on Inspection and Control," Woods Hole, Mass., 2 July 1962 (excerpts).

14. *Woods Hole Summer Study: Verification and Response in Disarmament Agreements: Summary Reports* annex and vol. II, (Washington, D.C.: Institute for Defense Analysis, 1962).

15. See table 10–2, *Restraints on Nuclear Weapons Testing.*
16. See the chapter by the U.S. representative to the MBFR talks, Ambassador Richard Staar.
17. Aleksei Myagov, *Inside the KGB* (New Rochelle, N.Y.: Arlington House, 1976), p. 121.
18. "How Russia Hides Its Missiles," *Foreign Report*, London, (5 March 1981): p. 2.
19. Robert L. Perry, *SALT: The Faces of Verification*, paper P-5986 (Santa Monica, Calif: Rand Corporation, 1977).
20. See the account of the Soviet military intelligence officer publishing under the *nom de plume* Victor Suvorov, "GUSM: The Soviet Service of Strategic Deception," *International Defense Review* 18(August 1985): pp. 1236–1237.
21. James T. Reitz, *Lexicon of Selected Soviet Terms Relating to Maskirovka (Deception)* (Washington, D.C.: Defense Intelligence Agency, October 1983).
22. Zell Stanley, *An Annotated Bibliography of the Open Literature on Deception*, Note N-2232-NA (Santa Monica, Calif: Rand Corporation, December 1985). Two of the most helpful overviews of the Soviet literature on *maskirovka* relating to arms control verification are Stuart A. Cohen, "The Evolution of Soviet Views on SALT Verification," Paper, UCLA, August 1979, revised in W.C. Potter, ed., *Verification and SALT* (Boulder, Colo: Westview, 1980), pp. 49–75; and Peter deLeon, *Soviet Views of Strategic Deception*, P-6685 (Santa Monica, Calif: Rand Corporation, September 1981). For earlier studies on continuing importance, see Herbert S. Dinerstein, *War and the Soviet Union*, Report R-326, ch. 6, "Surprise and the Initiation of War," (Santa Monica, Calif: Rand Corporation, 1976), pp. 167–214; Raymond L. Garthoff, "The Role of Surprise and Blitzkrieg," *The Soviet Image of Future War* (Washington, D.C.: Public Affairs Press, 1959), pp. 60–137.
23. On political aspects of Soviet deception relating to arms control practices, see Abraham S. Becker, *Strategic Breakout as a Soviet Policy Option*, Report R. 1097-ACDA (Santa Monica, Calif: Rand Corporation, March 1977); William Beecher, "Brezhnev Termed Detente a Ruse, 1973 Report Said," *Boston Globe*, 11 February 1979; Tom Tethell, "The Mugger's Deal in Geneva," *National Review* (26 March 1985): pp. 26–29; Vladimir Bukovsky, "The Peace Movement and the Soviet Union," *Commentary* (May 1982): vol. 73, pp. 25–41; Joseph D. Douglass, Jr., "Soviet Strategic Deception," *Defense Science 2002* August 1984, pp. 87–99; Joseph D. Douglass, Jr., "Soviet Disinformation," *Strategic Review*, vol. 9, No. 1 (Winter 1981), pp. 16–26; Colin S. Gray, "Moscow Is Cheating," *Foreign Policy* (Fall 1984): vol. 56, pp. 141–152; William R. Harris, "Breaches of Arms Control Obligations and Their Implications," in Richard Staar, ed., *Arms Control: Myth Versus Reality* (Stanford, CA: Hoover Institution Press, 1984), pp. 135–155; Wynfred Joshua, "Soviet Manipulation of the European Peace Movement," *Strategic Review* (Winter 1983): vol. 11, No. 1, pp. 9–18; MacKubin T. Owens, Jr., "Arms Control: Tracking Soviet Violations," *Journal of Contemporary Studies* (Fall 1983): pp. 101–113; Clive Rose, *Campaigns Against Western Defense: NATO's Adversaries and Critics* (New York: St. Martin's Press, 1985), Richard H. Shultz and Roy Godson, *Dezinformatsia: Active Measures in Soviet Strategy* (Washington, D.C.: Pergamon-Brassey's, 1984): Charles A. Sorrels, *Soviet Propaganda Campaigns Against NATO* (Washington, D.C.: Arms Control and Disarmament Agency, October 1983); Mark C. Storella, *Poisoning Arms Control: The Soviet Union and Chemical/Biological*

Warfare (Boston: Institute for Foreign Policy Analysis, June 1984); David S. Sullivan, "Lessons Learned from SALT I and SALT II: New Objectives for SALT III," *International Security Review* (Fall 1981): vol. 6, No. 3, pp. 26–41; David S. Sullivan, "Soviet Negotiating Deception and Treaty Violations in Arms Control," paper, September 1985, U.S. Senate Committee on Appropriations, *Hearings, SALT II Violations*, 98th Cong., 2d sess., 1984, Malcolm Wallop, "Soviet Violations of Arms Control Agreements: So What?" *Strategic Review* (Summer 1983): vol. 11, No. 3, pp. 11–20.

24. William R. Harris, "Counterintelligence Jurisdiction and the Double Cross System by National Technical Means," in Roy Godson, ed., *Intelligence Requirements for the 1980's: Counterintelligence* (Washington, D.C.: National Strategy Information Center, 1980), pp. 53–82; U.S. Senate Select Committee on Intelligence, prepared statement, "Counterintelligence Jurisdiction and the National Intelligence Act of 1980," S. 2284, April 1980.

25. "Trickery on Chemical War," *Washington Star*, 5 June 1978; Edward J. Epstein, "Incorporating Analysis of Foreign Governments' Deception into U.S. Analytical Systems," in Godson, *Intelligence Requirements*; Joseph D. Douglass, Jr., "The Growing Disinformation Problem," *International Security* 6, pp. 333–353.

26. Howard Stoertz, Jr., "Monitoring a Nuclear Freeze," *International Security* (Spring 1984): vol. 8, p. 92.

27. *GAC Report*, 10 October 1984, p. 10.

28. Stephen M. Meyer, "Verification and Risk in Arms Control," *International Security* (Spring 1984): vol. 8, p. 126.

29. U.S. Department of State, *Verification of SALT II Agreement*, Special Report 56, August 1979.

30. On the limited value of on-site inspection, and possible harm of ill-designed inspection systems, see Carnes Lord, "Rethinking On-site Inspection in U.S. Arms Control Policy," *Strategic Review*, Vol. 13, No. 2 (Spring 1985), pp. 45–50. Nevertheless, the right to on-site inspection may add credence to unilateral findings of treaty noncompliance, particularly if on-site inspection has been refused or impaired. See Louis Sohn, "Why We Need Inspection: A Dissent," in *Report of the Woods Hole Summer Study, Verification and Response in Disarmament Agreements*, annex vol. II (Washington, D.C.: Institute for Defense Analysis, November 1962), pp. 91–94.

31. *The President's Unclassified Report on Soviet Noncompliance with Arms Control Agreements* (Washington, D.C.: U.S. Government Printing Office, 23 December 1985), p. 11.

32. F.D. Froman, "Kiev and the Montreux Convention: The Aircraft Carrier that Became a Cruiser to Squeeze Through the Turkish Straits," *San Diego Law Review*, (14 April 1977): vol. 15, No. 3, pp. 681–717; Captain John Moore, "Not so Chicken Kiev," *Navy International*, (November 1976): vol. 81, No. 11, For the Soviet legal misanalysis, see Captain V. Serkov, "Legal Regime of the Black Sea Straits," (in Russian) in *Moskoy Sbornik (Naval Review)*, July 1976. It was the Soviet Foreign Commisar Litvinov who, in 1936, succeeded in banning passage of aircraft carriers through the straits. See A.R. Deluca, *Great Power Rivalry at the Turkish Straits: The Montreux Convention of 1936*, East European Quarterly, Monograph No. 77, 1981.

33. *New York Times*, 29 October 1985, p. 1; *Los Angeles Times*, 30 October 1985, pp. 1, 16.

34. Sidney N. Graybeal and Michael Krepon, "Making Better Use of the Standing Consultative Commission," *International Security* 10(Fall 1985): No. 1, pp. 183–199.

35. *GAC Report*, 10 Oct. 1984; William R. Harris, "Breaches of Arms Control," in Staar, *Arms Control*, pp. 134–153.

36. U.S. Department of State, *SALT I: Compliance and SALT II: Verification*, Selected documents no. 7 (Washington, D.C.: U.S. Government Printing Office, 21 February 1978), p. 7. Graybeal and Krepon cite this February 1978 report of Secretary Vance as their authority for the "success" of the SCC in excusing excess Soviet ballistic missile launchers during SALT I.

37. This "success" is also cited by Graybeal and Krepon, "Making Better Use," pp. 189–190.

38. See remarks of Senator James McClure, in *Congressional Record*, 1 November 1985, p. S14591.

39. U.S. Department of Defense and Department of State, *Soviet Strategic Defense Programs* (Washington, D.C.: U.S. Government Printing Office, October 1985), pp. 12, 16, 18–21.

40. W.K. Wark, *The Ultimate Enemy*, pp. 231–232.

41. Hermann Rausching, *Voice of Destruction*, (New York: Putnam's, 1940), p. 104. On opposition to sanctions and collective security measures, see Emile Girand, *La Nullite de la Politique Internationale des Grandes Democraties, 1919–1939 [The Nullity of the International Politics of the Democracies, 1919–1939]* (Montigeon, France: Recueil Sirey, 1948); and Keith Middlemas, *The Strategy of Appeasement: The British Government and Germany 1937–1939* (Chicago: Quadrangle Books, 1972).

42. U.S. Department of Defense, *Soviet Military Power*, (Washington, D.C.: U.S. Government Printing Office, April 1985), p. 23.

43. Ronald Buchanan, *Public Opinion and the Last Peace* (London and New York: Oxford University Press, 1944), p. 137.

44. J.H. Morgan, *Assize of Arms*, pp. 201–203.

11
Deception, Perceptions Management, and Self-Deception in Arms Control: An Examination of the ABM Treaty

Brian D. Dailey

The Treaty on Limitation of Anti-Ballistic Missiles (ABM) of 26 May 1972, continues to be considered by many as one of, if not the most, significant and successful arms control agreement between the United States and the Soviet Union.[1] Indeed, it is often referred to as the crowning achievement of détente and the arms control process.[2] This judgment is based on the assumption that Soviet objectives in negotiating the ABM treaty were compatible, if not identical, with those of the United States. The release since 1983, however, of five U.S. government reports on Soviet noncompliance with the ABM treaty, among other agreements, brings into question the validity of this assumption and, more importantly, the success of the treaty.[3] The evidence put forth in these five reports strongly suggests that the Soviets deceived the United States government and the West as to their actual objectives in negotiating limits on antiballistic missile defenses.

Whether, how, and to what extent the Soviets deceived the United States regarding the ABM treaty is important to the understanding of the changes in the U.S.-Soviet strategic nuclear balance since 1972. The quantitative and numerous qualitative changes in the offensive and defensive balance, from parity in the late 1960's to Soviet superiority in the 1980's, are dramatic. The consequences of these changes are important in the event deterrence fails and also for U.S. foreign policy and the future of the arms control process.

The ability of the United States to redress in the foreseeable future the disparity in so-called offensive nuclear systems is questionable given the number of open Soviet missile production lines and submarine construction facilities.[4] Although Soviet production of air and missile defense systems and components is equal to, if not greater than, that of their offensive systems, a near term opportunity probably does exist for Western technology to respond to Moscow's initiatives in this arena. The president's proposed Strategic Defense Initiative (SDI) has brought to the fore the issue of whether the United States should try to redress the strategic balance by developing defensive systems of its own. The SDI is presently an ambitious long-range research program. Even as such, decisions must soon be made about deployment of United States active defense systems. Additionally, decisions are required on precisely what the missile defense should protect, the number and character of the systems to be deployed, and the effect of such deployments on deterrence and stability. In order to do this, the question of the status of the ABM treaty, which currently restricts many aspects of full-scale development and deployment, and the effect on the arms control process of both SDI and Soviet noncompliance need to be resolved.

In making these judgments and decisions, it is important to pay proper attention to Soviet views and activities toward ballistic missile defense (BMD) and on their objectives in signing the ABM treaty. Those views are anything but straightforward. This chapter argues that Soviet motives for entering into an agreement on limiting ABM systems in 1972, were almost exclusively to slow down and hopefully halt altogether U.S. advances in ABM technology—an approach that would greatly facilitate their counterforce targeting objectives through U.S. agreement not to defend its intercontinental ballistic missiles (ICBMs).

Thus, we argue, the Soviets' deception *during* the negotiations of the ABM treaty consisted primarily of disguising their objectives, which were to ensure that Soviet development and production of the necessary components of an antimissile defense were not precluded explicitly by the terms of the treaty; and even if their objectives were revealed, the time required for the United States to detect illegal Soviet activities would be such that an effective compensatory response would be protracted and perhaps too late. An important element of this deception was a Soviet attempt to give U.S. negotiating officials the impression that their reasons for pursuing SALT I were very similar to those of the United States. The Soviets supported this charade during the negotiations through, inter alia, the use of disinformation to mislead the United States about the characteristics and quality of Soviet weapon systems.

This technical deception is not something that can be dismissed as merely a clever tactical Soviet negotiating technique used to enhance the terms of an agreement. It was certainly not the basis from which the United States entered into negotiations in 1969.[5] The United States made the Soviets clearly aware of their objectives with respect to what they hoped to achieve by establishing limitations on nearly all types of active defensive systems.[6] The U.S. thinking and objectives in negotiating an ABM treaty consisted of reaching a mutual acknowledgement and acceptance of the principles associated with Western theories of nuclear deterrence or assured mutual vulnerability, a U.S. precept of the treaty, and a firm belief that a treaty limiting defenses would "halt the arms race" as it is understood in Western terms. The Soviets, nonetheless, refused to express a rejection or acceptance of these U.S. objectives and understandings. Rather, the Soviets responded with the hackneyed statement that "nuclear war is tantamount to suicide," which was understood by U.S. negotiators as equivalent to Soviet acceptance of these principles.[7] The Soviets' signing of the ABM treaty, therefore, was seen by the United States as a codification of these U.S. deterrence principles.[8] The Soviets intended that it be so seen, knowing that this impression was false—hence deception.

In the years following the signing of the treaty, however, it was essential for the Soviets to modify their deception techniques. The most basic U.S. perception that required managing was that of actual Soviet military strategy. As this chapter will later demonstrate, this period of Soviet perceptions management *after* the signing of the ABM treaty included attempts to disguise, or at least obscure, the fact that Soviet military strategy continued to be based on military superiority and a reliance on a war-fighting strategy that combines offense and defense.

Protestations of the "suicidal nature of nuclear war" by Soviet party officials, propaganda organs, and some military officers, were and are designed for the express purpose of reinforcing the perception that the Soviet nuclear posture was only a deterrent. Indeed, the Soviets, beginning in the late 1970's, began professing an acceptance of the principles embodied in the U.S. assured-destruction theory even though the Soviet defense program did not reflect such a doctrine.[9]

In short, the bases on which the Soviets entered the negotiations were to, first, mask their objective of stopping or significantly curtailing the U.S. ABM research to buy time for the Soviet active defense program, and second, after 1972, to adjust the deception to reinforce Western perceptions and predilections of Soviet military strategy as a solely assured-destruction policy.

Perhaps the most interesting aspect of this deception is that much of the evidence necessary for identifying Soviet disregard for the principles supposedly embodied in the ABM treaty was pervasive during the negotiations. In other words, Soviet deception and perceptions management were not devilishly clever. Rather, self-deception has been arguably the principal factor contributing to the success of the Soviet ABM deception. Before, during, and after SALT I, copious evidence demonstrating a continuous Soviet interest in active and passive defensive systems was reflected in Soviet military writings on strategy and operational art, force planning and sizing, research and development, resource allocation, and civil defense efforts. Yet, it is increasingly clear that many in the United States (and elsewhere in the West) wanted to believe that the Soviet purpose in signing the ABM treaty was a reflection of their own biases or ethnocentric concepts of deterrence and stability. The relatively few open statements combined with a little intelligence deception were enough to tip the balance of Western judgment away from the preponderance of evidence. Consequently, an examination of American self-deception in the negotiations is a necessary adjunct to the study of Soviet deception.

We begin with an overview of the evolution of Soviet military strategy and the development of U.S. perceptions of that strategy and assured destruction deterrence theory. The next section addresses the historical sources of self-deception in order to facilitate a review of the elements that contributed to U.S. self-deception with respect to defenses in Soviet military strategy. Finally, we conclude with an examination of Soviet deception and perceptions management techniques as they pertain to arms control negotiations, and we illustrate these techniques with two examples.

U.S. Perception of Soviet Military Strategy

Soviet military writings in the 1950's and 1960's clearly articulated an operational art emphasizing the role of nuclear weapons and long-range missiles in the conduct of warfare. These weapon systems were to have revolutionized military thought without mitigating the possibility of war and the attainment of victory, should hostilities break-out. From such writings emerged strategies and tactics based on fundamental military principles incorporating the changes mandated by these new weapon systems. These principles, the desire to limit damage to the homeland and to develop forces capable of waging war (at whatever level of conflict) and achieving victory, have formed the basis of Soviet strategy ever since. An important element of this strategy was the understanding that damage to the homeland was best limited through the prompt destruction of enemy forces at the outset of hostilities.[10] Should a retaliatory strike occur, employment of active and passive defenses would limit damage to the leadership, population, and industry vital for postwar recovery.

During the time that this military strategy was being articulated, the Soviet Union was building forces that reflected and supported these stated doctrinal requirements. Western military analysts and leaders drew attention to this war-fighting strategy and to the accompanying force structure being built to support it.[11] During the 1960's, however, civilian military leaders, such as former Secretary of Defense, Robert S. McNamara (1961–68), ultimately rejected the notion of nuclear war fighting and damage limitation. They countered that such a strategy was destined to fail and that planning for a nuclear war contingency was hopelessly uncertain and could only be done when the situation arose.[12] Upon reading Soviet military writings on nuclear strategy, Secretary McNamara commented that he found nothing sophisticated in their thinking.[13] Reflecting the opinions of the systems analysts he had placed in influential positions in the Pentagon, McNamara postulated a concept of deterrence that eventually came to dictate a doctrinal requirement for the mutual vulnerability of each side's population. Labeled Mutual Assured Destruction (MAD), it postulated that the threat of retaliation against unprotected cities would constitute the highest level of deterrence.[14] Defenses of any kind that interfered with the targeting of cities or reduced the damage that could be inflicted on them would be destabilizing in as much as they would only encourage a further buildup in offensive weapons to achieve the requisite assured destruction capability.

It was this belief, in part, that dissuaded McNamara from supporting the production and deployment of the Sentinel ABM system, which was designed to protect American cities. McNamara presented his thinking to the Soviets at the 1967 Glassboro summit in expectation of convincing them that the MAD approach was the most stabilizing form of deterrence. He argued that if either side deployed an ABM system, the other country would be forced to build more offensive systems to maintain its assured destruction capability. It was, according to McNamara and other proponents of MAD, this very reaction to the adversary's deployment of ABM systems that constituted an arms race. Premier Kosygin harshly rejected McNamara's argument, insisting that protection of cities was not only strategically vital but morally responsible.[15]

While the Soviets quickly rejected the concept of MAD, influential U.S. members of government, academia, the civilian sector, and even some senior military officers were becoming increasingly attracted to it. Consequently, despite these early Soviet pronouncements against the concept of MAD, an attempt was made to formalize just such a situation in what would become the first SALT agreement. The U.S. negotiators saw as their mission the "education" of the Soviet military in the theory of deterrence articulated by McNamara and others. Indeed, the first and even second rounds of SALT were primarily seminars on deterrence, the objectives of which were to convince the Soviets that MAD was the most stable strategic relationship.[16] It was, as John Newhouse characterized it, an attempt to "raise the Soviet learning curve" on strategic thinking.[17] Subsequent events have demonstrated, though, that this display of arrogance and ethnocentric behavior on the part of U.S. negotiators did nothing to move the Soviets away from their offensive-defensive war-fighting strategy.

Sources of Self-Deception

The driving factors behind much of the assured destruction doctrine outlined above originate from an emotional belief that the importance and usefulness of military superiority in the nuclear age, at least between the major powers, is essentially irrelevant. A consequence of such a mindset has led to the virtual avoidance of systematic assessments of an adversary's military strategy, force posture, and actions as an indicator of his strategic calculations or intentions. This lack of appreciation for the importance of military superiority and the strategic balance, as it pertains not only to the perceived ability to successfully execute war but also its ability to support the day-to-day implementation of foreign policy, is particularly perplexing. The struggle for the perception of peacetime military superiority and the ability to obtain foreign policy objectives between the major powers has become, in a sense, the modern forehand for war in the nuclear age.

As such, how governments and individual officials perceive, for example, national interests, foreign military capabilities, differing state systems, and the external behavior of other states are critical factors affecting global stability. In effect, perception is an assessment of reality. The difference between policies and actions based on accurate versus inaccurate perceptions of reality in peacetime bears a direct relationship to whether and how wars occur.[18] It is, therefore, important to understand how decision makers form their perceptions of the external world, how and by whom these perceptions are managed, and who the targets of perceptions management are.

There are two systemic principles associated with the problem of perceptions management and self-deception as they pertain to the issues raised in this chapter. The first is a recognition that perceptions management is an important and effective tool in achieving politico-military objectives in peacetime; and the second is the recognition that if perceptions management is successfully employed by an adversary, the target state's military may be poorly prepared for war in terms of both capability and development of operational art. (This is particularly significant for democratic states, since they are prone to self-deception and myopic planning and, unlike totalitarian regimes, are unable to employ perceptions management systematically because of the democratic and competitive structure of government, free and divisive press, and the openness of the society.[19])

The danger lies in the foreign policy utility that an aggressive state may perceive available in its possession of a credible or apparently credible superior military capability. Edward Luttwak, in his book, *The Grand Strategy of the Roman Empire*, for example, analyzed the Roman use of military capability and found that the influence and success of their national strategy were derived:

> From the whole complex of ideas and traditions that informed the organization of Roman military force and harnessed the armed power of the empire to political purpose. . . . In the imperial period at least, military force was clearly recognized for what it is, an essentially limited instrument of power, costly and brittle. Much better to conserve force and use military power indirectly, as the instrument of political warfare. . . . Above all, the Romans clearly realized that the dominant dimension of power was not physical but psychological—the product of the others' perceptions of Roman strength rather than the use of this strength.[20]

Balancing the manipulation of a target state's perceived reality is a vital concern, however. In other words, while there are advantages in conveying or manipulating the target's perceptions of an adversary's actual military capability to further foreign policy objectives, it is important not to overstate that capability to the extent that it may incite the adversary to improve its own military capabilities.[21] The Soviets believe strongly in trying to achieve this balance of perceptions.[22] They have expended substantial resources in attempting to convince public opinion in the West, as well as a certain sector of the political and military leadership, that Soviet intentions are benign and that the source of tension in the world is located within Western governments. There are people in the West who are eager to believe this. Soviet perceptions management, therefore, does not have to be very good. At most, all that is needed is denial of proof to the contrary of Soviet themes.

One of the primary sources of this misperception/self-deception problem is found in U.S. assessments of intentions and capability in intelligence products. Within the analytical sector of the U.S. intelligence community, the primary approach taken in estimates and analyses is limited to assessment of a foreign state's *capabilities*. Rarely in intelligence analysis are intentions evaluated in the context of capability—let alone in the context of the aggregate military capabilities of a state. This is due to the near absence of human and technical sources that have anything authoritative to say on either subject. Hence, there is a license to indulge in personal prejudices.

There are notable exceptions, but they only serve to illustrate the proposition. One that is particularly relevant to this chapter is the issue over the capability and mission of the Soviet SA-5 interceptor and associated radar. U.S. intelligence by the mid- to late-1960's concluded that the SA-5 was capable of an ABM role if not actually ABM dedicated.[23] If the Soviets could use this system in either a dual-purpose or clandestine ABM role then it did not bode well for the prospects of successful arms control negotiations (originally scheduled in 1968).[24] Those predisposed to arms control and assured-destruction thinking, such as then Secretary of Defense Robert McNamara, DDR&E Herbert York and subsequent DDR&E Harold Brown did not technically dispute that the SA-5 and its radars were dual capable, or at least could be upgraded for the ABM mission in a few years, a situation that appears to have come about with testing of the SA-5 and SA-10 radars in an ABM mode in the 1980's; instead, they argued that Soviet technological inferiority mitigated these concerns.[25] In the end, politics and a belief in assured destruction, more than what U.S. intelligence knew and did not know about the SA-5's capability and mission, were factors that determined the missile and radar's role in the U.S. SALT position. The question of how the Soviets might choose to use an SA-5, or anything else with ABM capability, was simply not dealt with.

It is, to a large extent, this lack of data, politics, and the uncertainty associated with prediction of unquantifiable variables that account for the failure to incorporate intention analysis into capability assessments. This, in turn, essentially factors the question of intentions out of intelligence products. This prevailing attitude in Western intelligence, in particular U.S. intelligence, is unique in history. In the past, assessing the intentions of foreign states was considered the most essential task assigned to intelligence.[26] Trying to reduce the synergistic relationship of intentions and capability into an either/or proposition seriously dilutes the value of intelligence products. Capability almost invariably reflects intentions because nations acquire capabilities for some reason. Alternatively, capability acquired for one set of means may, in some instances, present possibilities or even lead to new intentions. Charles Burton Marshall elaborated on this relationship in a public letter to George Kennan in response to the latter's insistence that intentions and capability were dichotomous:

> Conceptual partitions between intentions and capabilities impress me as fallacious. . . . An intention denotes a desire translated from being an inert concept in the realm of wishing into an active purpose, or end, in the realm of phenomena. What converts desire into purpose is commitment of means for effectuating it. Besides the purpose or end, the intention must encompass whatever is perceived to be required for the realization. That is to say, an intention includes the quest as well as the goal. An intention embraces not only the end but also the means-to-the-end expressing the aspects for which, and the means including the aspects despite which, the intention is affirmed. . . . To state the matter as a theorem—a cognitive entity's impulsion to convert latent desires into active ones tends to vary expansively or contractively according to opportunities, temptations, and relative capabilities. Capabilities pertain to intentions as hops to beer.[27]

Ignoring intentions in intelligence assessments has deleterious consequences. It fosters mirror-imaging and inadequate intelligence products. Assessments that lack consideration of the regime's historical tradition and the dynamics and disparities of its polity vis-à-vis other states lead to static conclusions about military capabilities versus a more useful product that includes strategic capabilities *and* calculations. A by-product of mirror-imaging is that we tend to look for elements that reflect a Western predisposition while ignoring writings, activities, and weapon systems that conflict with that strategic mindset.[28]

Nowhere is the effect of this process more evident than in the logic of statements by some former and current high level government officials, academics, and national security analysts. During, for example, the hearings before Congress on the ratification of the ABM treaty and interim agreement on offensive systems, negotiators mirror-imaged that the Soviets, by signing the

ABM treaty, had accepted the deterrence concept of mutual assured destruction. Such statements were not limited to the ratification process. Indeed, proponents of MAD continue to misperceive Soviet military strategy and, if anything, the conviction of their belief appears to be increasing even though irrefutable evidence of their relentless push toward active and passive defenses keeps mounting. These people who mirror-image, such as those listed below, are so prejudicial that they will absorb and incorporate whatever the Soviets verbally offer and sell it to Western officials and the public almost despite what the Soviets do. The following quotes amply illustrate this point:

> The best evidence that they are moving in [the] direction [of the doctrine of assured destruction] is their acceptance of these very low levels of ABM's which, in effect indicates that they do not calculate that they can make a first strike and then handle a ragged retaliatory strike and keep it at tolerable levels. That, to my mind, is one of the most important things about this ABM agreement.[29]—*Ambassador Gerard Smith, Chief Delegate to SALT, before the Armed Services Committee, 18 July 1972*

> [The ABM Treaty] embodies a political decision of the first magnitude. For the Soviet Union, it represents a significant shift in strategic doctrine by accepting, in a formal international agreement, that Soviet territory is and will remain defenseless against U.S. land-based and sea-based nuclear missiles.[30]—*John B. Rhinelander, Legal Advisor to U.S. SALT Delegation, 1973.*

> [A] relatively stable but uneasy balance has resulted in the recent past, the state of Mutually Assured Destruction. This balance of terror, while morally repugnant to many, is a fact of modern life. The superpowers have recognized that the populations of the United States and the Soviet Union have become unavoidably hostage because of the ineffectiveness of defenses against nuclear-armed strategic weapons systems and so their 1972 agreement, and treaty, in effect terminated efforts at active anti-missile defenses.[31]—*Declaration to the President and Congress from the Union of Concerned Scientists, September 1977*

> The ABM Treaty represents a joint recognition that effective nationwide defense against nuclear weapons is technologically impossible and that a partial defense would be strategically destabilizing. These principles are as valid today as they were when the Treaty was ratified in 1972. The Treaty is as much in the mutual interest of the United States and the Soviet Union today as it was in 1972. . . . Without the ABM Treaty, our world will instantly become more dangerous and more threatening, less stable and less secure.[32]—*Senator Edward M. Kennedy, July 1984*

Particularly perplexing about this mindset is that while many Americans were extolling the virtues of this newly codified mutual vulnerability,[33] the Soviets were saying and doing things totally at odds with MAD.[34] In the area of research and development on defensive systems, the Soviets over the years have expended resources far in excess of any similar U.S. effort.[35] The overall Soviet active and passive defense program, including testing and deployment of legal and illegal programs (with respect to ABM treaty limitations), has no counterpart in the United States.[36] The unclassified comparative review of Soviet and U.S. active and passive defense efforts found in tables 11–1 through 11–9 dramatically illustrates this point.

There was, however, a major change that did occur following the ratification of the ABM treaty by both the United States and the Soviet Union. By 1973, Soviet writings on military strategy had begun to reduce the extent to which they discussed the *nuclear* aspect of their war-fighting strategy and, in particular, the role of defensive systems in that strategy. This was needed to deprive from U.S. proponents of antimissile systems evidence of Soviet military strategy, thus

Table 11–1
Evolutionary Testing of SAM Interceptors and Radars against Reentry Vehicles

Period	USSR	United States
1973–74	Testing the SA-2, the SA-5 and associated SA-5 radars over 50 times in an ABM mode (over 100,000 feet) over a period of 18 months.	No comparable activity
1970s	Continued upgrading, testing and deployment of the SA-5 radar and interceptor.	
Mid–late 1970s	Development of the SA-10 to counter SRAMs and cruise missiles, thereby giving the interceptor missile a significant capability for low altitude defense, including defense against ballistic missile reentry vehicles (RVs).	
1980	Testing of the SA-10 phased-array acquisition and tracking radar as a battle management system for low altitude defense against ballistic missile RVs.	
1980	Resume testing of the SA-5 and its upgraded radar in an ABM mode after supposedly having resolved this violation issue in the Standing Consultative Commission (SCC) five years earlier.	
1981	Begin testing the SA-12 in an ABM mode against ballistic missile RVs.	

Sources: Colin S. Gray, "SALT I Aftermath: Have the Soviets Been Cheating?" *Air Force Magazine*, November 1975; Clarence A. Robinson, Jr., "Soviet Treaty Violations Detected," *Aviation Week & Space Technology (AWST)*, 21 October 1974; Robinson, "Further Violations of SALT Seen," *AWST*, 3 February 1975; Robinson, "Soviet SALT Violations Feared," *AWST*, 22 September 1980; Robinson "Soviets Accelerate Missile Defense," *AWST*, 16 January 1984; Mark E. Miller, *Soviet Strategic Power and Doctrine* (Miami: Advanced International Studies Institute, 1982); Elmo Zumwalt, Testimony before the Senate Committee on Appropriations, *SALT II Violations* (Washington, D.C., 28 March 1984).

Table 11–2
Netting of Various SAM and ABM Radars

Period	USSR	United States
1975	Netting of mobile ABM radars at test sites at Sary Shagan and Kapustin Yar to other ABM radars for ABM interceptor launches.	No comparable activity
1984	Netting of C^3, air defense radars and ABM radars with battle management radars to tie together elements of a nation-wide strategic defense system.	
1986	Calibrating the SA-5 "Square Pair" radar to the ABM-3 battle management radar to allow the "handing off" of acquisition information to the SA-5 for interceptor launch.	

Sources: Clarence A. Robinson, Jr., "Further Violations of SALT Seen," *AWST*, 3 February 1975; Robinson, "Soviets Accelerate Missile Defense," *AWST*, 16 January 1984; Rowland Evans and Robert Novak, "ABM: A New Soviet Violation," *Washington Post*, 10 March 1986.

giving support to its opponents. This early period marked the beginning of what would become a more sophisticated employment of Soviet perceptions management. In one example, William Green has noted that:

> About 1973 the Soviet military press began to tighten the Filter in statements about nuclear weapons policy. Following SALT, the Soviet military found it necessary to be less specific in direct references to the possible strategic use of nuclear weapons from its publications; especially when they were discussed in terms of preemption. . . . By filtering its military publications, the Soviet leadership has been able to remove an important resource from the proponents of strengthened U.S. and NATO defenses. As the pre-1973 literature becomes increasingly older, it provides less support in Western policy debates for refuting assertions of Soviet willingness to accept strategic parity and a state of mutual vulnerability.[37]

In addition, to adjusting this "filter" on Soviet military writings, they also began to restrict the amount and kind of information the West would receive from the Soviet Union. On 27 May 1973, the USSR became a party to the Geneva Universal Copyright Convention (UCC) of 1952. By acceding to this convention, the Soviets were able to control the types of military writings authorized for translations and nongovernmental use (or public dissemination) in the West. Although there is no proof that the Soviet military deliberately sought accession to the convention specifically to control the flow of military writings to the West, they quickly saw its apparent value:

> It appears that the Soviet military was only alerted to this means of halting Western translation of its strategic literature as a result of VAAP's [The Soviet's All-Union Copyright Agency] attempts to receive author's permissions for

Table 11-3
Soviet Strategic SAM Characteristics and Numbers

System	First Deployed	USSR Slant Range (miles)	Ceiling (feet)	Warhead	Launch Site	Numbers Deployed	United States
SA-1	1956	25	60,000	HE/nuclear	Fixed	3,000	U.S. strategic SAMs in the continental United States were deactivated following the signing of the ABM Treaty.
SA-2	1958	30	medium–80,000	HE/nuclear	Fixed	2,900	
SA-3	1961	15	low–40,000	HE	Mobile	1,250	
SA-5	1967	175	100,000+	HE/nuclear	Mobile	2,020	
SA-10	1980	60	low–80,000	HE/nuclear	Mobile	520	
SA-12	1985	60	low–high	?	Mobile	?	
Total						9,690[a]	

Sources: John M. Collins, *U.S.-Soviet Military Balance 1980–1985* (New York: Pergamon-Brassey's, 1985); *The Military Balance 1984–1985* (London: IISS, 1984); U.S. Department of Defense, *Soviet Military Power 1986* (Washington, D.C., 1986).

[a] This number refers only to launchers, not to interceptor missiles. The SA-3 launcher carries 2–4 rails, the SA-10 carries 4, and the SA-12 carries 2 rails per launcher. Not counting reloads, this would amount to over 14,000 strategic SAM interceptors. Also, one must consider that the continued deployment of the SA-10 and SA-12 will dramatically influence the qualitative coloration of the SAM mix, greatly augmenting thereby its ABM capability.

Table 11-4
ABM Treaty Radar Violation Issues

Period	USSR	United States
1974	Development of a mobile ABM radar at the ABM test site in Sary Shagan.	No comparable activity
1975	Installation of a movable (rapidly deployable) ABM-X-3 radar at Kamchatka, a previously undesignated test site. The Soviets resolved part of this violation by simply declaring Kamchatka an official ABM test site.	
1975–present	Continuation of developmental activities pertaining to non-permanently fixed ABM radars.	
Early–mid-1970s	Decision to deploy a new large phased-array radar near Krasnoyarsk. R&D on this class of radar commenced in the 1960s.	
Early 1980s	Beginning of construction of the new large phased-array radar near Krasnoyarsk (Abalakova).	
Summer 1983	Discovery of the Krasnoyarsk radar after some two years of construction had already been completed.	

Sources: Testimony of Kenneth L. Adelman before the Senate Armed Services Committee, *Soviet Treaty Violations* (Washington, D.C., 20 February 1985); General Advisory Committee on Arms Control and Disarmament (GAC), *A Quarter Century of Soviet Compliance Practices Under Arms Control Committments: 1958–1983*, Summary (Washington, D.C., October 1984); U.S. Arms Control and Disarmament Agency, *Soviet Noncompliance* (Washington, D.C., 1 February 1986); U.S. Department of State, *SALT I: Compliance; SALT II: Verification*, Selected Documents No. 7 (Washington, D.C., 21 February 1978); Jake Garn, "The Suppression of Information Concerning Soviet SALT Violations by the U.S. Government," *Policy Review*, Summer 1979; Clarence A. Robinson, Jr., "Soviet Treaty Violations Detected," *AWST*, (21 October 1974).

copyright licenses. Yet once alerted, the Soviet military has proved itself adroit in using American law to cut off public access to a source that had been used with great effect in debates on public issues such as SALT II ratification. In short, the Copyright Convention . . . has resulted in the Soviet Union obtaining control, through the U.S. legal system, of an important means of affecting public perception of Soviet nuclear weapons policy.[38]

In support of Soviet attempts to manipulate Western perceptions through the dissemination of disinformation on Soviet arms limitation policy and publications on military strategy, they have utilized the USSR Academy of Sciences, "social science" institutes under the auspices of the Academy of Sciences, trade centers, and international front organizations.[39] The value of utilizing these organizations cannot be overstated. Western scholars, scientists, and peace groups frequently cite materials published by these institutions to buttress their claims concerning Soviet disarmament policy, military strategy, bureaucratic and individual struggles in decision-making circles, and so on.[40] Former KGB officer Stanislav Levchenko described the internal structure and purpose of these institutes as

> a large army of scientists and researchers, some of whom are full members of the Academy of Sciences, working on projects designated by the Central Committee of the Communist Party of the USSR (CC CPSU) and, more specifically by the International Department (ID) of the CC CPSU. . . . Two functions of the International Department CC CPSU are considered by the Soviet leadership as of utmost importance: (1) to work out long range tactical and strategic plans for the Soviet external policy (in cooperation with the Ministry of Foreign Affairs); (2) to plan and implement (in cooperation with KGB and GRU intelligence agencies) Active Measures aimed against the West.[41]

The influencing of public policy debates in the West is a fundamental objective of Soviet perceptions management strategy. The net effect of limiting the public flow of information on Soviet defense spending and military affairs, coupled with the increasing amount of writings and public exposure in the West of Soviet officials from these institutes and front organizations can be seen in U.S. public policy debates on national security issues.[42] Analysts and scholars concerned about Soviet military capabilities (and the intentions inherently implied in their capability) are faced with the difficult task of *publicly* supporting their arguments with hard evidence.

The Soviets have long understood the benefits of exploiting public policy debates in the West. With respect to SALT I and ABM, the Soviets demonstrated an insightful analysis of the internal division among U.S. policymakers, scholars, and scientists during the negotiations. Writing in the inaugural issue of *USA: Economics, Politics, Ideology*, Georgi Arbatov noted that " [t]he contemporary internal situation of the United States is a large and important subject which deserves special examination. In this case, only one of its aspects interests us—the effect which the aggravation of internal problems has on Washington's foreign policy."[43] From the Soviet's perspective, the source of this internal aggravation lies in the societal crisis, disarmament attitude, and internal budgetary constraints that exist in the United States. In fact, for the Soviets this breaking down of the internal U.S. consensus regarding the threat posed by the Soviet Union concomitant with the initiation of SALT in 1969 marked a favorable shift toward Moscow in the correlation of forces in the eyes of the Soviet leadership.[44] Elaborating on the significance of this change in the correlation of forces Mr. Arbatov continued:

> Meanwhile, one should not underestimate the importance of the activization of the opposition which is coming out for a reexamination of American foreign policy. Its strength is not only in the considerable number of votes in the Senate and in the support of many political and public figures and scientists who enjoy

Table 11-5
Ballistic Missile Early Warning, Target-Tracking, and Battle Management Radars

USSR	United States
HEN HOUSE Ballistic Missile Early Warning Radars: R&D started during the mid-1950s with deployment beginning in the early-mid-1960s. These 11 large radars are located at 6 sites on the periphery of the USSR and provide warning and target tracking data in support of the Soviet ABM system.	*BMEWS (Ballistic Missile Early Warning System)*: R&D started on this class of radar in the late 1950s. The first system became operational in December 1960 (the other two are Alaska and England). BMEWS would confirm ICBM attack and begin transmitting predicted impact locations. This system has little capability to count RVs and predict precise impact points. The radars in Greenland and England, however, are presently being upgraded with phased-array radars similar to PAVE PAWS.
DOG HOUSE and CAT HOUSE Battle Management Radars: R&D started on these radars in the mid-1950s with deployment beginning in the early-mid-1960's. Along with the TRY ADD missile control radars, these systems provide battle management for the Moscow ABM system. This system, however, is currently being upgraded.	*PAVE PAWS*: This phased-array radar system is intended to confirm SLBM warning data received from satellite warning systems. The two systems constructed in the 1970s in California and Massachusetts are presently being supplemented by two additional radars in Texas and Georgia. These radars will close the SLBM coverage gaps to the southeast and southwest. These radars, however, have limited ability to track and count MIRVs and predict their impact points.
Pechora Class Ballistic Missile Detection and Tracking Radars: R&D started during the mid-1960s with deployment commencing in the mid-1970s. Five of these modern large phased-array radars duplicate or supplement the HEN HOUSE network, greatly enhancing its capability. The sixth radar, now nearing completion near Krasnoyarsk, closes the final gap in Soviet ballistic missile early warning. In addition, two new LPARs are being constructed on the western periphery, bringing the total to eight.	*PARCS (Perimeter Acquisition Radar Control System)*: The sole portion of the SAFEGUARD ABM site in North Dakota still in service. Although this is the most accurate attack characterization sensor in operation, it does not view all ICBM windows and only few for SLBMs.
Pushkino Class Battle Management Radar: R&D having started some time in the 1970s, deployment of this radar commenced in the early-1980s. The new large radar, designed to control ABM engagements, form part of the modernized Moscow ABM system, provides 360-degree strategic defense coverage. The four-sided phased-array radar structure, 120 feet high and 500 feet wide, is about twice as large as those designed for the now deactivated U.S. SAFEGUARD ABM system.	*Cobra Dane*: This radar, situated on Shemya island, Alaska, was built in 1977 as part of the U.S. national technical means for monitoring Soviet missile tests. It can track dozens of warheads simultaneously. Cobra Dane would reportedly be activated for attack early warning purposes at defense condition 3 or higher.

Sources: U.S. Department of Defense, *Soviet Military Power 1986* (Washington, D.C., 1986); *Soviet Military Power 1983*; *The Military Balance 1984–1985* (London: IISS, 1984); Paul Bracken, *The Command and Control of Nuclear Forces* (New Haven: Yale University Press, 1983); Bruce G. Blair, *Strategic Command and Control: Redefining the Nuclear Threat* (Washington, D.C.: Brookings, 1985); Kenneth L. Moll, *Strategic Command and Control* (Congressional Research Service, 15 May 1980); Secretary of Defense Caspar W. Weinberger, *Annual Report to the Congress, FY 1987* (U.S. Department of Defense, 5 February 1986). John Walcott "US Analysts Find New Soviet Radars Possibly Complicating Arms-Pact Effort." *The Wall Street Journal*, 15 August 1986, p. 2.; Walter Pincus, "Soviets Believed Building Radar Sites," *Washington Post*, 16 August 1986, p. A20.

240 • Arms Control and Verification

Table 11-6
ABM Systems and Related Activities

Moscow System	U.S. System
Original system: Consisting of 64 above-ground reloadable launchers, the GALOSH exoatmospheric interceptor and the DOG HOUSE/CAT HOUSE/TRY ADD radar network. R&D started on this system in the mid-1950s with deployment beginning a decade later.	The single ABM site of 100 interceptors and associated radars allowed by the ABM Treaty was deactivated in 1975.
New system: Consisting of silo-based SH-04 modified GALOSH exoatmospheric interceptors and silo-based SH-08 GAZELLE high-acceleration endoatmospheric interceptors. This two-layer system, when complete in 1987, will consist of 100 underground reloadable ABM launchers with an unknown number of interceptor missiles. The older engagement, guidance and battle management radar system will be augmented by the new class, large engagement Puskino radar. R&D on the new system started in the early 1970s was not slowed down by SALT I, and deployment commenced late in the decade.	
June 1982: Testing of the new SH-08 hypersonic interceptor, controlled by the ABM-X-3 phased-array radar, in a fully integrated simulation of a nuclear war against ICBM RVs.	
Early–Mid-1980s: Testing the SH-08 interceptor in a rapid reload configuration by firing two of the missiles from the same silo. Observation that the second firing had happened occurred within 2 hours. The second firing itself could have occurred almost instantly after the last. The internal reload, rapid refire system appears to be a clear violation of the ABM Treaty, by allowing an unknown reserve of interceptors to be stored underground.	

Sources: U.S. Department of Defense, *Soviet Military Power 1986* (Washington, D.C., 1986); "Soviets Stage Integrated Test of Weapons," *AWST*, 28 June 1982; Clarence A. Robinson, Jr., "Soviets Accelerate Missile Defense," *AWST*, 16 January 1984.

Table 11–7
Development of Directed Energy Weapons and Other Advanced ABM Technologies

USSR	United States
	Pre-SDI Speech
Mid-late 1960s: Beginning of R&D for space-based BMD and ASAT lasers.	*Early 1960s:* Beginning of R&D in high energy lasers.
Late 1960s: Beginning of R&D for space-based particle beam weapons.	*Early-Mid 1960s:* Beginning of a program to study the application of particle beam weapons to BMD.
Late 1960s: Beginning of R&D for ground-based ASAT lasers.	*1973–76:* First successful tests of high energy lasers in engaging moving targets (winged and helicopter drones, and anti-tank projectiles).
Mid-1975: Testing of components designed for a ground-based proton beam device. This device will initially be for ASAT and eventually for BMD missions.	
Mid-Late 1970s: Developmental testing of a compact hydrogen fluoride high energy laser intended for space basing. Report of a Soviet achievement of 5.5 megawatts of continuous power in 1975.	**Post-SDI Speech**
Mid-late 1970s: Electron beam propagation experiments in space from manned Soyuz spacecraft, Salyut space stations and unmanned Cosmos spacecraft.	*Mid-1980s:* Research into the area of directed energy weapons (DEW), including high-power laser and particle beam generation, as part of the SDI program.
Early 1980s: Deployment of ground-based (prototype) lasers with a limited capability to attack satellites.	*Mid-1980s:* Development of kinetic energy weapons (KEW) as part of the SDI program. Electromagnetic launcher, or "rail gun," research continues to progress.
1981: Test of an optical pointing and tracking device aboard Salyut 7 against an SS-4 booster.	*June 1984:* Flight of the Army Homing Overlay Experiment (HOE) for the first time. Based on existing technology, the HOE demonstrated the ability to see a warhead (not a rocket) against the blackness of space, and to show the ability to maneuver in such a way as to hit the target directly. Such a system, if deployed, would be capable of intercepting targets in various stages of flight (not merely terminal defense).
Late 1970s–1980s: Development of tactical air defense lasers for defense of high value strategic targets in the USSR, for point defense of ships and for air defense of theater forces.	
1980s: Research into the use of strong radio frequency signals capable of destroying critical electronic components of ballistic missile warheads or satellites.	
1960s–present: Development of kinetic energy weapons using the high speed collision of a small mass with the target as a kill mechanism.	

Sources: U.S. Department of Defense, *Soviet Military Power 1986* (Washington, D.C., 1986); Clarence A. Robinson, Jr., "Soviets Push for Beam Weapons," *AWST,* 2 May 1977; Robinson, "Soviets Test Beam Technologies in Space," *AWST,* 3 November 1978; Robert R. Ropelewski, "Soviet High Energy Laser Program Moves Into Prototype Stage," *AWST,* 15 April 1985; Colin S. Gray, *American Military Space Policy* (Cambridge, Mass.: Abt Books, 1982); Keith B. Payne, ed., *Laser Weapons in Space* (Boulder, Colo.: Westview Press, 1983); Uri Ra'anan and Robert Pfaltzgraff, eds., *International Security Dimensions of Space* (Archon Books, 1984); Caspar W. Weinberger, *Annual Report to the Congress, FY 1987* (U.S. Department of Defense, 1986); U.S. Senate Appropriations Committee, *Department of Defense Appropriations, FY 1986,* Part 2 (Washington, D.C., 1985).

Table 11-8
Development of ASAT Capabilities

USSR	United States
Co-Orbital ASAT	
Mid-1960s: Beginning of R&D.	No comparable system
October 1968–December 1971: First test series of a radar guided system. 5 successful kills in 7 attempts.	
February 1976–May 1978: Second test series of both radar and optical guided systems. Demonstration of interception in first revolution after launch.	
1972–78: Operational deployment of co-orbital ASAT system.	
April 1980–June 1982: Third test series of both radar and optical guided systems.	
June 1982: ASAT test preceded and integrated with a strategic exercise simulating a nuclear war involving the firing of ICBMs, SLBMs, IRBMs and ABMs, all coordinated by C^3 over a seven hour period.	
Other ASAT Capabilities	
Mid-1950s: Beginning of R&D for a direct-ascent ASAT capability in the GALOSH ABM system.	*1964–68:* Maintenance in a semi-operational mode of Nike-Zeus AMB interceptors at Johnston Island previously tested for ASAT missions.
Early–mid-1960s: Deployment of a direct-ascent ASAT capability in the GALOSH ABM system.	*1985:* Flight testing of a miniature vehicle (MV) warhead mounted on a two-stage SRAM/Altair booster. This system was carried aloft and launched from a modified F-15. If deployed, the system will be capable of attacking satellites in low altitude orbits. Testing, however, has recently been halted.
1977: Demonstration of the capability to prepare for launch the SS-9 ASAT booster in less than 90 minutes. Such a large booster would also provide a direct-ascent capability great enough to threaten satellites in geosynchronous orbit.	
June 1981: Testing of a space-based ASAT battle station. The Kosmos 1267, docked to Salyut 6, is equipped with clusters of interceptor vehicles that may possess the capability to destroy satellites and other spacecraft. Some reports, however, have identified the "podded miniature attack vehicles" as fuel tanks.	
1986: Two separately located ground-based ASAT lasar facilities discovered near the Afghanistan border.	

Sources: U.S. Department of Defense, *Soviet Military Power 1986* (Washington, D.C., 1986); Robert daCosta, "ASAT Weapons," *Defense Science 2002*, August 1984; Uri Ra'anan and Robert L. Phaltzgraff, Jr., eds., *International Security Dimensions of Space* (Archon Books, 1984); "Soviet Killer Satellite System Confirmed," *AWST*, 10 October 1977; "Soviets Stage Integrated Test of Weapons," *AWST*, 28 June 1982; Colin S. Gray, *American Military Space Policy* (Cambridge, Mass.: Abt Books, 1982); *Report to the Congress on U.S. Policy on ASAT Arms Control*, House Document 98-197 (Washington, D.C., 31 March 1984); "White House Assesses Reports of Soviet ASAT Lasar Facilities," *AWST*, 15 September 1986, p.21.

Table 11-9
Developments in Civil Defense

Period	USSR	United States
1961	Civil defense reorganized on a national level and placed under the control of the Ministry of Defense.	The United States continues to maintain an extremely limited civil defense program. Federal spending on this program in FY 85 was estimated at $181 million. The budget request for FY 1986 has decreased to $119 million. This decrease, however, will partially be made up by state and local funding.
1967	Opening of the Moscow School of Civil Defense designed to prepare officers for mechanized civil defense units through a 3 year program.	
Late 1960s–1970s	Establishment of a program for the dispersal of industry to remote areas such as Siberia and an attempt to ban the construction of industry in large cities.	
1972	Just months after the signing of SALT I, General Colonel [Lt. General] A.T. Altunin became Chief of Civil Defense of the USSR and a Deputy Minister of Defense. Civil defense troops were hence listed on par with the other five services.	
1972	Emphasis moving away from pre-attack evacuation and dispersal of urban residents to shelters as the prime means of protecting the population with the stated goal being the development of a capability to "shelter the entire population in protective shelters."	
1975	Participation of some 23 million Soviet youth in massive military sports games in which survival training in simulated nuclear war conditions played a major part.	
1970s–1980s	The total Soviet annual investment in civil defense may be on the order of $6 billion in equivalent U.S. costs. This British, Swiss and Swedish estimate contrasts with a 1978 CIA figure of $2 billion. The CIA neglects to consider the cost of training and equipping more than 20 million part-time civil defense personnel, adopting dual-purpose installations as shelters, protective measures for industry and transportation, and mass production and stockpiling of civil defense equipment, supplies, construction material, food, fuel and many other items.	

Sources: Leon Goure, *Civil Defense in the Soviet Union* (Berkeley: University of California Press, 1962); Goure, *Shelters in Soviet Survival Strategy* (Miami: Advanced International Studies Institute, 1978); Harriet Fast Scott, "Civil Defense in the USSR," *Air Force Magazine*, October 1975; Major George Kolt, "The Soviet Civil Defense Program," *Strategic Review*, Spring 1977; *United States and Soviet Civil Defense Programs*, Hearings before the Subcommittee on Arms Control, Oceans, International Operations and Environment of the Senate Foreign Relations Committee (Washington, D.C., 16 and 31 March 1982); U.S. House Armed Services Committee, Defense Department Authorization and Oversight Hearings for FY 1986, Part 7, *Civil Defense* (Washington, D.C., 6 March and 17 April 1985).

a broad reputation and great authority in the United States. Even more important is the fact that the line of this opposition expresses the objective requirements of the situation and finds a response among broad public opinion. This converts it into a political factor which can affect the formation of Washington's foreign policy course to one degree or another.[45]

This assessment of American domestic constraints may help explain Soviet behavior in SALT I. Although not unlike that of past Soviet negotiating behavior, their attitude in SALT I was especially resistant to dialogue and substance. Instead, the negotiations served as a means for exploiting the mounting legislative and domestic pressures to reduce U.S. defense programs and, subsequently, the long-range strategic threat of the United States. For example, in 1969 to 1970, and again in 1972, there was a major increase in Soviet personnel lobbying U.S. officials. The focus of their efforts was on Congressmen, their staffs, and academicians. The objective was to spread disinformation that if the United States would take the initiative to ban MIRVs or ABMs, for instance, the Soviets would eventually follow suit. As it turned out, this strategy was arguably unsuccessful since many of the key SALT programs were funded, however, the voting was extremely close.[46] Although the nature of this type of activity makes the evaluation and extent of their success in exploiting domestic factors uncertain and debatable, it should not be dismissed lightly. The practice has not been terminated. Indeed, it has increased, become more overt, and sophisticated.[47] Thus, it should be brought to the attention of and examined seriously by policymakers and academicians.

The final section of this chapter examines two examples of Soviet deception and perceptions management during SALT I. Each of these examples illustrates a different aspect or technique employed by the Soviets to support foreign policy objectives and military planning.

Examples of Soviet Deception and Perceptions Management

The Myth of Soviet Adherence to MAD

The previous section demonstrates that many in the West believe, contrary to fact, that Soviet military strategy is guided by an assured destruction policy. Tables 11–1 through 11–9, on the other hand, cast strong doubt on this premise. The defensive programs, both legal and illegal, outlined in the tables are more than robust research programs designed to hedge against American bad faith or technological breakthroughs. A heavy burden lies on anyone who would attempt to make a coherent argument for a Soviet assured destruction policy.

The contention that the Soviets ceased to be interested in strategic defense, circa 1972, cannot be supported by references to what the Soviets have *done*, it can only be supported by what they *say*. With President Reagan's announcement of SDI, the Soviets have turned up the rhetoric on the dangers of defensive systems and their threat to strategic stability. Soviet polemics are remarkably similar to those of Western scientists, politicians, and academics opposed to defensive systems. In short, the Soviets are telling the West what it wants to hear. The themes are the basic tenets of MAD: defensive systems will inspire an arms race, destabilize the strategic balance, and in the final analysis, the system will not work with any degree of strategic significance.[48] Ironically, Soviet attempts at perceptions management and deception are straightforward—so much so that it can only succeed with someone who wishes it so.

For example, appearing on the television program *Nightline*, Stanislav Menshikov, Senior Advisor to the Soviet Central Committee, was questioned by Ted Koppel about Soviet concerns regarding SDI:

Koppel: Let me ask you one question, because it seems to be the great bugaboo as far as the United States and the Soviet Union negotiations in Geneva are concerned. I don't quite understand why it is on the one hand that the Soviet Union is so concerned about the development of Star Wars, and on the other hand tends to pooh-pooh the validity of the notion—in other words, says it's kind of a pointless system.
Mr. Menshikov: I realize that.
Koppel: Why are you so concerned about it then?
Mr. Menshikov: Well, I'll tell you. We are concerned about it because a beginning of actually putting space weapons into space will start a new phase in the arms race. We will have to retaliate in terms of larger numbers of strategic weapons, new kinds of strategic weapons and of course space weapons.
Koppel: Only if they're effective. I mean, if we put a bunch of marshmallows up there in space that are ineffective, that don't work, you've got nothing to worry about, do you?
Mr. Menshikov: Yes. Now, the other side of the equation, as you pointed out, there is this argument. But you see, the system is not effective as far as you can see it in terms of what it can do to defend the population of the United States, you see. As of now, I haven't seen any serious assessment, official or nonofficial, that would point to the fact that it can really protect the population of the United States. Now, what it can do, and everybody has been saying that and everybody agrees on that, that it can be effective in a few years in protecting the nuclear— well, the missiles, your strategic missiles. That is the important thing you see, and that makes it important because it sets up an additional military capacity, an additional potential to strike, and additional potential to defend from a second strike by the Soviet Union.[49]

The implications of this statement are profound. If it is examined closely, it is apparent that it contradicts Soviet propaganda statements on their official position regarding defensive systems. If the Soviets are to be taken at their word, that they adhere to the principles of MAD, then they should appreciate the necessity of protecting our strategic forces. A basic tenet of MAD is that vulnerability of strategic weapon systems is destabilizing, that such weapons should not be attacked or interfered with. The targeting emphasis should instead be cities, not retaliatory forces. Yet, Mr. Menshikov dismisses the importance of cities, instead concentrating his attention on the need to destroy American *strategic* forces. But many American opinion makers choose not to look at this and prefer instead the unexamined Soviet line.

In another revealing conversation, this time with a Soviet military attaché, the question again surfaced about Soviet ABM systems. Speaking privately to Dr. Michael Deane, in late June 1983, at the University of Miami's Advanced International Studies Institute in Washington, D.C., the Soviet attaché was asked why recent writings by air defense officials do not mention the role of ballistic missile defenses in Soviet military strategy. In a letter to an American intelligence official on his conversation with the Soviet attaché, Deane characterized his response as a

> simple assertion that Soviet military writings frequently discuss Soviet ABMs. I said that I was unfamiliar with such writings and asked if he could point some sources out.
>
> [The attaché's] response was to point to Koldunov's article in *Voyennyye znaniya*, specifically to the phrase *"zenitnykh raketnykh kompleksov"* therein, as such an example.
>
> I said Western and Soviet translators render that particular phrase as "anti-aircraft missile complexes" only.
> But he responded that the term also covers missiles with an *anti-ballistic missile capability*.
>
> I then asked if he meant that Soviet "anti-aircraft missiles" had a capability to hit U.S. ICBMs.
>
> He answered yes *and elaborated without any prompting that Soviet weapons builders had the knowledge to make "anti-aircraft missiles" effective against U.S. ICBMs and did so.*
>
> To check that we were in fact talking about the same thing, I noted that the 1972 ABM treaty and its revision permit each country with a limit of 100 ABM missiles. I asked directly if what he was saying meant that the Soviets had broken [sic] the Treaty.
>
> [The Colonel] responded with a question—what did you want us to do, not use the knowledge we had? . . .
>
> I asked again if he meant the Soviets had already broken [sic] the Treaty. This time he gave no verbal answer, merely shrugging his shoulders.[50] (emphasis added)

This conversation with the Soviet colonel illustrates the deception the Soviets have constructed in their writings to disguise explicit references to antiballistic missile capability. In this instance the "filter" was adjusted to deny Western analysts the ability to cite Soviet references on the role ballistic missile defense plays in Soviet strategy. But when this conversation was circulated within the United States government it affected no partisan of arms control. It should have.

An additional significance of this letter is the insightful look at Soviet attitudes toward the ABM treaty. Specifically, this raises the question: did the Soviets ever intend to abide by the terms of the agreement? In fact, the statement by the Soviet attaché helps explain the continued testing and modification, since 1972, of the SA-5 in an ABM mode and the development of the SA-12 and associated radar as a dual-purpose system suited for widespread mobile ABM deployment. The real Soviet attitude with respect to the ABM treaty is further illustrated by the seven Pechora-class LPAR's and by the one at Krasnoyarsk in particular. The decision by Soviet leaders to build the long lead-time Pechora-class radars on the periphery of the Soviet Union and the Krasnoyarsk Pechora-class radar away from the periphery had to have occurred in the mid- to-late-1960's and early-to-mid-1970's, respectively.

The most troubling aspect of the Soviet perceptions management program, today, however, is the contempt it has engendered for the United States among Soviet decision makers. This point was outlined by the Director of the Arms Control and Disarmament Agency Kenneth Adelman during testimony before the Senate Armed Services Committee on 20 February 1985. Adelman stated that the construction of the Krasnoyarsk radar is disturbing because "they embarked on a path that they knew was a violation, we knew was a violation, and second, they knew we would detect as a violation."[51] He continued stating: "It is a huge construction endeavor that must have been planned and begun in the early to mid-1970's. Now, this was right after the signing of the ABM Treaty in 1972. This was at the heyday of détente, and high hopes for arms control."[52]

When seen in totality, Soviet programs and activities logically point to one conclusion: their purpose in signing the ABM treaty was to halt or delay U.S. research and development on defensive systems and at the same time continue, unabated, Soviet programs designed to deploy a nationwide defense. Evidence of this supposition has become so strong that some supporters of arms control now admit that their military strategy and programs are at variance with the principles of MAD.[53] Nevertheless, because Soviet perceptions management played directly to the self-interest and self-image of U.S. officials and others, arguments still persist that the United States should not pursue defensive systems but continue to view arms control negotiations as the best means of enhancing strategic stability irrespective of the Soviet active and passive defense programs.

The Soviet Military and SALT:
Deception and Perceptions Management

One of the striking contrasts between the U.S. and Soviet approaches to negotiations is the importance and authority relegated to the Soviet military.[54] Yet the Soviets, in an interesting tactical deception, listed Deputy Foreign Minister Vladimir S. Semenov as head of their SALT delegation while the ranking Soviet military officer, Colonel-General Nikolai V. Ogarkov, was listed as the second-ranking member.[55] The objective, of course, was to mirror the Western organizational approach by giving the appearance that the Party or civilian members, and not the military, were in charge of the delegation. But clearly this was not the case—at least in Helsinki and Vienna, where the negotiations were being conducted. The Soviet military was the premier authority in SALT; the Ministry of Foreign Affairs had little influence during the negotiations. In fact, official Washington expressed anxiety over the rise in influence and power that the Soviet military enjoyed both on matters relating to the negotiations and in military decisions within the Kremlim.[56] In no other area was this more evident than in SALT. The U.S. delegation was bemused by the lack of quantitative and qualitative knowledge that members of the Foreign Ministry had about Soviet weapons systems. Foreign Ministry officials were confused about the characteristics of various American and Soviet weapon systems and proved unable to discuss even general issues relating to these systems. It was General Ogarkov who had to set U.S. officials straight on specific issues.[57] A striking example of the ignorance displayed by members of the Soviet Foreign Ministry and the importance of the Soviet military is best told by John Newhouse in his book, *Cold Dawn: The Story of SALT*, in which he describes Ogarkov as taking "aside a U.S. delegate [to explain that] there was no reason why the Americans should disclose their knowledge of Russian Military matters to civilian members of his delegation. Such information, said Ogarkov, is strictly the affair of the military."[58]

The authority of the military during SALT served to ensure that the information released by the Soviet delegation, however limited, would not reveal data on Soviet weapon systems and programs and any information that was released to the United States was disinformation designed to mislead the United States. It is reported that General Ogarkov was the head of the Principal Directorate for Strategic Deception of the General Staff during the SALT negotiations.[59] Formed in the late 1960's, this directorate probably controlled, to a large extent, the flow of military information divulged to the United States. On rare occasions when they did supply figures, they were such gross underestimations of what U.S. intelligence knew about Soviet force levels that the United States refused to accept them as part of the SALT database. The Soviets, for example, supplied disinformation on the numbers and types of weapons systems available in their arsenals. The Soviet refusal to submit a remotely realistic database compelled the United States to submit its own estimates of Soviet force levels and characteristics. On close examination of the numbers, the Soviet military accepted the U.S. figures as the basis for SALT. This unwillingness to release accurate data on their weapon systems denied U.S. officials information necessary for the formulation of sound arms control proposals.

The military also used the negotiations as a source of intelligence. The U.S. delegation, for example, had to submit intelligence data in order to keep the talks going—which afforded the Soviets a significant insight into the amount of information Western intelligence had on Soviet military organization and capability.

In the end, Russian negotiating behavior and duplicity, the general nature of the Soviet totalitarian system, the Soviet military's influence, and an absence of U.S. tenacity and patience were the primary factors that precluded the inclusion of specifics on the terms and wording of the treaty. This lack of specifics resulted in numerous questions regarding Soviet compliance in the 1970's and 1980's. In light of their ongoing active defense program, if specifics had been included, not even the most ardent partisans of Soviet "good faith" could argue before U.S. audiences that the Soviets have adhered to any parts of the treaty.

The Soviets refused to declare a second ABM test site during the negotiations and, in fact, the United States had to identify their first site at Sary Shagan. The Soviets simply accepted without comment our choice. It was not until several years later, when the United States had observed and protested the testing of SA-5 radars against ballistic missile reentry vehicles and the installation of a "movable" type of ABM radar at Kamchatka, that the Soviets declared this "long-time" test site as their second allowed under the terms of the treaty. If indeed it was a "long-time" test site, why did they not declare it during SALT? What was their motive in hiding the purpose of the site?

The Soviets also blocked attempts to define the term "tested in an ABM mode" and, in fact, Soviet insistance on ambiguous language forced the United States to define the term in a unilateral statement. Other ambiguous language was sought and obtained by the Soviets pertaining to the use of certain SAM radars for calibration, thus providing an excuse for the concurrent testing of SAM and ABM radars. Finally, the Soviets secured ambiguous language relating to "ABM systems based on other physical principles" in "Agreed Statement D."[60] The inclusion of the ambiguous wording in "Agreed Statement D" left the door open for the Soviets to continue research, development, and even testing of ABM systems based on technologies that, at the time, were uncertain or unknown.[61] Specific and comprehensive analysis of these and other complicated issues relating to Soviet violations of the ABM treaty have been well documented and thus need not be reiterated.[62] Suffice it to say that the Soviets approached the negotiations with the objective of building in as much ambiguity or outright exclusion of specifics as possible. This has enabled the Soviets to exploit the various factions in the West opposed to defensive systems, allowing these factions to focus the debate on legalistic interpretations rather than on the more pertinent question of Soviets' strategic military aims—not to mention specific intentions for negotiating the ABM treaty.

One of the more recent debates that has important consequences for the U.S. SDI is over the above mentioned issue of "Agreed Statement D." Debate over the interpretation had not surfaced in the past because of a perceived U.S. uncertainty regarding the nature and potential benefits of ABM technology and a lack of U.S. interest therein. Recent observance (and in the past by some perceptive U.S. intelligence analysts) of Soviet research and development, however, confirmed by U.S. research conducted under the SDI, verifies that technologies can, in the not too distant future, lead to significant ABM capability. In a review of the SALT negotiating record conducted by government lawyers, it was determined that the Soviets did indeed intend on and succeeded in obtaining ambiguous language regarding "Agreed Statement D". Citing a State Department report, Judge Sofaer, the legal advisor in charge of the review, stated:

> I reached the firm conclusion that, although the U.S. delegates initially sought to ban development and testing of nonland-based systems or components based on future technology, the Soviets refused to go along, and no such agreement was reached. The Soviets stubbornly resisted U.S. attempts to adopt in the body of the treaty any limits on such systems or components based on future technology; their arguments rested on a professed unwillingness to deal with unknown devices or technology. . . . The negotiating record also contains strong support for a reading of article II(1) that restricts the definitions of "ABM system" and "components" to those based on current physical principles. The Soviets specifically sought to prevent broad definitions of these terms, and our negotiators acceded to their wishes.[63]

Thus, the lack of specificity in the treaty and the scarcity of information and Soviet statements, has allowed those in the United States to believe what the evidence clearly contradicts.

In conclusion, it must again be emphasized that the success of Soviet deception and perceptions management is, to a large extent, attributable to the Soviets' ability to exploit U.S. cultural predilections and, above all, the personal stake that a whole class of U.S. officials and authorities have built into the position that antimissile defenses are bad, impossible to build effectively, and a dogmatic belief that arms control is the only means to achieve strategic stability. The Soviets have simply sought to bolster this influential faction to the U.S. internal debate, and this faction has accepted the help it has received in presenting to the rest of the American people positions that unwittingly support Soviet objectives.

At the same time, evidence to identify Soviet perceptions management and deception has and continues to be ubiquitous. The struggle, then, is not so much intellectual, but political—not so much international, as U.S. intramural. It is only the desire of many among us not to confront this reality that prevents us from combating a formidable force that reinforces dangerous misperceptions of reality—Soviet perceptions management. When Soviet military strategy and force posture are examined together, the evidence is incontrovertible: Soviet objectives are to develop a military capability designed to serve foreign policy goals in peacetime and military victory in wartime, irrespective of the potential destructive capability of nuclear weapons.

In the forthcoming debate over the future of SDI, its impact on deterrence and stability, and the efficacy of the ABM treaty, these factors should not be ignored. In addition, serious consideration should be given to Soviet motives for negotiating further limits on U.S. active defense programs.

Notes

1. Gerard Smith, *Doubletalk: The Story of SALT*, (New York: Doubleday, 1980), p. 455; Robbin F. Laird and Dale R. Herspring, *The Soviet Union and Strategic Arms*, (Boulder Colo.: Westview, 1984), p. 111; Roman Kolkowicz and Ellen P. Mickiewicz, *The Soviet Calculus of Nuclear War*, (Lexington, Mass.: Lexington Books, 1986), p. 146; Thomas Longstreth, et al. *The Impact of U.S. and Soviet Ballistic Missile Defense Program on the ABM Treaty*, (Washington, D.C.: National Campaign to Save the ABM Treaty, March 1985.), p. 65.

2. See Thomas Longstreth, et al., *The Impact of U.S. and Soviet Ballistic Missile Defense Program on the ABM Treaty*, p. 65.

3. The President's General Advisory Committee on Arms Control and Disarmament (GAC), Unclassified Summary Report, *A Quarter Century of Soviet Compliance Practices Under Arms Control Commitments: 1958–1983*, (Washington, D.C.: The White House, Office of the Press Secretary, 10 October 1984); *Report of the President on Soviet Noncompliance*, (Washington, D.C.: The White House, Office of the Press Secretary, 23 January 1984); *Report of the President on Soviet Noncompliance*, (Washington, D.C.: The White House, The Office of the Press Secretary, 10 June 1985); *The President's Unclassified Report on Soviet Noncompliance with Arms Control Agreements*, (Washington, D.C.: The White House, Office of the Press Secretary, 23 December 1985); United States Arms Control and Disarmament Agency, *Soviet Noncompliance*, (Washington, D.C.: U.S. Government Printing Office, 1 February 1986).

4. See Department of Defense, *Soviet Military Power 1986*, (Washington, D.C.: U.S. Government Printing Office, March 1986), pp. 106–108, 111–119.

5. Gerard Smith, *Doubletalk: The Story of SALT*, p. 85.

6. Ibid.

7. Ibid.

8. John B. Rhinelander, "The SALT I Agreements," in Mason Willrich and John B. Rhinelander, eds., *SALT: The Moscow Agreements and Beyond* (New York: Free Press, 1974), p. 127.

9. V. Chernyshev, *TASS*, 15 February 1985, *Foreign Broadcast Information Serv-*

ice, 15 February 1985; Interview with A. Kokoshin, A. Arbatov, A Vasilyev in *Der Spiegel*, 11 March 1985, pp. 138–148, *Foreign Broadcast Information Service*, 14 March 1985. In this interview the Soviets made the statement that "[a]t the time Kosygin made this remark [that it was strategically and morally imperative to have defenses] there was neither strategic parity nor the principle of mutual assured destruction. There was no missile defense system or any agreement on strategic arms. Things are quite different today."

10. V.D. Sokolovski, *Soviet Military Strategy*, The Rand Corporation, (London: Prentice-Hall, 1963); Maj. Gen. S. Branevskiy, "The Factors of Time and Space in Military Operations, 7(*Voyennaya Mysl'*, 1963), pp. 35–47; Colonel P.M. Derevyanko, ed., *Problems of the Revolution in Military Affairs* (Moscow: Military Publishing House, 1965); Gen. Maj. K.S. Bochkarev, "On the Character and Types of Wars in the Modern Era", *Communist of the Armed Forces*, June 1965; Colonel V.V.Glazov,"Some Features of Conducting Military Actions in Nuclear War", *Communist of the Armed Forces*, February 1964; Lt. Colonel, Ye. I. Ribkin, "On the Nature of World Nuclear Rocket War", *Communist of the Armed Forces*, September 1965; Colonel S.I. Kropnov, "According to the Laws of Dialectics, *Red Star*, 7 January 1966; Gen. Lt. I.G. Zavyalov, "On Soviet Military Doctrine", *Red Star*, 30 and 31 March 1967; William R. Kinter and Harriet F. Scott, *The Nuclear Revolution in Soviet Military Affairs* (Norman, Ok: University of Oklahoma Press, 1968). In addition to Soviet sources, see also the following Western sources: Joseph D. Douglass, Jr. and Amoretta M. Hoeber, *Soviet Strategy for Nuclear War*, (Stanford, Calif.: The Hoover Institution Press, 1979), pp. 71–107. Mark E. Miller, *Soviet Strategic Power and Doctrine: The Quest for Superiority*, (Washington, D.C.: Advanced International Studies Institute, 1982), pp. 208–217; William R. Van Cleave, "Soviet Doctrine and Strategy: A Developing American View," in Lawrence L. Whetten, ed., *The Future of Soviet Military Power* (New York: Crane Russak, 1976), pp. 41–58; Alfred L. Monks, *Soviet Military Doctrine: 1960 to the Present* (New York: Irvington, 1984), pp. 93–97, 140–144, 183–184, 215, 227–229; William T. Lee and Richard F.Staar, *Soviet Military Policy Since World War II* (Stanford, Calif.: The Hoover Institution Press, 1986), pp. 26–29.

11. H.S. Dinerstein, *War and the Soviet Union: Nuclear Weapons and the Revolution in Soviet Military and Political Thinking* (New York: Praeger, 1959); See also references under note 10.

12. Henry S. Rowen, "Evolution of Strategic Nuclear Doctrine," in Laurence Martin, ed., *Strategic Thought in the Nuclear Age* (Baltimore, Md.: The Johns Hopkins University Press, 1979), p. 151.

13. William W. Kaufmann, *The McNamara Strategy* (New York: Harper & Row, 1964), p. 97.

14. See Alain C. Enthoven and K. Wayne Smith, *How Much is Enough? Shaping the Defense Program, 1961–1969* (New York: Harper & Row, 1971) for an authoritative history of the evolution and thinking of mutual assured destruction.

15. U.S. Arms Control and Disarmament Agency, *Documents on Disarmament, 1967* (Washington, D.C.: U.S. Government Printing Office, July 1968), pp. 60–61, 270.

16. John H. Barton and Laurence A. Weiler, eds., *International Arms Control: Issues and Agreements by the Stanford Arms Control Group* (Stanford, Calif.: Stanford University Press, 1976), p. 180.

17. John Newhouse, *Cold Dawn: The Story of SALT* (New York: Holt, Rinehart and Winston, 1973), p. 4.

18. Two classic examples of how misperceptions have been a cause of war are, of course, the failure of Western nations to deal with the ascendancy of Adolf Hitler and, to a limited extent, the actions of states prior to World War I. Additional examples are French misperceptions leading up to the Franco-Prussian War in 1870 and the perpetuated belief by European nations that the Swiss were omnipotent well beyond the period in which they were truly a powerful and well-trained army. See Herbert Goldhamer, *Reality and Belief in Military Affairs: A First Draft (June 1977)*, R-2448-NA (Santa Monica, Calif.: The Rand Corporation, February 1979), pp. 1–4 for more examples of reality and misperceptions.

19. See Robert Bathurst's chapter, "On Soviet Linguistics: Expropriating Utopia," and Patrick J. Parker's "Soviet Strategic Deception and United States Vulnerability: A Net Assessment" in this book for a detailed discussion of the disparities between democratic and totalitarian state systems. See also Donald C. Daniel and Katherine L. Herbig, *Strategic Military Deception* (New York: Pergamon Press, 1982) for a discussion of the factors influencing the likelihood of deception, pp. 13–14; and Goldhamer, *Reality and Belief*, pp. 107–108.

20. Edward Luttwak, *The Grand Strategy of the Roman Empire: From the First Century A.D. to the Third*, (Baltimore, Md.: Johns Hopkins University Press, 1976), pp. 2–3.

21. One need look only as far as Nikita Khrushchev's miscalculation in boisterously declaring Soviet superiority in ICBMs during the late 1950's and early 1960's. The result was fear in the West about a missile gap. The effect of Khrushchev's invective was to give the United States an *additional* and important political incentive to produce and deploy its first generation ICBMs beyond the momentum that already existed because of the Soviet ICBM test in August 1957 and Sputnik I in October 1957. See, for example, Michael Mihalka, "Soviet Strategic Deception, 1955–1981," *The Journal of Strategic Studies*, (5 March 1982): pp. 46–49; also, Robert J. DeSutter, Jr., *Arms Control Verification: "Bridge" Theories and the Politics of Expediency*, Ph.D. dissertation University of Southern California, April 1983; Arkady Shevchenko, "Danger: The Networks are Misreading the Russians," *TV Guide* (9 August 1986) p. 4.

22. One of the more notable forms of perceptions management that the Soviets employ is called *reflexive control*. See Clifford Reid's chapter in this book, "Reflexive Control in Soviet Military Planning." "Reflexive Control" is not limited solely to military affairs, however. There are numerous examples demonstrating its discussion and use in influencing the general decision-making process of an adversary: V.A. Lefebvre and V.D. Lefebvre, *Reflexive Control: The Soviet Concept of Influencing an Adversary's Decisionmaking Process*, unpublished technical report, Englewood, Colo., Science Applications Inc., 1984, p. 7; V.A. Lefebvre, *Conflicting Structures [Konflixtuyushchiye struktury]* (Moscow: Soviet Radio Publishing House, 1973), translated by JPRS, JPRS–61332, 1974; V.A. Lefebvre and G.L. Smolyan, *Algebra of Conflict [Algebra Konflikta]* (Moscow, 1968), translated by JPRS, JPRS-52700 (March 1971); A. Berezkin, "On Controlling the Actions of an Opponent," *Military Thought [Voyennaya Mysl']*, (November 1972), no. 11, pp. 92–93, translated by FBIS, FPD 0049/73; V.A. Lefebvre and V.D., *Reflexive Control II*, unpublished technical report, Greenwood Village, Colo., Science Applications, Inc., 1985.

23. See Lawrence Freedman, *U.S. Intelligence and the Soviet Strategic Threat* (New York: Macmillan, 1977), p. 90–96; John Prados, *The Soviet Estimate: U.S. Intelligence Analysis and Russian Military Strength* (New York: Dial, 1982) pp. 155–171.

24. Ibid., p. 94.

25. Ibid., pp. 94–95; and Lee and Staar, *Soviet Military Policy Since World War II*, p. 123.

26. See Goldhamer, "Reality and Belief," p. 41, also see pp. 31–53 of Goldhamer for other examples of how intentions assessments have always played a critical role in military planning.

27. Letter to George Kennan from Charles Burton Marshall dated 25 February 1978, pp. 4–6.

28. Examples are many: dismissing Soviet civil defense activities as not serious and thus ignoring its indication of Soviet military strategy, intentions, and calculations; accepting Soviet arms control definitions of weapon systems irrespective of their gray area or dual-use capability; denigrating the significance and impact of ideological training in military and civilian education; assuming Soviet objectives in arms control are similar to ours, while Soviet defense spending, research and development, training, and force posture are all antithetical to the underlying principles associated with U.S. objectives. See Goldhamer, "Reality and Belief," pp. 22–26 for additional examples.

29. Testimony of Ambassador Gerard Smith before the U.S. Senate Armed Services Committee, *Military Implications of the Treaty on the Limitations of Anti-Ballistic Missile Systems and the Interim Agreement on Limitation of Strategic Offensive Arms* (Washington, D.C.: U.S. Government Printing Office, 18 July 1972), p. 384.

30. John B. Rhinelander, "The SALT I Agreements," in Mason Willrich and John B. Rhinelander, eds., *SALT: The Moscow Agreements and Beyond* (New York: Free Press, 1974), p. 127.

31. Letter to members of the Union of Concerned Scientists soliciting support for an attached declaration to the president and Congress, dated September 1977. The letter is signed by twenty-one notable supporters of the ABM treaty who are also prominent scientists, members of Congress, and former government officials: Hans A. Bethe, Mary Bunting, Owen Chamberlain, Bernard Feld, J. William Fulbright, John K. Galbraith, Donald Glaser, Donald Hornig, Carl Kaysen, Henry Kendall, James R. Killian, Jr., George B. Kistiakowsky, Salvador Luria, J. Carson Mark, Eugene McCarthy, Linus Pauling, George Rathjens, Herbert Scoville, Jr., Albert Szent-Gyorgyi, Victor F. Weisskopf, Jerome B. Wiesner.

32. Edward M. Kennedy, "Star Wars vs. The ABM Treaty," *Arms Control Today*, (14 July/August 1984): p. 24.

33. The degree to which political leaders supported the ABM treaty is reflected in the numbers of votes the treaty received in Senate ratification. On 3 August 1972, the Senate voted 88–2 in favor of the ABM treaty. Testimony in support of the ABM treaty was also overwhelming. In fact, only William R. Van Cleave, in official testimony, and Richard Pipes and Donald Brennan, in open public testimony, were against ratification, as opposed to the vast majority of scientists, academics, and former government officials who were in favor of the treaty. The testimony of those in favor of the ABM treaty focused on the basic principles of MAD: it will stop an arms race, a world without defenses is the most stable form of deterrence, and the system would not work anyway.

34. See Michael Deane, *Strategic Defense in Soviet Strategy* (Washington, D.C.: Advanced International Studies Institute, 1980), pp. 47–115 for a detailed analysis of the comprehensiveness of Soviet efforts in defensive systems during and after the signing of the ABM treaty; Marshal A.A. Grechko, "The Soviet Armed Forces of the Soviet State: A Soviet View," *Soviet Military Thought*, no. 12, translated and published under the auspices of the U.S. Air Force, (Washington, D.C.: U.S. Government Printing Office, 1975) especially pp. 88–93; U.S. Senate, Joint Hearing before the Committee on Appropriations and Committee on Armed Services, Subcommittee on Strategic and Theater Nuclear Forces, *Soviet Strategic Force Developments*, (Washington, D.C.: U.S. Government Printing Office, 26 June 1985) 99th Congress, 1st Session, pp. 15–20, 41–43, 47–51.

35. The following figures were supplied by the Department of Defense through Senator Malcom Wallop's office. They dramatically illustrate the decline in U.S. research and development in antimissile systems after SALT I.

Impact of the Signing of the ABM Treaty on Funding for the Army Ballistic Missile Defense Program
($ in millions)

	1971	1972	1973	1974	1975	1976
Procurement[a]	620	599	264	124	2	0
R&D[b]	490	450	471	351	241	197
Total	1,110	1,049	735	475	243	197

[a] Sentinel/Safeguard
[b] Includes: Safeguard Program, System Technology Program; and Advanced Technology Program.

See also U.S. Congress, Senate Armed Services Committee Hearings, Department of Defense Authorization for Appropriations for fiscal year 1985, part 6, *Strategic Defense Initiative* (Washington, D.C.: U.S. Government Printing Office, 8, 22 March 1984; 24 April 1984) pp. 2928–2930, 2952; See also John M. Collins, *U.S.-Soviet Military Balance, 1980–1985* (New York: Pergamon-Brassey's, 1985), p. 154. for a statement that the United States spends hardly anything on defensive systems and civil defense.

36. William R. Van Cleave, *Fortress USSR: The Soviet Strategic Defense Initiative and the U.S. Strategic Defense Response* (Stanford, Calif.: The Hoover Institute Press, 1986); U.S. Department of Defense and Department of State, *Soviet Strategic Defense Programs* (Washington, D.C.: U.S. Government Printing Office, October 1985); "In Strategic Defense, Moscow is Far Ahead," Backgrounder (Washington, D.C.: The Heritage Foundation, 21 February 1985); Defense Intelligence Agency, *Soviet Military Space Doctrine* (Washington, D.C., U.S. Department of Defense, 1 August 1984); and U.S. Senate, *Soviet Strategic Force Development*.

37. William C. Green, *U.S. Interpretations of Soviet Publications on the Nuclear Weapons Policy of the USSR, 1950–1980*, Ph.D. dissertation, University of Southern California, May 1986, pp. 269–270.

38. Ibid., pp. 284–285.

39. See chapter in this book by Richards Heuer, Jr.; Igor S. Glagolev, *Post-*

Andropov Kremlim Strategy (Washington, D.C.: Association for Cooperation of Democratic Countries, 1984), pp. 76–80; John Baron, "The KGB's Magical War for Peace," *Reader's Digest*, (October 1982), p. 211; *Soviet Covert Action*, Hearings before the Subcommittee on Oversight of the Permanent Select Committee on Intelligence, House of Representatives, 96th Congress, 1st session, Washington, D.C., 6 February 1980, pp. 59–87; William Green, *U.S. Interpretations of Soviet Publications*, pp. 290–297; William Lee and Richard Staar, *Soviet Military Policy Since World War II*, pp. 31–34; Nora Beloff, "Escape from Boredom: A Defector's Story," *Atlantic Monthly*, (December 1980): p. 48, and Barbara Dash, *A Defector Reports: The Institute of the USA and Canada* (Falls Church, Va.: Delphi Associates, May 1982) both of which are cited in William Lee and Richard Staar, and Arkady Shevchenko, *Danger*, p. 8.

40. For example see Anne T. Sloan, "Soviet Positions on Strategic Arms Control and Arms Policy: A Perspective Outside the Military Establishment," in Roman Kolkowicz and Ellen Popper Mickiewicz, eds., *The Soviet Calculus of Nuclear War* (Lexington, Mass.: Lexington Books, 1986), pp. 115–141; Robert L. Arnett, "Soviet Attitudes Towards Nuclear War: Do They Really Think They Can Win?", in *Soviet Strategy*, edited by John Baylis and Gerald Segal (London: Croom Helm, 1981), pp. 55–74; Dimitri Simes, "Deterrence and Coercion in Soviet Policy," *International Security*, 5(Winter 1980/1981), pp.80–103; Paul Dibb, *The Soviet Union: The Incomplete Superpower* (London: Macmillan, 1986); Samuel B. Payne, Jr., *The Soviet Union and SALT* (Cambridge, Ma: The MIT Press, 1980).

41. Stanislav A. Levchenko, "Unmasking Moscow's 'Institute of the U.S.A.' ", *Backgrounder* (Washington, D.C.: The Heritage Foundation, 17 December 1982): p. 2.

42. John Weisman, "What T.V. Isn't Telling Us about those Soviet Spokesmen", *TV Guide*, (26 April 1986): pp. 3–5; Arkady Shevchenko, "The Networks are Misreading the Russians", *TV Guide* (9 August 1986), pp. 3–8; Sir James Goldsmith, "Soviet Active Measures V. the Free Press", in "Soviet Disinformation and the News", *Backgrounder*, (Washington, D.C.: The Heritage Foundation, 28 October 1985): pp. 43–52.

43. G.A. Arbatov, "American Foreign Policy at the Threshold of the 1970's", *USA: Economics, Politics, Ideology*, (1 January 1970), translated by JPRS, 49934, 26 February 1970, p. 22.

44. J.K. Grange, et al., "Net Assessment of U.S. and Soviet Approaches to Arms Control Analysis: Phase II" (U), Foreign Systems Research Center, (Science Applications International, 31 March 1984, Secret), p. 2:15.

45. Arbatov, "American Foreign Policy," p. 24.

46. In the end, however, the cost to the Soviets for accepting limitations on defensive systems would be minimal since aspects of their ABM program were deficient and since the offensive element of SALT did not restrict, in any meaningful way, their ICBM modernization program, in particular, the deployment of large, mirved, SS-18 and SS-19. Having successfully stopped the U.S. ABM program in its tracks, the Soviets ceased to deploy or upgrade the then relatively ineffective Galosh ABM system surrounding Moscow (and adjacent ICBM fields) with technology of the 1960's. This hiatus allowed them to begin construction on long lead-time ABM components, such as the Pechora-class large phased array radars (LPAR) (including the illegal *Krasnoyarsk* radar complex) and the deployment of various radars and support systems necessary for the netting of these components for data distribution and other battle management tasks.

This ABM system would be superior to the U.S. design propagated in the 1960's and stopped by the ABM treaty. In short, the hiatus allowed the Soviets to skip two full generations in their antimissile work and to leap frog the United States effort.

47. In a recent press report, for example, it was stated that the Kremlin is attempting to bypass President Reagan on arms control by going directly to Congress. The issues specifically mentioned were the nuclear test moratorium (which has crucial implications for SDI) and saving the SALT II treaty. The article reported that a joint resolution by the two houses of the Soviets' so-called legislative parliament was being sent to Congress urging a meeting soon to discuss the unratified SALT II treaty. Quoting from a speech presented to the Soviet parliament on this issue, former Soviet ambassador to the United States and now head of the CPSU's International Department Anatoly Dobrynin stated: "The United States Congress can and must play a role here. We would like to express the hope that the United States Congress and its members join in the demands that the government of the United States strictly comply with the existing Soviet-American agreements and refrain from the renunciation of international legal documents supporting the arms limitation process." Roxinne Ervasti, "On Test Moraturium, SALT II Soviets Trying to Bypass Reagan," Associated Press Report, *The Herald*, 21 June 1986, p. 2.

48. See for example: "On the United States' So-called 'Strategic Defense Initiative'," *Izvestiya*, 25 January 1985, translated in FBIS Daily Report: Soviet Union, 25 January 1985; A. Kokoshin, "Space and Security," *Pravda*, 29 January 1985, p. 4, translated in FBIS Daily Report: Soviet Union, 30 January 1985; V. Falin, "Fact and Fancy," *Izvestiya*, 10–11 April 1985, p. 5, translated in *FBIS Daily Report*: Soviet Union, 15,18 April 1985; A. Gromyko, *Pravda*, 20 February 1985, p. 2, *FBIS Daily Report*, 20 February 1985; V. Falin, *Izvestiya*, 14 July 1985, p. 5, *FBIS Daily Report*, 19 July 1985; A. Arbatov, "Limitation of ABM Systems: Problems, Lessons, and Prospects," *SShA: Ekonomika, Politika, Ideologika*, (December 1984), no. 12: pp. 16–18.

49. ABC News, *Nightline*, "Gorbachev and the Media," 3 October 1985, transcript of show #1139, pp. 5–6.

50. Letter from Michael Deane dated 19 July 1983 to an American intelligence official recounting his conversation with a Soviet military attaché. Dr. Deane is an expert on Soviet strategic defense and is the author of *Strategic Defense in Soviet Strategy*. The attaché was a regular visitor at Dr. Deane's office. According to Deane, the attaché stopped by approximately every four to six weeks. For those questioning whether language was a problem, causing misunderstanding about what was being discussed, Dr. Deane closed his letter with the following statement: "While I make no attempt to evaluate either the truth or the intent of his statements, I got the impression that the attaché was fully aware of what he was saying. His English is excellent. He made no attempt to dissuade me from the idea that the Soviets had broken [sic] the ABM Treaty." Selected sections of this letter can also be found in the Senate *Congressional Record*, 1 November 1985, p. S-14591.

51. Testimony of Ambassador Kenneth Adelman before United States Senate, Committee on Armed Services, *Soviet Treaty Violations*, (Washington, D.C.: U.S. Government Printing Office, 20 February and 7 May 1985), 99th Congress, 1st Session, p. 11.

52. Ibid.

53. Roman Kolkowicz, "The Soviet Union: The Elusive Adversary," in Kolkowicz and Mickiewicz, *The Soviet Calculus*; Robin F. Laird and Dale R. Herspring, *The Soviet Union and Strategic Arms* (Boulder, Colo.: Westview, 1984).
54. Newhouse, *Cold Dawn*, pp. 52–53.
55. Ibid., p. 53.
56. Ibid., p. 55.
57. Ibid., p. 56.
58. Ibid.
59. Viktor Suvorov, "GUSM: The Soviet Service of Strategic Deception," *International Defense Review*, 8(1985): p. 1237; Lee and Staar, *Soviet Military Policy*, p. 31; and Richards Heuer's chapter in this book. It is interesting to note that Suvorov alleges in his article that Lt. General K. Trusov was also a member of the Directorate for Strategic Deception. General Trusov was the second-ranking member of the SALT delegation and the officer who assumed General Ogarkov's duties when he did not return to round four of SALT. The reason for Ogarkov's absence in round four is interesting and may have been related to the opening of the "back channel".

John Newhouse's partial explanation in *Cold Dawn* for Ogarkov's absence is that between round three and four of the negotiations, the Party Congress was held in the Soviet Union and that Ogarkov was promoted from candidate member to full membership in the Central Committee. Also, according to Newhouse, he was known to be in the running for the job of chief of staff. Thus, in Newhouse's opinion, "Ogarkov. . . had became too important for SALT" (p. 212). Given the importance the military placed on SALT, at least to the extent they desired to control the negotiations, this may not have been the case. There may be an alternative explanation. The "back channel," which was set up between Soviet Ambassador to the United States Anatoly Dobrynin and Assistant to the President for National Security Affairs Henry Kissinger after the third round of SALT. This "channel" was initiated to discuss issues in a more informal and direct manner—in particular, issues that stalemated the official negotiations. It has been revealed through numerous memoirs of government officials that this back channel proved to be the factor that helped consummate SALT I. Thus, an alternative explanation for his absence may be that with the initiation of the back channel between rounds three and four, Ogarkov opted to stay in Moscow and monitor the talks between Dobrynin and Kissinger.

60. U.S. Arms Control and Disarmament Agency, *Arms Control and Disarmament Agreements: Texts and Histories of Agreements* (Washington, D.C.: U.S. Government Printing Office, 1982) p. 143.
61. U.S. Department of State, Bureau of Public Affairs, *The ABM Treaty and the SDI Program*, Current Policy No. 775 (Washington, D.C.: U.S. Government Printing Office, 22 October 1985).
61. See note 3 for violation studies. See also U.S. Senate, Committee on Armed Services, *Soviet Treaty Violations*, (Washington, D.C.: U.S. Government Printing Office, 20 February; 7 May 1985) 99th Congress, 1st Session; U.S. Senate, Special Hearing before the Committee on Appropriations, *SALT II Violations* (Washington, D.C.: U.S. Government Printing Office, 28 March 1984); U.S. Senate, Hearings before the Committee on Armed Services, *Soviet Treaty Violations* (Washington, D.C.: U.S. Government Printing Office, 14 March 1984); U.S. Senate, Hearings before the Committee on

Foreign Relations, *Briefing on SALT I Compliance* (Washington, D.C.: U.S. Government Printing Office, 25 September 1979); U.S. Senate, Hearings before the Committee on Armed Services, Subcommittee on Arms Control, *Soviet Compliance with Certain Provisions of the 1972 SALT I Agreements* (Washington, D.C.: U.S. Government Printing Office, 6 March 1975).

63. United States Department of State, Bureau of Public Affairs, *The ABM Treaty and the SDI Program*, p. 3.

12
Soviet Deception at MBFR: A Case Study

Richard F. Staar

> Negotiation with the Russians does occur, from time to time, but it requires no particular skill. The Russians are not to be persuaded by eloquence or convinced by reasoned arguments. They rely on what Stalin used to call the proper basis of international policy, the calculation of forces. So no case, however skillfully deployed, however clearly demonstrated as irrefutable, will move them from doing what they have previously decided to do; the only way of changing their purpose is to demonstrate that they have no advantageous alternative, that what they want to do is not possible. Negotiations with the Russians are therefore very mechanical; and they are probably better conducted on paper than by word of mouth.[1]
>
> —Sir William Hayter

In one of his weekly radio broadcasts, Ronald Reagan told the audience that the USSR refuses to admit existence of its own strategic defense program on which about 10,000 Soviet scientists and engineers are working. To quote the President:

> . . . This is not only deception, it is dangerous deception, for without a full picture of what is going on, the people of the world cannot know what they need to know to keep the peace.[2]

President Reagan gave a current illustration of strategic deception, past examples of which have included the 1962 official government statement via TASS that "there is no need for the Soviet Union to set up in any other country—Cuba, for instance—the weapons it has for repelling aggression, for a retaliatory blow."[3] At that very moment, Soviet intermediate-range nuclear missiles were being installed on Cuban soil. In two other cases of strategic deception, the USSR military invasions of Czechoslovakia (1968) and Afghanistan (1979), allegedly the Soviets had been invited by their respective communist party/government leaders. In the first instance, no such persons could ever be found; in the second, all were murdered by Soviet commando units.[4]

This chapter will be restricted to the tactics of deception and surprise, as the USSR and its client states in Eastern Europe have practiced them during the Mutual and Balanced Force Reduction (MBFR) talks at Vienna, Austria (now in their fourteenth year). Such tactics represent only a small part of the strategic relationship between arms control and deception. For example, then General N.V. Ogarkov held dual roles as military representative at the SALT II negotiations and as head of the chief directorate for *maskirovka* (deception) under the USSR General Staff in Moscow.[5]

That relationship exists on two levels at the MBFR talks in Vienna: (1) the petty intrigue, designed to make Western delegations more amenable at the game of negotiations in general, and (2) the role of these negotiations themselves in overall Soviet strategy. In terms of the latter, between 1981 and 1983, the USSR applied certain political tactics in the same manner at both the Intermediate-range Nuclear Force (INF) negotiations and the Strategic Arms Reduction Talks (START) in Geneva. According to the former chief Soviet INF negotiator, Iu. A. Kvitsinskii, a body subordinate to the Politburo dealt with arms control on a daily basis. He reportedly revealed that it included representatives from the military, the ruling party's central apparatus, the Foreign Affairs Ministry, and the State Security Committee (KGB).[6]

Although this group probably functions as a coordinating mechanism for external propaganda, the most important decisions regarding arms control negotiations are undoubtedly made by an ad hoc committee of five Political Bureau members, including CPSU General Secretary M.S. Gorbachev, Supreme Soviet Presidium Chairman A.A. Gromyko, KGB Chief V.M. Chebrikov, Foreign Minister E.A. Shevardnadze, and Defense Minister S.L. Sokolov.[7]

Framework for MBFR

The talks in Vienna began on 30 October 1973 among twelve delegations from the North Atlantic Treaty Organization (NATO) and seven from the Warsaw Treaty Organization (WTO), with the agreed objective of reducing conventional ground and air forces stationed in central Europe. The applicable area includes Belgium, the Netherlands, Luxembourg, and the Federal Republic of Germany in the West; and Czechoslovakia, the German Democratic Republic, and Poland in the East. Indigenous armed forces and those from other alliance members stationed in these countries would be subject to reductions.[8]

The main Western objective has been to eliminate the existing disparity in military personnel and to bring both sides down to equal levels. The most recent data in the public domain indicate that WTO has deployed 57 ground divisions with about 960,000 men, of whom approximately 475,000 are Soviet. By contrast, NATO has 25 divisions and about 790,000 troops, including approximately 200,000 Americans.[9] To rectify this destabilizing situation is the primary

Table 12-1
Disparity between Forces of Eastern and Western Direct Participants in the Reduction Area, 1 January 1981

Western Estimates	NATO Estimates of WTO Forces	NATO Figures of Western Forces	Disparity
Ground	960,000	790,000	170,000
Air	230,000	200,000	30,000
Total	1,190,000	990,000	200,000

Eastern Estimates	WTO Figures of WTO Forces	NATO Figures of Western Forces	Disparity
Ground	800,000	790,000	10,000
Air	180,000	200,000	-20,000
Total	980,000	990,000	-10,000

Source: U.S. Delegation to MBFR, appendix to "Mutual and Balanced Force Reductions" (Vienna, July 1983), mimeographed and unclassified report.

objective of the United States and its NATO allies at the Vienna talks. They think, perhaps naively, that parity can be attained, and they point to the East's acceptance of collective ceilings as a principle for each side: 700,000 ground, and 900,000 if air forces are included.

This agreement had been attained "in principle" after many years of frustrating talks that resulted in nothing tangible. Hence, the generality became an acceptable substitute for specificity. In practice, the USSR continued to pursue its original goals, and never has agreed to any details required for a mutually beneficial settlement. Such deception is not new; it has been experienced since World War II by numerous American officials.[10]

In order to finally begin negotiations, after nine long years of frustration, NATO approved a comprehensive draft treaty, which was submitted formally to the East in July 1982.[11] It provided for one agreement under which all direct participants would obligate themselves to reach the above-mentioned combined collective ceilings. Reductions would occur in stages, each fully verified by the other side. One agreement, instead of two, involved a concession by NATO, because each direct participant would specify the exact number of troops to be demobilized or sent back to its own country in the final treaty.

It remained for the East to respond with a new proposal that would settle one or both of the two major existing problems: data on numbers of ground and air personnel and associated measures. The only "achievement" on the data question had been reallocation of 20,000 to 30,000 Soviet troops from ground to air defense units.[12] The latest officially exchanged figures indicate an overall discrepancy totaling some 200,000 men (see table 12-1). Without agreement on data, it would be impossible to establish residual manpower levels.

Associated measures, including those of a confidence-building nature, are the other major obstacles to an agreement. In the West's draft treaty, these are enumerated as follows:[13]

1. Each side would notify the other in advance about out-of-garrison activity by one or more division-size formations. An exception, alert activities, would be announced only at the time when they begin.
2. The right to send observers to prenotified, out-of-garrison activities would be guaranteed to both sides.[14]
3. Major military movements by ground forces of those direct participants, whose home territory is outside the reduction area, into the area of reductions would also be prenotified.
4. Each side would have the right to conduct an annual quota of inspections on the territory of the other side in the area of reductions. Inspection teams would conduct their surveys from the ground, air, or both.
5. Permanent exit/entry points would be established to monitor military movements into and out of the area. Observers would be stationed at these points for the duration of the treaty.
6. Information would be exchanged on forces to be withdrawn. There would be continuing periodic exchanges of information on personnel strength and organization of forces in the reduction area.
7. A provision would prohibit interference with national technical means of verification (that is, photography from reconnaissance satellites).[15]

In addition, the West indicated that participants should consider establishment of a consultative group to oversee implementation of the provisions in the agreement. If the model were to become the United States-USSR Standing Consultative Commission (SCC), established in 1972 for monitoring adherence to the first Strategic Arms Limitation Treaty (SALT I), such a group would meet only twice a year.[16] Even that arrangement has not worked out, because the USSR representatives refuse to discuss their government's arms control violations, which they deny ever having taken place.

Contrary to Western expectations that the Soviet Union and its client states in Eastern Europe would accept the NATO draft treaty as a basis for serious negotiations, Warsaw Pact representatives spent a full year criticizing it for various imaginary shortcomings. They refused to engage in any discussion of specific provisions. The West's proposal was finally rejected as the basis for an agreement, even though it had never been presented on a take-it-or-leave-it basis.[17]

Why do the Soviets bother to remain at the talks in Vienna? It is known that they came unwillingly, as a price for the Conference on Security and Cooperation in Europe (CSCE), which resulted in the 1975 Final Act at Helsinki. However, they refuse to negotiate an equitable MBFR agreement that would provide a measure of security for both sides by reducing ground and air forces to equal levels. The USSR idea of associated measures includes:

No first use of weapons,

Prohibition of attacks against countries outside the two alliances,

A ban on threats to international communications and on surprise attacks,

Exchange of military visits, and

Increased support of the United Nations.[18]

These are all general propositions, many of which have been written into the UN Charter and the CSCE agreement.

Whether such declaratory statements have any relevance to the situation in Central Europe is not really important. They are advanced by the East to project the deceptive image of a peace-loving Warsaw Treaty Organization that is threatened by an aggressive NATO preparing to attack the Soviet Union. Apart from the marking of time at MBFR, attempts have also been made to split the Western alliance and to use the talks as a propaganda forum from which adversaries are accused of doing exactly what the USSR itself does. In short, none of these activities has anything to do with concluding an agreement in Vienna. An agreement is always possible, of course, on Soviet terms.

Examples of Deception

Deception schemes predate the communist regime, and examples can be found from the time of imperial rule in Russia. At the early nineteenth century Congress of Vienna, Tsar Alexander called for complete and general disarmament.[19] He did not expect, of course, that any European government would respond positively. The Soviets also have repeated earlier tsarist proposals made at the 1899 Hague Conference for a temporary freeze on armed forces and for government appropriations to be allocated to disarmament. The propaganda dividends from these tsarist and communist proposals have been significant. However, their lack of practicality has resulted in the antithesis to disarmament, as evidenced in two successive world wars during the first half of the twentieth century.

When the Soviets refused to set the time for the next round of MBFR talks in Vienna before the December 1983 break, as had been customary in the past, they were simply following the pattern established earlier at INF and START in Geneva. The fact that NATO did not see through this deception (that is, the

West thought it had to pay a price for a return to the negotiating table) seems obvious from what followed. Secretary of State George P. Shultz met with Foreign Minister Andrei A. Gromyko in January 1984 at the opening of the Conference on Disarmament in Europe (CDE) in Stockholm, and they agreed that MBFR would be resumed during mid-March. It can only be speculated whether or not Gromyko had been told of the next concession.

A month later, the West submitted a new proposal that provided for an exchange of data only on ground combat and combat support forces.[20] This excluded ground combat service support elements and air force personnel. NATO offered to accept the Warsaw Pact's own figures for the latter's ground troops within an "acceptable range" of Western data estimates (between 5 and 10 percent), rather than reaching a full agreement on precise figures. The exchange of information would be preceded by definitions of new categories for the data breakdown, altering the framework under which ground forces would be counted by both sides.

The East's deception (that agreement could be reached if NATO made only one more concession) dispelled itself seven months later when the Soviet ambassador to MBFR made the following statement:

> . . . The NATO April [1984] proposal not only doesn't remove previous obstacles barring progress, but also erects additional ones. It does not lead to an agreement. The materialization of it would bring about accelerating the arms race [sic] and new difficulties rather than lowering military confrontation and improving the situation in Europe.[21]

The heads of Warsaw Pact delegations at MBFR showed a preference for dissembling rather than outright lies, something they probably learned from their USSR mentors.[22] Soon after our arrival in Vienna, the Soviet and East European ambassadors all assured me that an agreement would be reached within the two years of our stay, which, as they had found out, would be limited to the period allowed by Stanford University regulations for leave-of-absence. The purpose behind this low-level deception obviously involved an attempt to make one anxious to cooperate in achieving agreement at any cost.

This question of time is based on completely different concepts. Soviet and East European representatives at MBFR were more than willing to meet their Western counterparts and repeat meaningless phrases that had been memorized. Certain diplomats from NATO countries, after delay and boredom, tended to want an agreement that would postpone resolution of the key issues. The point is that "one cannot negotiate successfully with Soviet representatives against a fixed deadline."[23]

Another case of attempted low-level deception occurred when the chief of the USSR political section, V.M. Baskakov, arrived at our residence, inebriated, about a half-hour before the traditional reception opening the autumn negotiating round was to begin. He requested a private conversation in the library. Baskakov stated that no agreements would be reached in either Vienna or Geneva, because President Reagan had made the Soviet leaders look like "fools."[24] When asked who in Moscow had made the decision, he claimed that the following agencies involved in the decision making process had arrived at a consensus: the Ministry of Foreign Affairs (First Deputy Minister G.M. Kornienko); the General Staff's International Treaty Department (Colonel General N.F. Chervov);[25] the CPSU central apparatus (L.M. Zamiatin, the head of the International Information Department; and possibly V. V. Zagladin, the First Deputy Chief of the International Department); and the KGB (either G.K. Tsinev or N.P. Emokhonov, both First Deputy Chairmen).[26]

Baskakov's slurred "warning" involved deception, because at the ensuing party he repeated the same story to other United States delegation members in the presence of a Czech. The head of the Soviet political section must have had good connections with the KGB, because his notorious drunkenness and womanizing reportedly had never been punished by means of a recall to Moscow. It should be noted that other USSR diplomats transmitted similar warnings at about the same time to U.S. Ambassadors Paul Nitze at INF and Edward L. Rowny at START, both in Geneva.

An example of high-level deception occurred when a top official from Washington, D.C., visited Vienna. He showed greater interest in, and more knowledge of, MBFR than on his previous visit. A luncheon at an elegant hotel, paid from U.S. delegation funds, provided the setting for USSR Ambassador Mikhailov to float an old idea concerning token and asymmetrical reductions: the Soviets would withdraw 20,000 troops from East Germany if the Americans removed only 13,000 from West Germany. Once that had taken place, data and associated measures would be quickly agreed upon.

Despite a warning that all of this had been proposed to my predecessor and really involved nothing new, the Washington official became euphoric and even suggested to our Soviet guests that he and I travel to Moscow for a meeting with his counterpart. A one-page reconstruction of Mikhailov's proposal, sent to the USSR ambassador's Vienna office by the Washington official, came back initialed, with only a single comma added. Of course, nothing was ever heard from Moscow. The ploy did accomplish something: it wasted the time of many high-ranking Americans among whom the deceptive "proposal" had circulated in the executive branch of government.

Inversions of Truth

One day, in the course of the informal weekly meeting between three Western and three Eastern heads of delegations, the USSR representative asked a series of questions about the latest United States, British, and Federal Republic of

Germany deployments in the reduction area. He promised that the Warsaw Pact would answer corresponding inquiries. It took considerable time to obtain the answers from the Western capitals involved, where the interagency coordination process applies. Before reading this unclassified information, prepared in the form of three papers to be delivered at one of the weekly informal meetings, the NATO ad hoc group agreed upon a corresponding series of questions about Soviet deployments in East Germany. Details were requested concerning developments that had been reported in the public domain. The Soviet ambassador to MBFR told us that he would send the queries to Moscow. Needless to say, the West is still waiting, more than three years later, for the answers. So much for reciprocity and good faith.

The leitmotif in all exchanges with the East has included the phrase "political will," which, translated into understandable English, simply means "make yet another concession." The NATO draft treaty of 8 July 1982 initially evoked an impromptu comment at the formal weekly meeting in the Hofburg by Ambassador Mikhailov that this represented "a step in the right direction." That phrase has never been repeated, and it is possible that the Soviet head of delegation may have received a reprimand in Moscow during the summer recess—or, it could have been yet another example of gross deception, hinting at future flexibility by the USSR.

When the talks resumed in September, the East began an orchestrated and methodical attack (mentioned in the foregoing) on the NATO draft treaty that lasted a full year. Warsaw Pact spokesmen found nothing positive in a document that exemplified the goodwill of the West, probably a naive American attitude in retrospect. Finally, on 21 July 1983, a spokesman from Czechoslovakia rejected the draft treaty as a basis for agreement.[27] Throughout this period, the East dropped hints that it would allow on-site inspections if the West eased its stance on data. As noted previously, the new (April 1984) NATO concession on this issue received a prompt rejection. One wonders where a senior associate at the Carnegie Endowment for International Peace in Washington, D.C. found the basis for a report that the Soviets have agreed to "more on-site inspections" at MBFR in Vienna.[28]

Another instance of blatant falsehood at one of the weekly informal meetings included the charge that American nuclear weapons had been pre-positioned in Norway. The Soviets knew that this was a lie. Even if the United States had wanted to place such weapons on Norwegian territory, the official and openly proclaimed policy in Oslo against such pre-positioning would have represented an insurmountable obstacle.

On other occasions, the rule of confidentiality that had been agreed upon between West and East was breached by Warsaw Pact spokesmen in the Thursday afternoon press conferences at the Hofburg. Frequently, matters that had been discussed *in camera* surfaced in the press briefings given by Eastern public affairs officials. Their target, of course, were the journalists from Western

Europe and the United States who attended these press conferences. Any distortion that appeared in a non-communist newspaper represented a net advantage to the USSR.

Attempts to Split NATO Unity

One sustained effort on the part of Soviet and East European representatives involved a diplomat from a NATO country who had spent many years in Vienna at MBFR. This man honestly believed that he had built a reservoir of credibility with Warsaw Pact delegation heads. To maintain this obvious self-delusion, he frequently would block decisions at the ad hoc group meetings, where consensus actually meant unanimity. An informal protest from the U.S. Department of State may have contributed to this diplomat's subsequent transfer to another country.

A less complicated effort to accomplish the same objective occurred when the West German embassy in Moscow received an invitation from the USSR Ministry of Foreign Affairs to begin bilateral negotiations on MBFR. The Bonn government rejected this overture, which would have been implemented within the framework of the Soviet-West German Commission, because the latter only dealt with economic and scientific cooperation.

An occurrence at the home of an East European ambassador could have led to this writer becoming a target. After a heavy dinner, the northern tier (Czechoslovakia, East Germany, and Poland) representatives conducted a long debate about the MBFR negotiations. They attempted to convey the impression that each had a position independent from that of the Soviet Union, whose ambassador conveniently had not been invited to the dinner. The Czech even went so far as to suggest that the U.S. delegation might want to avail itself of him as an intermediary for passing on messages to the USSR delegation, as if we were incapable of talking directly to Ambassador Mikhailov.

Conclusions

Why does the USSR favor arms control talks? Some contend that the possibility of a new detente or resumption of the seven-year period after 1972 in Soviet-American relations may be the objective. This allegedly would provide for renewed access to trade and technology from the West, and such agreements could place restraints on an "unpredictable" United States. Under these circumstances in the past, the USSR always obtained the better end of the bargain. The reason it is so difficult to negotiate with the Soviets is because they

> . . . have always had a fundamentally different approach toward diplomacy from that of their Western colleagues. To them diplomacy is more than an

instrument for protecting and advancing national interest; it is a weapon in the unremitting war against capitalist society. Diplomatic negotiations, therefore, cannot aim at real understanding and agreement; and this has profound effects upon their nature and techniques.[29]

This basic world outlook colors the USSR approach to negotiations with the West. The Soviet diplomat functions as "a mechanical mouthpiece for views and demands formulated in Moscow."[30] He is a functionary, bound by rigid instructions, who does not search for "compromise" (as a matter of fact, that word does not exist in the native Russian vocabulary). Rather than admit the foregoing, USSR negotiators engage in constant deception on this score.

A retired American career foreign service officer, who is considered one of the foremost experts on the Soviet Union, has written some rules of behavior that are based on his many years of experience. His rules include the following:[31]

1. Do not attempt to form close friendships with the Soviets.
2. Do not assume a "community of aims."
3. Do not make goodwill gestures.
4. Make our displeasure felt when requests are rejected.
5. Support our lower-level officials in their dealings with Kremlin bureaucrats.
6. Do not initiate high-level conferences unless 50 percent of the initiatives come from the Russian side; and
7. Do not be afraid to take strong stands on "minor" issues.

In view of this, what does one do when faced with deception? Pretending that it is nonexistent or making excuses for the USSR has only led to strengthening the contempt in which the United States is held. The American negotiator must tell his counterpart that he sees through the deceptive techniques and must expose them openly at the conference table.

Notes

1. Sir William Hayter [former British Ambassador to Moscow], "Goldfish in Moscow," *The Observer* (London) 2 October 1960, p. 5.
2. Cited in *The New York Times*, 13 October 1985, p. 16.
3. TASS Statement in *Pravda*, 12 September 1962, pp. 1–2.
4. Richard F. Staar, *USSR Foreign Policies After Detente* (Stanford, Calif: Hoover Institution Press, 1985), pp. 6–7.
5. Richards J. Heuer, Jr., "Soviet Organization and Doctrine for Strategic Deception," chapter 2 in this book. See also Roger Beaumont, *Maskirovka: Soviet Camouflage, Concealment and Deception*, Stratech Study Series No. SS82-1 (College Station: Center for Strategic Technology, Texas Engineering Experiment Station, Texas A&M University, November 1982).

6. Quoted by Paul Nitze, "Living With the Soviets," *Foreign Affairs* 63 (Winter 1984/85), p. 362.

7. Listed as having met with the three chief USSR negotiators from the Geneva talks, in order to issue "the necessary directives" for the next round. TASS Report, "In the CPSU Central Committee," *Pravda*, 17 September 1985, p. 1.

8. Richard F. Staar, "The MBFR Process and Its Prospects," in R. F. Staar, ed., *Arms Control: Myth versus Reality* (Stanford, Calif: Hoover Institute Press, 1984), pp. 47–58.

9. International Institute for Strategic Studies (IISS), *The Military Balance, 1985–1986* (London: IISS, November 1985), pp. 182–187.

10. Philip E. Mosely, "Soviet Techniques of Negotiation," in Raymond Dennett and Joseph E. Johnson, eds., *Negotiating With the Russians* (Boston: World Peace Foundation, 1951), p. 289.

11. The West's draft treaty is summarized in U.S. Congress, House Committee on Foreign Affairs, Subcommittee on International Security and Scientific Affairs, *East-West Troop Reductions in Europe: Is Agreement Possible?*, Report prepared by the Foreign Affairs and National Defense Division, Congressional Research Service, Library of Congress, 98th Cong., 1st sess., Committee Print (Washington, D.C.: U.S. Government Printing Office, 1983), appendix A, pp. 21–25.

12. Lothar Ruehl, "MBFR: Lessons and Problems," *Adelphi Papers*, no. 176 (London: IISS, Summer 1982), p. 29.

13. R.F. Staar, *Arms Control*, pp. 52–54; and Richard E. Darilek, "Separate Processes, Converging Interests: MBFR and CBM's," in Hans Guenter Brach and Duncan L. Clarke, eds., *Decisionmaking for Arms Limitations: Assessments and Prospects* (Cambridge, Mass: Ballinger, 1983), pp. 237–257.

14. NATO proposed that measures one and two cover territory of all European participants in the Vienna talks, not only those in the reduction area, and that they should include a considerable part of the western Soviet Union.

15. Hans-Joachim Schuetz, *Militaerische Vertrauensbildende Massnahmen aus Voelkerrechtlicher Sicht* [*Military Confidence Building Measures from the Point of View of International Law*] (Berlin: Duncker & Humblot, 1984), pp. 107–111.

16. "Treaty Between the United States of America and the Union of the Soviet Socialist Republics on the Limitation of Anti-Ballistic Missile Systems: Article XIII," in U.S. Arms Control and Disarmament Agency, *Arms Control and Disarmament Agreements: Texts and Histories of Negotiations* (Washington, D.C.: ACDA, 1982), pp. 141–142.

17. This occurred at an end-of-round press conference in the Vienna Hofburg. For details, see *Transcript* (21 July 1983), pp. 22–23, prepared by the U.S. Delegation to MBFR in Vienna, Austria; mimeographed and unclassified.

18. Listed by O.N. Bykov, *Mery doveriia* [*Confidence Building Measures*] (Moscow: Nauka, 1983), p. 71; and V.L. Shvetsov, *Voennaia razriadka i mery doveriia* [*Reduction of Military Tensions and Confidence Building Measures*] (Moscow: Mezhdunarodnye otnosheniia, 1984), pp. 71–84.

19. Harold G. Nicolson, *The Congress of Vienna: A Study in Allied Unity, 1812–1822* (New York: Harcourt Brace, 1946), 312 pp.

20. *The New York Times*, 19 April 1984, pp. 1 and 12.

21. V.V. Mikhailov, quoted in USSR press release, 15 November 1984; USSR embassy, Vienna, Austria.

22. William T. Shinn, Jr., "On the Russians and Their Ways," *Washington Quarterly* 8(Winter 1985): pp. 5–6.

23. Arthur H. Dean, "Soviet Diplomatic Style and Tactics," in U.S., Congress, Senate, Committee on Government Operations, Subcommittee on National Security and International Operations, *The Soviet Approach to Negotiations: Selected Writings*, 91st Cong., 1st Sess. (Washington, D.C.: U.S. Government Printing Office, 1969), p. 63.

24. Baskakov actually used a vulgar Russian expression.

25. Private conversation with the U.S. Ambassador to the Soviet Union, Arthur A. Hartmann, who gave this writer Chervov's name.

26. Former INF negotiator, Iu. A. Kvitsinskii, revealed that a body subordinate to the Politburo deals with arms control on a daily basis, and includes these constituencies. Nitze, "Living With the Soviets," p. 362. The names appear in R.F. Staar, *USSR Foreign Policies After Detente*, figure 5.1, pp. 90–91.

27. *Transcript*, pp. 22–23; cited in Note 17.

28. Michael Krepon in *Christian Science Monitor*, 8 August 1985, p. 6.

29. Gordon Craig, "Totalitarian Approaches to Diplomatic Negotiation," in A.O. Sarkissian, ed., *Studies in Diplomatic History and Historiography in Honour of G.P. Gooch* (London: Longmans, Green, 1961), p. 119; cited by U.S. Congress, House of Representatives, Committee on Foreign Affairs, *Soviet Diplomacy and Negotiating Behavior: Emerging New Context for U.S. Diplomacy* 1, House Doc. no. 96–238, 96th Cong., 1st sess., Special Studies Series on Foreign Affairs Issues, prepared by the Senior Specialists' Division, Congressional Research Service, Library of Congress (Washington, D.C.: U.S. Government Printing Office, 1980), pp. 5–6, 10.

30. Mosely, "Soviet Negotiating Techniques," p. 229.

31. George F. Kennan, *Memoirs*, vol. 1 (Boston: Little, Brown, 1967), p. 291, cited in *Negotiating With the Russians*, pp. 235–237.

Part IV
The Soviet Military and *Maskirovka*

13
The Role of Deception in Soviet Military Planning

Notra Trulock III

Introduction

The role of deception in Soviet military planning is a subject of increasing importance for U.S. and NATO decision makers and defense planners. Soviet military theory has long valued the role of deception; a number of recent Western defense initiatives, however, would seem to have greatly enhanced Soviet incentives to further develop deception techniques. In recent years, efforts have been undertaken to modify strategies and concepts governing the employment of both strategic nuclear and theater-level forces. Many of these concepts, however, would appear to be especially susceptible to Soviet deception efforts.

The degree to which the Soviets value deception has been well documented by Western analysts.[1] Much of this analysis has dealt with specific examples of Soviet deception attempts in a somewhat anecdotal fashion. These analyses have been devoted, in large part, to Soviet attempts to evade arms control compliance or to conceal actual capabilities of, for example, their strategic nuclear systems.[2] Although extremely valuable, these analyses provide few insights into the Soviet theory of deception or the Soviet view of the potential contribution of deception to military success.

Considerable attention has also been devoted to detailed descriptions of the specific methods, techniques, and materials that might be employed in Soviet deception efforts.[3] These analyses have tended to focus somewhat more upon the tactics of Soviet deception and less upon the operational dimensions of Soviet deception theory. Again, although enormously useful, especially to operators in the field, these analyses reveal little with regard to Soviet deception theory.

The objective of this chapter, therefore, will be to provide some insights into the Soviet view of the role of deception in military planning. It will identify the key elements of the Soviet theory of deception, its role and place in military planning, and potential deception objectives. Soviet criteria and requirements for evaluating the effectiveness of deception planning will also be discussed. In particular, it will attempt to depict the degree to which the Soviets have systematized a theory of deception. Finally, some possible implications for Western defense planning will be discussed.

Sources

Obviously, given the nature and sensitivity of the subject, the Soviets are not exceedingly forthcoming about their theory and practice of deception. Nevertheless, increasing Soviet interest in the subject in recent years has led to the publication of a number of articles in Soviet military journals as well as several book-length treatments of operational deception—some by prominent Soviet military theoreticians. The former editor of the important Soviet journal, *Military-Historical Journal*, published a book and several articles on deception in the mid-to-late 1970's. In 1982, the chief of the Frunze Academy published a major article on operational deception, and the Soviet Ground Forces journal, *Military Herald*, has devoted articles to deception—especially during its 1984 thematic discussion of combat support activities. Scattered references to the role of deception also may be found in other Soviet works setting forth Soviet conclusions on military art and military science, as well as Soviet perceptions of Western military theory and practice.

It is not surprising that none of these publications provide detailed descriptions of current Soviet intentions and deceptive practices. Instead, these analyses have focused on the Soviet wartime experience with deception in considerable detail. The reasons for this approach should be quite clear. The shift in Soviet military thinking away from an excessive preoccupation with global nuclear warfare to a more flexible approach to military planning created a requirement for renewed attention to historical experiences. Soviet interests in and incentives for conventional warfare have increased to the point that a prominent Soviet military scientist recently declared that a "comparatively long conventional war" with the West is considered a distinct possibility.[4] The Soviets believe that their experiences in the Great Patriotic War are useful for the investigation of modern concepts for strategic leadership, operational maneuver groups, strategic operations, and other characteristics of the contemporary Soviet approach to theater warfare. Similarly, the Soviets have concluded that their use of deception in the Great Patriotic War offers a rich data base for modern deception efforts.

Lest the reader miss the point, Soviet authors always include a reminder of the relevance of the wartime experience for contemporary operations. Soviet military spokesmen all agree on the importance of careful attention to their wartime experience. General Matsuylenko, for example, concluded his major study of operational deception, published in 1975, with the following observation: "The experience of the conduct of operational maskirovka in operations of the former war has urgent significance for the combat preparation of troops in the contemporary stage."[5] Similarly, General Mel'nikov concluded, in 1982: "The experience of the organization and conduct of operational maskirovka in the years of the Great Patriotic War has the greatest value for contemporary military art."[6] Contemporary military theoreticians and field commanders are exhorted to study and analyze this experience for its relevance to modern battlefield conditions.

> The rich experience of the Great Patriotic war must be studied in detail, generalized and used in the course of combat and political preparation of all the arms of service and services of the Armed Forces taking into account the development and qualitative changes in the means of armed conflict.[7]

In particular, the Soviets have derived a set of criteria and requirements from their wartime experiences by which to judge the potential effectiveness of contemporary deception efforts.

It would seem useful, therefore, to focus upon these Soviet analyses to understand the lessons Soviet military theoreticians have derived from this experience. Soviet accounts of their experience with deception in exercises conducted during the postwar period are equally interesting, but much more scarce. The formerly classified Soviet General Staff journal, *Voyennaya Mysl'* also published a number of articles on the general subject of deception during the late 1960's and early 1970's. These articles tended to reinforce the basic Soviet premise that deception is an integral part of any successful military operation.

Development of Soviet Deception Theory

Soviet military planners have long appreciated the potential contribution of successful deception to the favorable outcome of battles, operations, and even entire military campaigns. Contemporary Soviet sources indicate that the Soviet military had elaborated a theory of deception as early as the 1920's. Many of the most prominent Soviet military theoreticians of the period participated in deception research. In particular, Marshals Tukhachevskiy and Svechin are often cited for their contributions to the development of Soviet deception theory. Much of this theory was developed as part of the wider analyses of the experiences of both World War I and the Civil War that contributed to the overall development of Soviet military theory. Deception research progressed rapidly, however, and by the mid–1920's, the Soviets had concluded that the "basic method for the achievement of surprise was operational deception."[8]

Further, the Soviets elaborated and published, in 1924, the basic principles for the conduct and organization of operational deception in future wars.[9]

The value of deception was apparently a subject of considerable controversy during this early period. Some in the Soviet military believed that the advent of maneuver warfare in the late 1920's and early 1930's would reduce the value of strategic deception, in particular. For example, the reduced role of deception in modern warfare was discussed in a 1936 analysis of strategic surprise and reconnaissance. The author, M.P. Galaktionov, believed that the potential for deception in the deployment of mass armies had been greatly reduced in comparison with past wars.[10] According to Galaktionov, this was the result not only of improving reconnaissance and communication capabilities but also of the increased maneuver capabilities of the potential enemy, which reduced his reaction times.

Prior to the war, however, the Soviets received some practical experience in the conduct of deception that served to dispel any doubts as to its future role in military planning. In particular, the use of deception at the battle of Khalkin-Gol River ensured the success of Soviet operations against the Japanese. Many of the principles and organizational methods later employed in the Great Patriotic War were first tested at Khalkin-Gol. In particular, the Soviets gained experience in the cover and concealment of the preparations for offensive operations, including the regrouping and concentration of forces, the preparation of assembly areas, and the selection of the main axes of attack.[11] The Soviets went to considerable lengths in devising their disinformation campaign, the objectives of which were to persuade the Japanese that Soviet preparations were of a strictly defensive nature.

According to Marshal Zhukov's account of the battle:

> We attempted to create by these [deception] measures the impression on the enemy of the absence on our side of any type of preparations of an offensive character, to show that we were conducting wide spread work on the construction of defenses, and only defenses.[12]

To this end, the Soviets conducted a number of activities, including the preparation of defensive positions and the widespread distribution of a pamphlet entitled "What the Soviet Soldier Must Know in Defense."[13]

As a result of this experience as well as of their theoretical research, the Soviets had succeeded in developing the basic principles of the organization and conduct of deception well before the Great Patriotic War. Many of these principles were incorporated in both the Draft Field Regulations of 1936 and the Field Regulations of 1940. These, in turn, were updated on the basis of the wartime experience in 1943 and 1944.[14]

Contemporary Soviet sources organize their analyses of the wartime experience in accordance with the Soviet characterization of the three periods of the war. The evolution of the Soviet approach to deception was characterized during the war by:

An increase in both the scope and the scale of employment of deception,

The steady improvement of the methods and organizational procedures for deception,

The gradual adoption of an integrated approach to deception measures in the place of individual, uncoordinated activities,

The emergence of special planning activities and the creation of special planning groups to direct deception in place of the ad hoc approach of the beginning of the war.

Retrospective Soviet analyses reveal a high degree of satisfaction with the wartime experience with deception. The Soviets have used this experience to draw certain conclusions regarding the overall application of deception in modern warfare. According to General Matsuylenko's 1975 study of operational deception:

The experience of the Great Patriotic war shows that the skillful application of integrated measures for operational deception is the most important means of achieving surprise; it enables the successful fulfillment of combat missions in defensive and offensive operations, it reduces personnel and military equipment losses, [and] it forces the enemy to make wrong decisions which lead him to destruction.[15]

It is to this data base that the Soviets turn for their analyses of the role of deception in modern military planning.

Contemporary Soviet Views on Deception

A starting point for investigation of contemporary Soviet views on military deception would appear to be current Soviet definitions of related terminology. The Soviets use the nearly untranslatable Russian word *maskirovka* to convey what Western analysts mean by deception. The Soviet concept is, however, broader and includes camouflage, cover, and denial. The most recent Soviet reference work, the 1983 *Soviet Military-Encyclopedic Dictionary*, defines *maskirovka* as "A complex of measures for misleading the enemy with regard to the presence and disposition of troops [forces], military objectives [targets], their status, combat readiness and activities and also the plans of the command."[16]

Soviet military reference works consistently define *maskirovka* as a type of combat support activity. These activities are designed to create favorable conditions for the successful conduct of operations [battles], the effective use of the means of armed struggle, the preservation of high combat readiness, the prevention or warning of an enemy surprise attack, and also a reduction in the effectiveness of his strikes on friendly forces.[17]

Other types of combat support activities include reconnaissance, defense against weapons of mass destruction, and radioelectronic combat. The categorization of *maskirovka* as a combat support activity has a number of implications for the comprehension of the modern Soviet view. In particular, as a support activity, the objectives of the *maskirovka* plan would be coordinated with the overall plan for the campaign, strategic operation, or frontal forces offensive operation. Soviet military commanders, as a result, would not allow *maskirovka* planning to override the basic military requirements associated with operational planning. Instead, *maskirovka* planning would be designed to ensure the success of the overall operational plan.

Soviet military theoreticians have identified three basic objectives for successful *maskirovka* planning. First, it must contribute to the achievement of surprise. Second, it must contribute to the preservation of the combat effectiveness of Soviet forces. Third, it must contribute to the survivability of Soviet forces. The Soviet organization, planning, and implementation of *maskirovka* parallels the structure of Soviet military art, which comprises strategy, operational art, and tactics. Accordingly, *maskirovka* may be planned and conducted at strategic, operational, and tactical levels. The objectives of each are described in Soviet sources as follows:

> Strategic *maskirovka* . . . preserve the secrecy of preparations for operations and campaigns, and also for the disorientation of the enemy with regard to the actual intention and actions of the armed forces.
>
> Operational *maskirovka* . . . support the secrecy of the preparation of operations.
>
> Tactical *maskirovka* . . . conceal the preparations of battle or the presence [disposition] of targets.[18]

By definition, therefore, the demands on *maskirovka* would appear to be most intense prior to the initiation of the battle, engagement, or strategic operation. One of the key tenets of the Soviet approach, however, is that *maskirovka* must be planned and conducted for the entire duration and entire depth of the operation.

Beyond the objectives stated in Soviet military reference works, however, the Soviet view of the basic objective of *maskirovka* would appear to focus primarily on the exercise of control over the perceptions and actions of an opponent. The establishment and maintenance of control ranks as one of the preeminent objectives of Soviet military planning. Soviet military theoreticians have elevated the role of control to a place of decisive importance in contemporary military affairs. In particular, the Soviets believe that the correlation of forces of the opposing sides is determined not just by the relative *potentials* of the sides, but the degree to which these *potentials* may be converted into actual military capabilities. This, in turn, depends primarily upon the effectiveness of the system of control.[19]

In the development of these views, Soviet attention is focused not just on control of their own forces and actions but also on control of the actions of their opponents. This is a principle long recognized in Soviet military planning; by the 1930's, Soviet military theoreticians had already concluded that it was a key to military success:

> Genuine control of a combat engagement should constitute control of the entire process of combat, that is, not only of one's own actions but to a certain degree the actions of the opponent as well, forced upon him by our actions.[20]

The Soviets have identified a number of methods to achieve this objective, including early seizure of the initiative, continuous pressure on the battlefield, or the unanticipated introduction of new weapons and combat methods.

One of the primary methods, however, is the use of deception and concealment. "In warfare, control of an opponent's actions is achieved by deluding the enemy as to one's intentions, capabilities, state, and actions of troops; concealment of their actual position by means of dummy, decoy, feinting actions."[21] Soviet attention to the role of *maskirovka* in modern warfare, therefore, would appear to be stimulated primarily by the potential it affords for the introduction of uncertainty into enemy decision making and the accompanying delay in decision cycles.

Soviet investigations into the impact of *maskirovka* on enemy decision making have focused primarily on this dimension. In a 1971 article in the General Staff journal *Voyennaya Mysl'*, the author argued that a well-planned *maskirovka* campaign could disrupt the effectiveness of the enemy's decision-making cycle.

> Neutralization of the opponent's deduction, increasing the uncertainty of our intentions, on the one hand makes it more difficult for the opponent to shape the objectives of his actions, and on the other hand disrupts the algorithm [sequence] of his decision making, requiring additional effort and more time to reach a well-founded decision.[22]

Soviet military theoreticians have long believed that the nature of modern armaments has greatly reduced the time available to an opponent to react to a Soviet strike or maneuver; even a moderately successful *maskirovka* effort would appear to have a multiplicative effect in this regard. Beyond this, however, the Soviets have clearly concluded that it is possible to conceal the overall intent of a strategic operation until very late in the operation. This article refers to a number of techniques for the achievement of this objective, including the introduction of "a large number of possible variants [of Soviet action], all of which, in spite of their diversity, should be more or less equally probable."[23]

One example of this approach was given as the "movement of a large number of hostile aircraft into an area which does not contain air defense installations, but which does open up routes to two or three important areas presents commanders with a difficult logical problem of determining the opponent's real intentions."[24]

Another approach might involve the selection of a secondary strategic axis which, nevertheless, contains important objectives. The value of this approach lies in the fact that it "enhances the value of the plan of operations by compelling the opponent to scatter his forces for defense."[25]

Maskirovka, therefore, appears to be valued primarily for its contribution to the disruption and delay of the enemy's decision-making cycle and the prevention of the development of a "well-founded decision." Successful fulfillment of this objective would not only enhance surprise but would also contribute directly to the survivability of Soviet forces and the preservation of combat effectiveness.

Soviet planning for the organization and implementation of *maskirovka* is conducted in accordance with the categories of strategic, operational, and tactical deception. There appears to have been some controversy in the late 1960's within the Soviet military as to the overall responsibility for deception. At the strategic level, it has been reported that responsibility was shifted from the Main Operations Directorate of the Soviet General Staff to a new General Staff directorate created especially to oversee *maskirovka* efforts.[26] According to this account, this reorganization of the Soviet management of *maskirovka* was undertaken to increase the creativity of the Soviet approach and also in recognition of the increasing importance of its role in modern military planning.[27]

Soviet sources indicate that wartime strategic *maskirovka* would be planned and executed by the STAVKA of the Supreme High Command (VGK). This strategic command echelon is solely responsible for the direction of the planning and execution of the activities of the Soviet Armed Forces. Articles in the Soviet military press have referred repeatedly to the role of the STAVKA VGK in the conduct of the successful strategic *maskirovka* efforts of the Great Patriotic War. Marshal Kulikov, the commander-in-chief of the Warsaw Pact, has credited the STAVKA VGK with planning responsibilities for both the "strategic disinformation of the enemy" and the development of the operational *maskirovka* plan.[28] More recently, army General Mayorov, the First Deputy Commander in Chief of the Ground Forces, has written of the measures taken by the wartime STAVKA VGK to mislead the enemy and to ensure the success of Soviet strategic plans. According to Mayorov, these included:

The preservation in secret of Soviet intentions, through operational maskirovka, secrecy of the concentration of forces, disinformation of the enemy, support of force actions on sectors, where the enemy did not anticipate an offensive, the use of dummy regroupings [of forces], and the use of methods of combat activities unanticipated by the enemy.[29]

The memoirs of senior Soviet wartime commanders such as Marshals Zhukov and Vasilevskiy also provide insights into the Soviet approach to the planning and execution of strategic deception. All of the major campaigns and strategic operations of the war featured major *maskirovka* efforts. Moreover, before the initiation of the Manchurian Campaign in 1945, the Soviets undertook a major transfer of forces from the western to the eastern part of the USSR under the complete cover of a strategic deception plan.[30]

The Soviets emphasize that the number of participants in the development of the strategic *maskirovka* plan was always extremely limited. In the planning for the Belorussian strategic operation in 1944, only three individuals—the Deputy Supreme Commander in Chief, the Chief of the General Staff, and the First Deputy Chief of the General Staff—were aware of the full dimensions of the *maskirovka* plan.

The role of strategic disinformation has also received some recent attention in the Soviet military press, although the focus has been on its use by the Germans and the Soviet's U.S. and British allies.[31] The lesson of this experience, however, is the potential value of strategic disinformation, especially if thoroughly planned and carefully executed by the strategic leadership. Strategic disinformation is one of the key techniques identified by Soviet sources as part of an effort to control the actions of a potential opponent. In particular, a successful strategic disinformation campaign can produce significant results at the outset of a military operation, since the potential opponent may be misled with regard to the axis selected for the main attack or even the overall intentions of attacking side. The Soviet technique of depicting defensive preparations, while actually preparing for offensive operations, during the Khalkin-Gol River operations and later against the Germans, is instructive in this regard. More contemporary Soviet sources discuss the use of exercises to mislead the potential opponent with regard to Soviet objectives. Again, in the formerly classified Soviet General Staff journal, *Voyennaya Mysl'*, for example, a Soviet major-general noted the utility of exercises for creating misperceptions on the part of the potential opponent.

> The group of techniques for shaping the opponent's decision-making algorithm requires substantial expenditure of effort, particularly the technique of regular conduct of strategic-scale exercises on one plane with the aim of decisive actions on another plane which sharply differ from the training exercise.[32]

This article also took note of the use of open-source publications as a means to influence the perceptions of an opponent. In a discussion of Western views of deterrence theory, the Soviet author concluded that these publications "may also constitute a technique of influencing the opponent, aimed at forming in him appropriate doctrines and decision-making algorithms."[33]

An analogous role appears to be one of the primary functions of the publications of the Soviet Institute of the United States and Canada, especially those discussions concerning Soviet perceptions of Western doctrinal developments. Soviet efforts to influence Western decision makers and elites on the question of controlled nuclear warfare would also fall into this category.[34]

Similar controversy over the responsibility for operational-level deception planning also appears to have taken place in the 1970's. Apparently one school of thought took the view that *maskirovka* was to be organized and conducted by the Chief of the Engineering Troops of the front or army. This view was sharply rebutted by General Dashevskiy in 1980.[35] Soviet specialists on the role of *maskirovka* apparently were concerned that field operators were viewing deception simply as a set of technical measures. These specialists did not deny the role of the engineering troops in the implementation of these measures, nor the fact that subordinate to the chief of these troops were specialists in the creation of mock-ups and camouflage to mislead the enemy.

Instead, Dashevskiy argued that field forces could not afford to take such a mechanistic approach and that only the commander and his operations staff would be able to develop a truly creative *maskirovka* plan. Again, the emphasis was on the fact that the *maskirovka* plan takes its cue from, and is subordinate to, the overall operational plan and the mission of the forces. This attitude further explains the relegation of *maskirovka* planning to the function of a combat support activity.

At the operational level, *maskirovka* would be planned and executed by the responsible front and army commanders and their staffs. Responsibility for developing the *maskirovka* plan would probably fall to a group formed from the operations directorate, of the department of the Chief of Staff. On the basis of the wartime experience, it appears that a "special *maskirovka* group" headed by the deputy chief of the operations department would be established to develop the *maskirovka* plan.[36] According to one account, this group would be responsible for all dimensions of the *maskirovka* plan and also for conducting systematic ground and air reconnaissance of all concealed objectives, artillery fire positions, and force groupings. The objective of this plan would focus primarily on concealment of Soviet intentions with regard to the selection of the main axes of attack and the concentration of the forces and means on those axes at the decisive moment in the operation.

The *front* commander's decision on the operational *maskirovka* plan would usually specify the concept of the *maskirovka*, the quantity of forces and means for its execution, the period of preparation and the sequence of measures for the implementation of the plan, and, an especially important factor for the Soviets, the verification measures to ensure its proper conduct.[37] As with the planning of strategic *maskirovka*, the circle of individuals involved would be limited. The front commander would be responsible not only for the decision on the front but also for the decision on the army plan.

An important characteristic of the operational deception plan is that it is to encompass not only activities prior to the initiation of the operation, but also activities to the entire depth of the anticipated operation. Selection of routes and river crossings to achieve army secondary objectives or the advance of second echelon and reserve forces from the rear, for example, would require considerable *maskirovka* efforts. The introduction of deep strike, high-technology weapons in NATO arsenals would only serve to intensify this requirement. Moreover, Soviet concerns in this regard seem to focus on the potential for outrunning their *maskirovka* measures, just as Soviet commanders feared outrunning their fire support in an earlier period.

Finally, at the tactical level command and staff efforts would center less on planning and more on the execution of the specific *maskirovka* measures. Attention here would be focused on the application of the various techniques of camouflage and cover.[38] The objectives at this level would include:

Concealment of installations and small units,

Simulation of individual installations,

Feigned tactical activity.[39]

Although activity at this level would appear to focus primarily on the technical aspects of deception, Soviet military sources reflect the conclusion that success at higher levels is critically dependent on the "strict observance of tactical camouflage measures." [40]

The basic methods of *maskirovka* to implement the plans of each of the command echelons responsible for *maskirovka* include the use of concealment, *maskirovka* measures or feints, simulation, and disinformation. Each of these methods has, as its primary objective, the maintenance of secrecy for the overall plan of operations and is carried out through a variety of technical means and troop activities. These could include the dissemination of false information by radio transmission and the use of decoys, dummy weapons deployments, corner reflectors, and diversionary actions. In particular, the Soviets seem to value highly the use of false troop deployments and groupings to mislead the opponent as to the selection of the main axes for attack. To achieve this objective, the Soviets would not only employ various technical means but also would attempt to exploit both weather and terrain conditions.

As the capabilities of modern weapons systems have improved, the role and importance of deception in Soviet military planning have steadily increased. At the same time, however, the Soviets recognize that the development of aerial photography and various types of sensors have greatly complicated the execution of *maskirovka* plans. In effect, the application of the Marxist law of the negation to military affairs, as explained by Marshal Ogarkov in his 1982 pamphlet, operates fully in the interaction between reconnaissance and *maskirovka*.[41]

> There exists a dialectical interrelationship between camouflage and hostile reconnaissance. The essence of this interrelationship consists in the fact that reconnaissance constantly seeks to detect targets and to determine their nature, and this engenders in the opposing side an objective necessity and effort to resort to various forms of camouflage and concealment (active and passive).[42]

In particular, the complexity of *maskirovka* is magnified by the "increasing sophistication of . . . space reconnaissance and utilization of high-accuracy intelligence-gathering devices."[43] A number of prominent espionage cases during the 1970's, both in the United States and NATO, undoubtedly strengthened Soviet convictions in this regard. Soviet comprehension of the scope and capabilities of U.S. intelligence collection systems was probably greatly facilitated by the Kampiles and Boyce cases. A considerable amount of information on the capabilities of reconnaissance systems is also openly published in the West. Much of this material finds its way into Soviet military journals, such as *Foreign Military Review*, which informs Soviet officers on opponent capabilities and concepts.

Although the existence of these intelligence collection systems has clearly complicated Soviet *maskirovka* planning, information regarding the capabilities of these systems could actually facilitate this planning. Obviously, it provides the Soviets with a better understanding of the capabilities of these systems, thus facilitating the development of Soviet deceptive activities. Perhaps more important, however, it provides insights into the types of information that can be collected in support of the potential opponent's development of an estimate of the initial situation. It is the potential impact on this aspect of the opponent's military planning that is most useful for establishing control over the actions of the opponent.

> In order to ensure control of the opponent's actions, reconnaissance and intelligence-gathering are required on a broader scope, encompassing in addition not only the organizational aspect but also the morale-psychological state of enemy command personnel and troops and determination of the effectiveness of psychological techniques employed.[44]

Knowledge of the types of information the potential enemy believes to be accessible would provide the Soviets with an immeasurable advantage in shaping and influencing that opponent's estimate of the initial situation.

The introduction of modern weapons systems has also significantly increased the value of *maskirovka* for the preservation of the combat effectiveness and survivability of Soviet forces. The use of successful *maskirovka* techniques would deny enemy fire controllers positive identification of Soviet targets and either delay fire decisions or force enemy fire to be, in effect, wasted on false targets. The Soviets know that NATO stocks of reserve munitions are already dangerously low; the expenditure of these munitions on false targets would also seem to have a force-multiplier effect. At the same time, Soviet sources acknowledge that the tasks of *maskirovka* have become increasingly difficult as the result of improved reconnaissance capabilities, and of two other major characteristics of contemporary warfare.

First, the Soviets believe that the increases in weapons and combat and transport material in combat units necessitated by the nature of modern combat have sharply increased the level of observable signatures. The Soviets appear to believe that the fire and support requirements that could result from anticipated attrition have greatly complicated the tasks of concealing Soviet combat preparations.

Second, the Soviets believe that, although there has been a sharp increase in combat material requirements, there has been a corresponding decrease in time available for combat preparations. After the Soviets were able to overcome the initial disasters of the early days of the war, Soviet strategic planners often had several months to plan and prepare the next strategic operation. As a result, *maskirovka* practices could be elaborately worked out and implemented. Contemporary warfare, however, would be characterized by continuous combat with only brief, if any, pauses between strategic operations.[45] Although *maskirovka* has retained and perhaps increased its significance for the initial operation of a future war, the increased pace of modern combat would appear to sharply reduce the time available to support subsequent *maskirovka* planning.

This change has been accompanied by a dramatic increase in attack tempos and the creation of rapidly changing combat situations. Soviet concerns in this regard appear to focus on the potential for outrunning their *maskirovka* measures. Additionally, the Soviets are concerned that rapidly changing situations could negate much of their preplanned *maskirovka* campaign and leave little time for them to react to these situations.

In order to overcome these characteristics of modern combat, the Soviets have attempted to develop a set of criteria and requirements by which to evaluate the potential effectiveness of their deception planning. These requirements were developed on the basis of their wartime experience and the application of *maskirovka* during exercises conducted since the war. For example, Soviet analyses of the wartime experience with simulation indicated that, although the simulation efforts must not be too transparent, the *maskirovka* was most successful when the enemy discovered not less than 20-to-25 percent of the simulated force grouping.[46] Moreover, the simulated grouping should be located at a distance not less than 20 kilometers from the real force grouping or target.[47] Similarly, the simulation should bear a close resemblance to both the appearance and actual operations of the actual objective. "Display of one installation in the guise of another should be accompanied by display of appropriate relations between analogous installations."[48] The example provided is that of a "dummy command post" that would operate in much the same fashion as a real command post. Along the same lines, the Soviets stipulate that a *maskirovka* is more effective if measures are taken to simulate efforts to disguise the *maskirovka*. "A dummy installation will be more readily accepted as genuine if, when it is displayed, steps are taken to hinder the reconnaissance effort."[49]

The Soviets have also identified a set of basic requirements that they consider fundamental to a successful *maskirovka* campaign. According to General Mel'nikov, these include

> Consideration of the realistic potential of all types of reconnaissance of the enemy and constant countermeasures against it,
>
> The elaboration of the *maskirovka* plan on the basis of the concept of the given operation and the correspondence of the concept and the basic *maskirovka* measure with the realistic potential of one's own forces in its implementation,
>
> Activeness, persuasiveness, and continuous and multifaceted *maskirovka* measures conducted systematically using different methods of deception,
>
> Initiative and creativity of the commanders organizing and conducting the deception measures.[50]

In particular, the Soviets stress the importance of initiative and creativity in the development and implementation of the *maskirovka* plan. According to the Soviets, this entails detailed knowledge of the enemy forces and capabilities, including his concept of operations and methods of combat activities. A key ingredient in this would be the Soviet commander's knowledge and familiarity with his counterpart's views on the character and content of Soviet operational behavior.

As noted at the beginning of this chapter, efforts have been undertaken in recent years to modify strategies and concepts governing the employment of both U. S. strategic nuclear and theater-level forces. The potential success of many of these concepts is critically dependent upon precise locational data to support effective targeting and force operations. The collection of such data, both in peacetime and especially in the context of actual military operations, would be enormously complicated by Soviet efforts to conceal critical leadership and force facilities. The U.S. intelligence community and defense planners are gradually becoming aware of the magnitude of Soviet efforts at concealment of critical Soviet targets.

Soviet incentives for concealment and deception are perhaps even greater at the level of theater warfare. For some time, NATO has been in the process of revising its operational strategy to increase the effectiveness of the overall Flexible Response doctrine. This change has taken the form of NATO's acceptance of the SHAPE Follow-on Forces Attack concept and the U.S. Army's adoption of the AirLand Battle concept. Many of these concepts rely extensively on a somewhat stylized portrayal of Soviet operational behavior, which would seem to make these concepts especially susceptible to Soviet deception efforts. In particular, an excessive reliance on the use of templating in the AirLand Battle concept would seem to enhance the potential value of deception in Soviet military planning.

A trend of particular importance to the Soviets is the development in the West of new high-technology conventional weapons systems designed, in part, to support the implementation of these concepts. The Soviet military press has focused an enormous amount of attention on the development of weapons systems that link in real or near-real time target detection and acquisition capabilities to weapons platforms. Termed "reconnaissance-strike complexes" by the Soviets, these systems have characteristics that would appear to provide little (if any) time for Soviet forces to maneuver out from under attack once detected. A prominent Soviet military tactician has recently argued that the entire detection-destruction cycle for these systems requires no more than six to ten minutes.[51] Given the difficulty of maneuvering away from attack, the primary alternatives open to the Soviets would appear to be to destroy these weapons systems preemptively, or to conceal successfully the primary targets for these systems. Modifications to Soviet fire support doctrine undertaken about 1982 seem designed to fulfill the first requirement. The Soviets have focused an increasing degree of attention on the value of deception for the survivability of Soviet forces in response to the second requirement.

In summary, Soviet views on the role of deception in military planning seem based primarily upon their experience in the former war, but are updated to take into account the new capabilities of intelligence collection systems. The primary objective of modern Soviet deception efforts appears to be the establishment of a degree of control over the plans and actions of the potential opponent. To further this objective, Soviet strategic planners and field commanders are constantly reminded of the necessity for creativity and the continuous application of deceptive measures throughout the course of their peacetime activities and in the event of actual military operations. Although the Soviets are fully aware of the difficulties associated with the conduct of contemporary deception efforts, they also appear to believe that these difficulties may be overcome through the combination of creativity and the increasing use of automation and other decision-making aids. The Soviets clearly believe that even a moderately successful deception campaign could introduce just enough delay in the enemy's decision cycle to ensure Soviet success on the battlefield.

Notes

1. See, among others, Michael Mihalka, "Soviet Strategic Deception, 1955-1981," *The Journal of Strategic Studies* 5(March 1982): pp. 40–93; Roger Beaumont, *Maskirovka: Soviet Camouflage, Concealment and Deception* (College Station, Tex.: Center for Strategic Technology, 1982); Jiri Valenta, "Soviet Use of Surprise and Deception," *Survival*, 24(March/April 1982): pp. 50–60; and Robert B. Vosilus, *Soviet Strategic Maskirovka and Active Measures* (Washington, D.C.: The National War College, 1985).
2. See, for example, Robert M. Gates and Lawrence K. Gershwin, "*Soviet Strategic Force Development*," testimony before a Joint Session of the Subcommittee on Strategic and Theater Nuclear Forces of the Senate Armed Services Committee and the Defense Subcommittee of the Senate Committee on Appropriations, 26 June 1985, p. 7; and *Soviet Strategic Defense Programs* (Washington, D.C.: U.S. Government Printing Office, 1985), p. 21.
3. See, especially, Beaumont, *Maskirovka*.
4. M.A. Gareyev, *M.V. Frunze-Voyennyy Teoretik* [M.V. Frunze–Military Theoretician] (Moscow: Voyenizdat, 1985), p. 240.
5. Major-General Y.A. Matsulenko, *Operativnaya Maskirovka Voysk* [Operational Maskirovka of the Forces] (Moscow: Voyenizdat, 1975), p. 180.
6. Colonel-General P. Mel'nikov, "Operational *Maskirovka*" *Voyenno-Istoricheskiy Zhurnal* (Military-Historical Journal, hereafter *Vizh*) (April 1982): p. 18.
7. Lt.-General N. Orlov and Colonel G. Tvardovskiy, "Methods of the Support of the Cover of the Preparation of Operations and Surprise of the Actions of the Forces in the War Years," *Vizh*, (September 1981): p. 24.
8. Mel'nikov, "Operational *Maskirovka*," p. 18.
9. Ibid.
10. M.V. Zakhorov, *Voprosy Strategii i Operativnogo Iskusstva v Sovetskikh Voyennykh Trudakh* (1917-1940) [Problems of Strategy and Operational Art in Soviet Military Works] (Moscow: Voyenizdat, 1965), p. 541.
11. MSU G.K. Zhukov, *Vospominaniya i Razmyshleniya* [Reminiscences and Reflections] vol I, (Moscow: UZD.APN, 1975), pp. 172–174.
12. Ibid.
13. John Erickson, *The Soviet High Command*, (Boulder, Colo. and London: Westview Press, 1984), p. 533.
14. Mel'nikov, "Operational *Maskirovka*", p. 22.
15. Matsulenko, *Operativnaya Maskirovka Voysk*, p. 179.
16. "Maskirovka," *Voyennyy Ehntsiklopedicheskiy Slovar'* [Military-Encyclopedic Dictionary] (Moscow: Voyenizdat, 1983), p. 430.
17. A.A. Beketov, A.P. Belokon, S.G. Chermashentsev, *Maskirovka Deystiviy Podrazdelen'y Sukhoputnykh Voysk* [Maskirovka of the Actions of Subunits of the Ground Forces] (Moscow: Voyenizdat, 1976), p. 2.
18. V.A. Efimov and S.G. Chermasentsev, "*Maskirovka*" *Sovetskaya Voyennaya Ehntsiklopediya* [Soviet Military Encyclopedia-hereafter SVE], vol. 5, p. 175.
19. Colonel-General P.K. Altukhov, ed., *Osnovy Teorii Upravleniya Voyskami* [Principles of the Theory of Troop Control] (Moscow: Voyenizdat, 1984), p. 1.
20. Attributed to Marshal Tukhachevskiy in Major-General M. Ionov, "On the

Methods of Influencing an Opponent's Decision," *Selected Readings from Military Thought 1963-1973*, vol 5, part II, (Washington, D.C.: U.S. Government Printing Office), p. 164.

21. Ibid.
22. Ibid., p. 167.
23. Ibid., p. 166.
24. Ibid.
25. Ibid., pp. 166–167.
26. Viktor Suvorov, "GUSM—The Soviet Service of Strategic Deception," *International Defense Review*, (1985), no. 5: p. 1237.
27. Ibid.
28. V. Kulikov, "Strategic Leadership of the Armed Forces," *Vizh*, (1975), no. 6: p. 21.
29. Army General A.M. Mayorov, "Strategic Leadership in the Great Patriotic War," *Vizh*, (1985), no. 5: p. 38.
30. K.A. Meretskov, *Na Slyzhbe Narody* [In the Service of the People] (Moscow: Politizdat, 1969), pp. 410–411.
31. Colonel-General V. Meshcheryakov, "Strategic Disinformation in the Achievement of Surprise According to the Experience of the Second World War," *Vizh* (1985), no. 2: pp. 74–80.
32. Ionov, "On the Methods of Influencing an Opponent's Decision," p. 167.
33. Ibid., p. 170.
34. See, for example, Notra Trulock, "Soviet Perspectives on Limited Nuclear War," in Fred Hoffman, Albert Wohlstetter, and David Yost, eds., *Swords and Shields: New Choices for Offense and Defense*, In Press.
35. Lt.-General Ya. Dashevskiy, "Organization and Conduct of Operational *Maskirovka*," *Vizh* (1980) no. 4: pp. 47–48.
36. A.K. Blazhey, *V Armeyskoy Shtabe* [On the Army Staff] (Moscow: Voyenizdat, 1967), p. 152.
37. Matsulenko, *Operativnaya Maskirovka Voysk*, p. 180.
38. See, for example, B. Varenyshev, "Means of *Maskirovka*," *Voyenyye Znaniya*, (October 1979) no. 10.
39. See, ENGR-LTC Kh. Adam and LTC R. Geble, "Military Camouflage," *Selected Readings from Military Thought*, vol. 5, part II, p. 157.
40. Ibid.
41. N.V. Ogarkov, *Vsegda v Gotovnost' k Zashchite Otchestva* [Always in Readiness for Defense of the Motherland] (Moscow: Voyenizdat, 1982), pp. 41–44. According to Ogarkov, this law expresses the continuous conflict between ongoing forces. It is the operation of this law, manifested in the ongoing struggle between offensive and defensive means, which produces most of what is "new" in military affairs.
42. Adam and Geble, "Military Camouflage," p. 157.
43. Ibid., p. 163.
44. Ionov, "On the Methods of Influencing an Opponent's Decision," p. 167.
45. Ogarkov, *Vsegda v Gotovnost'*, p. 35.
46. Mel'nikov, "Operativnaya *Maskirovka*," p. 19.
47. Ibid.

48. Ionov, "On the Methods of Influencing an Opponent's Decision," p. 167.
49. Ibid.
50. Mel'nikov, "Operativnaya *Maskirovka*," p. 26.
51. Major-General I. Vorob'yev, "Time in Battle," *Krasnaya Zvezda*, 9 October 1985, p. 2.

14
Reflexive Control in Soviet Military Planning

Clifford Reid

Reflexive Control is a Soviet construct that stemmed from Soviet interests in cybernetics in the late 1950's. At that time, research on military cybernetics was being conducted in the First Computer Center of the Soviet Ministry of Defense (also known as Military Unit 01168) located in Moscow. A primary objective of the research underway at the institute was the development of methods for optimizing military decisions, drawing on the technology of the digital computer.

One of the Soviet researchers assigned to Unit 01168 was a young mathematical psychologist named Vladimir Lefebvre. As part of his research on military decision making, he concluded that the approaches that were currently under investigation were incomplete. He believed that to incorporate cybernetic concepts properly in Soviet military decision making, it was necessary to develop a "modeling system which consisted of three subsystems: a unit to simulate one's own decisions, a unit to simulate the adversary's decisions, and a decision making unit."[1] Upon further study, Lefebvre concluded that this construct provided a method of influencing an adversary in ways that were favorable to Soviet decision making. He argued that

> . . . in making his decision the adversary uses information about the area of conflict, about his own troops and ours, about their ability to fight, et cetera. We can influence his channels of information and send messages which shift the flow of information in a way favorable for us. The adversary uses the most contemporary method of optimization and finds the optimal decision. However, it will not be a true optimum, but a decision predetermined by us. In order to make our own effective decision, we should know how to deduce the adversary's decision based on information he believes is true. The unit modeling the adversary serves the purpose of simulating his decisions under different conditions and choosing the most effective informational influence.[2]

This new approach of Lefebvre's required a change in the underlying views on conflict between two opposing military forces. Instead of looking at conflict as the interaction between, for example, two opposing tank battalions, the Lefebvre model viewed conflict as the interaction between the decision processes governing the actions of each tank battalion. In this model, conflict is viewed as reflexive interaction between two opponents, where *reflexion*, in this context, is a psychological term that denotes that each opponent bases his decision on a "model" of both himself and his adversary.

Since the end of 1963, Lefebvre has continued his research on the study of reflexive processes and the formal development of the theory of reflexive control. This research has included the development of a formal algorithmic structure for studying reflexive interactions. Soviet military literature written since 1963 indicates that other Soviet theoreticians have also apparently studied the theory of reflexive control for its application to military decision making problems.

This chapter does not develop the full theory of reflexive control with the richness obtained by Lefebvre. It does not develop the algorithmic structure by which one can study reflexive processes.[3] It does not develop the complexities of the hierarchy of reflexive interactions that can exist in practice. Rather, its purpose is to summarize and interpret the main elements of the theory of reflexive control. To this end, the concept of reflexive control and its main elements will be summarized, followed by a discussion of several types of reflexive interactions, which have military implications within the context of reflexive control. Finally, evidence of continuing Soviet interest in the practical applications of reflexive control is discussed.

This chapter is based principally on the works of Lefebvre. It is also based, to a much lesser extent, on a few Soviet military texts available in the West in which reflexive control is explicitly discussed.

The Concept of Reflexive Control

In its most simple form, *reflexive control* is that branch of the theory of control related to influencing the decisions of others. In a military context, it can be viewed as a means for providing one military commander with the ability to indirectly maintain control over his opponent commander's decision process. K.V. Tarakanov, writing in 1974, gives a simple definition:

> Reflexive control is understood as the process of one of the sides giving reasons to the enemy from which he can logically infer his own decision, predetermined by the first side. . . . The term "reflexive control" should be understood as the reflection by the opposed sides in the thoughts of their discussions with each other.[4]

Lefebvre makes it clear that control over an opponent is indirect:

> Control of an opponent's decision, which in the end is a forming of a certain behavioral strategy on him through reflexive interaction, is not achieved directly, not by a blatant force, but by means of providing him with the grounds by which he is able logically to derive his own decision, but one that is predetermined by the other side.[5]

Hence, reflexive control is a process for providing an opponent with a basis for making decisions that are favorable to the side attempting to exert reflexive control. For example, if a Soviet tank commander would prefer that the enemy commit his reserve on the left axis of engagement, then reflexive control would be a process to encourage the enemy tank commander to make a decision to commit his reserves on the Soviet left, rather than on the right or on the center.

It follows that the successful employment of reflexive control requires a detailed understanding of the opponent's decision process and the factors that influence it, including his policies, ideologies, military doctrine, goals, the status of his forces and organizations, psychology, the personal qualities of his leadership, interrelations and emotional makeup.[6] Even though it is an established military principle that a commander must, to the extent possible, know his enemy, reflexive control is somewhat more axiomatic. The Soviet theory argues that the decision process can be decomposed into four different elements, each of which can be the subject of reflexive interactions: the opponent's (1) perception of the situation, (2) goals, (3) solution algorithm, and (4) decision.

The *perception of the situation* is that element of the decision making process that includes the specific descriptors of the forces and the nature of the conflict itself. Some elements of the perception of the situation include:

The size and characteristics of one's own forces,

The size and characteristics of the opponent's forces,

The physical environment within which conflict occurs,

The history of actions by the two sides,

The current evolution of events, and

The objectives and constraints of the opponent.

Methods of influencing the perception of the situation are standard ones normally associated, in the West, with the terms *camouflage, concealment,* and *disinformation.*

The *goals* also comprise an important element of the decision making process of an opponent. Goals can be formulated in both peacetime and wartime. In peacetime, examples of goals include force structure requirements, military readiness objectives, and technological developments. In wartime, examples of goals include the control of military regions, the attainment of a prescribed level of damage to enemy forces and facilities, and the prescribed timetables for military operations.

Soviet literature suggests at least three approaches to shaping the opponent's goals. One is through a show of force to convince the enemy that a specific objective is unobtainable. A second is to demonstrate a threat of such significance that the countering of that specific threat dominates the goals of the opponent. The third is to present the opponent with such a spectrum of uncertainties about your own actions that he is unable to define any objective that has a satisfactory outcome for all plausible sets of events. Soviet literature also cautions that the techniques to influence the goals of the opponent are "more difficult to spot, and for this reason they are more insidious and dangerous than techniques . . . of shaping the initial situation estimate."[7]

The *solution algorithm* (also called *doctrine*) consists of the behavioral conventions of the opponent, his analytical procedures, his methods for displaying and evaluating the situation, and his prepared contingency plans. It is manifested in standard conventions, methods and operating procedures, training, and the experience of the military officers themselves. Hence, the solution algorithm is difficult to influence directly by means of reflexive control. However, one Soviet author argues that the solution algorithm can be influenced primarily through "techniques for influencing the choice of the decision making moment."[8] A principal means for achieving this influence is through the use of surprise.

Soviet literature argues that the last element of the decision process, the decision itself, is very difficult to influence indirectly. Conversely, the first two elements (perception of the situation, and goals of the opponent) are the most frequent objects of reflexive attempts to control the opponent.

Types of Reflexive Interactions

According to Soviet literature, there are several different types of reflexive interactions that can be pursued as a means to exercise reflexive control. This section discusses the principal types, using examples given in Soviet literature.

Transfer of an Image of the Situation

Probably the most common form of reflexive control is accomplished by providing the opponent with an erroneous or incomplete image of the situation. For reflexive control of this type, the flow of information is not usually curtailed, but there is not an adequate basis for determining which pieces of information are false.[9]

Most often, this procedure is summarized as a disguise of one's objects. Disguise has the purpose of giving the opponent very specific information without curtailing the flow of information in general. This is a means for transferring the information "there is nothing at the location" to the opponent. Another side of this procedure is the fabrication of false objects. These could be false troop concentrations or ground or aerial targets whose purpose is to hide the true threat of the nonexistent armaments used. Many examples of practical military proficiency are, as a rule, a combination of camouflaging procedures and fabrication of false objects.[10]

The use of decoys to cause a virtual increase in the number of targets to be attacked is an example of this type of reflexive control. The usual effect is to decrease the effectiveness of the opponent's weapons by making it impossible to use the weapons to maximum effect. This impact is represented as especially important with modern weaponry because

> The more powerful the means of attack are that the enemy intends to use, the more important it is to force him to expend them on dummy objectives. It should be recalled that *maskirovka* has been used since time immemorial as one of the most effective means of defense.[11]

This type of reflexive control usually relies on a combination of several techniques, each applying a different kind of influence on the opponent's thought processes.

> For example, display of one installation in the guise of another should be accompanied by display of appropriate relations between analogous installations. A dummy command post should maintain radio communications with the same patterns as a real command post. In like manner, a dummy installation will be more readily accepted as genuine if and when it is displayed if steps are taken to hinder the reconnaissance effort. Considerable influence on shaping an initial situation estimate is also exerted by the element of surprise in employing new forces.[12]

Examples of this use of deception appear quite frequently in the operations research textbooks in discussions of estimates of weapon system effectiveness. Two such examples follow:

> *Problem.* There are 18 interceptors at the airfield. To assure high combat readiness and survivability with enemy action at the base airfield, all interceptors are dispersed uniformly throughout the airfield, and in addition, there are 18 dummy interceptors. The enemy raids the airfield and bombards, at random, half of the aircraft (18 of the total of 36 real and dummy airplanes). During the bombardment, each bombarded interceptor is damaged with a probability of 0.2.

Determine the expectation of the number of damaged interceptors. How does this number decrease if we double the number of dummies?[13]

The text then solves the basic problem in combinatorics associated with the probability distribution of the number of damaged interceptors, and uses that information to calculate the desired expectations.

A second example involves concealment against weapons fire:

> *Example.* Fire is being delivered at a camouflaged or concealed target 2_y = 0.60m in dimensions. The precise location of the target is not known. It is known only that the target is located in a frontage interval $2L_y$ = 6.0m in length. Mean firing errors are: E_y = 0.50m; ^YE_z = 0.2m; $B_{b1}B_v$ = 0.15m. Determine the number of rounds necessary to attain a target description probability of P = .050.[14]

The text then uses basic probability theory to calculate the required ammunition level.

In addition to the use of camouflage and of dummy equipment or installations, means for implementing this type of reflexive control include such approaches as "distribution of leaflets, radio propaganda, and others."[15]

Reflexive control by means of transferring an image of the situation is very complex. It consists of conducting a variety of measures over a period of time to condition the opponent to the implications of various situations.

> Systems of reflexive control that are achieved through time are of a special class. In certain cases, one opponent provides another with his "pseudohistory" in order that the other extrapolates this false history, makes a prediction about the future condition of the opponent that is correct from his point of view, and makes a decision based on his prediction. . . . Any sharp change in a schedule of activity that is generated by a conviction that the opponent knows this schedule can serve as an example.[16]

This form is probably primarily a peacetime function. Such interactions as the exchanges of data and policy statements in conjunction with arms control negotiations could be one way to accomplish at least a portion of the establishment of a pseudohistory.

Creation of a Goal for the Opponent

Putting the opponent into a position such that he is forced to select a goal in your favor is perhaps the second most common form of reflexive control. Two ways in which this may be accomplished are (1) the massing of superior force to support the direct imposition of a goal and (2) provoking the enemy with a threat for which the only rational response is the desired one. Tarakanov presents an example of the first form:

> The essence of this transformation is while taking into consideration the law-governed patterns of war, to convince the enemy of the impossibility of achieving his goals by unleashing a nuclear war. By taking steps which guarantee the delivery of a reciprocal strike, the other side should form the enemy's goal: to restrain [him] at least from delivering a massive strike.[17]

Various acts of deception could be employed to support this type of reflexive control, but the capability to enforce the imposition of the desired goal must almost certainly be substantially grounded in fact.

The second form of implementation of this type of reflexive control consists primarily of exploiting uncertainty, which can be created in the minds of the opponent's decision maker, causing him to waste resources by being forced to select strategies to counter threats that may not materialize. These may be very difficult to detect. Ionov gives an example of this:

> Some techniques can be revealed only after a considerable amount of effort of a scientific research type. The following example is notable in this respect. U.S. Air Force leaders, substantiating a request for funds to develop a new low-altitude attack aircraft, emphasized that the USSR would have to spend approximately $21 billion dollars over a period of five years in order to improve air defense to cope with the new aircraft, while organization of air defense without the necessity of countering the performance of the new aircraft (as part of a program of continuous upgrading) would require, in the opinion of the Americans, an expenditure of only $6 billion dollars during the same period. Although the U.S. Secretary of Defense did not approve the request, he ordered development of certain assemblies and the engine for this aircraft.[18]

Because techniques of this type rely principally on the creation of uncertainties for the decision maker, "they are more difficult to spot, and for this reason they are more insidious and dangerous" than techniques to create a false image of the situation.[19] The principle on which this type of control is based is that the thinking of the decision maker

> . . . is based primarily on the deductive method. He draws his conclusions, particularly in determining the opponent's plan, as a rule on the basis of incomplete, fragmentary, frequently contradictory data, utilizing not only direct information, but various indirect indications as well.[20]

A special case of this category of reflexive control is the creation of a situation so laced with uncertainties that the opponent is unable to establish any goal until well into the conflict. This is referred to as "neutralization of an opponent's deductions."[21] This may be desirable when it is not possible to conceal the substance of the situation, but it is possible to simulate the actions of "a large number of possible variants, all of which, in spite of their diversity, should be more or less equally probable."[22] This creates a situation in which the opponent has the options of (1) deferring actions until additional evidence on the authenticity of the variants can be obtained, (2) fragmenting his forces to provide a thin defense against each variant, or (3) concentrating his forces against one of the variants, with the possibility of having selected the wrong one. One example of neutralization of the opponent's decision is given by Ionov:

> For example, movement of a large number of hostile aircraft into an area which does not contain air defense installations, but which does open up routes to two or three important areas faces commanders with a difficult logical problem of determining the opponent's real intentions. The selection of a minor strategic axis, containing several important targets, enriches and enhances the value of a plan of operations by compelling the opponent to scatter his forces for defense.[23]

A second example is from Lefebvre and Smolyan:

> An example of such an operation having the goal of neutralizing the opponent's deductions is the German breakthrough at Sedan on the French front on 15 May 1940. Here is how Liddell Hart describes this operation: "Movement of the stream of German tanks was made easier because the French command did not know precisely the direction in which they were going to move. The special advantage of the German breakthrough of the front at Sedan was that it was made at the center of the front, and afforded the Germans the possibility of working in any direction thus creating a threat against several positions simultaneously. And so the French did not know whether the Germans were planning to move to the shore of the English Channel or had decided to march directly on Paris. Even though the advance of German troops appeared to be directed West, the French feared that the Germans could at any time turn to the South, in the direction of Paris."
>
> Inasmuch as the Germans (Y) were unable to hide the movement of the tanks from the French (X), then the selection of a breakthrough at the center was backed by the fact that two goals of equal probability could be deduced.
>
> It was namely this circumstance that placed the French command in a most difficult position.[24]

Thus, the variant might be more properly labeled "denying the enemy a goal." A major effect is that the establishment of the goal is so delayed that it is impossible to organize properly and conduct the actions required to support the attainment of the goal.

Transfer of a Decision

Reflexive control by transferring a decision cannot be implemented frequently. It requires a level of trust between the sides. An example of this form is "a false hint during a lesson given by one student to another to get even with him."[25] Tarakanov, however, indicates that this is the type of control that underlies the concept of an assured retaliatory capability as a foundation for nuclear deterrence.

> The essence of this transformation is the second party giving the enemy its decision on a retaliatory strike. This may be carried out by conducting appropriate measures which convince the enemy of the fact that the second side will unfailingly conduct a specific policy as a result of which the enemy will be punished.[26]

Formation of a Goal by Transferring an Image of the Situation

The preceding three sections have discussed "simple" techniques for reflexive control that directly attempted to affect the opponent's image of a specific part of the decision process (that is, the perception of the situation, the goal, the decision). The remainder of the strategies that will be discussed are more complex, because they attempt to modify one portion of the decision process by controlling the opponent's image of another part. Successful implementation of these strategies necessarily requires a very good understanding of the actual process through which the opponent makes decisions.

Creating a false picture of the situation is probably the easiest way to influence the goal of the opponent. Feigning weakness in some sector may induce the enemy to direct his forces against a strong point and thus suffer unanticipated attrition.[27] Alternatively, a deceptive display of strength may cause the opponent to back off.

> For example, if the enemy knows that the availability of N_k quantity of nuclear weapons carriers would guarantee the infliction on him of assured destruction [sic] and, in fact, in the event of a preventive attack by him this quantity would not remain, then conducting decoy measures and camouflage steps by the other side may give him the basis for evaluating his forces in the direction desired by the other side.[28]

Druzhinin and Kontorov indicate that inducing the enemy to select a goal that imposes an inappropriate level of combat readiness may be one of the reasons to employ this type of reflexive control.

Combat readiness control is one of the most crucial and complex control problems, one which involves identification of situations and distribution of resources and forces. There is a definite number of fixed states of combat readiness, and one of them must be selected depending on the situation. The cost of both understanding as well as unjustifiably overestimating combat readiness (above set requirements) can be very great; therefore, control should strictly regulate the composition of information upon which decisions on a change in combat readiness are made. The enemy will attempt to create a false image of the situation in order to stimulate a useless expenditure of forces and means by the other side. One of the methods of disinformation is a gradual involvement in a complex situation or simulated peril: the symptoms of the peril are increased slowly and almost imperceptibly, but after a certain period of time one of the sides can be faced with an intolerably low or unjustifiably high combat readiness, which wears out the forces.[29]

In many cases, it is impossible to create a complete image of the situation for transfer to the opponent. If the methods used by the opponent to interpret data are known, then it is possible to merely transmit "benchmarks" from which the opponent will then reconstruct the complete image of the situation. An example of this is given by Lefebvre:

In 2000 B.C., the famous general Gideon used lamps as a means of reflexive control of his opponent—the armies of the Midianites. According to the official standards of his time, every hundred warriors had one trumpeter and one torch-bearer. Gideon proceeded from the fact that the leaders of the Midianites were familiar with this standard, and furthermore they knew at least the fundamentals of arithmetic. Gideon equipped each of his 300 warriors with a lamp and a trumpet. He assumed that the opponent would make the following computation: $300 \times 100 = 30,000$, the same number of men as the opposing army, whence comes the goal of avoiding armed encounter. [As we know, the Midianites took flight.][30]

Transfer of an Image of One's Own Perception of the Situation

Reflexive control over an intelligent opponent (who presumably is trying to attain some level of understanding of one's own decision process) may provide an opportunity to influence the opponent's decision process by providing him with false information (or perhaps even selected portions of the truth) on one's own perception of the situation. This type of control would probably consist primarily of careful leaks of intelligence data (made appropriately difficult to obtain). Some of the types of information that might be made available could, for example, serve the function of

. . . providing support to the idea of one side that the opponent's camouflaged objects are hidden from view (even though in reality they are not hidden from view), and that false objects are thought to be real ones even though in reality that side knows that they are false.[31]

Other types of information that could be made available include one's alleged view of the opponent's plan and a view of one's supposed plans for force deployment.[32]

Transfer of an Image of One's Own Goal

A feint by a basketball player is a classic example of this type of reflexive control. The objective is to attempt to induce the enemy to lower his defenses against the actual goal by creating the impression that either he should defend against a different goal or that he need not worry about defense. The following two examples discuss the use of this type of strategy in wartime to divert the enemy's attention.

> For example, in the summer of 1944 the German Command had surmised that an offensive by Soviet forces in Belorussia was a possibility, but was unable to determine the sector of the main thrust. In order to mislead the enemy, the troops engaged in defensive work constructing barbed-wire entanglements in front of the forward edge, and mining the terrain. Personnel were issued instructions and memoranda on the organization of defense. Troop movements took place only at night, while during the day their camouflage was checked from the air by responsible staff officers of the front, as well as by officers of the General Staff. In order to hold the enemy's operational reserves on other sectors of the Soviet-German front, the 3rd Ukrainian Front was instructed to simulate a large-scale concentrations of forces, ostensibly preparing for an offensive against Kishinev. . . . As a result of these measures, the enemy failed to discover the real purpose of these activities, and not only did he not send his reserves into Belorussia, he even reinforced the first echelon troops facing the 3rd Ukrainian Front.[33]
>
> During the civil war, S.M. Budenniy gave the White general, Mamontov, a warning about the predicted time and place of an attack (in a letter delivered by Aleko Dundich). This put the opponent into total confusion. The objective was accomplished and the enemy forces were decomposed.[34]

Chuyev and Mikhaylov indicate that, for this type of reflexive control to succeed, it must be carefully supported by an appropriate image of the situation. They cite a case in which an analysis of a false goal in light of actual actions not only revealed the falsification of the goal but also gave important information on the actual goal.

We can cite the process of the exposure by the Russian Command of an important forged document put out by the German General Staff prior to World War I. The Germans, through their agents, planted in the Russian General Staff a photocopy of a false "Memorandum on the Distribution of German Combat Forces in the Event of War." This was a distortion of Schlieffen's plan, adopted by the German General Staff, based on the idea of defeating first France, against which seven armies were deployed, then Russia, against which at first only one army would operate. The main thrust in the West was to be through Belgium, whose neutrality would be violated. In the false Memorandum, the main points of this plan were presented in the following form: "The war on three fronts is to be waged as follows: four armies on the French frontier, one army on the coast, three armies on the Russian frontier." The Memorandum was intended to convince the Russians and the French that approximately equal forces would be arrayed against them, and that the main thrust in the West would be made not by the right, but by the left flank.

The Memorandum was analyzed very carefully at the Russian General Staff Headquarters by Colonel V. Ye. Skalon. To answer the question of the most likely concentration of the German Armed Forces, Skalon put himself in the place of the enemy and tried to find the most expedient solution from the enemy's point of view. The results of his work were embodied in a document entitled "Notes on the Most Probable Concentration of the German Armed Forces on the Russian Frontier" in which it was not only proved that the Memorandum was a fake, but a forecast was made of the enemy's main operational-strategic plan.[35]

The long lead times required for the development of new weaponry make this type of strategy of reflexive control an especially attractive one for the use in long-term armament competition in peacetime. By the time data on "the situation," which would contradict stated goals, became available, one side may have accomplished a substantial lead. A model of peacetime competition in armament and industrial development, which was presented in a 1969 article in *Tekhnicheskaya Kibernetika* suggests some ways in which deception could be used to achieve a long-term advantage in an "arms race."[36] In this model, formulated as a formal problem in control theory, two hypothetical countries, referred to as Greece and Rome, are in a long-term competition, which is measured by an aggregate armament level. It is assumed that the ability of either country to develop armament is a function of the size of the industrial base (with armament development occurring more rapidly with a large industrial base) and the efficiencies of the economy.

At the initial conditions, Greece leads Rome in both industrial level and armament level, but Rome has a more efficient economy. The objective of Rome is to achieve parity with Greece in armament level as soon as possible, while Greece tries to select strategies for investment in industry and armament that will delay the attainment of parity for as long as possible. In two of the cases discussed, advertisement of a false goal is cited as one means to achieve advantage. If Greece has a slight lead, and Rome has significantly greater efficiencies, the optimal strategy for Rome is to maintain her existing industrial base and build armament as rapidly as possible. At the same time, Greece should first develop her industrial base further (to compensate for the greater Roman efficiencies) and begin to build up the armament level at a later date.

Threatening Roman propaganda, which would cause Greece to begin building armament too soon, could help Rome to achieve parity faster. On the other hand, if Greece has a substantial lead, Rome may require a prolonged period of industrial development before attempting to match the armament level of Greece. Rome may gain substantially by advertising peaceful intentions during this early period to convince Greece that her initial lead in armament will never be threatened. During this period, Rome would like to see Greece increase consumption to minimize investment in either industrial or armament development.

Transfer of an Image of One's Own Doctrine

Providing the opponent with a false view of one's own procedures and algorithms for making decisions may invite him to attempt to exploit perceived weaknesses that do not, in fact, exist. Ionov indicates that exercises may provide one means for transferring this type of information.

> The group of techniques for shaping the opponent's decision making algorithm requires substantial expenditure of effort, particularly the technique of regular conduct of strategic-scale exercises on one plan with the aim of decisive actions on another plan which sharply differs from the training exercises.[37]

Any leaks of falsified details of contingency plans could accomplish this same objective.

Transfer of One's Own Image of a Situation to Make the Opponent Deduce His Own Goal

For many of the circumstances in which one side might wish to present the other side with an incorrect image of the goal, there is no credible way to provide the information directly. Thus, it is necessary to accept some additional level of risk by choosing to present a false image of one's own perception of the situation, with the expectation that an erroneous goal will be assumed. This type of control is seen primarily in troop battle operations, and, according to Lefebvre and Smolyan, "this procedure lies at the basis of one of the unwritten laws of conflict which argues that the threat is stronger than the act."[38] Several examples of this are given in Soviet literature. One example illustrates the deceptive use of artillery:

For example, Y concentrates his artillery not with the goal of attacking, but with the purpose of forcing his opponent to arrive at the conclusion that Y is making ready to attack.[39]

A second example discusses firing tactics to compensate for use of this form of reflexive control by an opponent.

> [For air defense] target-assignment by the mathematical expectation of the number of targets shot down sometimes leads to several targets not being fired at. This occurs when the probability of hitting certain targets is so small, that it is more useful not to use a weapon by itself, but with the help of other ones. Target-assignment, based upon such a principle can lead to the enemy, having understood our tactics, deliberately drawing our fire away from important targets to less important ones, placing the latter into situations where the effectiveness of firing at them will be high. Therefore, it is necessary also to have other principles of target-assignment, which contain a limit to the number of targets which pass through without being fired upon. It is efficient to make the following demand: to fire at every target, if it is possible, and to concentrate the fire of several weapons on one target only when all possible targets have been fired upon one time.[40]

Reflexive Control of Bilateral Engagement by a Third Party

Although he does not consider it a major class of reflexive control, Tarakanov indicates that, because reflexive control is targeted for the decision processes rather than directly toward military forces, reflexive control may be exercised in a bilateral engagement by a third party.

> The essence of this transformation is that the third party, conducting nuclear provocation in the guise of the basic enemy, will have his goal to conflict two great powers if the goal of the second party will be a massive strike against the actions of the opposed party.[41]

Reflexive Control over an Opponent Who Is Using Reflexive Control

Just as reflexive control is exercised by attempting to imitate the decision process of the opponent, it is also possible to exploit opportunities that may be identified through imitation of his process of reflexive control. Thus, it is possible to negate reflexive control, or to turn it against the one attempting to use it.

> Relex control is of a probability nature, since the opponent may "not be taken in" by our device, promptly determining its real significance with the aid of

reconnaissance or intelligence: he may ignore it, if the device is ineffective in his estimation; finally, he may attempt to utilize it to our detriment.

Selection of a given method of reflex countercontrol is determined by the enemy's skill and experience, his estimate of the effectiveness of the device utilized, which may be diametrically opposite for opposing sides. . . . [In] forming such estimates, one must take into consideration not only psychological, but also political and social aspects.[42]

The use of reflexive control creates some additional vulnerabilities because, in general, it is necessary to provide the enemy with additional data to try to influence his decision process. To the extent that he is able to assess accurately the truth of that data (or infer the truth from the form of deception), additional channels for reflexive control may be opened. For example:

> It is by far easier for a chess player to catch his partner in a trap if this trap is fabricated on the defects of the reasoning of the partner, who himself is trying to set a trap.[43]

Thus, one who plans to employ reflexive control should be cautioned that "attempts at outwitting a sufficiently cunning enemy leads to disaster more rapidly than 'passive resistance'."[44]

Reflexive Control over an Opponent Whose Doctrine Is Game Theory

The techniques of game theory provide a very convenient and powerful framework for the evaluation of conflict situations. As a result, a large number of analytic tools that are used to support decision making are derived from game theoretic constructs. Unfortunately, the game theoretic approaches that are best understood and most computationally tractable (and that, consequently, provide the basis for most real applications) are two-player, zero-sum games with complete information. These assume that every image of the situation developed by one opponent is also seen by the other, and that both sides identically perceive all possible strategies. Further, for all possible solutions, the gain for one side is equal to the loss of the other.

> A player has such a model of his opponent in which any thought of X (from his point of view) is imitated by opponent Y who makes a decision based on the results of the imitation. Naturally such a model imparts advantage to the "least destructive thought." Player X will follow that strategy which is known beforehand, and, making the best decision, player Y will do the least harm to X. This is the minimax principle.[45]

Since this framework is fairly rigid, and the resultant strategies are generally quite conservative, there exists the potential for causing the opponent to act to his disadvantage if it is known that he is using game theory for his decision making.

> Reflexive control of the enemy is possible in essence in any case, no matter what scientific methods he uses. This may be successful when the gaming theory, for example, is the enemy's scientific doctrine. In this case, there is always the potential capability of disinformation of the enemy on the basis of which he makes a calculation leading him to a loss.[46]

Even if formal game theoretic analytical approaches are not used, the same reasoning applies if the opponent is cautious in his evaluation of potential outcomes. For example, even though the use of game theory would normally appear to guarantee a preplanned minimum, its very rigidity creates a potential susceptibility to reflexive control. Lefebvre and Smolyan provide a detailed and rather lengthy example of how reflexive control can be used in this way.[47]

These discussions indicate that it is possible to gain a substantial advantage over an opponent who has selected the rather conservative doctrine of game theory to support his decision making process. The greatest benefit can be obtained by causing him to fail to recognize one's own promising strategies, although substantial benefits may also be achieved by causing him to assess the effectiveness of the options erroneously.

Continuing Soviet Research

The theoretical work of Lefebvre has apparently been the object of military research. Specific examples of the potential application of reflexive control to military problems appear in Soviet literature. Examples include the works of Ionov, Berezkin, Tarakanov, Druzhinin, and Kontorov. These examples were analyzed in Lefebvre and Lefebvre in 1984 and 1985.[48] The main points of the Lefebvre analysis are summarized here.

The Ionov and Berezkin discussions appear in *Voyennya Mysl'*—the journal of the Soviet General Staff. Ionov conducted a detailed analysis of the utility of reflexive control from a military point of view. He classifies the various military methods of reflexive control into several categories. One category he terms "power pressure" includes such actions as a military show of force to convince an opponent to avoid combat. Another category focuses on the enemy's situation estimate and includes such measures as camouflage, disinformation, and the use of surprise to change the situation abruptly. Still another category involves the careful presentation to the enemy of a number of equally likely options for its own actions, thereby forcing the enemy to take more time to make a good decision. Ionov also talks of reflexive control techniques for shaping the opponent's decision making algorithm itself, "particularly the technique of regular conduct of strategic-scale exercises on one plane with the aim of decisive actions on another plane which sharply differ from the training exercise."[49] Ionov also argues for the need to use several methods in combinations.

The Berezkin article is a comment on the Ionov article. Lefebvre concludes that this article indicates that the concept of reflexive control was accepted in Soviet military circles at that time.

One example developed by Tarakanov focuses on the problem of a nuclear power attempting to influence the decision process of an enemy with respect to a nuclear strike by the enemy. By reflexive control methods, it is suggested that it is possible to lead the enemy to incorrect conclusions about the nature of one's own forces and also to convince the enemy that he cannot attain high enough levels of damage against one's own forces to prevent a guaranteed retaliation. It is also suggested that a third party, using reflexive control methods, can convince one of the main parties that the other party executed a nuclear strike, and hence have the two main parties engage each other with nuclear weapons.[50]

The works of Druzhinin and Kontorov show a continuing interest in the potential application of reflexive control to a variety of military decision problems. They state explicitly that "in military affairs, reflexive control brings especially good results in training troops (formulating orientation problems, stimulating the activity, using prestige incentives) and mainly in control of the adversary."[51]

Notes

1. V.A. Lefebvre and V.D. Lefebvre, *Reflexive Control: The Soviet Concept of Influencing an Adversary's Decisionmaking Process*, (Englewood, Colo.: Science Applications Inc., 1984), p. 7.

2. Ibid., p. 9

3. V. A. Lefebvre, *Conflicting Structures [Konflixtuyushchiye struktury]* (Moscow: Soviet Radio Publishing House, 1973; trans. by JPRS, JPRS-61332, 1974). See V.A. Lefebvre and G. L. Smolyan, *Algebra of Conflict [Algebra Konflikta]* (Moscow, 1968). Trans. by JPRS, JPRS, 52700 (March 1971).

4. K.V. Tarakanov, *Mathematics and Armed Combat [Matematika i Vooruzhennaya Bor'ba]* (Moscow: Voyenizdat, 1974), pp. 298-299; trans. by FTD, FTD-ID (RS)T—577-79 (August 1979).

5. Lefebvre and Smolyan, *Algebra*, pp. 33-34.

6. V.V. Druzhinin and D.S. Kontorov, *Problems of Military Systems-Engineering [Voprosy Voyennoy Sistemotekhniki]* (Moscow: Voyenizdat, 1975), p. 191.

7. M. Ionov, "On the Methods of Influencing an Opponent's Decisions, *Military Thought [Voyennaya Mysl']*, (1971), no. 12d(1971), p. 24. Translation Foreign Broadcast Information Service (FBIS).

8. Ibid.

9. Tarakanov, *Mathematics and Armed Combat*, p. 300.
10. Lefebvre and Smolyan, *Algebra*, p. 35.
11. A. Limno and A. Gorkin, "The Effectiveness of *Maskirovka*," *Voyennaya Vestnik*, (1980) no. 5, pp. 83-85.
12. Ionov, "On the Methods," p. 60.
13. V. R. Durov, *The Combat Use and Combat Effectiveness Fighter-Interceptors* (Moscow: Voyenizdat, 1972), pp. 231-234. Translation by FTD.
14. N. M. Fendrikov and V. I. Yakovlev, *Methods of Calculating Combat Effectiveness of Armament* [*Metody Raschetov Boyevoy Effektivnosti Vooruzheniya*] (Moscow: Voyenizdat, 1971). Trans. by JPRS, JPRS-56 631 (July 1972), p. 89.
15. Lefebvre and Smolyan, *Algebra*, p. 50.
16. Ibid., p. 43.
17. Tarakanov, *Mathematics and Armed Combat*, p. 302.
18. Ionov, "On the Methods," p. 60.
19. Ibid.
20. Ibid., p. 61.
21. Lefebvre and Smolyan, *Algebra*, p. 61.
22. Ionov, "On the Methods," p. 61.
23. Ibid.
24. Lefebvre and Smolyan, pp. 30-40.
25. Ibid., p. 36.
26. Tarakanov, *Mathematics and Armed Combat*, p. 300.
27. Lefebvre and Smolyan, *Algebra*, p. 36.
28. Tarakanov, *Mathematics and Armed Combat*, p. 300.
29. Druzhinin and Kontorov, *Problems of Military Systems-Engineering*, p. 190.
30. Lefebvre, *Conflicting Structures*, p. 53.
31. Lefebvre and Smolyan, *Algebra*, p. 37.
32. Tarakanov, *Mathematics and Armed Combat*, p. 302.
33. Yu. V. Chuyev and Yu. B. Mikhaylov, *Forecasting in Military Affairs* [*Prognozirovaniye v Voyennom Dele*] (Moscow: Foyenizdat, 1975), p. 55. Trans. and issued by USAF, *Soviet Military Thought* series, no. 16.
34. Druzhinin and Kontorov, *Problems of Military Systems-Engineering*, p. 193.
35. Chuyev and Mikhaylov, *Forecasting*, p. 199.
36. Ye. B. Ivanilov, "A Model of Competition Between Two Countries," *Engineering Cybernetics* [*Tekhnicheskaya Kibernetika*], (1969) no. 1, pp. 19-30.
37. Ionov, "On the Methods," p. 61.
38. Lefebvre and Smolyan, *Algebra*, p. 39.
39. Ibid.
40. I.I. Anureyev and A.Y. Tatarchenko, *Application of Mathematical Methods in Military Affairs* [*Primeneniye Matematicheskikh Metodov v Voyennom Dele*] (Moscow: 1967), p. 53. Chaps. 2, 4, and 5 trans. by FSTC (AD 757 236) (Charlottesville, VA: January 1973); Chaps. 1, 3, and 6 trans. by JPRS, JPRS-42-069 (August 1967).
41. Tarakanov, *Mathematics and Armed Combat*, p. 302.
42. A. Berezkin, "On Controlling the Actions of an Opponent," *Military Thought* [*Voyennaya Mysl'*], (November 1972) no. 11, pp. 92-93. Trans. by FBIS, FPD 0049/73.
43. Lefebvre and Smolyan, *Algebra*, p. 40.

44. Ibid., p. 41.
45. Ibid., p. 32
46. Tarakanov, *Mathematics and Armed Combat*, p. 302.
47. Lefebvre and Smolyan, *Algebra*, pp. 41- 43.
48. V.A. Lefebvre and V.D. Lefebvre, *Reflexive Control II*, (Greenwood Village, Colo.: Science Applications Inc., 1985).
49. Ionov, "On the Methods," p. 167.
50. Tarakanov, *Mathematics and Armed Combat*), pp. 183-197.
51. Druzhinin and Kontorov, *Problems of Military Systems-Engineering*, p. 192.

15
Postwar Soviet Strategic Economic Deception

Steven Rosefielde

Introduction

Strategic economic deception is a form of economic warfare in which fundamental national security objectives are pursued through deceptive economic means. The concept applies to a relatively narrow set of activities. It excludes deceptive economic practices designed to achieve commercial or tactical geopolitical goals. By definition, strategic economic deceptive activities are intended to facilitate the attainment of the principal national security policy objectives of a country: (1) by constraining an adversary's ability to prosecute a war, (2) by degrading its defense capabilities prior to the initiation of hostilities, and, (3) by deceiving it into desisting or capitulating before military operations are required. Any activity that satisfies these criteria, whether implemented for offensive or defensive purposes, may be classified as a strategic economic deception, providing it involves economics in some meaningful way.

This chapter seeks to evaluate whether postwar Soviet-American national security relationships have been affected by Soviet strategic economic deception. It will be shown with varying degrees of certainty that the Soviets have successfully engaged in strategic economic deception, and that these efforts will almost certainly persist. If the Soviet's ultimate goal is defensive, these actions are of subsidiary concern; if they are not, strategic economic deception could have major geopolitical repercussions in Europe and other areas of global concern.

The Soviet Defense Budget

Opportunities for Soviet strategic economic deception in the postwar period have been restricted to constraining Western defense capabilities and creating an environment conducive to allied geopolitical accommodation. Assuming, as Soviet military doctrine ideology and force developments suggest, that Soviet actions are motivated by strategic considerations, at least two instances of strategic economic deception can be identified as being aimed at restricting NATO's military potential.[1] One involves the falsification of the Soviet defense budget,[2] the other concerns SALT treaty provisions governing ballistic missile modernization.

The objective of the first deception was to prevent the West from responding to the postwar Soviet arms buildup begun in the early 1960's by manipulating perceptions of Soviet defense spending. The feasibility of this endeavor depended, for the most part, on the measures used by Western intelligence agencies to gauge the magnitude of the aggregate Soviet military effort and on the effect their assessments had on the level of allied defense appropriations. The Soviets could only manipulate perceptions (propaganda aside), if Western intelligence estimates were either directly or indirectly tied to official Soviet economic statistics and legislators heeded their appraisals.

Fortunately for the Soviets, these preconditions were satisfied during the 1960's and much of the 1970's. The costing methodology utilized by the CIA in this period was closely linked to official Soviet budgetary statistics.[3] Expenditures on military research, development, testing, and evaluation (RDT&E) were partly imputed as a share of the official science budget.[4] Procurement construction, manpower, and operations and maintenance were estimated independently with the building block method,[5] but yielded estimates that appeared to be confirmed by official Soviet defense budgetary outlays. As a consequence, the CIA's independent estimates, which were the sum of these outlays and other relatively minor budgetary items, closely paralleled official Soviet budgetary series. The data in table 15–1 show that CIA estimates of total Soviet defense spending grew 4 percent per annum from 1960 to 1974, while the official defense budget increased slightly faster, at 4.7 percent per annum.[6]

The reasons for this correspondence are bureaucratically complex and may involve Soviet penetration of the CIA's costing activities,[7] but perhaps the single most important factor was historical. Published Soviet defense statistics from the late 1930's until the early 1960's (including the war years) appeared to behave plausibly and were compatible with the broad tapestry of Soviet economic statistics.[8] The CIA, thus, was justified in linking its estimates to official Soviet budgetary series, but was also ripe for deception.

It is not known when the Soviets first recognized the vulnerability of the CIA, but data obtained directly from the books of the Soviet Ministry of Defense in 1975 proved beyond any doubt that the Soviets began manipulating their official defense budgetary statistics in the early 1960's.[9] This is easily confirmed by comparing the CIA's revised figures based on the "new information" and the official defense expenditure growth rates from 1960 to 1975 in table 15–1. The

Table 15–1
Real Soviet Defense Expenditures, 1960–1985
(billions of rubles)[a]

	CIA[b] (1)	Rosefielde (2)	Official (3)
1960	14.3	14.3	9.3
1961	14.9	15.5	11.6
1962	15.5	16.9	12.6
1963	16.1	18.3	13.9
1964	16.7	19.8	13.3
1965	17.4	21.7	12.8
1966	18.1	23.7	13.4
1967	18.8	26.7	14.5
1968	19.8	28.7	16.7
1969	20.8	31.6	17.7
1970	21(42)[c]	43.5	17.9
1971	21.8	46.7	17.9
1972	22.5	50.2	17.9
1973	23.8	55	17.9
1974	24.8	59.7	17.7
1975[d]	51.5	64.7	17.4
1976	53.5	69.2	17.4
1977	54.4	73.7	17.2
1978	55.5	78.6	17.2
1979	56.6	83.8	17.2
1980	57.7	89.4	17.1
1981	58.8	94.3	17.1
1982	60.0	99.5	17.1
1983	(61.2)[e]	105.1	17.1
1984	(62.4)[e]	110.9	17.1
1985	(63.6)[e]	(117.0)[e]	19.1
Compound annual rate of growth			
1960–1974	4.0%	10.7%	4.7%
1960–1975	8.9	10.6	4.3
1970–1985	2.8	6.8	0.4

Sources: Steven Rosefielde, *False Science: Underestimating the Soviet Arms Buildup*, second ed. 1985, tables R5, 13.11, and 19.2; *Narodnoe khoziaistvo SSSR 1983*, p. 547. International Institute for Strategic Studies, *The Military Balance 1985–1986*, p. 18.

[a] The CIA's and the author's estimates are expressed in constant 1970 ruble prices. The official defense budgetary statistics are measured at current ruble prices.

[b] Estimates for the subperiod 1960–74 refer to CIA statistics computed prior to the receipt of the "new information" in 1975.

[c] The bracketed entry for 1970 is the CIA's postrevision estimate.

[d] Figures after 1974 are based on the Agency's revisions reported in *Allocation of Resources in the Soviet Union and China–1983*, JEC, 1983.

[e] The bracketed entries for 1983, 1984 and 1985 are extrapolations. See CIA, *Policy Implications of the Slowdown in Soviet Economic Growth (U)*, SOV-84-10104, July 1984 (Secret), p. vii. Also see Senator William Proxmire, *Joint Economic Committee Press Release*, 21 February 1985 "Soviet defense spending has been growing at a 2 percent rate since the end of 1976. There is recent evidence of some acceleration according to the CIA, but this conclusion is tentative."

implied true CIA growth rate is 8.9 percent per annum—more than double the official rate.[10]

The official figures were falsified in two phases. From 1960 to 1970, the Soviets merely understated the level and rate of military outlays. From 1970 to 1985, they grew bolder, distorting the trend so that it erroneously indicated that Soviet defense appropriations had steadily declined after 1970.[11] The CIA's own statistics for this period did not slavishly follow the official example, but they were strongly downward biased. Instead of growing 6.8 percent per annum, influenced by the official series, they grew only 2.8 percent per annum. (See table 15–1, column 2.)

The success of these machinations is readily apparent in the behavior of American defense outlays, which fell sharply between 1968 and 1973 and then leveled off for the rest of the 1970's[12] despite mounting evidence that the CIA prerevision estimates masked a Soviet military buildup of immense proportions. Its residue can also be found in the biased CIA estimates of Soviet procurement from 1976 to 1984 (table 15–2), which display no growth;[13] and largely parallel the behavior of the official Soviet defense budget and replicate its prerevision ruble procurement estimates from 1960 to 1974.[14] These latest CIA estimates, which are strikingly at variance with DIA statistics,[15] have not yet halted the West's belated response to the Soviet military buildup, but they are apt to do so soon, testifying to the enduring success of this strategic economic deception.

Ballistic Missile Modernization

The second Soviet strategic economic deception involves a negotiating ploy that onesidedly impeded American landbased ballistic missile modernization by imposing SALT compliance costs on the United States which the Soviets themselves circumvented. It is widely understood, that during the 1970's, the United States entered into a series of treaties with the Soviet Union that undermined the survivability of its land-based ICBMs. The Treaty on Anti-Ballistic Missile Systems (26 May 1972) prevented the United States from defending its land-based ballistic missiles jeopardized by improvements in Soviet ICBM accuracy.[16] The Interim Agreement on the Limitation of Strategic Offensive Arms (signed concurrently) increased American ballistic missile vulnerability by making silo launchers the effective unit of SALT verification.[17] Although SALT I did not explicitly prohibit mobile or moveable systems such as the MX/MPS (multiple protection shelter) program, the silo-launcher verification requirement created a serious impediment to achieving secure land-based ICBM deployments. This obstacle was intensified by the Treaty on the Limitation of Strategic Offensive Arms and the Protocol to the Treaty (18 June 1979, concluded in Vienna), which barred the development, testing, or deployment of mobile launchers of heavy ICBMs (article IX, d), and the deployment of mobile

Table 15-2
U.S. and Soviet Defense Procurement, 1976-1984
(*billions of 1978 dollars*)

	Soviet		U.S.
	CIA[a] (1)	Rosefielde (2)	DOD (3)
1976	37.3	57.5	18.6
1977	37.3	61.9	20.1
1978	37.3	66.6	21.3
1979	37.3	71.7	25.0
1980	37.3	77.2	25.2
1981	37.3	81.8	28.9
1982	37.3	86.7	32.0
1983	37.3	91.8	35.9
1984	37.3	97.3	40.3
1976-84	335.7	692.5	247.3
Compound annual rate of growth	0%	6.8%	10.1%

Sources: Rosefielde, *False Science: Underestimating the Soviet Arms Buildup*, second edition, table R1.

[a] This is the CIA's adjusted 1978 series. See "Allocation of Resources in the Soviet Union and China-1983," JEC September 1983, p. 306, and Rosefielde, *False Science*, table 13.2, p. 162. Cf. CIA, *Policy Implications of the Slowdown in Soviet Economic Growth (U)*, SOV-84-10104, July 1984 (Secret), p. vii. Also see Senator William Proxmire, *Joint Economic Committee Press Release*, 21 February 1985 "Soviet military procurement has grown little, if at all, throughout this period, although there may have been some modest growth in 1983 over 1982." This statement is quoted from closed CIA testimony before the JEC 21 November 1984. Data are obtained from the Department of Defense (Outlays) computer printout, base year 1985, and have been converted from a fiscal to a calendar year basis.

ICBM launchers or the flight-testing of ICBMs from such launchers (Protocol, article I).[18]

In signing these accords, Presidents Nixon and Carter believed that they had reached balanced agreements that did not require additional negotiated assurances of noncircumvention. They were convinced that the treaties constrained Soviet land-based deployments, while allowing the United States to modernize its landbased ballistic missile forces, subject to an expensive, but manageable SALT compliance penalty.[19] Only two weeks before the SALT II agreement was finalized, President Carter decided to proceed with the development of the MX missile in a multiple protective shelter basing mode.[20]

As events subsequently revealed, however, Nixon and Carter were mistaken. First, the absence of explicit provisions effectively controlling ballistic missile reserves and reloads not only enabled the Soviets to flaunt the implied ceilings on missiles and warheads while adhering to SALT II launcher restrictions, but allowed them to modernize their land-based ballistic missile forces (including SS-25s) without concern for their vulnerability or for the compliance costs they should have borne, had they honored their informal assurances on noncircumvention.[21] Second, the compliance costs of the MX/MPS system— approximately $10 billion measured in 1978 prices, $16 billion today—when coupled with doubts about its long-term effectiveness proved to be politically unacceptable.[22] Within a year the program was dead; the United States was left without a survivable land-based ballistic missile force for the 1980's and agreements that effectively constrained the Soviets.

It is readily seen from the foregoing review that the Soviets used the SALT process not only to obtain by deception a decisive advantage in land-based ballistic missiles,[23] but also to obstruct American ICBM modernization. The strategy of this deception primarily involved physical restrictions on defensive and offensive systems, which were circumvented on the Soviet side by evading controls on missiles, while adhering to those on launchers. The deception could not be consummated by physical restrictions alone, because, as President Carter clearly understood, the Senate would not ratify SALT II if all multiple aim point (MAP) systems were precluded.[24] Therefore the Soviets did everything in their power to limit U.S. basing options to the most expensive alternatives. They coaxed the American side into prohibiting mobile systems, and rejected vertical silo basing as a violation of SALT silo-launcher ceilings.[25] These actions together with their informal assurances of noncircumvention induced the U.S. to choose the compliance cost intensive MX/MPS system. The Soviets, of course, could not have been certain that these compliance costs would scuttle the program, but as events ultimately proved, they had good grounds for optimism. The compliance costs imposed in a one-sided manner on the United States helped kill MX/MPS and assured that the deployment of a survivable land-based American ballistic missile system was indefinitely postponed, while the Soviets were left free to vigorously expand their own ICBM forces.

Economic Détente

The direct forms of strategic economic deception discussed above may have been supplemented in the postwar period by a host of indirect activities conveniently subsumed under the rubric of economic détente. To the extent they occurred, these activities operated primarily on factors conditioning Soviet strategic prospects and had two distinct objectives: constraining Western military capabilities and promoting the attainment of Soviet geopolitical ends through nonviolent means. The methods employed to achieve these goals were largely commercial and dual-optioned, in the sense that the Soviets benefited regardless of whether they chose to exploit or refrained from exploiting, the strategic advantages conferred by their policies.

Unfortunately, this latter property makes it exceedingly difficult, if not impossible, to distinguish commercial activities designed to influence the achievement of strategic policy goals from those pursued for profit.[26] The net benefit obtained from subsidized loans (for example, favorable natural gas contract prices and COCOM-sanctioned technology transfers) provide no clue, in and of themselves, because they neither constrain Western military capabilities, nor promote accommodation, even though they may indirectly enhance Soviet military capabilities by increasing real GNP. It may be reasonable to infer from the strength of Western European opposition to increased defense spending and accommodationist sentiment that economic détente effectively served Soviet geostrategic purposes;[27] but this cannot be proven, because other noneconomic factors may provide an adequate explanation. Thus, while the evidence does not disconfirm the hypothesis that economic détente was pursued to further Soviet strategic ends, all that prudently can be concluded from the strong correlation between Soviet doctrine, deployments, and commercial policy on one hand, and West European military-political behavior on the other, is that the relationship may not be coincidental and could be attributable to strategic economic deception.

The Next Quinquennium

The enormous gains realized by the Soviets in the postwar period through the deft and virtually costless use of strategic economic deception suggests that they will almost certainly try to achieve further successes in the next quinquennium. Recent activities in the American academic and commercial communities indicate that the Soviets are laying the foundation for a coordinated revival of economic détente, stressing the benefits of commercial interdependence and Western arms restraint. As in the past, an initiative of this sort is likely to succeed without producing certifiable proof of deceptive intent.

Soviet falsification of their official defense budgetary statistics is also likely to persist, but may take several novel forms. The growing divergence between the dollar estimates of the DIA and the CIA of Soviet procurement from 1982 to 1985, and the much larger disparity between their respective ruble estimates from 1965 to 1985, could induce the Soviets to manipulate their machine-building statistics in the CIA's favor.[28] This could be accomplished by suppressing the data upon which the DIA's estimates depend, falsifying them by exaggerating the civilian share of aggregate machine building/metalworking (MBMW) production, or by releasing information that ostensibly confirms the CIA's position on hidden inflation in the military machine-building sector.[29] The first two alternatives are the most likely because they would be relatively unobtrusive, would be consistent with the treatment of machinery production in Soviet input-output tables,[30] and would have the ancillary benefit of exaggerating aggregate Soviet consumption.

It should be anticipated that the effectiveness of the Soviet budgetary deception, with or without embellishment, will increase as allied politicians become increasingly aware that the Soviet advantage and Soviet weapons expenditures in defense spending, as calculated by the CIA, have been ostensibly reversed. Although a powerful case for increased American defense spending can be sustained on the basis of production, order of battle, and related technical data,[31] it would not be surprising if this physical evidence were again overshadowed by official Soviet and CIA economic statistics that showed the U.S. outspending the Soviets.[32]

Finally, the Soviets can be expected to fashion a new economic deception to encumber the strategic defense initiative in much the same way they degraded the MX program.[33] The preconditions for an action of this sort are already partly in place. The attention of American policy makers is riveted on CONUS, with little appreciation that the immediate focus of Soviet concern is tactical ballistic missile defense in the West European theater.[34] Costing estimates are being devised on the basis of nominal Soviet ballistic missile deployments without regard for the total force capabilities disclosed by DIA, ICBM, SLBM, and LRINF production statistics. Little, if any, attention is being paid to the potential damage to the viability of SDI that could arise if the costs of an adequate system are significantly underestimated, or are distorted by unanticipated compliance obligations. The Soviets may not be able to exploit these vulnerabilities, but it would be uncharacteristic of them not to try.

Conclusion

Western experts recognize that the Soviets occasionally falsify their statistics to manipulate perceptions; that they are capable of adroitly employing other economic instruments to further their purposes; and that their military doctrine sanctions the use of these means to gain their strategic ends. Despite these realizations, little serious attention has been paid to the subject of Soviet strategic economic deception. This exploratory review shows that this is a grave oversight; that in at least two instances during the postwar period, the Soviets successfully constrained and/or degraded Western military capabilities. Moreover, it has been demonstrated that the conditions that facilitated these actions have not been redressed, leaving the Western alliance vulnerable to a new wave of Soviet strategic economic deception.

Notes

1. Glenn Skaggs, Glenn Bailey, and Steven Spayed, *Surprise and Preemption in Soviet Nuclear Strategy* 83–015, DTIC (Washington, D.C.: National War College, 1983).

Patrick Parker and Steven Rosefielde, "Soviet Arms Procurement Strategy in the Eighties: Conflicting Perceptions of the Soviet Arms Buildup, *Russia* 12 (1986).

2. The Soviets overtly attempted to use budgetary means to control Western defense spending on numerous occasions. "Between 1948 and 1964, the Soviet Union alone made 20" proposals to curb the arms race by budgetary freezes. John Barton and Lawrence Weiler, eds., *International Arms Control* (Stanford, Calif: Stanford University Press, 1976), p. 247; Cf. Abraham Becker, *Military Expenditure Limitation for Arms Control: Problems and Prospects* (Cambridge, Mass: Ballinger, 1977).

3. Central Intelligence Agency (CIA), *The 1960 Soviet Defense Budget* (November 1960); CIA, *The Soviet Defense Budget for 1961* (June 1961); CIA, *The Soviet Defense Budget for 1962* (November 1962); Abraham Becker, *Soviet Military Outlays Since 1955* (Santa Monica, Calif: Rand Corporation, July 1964).

4. See note 3.

5. Steven Rosefielde, *False Science: Under-Estimating the Soviet Arms Buildup*, 2d ed., ch. 3, (New Brunswick, N.J.: Transaction, 1986).

6. CIA statistics are valued in constant prerevision 1970 ruble prices, which are essentially 1955 ruble prices. The official series are in current rubles, but open inflation between 1960 and 1970 was negligible.

7. Rosefielde, *False Science*, pp. 252–254.

8. Abram Bergson, *The Real National Income of Soviet Russia Since 1928* (Cambridge: Harvard University Press, 1961), pp. 68–76; Raymond Hutchins, *The Soviet Budget* (Albany: State University of New York Press, 1983), pp. 120–139; Peter Wiles and Moshe Efrat, *The Economics of Soviet Arms* (London: Suntory-Toyota International Centre for Economics and Related Disciplines, 1985), p. 72. Michael Kaser still believes that the official defense budget is unfalsified. See Archie Brown and Michael Kaser, eds., *Soviet Policy for the 1980s* (London: Macmillan/ St. Anthony's, 1982). For an analysis of Wiles estimates, see Steven Rosefielde, "The Integrity of Official Soviet Defense Budgetary Statistics," unpublished manuscript, November 1985.

9. The CIA acknowledges that the Soviets are manipulating their defense budget for deceptive purposes. See Robert Leggett and Sheldon Rabin, "A Note on the Meaning of the Soviet Defense Budget," *Soviet Studies* 30(October 1978): pp. 557–566. On the "new information," see Rosefielde, *False Science*, ch. 1.

10. The 8.9 percent rate is computed using the CIA's 1960 estimate in prerevision 1970 ruble prices, and its 1975 estimate measured in postrevision 1970 ruble prices. Soviet price indexes indicate that these statistics should be comparable, but the CIA makes other adjustments for hidden inflation. See Rosefielde, *False Science*, table 13.10, p. 184.

11. The official Soviet defense budget for 1985 is 19.1 billion rubles. The growth rate from 1970 to 1985 is 0.4 percent per annum. The corresponding CIA estimate is 2.8 percent per annum. See *The Military Balance 1985–1986* (London: International Institute for Strategic Studies, 1985); See table 1 and other reference, in this chapter.

12. Rosefielde, *False Science*, table 13.10, p. 184.

13. According the the CIA, Soviet defense spending has increased 2.0 percent per annum since 1976, with weapons procurements displaying no growth through 1981, and presumably beyond. See, Joint Economic Committee (JEC) Report, *Allocation of Resources* (September 1983), p. 306; JEC, *Allocation of Resources in the Soviet Union and*

China—1983 (November 1984), pp. 12, 18; Cf, CIA, *A Comparison of Soviet and U.S. Defense Activities—1972-81 (U)*, SOV83 10035 (S), February 1983; CIA, *Policy Implications of the Slowdown in Soviet Economic Growth (U)*, SOV-84-10104 (S), July 1984, p. vii. The official defense budget declined negligibly during the same time period (see table 15-1). Also see Senator William Proxmire, *Joint Economic Committee Press Release*, 21 February 1985: "Soviet military procurement has grown little, if at all, throughout this period, although there may have been some modest growth in 1983 over 1982." CIA, *A Comparison of Soviet and U.S. Defense Activities, 1976–1985 (U)*, SOV 86-10028, May 1986.

14. Rosefielde, *False Science*, ch. 1.

15. Defense Intelligence Agency (DIA), *USSR: Military Economic Trends and Resource Allocation—1984 (U)*, DDB-1900-89-85 (S), April 1985; DIA, *The Defense Intelligence Agency and Central Intelligence Agency Ruble Estimates of Soviet Defense Expenditures (U)*, DDB-1900-63-83 (S), August 1983; DIA, *USSR: Military Economic Resource Allocations—1984*, DDB-1900-88-85 (March 1985). The CIA has decided to suppress its dollar estimates. The official rationale is provided in CIA, *Allocations of Resources in the Soviet Union and China—1984*, pp. 18–19.

16. Roger Labrie, ed., *SALT Handbook* (Washington, D.C.: American Enterprise Institute, 1979), pp. 15–19.

17. Ibid., pp. 20–22. Cf. Colin Gray, *The MX ICBM and National Security* (New York: Praeger, 1981), p. 65:

"For reasons of contemporary technical detail, and diplomatic habit, there is a SALT negotiating history that could be held to have established [through implicitly agreed usage] that an ICBM silo is an ICBM launcher."

18. Labrie, *SALT Handbook*, pp. 645, 651.

19. SALT II precluded the deployment of the SS-16. See Herbert Scoville, *MX: Prescription for Disaster* (Cambridge: MIT Press, 1981), p. 96.

20. John Edwards, *Superweapon: The Making of MX* (New York: Norton, 1982), p. 199.

21. Steven Rosefielde, "National Security Implications of the Soviet Arms Buildup 1975–1984", in Alexander J. Matejko and Agit Jain, eds., *From Brezhnev to Gorbachev* (New York: Praeger forthcoming table 3; Cf. Seymour Weiss, "SALT Verification," in John Lehman and Seymour Weiss, *Beyond the SALT Failure* (New York: Praeger, 1981), p. 69. The evidence suggests that the Soviets have several thousand MIRVed ICBM reserves including SS-18 reloads. Most authorities state that the U.S. has no reserves, but Secretary of the Navy John Lehman acknowledges that the U.S. had 100 Minuteman IIIs stockpiled in the early 1980's. See Lehman and Weiss, *Beyond the SALT Failure*, p. 148.

22. As of September 1979, facility design and construction for the MX/MPS system were pegged at $10.8 billion, with $4.9 billion allocated for operations and maintenance. I have arbitrarily assumed that roughly two-thirds of these outlays represent excessive compliance costs. See Scoville, MX table 15.1, table 15.1, p. 162.

23. See note 20.

24. Edwards, *Superweapon*, ch. 7, pp. 171–199.

25. See William Van Cleave, "U.S. Strategic Forces in the 1980s," in Gordon J. Humphrey et. al., *SALT II and American Security* (Cambridge, Mass: Institute for Foreign Policy Analysis, October 1980), p. 17. Cf. Gray, pp. 26, 50–53; Edwards, *Superweapon*, p. 219; Scoville, MX, p. 109.

26. The classic case of commercial economic deception was the "Great Grain Robbery" of 1972, when the Soviets purchased millions of bushels of American wheat at discount prices before the market recognized that the Soviets were having a catastrophic harvest. The United States may have suffered a windfall loss of more than $1 billion as a result of this deception. However, as large as this loss was, it does not appear to have been intended to constrain American military power, or to achieve some related strategic objective.

27. David Yost, *France's Deterrent Posture and Security in Europe: Part I, Capabilities and Doctrine*, Adelphi Paper no. 194, International Institute for Strategic Studies (Winter 1984/1985); *France and Conventional Defense in Central Europe*, EAI Paper No. 7, European American Institute for Security Research (Spring 1984).

28. DIA, *The Defense Intelligence Agency and Central Intelligence Agency Ruble Estimates of Soviet Defense Expenditures (U)*, DDB-1900-63-83 (S), April 1985.

29. Rosefielde, *False Science*, appendix 7.

30. In my view, weapons are included mostly in final MBMW consumption in the 1966 and 1972 Soviet input-output tables, not in investment as Treml believes, or repair and replacement as Wiles hypothesizes. See Wiles and Efrat, *The Economics of Soviet Arms*.

31. Steven Rosefielde, "National Security Implications of the Soviet Arms Buildup, 1975–1984."

32. Senator William Proxmire, *JEC Press Release*, 21 February 1985:
"It is time for Washington to take official notice that Soviet military procurement has been stagnent for the past seven years, and to stop acting like nothing has changed."

33. CIA, *Possible Soviet Responses to the U.S. Strategic Defense Initiative (U)* NIC-M-83-10017 (S), 12 September 1983; Benjamin Lambeth, *Arms Control and Defense Planning in Soviet Strategic Policy*, P-664 (Santa Monica, Calif: Rand Corporation, July 1981).

34. James Fletcher, *Eliminating the Threat Posed by Nuclear Ballistic Missiles (U)*, Vol. II, *Surveillance Acquisition, Tracking and Kill Assessment (U), Part I*, Defense Technical Information Center (S), February 1984; James Fletcher, *Eliminating the Threat Posed by Nuclear Ballistic Missiles (U), Vol. VI, Systems Concepts, Part I*, Defense Technical Information Center (S), February 1984; James Fletcher, *Eliminating the Threat Posed by Nuclear Ballistic Missiles (U), Vol. VII, Soviet Countermeasures and Tactics (U)*, Defense Technical Information Center (S), February 1984; Fred Hoffman, *Ballistic Missile Defense and U.S. National Security (U), Vol. I, Summary Report and Main Report (U)*, Future Security Strategy Study (Alexandria, Va: Institute for Defense Analyses, October 1983). Cf. Stephen Meyer, "Soviet Strategic Programmes and the U.S. SDI," *Survival* 27(November/December 1985), pp. 274–292.

16
Chemical and Biological Warfare: The Covert Dimension

Joseph D. Douglass, Jr.

In the mid-1950's, the Soviets decided that chemical and biological weapons were an area where they could get the West to unilaterally disarm. To do so, they reasoned, it was important that the West perceive the Soviets as complying with the 1925 Geneva Protocol. Accordingly, Soviet offensive chemical and biological programs were placed under the highest security protection, and a cover and deception program was developed to hide their interests and programs.

Also during the 1950's, Soviet military development efforts were concentrated in nuclear weapons and long-range means of delivery. Other areas, including chemical and biological warfare, were low on the priority list. By 1960, the nuclear revolution was well underway and under control. Shortly thereafter, other areas began to reemerge. One of the first to have its priority greatly increased was chemical and biological warfare. Research institutes were built, and espionage in these areas was made a top priority activity.

In 1963, high-level Soviet officials were explaining the important role of chemical and biological warfare in a European context and in a war against China. At that time, chemical and biological weapons were as important as nuclear weapons in Europe and more important for a war against China. In 1965, a major twenty-year plan to coordinate efforts throughout the Warsaw Pact was initiated. The first phase, preparation for production, was from 1966 to 1971; phase two, expanded production, was from 1971 to 1976. A qualitatively new family of both chemical and biological weapons was scheduled to enter the inventory in 1985.

This background of strong Soviet interest, coupled with a major program of development and expansion and challenging objectives is essential to understand what began to happen in the mid-1970's, because this is when one of the greatest revolutions in science and technology began. This is the revolution in the life sciences—recombinant DNA, immunology, toxicology, neuropharmacology, and the more popularized biotechnology and genetic engineering. While the effects of the revolutionary advances in these areas can be compared with the nuclear revolution, they really go beyond the nuclear revolution in terms of their potential impact, because of the qualitative advances (selectivity, flexibility, and controllability) that accompany the enormous quantitative advancements, and because of the rapid technology transfer to different nations, cultures, and educational levels that has been proceeding at a very brisk pace.

With the technology that is now available, agents can be tailored to produce very specific results and do so with the greatest efficiency. Agents can be externally manufactured, packaged in minute capsules, and delivered by a variety of means. Alternatively, organisms can be turned into miniature production facilities that manufacture the desired toxic substances, and delivery then becomes a problem of depositing the minute organisms so that they are carried naturally and unobtrusively into the target body. Additionally, the same technologies that make possible these new approaches also can be used to make many of the classic agents (both chemical and biological) far more simple to manufacture, easier to deliver, and more effective, while at the same time eliminating undesirable side effects.

All this emerged at a time when the Soviet Union was both poised and motivated to take the developments and exploit them for their total potential to military, political, intelligence, and economic warfare. And, it is interesting to note (perhaps as a testament to their success in keeping secret the nature of their offensive programs and capabilities) that as recently as 1983, the perception of the Department of Defense of the Warsaw Pact chemical and biological threat was not much different from that of the late 1960's; it was not until 1984 that official concerns of a far improved and quite different threat began to emerge.

The nature of the Soviet chemical and biological threat is still far from understood. Moreover, it will be exceedingly difficult to develop any broad acceptance of its possible range because, while directed at the heart and mind of national security, it falls outside the mainstream of traditional military thinking. It involves a whole host of new scientific and technical developments, and brings into question the whole range of ongoing chemical defense and offense programs. Moreover, while with the application of modern technology, whereby the traditional chemical threat to forces in Europe is greatly exacerbated, the real impact is in a whole range of "new" possibilities, including: terrorism, proliferation and Third World nations, *spetsnaz* (or special forces) operations, and, most sinister, covert intelligence operations.

To provide a partial glimpse into where the Soviets might seek to apply this technology, the following material draws upon Soviet statements and prior practices where the recent scientific advances appear to hold great promise. The areas examined are sabotage in preparation for war and intelligence operations conducted in peacetime against a variety of different enemies. It should not take much imagination to visualize the use of these concepts as a part of a wide variety of covert activities.

Sabotage

Sabotage generally refers to covert, behind-the-lines military operations undertaken before or during a war. Here attention is directed only to acts performed before the war starts, or at its very start, to disable the enemy's ability to go to war. In the rapidly moving context of modern day conflict, this sabotage is considered far more important than the World War II type that takes place during war.

Sabotage is a major weapon in Soviet strategy. According to the former high-level Communist official, Jan Sejna, all important targets are planned for attack in different ways, the first of which generally is sabotage. Chemical and biological weapons have been used for sabotage on several occasions in the past and, according to the same source, are part of Soviet sabotage plans for war. The number of sabotage teams that are part of Soviet plans for war in Europe alone very likely number several hundred.[1] The number planned for action in the United States might well be comparable, if not greater.

Notwithstanding the severity and diversity of this threat, it is only in the last five years that it has begun to receive widespread attention.[2] In the United States, there is still little appreciation of the potential severity of the sabotage threat. In all likelihood, the severity of the threat has advanced considerably over the past ten years.

The rationale behind this conclusion is the self-destruction of the U.S. internal security capabilities that took place in 1973 to 1976, especially when it is coupled with a parallel influx of tens of thousands of emigres and refugees from Communist regions during the 1970's and 1980's. As an indication of diminished U.S. capabilities to monitor potential problems, the number of cases of "subversives and extremists" under investigation by the FBI went from 55,000 in 1974, to roughly 20,000, by the summer of 1975, to slightly over 100 in 1977, to 17 in 1982–83.[3] This helps to explain why Arnaud de Borchgrave testified before Congress in 1983 that the Soviet KGB and its subsidiary, the Cuban DGI, operate freely in the United States, and that "the DGI regards internal security in the U.S. as a joke."[4]

Both the KGB and the GRU have sabotage departments—in all Communist client states as well as in the Soviet Union. The work normally is divided up. The KGB generally takes action against political and civilian targets. The GRU-trained officers, attached to military commands and high-level staff organizations, handle military, military-industrial, and military-economic targets. Both KGB and GRU have training facilities. Recruits of all nationalities, including Americans are trained.[5] Basic training for non-Soviets takes place in many

Communist countries, but advanced training for those that excel, both substantively and ideologically is conducted exclusively within the Soviet Union.[6] There are special camps where trained personnel live for extended periods of time. These camps model the target country. The language and currency of the target country are used, and training is specifically target-intensive.[7]

Over the past five years, due to a number of defections and strong nationalist concerns for Communist penetration, a large-scale effort to employ Latin Americans in this role has come to light. For example, there is now reported to be a Latin American sabotage army resident in Sweden numbering six to eight thousand Soviet and Cuban trained revolutionaries. This army is linked to Moscow, and members receive training each year in various Eastern European countries and the Soviet Union. Their targets are believed by Swedish counterintelligence officials to be Western Europe and Great Britain. Similar Latin American enclaves in Eastern Europe and the Soviet Union have also been identified.[8] Their possible relevance to the United States, or more likely parallel organizations in Cuba or Mexico, needs no elaboration.

The organization of sabotage is carefully constructed to utilize Soviet and surrogate, in-place and inserted, sabotage agents with proper regard for ideology and national feelings as well as technical training. Many agents are already in the targeted countries, as are most of the required weapons and supplies. Given the ease of penetrating U.S. borders, there would be little problem for an enemy to bring explosives and large quantities of chemical and biological agents into the United States or other NATO countries. Additional agents are to be inserted into the various countries before a war starts.

Sabotage groups may be as small as one or two individuals in very specific tasks, generally assassinations, to as large as 1,000 in the attack of a major complex. The normal size group contains five or six members. Control is exercised through Soviet agents in-place, and where possible, Soviets will lead the sabotage groups. In any one country, there are several independent GRU and KGB nets to preserve security.

In periods of crisis, when war is considered imminent, preparations are carried to the point at which operations can be put into action on a moment's notice. Targets are not necessarily coincident with an agent's location in peacetime, particularly when agents are very close to a given target. To guard against discovery and arrest during crisis preparations, agent targets often are at different locations. In a parallel fashion, agent groups that are collected together in one place, such as Sweden, generally are viewed as targeted against other countries such as Germany, Belgium, and England (in the case of those based in Sweden).

Sabotage would be directed at military units and facilities, political or administration elements, military-industrial facilities, and specific people. Their broad objective would be to cripple the enemy's ability to mobilize and go to war. Sabotage can take place right at the start of the war, or days to weeks or months earlier.

In Soviet terminology, sabotage often is referred to as diversionary, special, or *spetsnaz* operations. A particularly good description, where the subject is "special reconnaissance," is presented in the *Soviet Military Encyclopedia*. Special reconnaissance

> is carried out to subvert the political, economic, military, and moral potential of a probable or actual enemy. The primary missions of special reconnaissance are: acquiring intelligence on major economic and military installations and either destroying them or putting them out of action; organizing sabotage and acts of subversion and terrorism; carrying out punitive operations against patriotic forces; conducting hostile propaganda; forming and training insurgent detachments, etc.[9]

Now and for the foreseeable future, it is inconceivable to most defense analysts that the United States would strike first, independent of Soviet actions. On the other hand, in their planning the Soviets assume the enemy is prudent. They might well believe that, in the event of war, the only course of action for the United States—because of the vulnerability of its forces—is to strike first. This would be true if it were not for the fact that war will not be seen in the United States as a certainty.

Soviet strategy calls for a preemptive first strike if they believe the United States has decided to strike.[10] Alternatively, their strategy calls for deceptive actions designed to mislead the West into lowering its guard while the Soviets covertly go to maximum readiness to strike first. To confuse matters further, as this takes place, Soviet strategy calls for indigenous forces in the capitalist world in a crisis situation to rise up and revolt to prevent "their aggressive leaders from unleashing war."

As part of this process, the Soviets could initiate a massive covert biological and chemical war that would be confusing for the U.S. leadership to analyze—possibly impossible to know the certain cause. This process could effectively disable U.S. forces and the civilian population and make it impossible for the U.S. to go to war, except as an extreme act of desperation.

Of disturbing relevance, the mission of sabotage is repeatedly coupled with toxins and biological weapons in Communist military literature.[11] For example, the *Soviet Military Encyclopedia*, in a discussion of neurotropic toxins, "the most toxic chemical substances of all known toxic agents," explains that these agents can be used as an aerosol or in solid or liquid state, and that "they can also be used for sabotage purposes."[12]

A particularly good example from East German literature is the following discussion from a 1967 military chemistry manual on the significance of psychotoxins:

> Besides their tactical significance, the psychotoxins are credited with strategic importance as diversion and sabotage poisons. With relatively small amounts, if

the actions are well-planned, great effects can be achieved in the interior. By poisoning water-supply facilities and the like, large portions of the population can be made incapable of action for a certain period of time. Breakdowns in sensitive production areas, anxiety, uncertainty, and unpredictable actions would be the results.[13]

The East German text also points out that psychotoxins have special advantages not shared by other chemical warfare agents. Incapacity is brought about

> by extremely slight doses or concentrations too small to be detected with conventional methods of detection. [Moreover, the agents are] . . . colorless, odorless, and tasteless. They can be used both as combat chemical agents and as sabotage poisons for the poisoning of water, foodstuffs, and luxuries. The compounds chosen are extremely stable in the atmosphere, and even in water.[14]

Toxins also are described in a 1977 East German *Textbook of Military Chemistry* as many times more toxic than soman, seven orders of magnitude more toxic in an included table. They are said to be simple to produce "in large amounts, using continuous processes,"—a specific example of the application of biotechnology to chemical and biological warfare.[15] And again, militarily, they distinguish between temporarily immobilizing and lethal toxins, and between combat and sabotage applications.

Many of the same advantages and contexts of usage associated with toxins also dominate the discussions of biological warfare. In the 1983 *Soviet Military Encyclopedia*, biological weapons are said to have high combat effectiveness because of the smallness of the required dose, the possibility of concealed employment over a large terrain, the difficulty of detection, the selectivity available (only on humans, or given types of animals, and so forth), the strong psychological pressure, the amount deployed, and the difficulty of biological protection of troops and population, and liquidation of their effects.

Biological weapons also are part of the Soviet discussions on sabotage. For example, in the previously mentioned *Soviet Military Encyclopedia*, in the discussion of *special reconnaissance*, the operations are described as set up by military and special services, "conducted by the forces of covert intelligence and special purpose troops." Among the special weapons listed for use in special reconnaissance are "biological weapons, narcotics, and poisons."[16]

Within the sabotage area, the same increased lethality and incapacitation objectives previously highlighted as a traditional military requirement would seem to be important. Additionally, where sabotage takes place well in advance of hostilities, considerable value would be placed on having agents or substances that were, in the first place, hard to detect and, in the second place, hard to identify. It is best to have an event appear to be the result of a natural cause. Alternatively, it probably is adequate for events simply to be designed so that security professionals are unable to explain with assurance what has happened.

The difficulties involved in detecting and identifying what has been happening and the value (or problem) of these difficulties can be seen in the Vietnam and Afghanistan experiences. Moreover, as detailed in the Hirsch report on Soviet CBW during and prior to World War II, the Japanese used chemical agents in World War II and, accompanying that use, had associated instructions that all evidence of the use was to be carefully destroyed following the use.[17] Many people have also pointed out that, in the suspected Soviet use of agents in the 1960's and 1970's, these uses were in hard-to-access locations, in areas of difficult terrain, and, accordingly, in areas where collecting evidence was extremely difficult. Most recently, stories emanating from Afghanistan have Soviets wearing gas masks entering target areas three to four hours following attacks with chemical munitions and carrying off the dead bodies.

Also, for sabotage, the development of an agent that can act through the water supply would be a desirable objective because of the ease and covertness of delivery. One can envision a range of acceptable options, from gradual cumulative effects to rapid, but short, duration effects. Poisoning the water supply that services important political-administration areas has been a reported Soviet plan. Also, one might add, many important military and political installations are critically dependent on water supply from external sources that are easily accessible to efficient sabotage.

A most challenging Soviet sabotage target would be closed facilities, both military and political, during a crisis. Obvious targets include the White House, presidential and successor relocation facilities; military command/control centers such as NORAD, Ft. Ritchie, and Omaha; air bases; Minuteman wing control centers and launch facilities; and especially submarines. During a crisis, such facilities become semi-closed citadels—no one goes in or out without high priority need. In-place agents would be an obvious enemy asset. On the other hand, they may be considered undependable because, in such a crisis, a prudent planner assumes that all suspect agents will be arrested and detained.[18]

For each of the above targets, the question is how to sabotage them. The time available could be as short as days or weeks, but more likely would be months. In all cases, a few people (fewer than 50) are closely together in a closed area for an extended period of time. Disabling only a few of them would be inadequate. The modern biochem possibilities for accomplishing these tasks are limited mainly by one's imagination.

Over the past quarter of a century, most attention in the West has been directed to the impossibility of nuclear war. Very little attention or effort has been directed to its possibility. The belief that nuclear war is impossible is also interpreted as a Soviet belief. That is, because we know it is impossible, surely the Soviets also must understand that to be the case. Thus, almost any action the Soviets take in nonnuclear areas is interpreted as a deliberate shift away from nuclear, except the improvements in nuclear forces, which are attributed to the effect of blind bureaucratic momentum.

The problem with these analyses is that they ignore the basic principles of Soviet strategy, such as using all forces and means, each to its best advantage, and not regarding nuclear weapons as absolute weapons. Whatever weapon is best for the job is the weapon to be used. There are many cases where weapons other than nuclear weapons are considered more effective, including biological and chemical weapons. Thus, it is not that the Soviets are afraid of nuclear weapons or understand the impossibility of nuclear war, but rather that they do not view nuclear weapons as absolute, that they believe the best weapon for the job is the one to use. As indicated earlier, nuclear weapons can be counterproductive if they interfere with one's own troop operations or if they destroy the war booty—for example, industrial plants, and so forth. Thus, the so-called shift, is not so much a shift away from nuclear war as it is a constant refinement and improvement of their plans for war using all forces and means.

In the consideration of the potential associated with modern biochem weapons, major significance is attached to their use in sabotage by special forces. This use could figure prominently in Soviet pre-attack war plans. As an alternative to nuclear weapons where their use is militarily or politically undesirable, or to deny the enemy the ability (as they would say) to unleash nuclear war, certainly, possible Soviet CBW objectives likely would be important incentives in a Soviet offensive biochem agent engineering program.

As new weapons that are more effective than, or better alternatives to, nuclear weapons in performing certain tasks enter the Soviet inventory, they should be expected to be put to use by the Soviets in pursuing those tasks. In many regards, from a defender's point of view, the increased use of chemical and biological weapons to perform tasks formerly accomplished with nuclear weapons is not (or should not be regarded as) a welcome relief.

Political and Intelligence Requirements

While military forces and objectives are important in Soviet strategy, the main thrust has been on political, ideological, intelligence, and economic warfare. These forms of warfare define what the Soviets call "peaceful coexistence." Together, they are designed to produce the well-known pattern of events: infiltration, subversion, revolution, and takeover. In this dimension of Soviet strategy, military forces mainly provide the intimidation used to ease or speed the process, and to secure the takeover at the appropriate time.

Accordingly, there is another set of objectives related to political, intelligence, and economic warfare that might be even more important than the military and paramilitary objectives. While these objectives are not viewed as direct military objectives (as the term is used in the West), it should be appreciated that military forces and capabilities are principal targets in this "peaceful" or less violent form of warfare. They can act directly, through attacks designed to demoralize the troops, erode discipline, or disrupt the chain of command, and indirectly, through actions designed to discredit the military and erode its base of popular support.

In Soviet subversion strategy, infiltration is usually the first step taken against an objective country. Moscow chooses its targets with surgical precision. The priority targets include:

> organizations that study the Soviet Union and communism, such as counterintelligence and Soviet studies programs in universities;
>
> centers for records, information, and statistics, such as commerce and personnel departments;
>
> government administration, military, and police;
>
> trade unions and other mass organizations;
>
> media;
>
> religions;
>
> private industry;
>
> scientific, technological, and research institutes; and
>
> centers of power and influence, such as life insurance companies and financial institutions (for example, banks).

The latter are especially important Soviet targets because the life insurance and financial institutions are known to have considerable control over industries. Therefore, to the Soviets, they are seen as the single most effective instrument to use in nationalizing the means of production, which is one of their priority objectives in the revolutionary process.[19]

Carefully selected cadres, trained in Communist ideology, organization, and tactics, are directed to infiltrate various organizations. They work over the years to build up the Communist infrastructure and to achieve positions of power. Their objective is to exploit the organizations within which they operate as bases for sabotage of capitalism, and for support of the Communist cause.

The long-term nature of this process may be the single most important aspect of the character of Soviet strategy. The Kremlin's planning includes designs that extend well beyond fifteen years. This process generally receives miniscule attention within the United States. The idea of a foreign government infiltrating the public and private sector in the United States is an issue that is avoided. One reason for not recognizing this pattern is one feared consequence: increased internal government surveillance and a resurgence of McCarthyism.

There is, however, an even more important reason that the activity receives little attention. The activity is the centerpiece of Soviet long-range plans; but, there is no place in the U.S. national security community where Soviet long-term plans and strategy are studied. This is a fundamental characteristic of the U.S. intelligence and policy-planning process that has been repeatedly stressed by several authorities, most notably by Richard Pipes.[20] When coupled with the aforementioned destruction of U.S. internal security capabilities, this further brings out the large inherent vulnerability of the United States to Soviet manipulation and sabotage.

The sabotage or destruction of certain individuals is one of the most important tactics utilized by the Soviet state in the process of destroying all opposition, that is, enemies of the Soviet state. As part of this tactic, the Soviets have a massive effort to identify and classify individuals in all countries, especially their main enemies—the United States and Great Britain.

Basically there two categories of people in the Soviet classification scheme: realists and radicals or reactionaries. The realists understand the course of history and are perceived as being available to assist the Soviet cause—either wittingly or unwittingly. These people are courted or supported, directly or indirectly. The reactionaries or radicals are considered unsalvable enemies of the Soviet state and are earmarked for destruction or neutralization.[21]

The use of chemical and biological agents by the Soviets in political and intelligence warfare has gone on for over forty years. From all indications, these Soviet efforts have been increasing in both breadth and depth and also have been buttressed by a gradually expanding research and development effort. Consider, for example, the following historical record of Soviet interests and activities.

Assassinations

Individuals who are effectively disrupting Soviet strategy or who represent a special threat are assassinated. Chemical and biological agents have been important tools in this trade. Known victims of a Communist ricin poison dart include the two Bulgarian emigre activists, Markov and Kostov; a CIA double agent, Boris Korczak, who was hit at Tyson's Corner, Virginia;[22] and a well-known African leader.

There are many cases involving the use of bacteriological techniques never proven. One good example is the unusual sickness and death of the British labor leader, Hugh Gaitskell, following his partaking of biscuits and tea at the Soviet Embassy.[23] In terms of intended targets where chemicals were planned, but other methods employed, there are the cases of Orlando Letelier[24] and Hafizulla Amin.[25] There are many other examples.[26]

Drugging and Kidnapping

A well-practiced Soviet tactic is to drug important individuals who are to be used politically and then transport them to Soviet controlled territory. A typical example is the Czechoslovakian emigre Bohumir Laushman, who was well known and respected in Czechoslovakia. With threats against his wife and daughter, he was forced to read a speech denouncing capitalism. By the time his speech was broadcast, he (along with his wife and daughter) was already in jail.[27]

Drugging Diplomats

As an act of recruitment, intimidation, or simply to discredit the person, the Soviets will drug an individual and then place the person in an incriminating situation (drunken rowdiness, incompetent espionage, or public behavior unbefitting an official). This has happened repeatedly to "unfriendly enemies" (that is, military attachés, unsympathetic journalists, and security personnel serving in or visiting the Soviet Union and other Communist countries).

A characteristic of this activity that should be of great concern among the more developed nations, such as the United States, is that these events tend to be ignored, kept quiet, accepted as a condition of doing business with the Soviets, or worse still, solved by shifting the blame onto the individual victim. As it is described by a former U.S. defense attaché,

> Whenever an American in Moscow is drugged, the individual somehow is judged guilty. The State Department attempts to keep the matter as closely held as possible because, if it were generally known, it might "hurt relations."[28]

Although there have been occasional exceptions, an American who is drugged usually is set back in his career, or his career is entirely ruined.

Drug and Narcotics Running

It goes without saying that the United States Armed Forces present a high priority target for Soviet subversion. Moscow's support of international drug-running may have several complementary objectives, but weakening of the force's morale and undermining the command structure are clearly very important.

The major effort to weave drugs into the fabric of the U.S. Army in Europe took place in the 1960's, especially the latter half. This is another activity that was pursued while U.S. attention was focused on Vietnam. By 1971, the conditions were so serious in Europe that the U.S. Army was experiencing a breakdown in command. The drug dealers were calling the shots, rather than the officers in charge of the units. Major disciplinary actions had to be undertaken to reestablish command authority. This also had the effect of exacerbating U.S.-German relations because of drug-related civil problems. Further, political problems resulted from reports of individuals with drug problems at nuclear bases.[29]

In its effort to flood NATO countries with easily available drugs, the Soviet KGB relies on the complete support of other Soviet bloc services. Notorious among them is Bulgaria, which operates through a front called KINTEX, a "business" firm fully controlled by *Darzhavna Sigurnost*, the Bulgarian Intelligence Service, well-known for its involvement in the attempt to assassinate the Pope. Also, it has been documented that 95 percent of all heroin consumed in West Germany, and all heroin reaching West Berlin, comes through East Germany. Needless to say, such smuggling could not take place unless it was a Soviet scheme.

Closer to home, in the 1980's it has become clear that Communist Parties (in Cuba and Columbia in particular) were deeply involved in the running of drugs into the United States. It has been documented that drug-running in Cuba is personally supervised by a member of the Central Committee in Havana, and a vice admiral of the Cuban Navy.[30] This pattern is global, with North Korea playing the major role in the Far East.

It is an almost trivial exercise to extrapolate the foregoing types of Soviet activities, to include the use of new sophisticated drugs and agents. Consider, for example, the effect of a growing history of military plane crashes as being the result of covert dissemination of chemical agents that could lead to mechanic or pilot error. As another example, consider the effect of the gradual spread of a new, difficult to treat, venereal disease whose origin could be traced back to various U.S. military installations; or the problems that would emerge following the outbreak of an AIDS-like problem at U.S. military installations overseas—or even worse, in the United States.

Of perhaps greatest long-term concern in the Soviet's practice of political warfare is the possible development of drugs for various forms of mind control. The Soviets have believed in the potential of this practice, and have extended considerable effort in this direction—an activity that goes hand-in-hand with their psychological theories and, more importantly, their ideology. This can be seen quite noticeably in the Soviet treatment of political prisoners. Doctors in Soviet mental hospitals have the task of teaching dissidents that they are mentally ill; and to this end, they use drugs that impede judgment, thinking, and memory, and eventually cause lasting mental derangement.

Considerable publicity arose, in 1983, when the World Psychiatric Association (WPA) threatened to expel the Soviets for their unethical practices. A resolution condemning Soviet practices was adopted at the 1977 meeting of the WPA, and, in February 1983, it was clear that the expulsion of the Soviets would be called for at the next meeting. Accordingly, in anticipation of the WPA disciplinary action, the Soviet All-Union Society of Psychiatrists and Neuropathologists withdrew its membership in the WPA.[31] In the attack on Soviet psychiatric practices, attention was focused on the so-called punitive medicine practiced in the Soviet Union.[32]

Unfortunately, little was said of what might be a more fundamental reason behind these medical practices—the Soviet doctrinal precept that an individual's basis is strictly physico-chemical, and therefore, open to intervention. While punishment and reward are ingrained in the Soviet approach to determining the behavior of individuals, so is the ability to manipulate behavior through chemicals. As difficult as this is to believe in the West, dissidents are considered sick, and the associated existence of medical research into "cures" should be considered likely.

The development of drugs for large-scale mind control as a natural component of Soviet biochem research and development is almost undoubtedly a major Soviet objective. As pointed out in the 1967 East German textbook, on military chemistry, the field of psychotoxins

> is by no means a closed subject; rather it is the beginning of a development that is directed toward a complete influence and control over human consciousness.[33]

Almost identical comments are also present in papers prepared for a "disarmament" conference of scientists that was held in East Berlin, in 1971. In both cases, the statements almost seem as though they were deliberately planted as a warning to the West.

A likely major Soviet research and development objective is further development or refinement of chemical or biological tools that can be used covertly to assist the Soviet process or subversion in both developed (that is, the United States, Europe, Japan, Canada, and so forth) and undeveloped countries. The types of tools that would be desired should enable an individual (or a small group of individuals) to assassinate or cause an individual (or a group of individuals) to be discredited, to discredit or neutralize organizations, to disturb or distort decision makers' mental processes, to put a region to "sleep," and so forth. The possibilities here are almost unlimited. In most cases, access to the target may be straightforward and simple; effects need not be overly dependable because, in the long-term, timing is not that critical. What is critical is covertness and the availability of natural explanations. This is an obvious Soviet biochem research and development objective, and one that poses a long-term threat of great danger to the Free World.

Notes

1. John J. Dziak, "The Soviet Approach to Special Operations," in *Special Operations in U.S. Strategy* edited by Frank R. Barnett, B. Hugh Tovar, and Richard H. Shultz (Washington, D.C.: National Defense University Press, 1985), ch. 3; Manfred Schell, "The Saboteurs of the East Wait for Orders on D-Day: Moscow and East Berlin Work Hand in Hand," *Die Welt*, 11 August 1978; and Viktor Suvorov, "*Spetsnaz*: The Soviet Union's Special Forces," *International Defense Review* 9, 1983.

2. Dziak, "The Soviet Approach," p. 97.
3. Joseph D. Douglass, Jr. and Neil C. Livingstone, "Terrorists Find the U.S. Offers Inviting Targets," *Detroit News*, 29 April 1984, p. 23. A discussion of the many events from 1973 to 1977 that emasculated U.S. internal security.
4. J. Michael Wailer, "Author Details Cuban Intelligence Activity in U.S.," *Washington Times*, 9 Mar. 1984.
5. The Soviet focus since 1955 for recruiting revolutionary agents in the United States has been minorities: blacks, Hispanics, American Indians, and so forth. As one example, see the testimony of Robert Moss in U.S. Congress, Senate, Committee on the Judiciary, *Terrorism: The Role of Moscow and Its Subcontractors*, hearing before the Subcommittee on Security and Terrorism, 26 June 1981 (Washington, D.C.: U.S. Government Printing Office), p. 27.
6. Interview with Jan Sejna.
7. Schell, "The Saboteurs of the East."
8. Neil C. Livingstone and Joseph D. Douglass, Jr., *CBW: The Poor Man's Atomic Bomb*, National Security Paper Series (Institute of Foreign Policy Analysis, Cambridge, Mass., 1984); and "Additional Details on USSR '*Spetsnaz*' War Role in Sweden," *Svenska Dagbladet*, 13 October 1983.
9. *Soviet Military Encyclopedia*, vol. 7 (Moscow: 1979), p. 493.
10. Joseph D. Douglass, Jr. and Amoretta Hoeber, *Soviet Strategy for Nuclear War* (Stanford, Calif: Hoover Institute Press, 1979).
11. Communist writings on offensive chemical, and biological intentions and capabilities are invariably couched as reports on what the enemy (the United States) is doing. This is a common technique used by the Soviets and their surrogates to treat important topics without violating their strict secrecy requirements. The excerpts used in this chapter were selected to demonstrate clear Soviet awareness of the subject matter. Further, the context in all cases is such that it is believed more likely that the material refers to Soviet interests, capabilities, or intentions than to Soviet concern over "reported" U.S. interests, capabilities, or intentions.
12. *Soviet Military Concepts*, no. 2–82, no. 3–82, trans. by Directorate of Soviet Affairs, Air Force Intelligence Services, 1982, p. 530.
13. *Manual of Military Chemistry*, Deutscher Militarverlag, East Berlin, 1967, trans. JPRS CN-787-67, p. 298.
14. Ibid.
15. *Textbook of Military Chemistry*, AD-B0629131L, (Berlin, 1977).
16. *Soviet Military Encyclopedia*, vol. 7, Voyenizdat, Moscow, 1979, p. 493.
17. Dr. Walter Hirsch, *Soviet BW and CW Preparations and Capabilities*, trans. by Zaven Nalbandian, Intelligence Branch, Office of the Chief, Chemical Corps, 1951.
18. Schell, "The Saboteurs of the East."
19. Interview with Jan Sejna.
20. U.S. Congress, House, Hearings before the Subcommittee on Oversight of the Permanent Select Committee on Intelligence, 7 and 20 February 1980, *Soviet Strategic Forces* (Washington, D.C.: U.S. Government Printing Office, 1980), p. 34; and more recently, in Richard Pipes, *Survival Is Not Enough* (New York: Simon and Schuster, 1984), pp. 276–277.
21. Interview with Jan Sejna.

22. "The Metal Ball Technique," *Clandestine Tactics and Technology* 7, no. 6, (International Association of Chiefs of Police, 1981, p. 9.

23. Chapman Pincher, *Too Secret Too Long* (New York: St. Martin's, 1984), p. 473.

24. John Goshko, "Nerve Gas Brought into U.S. in Letelier Plot, Townley Says," *Washington Post*, 13 December 1981, p. 1.

25. "Defectors Elaborate on Secrets of Soviet Coup Operations," *Neue Zuericher Zeitung*, 30 December 1982, pp. 3–4.

26. John Barron, *KGB: The Secret Work of Soviet Secret Agents* (New York: Bantam Books, 1974), p. 195.

27. "General Sejna on Soviet Deception," *Congressional Record*, 20 December 1979, p. S19538.

28. A current example of this practice is the recent deliberate shooting of U.S. Army Major Arthur Nicholson and reported guidance from the U.S. State Department official, Richard Burt, to the Soviets on what to do and not to do to avoid derailing efforts to improve Soviet-American relations. Alan McCouagha, "Killing of Major Was Part of Soviet Plot, Says NSC," *Washington Times*, 5 April 1985, p. 1.

29. R. W. Apple Jr., "Drugs at U.S. Bases an Issue in Britain," *New York Times*, 25 March 1984, p. 3.

30. "A World of Drugs: America as Target," *New York Times*, 13 September 1984, p. A–17.

31. W. Herbert, "Soviet Psychiatrists Make Preemptive Bid, Quit World Body," *Science News*, 19 February 1983.

32. Alexander Podrabinek, *Punitive Medicine* (Ann Arbor, Michigan: Karoma, 1980); Harvey Fireside, *Soviet Psychoprisons* (New York: W. W. Norton & Co., 1979); and Victor Nekipelov, *Institute of Fools* (New York: Farrar, Straus, & Giroux, 1980).

33. Siegfried Franke *Manual of Military Chemistry*, Deutscher Militarverlag, East Berlin, 1967, trans. JPRS CN-787-67.

Part V
Regional Deception

17
The Soviet Campaign against INF in West Germany

David S. Yost

In December 1979, the North Atlantic Council approved what became known as a "two track" decision: to deploy U.S. Pershing II ballistic missiles and ground-launched cruise missiles (GLCMs) in Western Europe beginning in November-December 1983, and to seek an arms control arrangement with the Soviet Union that could modify the scope of the planned deployments, or make them entirely unnecessary.[1] Even prior to December 1979, the Soviet Union had foreseen the decision on what NATO termed intermediate-range nuclear forces (INF), and had begun to set forth an array of propaganda themes intended to influence Western thinking about its implementation, with special attention to West Germany. To some extent, of course, these arguments represented updated versions of older themes of Soviet public relations efforts in Western Europe. However, during the four-year period from December 1979 to November 1983 (the arrival of the first INF in Western Europe), the USSR held to a certain set of arguments and behaved with a fair degree of consistency in an intense effort to sway West European opinion and thus prevent deployment of U.S. INF in Western Europe.

The Soviet campaign against implementation of NATO's INF decision therefore offers unusually rich material for a case history. The evidence of Soviet activities is ample. The principal goal of Soviet efforts was precise: to prevent implementation of a specific decision, with a definite time schedule. This would seem to make the anti-INF campaign a relatively clear-cut test of the effectiveness of Soviet capabilities to affect the perceptions of foreign publics.

The views expressed are those of the author alone, and should not be construed to represent those of the Department of the Navy or any U.S. Government agency.

The case also stands out as one of great intrinsic importance for Western security. As the head of the Planning Department in the West German Foreign Ministry, Konrad Seitz, pointed out in 1982:

> The threat engendered by Soviet over-armament is not only of a military nature. It is also of a politico-psychological nature. The Soviet weapons are intended to project a political shadow, and in actual fact do project this shadow over Europe. Today the primary danger in Europe is not aggression and open warfare. *We risk rather to see permanently modified, to the advantage of the Soviet Union, the force balances in Europe and the world.* At the end of this process, the European democracies would see themselves constrained to self-neutralization. *The Soviet Union would have won political control over Western Europe without having had to fire a shot.*[2] [Emphasis added.]

NATO's cohesion, its ability to make and implement defense decisions, and its overall deterrent credibility were thus at stake. The Soviet Union attempted to break down the will of West European governments to implement a decision that these governments had originated and approved by remonstrating with them directly, and more significantly, by appealing over their heads to Western public opinion.

West Germany received special attention from the Soviets because they recognize its unique importance. The United States has no ally, within or outside the Atlantic alliance, more important than the Federal Republic of Germany (FRG). On geostrategic grounds alone (without considering the moral, political, and economic foundations of the alliance), it is obvious that the Western position in Europe would be untenable without a strong and reliable partnership with West Germany. The Federal Republic is the host country for the bulk of U.S. military forces in Europe, has the largest gross national product in Western Europe, and is the strongest nonnuclear power in Europe.

As might have been expected, therefore, the two most prominent interviews given by Soviet Presidents regarding INF (Brezhnev in November 1981, and Andropov in April 1983) appeared in the weekly West German magazine *Der Spiegel*. The degree of Soviet interest in Western Europe, and West Germany in particular, is also suggested by the backgrounds of key Soviet personnel: the Deputy Head of the International Department of the Central Committee of the Soviet Communist Party, Vadim Zagladin, is a specialist on Western Europe, fluent in German, French, and English; Valentin Falin, Soviet Ambassador to Bonn (1971–78) was Zagladin's First Deputy Chief until early 1983; and Nikolai Portugalov, a "consultant" to the CPSU Central Committee (frequently interviewed in the West German media), is one of the USSR's top German area specialists, and was a *Novosti* correspondent in West Germany from 1972 to 1978. The head of the Soviet delegation to the INF negotiations from 1981 to 1983, Yuli Kvitsinsky, is a German area specialist as well. Prior to this appointment, Kvitsinsky was the Minister Counselor, or Deputy Ambassador, in the

Soviet Embassy in Bonn. His previous service included the Soviet Embassy in East Berlin, while his doctorate concerned West Berlin. Soviet sources indicate that the Soviets took a great deal of interest in the impact of their declarations in West Germany:

> Soviet peace initiatives show West Germans that despite all the slander against the USSR, it in fact seeks to halt the arms race and the growth of the danger of war in Europe. A truly tremendous response was elicited in the FRG by the important initiative which the USSR put forward in mid-June [1982] by unilaterally making a solemn promise not to be the first to use nuclear weapons.[3]

Apparent Failures and Successes

At first glance, this episode would seem to be an open-and-shut case of Soviet failure on two key grounds. First and above all, the initial missile deployments took place as scheduled in West Germany, Britain, and Italy. Second, the leaders of three of the principal countries of Western Europe (Thatcher, Kohl, and Mitterrand) were clearly more skeptical regarding the benevolence of Soviet intentions in 1983 than those in office when the INF affair began. Thatcher and Kohl were confirmed in office in 1983 elections which were seen (to some extent) as referenda on INF.

To emphasize only these facts could, however, overstate the degree of Soviet failure by overlooking three key successes—developments that, if not directly and exclusively attributable to Soviet behavior, may be seen as objectively favoring the USSR in the political and psychological correlation of forces.

First, Socialist and Social Democratic parties throughout northern Europe (above all the British Labour Party and West Germany's Social Democratic Party, the SPD) and elsewhere (for example, Greece) have adopted key elements of the Soviet position on INF issues, and endorse other policies that would have the de facto effect of aiding the USSR in the consolidation of its military preponderance in the European region—most conspicuously, the creation of nuclear-weapons-free-zones and (in Britain's case) unilateral nuclear disarmament. The destruction of the previous consensus on defense in West Germany includes the emergence of an explicitly anti-NATO and pro-neutrality political party (the Greens) that outpolled the Free Democratic Party (FDP) in the March 1983 national elections and in the June 1984 European elections. The SPD's change of course is even more significant, because it is the principal opposition party and more likely to form a government in the future. The SPD professes loyalty to NATO, but has rejected NATO policy on INF deployments and on the requirements of deterrence; in addition to endorsing the creation of nuclear-weapons-free and chemical-weapons-free-zones in Central Europe, the SPD holds that NATO should adopt a policy of "no-first-use" of nuclear weapons without increasing its conventional defense capabilities. Leading figures of the SPD (for example, Willy Brandt and Hans-Jochen Vogel) hold that the United States should have accepted the Soviet terms for an INF agreement in order to prevent the U.S. deployments.[4]

Second, opinion polls and interview findings suggest that the Soviet-preferred definition of some of the issues at stake in the INF affair won a great deal of popular sympathy—for example, the contention that the USSR deserves compensation from the United States for the existence of the British and French nuclear forces. Although poll findings differ and are always subject to qualification, some polls suggest that some 70 percent of the West German public (including a majority of the more conservative Christian Democratic Union/ Christian Social Union—CDU/CSU—voters) believe that the United States and USSR were both at fault for the failure to achieve an arms control agreement precluding the need for INF deployments in West Germany. Opponents of implementation of the NATO INF decision have argued that the deployments are being carried out against the will of the people and are therefore illegitimate.[5]

If the first success may be described as a polarization of political party orientations leading to a breakdown of national defense consensus among elites in key West European countries, the second may be described as a certain delegitimization of the U.S. nuclear presence in Western Europe and of the Western approach to nuclear arms control. Large sectors of the public have a renewed awareness of nuclear vulnerabilities and dilemmas, and yearn for solutions that would involve no actual deployments of nuclear weapons and no consideration of nuclear employment options, even in the interests of deterrence.

Third, the INF affair has served as a vital socialization experience for many members of the successor generations in West Germany. Studies of the younger generations indicate that they furnished a high proportion of the participants in the anti-INF demonstrations and protest movements; that they feel increasingly distant from the United States and less convinced than their elders about the reality of the Soviet threat to Western Europe's freedom; and that they are, to a high degree, attracted to concepts of neutralism. Given the emergence of the Greens and the content of the resolutions adopted by the youth organizations of the SPD, FDP, and CDU (critical of U.S. policy in general, especially regarding INF, and sympathetic regarding Soviet concerns), the INF affair may be expected to leave important and enduring political aftereffects.[6]

These three developments—which might be summed up as significant polarization, delegitimization, and socialization—work against the maintenance of a solid defense consensus in Western Europe, could well hinder the realization of future NATO decisions, and objectively favor Soviet interests. To what extent, however, do Soviet activities account for these developments? To what degree could non-Soviet factors explain the trends that appear to be successes objectively favoring Soviet interests? These questions are central to any assessment of Soviet effectiveness, and must be considered after the main features of the anti-INF campaign have been outlined.

Soviet Efforts to Influence West German Perceptions

Overt Efforts

Some of the Soviet efforts to influence West German opinions and decision making about INF were overt and relatively uncontroversial. The most obvious and traditional means of overt communication were broadcasts (Radio Moscow), releases from press agencies (Tass and Novosti), and publications clearly emanating from the USSR. Of the latter, the following titles from Progress Publishers (available in German, English and other languages) seem to have been the most widely distributed:

> *The Lie of a Soviet War Threat*, 1980, chapters by Lenin, Brezhnev, Gromyko, Ustinov, Ogarkov, and Yepishev
>
> Soviet Committee for European Security and Cooperation, *The Threat to Europe*, 1981
>
> Dmitri Volkogonov, *Mythical "Threat" and the Real Danger to Peace*, 1982
>
> Soviet Committee for European Security and Cooperation, *How to Avert the Threat to Europe*, 1983

Other readily available publications include:

> *Truth About Intermediate Range Nuclear Missiles: Answer to Authors of the USIA booklet*; *Intermediate-Range Nuclear Forces: Questions and Answers* (Moscow: Novosti Press Agency Publishing House, 1983)
>
> *Whence the Threat to Peace*, 2nd ed., supplemented (Moscow: Military Publishing House, 1982)—The Soviet response to the first edition of the U.S. Department of Defense's assessment entitled *Soviet Military Power* in 1981

West German interview sources judged these publications less effective than other overt communications means because they were so obviously one-sided and tedious.

Georgi Arbatov's book, *The Soviet Viewpoint*, falls into a separate category, partly because of its high degree of sophistication and partly because it was commercially published in West Germany and elsewhere.[7] When the book first appeared in March 1981, Arbatov gave two interviews on West German television to promote its sales and to urge West Germans to accept the Soviet proposal for a "moratorium" on new INF deployments. Although a number of other Soviet spokesmen (articulate in German) appeared on West German television, West German interviewees considered such spokesmen more effective in print than live on television. Published interviews in *Der Spiegel* and other magazines included Soviet experts such as Valentin Falin, Georgi Arbatov, and Nikolai Portugalov.[8] Portugalov and Vadim Zagladin even contributed articles to *NATO's Fifteen Nations*, while left-leaning newspapers, such as *Frankfurter Rundschau*, included interviews with Soviet generals and Soviet Defense Minister Dimitri Ustinov.[9]

Aside from using the print and broadcast media, the Soviets also sent spokesmen to university seminars and other public discussions. In early 1983, the Soviets reportedly dispatched spokesmen to West German universities at a rate of twenty per month.[10] Perhaps the most politically important of the seminars was held at the SPD's Friedrich Ebert Foundation (October 1982) and devoted to the theme of "East-West relations and European security." The twenty-person Soviet delegation included Falin, Portugalov, General Chervov, and the Soviet Ambassador to Bonn, Vladimir Semionov. Several West German officials participated, including top-level members of the Bundestag such as Egon Bahr and Hans Apel.[11]

More directly personal Soviet attempts at influence were also reported. In September 1983, for example, Andropov sent letters to fifty-seven SPD members of the Bundestag to urge them to oppose the projected U.S. INF deployments.[12] Some West German reports suggest that the Soviets made threats to specific personalities selected for maximum possible impact:

> Disinformation and intimidation are also the aims of the assertion that there is an urgent threat of war being waged on the backs of a handful of carefully chosen and strictly limited Europeans.[13]

A final overt method of communication worth noting is the welcoming of opinion leaders to Moscow. Those seeking enlightenment as to Soviet perceptions may, of course, receive the insights the Soviets prefer to see disseminated. For example, in March 1983, Theo Sommer (one of the editors of *Die Zeit*), visited Moscow for a week. He then published a long, two-part article entitled "Do the Russians Want War? Their Answer: 'No, but the West Wants Hegemony.'"[14] In other words, the Soviets successfully conveyed the themes of defensiveness and fear of encirclement to evoke sympathy. In addition to according red-carpet treatment to prominent journalists, the Soviets have welcomed West German politicians of all major parties to Moscow.

Covert Efforts

In addition to using these overt means of communication, the Soviets employed two main covert means. The first consisted of what the Soviets call "active measures," including disinformation, the spreading of false rumors, forgeries, efforts to control foreign media, blackmail, and so forth—activities planned and implemented by the First Directorate of the Committee for State Security (KGB), with the participation of the International Department of the Central Committee of the Communist Party of the Soviet Union, and with possible additional assistance from the International Information Department.[15]

The same organizations were responsible for the second main covert activity—exploiting the potential of local Communist parties and front organizations. How significant were these relatively indirect proxy activities in the overall Soviet perceptions management effort? Of the numerous statements on this subject by the West German government in 1981 and 1982, the following points stand out: there was no evidence that peace movements in West Germany were controlled by the KGB or that direct financial assistance had come from Moscow; the West German Communists (DKP) and their collateral organizations constituted a "most active" minority in the peace movement; and the "overwhelming majority of the participants in the demonstration of October 10, 1981 reject Communist aims and objectives."[16]

In light of these official assessments, Professor Günther Schmid of the University of Munich concluded in 1982 that

> . . . the movement, which has now apparently grown to well over 2 million "members" and activists, has long since become too large and (politically) too diverse for it to be in any way "remotely controlled" by any one side. . . . All known attempts by the DKP (primarily its younger members) to dominate "peace groups" have thus far—as far as one can tell—failed. . . . Communists are involved; they join in marching and organizing, but they neither define the overall view of the peace movement nor have they given the movement its impetus.[17]

While several other U.S. and West German experts agreed that the USSR's roles in initiating and directing the peace movement were quite secondary,[18] Gerhard Wettig of the Federal Institute for Eastern and International Studies in Cologne estimated a somewhat greater degree of indirect Soviet involvement, including finance:

> The "Krefeld Appeal" (which was allegedly signed by two million people and which unilaterally condemns NATO's Euro-strategic armament) came about under the influence of the DKP and its subsidiary organizations, especially the *Deutsche Friedens-Union* [German Peace Union]. At the same time, the CPSU

[Communist Party of the Soviet Union] and SED—[Socialist Unity Party, which governs East Germany] dominated West German communists earned themselves a good reputation as fellow fighters in the peace movement, enabling them considerably to expand their influence. This is due (among other things) to the fact that *the funds available to the Moscow-oriented Communists and their organizational ability are largely lacking in the peace movement and thus exert a very considerable attraction.*[19] [Emphasis added.]

By 1983, the West German government had apparently revised its estimate of the degree of DKP influence in the various protest movement organizations. Friedrich Heuer, director of domestic security at the West German Interior Ministry, suggested that about half of the decision making positions were under DKP control, even though leftist extremists constituted 20 percent, at most, of the protest movement.[20] One West German interview source in 1983 offered a similar rough estimate—perhaps 40 percent of the influence on the anti-INF campaign came from Communist sources (including front organizations and the DKP), of which the overt Soviet portion was no more than 5 percent. While the West German Government statements in 1981 and 1982 had specifically excluded Soviet financial aid to the protest movements, a West German government statement in 1983 indicated that the DKP must have received more than 60 million Deutschemarks from the German Democratic Republic (GDR) in 1982 to support its protest movement activities.[21]

The DKP and its various front organizations played four key roles in addition to supplying dedication, organization, money, and clear objectives. First, they used the "minimum consensus" principle to block, to the maximum extent possible, any criticism of the USSR with respect to Poland, Afghanistan, the SS-20 missile buildup, and so forth. Second, they sought to broaden the appeal of the movement by drawing in diverse groups (labor unions, churches, professional societies, and so forth), and by working with SPD leaders—in opposition to the Greens and other purists who wanted to avoid working with the established political parties and other elements of an industrial society they reject. Third, they supplemented Soviet intelligence efforts by monitoring the concerns of West European publics, so that Soviet propagandists could provide statements conforming to what the protestors were predisposed to hear concerning the benign intentions of the USSR and the risks of nuclear war. Fourth, they worked to spread the Soviet-preferred point of view without it being directly attributable to Soviet sources.

Themes for Western Audiences

Several surveys of the themes regarding INF employed by the USSR for the consumption of Western audiences have been made. Of these, the best periodic reports appear to be those prepared by the Foreign Broadcast Information

Service and by Radio Liberty, Munich.[22] A concise survey of almost all the major arguments set forth by the Soviets during the INF affair was published by the U.S. Arms Control and Disarmament Agency (ACDA) in October 1983, *Soviet Propaganda Campaign Against NATO.* This survey included citations from Soviet sources for each theme, and facts from Western sources to refute or otherwise respond to it. The table of contents of the ACDA survey illustrates the range of issues about which the Soviets sought to mislead Western audiences:

Assertion about the Military Balance
A balance currently exists in intermediate-range nuclear forces in Europe.

Assertions about Soviet Military Doctrine
The Soviet Union does not seek military superiority in the INF balance.
The Soviet Union, in contrast to NATO, pledges no first use of nuclear weapons.

Assertions about U.S. Motives for INF Deployment
The United States seeks superiority over the Soviet Union through deployment of INF missiles in Western Europe.
The United States has a preemptive strike doctrine, and U.S. INF missiles will have a short-warning, first-strike capability against Soviet strategic systems, thereby performing a strategic role.
The United States' motive for deploying INF missiles is to "Europeanize" or limit nuclear war to Europe, leaving U.S. territory as a sanctuary.
The U.S. is not interested in arms control.

Assertions about Military/Diplomatic Consequences of Nato's Proceeding with Deployment of INF Missiles
NATO's planned INF deployment will stimulate a new round in the arms race.
NATO's planned INF deployment will prompt Soviet counterdeployments.
NATO host countries for U.S. INF missiles will become targets for a Soviet strike.
NATO's deployment of INF missiles will increase the likelihood of a conflict.
NATO's pursuit of planned INF deployment will reduce Western Europe's future trade potential with the Soviet Union.
NATO's decision approving deployment of INF missiles will make impossible or complicate arms control negotiations.

Assertions about Soviet Arms Control Efforts
The Soviet Union seeks disarmament/an "end to the arms race."
Claimed unilateral moratorium on deployment of SS-20s in the European part of the USSR.[23]

Although each of the above themes merits extensive analysis, two examples may suffice: Soviet threats regarding nuclear war and the USSR's portrayal of its behavior in the INF negotiations.

Nuclear War Threats. Threats to the effect that U.S. INF would constitute targets for Soviet strikes were variations on an old theme, first articulated by Khrushchev in the late 1950's, when the U.S. first deployed tactical nuclear weapons to Europe.[24] A typical formulation was the nuclear-weapons-free-zone argument put forth by Vadim Zagladin in an interview in *Der Spiegel*:

> . . . But if there are no medium-range nuclear weapons on the territory of the Federal Republic any longer, there will not be any missiles targeted on it either.[25]

Western governments supporting INF modernization argued that it would help to deter war, because the risks of aggression for the Soviets would be raised through the recoupling of U.S. strategic nuclear forces to European security. Protest movement leaders rejected this argument on the ground that deterrence could fail, and its failure could lead to an uncontrollable nuclear war. In seeking to capitalize on this fear, the Soviets emphasized the notion of inevitable escalation to global apocalypse. In the words of Leonid Brezhnev,

> . . . there can be in general no "limited" nuclear war. If a nuclear war breaks out, . . . it would inevitably and unavoidably assume a worldwide character.[26]

In other words, the Soviets simultaneously misrepresented their own military policy (for they would almost certainly prefer to wage limited and controllable wars, if war cannot be avoided in the pursuit of their aims) and the rationale for NATO's INF decision. To the extent that NATO's INF deployment had a strategic rationale (it was intended in part, somewhat ironically, as a political reassurance program for the West European governments that first proposed it), it resided in recoupling U.S. strategic nuclear forces to European security. But the Soviets represented it as a U.S. plot for limited nuclear war in Europe, which they would frustrate by making sure any nuclear war would be unlimited. In making this threat, the Soviets assured the West Europeans they were doing their best to avert any war; but, they added, the risk of nuclear war would be more unquestionably reduced if the U.S. nuclear presence in Europe were eliminated. The theme that any use of nuclear weapons would lead to uncontrollable escalation and universal destruction was intended to exacerbate public doubts about the validity of NATO's "flexible response" strategy (because it does in fact posit deliberate and controlled nuclear escalation as an option), and to bolster the argument that Western Europe would be safer without a U.S. nuclear presence.

Negotiations Behavior. Soviet INF proposals demonstrated great inflexibility and prescribed Soviet regional nuclear dominance; but the Soviet presentation of their behavior was oriented toward communicating an image of flexibility and fairness.

The first formally presented Soviet proposal (in February 1982) provided for a two-phase limitation on longer-range INF deployed in Europe or "intended for use" in Europe, to be completed by 1990, in which each side would reduce its arsenal to 300 systems (aircraft and missile launchers) and would observe a deployment moratorium in Europe during the negotiations. This offer had at least four major flaws:

1. It assumed an existing balance of approximately 1,000 INF on each side, excluding Soviet systems comparable to the included U.S. systems, and otherwise distorting reality.[27]
2. It included British and French systems with U.S. totals.
3. It sought not only to prohibit the projected deployments of Pershing IIs and GLCMs, but to force the withdrawal of most other U.S. nuclear systems of INF range in Europe.
4. It would not have required the elimination of a single SS-20 launcher and would have permitted unlimited missile reload manufacture and unlimited SS-20 deployments east of the Urals.

Since the Soviet Union attributed 255 longer-range INF to Britain and France as part of United States totals, the United States would have been allowed only 45 longer-range INF systems in Europe; since most of these so-called "forward-based systems" were aircraft capable of carrying conventional as well as nuclear arms, NATO's deterrence and defense capabilities would have been weakened in both conventional and nuclear terms.

In December 1982, the Soviet Union proposed again that no Pershing IIs or GLCMs be deployed, in return for which the USSR would limit its SS-20 launchers in Europe to no more than the 162 that the Soviets deemed equivalent to British and French missiles. This "third country compensation" argument was disingenuous on numerous grounds, including the fact that the United States does not control British or French forces and has no operational release authority over them. The British and French systems can—at best—only protect Britain and France. Neither country could credibly threaten limited nuclear strikes against the USSR, nor could either offer a nuclear guarantee to non-nuclear allies in Europe.[28]

Despite the dramatic breadth of the Soviet proposals for Soviet regional nuclear dominance, the Soviets claimed that the Americans were seeking nuclear superiority in the face of Soviet reasonableness. The Soviets sought to convey an impression of flexibility by making superficial amendments in the initial proposal of February 1982. These included the December 1982 initiatives, the May 1983 proposal to make warheads-on-launchers the unit of account, the August and October 1983 proposals implying a willingness to destroy some SS-20 launchers (without accepting any missile inventory limits), and the November 1983 proposal (since disavowed) to reduce Soviet INF in Europe by 572 warheads. Yet there was no substantial change in the Soviet negotiating position. All the Soviet INF proposals were aimed at reducing the credibility of U.S. guarantees to allies by banning the Pershing II-GLCM deployment, expelling almost all U.S. intermediate-range nuclear systems from Europe, and establishing a permanent ceiling or ban on future INF deployments by the United States. In contrast, Soviet INF systems (notably INF missiles) could have been modernized and increased in number, and Western Europe would have found growing Soviet INF superiority sanctioned by international treaty.[29]

Themes for West Germany

While all of the general themes for Western audiences were transmitted to West Germany as thoroughly as possible, others were devised with the West German public especially in mind. Four sets of interrelated themes particularly tailored for West German consumption stand out: (1) those directed toward the special nuclear sensitivities of the Federal Republic; (2) threats to the future development of inter-German relations; (3) appeals to specific political parties; and (4) those playing on German feelings of guilt regarding World War II.

Special Nuclear Sensitivities. West Germany is especially sensitive to the more general themes articulated by the USSR because of its acute sense of vulnerability to nuclear attack: for geographical reasons (its front-line position); military reasons (the high concentration of nuclear warheads and other attractive targets in West Germany) and political reasons (the special fear of the Germans that the Soviets insistently profess, and West Germany's dependence on the United States for nuclear deterrence).

In addition, although the Federal Republic has made a commitment to its principal West European allies not to manufacture nuclear weapons (the London and Paris agreements of the Western European Union in 1954) and to the other signatories of the 1968 Nonproliferation Treaty (including the USSR) not to seek nuclear weapons, the question of possible West German control over nuclear weapons remains politically sensitive enough for the Soviets to exploit. To do so, the Soviets simply profess fear regarding the prospect of German control over nuclear weapons, owing to past experiences of German aggression. The Soviets can thus claim to be an aggrieved party. Some West Germans (and other West Europeans) are then led to wonder if they should not try to assuage possibly dangerous Soviet misperceptions by avoiding the "provocation" of accepting U.S. nuclear weapons deployments on West German soil. The Soviets exploited this theme by suggesting that, through the U.S. INF deployments, West Germany might "receive certain nuclear privileges from its senior partner, and . . . become the USA's chief nuclear agent in Western Europe,"[30] and by charging that "the essence of the matter is that the FRG is laying claim to its own nuclear missile equality with the Soviet Union, independently of the American deterrent."[31]

Before NATO agreed on the INF decision in December 1979, West German Chancellor Helmut Schmidt tried to forestall such Soviet accusations and expressions of anxiety by making it clear that the Federal Republic wanted the U.S. to be solely responsible for control of the new INF because their range could reach Soviet territory.[32] However, the lack of any West German veto power in the form of a special U.S.-West German bilateral consultation agreement of some kind came back to haunt Schmidt and other West German officials, because it was then possible for protestors to argue that West Germany's sovereignty and survival were in the hands of a U.S. President who might see advantages in keeping any eventual war limited to German soil. While the Soviets naturally never argued for autonomous West German control over nuclear weapons, they did try to underline the disadvantages for West Germany that could reside in U.S. control over nuclear weapons on West German soil.

Historians of the INF decision making process in NATO generally agree that 108 Pershing IIs were planned because there were 108 Pershing IAs under U.S. control in West Germany, and the substitution of the former for the latter could be readily understood by West European publics as simply a modernization of existing capabilities. In practice, however, the fact that Pershing IIs were to be deployed only in West Germany allowed the Soviets to place special emphasis on them and, to some degree, to isolate West Germany in their propaganda efforts. Although some Soviet spokesmen claimed that even cruise missiles could be used as first strike strategic weapons offering the USSR very little warning time,[33] most concentrated on the Pershing II, which was falsely portrayed as capable of destroying the Soviet strategic nuclear command system.[34]

Threats to Inter-German Relations. The USSR's leadership is well-aware of the value the West Germans place on the various accords reached during the era of détente and *Ostpolitik*—above all, those having to do with improved inter-German relations (the 1972 Basic Treaty between the FRG and the GDR) and the status of Berlin (the 1971 Quadripartite Agreement). The Soviet Union warned West Germany that the USSR would regard U.S. INF deployments in the Federal Republic as inconsistent with the 1970 Soviet-West German treaty renouncing the use or threat of force in their mutual relations. This treaty preceded the key *Ostpolitik* agreements. While some Soviet threats to inhibit the future development of inter-German relations were relatively subtle, others were more explicit. Andropov, for example, declared that Soviet medium-range missiles

... are not aimed against the West German Armed Forces. But if American missiles are deployed on West German soil, the situation will change. The military threat for West Germany will grow manifold. Relations between our two countries will be bound to suffer certain complications as well. As for the Germans in the FRG and GDR, they would have, as someone recently put it, to look at one another through thick palisades of missiles.[35]

Appeals to Specific Political Parties. Soviet sources have been categorical in characterizing specific West German political parties and leaders. The CDU/CSU is regularly described as "a party of the cold war and the arms race, revanchist ambitions, and pathological anti-Sovietism."[36] Kohl has been portrayed as blocking the will of the West German people by following through with the INF deployment, and criticized because he

> ... asserted without any ground whatsoever that allegedly the USSR "threatens the security of its neighbors" by its "excessive armaments."[37]

The FDP party leader and Foreign Minister Hans-Dietrich Genscher was vilified as being more zealous regarding U.S. INF deployment than Washington.[38]

In contrast, the Soviets have consistently described the Greens and the SPD in more positive terms. The Soviets clearly followed the proceedings of the SPD's December 1979 Party Congress in Berlin with care, for they accurately summarized its INF decision:

> It is known that the Congress of the Social Democratic Party in December 1979 consented, under strong pressure from the party leadership, to *Nachrüstung* [counter-armament] under three conditions: if the new American missiles appeared not only on West German soil; if the SALT-2 Treaty was "immediately" ratified; and if the disarmament talks acquired "political priority."[39]

The Soviets, moreover, welcomed the changes in SPD positions after 1979 (SPD support for the Soviet view on counting British and French nuclear forces with those of the United States, on postponing deployment of U.S. INF, and so forth) and clearly endorsed the SPD's candidate for chancellor in the March 1983 elections—Hans-Jochen Vogel.

Playing on German Guilt Feelings. West German interviewees stressed Soviet use of the theme of German guilt for World War II. Although the renunciation of force agreements that Bonn concluded in the early 1970s with Moscow, Warsaw, and Prague were partly intended to neutralize the standard Soviet claims of fear of German "revanchism," the Soviets still find it profitable to introduce the idea that U.S. INF deployments could "once again" lead to

Germany-based aggression against Russia. When Kohl visited Moscow in July 1983, Andropov declared:

> It is planned to turn West German territory into a launching site for American first-strike nuclear missiles aimed at the Soviet Union and its allies. This would actually mean the revival of the threat of war against the USSR being unleashed from German soil.[40]

Use of the theme evokes a certain guilt regarding the suffering caused by Germany in the past, and promotes suggestions that something be done to assuage Soviet anxieties.

Interpretive Uncertainties

In trying to assess the impact of the Soviet anti-INF campaign,[41] it is important to look beyond hasty conclusions as to Soviet efforts having completely failed. As noted at the outset, three developments in the INF affair—summed up in the words polarization, delegitimization, and socialization—may be seen as successes from the point of view of Soviet interests.

The Soviet explanation for their failure to prevent the confirmation in office of Chancellor Helmut Kohl in the March 1983 elections presaged their explanation for their failure regarding the missiles. The Soviets attributed the SPD's defeat to its vacillating and ambiguous positions on INF, and to a failure to mobilize the potential of the protest movements. The CDU/CSU's victory was explained by its alleged control of the mass media and the backing of industry. From the Soviet point of view, the Greens won representation in the Bundestag because of their anti-INF policies:

> . . . the decisive and uncompromising position of the Greens on the issue of deploying American medium-range nuclear weapons, their categorical "no" to missiles and their intention to continue the struggle against their deployment, both inside parliament and outside its walls, brought success to the party.[42]

Soviet explanations of their successes and failures are inadequate, not merely because they are self-serving but also because they oversimplify complex realities. It would be simplistic and reductionist to attribute the polarization of attitudes in West German party politics, the changing views of successor generations, and the partial delegitimization of NATO nuclear policy in public perceptions to an uncomplicated endorsement of Soviet propaganda themes by large sectors of society. The effects of Soviet efforts should ideally be sought in a broad framework of analysis including, at the least, the political forces and trends at work in West Germany independent of the INF affair, the overall political-military situation of the Atlantic Alliance aside from the INF affair, and West Germany's fundamental situation of geostrategic vulnerability and political dependence—again, apart from INF. Such an analysis would try to distinguish the effects of various Soviet and non-Soviet factors.

The identification of causative factors is, however, rarely easy and always provisional—especially in the study of human behavior. The difficulty is compounded by the scarcity of positive theoretical knowledge about this type of case. Most research in strategic deception has focused on the deliberate misleading of foreign governments and military elites to achieve surprise or other practical operational advantages (for example, a wasteful diversion of scarce military resources) immediately prior to a war, or prior to a campaign or battle within a war. Less attention has been devoted to attempts to influence the behavior of foreign governments in peacetime by modifying and managing their perceptions, and the perceptions of the elites and mass publics of their societies. The Soviet anti-INF campaign was an attempt to profit from the psychological and political impact of military power during peacetime. The long-term implications concern potential operational contingencies in war and the Soviet ability to coerce adversaries in situations short of war.

Strategic deception in war should be seen as a crucially important subset of activities within the much broader field of influencing foreign perceptions for competitive advantage. This broader field (the master category, as it were) might be called "perceptions management." It involves not only strategic military deception (including the duping of national technical means and other governmental information sources) but also propaganda (one-sided advocacy, including facts as well as half-truths and lies) and disinformation (deliberately false and misleading messages, including such active measures as forgeries and rumors) aimed at mass publics as well as governing elites. Above all, perceptions management also encompasses what might be termed "reality management"—trying to change objective military conditions and force relationships so that messages of persuasion and coercion may be more clearly understood. As Herbert Goldhamer noted, "the opinion to be cultivated or inspired in the enemy does not always involve deception. Indeed, in some cases, intimidation or deterrence may require that the enemy know the real facts of the situation . . . ." In Goldhamer's view, if perceptions and objective force relationships could be managed skillfully enough, wars could

> be entirely avoided . . . while nonetheless achieving the political-military gains that national policy pursued. . . . In all ages, military forces have often been used primarily to induce desired behavior rather than as military instruments. This lesson has . . . acquired special importance in the nuclear age.[43]

This conceptual framework suggests that Soviet policy could well simultaneously encompass several types of perceptions management efforts designed to strengthen the USSR's position and erode that of the West in the long-term competition. All involve trying to influence and exploit perceptions while controlling the supply of accurate information. A case such as the anti-INF campaign is especially important because (even more than strategic deception in war) it concerns the West's ability to compete in the long-term—that is, to maintain a credible deterrent posture to avert war, and to be prepared for contingencies of conflict.[44] In all probability, the Soviets would prefer to achieve political hegemony in Europe without war by demoralizing public opinion with the display of superior military power, and by making it impossible for Western governments to maintain adequate deterrent postures. As Hannes Adomeit has argued, one of the principal purposes of the Soviet military buildup is "to influence Western perceptions . . . to convey the impression that Western Europe *cannot* and therefore, *will not* be defended."[45] (emphasis in original)

This is the "reality management" component of perceptions management. If objective realities could be made to resemble the desired perceptions, it would be more feasible to persuade people of the accuracy of the perceptions of reality that would serve Soviet political intimidation purposes. Some West Germans judge that changing U.S.-Soviet force relationships have eroded the credibility of U.S. "extended deterrence" guarantees, since the USSR has steadily improved its capabilities to retaliate in kind for any U.S. nuclear employment against Soviet interests. This might grant the Soviet Union an ability to deter U.S. nuclear employment and thus enable the Soviet leadership to exert control over the process of nuclear escalation in war, with intimidating effects in peace.

Some observers have rejected concepts of "escalation control" and "escalation dominance" with the argument that relative degrees of operational superiority are meaningless in the nuclear age; but Soviet and Western assessments of comparative strengths and vulnerabilities could have an undeniable influence on decisions in concrete circumstances. In a practical sense, "escalation control" effects are present if government officials perceive them to be operative. According to Hans Rühle, the head of the Planning Staff in the West German Ministry of Defense,

> The previous clear-cut superiority of the U.S. in the realm of strategic nuclear weapons has been replaced by an approximate parity. . . . In the sphere of intermediate-range nuclear systems the Soviet Union has come to enjoy a clear superiority—even when all the NATO states will have implemented the dual-track decision of 1979. The nuclear escalation dominance of the U.S. has thus been lost, while escalation control has become extremely difficult [for the U.S.]. The effectiveness of extended deterrence has thereby necessarily been diminished. . . . This implies on the other hand that the Soviet Union's ability to threaten Western Europe militarily and intimidate it politically has increased considerably.[46]

Because perceptions management efforts such as the Soviet anti-INF campaign have not received much analytical attention, no recognized theoretical framework for organizing and interpreting the empirical data exists. Even if such a framework were available, the case at hand poses virtually insoluble problems of causative interpretation, owing to the complexity of the interactions among multitudes of actors. It appears, for example, that constant interactions took place between the Soviet Union and West European protest movements, not least on the level of ideas. Soviet intelligence agents appear to have monitored Western trends of thought closely so that the Soviet Union's public positions would reflect, to some degree at least, what West Europeans wanted to hear about Soviet intentions. Soviet statements could also be tailored to confirm West European fears about the implications of Western INF policy. For some observers, these statements were evidence of Soviet propaganda and disinformation influencing West European protest movements, although the sources originating certain themes seem at times to have been in Western Europe. In other words, it is not always clear whether the Soviets incited specific protest movement activities, or whether the existence of such activities incited the Soviets to take supportive steps.

Moreover, the relevant data exceed any practical grasp. Günther Schmid has, for example, noted that over 600 books were published on INF and the general issue of "peace" in West Germany during the early 1980s.[47] Even the information that would seem to be relatively precise (for instance, opinion poll results) offers little more than inferential suggestions about the origins of the opinions held. Little insight about the effectiveness of the Soviet anti-INF campaign, in comparison to other possible causative factors, can be drawn from such data.

An attempt to elucidate all the relevant causative factors would risk being diagrammatic and imposing an analytical structure unjust to the facts. Interpretations stressing the impact of the Soviet campaign should consider at least a brief inventory of the principal non-Soviet factors that contributed to the polarization, delegitimization, and socialization that became evident during the INF affair. Non-Soviet factors qualify the importance of the Soviet campaign.

Within the Federal Republic of Germany, for example, it can be argued that German political culture—marked by a propensity to feelings of insecurity and a relatively low tolerance for uncertainty and disorder—helped to predispose West Germans to political polarization.[48] Key activists of the anti-INF protest movements led anti-nuclear energy movements and championed other anti-establishment causes well before INF gave them a new focus of concern. Participants in the anti-INF movements were often motivated by divergent ideological and personal incentives—many with little obvious linkage to Soviet behavior.[49]

Intraparty politics (notably within the SPD) and interparty conflicts (particularly between the SPD and CDU/CSU) probably heightened the polarization regarding INF. INF issues were used as instruments in internal competitions for power, and exploited in a polarization already underway for other reasons. Moreover, it should be noted that the leading figures of the SPD would deny being in any way uninformed about Soviet military capabilities and political aspirations. They would contend, however, that their theories about how to manage Soviet power and pursue West German national interests are more sensible than those typically formulated in the CDU/CSU. Paradoxically, those most convinced of the practical importance of relative increases in Soviet military power are least inclined to accommodation (CDU/CSU), while those who disparage the political and operational utility of Soviet military power are most dedicated to perpetuating the détente policies of the 1970's (SPD).[50]

Intra- and interparty factors inevitably overlap with the internal politics of the Atlantic Alliance—above all, with West German assessments of U.S. policy and of the unwitting role played by the United States in stimulating anti-INF protests. Konrad Seitz remarked in 1982 that:

> . . . the Soviet Union . . . is waging psychological combat with superb skill. But, whether the United States is participating in this battle can seem doubtful at times; or, if so, it can happen sometimes that its battalions of psychological warfare inadvertently fight on the side of the Soviet Union.[51]

West German experts of various political orientations consider U.S. behavior (particularly after January 1981) to have been just as important as (if not more important than) Soviet efforts in contributing to political polarization, the socialization of successor generations, and the delegitimization of NATO nuclear policy in Western Europe. In their view, the way in which the Reagan administration argued the need for Western rearmament efforts deprived the U.S. of public support in Europe. It reinforced the image of the U.S. that the USSR has tried to project—namely, that the U.S. is the engine of the arms race, and the truly dangerous superpower. The most harmful U.S. declarations appear to have been those having to do with types of nuclear wars—particularly those made in 1981 by President Reagan, Secretary of State Haig, and Secretary of Defense Weinberger. These could be exploited by the Soviets, by their front organizers, and by anti-INF protestors of all types.

The general intra-Alliance debate about nuclear policy also stimulated the protest movements, quite aside from Soviet activities. Some West German experts, for example, judge Henry Kissinger's September 1979 speech in Brussels to have been more detrimental to the credibility of extended deterrence than any Soviet statement.[52] A no-first-use of nuclear weapons proposal by four prominent Americans preceded the Soviet policy declaration to this effect, and may have influenced its timing.[53] Some West German observers have stressed the pivotal importance of the polarization of the U.S. security debate in the post-Vietnam period, with the collapse of what had passed for a defense consensus most obvious in the intense campaigns for and against ratification of the 1979 agreements in the Strategic Arms Limitation Talks (SALT). In their view, this continuing polarization (which became intense immediately before the INF affair) promoted a similar pattern in West Germany; that is, West Germans were encouraged by trends within the U.S. and general Western debate to align themselves with one wing or another of the debate, with direct linkages between like-minded interest groups and political forces on both sides of the Atlantic. This interpretation highlights the role of intra-Western divisions in explaining developments that objectively favor Soviet interests.

Why the Successes?

A tentative hypothesis in need of further research and analysis may be set forth. It appears that several fundamental causes of polarization, delegitimization, and socialization were not originated by Soviet anti-INF efforts, even though the Soviets tried to exploit them. It may be hypothesized that the truly important Soviet contribution to these three developments is not to be found in the USSR's anti-INF campaign, but in the perceptual foundations laid during the 1960s and 1970s. These foundations were détente and the USSR's continued military buildup—both of which were perceived somewhat differently in Western Europe and the United States.

In Western Europe, more than in the United States, the Soviets succeeded during the détente era in improving their image. The Soviet presence in Central Europe was seemingly legitimized, and the subject (for many West Europeans) was shifted away from conflictual issues of political order in Europe, to dialogue, arms control, and "security partnership" in order to preserve peace and avert nuclear war. For West Germany, détente had especially practical benefits in that Berlin's status seemed to have been made more secure, while relations with the GDR improved.

At the same time, the continuing Soviet military buildup underlined (with relatively few words) an almost subliminal message for Western Europe: the structural conditions of West European security are increasingly precarious; any war in Europe would be fatally destructive (especially for Germany); armed resistance would be futile and suicidal; U.S. nuclear guarantees are less and less likely to be honored; and so forth. Some West German experts judge that the Soviets succeeded in conveying such an intimidating message. Hans Rühle has written that

> If, as all empirical data demonstrate, at the turn of the decade 1979/1980, 50 percent of the West German people considered the Soviet Union to be the world's strongest power, and just 10 percent the leading power of their own alliance, the U.S., then this explains much of what at the present appears as fear and evident readiness to accept "peace at any price," to adopt "preventive capitulation."[54]

These military trends—symbolized by U.S.-Soviet strategic "parity" in the SALT process and growing Soviet regional nuclear superiority in non-SALT-counted forces—led to both a reaffirmation of commitment to détente in Western Europe and to a proposal by West European governments (chiefly West Germany and Britain) to recouple U.S. strategic nuclear forces to European security—an initiative that resulted in the December 1979 INF decision. However, with the long experience of détente (made all the more attractive by its practical benefits and the increase in Soviet military power) its continuation and appropriate arms control accords had become expected features of the international scene for many members of the SPD, the successor generations, and the public at large in Western Europe.

In short, what happened in Western Europe in the period of the INF affair (especially in West Germany) was that U.S. policy, and the policies of most NATO governments, shocked the assumptions firmly embraced during the détente era—that is, that one may readily choose an "arms control priority" instead of re-arming to compensate for the military buildup of the USSR; that the USSR is open to fair and reasonable proposals making counterarmament unnecessary; that counterarmament provides no real security and only propels the arms race forward; that counterarmament contradicts détente and raises the risks of a suicidal and apocalyptic war; that security is only to be found in more détente and more mutual political confidence-building; and so forth. These assumptions were so firmly embraced during the period from the mid-1960s to 1979 that most members of the SPD and many members of the public (especially the successor generations) refused to abandon them during the INF affair and blamed the shock to their preferred attitudes on the most obvious target, the refusal of the U.S. government to continue conforming to the détente policies of the late 1970's. The U.S. was then accused of adopting "aggressive" and "confrontational" policies. This probably helped to erode West European confidence in U.S. foreign policy.[55] As Pierre Hassner has noted, détente

> meant taking for granted the decline of the East-West conflict and the obsolescence of military force and the emergence of new priorities: Third World, environment, women's movement, or just psychological and social self-fulfillment. To be told that the party is over and that it is time to return to the priority of the Soviet threat and of military budgets just when economic scarcity and austerity also attack the new priorities based on affluence provokes disbelief and revolt. This is the well-known Tocqueville effect, according to which the reversal of a favorable trend is much less easily accepted than the original situation this trend had begun to change.[56]

It may also be hypothesized that no more than a minor role was required of Soviet propaganda and disinformation in the INF affair; the real work was done during the 1960's and 1970's. The attitudes of faith in détente as the only road to peace, and in arms control as an available "priority" (a means of security that could be chosen instead of counterarmament and deterrence) were well-entrenched by Soviet behavior from the Partial Test Ban Treaty of 1963 to SALT II in 1979. These attitudes were not established by the Soviets alone, of course.[57] Western governments also contributed heavily to their establishment by exaggerating the substantive merits of the arms control and détente accords they reached with the USSR, partly for domestic electoral advantage and partly out of wishful thinking.

During the INF affair, the Soviets had only to outline a position that sounded reasonably fair (equality and equal security) to persuade those *already convinced* of the dangers of "arms race" counterarmament, and of the availability of means to avoid it—more détente and arms control. The SPD as a whole endorsed elements of the Soviet INF position, the vast majority of the party opposed NATO's INF deployments, and leading figures of the party recommended that NATO accept the Soviet terms for an INF accord—terms which would have precluded any NATO deployments. Elements of the Soviet position also won sympathy in the protest movements, in the successor generations, and in the public at large.

It may be conjectured that these successes did not stem so much from the skill and content of Soviet perceptions management efforts during the INF affair as from the attitudes that had been built up during the preceding period of détente (roughly 1963 to 1979) with a large degree of Soviet assistance. In other words, one of the central propositions of the theory of strategic deception in war may apply to peacetime perceptions management as well—that is, the most effective campaigns are those that reinforce existing perceptions and predispositions.

The role of INF-specific Soviet perceptions management efforts during the 1979–83 INF affair was, therefore, probably secondary in relation to both (a) various important indigenous factors that helped to cause the polarization, delegitimization, and socialization at issue, and (b) the crucial attitudinal factor during the preceding détente experience—namely, the commitment to détente and arms control. This commitment was especially profound in West Germany, owing in part to the enhanced geostrategic vulnerability of the Federal Republic to Soviet military power, and in part to the Soviets having permitted practical improvements in the status of Berlin and better West German relations with East Germany.

Why the Failures?

If this hypothesis provides a plausible, albeit tentative and rough-hewn, explanation for the developments objectively favoring the USSR, what accounts for the Soviet failure to prevent the initial INF deployments? First, as with the successes, indigenous factors unrelated to Soviet behavior help to explain Soviet failure—for example, the German political culture's tradition of obedience to established secular authority. The INF decisions were taken by the best-established representative democracy in German history, with the legitimacy of its policy making bolstered by the concurrence of numerous democratic allies.

Second, as with the successes, the role played by INF-specific Soviet perceptions management efforts in the Soviet failure appears to have been secondary. It should be noted, however, that these efforts may well have been counterproductive (from the Soviet viewpoint) in the cases where West Germans pondered the implications of the Soviet position. In fact, the Soviets were relatively sincere (despite their lies and misrepresentations about the state of the INF balance, U.S. policy, and so forth) in declaring their view that the USSR should have a monopoly in long-range INF missiles, and that existing U.S. nuclear capabilities in Europe should be drastically reduced. Some West European governments were able to use the Soviet position to demonstrate the arrogance of the Soviet demand that the USSR not face any threat from Europe comparable to the threat it poses to Europe.

It may even be argued that the Soviets committed serious blunders in their propaganda and disinformation campaign. For example, the March 1982 moratorium on SS-20 deployments the Soviets claimed to have instituted was shown to be fraudulent, and the Soviets lost credibility. The "nuclear war limited to Europe" argument was less successful as West Germany and other NATO governments emphasized the recoupling function of U.S. INF, and called attention to convoluted and inconsistent Soviet uses of this argument. The Soviet failure to capitalize on the "walk in the woods" episode of summer 1982 (especially the implicit U.S. willingness to forego Pershing II deployments) also remains puzzling.

Some have speculated that the Soviets were overconfident during the INF affair, owing to an exaggerated assessment of their own importance in influencing Western views during the 1977–1978 "neutron bomb" controversy. This may explain their failure to exploit some opportunities. Others conjecture that the rigidity in Soviet policy during the INF affair may be partly explained by the leadership succession crisis during the years in question. This situation, it has been suggested, made imaginative shifts in policy difficult to undertake.

A more basic reason for the Soviet failure was that, in accepting the initial NATO INF deployments, West Germany could continue with both of the pillars of her security policy: détente with the East and U.S. nuclear guarantees. The latter pillar is more important, but the former should not be minimized. The GDR's refusal to cooperate with the Soviet threats to inter-German relations has greatly facilitated the INF deployment process in West Germany, because it has kept a semblance of détente alive with the state to the East that West Germans care about most. Although the Soviet propaganda line has implied that the Soviets oppose this state of affairs, it is quite possible that the Soviets have discreetly used GDR-FRG relations to help maintain the continuity of the Federal Republic's commitment to détente.[58]

The most fundamental reason for the Soviet failure is that the developments favorable to Soviet interests (polarization, delegitimization, and socialization) did not affect a decisive political majority. The decisive political majority in West Germany turned against the politicians and movements championing ideas congruent with Soviet objectives, partly because of their policies on INF, and partly for reasons extraneous to INF (for example, judgments that the SPD's economic policies were inferior to those likely to be pursued by the CDU/CSU). The decisive political majority in West Germany, the CDU/CSU-FDP coalition, determined that implementing the NATO INF decision was essential to preserve alliance cohesion, to retain U.S. nuclear guarantees, and to show that the West would not capitulate to Soviet blackmail—in short, to maintain the security of West Germany's freedom.[59] In the words of Chancellor Kohl in December 1982:

> The great majority of our people understand the issue and share my conviction that we must not be open to [Soviet] blackmail and pressure. . . . for us peace and freedom for the Federal Republic is the dominant issue. Everything else takes second place.
>
> And so we must do everything we can to keep the alliance intact.[60]

The Anti-INF Campaign in Perspective

It appears useful to distinguish between the anti-INF campaign of 1979–83 and the impact of Soviet behavior in the preceding era of détente (1963 to 1979). The latter behavior involved a large element of "reality management" in that the Soviet capacity to physically threaten Western Europe was greatly augmented (and this was noted by West Europeans, at varying levels of consciousness) and in that concrete ties between Western Europe and the countries to the East (involving West Germany in particular) were greatly expanded—all in a climate of U.S.-Soviet concord on fundamental issues of nuclear arms control.

During the détente era, the Soviets encouraged the Western (especially West European) tendency to adopt concepts of détente, arms control, and arms races, that would constitute a barrier to the realization of Western programs supporting unilateral means of security—deterrence and defense. Soviet behavior helped to establish the prominence of "mutual interests" approaches to security that exaggerate the willingness of the USSR to accept mutual vulnerability or fixed spheres of interest on a long-term basis. The mutual interests model then became a prescription for Western restraint for fear of generating a dangerous "arms race," or undermining détente, or "provoking" the USSR into rash actions. Relatively few in the West pointed out that properly directed Western counterarmament would be stabilizing, would promote Soviet restraint, and would be less dangerous than inaction in the face of Soviet force expansion.

The 1963 to 1979 experience affected the perceptions of many in the SPD and the successor generations so decisively that INF-specific propaganda and disinformation did not need to have a great impact; it was enough if the Soviets conveyed the impression that their INF proposals were flexible, fair, and oriented toward continuing détente. The Soviet INF campaign probably convinced most readily those already disposed to believe. The impact of the Soviet campaign against INF was much smaller than that of the interpretation of Soviet behavior purveyed by NATO governments in the preceding era of détente, combined with the shock that came with the Soviet invasion of Afghanistan, the non-ratification of SALT II, the intensity of intra-Western defense debates, the rhetoric of the Reagan administration, and so forth.

The decisive variable in one hypothesis may be a trivial epiphenomenon in another framework of analysis. The tentative hypothesis advanced in this case study is, however, consistent with theoretical analyses of strategic military deception—the most effective perceptions management reinforces preexisting views. A key novelty in peacetime perceptions management (in contrast to the relatively fast-moving pace of strategic deception in war) is that it may be able to structure and cultivate perceptions far in advance for exploitation on a later occasion. The hypothesis may exaggerate the degree of conscious Soviet complicity with Western wishful thinking and self-deception during the era of détente, but—however crudely—it seems to account for many of the facts.

Conclusion

From a Soviet viewpoint, the results of the INF affair were not entirely discouraging. In West Germany and elsewhere in Western Europe, the political polarization, delegitimization of NATO nuclear policy, and socialization of successor generations could all be considered positive developments at least partially attributable to INF-specific Soviet propaganda and disinformation and to the attitudes established with Soviet encouragement during the 1963–79 era of détente. These developments constitute a hindrance to further NATO military modernization projects.[61]

In assessing the results of the INF affair, the Soviets probably rate the destruction of the West German defense consensus (above all, the conversion of many in the SPD away from key NATO policies) as their most significant accomplishment. The Soviets may well underestimate the importance of indigenous and non-Soviet factors in bringing about this situation, but they have ideological reasons for considering the division of the SPD and the conversion of many SPD members to policies at variance with those of NATO more significant than the emergence of the protest movements. Soviet ideology holds that change in the SPD is likely to be of more durable importance than the relatively ephemeral, amorphous, and "classless" protest movements.[62]

This consideration overlaps with the structural factors in the East-West competition that encouraged the Soviets to return to "détente" and perceptions management efforts as carried out prior to November 1983. The return became official in March 1985 with the opening of U.S.-Soviet nuclear, space, and defense arms control talks in Geneva. Three important incentives stand out.

First, without a climate of détente, Western governments could point to the hostile attitude of the USSR and its intransigent refusal to negotiate arms control as justifications for higher levels of defense effort. During the period from December 1983 to the U.S.-Soviet meeting in Geneva in January 1985 (which chartered the arms control talks that opened in March 1985), West Germany and other allies were impelled to move closer to the United States by the chill from Moscow. The continued expansion and modernization of Soviet military capabilities could well cause more divisive debates in the West regarding what to do in response during a nominal détente than during a period of overt Soviet hostility. The Soviet "cold shoulder" in 1984 made it clear that counterarmament was virtually the only option. For this reason, a Soviet return to Geneva was predictable, even without the incentive of trying to interdict the U.S. Strategic Defense Initiative.

Second, the West was generally disposed to welcome another détente era whenever the Soviets were ready for one. According to Uwe Nerlich, the durable Soviet theme of the "irreversibility of détente" dovetails with the West German commitment to détente in a manner that is bound to be attractive to the Soviets:

> . . . Soviet diplomacy has locked West Germany into a situation in which it is engaged in a continuous effort to maintain some momentum in the process of East-West cooperation in Europe. . . . West Germany's commitment to continuity of East-West cooperation meets the Soviet interest in projecting the image of "irreversibility of détente," whereas . . . the growing need and shrinking political capacity for allied military cooperation will channel East-West cooperation to maximize the political bargaining power of Soviet military preponderance in Europe.[63]

The third and final reason why the Soviets were likely to return to détente is that propaganda and disinformation opportunities represent an East-West asymmetry that is too lucrative for the Soviets to abandon. In conjunction with arms control negotiations, perceptions management efforts could be (and perhaps have already been) of enormous assistance in cutting the cost of Soviet military procurement. Affecting Western decision making about military requirements could be inexpensive in comparison to spending more to achieve comparable levels of relative capability.

Moreover, the personnel, infrastructure, and ideology for renewed perceptions management efforts in the détente framework are at hand, and have steadily matured in sophistication since Soviet institutions such as the Institute for the Study of the USA and Canada were founded (1967). John Van Oudenaren has pointed out the progress made by figures such as Zagladin, Zamyatin, and Arbatov in reaching high levels of the CPSU during the 1970s:

> The fact that these individuals are now moving into the actual power structure of the Soviet state is significant not only for what it says about the quality of foreign-area expertise in the upper reaches of the CPSU, but for what it says about the importance of the media, propaganda, and press affairs in the USSR.[64]

Perceptions management may well be one of the single most important (and most neglected) areas in national security studies. Few courses of action could be more profitable for the Soviets than undermining the Western will to build countervailing military capabilities and, more fundamentally, to resist the expansion of Soviet political influence. If they could do so, Western programs such as INF could be rendered irrelevant.

Herbert Goldhamer once argued that,

> In the present condition of Europe, it seems likely that an increased ability to convince the Soviet Union of a German and European will to resist aggression to the full would have a greater deterrent effect than the improved military capability that is usually sought.[65]

Soviet analytical frameworks concur with this common sense judgment; the Soviets regard "political will" as a key element in their assessments of the East-West "correlation of forces."

If the full scope of the Soviet challenge to Western security interests is to be understood, it will be necessary to stop dismissing Soviet perceptions management efforts, both overt and covert, as elements of Soviet policy too marginal in their impact to be worthy of serious analysis. The Western tendency to discount the impact of such Soviet activities could be a form of self-deception that will facilitate future Soviet efforts. One is reminded of Pierre Hassner's observation that:

> One of the least unsatisfactory definitions of "Finlandization" is the constant need to adopt the most reassuring interpretation of Soviet behavior because one cannot face a more disquieting one or cannot afford to take actions that would follow from it. The apparent or conscious optimism is based in this case, on a deeper or less conscious pessimism.[66]

Notes

1. For background, see David S. Yost, "European-American Relations and NATO's Initial Missile Deployments," *Current History* 83 (April 1984).

2. Konrad Seitz, "Deutsch-franzosische sicherheitspolitische Zusammenarbeit," *Europa-Archiv* 37 (25 November 1982): p. 663.

3. Yu. Yakhontov, "FRG: Time Waits Not," *Pravda*, 3 Dec. 1982, in *Foreign Broadcast Information Service (FBIS) Soviet Union (SU)*, 13 December 1982, p. AA6.

4. See the resolutions adopted at the SPD Conference on Peace and Security, Cologne, 19 November 1983; and at the SPD Federal Party Conference, Essen, 17–21 May 1984. See also Vogel's speech at the Cologne conference, and Brandt's speech before the Bundestag on 22 November 1983.

5. Among other polls and analyses thereof, see Arnim V. Manikowsky, "Angst vor den Raketen", *Stern*, 20 October 1983, pp. 71–76; Werner Hagstotz, *Von Doppelbeschluss bis zum "Heissen Herbst": Das Meinungsbild zur NATO-Nachrüstung in der Bevölkerung und bei Anhängern der Friedensbewegung* (Mannheim: Zentrum fur Umfragen, Methoden und Analysen, November 1983); Peter Schmidt, *Public Opinion and Security Policy in the Federal Republic of Germany: Elite and Mass Opinion in a Comparative Perspective*, P-7016 (Santa Monica, CA: Rand Corp., September 1984).

6. The single best source is Stephen F. Szabo, "West Germany: Generations and Changing Security Perspectives," in Szabo, ed., *The Successor Generation: International Perspectives of Postwar Europeans* (London: Butterworths, 1983), pp. 43–75. For an intriguing brief discussion of the next "successor generation," people now in their late teens and early twenties, see James M. Markham, "For West Germany's Young, the Trend Is Conservative," *New York Times*, 19 January 1986, pp. 1, 12.

7. Georgi Arbatov, *Der Sowjetische Standpunkt: Uber die Westpolitik der UdSSR* (Munich: Rogner und Bernhard, 1981).

8. Examples of INF-related interviews in *Der Spiegel*: Falin, 15 December 1980, pp. 94–104; Arbatov, 23 March 1981, pp. 128–134; Portugalov, 5 June 1980, pp. 27–37.

9. Nikolai Portugalov, "European Nuclear Balance—A Soviet View," *NATO's Fifteen Nations* 26 (October-November 1981), pp. 40–43; Vadim Zagladin, "The Western Threat to the Soviet Union," *NATO's Fifteen Nations* 27 (August-September 1982), pp. 22–26; General Konstantin Michailow in *Frankfurter Rundschau*, 3 November 1982; Ustinov in *Frankfurter Rundschau*, 8 September 1982.

10. Charles A. Sorrels, *Soviet Propaganda Campaign Against NATO* (Washington, DC: U.S. Arms Control and Disarmament Agency, October 1983), p. A–8.

11. *Medienecho zum Deutsch-Sowjetischen Expertengespräch am 21 und 22 Oktober 1982 in Bonn, Generalthema: Ost-West-Beziehungen und Europäische Sicherheit* (Bonn: Studiengruppe Sicherheit und Abrüstung in Forschungsinstitut der Friedrich-Ebert-Stiftung, November 1982).

12. *New York Times*, 21 September 1983.

13. Hans-Joachim Nimitz, *Frankfurter Neue Presse*, 2 April 1983.

14. *Die Zeit*, 11 March 1983; 18 March 1983.

15. All three of the following reports are available from the U.S. Department of State, Bureau of Public Affairs: *Forgery, Disinformation, Political Operations*, Special Report no. 88, October 1981; *Soviet Active Measures: An Update*, Special Report no. 101, July 1982; *Soviet Active Measures*, Special Report no. 110, September 1983.

16. Günther Schmid, *Sicherheitspolitik und Friedensbewegung* (Munich: Günther Olzog Verlag, 1982), p. 73.

17. Ibid., pp. 73–74.

18. For example, Wilfried von Bredow, "Zusammensetzung und Ziele der Friedensbewegung in der Bundesrepublik Deutschland," *Aus Politik und Zeitgeschichte*, (19 June 1982) no. 24, p. 11.

19. Gerhard Wettig, "The New Peace Movement in Germany," *Aussenpolitik* 33, no. 3, (1982), p. 231.

20. Heuer cited in *Wall Street Journal*, 19 October 1983, p. 34.

21. Statement by Secretary Frohlich to the Bundestag on 27 May 1983, offprint 10/141, *Deutscher Bundestag, Stenographischer Bericht, Plenarprotokoll*.

22. For examples, see the FBIS Special Memorandum of 13 August 1980, *Soviet Public Statements on U.S. Forward-Based Systems Since the June 1979 Vienna Summit*; and Sallie Wise, *The Soviet Peace Offensive: A Chronology*, RL 180/82 (Munich: Radio Liberty Research, 3 May 1982).

23. Sorrels.

24. Thomas W. Wolfe, *Soviet Power and Europe, 1945–1970* (Baltimore: Johns Hopkins University Press, 1970), pp. 83–84, 143.

25. Zagladin interview in *Der Spiegel*, 9 June 1981, cited in Sorrels, *Soviet Propaganda*, p. 25.

26. Brezhnev's interview in *Der Spiegel*, 2 November 1981, in *Survival* 24(January-February 1982), p. 32. Brezhnev's statement and similar Soviet declarations appear to be intended for Western consumption, in order to encourage feelings of demoralization. Soviet military doctrine has for over two decades explicitly recognized the desirability of retaining control over nuclear operations, and has posited the possibility of limited and selective employment of nuclear weapons. For background, see Notra Trulock III, "Weapons of Mass Destruction in Soviet Strategy," a paper presented at the conference on Soviet Military Strategy in Europe, sponsored jointly by the Boston Foreign Affairs Group and the Royal United Services Institute, Oxfordshire, England, 24–25 September 1984.

27. For details, see Gerhard Wettig, "The Soviet INF Data Critically Reviewed," *Aussenpolitik* 34, no. 1 (1983), pp. 30–42.

28. The history of Soviet attempts to count British and French forces with those of the United States, and the ten principal reasons why Western governments have rejected such Soviet arguments are reviewed in David S. Yost, *France's Deterrent Posture and Security in Europe, Part II: Strategic and Arms Control Implications*, Adelphi Paper no. 195 (London: International Institute for Strategic Studies, Winter 1984/85), pp. 55–60.

29. Paul Nitze has discussed the institutional relationships between Soviet decision making bodies for arms control negotiations and those for propaganda and "political action," in "Living with the Soviets," *Foreign Affairs* 63 (Winter 1984/1985), p. 362.

30. N. Polyanov, "Europe at the Turn of the Decade," *International Affairs* (Moscow: April 1980), p. 92.

31. *Literary Gazette*, 14 May 1980, in *Soviet World Outlook* 5, no. 6, 15 June 1980, p. 2.

32. Flora Lewis, *New York Times*, 1 November 1979. Two strategic reasons have been advanced to justify the lack of U.S.-West German consultation arrangements supplementing those in the 1962 Athens guidelines and NATO Nuclear Planning Group practices: (a) U.S. nuclear employment commitments, or "guarantees," are regarded as more credible if prospects for delays in implementation owing to consultation obligations

are held to a reasonable level; and (b) U.S. control may promote continuity between U.S. INF and U.S. central strategic systems in Soviet perceptions. The latter judgment underlines the intended "recoupling" function of U.S. INF.

33. Radio Moscow broadcast of 5 October 1983, in *FBIS (SU)*, 7 October 1983, p. AA–4.

34. Interview with Yevgeniy Velikhov, in *l'Unita*, 22 August 1983, in *FBIS (SU)*, 25 August 1983, p. AA–3; Zagladin interview in *Der Spiegel*, 9 June 1981, in Sorrels, p. 13.

35. Andropov remarks reported by TASS, in *Soviet World Outlook* 8, no. 7, 15 July 1983, p. 3.

36. A. Grigoryants, "Bonn Faces Complex Problems," *International Affairs* (Moscow) (July 1982): p. 109.

37. TASS dispatch, 5 May 1983, in *FBIS (SU)*, 6 May 1983, p. G–1.

38. TASS dispatch, 15 September 1983, in *FBIS (SU)*, 16 September 1983, p. G–4.

39. A. Grigoryants, "The FRG in the Snares of 'Nachrüstung,' " *International Affairs* (Moscow), June 1981, p. 104.

40. Andropov remarks reported by TASS, in *Soviet World Outlook* 8(15 July 1983): p. 3.

41. Alexander R. Alexiev has provided a useful survey of the events in *The Soviet Campaign Against INF: Strategy, Tactics, Means*, N-2280-AF (Santa Monica, Calif: Rand Corporation, February 1985).

42. TASS dispatch in *FBIS (SU)*, 8 March 1983, p. G–3.

43. Herbert Goldhamer, *Reality and Belief in Military Affairs: A First Draft (June 1977)*, Joan Goldhamer, ed., R-2448-NA (Santa Monica, Calif: Rand Corporation, February 1979), pp. 8–9.

44. A basic point of consensus in the Western alliance is that military strength is essential for acceptable diplomatic relations with the Soviet Union and its allies. As was pointed out in the 1967 Harmel Report, the Atlantic Alliance has two main roles. The first is to maintain sufficient military strength to deter aggression and attempts at coercion, to defend the allies in the event of aggression, and "to assure the balance of forces, thereby creating a climate of stability, security, and confidence." Fulfillment of the first role creates a basis for the second role: "to pursue the search for progress towards a more stable relationship in which the underlying political issues can be solved." See "The Future Tasks of the Alliance (Harmel Report)," Report of the Council, Annex to the Final Communiqué of the Ministerial Meeting, December 1967, in *The North Atlantic Treaty Organization: Facts and Figures*, 10th ed. (Brussels: NATO Information Service, 1981), pp. 288–290.

45. Hannes Adomeit, "The Political Rationale of Soviet Military Capabilities and Doctrine," in *Strengthening Conventional Deterrence in Europe: Proposals for the 1980's*, Report of the European Security Study (London: Macmillan, 1983), p. 95.

46. Hans Rühle, "Die Zukunft der NATO," in Günther Wagenlehner, ed., *Die Kampagne gegen den NATO-Doppelbeschluss: Eine Bilanz* (Koblenz: Bernard und Graefe Verlag, 1985), pp. 197–198.

47. Günther Schmid, "Die öffentliche Diskussion um Frieden und Sicherheit," *Oesterreichische Militaerische Zeitschrift*, no. 4, 1983, pp. 294–295.

48. On German political culture, see Richard Lowenthal, "Why German Stability

Is so Insecure," *Encounter*, (December 1978); and Gordon A. Craig, *The Germans* (New York: G. P. Putnam's Sons, 1982), pp. 16–17, 22–23, 290–297.

49. For a useful and concise survey, see Gottfried Linn, "Die Friedensbewegung in der Bundesrepublik Deutschland", in Günther Wagenlehner, ed., *Die Kampagne gegen den NATO-Doppelbeschluss*, pp. 131–146.

50. For background, see David S. Yost and Thomas C. Glad, "West German Party Politics and Theater Nuclear Modernization Since 1977," *Armed Forces and Society* 8 (Summer 1982).

51. Seitz, "Deutsch-französische," p. 663.

52. Henry Kissinger, "The Future of NATO," *Washington Quarterly* 2(Autumn 1979).

53. McGeorge Bundy, George F. Kennan, Robert S. McNamara, and Gerard Smith, "Nuclear Weapons and the Atlantic Alliance," *Foreign Affairs* 60(Spring 1982).

54. Hans Rühle, "Wunschträume statt Alpträume: Bedrohungsanalysen mit Zweierlei Mass," *Europäische Wehrkunde* 33(November 1984), p. 612.

55. For a valuable analysis of the tendency in some sectors of West European opinion toward "equidistancing" in perceptions of the U.S. and the USSR, see Stephen F. Szabo, "European Opinion After the Missiles," *Survival* 27(November/December 1985), pp. 269–272.

56. Pierre Hassner, "Arms Control and the Politics of Pacifism in Protestant Europe," in Uwe Nerlich, ed., *The Western Panacea: Constraining Soviet Power through Negotiation*, vol. II of *Soviet Power and Western Negotiating Policies* (Cambridge, Mass.: Ballinger Publishing Co., 1983), p. 125.

57. The last year of the Kennedy administration, 1963, has been identified by various scholars as marking the beginning of a period of ascendancy for nuclear arms control priorities in U.S. (and general Western) policies toward the Soviet Union. See, for example, Catherine Kelleher, "America Looks at Europe," in Lawrence Freedman, ed., *The Troubled Alliance* (London: Heinemann, 1983), p. 50; and John Van Oudenaren, "U.S.-West German Relations and the Soviet Problem," in Uwe Nerlich and James A. Thomson, eds., *The Soviet Problem in American-German Relations* (New York: Crane, Russak and Co., 1985), pp. 100–102.

58. For a useful discussion of the GDR's behavior and the Soviet-FRG-GDR triangle in the post-November 1983 period, see Roland Smith, *Soviet Policy Towards West Germany*, Adelphi Paper no. 203 (London: International Institute for Strategic Studies, 1985), pp. 25–30.

59. For an extensive analysis of how the anti-INF campaign failed to dislodge the decisive political majority in West Germany, despite its impact in certain sectors of society, see Hans Rattinger, "The Federal Republic of Germany: Much Ado About (Almost) Nothing," in Gregory Flynn and Hans Rattinger, eds. *The Public and Atlantic Defense* (London: Croom Helm, 1985), pp. 101–174.

60. Kohl interview in *Economist*, (18 December 1982), pp. 39, 44.

61. According to a Congressional staff report, "The anti-military and especially anti-nuclear constituency in Europe has become a permanent factor affecting the arms control and force modernization programs of Alliance governments." *Post-Deployment Nuclear Arms Control in Europe*, a Staff Report Prepared for the Committee on Foreign Relations, United States Senate (Washington, DC: US GPO, 1984), p. 7.

62. Gerhard Wettig, "The Western Peace Movement in Moscow's Longer View," *Strategic Review* 12 (Spring 1984), p. 52.

63. Uwe Nerlich, "The Enduring Competition with the Soviet Union: Western Political Strategy Reconsidered," in Uwe Nerlich and James A. Thomson, eds., *The Soviet Problem in American–German Relations* (New York: Crane, Russak and Co., 1985), p. 360.

64. John Van Oudenaren, *Political Change and Detente in Europe: Soviet Policy, 1969–1976*, unpublished Ph.D. dissertation, Department of Political Science, Massachusetts Institute of Technology, January 1983, p. 272. [Cited with the author's permission.]

65. Goldhamer, *Reality and Belief*, p. 112.

66. Pierre Hassner, "Western European Perceptions of the USSR," *Daedalus* 108(Winter 1979), p. 114.

18
Seizing Power: Deception in the Nicaraguan Revolution

David Blair

Communist Deception Strategy and the Broad Front

The Cuban and Nicaraguan revolutions were mass uprisings by broad coalitions against corrupt dictatorships. Many, probably most, of the revolutionaries were democrats who received substantial support from democratic Latin American states, as well as from Western Europe and the United States.

The Communist leaders of the 26 July Movement and the Sandinista National Liberation Front faced a dilemma during and immediately after the revolutions against Batista and Somoza. How could they establish total Communist control while most of their support had to come from non-Communists? They faced the following conditions: (1) The guerrilla armies *per se* were far inferior numerically to Batista's Army or Somoza's National Guard and could not hope to win without mass support from the general population. The East European model, where Communist power was established at the point of a Red Army bayonet, could not apply directly to Cuba or Nicaragua until after a transition period when the Communists were consolidating their power. (2) Large portions of the guerrilla armies themselves were non-Communist, and important guerrilla commanders were anti-Communist (for example, Huber Matos and Edén Pastora). (3) The civilian opposition to Batista and Somoza was certainly non-Communist—much of it was middle-class and explicitly anti-Communist. (4) The democratic Latin American supporters of the revolutions were very much anti-Communist. And, (5) the United States might intervene to prevent an explicitly Communist revolution.

The solution to this dilemma was a strategy that hid the communism of the guerrilla leaders until they were able to consolidate their power sufficiently so that the domestic anti-Communists were unable to dislodge them, and the U.S. was unwilling to use sufficient military force to do so. Several recent Cuban documents have explicitly outlined this strategy. Fidel Castro recently called for:

> . . . the formation of a broad front to fight for social changes in Latin America to include Christians, Marxists, workers, and military officers. . . . I truly believe the message must be broad, and to be broad it cannot be a radicalism that isolates people and the revolutionary movement. . . . If the Nicaraguan revolution had proclaimed socialism it would not have helped the revolutionary movement in Central America and Latin America.[1]

Similarly, the 1980 2nd Congress of the Communist Party of Cuba adopted a resolution stressing

> . . . the importance of continuing to promote the consolidation of a common front to back the indispensable structural transformations required by the region. This process is backed by the active, large-scale incorporation of Christian groups and organizations in the struggles for national liberation and social justice, as has occurred in Nicaragua and El Salvador.[2]

This "large-scale incorporation" of non-Communist opposition groups within broad alliances directed by Communists was essential to the success of the Communists in seizing power in Nicaragua and Cuba. However, this strategy should not be misinterpreted to mean that the Communists had any intention of incorporating these groups into the government (except as powerless and temporary spokesmen) after the revolution.[3]

The 1977 "General Political-Military Platform of the Sandinista Front for National Liberation," written primarily by Humberto Ortega, called for a platform "without leftist rhetoric" designed to appeal to, and radicalize, the moderate opposition while promising political pluralism, a mixed economy, and international nonalignment.[4] Yet, as H. Ortega was quick to point out in a 1979 letter to a guerrilla colleague, this strategy was adopted only as a means of seizing power, and implied no wavering from the goal of total Communist control:

> We have mounted this great insurrection . . . without losing for one moment our Marxist-Leninist, Sandinista principles to draw all our people behind the FSLN. . . . We are the ideological representatives of the exploited, the working class, which historically is destined to bury capitalism and imperialism. . . .
>
> The art is in our causing the changes . . . in carrying out our undertaking, which, founded on a Marxist-Leninist ideology, can guide a backward people, imbued with anti-communist propaganda, precisely toward the objectives of the Sandinista revolution, toward national and social liberation. . . .
>
> Many of our young militants come to the struggle with some training in

Marxist theory; this is good, and it is a long step forward compared to the recent past. . . . Some do not understand the politics of tactical alliances . . . they become extreme in public when presenting our position (becoming very red).
. . .
Our movement demands more in terms of standards and commitment, more in class consciousness and clarity in Marxist ideology, but let us not do this openly and before the masses lest we run the risk of sectarianizing and isolating ourselves from the masses.[5]

The *Platform* itself admitted that the pluralistic promises were made because "strategic and tactical factors make it impossible, both nationally and internationally, to adopt socialism openly during this phase."[6]

There has long been a debate about whether Castro originally intended to set up a Communist dictatorship or was "forced into it" by the United States. In a recent interview with *Le Figaro Magazine*, Castro himself left no doubt that he planned a Communist state from the start—his moderate image was just a ruse:

Figaro: In 1959 you made a statement in the United States that was regarded as totally anticommunist.

Castro: The United States wanted us to make a strategic and tactical error and proclaim a doctrine as a communist movement. In fact, I was a communist. . . . I think that a good Marxist-Leninist would not have proclaimed a socialist revolution in the conditions that existed in Cuba in 1959. I think I was a good Marxist-Leninist in not doing that, and when we did not make known our underlying beliefs. What the United States wanted was to judge, to know what we thought, and we did not want to allow ourselves to be maneuvered or manipulated by it. I think it was an excellent thing that we did not proclaim the Marxist-Leninist or socialist nature of the revolution at the time.[7]

Anyone fighting against Batista or Somoza started with a large supply of goodwill from democrats in the U.S. and Latin America. These democrats did not need to be absolutely convinced that the rebels were not Communists—they only needed to be convinced that there was enough opportunity for a democratic outcome of the revolution to make it worth taking a chance on supporting the rebels. Within Nicaragua and Cuba, the rebels followed the dual strategy of: (1) attempting to provoke the dictatorship to more violent repression while (2) promising a democratic and moderate revolution. Thus, the non-Communists could be convinced that their best option was to back a guerrilla-led revolution and hope that the guerrillas would keep their promises of a pluralistic democracy. To seize power through this strategy, the Communists had to be sure that no compromise solution could be reached in which the dictator was thrown out before the guerrilla army was the sole surviving military force.

Promises of Pluralism

The Sandinistas' elaborate scheme for deceiving democrats about the likely nature of the regime that would result from a Sandinista victory consisted of five major techniques: (1) The Sandinista leaders, while sometimes stating that some of them were Marxists (never using the word *Communist*), repeatedly promised that the goal of the revolution was a pluralistic democracy. (2) They created the myth that the Sandinista directorate of nine commandantes was split into a Marxist group and a democratic, Christian group. (The implication was that the moderate group could get the upper hand if democrats gave it enough support.) (3) The Sandinistas were careful to include priests and other Christians in highly visible places in their government. (4) Similarly, important non-Communist Nicaraguan businessmen were placed in prominent but powerless positions in the government. (5) Finally, the Sandinistas were able to gain the support of democratic Latin American countries such as Venezuela and Costa Rica—largely because both these countries hated Somoza, and both believed that Edén Pastora would be the leader of a Sandinista government.

In the months before the Sandinista victory on 19 July 1979, leading Sandinistas were adamant in their claims that they had no intention of establishing a Communist state. These claims were widely repeated in the U.S. press. For example, on 30 May, The *Washington Post* reported:

> In an interview broadcast yesterday on Costa Rican television, Tomás Borges [sic], one of a nine-member Sandinista council of directors, said, "The offensive has begun." He vowed it would "soon spread to a nationwide insurrection" to overthrow Somoza. Borges [sic] had been considered one of the doctrinaire Marxists within the Sandinista leadership. Yesterday, however, he pledged that the Sandinistas "do not promise a socialistic scenario, but rather a democratic one," with early elections.[8]

(The *Post*'s lack of knowledge about Nicaragua, and therefore its vulnerability to disinformation, is indicated by its misunderstanding of the name Tomás Borge—a mistake that was repeated on June 2. Presumably, the reporter had not previously heard of this prominent and well-known Sandinista.)

Such promises were common at the time from prominent Sandinistas. Ernesto Cardenal, now Sandinista Minister of Culture, gave an interview to the *New York Times* where he repeated the common line:

> Among the Sandinistas, there are Marxists, but there are others who are not. We don't want to be a second Cuba. We want to establish a first Nicaragua.[9]

Then he proceeded to promise that the Sandinista revolution meant democracy, and that non-Somoza private property would not be nationalized.

Sergio Ramirez, now Vice-President of Nicaragua, and then considered "the apparent leader of the five-member provisional junta proclaimed by the rebels," reportedly

> ... said his group would create a democratic regime with a foreign policy of nonalignment. It would adhere to the human rights resolutions of the United Nations and the Organization of American States, he said, recognize the separation of executive, legislative, and judicial powers and guarantee freedom of speech, religion, and assembly.[10]

Later, he promised that elections for both the local and national government, including the President, would be held within two years.[11] Immediately after the Sandinista victory, Ramirez forecasted good relations with the United States:

> What would make them react against us? If we were to say we were Marxist-Leninist, but we're not going to do that. If we were to expropriate U.S. companies, but we're not going to do that either. If we announced we were joining the Soviet bloc, but that won't happen. If we intervene in El Salvador's affairs, but that isn't going to happen either.[12]

Many accounts quoted unnamed Sandinistas who repeated the pluralistic promises. The following paragraph from the *New York Times* is typical:

> The rebels say that while several top guerrilla leaders are Marxists, their immediate objective is the restoration of democracy to Nicaragua, which has been ruled by the Somoza family for 46 years. They say that their first measures once in power would be the expropriation of the Somoza family's $500 million business empire, and the reorganization of the National Guard. Free elections would follow soon after, they say.[13]

One week before taking power, the junta of five appointed by the Sandinistas to be the official government of Nicaragua (which included current Sandinista President Daniel Ortega and Vice President Sergio Ramirez) wrote a letter to the Organization of American States (OAS) promising free elections at the municipal, constituent assembly, and presidential level. Violeta Chamorro, then a member of the junta, recently wrote another letter to the OAS that shows the value of such Sandinista promises:

> Six years ago, I and my then fellow members of the Nicaraguan provisional government signed a letter commitment dated July 1979 and addressed to the OAS. According to this document, the new government pledged to establish a regime that would ensure nonalignment, political pluralism, and a mixed economy . . . enough time has elapsed for me to see beyond any possible doubt that those principles for which we all fought until we succeeded in ousting Anastasio Somoza Debayle from power have been flagrantly betrayed by the ruling party, namely the FSLN.

For this reason, I feel it is my duty to denounce the fraud committed by the FSLN, which abusing the trust we placed in its leaders, has perverted the democratic foundations and led Nicaragua down the path of Marxism-Leninism, a doctrine that clashes with our Christian and Democratic principles. . . . I hereby propose that you—based on the letter-commitment I have mentioned—the OAS, demand that the Nicaraguan government fulfill its previous pledge.[14]

The Formation of the Front Organizations

One way the Sandinistas sought to give credibility to their promises was to organize broad groups of non-Communists who would endorse the Sandinista fight.

Los Doce

In October 1977, a group of twelve Nicaraguan businessmen, clergy, academics, and professionals publicly announced their support for the FSLN in its fight against Somoza. This group, known as Los Doce [the twelve], included the Cardenal brothers and Sergio Ramirez, who were then secretly Sandinistas, as well as moderate businessmen such as Arturo Cruz. Los Doce was considerably to the left of the traditional opposition parties and the private business organization, COSEP. Nevertheless, it provided a legitimizing non-Communist patina that allowed the Sandinistas to raise money from Nicaraguan businessmen and foreign democrats.

Carlos Tunnerman, a member of Los Doce who coordinated Sandinista finances during the war, said that Los Doce's declaration of support was a key factor in helping the Sandinistas gather $5 million from European and Venezuelan supporters, with the help of Willy Brandt, Olaf Palme, and Venezuelan President Luis Herrera Campins. After the assassination of Pedro Joaquin Chamorro, Tunnerman said, Los Doce funneled even more than $5 million from Nicaraguan "members of the Chamber of Commerce, people who before called the Sandinistas Marxist-Leninists . . ."[15] Essential logistical aid from the anti-Communist Costa Rican and Panamanian governments would not have been available if the Sandinistas had not put forward an apparently non-Communist front.

In mid-1978, Los Doce, along with the Conservative and Social Christian opposition parties and some Christian Democratic labor unions, formed an umbrella organization known as the Broad Opposition Front, which called for Somoza's resignation and the depoliticization of the National Guard. The Sandinistas used Sergio Ramirez's position in the Broad Opposition Front, where he represented Los Doce, to quash October 1978 negotiations that might have led to Somoza's resignation before a total Sandinista military victory.[16]

The Junta

In June 1979, the Sandinistas appointed a junta of five, (Daniel Ortega, Sergio Ramirez, Moises Hassan, Alfonso Robelo, and Violeta Chamorro) who were to be the official government of Nicaragua after a Sandinista victory. There was much confusion about the ideological orientation of the junta. For example, the *Washington Post* reported that "the junta's five members range from middle-class centrists to a leftist who says he is not a Marxist,"[17] and that Hassan and Ramirez were considered to be "social democrats or socialists."[18] The *Christian Science Monitor* reported that none of the five members of the junta had been "directly involved in the guerrilla cause."[19] It wrote that Moises Hassan was "not a Sandinista himself," and that he " was one of the key moderates whose presence is supposed to reassure the United States Government that post-Somoza Nicaragua will not rush to the extreme left."[20]

On the other hand, the *New York Times* saw Hassan as leftist and Sergio Ramirez as the centrist "bridge within the group, balancing two members of the Nicaraguan establishment with two leftists."[21] The *Los Angeles Times* described the junta and the cabinet it appointed as a "model of moderation."[22]

The truth was that Hassan and Ramirez were secret members of the Sandinista leadership and that Ortega was the leader of the Tercerista branch of the Sandinistas.[23] Still the Sandinistas were able to establish a deception that at least allowed democrats to hope for the best. This was enough to prevent the U.S. from taking decisive action and to convince the Broad Opposition Front and COSEP, the Nicaraguan business organization, to endorse the junta.[24]

The Terceristas

The Sandinistas also deceived democrats about the ultimate regime that would result from the revolution by circulating the story that one branch of the Sandinistas, the Terceristas, was not Marxist. This also led some democrats to believe that they should aid the Terceristas in order to avoid the "extremists." This lie was widely repeated in the U.S. press. The *Los Angeles Times* editorialized:

> The world would not come to an end if the Somoza government were succeeded by the Sandinistas. The guerrilla movement is split into moderate and anti-U.S. Marxist factions, and it is by no means clear that the pro-Castro elements would prevail.[25]

Similarly, the *New York Times* described Daniel Ortega as the "leader of the group that sponsored the coalition of Marxists and bourgeoisie to overthrow the dictatorship and install democracy:"[26]

> Even within the Sandinista Front there are three vying factions which joined forces earlier this year to overthrow General Somoza. But, while the moderate "insurrectional" [Tercerista] group is merely seeking to restore democracy, the so-called "Proletarian Tendency" and "Prolonged Popular War" factions favor more rapid transition toward socialism. . . .
> If Washington fears a "second Cuba," many Latin Americans believe that Washington created the "first" Cuba by alienating the young Castro regime.
> Significantly, despite the anxiety of the United States, Cuba has deliberately avoided immediate advantage from the Nicaraguan turmoil. President Fidel Castro appears to view Nicaragua as a case study in liberation from dictatorship rather than a transition to socialism. But an isolated regime that turned to Havana for assistance could not expect to be rebuffed.[27]

The *Miami Herald* described the Terceristas as "a combination of various democratic and Christian persuasions with a vague ideology that never has crystalized," and which "publicly rejects any single party dictatorship."[28] This was complete nonsense. The Ortega brothers had received extensive training in Cuba, and their only dispute with the other factions of the Sandinistas was about the efficacy of different means of taking power—not the type of regime that should follow the seizure of power.[29]

The Cabinet

On 14 July, the Sandinistas created one more facet in the elaborate deception about the likely nature of their regime. The junta appointed a cabinet that was intended to reassure democrats who might doubt the democratic promises. The economics offices were held by respected bankers Joaquin Cuadra Chamorro and Arturo Cruz, and the defense minister was Lieutenant Colonel Bernardino Larios, a National Guard officer who had been arrested for plotting against Somoza. Foreign Minister Miguel D'Escoto and Culture Minister Ernesto Cardenal were secretly members of the FSLN. The only known FSLN member was Tomás Borge, who was given the Ministry of the Interior, *which controlled the police*.[30] This control of the police, plus the Sandinista commandantes' effective control of the army, was sufficient to allow the Communists to consolidate their control.

The Church

The Catholic Church hierarchy, led by Archbishop Obando y Bravo, strongly supported the Sandinistas during the revolution. In May 1979, Obando y Bravo headed a "national reflection committee" that recommended that the Sandinistas respect the lives of prisoners and children, and observe International Red Cross procedures. The Sandinistas publicly agreed. Somoza publicly condemned this as a tacit alliance between the church and the Sandinistas.[31]

In 1978, the church hierarchy called on Somoza to resign[32] and, in June 1979, pledged its support for the Sandinistas and said that the guerrillas' military push was justified.[33] The junta did not officially take office in Managua until it received a public benediction from the Archbishop.[34]

Of course, the Sandinistas did not live up to their promises of religious freedom any more than any of their other promises of democracy. But their ability to deceive the church during the revolution was instrumental in helping them to deceive other Nicaraguans and foreigners. How could a guerrilla group be bad if it had the support of Archbishop Obando y Bravo?

Edén Pastora

The famous Commander Zero was both an important part of the Sandinistas' international and domestic appeal, and a threat to the ability of the Communists to establish their total control in Nicaragua. Pastora lived in Costa Rica for many years, and he became close friends with General Omar Torrijos of Panama and President Carlos Andres Perez of Venezuela. Their belief that he was the supreme leader and their confidence that he was non-Communist was a crucial factor in the decision of the Latin American democracies to provide aid and bases for the Sandinistas.[35] The Communist leaders of the Sandinistas were put in a position in which they had to use Pastora's popularity without allowing him to establish himself as the head of a non-Communist revolutionary government.

Part of the deception strategy was to allow anti-Communists to believe that Pastora was actually the chief leader of the Sandinistas—although the Sandinistas never explicitly stated this. As late as June 1979, the *Financial Times* reported that Pastora was the "overall Sandinista commander" and that:

> He is understood to be committed to the holding of genuine elections and to oppose the ideas of some members of the smaller factions which have wanted to thrust undiluted Marxism-Leninism down Nicaraguan throats.[36]

However, other newspapers realized that Pastora certainly had rivals and was not in overall control of the Sandinistas.

Pastora was the commander of an army that invaded southern Nicaragua from Costa Rica in May 1979. Somoza's National Guard fiercely resisted this invasion and inflicted very heavy casualties on Pastora's force. Shirley Christian reports that Pastora sent a message to the United States (through Costa Rica) asking that Somoza withdraw his troops in the south, so that Pastora, rather than the other Sandinistas, could reach Managua first.[37] However, the U.S. refused to do this, and Pastora remained bogged down in the south against heavy National Guard resistance while the Communist-led guerrillas took Managua. In late June, after it had become clear that a Sandinista victory was inevitable, the United States did send a message that the State Department would like to talk to Pastora. The Sandinistas "replied that they would decide whom the Americans could talk to, and when."[38]

Although Pastora was clearly the most popular of the commanders at the time of the victory (he was repeatedly greeted by cries of "Zero, Zero, Zero" when he entered Managua after the revolution), he lacked troops in Managua, and thus could be shunted off into the powerless post of Deputy Defense Minister.[39] The southern army was loyal to Pastora personally, and Leonel Poveda, his deputy commander, did not want to hand over command to Tomás Borge, as ordered by the Sandinista Directorate. However, he did hand over command when ordered to do so by Pastora.[40]

The U.S. Attempt to Create a Moderate Government

The chief goal of the United States was to arrange a moderate, democratic government to replace Somoza, thereby preventing a total military victory by the Sandinista guerrilla armies. The Carter administration apparently fully realized that a Sandinista military victory was likely to lead to a Communist dictatorship. However, they did not take actions to replace Somoza soon enough to prevent the Sandinistas from gaining widespread popular support for the goal of overthrowing him by force. Then, the U.S. government's options were very constrained by its unwillingness to use military force to prevent a complete Sandinista victory. The U.S. was left hoping against odds that our economic generosity would convince the Sandinistas not to impose a Communist, pro-Soviet regime.

In retrospect, it is clear that the formation of Los Doce in October 1977 and the assassination of Pedro Joaquin Chamorro in January 1978, heralded the end of the Somoza regime. But the U.S. did not understand this until later in 1978. U.S. envoys refused to meet Los Doce and cultivated contacts with conservatives whom they expected to succeed Somoza in 1981.[41]

The U.S. first tried to arrange Somoza's resignation in the fall of 1978, after the failed September Sandinista uprising.[42] Somoza revealed later that the U.S. privately requested his resignation during the September campaign.[43] As the representative of Los Doce on the Broad Opposition Front, Sergio Ramirez was able to kill these negotiations by refusing to participate.[44] Thus the Sandinistas managed to preclude a democratic government that would have eliminated their chance for seizing power. In June 1979, however, William Bowdler of the State Department publicly blamed Somoza for the failure to arrange a negotiated solution.[45]

In January, Somoza refused to permit an internationally supervised plebiscite and the U.S. cut off all aid to his regime and cut its embassy staff in half.[46] The United States then apparently forgot about Nicaragua until fighting broke out again on May 28, 1979.

The United States government, or at least major parts of it, were not deceived by the Sandinista promises of pluralism. The Carter administration reportedly believed that hard-core Marxists would quickly neutralize the moderates within the junta after a total Sandinista military victory.[47] Reportedly at National Security Advisor Zbigniew Brzezinski's insistence, the U.S. requested an OAS Foreign Minister's Conference where it called for an OAS peacekeeping force, similar to the U.S. solution to the Dominican Republic crisis of 1966.[48] This force was quickly rejected by the OAS, which interpreted it as an attempted U.S. intervention (at a time when nonintervention was a sacrosanct OAS principle).[49]

The Assistant Secretary of State for Inter-American Affairs, Viron Vaky, quickly denounced Somoza and proclaimed publicly that the U.S. would "not contemplate" either direct or indirect military intervention.[50] Perhaps realizing the limited remaining options, he expressed confidence that Somoza's overthrow would not lead to a "second Cuba" ruled by a Marxist dictatorship.[51]

The United States attempted to convince the Sandinistas to increase the size of the junta from five to seven, giving the moderates (two new members plus Alfonso Robelo and Violeta Chamorro) a four-to-three majority. The other chief goal of the United States was to arrange some form of survival of the National Guard as an institution, preventing the Sandinistas from becoming the sole surviving armed force. Yet the U.S. had few bargaining cards and was unable to achieve either of these two goals.

The U.S. obtained Somoza's resignation in late June and told the Sandinista junta that it would invoke it when it felt secure about the nature of the new government. An earlier Somoza resignation would have saved thousands of Nicaraguan lives, but the Sandinistas were not willing to forego a total military victory, and the U.S. continued to hope that the National Guard would hold up long enough to force the Sandinistas into a compromise agreement. As it turned out, the Sandinistas did win a total military victory, and the only compromise they made was writing the letter to the OAS promising pluralism and pledging to set up safe havens to protect the National Guardsmen who surrendered. U.S. envoy William Bowdler told the junta on July 15: "You are the government of Nicaragua."[52]

Economic Aid

The Sandinistas encouraged the delusion that they would not be able to implement Marxist policies because they needed economic aid from the United States and democratic Latin American countries. For example, Sergio Ramirez told reporters:

> Nobody denies that in Nicaragua there are Marxists. But there are limits on them, and on radical solutions. Moreover, the people who are Marxists are realists . . . they realize that radical change is impossible in a destroyed nation.[53]

Editorials in many U.S. newspapers concluded that the Sandinistas would be constrained by their need for this assistance. The *Los Angeles Times* editorialized:

> The logical sources of help for Nicaragua's economic reconstruction are the United States, Europe, and Japan. A flagrant display of Castro-style Marxism would not be helpful, to say the least.[54]

The *Washington Post*'s editorial said:

> Nicaragua is small and devastated and contiguous to other Latin countries—all conditions tending to open it to close relations with them. Its need for vast economic repair ensures a respect for its neighbor's anti-Communist sensitivities. It is inconceivable, moreover, that Moscow will take on another billion-dollar baby.[55]

And the *New York Times* reported:

> On a practical level, the junta is obliged to deal with the United States. The United States says it can induce Mr. Somoza to step down, and the junta will need American help in the $4 billion job of reconstructing the war-shattered country.[56]

The United States government tried to use economic aid to convince the Sandinistas not to follow a pro-Soviet course. After they took power, American Ambassador Lawrence Pezzulo returned to Managua aboard a plane of the U.S. Agency for International Development, which carried gifts of medicine and baby formula.[57] Over the next year and a half, the U.S. provided the Sandinistas with aid totalling about $125 million—by far the most of any country. Secretary of State Edmund Muskie cut off this aid in January 1981 after he received evidence that the Sandinistas were shipping arms to the Salvadoran FMLN guerrillas for their attempted "final offensive" of that month.

The futility of these hopes that economic aid will convince Communists to loosen their grip on power is best illustrated by Sandinista Commandante Bayardo Arce's May 1980 statement that the Sandinistas would do nothing that might lead to their giving up power, even if it meant that Nicaraguans had to eat grass.[58] In fact, the United States has had enough experience in the last ten years to conclude that economic aid cannot wean clients away from the Soviets. For example, the West provides large amounts of economic aid to the military dictatorship in Ethiopia—the Soviets provide almost none. But the Soviets and Cubans do provide the military assistance and apparatus for internal repression that is necessary to keep Mengistu in power. The West cannot match the Soviets in providing this kind of ruthless support. It is obvious which type of assistance is most likely to gain a dictator's loyalty.

The Latin American Reaction

The Sandinistas could not have defeated Somoza without the active support of the democratic Latin American countries, particularly Venezuela, Panama, and Costa Rica. These three countries provided essential arms and bases.[59] Mexico, Costa Rica, Panama, and Ecuador early on broke diplomatic relations with Somoza,[60] and the Andean Pact declared the Sandinistas to be legitimate belligerents in June 1979.[61]

Costa Rica broke diplomatic relations with Somoza in November 1978, after two Costa Rican Civil Guardsmen were killed by gunfire from the Nicaraguan National Guard.[62] In June 1979, Somoza repeatedly threatened to invade Costa Rica because the Costa Rican government was allowing the Sandinistas to operate from its territory.[63] Venezuela and Panama publicly pledged that they would come to Costa Rica's aid against such Nicaraguan aggression.[64]

The situation in 1985 looks eerily familiar, except that the current threat to Costa Rica is not Somoza, but the Sandinistas. On 31 May 1985, two Costa Rican Civil Guardsmen were killed in a Sandinista attack on Costa Rican territory at Las Crucitas. Costa Rica has called for an OAS denunciation of Nicaragua and has refused to receive a Nicaraguan ambassador.[65] Nicaraguan troops and planes repeatedly violated Costa Rican territory, and the Costa Rican Public Security Minister reported that 700 Costa Rican leftists have received terrorist training in Cuba.[66] Costa Rican President Monge reportedly asked for, and received, promises that Venezuela and Panama would come to Costa Rica's aid in the event of a Sandinista attack.[67] And Costa Rican Foreign Minister Gutierrez publicly stated that Central America cannot live with a Communist regime.[68]

After six years, it is clear that the democratic Latin Americans made a mistake in believing the democratic promises of the Sandinistas. Their hatred of Somoza made them willing to hope for the best outcome for a Sandinista-led revolution. Just before the Sandinistas took power in Managua, the democratic

Latin Americans began to worry that they had been instrumental in creating a second Cuba. On 8 July 1979, Costa Rican President Rodrigo Carazo Odio and former Venezuelan President Carlos Andres Perez warned the Sandinistas that the Latin American countries would cut off support unless the junta was expanded to include more moderates and there was agreement that the basic structure of the National Guard would be preserved.[69] The Sandinistas promptly rejected these threats, which in any case came too late to affect the outcome of the revolution. Panama sent teachers and doctors to Nicaragua immediately after the revolution, but the Panamanians received a much less enthusiastic welcome than did Cubans who brought "humanitarian" assistance. Latin American democrats were left hoping that economic aid would convince the Sandinistas to honor their promise of pluralism.

U.S. Apologists for the Sandinistas

One important factor in constraining U.S. opposition to the Sandinista and Castro consolidation of power after the revolutions was the support that those governments received from many people in the United States. The Castro government had many partisans in the United States—typically Marxist academics. For example, in 1960, Professor C. Wright Mills of Columbia University wrote *Listen, Yankee!*. Theodore Draper described it as follows:

> It purports to be "the voice of the Cuban revolutionary," not that of its author. From the conversations I had in Cuba in April, 1960, I can testify that the Castro leaders talked in much the same way Mills recorded them. Sometimes the words in the book were so close to those I had heard that I felt I knew the name of the source. To this extent, Mills made himself the vehicle of the purest and most direct propaganda, unlike the others who talked to more or less the same people, but passed on in their own name what they had been told.[70]

The Sandinistas are much more successful than were the Cubans in creating groups of Americans who eagerly spread the Communist line as if it were their own personal testimony. The most successful technique the Sandinistas have for creating this formidable publicity department is the guided tour of Nicaragua. Such tours are usually organized by members of mainline protestant churches who want to see the situation for themselves. Typically, the itineraries of these tours are scheduled and the guides are provided by the Sandinista-affiliated but outwardly religious Centro Antonio Valdivieso (which has an office at Georgetown University), or the so-called protestant umbrella CEPAD in Managua. Both of these Sandinista organizations receive funding from the National Council of Churches.[71]

Over 17,000 Americans have gone to Nicaragua for short visits since the revolution. The alumni of the tours are testimony to their persuasive powers. Most people who attend the tours speak little or no Spanish, they are constantly guided, and usually have very little previous knowledge of Nicaragua, but tend to be generally opposed to President Reagan and suspicious of his policies. On arriving in Nicaragua, they are put up not in hotels, but in the homes of "ordinary people." Typically, most of the tourists have never before been in a Third World country (except perhaps Acapulco) and will be shocked at the poverty of the Nicaraguans, but just as shocked at their tremendous hospitality. Each tour group will meet humble Nicaraguans who will tell of their son who was killed by the Contras, who, of course, are supported by President Reagan. This is truly a very emotional experience.

The Sandinista technique for impressing visitors is much more powerful than the old Soviet technique of the 1930's. The Soviets always tried to convince visitors of the economic success of socialism—giant dams and scores of tractors. The Sandinistas have found that it is much easier to arouse visitors sympathy than their admiration—thus Nicaraguan tourists will be shown poor barrios populated by proud people who only want to be left in peace so they can learn to read.[72]

When the pilgrims return home, they will be asked to show their slides and tell their story at innumerable small church and civic group meetings and to write for innumerable church newsletters. Seemingly at random, they will have heard the Sandinista line from many of the Nicaraguan friends they met on the tour. The Sandinista line has become so routine that it can easily be summarized by a few quotes from American pilgrims.[73]

It is especially important for the Communists to maintain the illusion that there is pluralism in Nicaragua. Thus, for example, there are billboards advertising opposition parties (really just posting their names) on the highway between the airport and the downtown Managua hotels—none elsewhere.

The *Presbyterian Outlook* reported that there is:

> . . . little evidence to support the charge of a "communist takeover" of Nicaragua. While there are communists within this country, the national leaders represent other parties, including the hardline conservatives, and many are devout committed Christians.[74]

This was also an important line during the Cuban Revolution, when Castro wore a rosary and was sure to have his men photographed wearing crucifixes. Similarly, Tomás Borge spends much of his time greeting American visitors in an office with a collection of crucifixes on the wall. The "people's masses" and the three priests in government are sufficient to convince many American visitors that the Nicaraguan government just cannot be Communist. Many religious visitors may even hold out the hope that they can convert the commandantes who already appear to be doing the work of Christ.

Liberation theology provides the theoretical underpinning for the participation of "religious" people in the Sandinista government. So Rhode Island Episcopal Bishop George N. Hunt, III, concludes that "it is possible for Marxist ideology to evolve in such a way that both the church and Marxist ideology can live compatibly in the same person."[75] Of course, all this neatly supports Castro's call for a broad front to fight for social changes in Latin America to include Christians, Marxists, workers and military officers.

In fact, however, many of the pilgrims are not so concerned about "democracy" in Latin America. In a not-so-subtle racism, they believe that democracy may be well and good for the United States (although the election of Reagan may make them question even that), but that there cannot be any real hope for democracy in Latin America—which requires repeated denial of the democratization of the continent that has taken place in the last ten years.

One prime tactic for eliminating any sympathy for Nicaraguans persecuted by the Sandinistas is to claim that these people must just be wealthy people longing for the good old days under Somoza. For example, Bishop Hunt acknowledges that there is "a class of people who are unhappy with the Communists."[76] But he finds it "helpful and persuasive to realize that those who are anti-Communist are usually those who have lost their privileged status." Similarly, United Methodist Bishop James Armstrong, who was President of the National Council of Churches in 1983, and Reverend Russell Dilley say that, while the Sandinistas and Cubans might have violated some human rights,

> . . . there is a significant difference between situations where people are imprisoned for opposing regimes designed to perpetuate inequities [as in Chile and Brazil, for example] and situations where people are imprisoned for opposing regimes designed to remove inequities [as in Cuba].[77]

Thus some prominent American churchmen have declared in advance that they will lend no credence to any statements of anti-Communists.

The Sandinistas have also succeeded in getting Americans to repeat a line designed to forestall complaints about the violations of human rights, while the same people would protest loudly if these actions were perpetrated by, say, the Salvadoran Government.

The Miskitos

For example, the Sandinistas acknowledge "mistakes" in dealing with the Miskito Indians. Once accepting this confession and offering absolution, the Sandinistas' publicists in the United States lay the real blame on the U.S. Government. An April 1984 Americas Watch Report concludes:

> We believe that the United States Government deserves some of the blame for

abuses by the government of Nicaragua because the activities sponsored by the United States leads to such matters as the forcible relocations of the Miskitos. . . . Under these circumstances, we cannot conclude that the decision to evacuate these villages was not justified by the military need to defend borders and facilities against attack.[78]

And Ronald Sider, President of Evangelicals for Social Action said that "if the U.S. continues to manipulate them for larger geo-political designs, large numbers of the Miskito Indians will continue to suffer and die."[79]

Elections and Press Freedom

Control of the press and lack of free elections is an essential part of the Sandinista plan for gaining total control of Nicaragua. Some of their American supporters say that such restrictions might be a good thing. Dale Lindsey, associate pastor of the Cleveland United Methodist Church, and Vice-Chairperson for the Cleveland Clergy and Laity Concerned, spread the party line in the *United Methodist Reporter*:

> While there is some censorship of the media, Nicaraguans from many walks of life support this. They feel that some restrictions are necessary to prevent the spread of false information and/or malicious interpretation of the news.[80]

The line about elections is that the Sandinistas are moving toward free elections, though it is understandable that this movement has been rather slow. Thus the *Texas Methodist* reported the line that any visitor to Nicaragua will be told:

> When asked about free elections, we were reminded that the United States consolidated its revolutionary efforts for nine years before our first national election was held.[81]

The *United Methodist Reporter* repeated this line:

> President Reagan faults the Sandinistas for not having held elections four years after the fall of Somoza. Someone forgot to tell him that after we defeated the British, several years passed before we elected George Washington.[82]

Finally, the same line is heard from Reverend Jesse Jackson:

> . . . their revolution was five years ago, and I had to remind myself that the gap between American independence, a revolution from Britain in 1776, and a President being elected in 1789, was 13 years. So, they are going through a painful transition, but when you compare it with ours, they are making faithful steps in the right direction.[83]

Cubans and Soviets in Nicaragua

It is difficult for the Sandinistas to deny the large Cuban and Soviet presence in Nicaragua. The operational line in reply to any worries was stated in the Dominican newsletter, *Contact*, by Sister Helena Sause when she concludes "that the USA is forcing Nicaragua toward Soviet dependence—something they do not want, and we say we don't."[84]

Democrats' Response to Ambiguous Warning

The Sandinistas never had to deceive fully the United States government or democratic Nicaraguan opponents of Somoza. They only had to create enough doubt and ambiguity about the likely outcome of the revolution to paralyze the anti-Communists from taking decisive action during the vulnerable stage when the Communists were consolidating their power.

This was particularly easy against a dictator like Somoza, who had become a symbol of tyranny for the democratic countries in the Caribbean, and who was easily made the focus of hatred. The choice the Sandinistas presented to the public was either: (1) the bully Somoza, or (2) the group of brave young men who talk a lot about democracy and love baseball. They only had to convince the democrats to take a chance on option (2). It was essential to their strategy that there never appeared to be an option (3)—a true democratic revolution. Thus they had to be sure to squelch any agreement that would have established a democratic government before the Sandinistas were able to win a complete military victory.

The U.S. has no strategy for dealing with such guerrilla threats. In both Nicaragua and Cuba, the U.S. did not begin to deal with the problem until it had become a serious crisis. No strategy whatsoever was decided on until the Communists were well-established in power.

The left often describes Latin American dictators as satraps of the United States, but this is wildly inaccurate. The U.S. does not determine the domestic policies of these dictators and certainly cannot order them to resign. However, the U.S. does have the power to weaken them seriously by publicly withdrawing our support.

In the case of Cuba and Nicaragua, the U.S. policies were the worst choices imaginable. After providing years of support for the dictator, the U.S. belatedly realized that a crisis was at hand. Rather than taking decisive action either to remove him and replace him with a democratic government or to back him fully, the U.S. followed the indecisive strategy of publicly condemning him and cutting off military aid without actually using our resources to remove him from power. Thus the U.S. was largely responsible for creating the period of ambiguity when the Communists were able to establish their military power.

A general rule cannot be established about the correct U.S. policy in response to a revolutionary threat to a pro-U.S. dictator. Probably much stronger backing should have been provided for the Shah of Iran. On the other hand, the U.S. probably could have established democratic governments in Cuba and Nicaragua if it had acted sooner and more forcefully. The one policy that certainly will not work is a half-hearted condemnation of a dictator that allows him to hold power, weakly, just long enough for guerrillas to become a militarily viable and, apparently, politically acceptable alternative.

Notes

1. Foreign Broadcast Information Service, *Daily Report, Latin America*, 24 June 1985, p. Q–2, quoting Havana International Service 1007 GMT, 22 June 1985.

2. Prensa Latina, *Direct from Cuba*, 31 December 1980. Quoted in Institute on Religion and Democracy, *A Time For Candor: Mainline Churches and the Radical Social Witness*, Washington, D.C., p. 30.

3. For a good discussion of the application of this strategy by the communist guerrillas in the Philippines, see Leif Rosenberger, "Philippine Communism and the Soviet Union," *Survey*, Spring 1985, pp. 113–145.

4. Shirley Christian, *Nicaragua: Revolution in the Family*, (New York: Random House, 1985), p. 37.

5. Quoted in Letter to the Editor, from Ian R. MacKenzie, Director, Nicaraguan Government Information Service, *New York Times*, May 28, 1979, p. A12.

6. FSLN National Directorate, *Nicaragua: On the General Political-Military Platform of Struggle of the Sandinista Front for the Triumph of the Sandinista Revolution*, 1977. This document is cited in the excellent article by Douglas W. Payne, "The 'Mantos' of Sandinista Deception," *Strategic Review*, Spring 1985, pp. 9–20. The works of Payne and Christian are essential sources on Sandinista deception techniques, and heavily influenced this chapter.

7. *Le Figaro Magazine* (Paris), 14–20 June 1986, pp. 118, 120. Translated in *FBIS (LA)*, 20 June 1986, p. Q–1.

8. Karen DeYoung, "Nicaragua Says 300 Irregulars Attack From Costa Rica," *Washington Post*, 30 May 1979, p. A18.

9. Merle Linda Wolin, "Nicaragua's Revolution," *The New York Times*, June 30, 1979, p. 19.

10. Warren Hoge, "Sandinista Chiefs Express Anger at the United States for not Making Contact," *New York Times*, June 28, 1979.

11. See Terri Shaw, "Junta's Peace Plan Was Turning Point for U.S. Mediator," *The Washington Post*, July 21, 1979, p. A2. And, Alan Riding, "Nicaragua Must Rebuild, But Who Will Lead—And Where?," *The New York Times*, July 22, 1979, section 4, p. 1.

12. Warren Hoge, "Junta Moves to Feed Nicaraguans and Bids Civilians Surrender Arms," *The New York Times*, July 22, 1979, p. 12.

13. a. Alan Riding, "Nicaraguan Rebels Begin Major Drive," *The New York Times*, June 2, 1979, pp. 1, 2.

For almost identical wording see the following newspaper articles:

    b. William R. Long, "Viva Sandino! Principles of Executed Rebel Unify Revolutionary Movement," *The Miami Herald*, June 24, 1979. (Reproduced in *Information Services on Latin America*, p. 67.)
    c. David Buchan and Hugh O'Shaugnessy, "End of The Banana Republics, "*The Financial Times*, June 27, 1979. (Reproduced in *Information Services on Latin America*, June 1979, pp. 68–69.)
    d. Jaime Flores-Lovo, "The Final Battle," *Manchester Guardian* and *Le Monde*, June 24, 1979. (Reproduced in *Information Services on Latin America*, June 1979, p. 81.)
    e. " 'Final' Offensive in Nicaragua," *The Christian Science Monitor* (editorial), June 4, 1979. (Reproduced in *Information Services on Latin America*, June 1979, p. 81.)
    f. Alan Riding, "In Nicaragua's Embattled Cities, Rebellion Becomes a Way of Life," *The New York Times*, June 11, 1979, pp. 1, A9.
    g. "The Battle of Nicaragua," *The New York Times* (editorial), June 12, 1979, p. A14.
    h. Karen DeYoung, "Andean Nations Provide Sandinistas a Diplomatic Opening," *The Washington Post*, June 18, 1979, p. A20.
    i. "Nicaragua: It May Be Too Late," *The Los Angeles Times* (editorial), June 20, 1979, part II, p. 6.

14. San Jose Radio Impacto, 1830 GMT August 20, 1985. Translated in FBIS, *Daily Report Latin America*, August 27, 1985, p. P14.

15. Barbara Koeppel, "How Sandinistas raise funds to pay for their war," *Christian Science Monitor*, July 17, 1979. (Reproduced in *Information Services on Latin America*, July 1979, p. 122.)

16. Shirley Christian, *Nicaragua: A Revolution in the Family*, pp. 60–74.

17. Terri Shaw, "Junta's Peace Plan Was Turning Point for U.S. Mediator," *The Washington Post*, July 21, 1979, p. A2.

18. Karen DeYoung, "Somoza Reportedly Close to Resigning: U.S. Offers Plan Seeking Expanded Junta," *The Washington Post*, July 6, 1979, pp. 1, A10.

19. "Profiling the Sandinista Guerrillas" (no by-line given), *The Christian Science Monitor*, June 22, 1979. (Reproduced in *Information Services on Latin America*, June 1979, p. 62.)

20. Helena Cobban, "PLO Hopes Ties to Nicaragua Will Leave Israel Out in Cold," *The Christian Science Monitor*, July 26, 1979. (Reproduced in *Information Services on Latin America*, July 1979, p. 313.)

21. "Sergio Ramirez Mercado" (no by-line given), *New York Times*, July 16, 1979, p. A3.

22. Stanley Meisler, "Nicaragua 1979 and Cuba 1959: Their Similarities Are Scant," *The Los Angeles Times*, July 29, 1979, part V, p. 2.

23. Payne, "The 'Mantos' of Sandanista Deception," p. 17.

24. Alan Riding, "Unable to Force Out Somoza, U.S. Lacks Clout With Foes," *The New York Times*, July 1, 1979, p. E3.

25. "Nicaragua: It May Be Too Late" (editorial) *The Los Angeles Times*, June 20, 1979, part II, p. 6.

26. Alan Riding, "Rebels in Nicaragua Name Five to Form Provisional Junta," *The New York Times*, June 18, 1979, pp. 1, A8.

27. Alan Riding, "After Somoza, Who Will Have Power to Fill the Vacuum?," *The New York Times*, July 8, 1979, p. E3.

28. Guy Gugliotta, "Somoza's Foes: 2 Parts Marxist, 1 Part Moderate," *The Miami Herald*, June 17, 1979. (Reproduced in *Information Services on Latin America*, June 1979, pp. 55–57.)

29. Payne, "The 'Mantos' of Sandinista Deception," pp. 14–15.

30. Alan Riding, "Nicaraguan Junta Selects Its Cabinet," *New York Times*, July 15, 1979, pp. 1, 12.

31. "Nicaragua Regime Assails Church, Dissident Links" (from UPI), *The Los Angeles Times*, May 13, 1979, part I, p. 9.

32. Alan Riding, "Nicaraguan Archbishop Appeals to the World for Help for Refugees," *The New York Times*, June 17, 1979, p. 7.

33. James Nelson Goodsell, "Nicaraguan Economy in Tailspin," *The Christian Science Monitor*, June 6, 1979. (Reproduced in *Information Services on Latin America*, June 1979, p. 83.)

34. Stanley Meisler, "Junta Greeted in Managua, Has Kind Words for U.S.," *The Los Angeles Times*, July 21, 1979, part I, p. 8.

35. See Shirley Christian, *Nicaragua*, p. 70.

36. David Buchan and Hugh O'Shaugnessy, "End of the Banana Republic," *The Financial Times*, June 27, 1979. (Reproduced in *Information Services on Latin America*, June 1979, pp. 68–69.)

37. Christian, *Nicaragua: A Revolution in the Family*, p. 105.

38. Warren Hoge, "Sandinist Chiefs Express Anger at U.S. for not Making Contact," *New York Times*, June 28, 1979, p. A3.

39. Stanley Meisler, "Junta Greeted in Managua, Has Kind Words for U.S.," *The Los Angeles Times*, July 21, 1979, part I, p. 8.

40. Christian, *Nicaragua: A Revolution in the Family*, p. 123.

41. Alan Riding, "Nicaragua Crisis: Was the U.S. Off Guard?," *The New York Times*, June 27, 1979, p. A3.

42. Terri Shaw, "Junta's Peace Plan Was Turning Point for U.S. Mediator," *The Washington Post*, July 21, 1979, p. A2.

43. Alan Riding, "Nicaraguan Rebels Reject U.S. Request For an O.A.S. Force," *The New York Times*, June 23, 1979, p. A1.

44. Christian, *Nicaragua: A Revolution in the Family*, p. 74.

45. "Negotiator Critical of Somoza" (no by-line given), *The New York Times*, June 6, 1979, p. A13.

46. Alan Riding, "Nicaraguan Rebels Begin Major Drive," *The New York Times*, June 2, 1979, pp. 1, 2. Alan Riding, "Nicaragua Crisis: Was the U.S. Off Guard?," *The New York Times*, June 27, 1979, p. A3.

47. John M. Goshko, "U.S. Walking Softly," *The Washington Post*, July 25, 1979, p. A1, A16.

48. Christian, *Nicaragua: A Revolution in the Family*, p. 103.
49. Graham Hovey, "U.S. Proposals on Nicaragua Crisis Meet Sharp Criticism From O.A.S.," *The New York Times*, June 23, 1979, p. 3. See also, John M. Goshko, "OAS Votes for Ouster of Somoza," *The Washington Post*, June 24, 1979, pp. 1, A13.
50. "U.S. Says Somoza's Ouster Needed for Nicaragua Peace," *The Washington Post*, June 27, 1979 (from the Associated Press), p. A18.
51. Graham Hovey, "U.S. Official Says Somoza's Ouster Would Not Lead to 'a Second Cuba'," *The New York Times*, June 27, 1979, p. A3.
52. Warren Hoge, "Nicaragua Rebels Say U.S. Is Ready to Back Regime Led by Them," *The New York Times*, July 16, 1979, pp. 1, A3.
53. Wiliam D. Montalbano, "Moderates, Marxists Unite in Fight Against Somoza," *The Miami Herald*, July 16, 1979. (Reproduced in *Information Services on Latin America*, July 1979, p. 226.)
54. "Out of Oppression, Hope" (editorial), *The Los Angeles Times*, July 18, 1979, part II, p. 4.
55. "Nicaraguan End Game" (editorial), *The Washington Post*, July 5, 1979, p. A18.
56. Warren Hoge, "U.S. Keeping Up Pressure on the Nicaraguan Junta," *The New York Times*, July 15, 1979, p. 11.
57. Graham Hovey, "U.S. Envoy goes Back to Nicaragua With Planeload of AID Supplies," *The New York Times*, July 29, 1979, p. 2.
58. Shirley Christian, *Nicaragua: A Revolution in the Family*, p. 155.
59. Guy Gugliotta, "Nicaragua Foes Honing Tactics," *The Miami Herald*, May 8, 1979. (Reproduced in *Information Services on Latin America*, May 1979, pp. 86–87.) See also Graham Hovey, "U.S. Proposals on Nicaragua Crisis Met Sharp Criticism From O.A.S.," *The New York Times*, June 23, 1979, p. 3.
60. Graham Hovey, "U.S. Proposals on Nicaragua Crisis Meet Sharp Criticism From O.A.S.," *The New York Times*, June 23, 1979, p. 3.
61. "Nicaragua Talks Sought by U.S.," *The Los Angeles Times* (no by-line given), June 19, 1979, pp. 5, 9.
62. Guy Gugliotta, "Carazo Message Details Plans, Issues Warning to Costa Rica," *The Miami Herald*, May 5, 1979. (Reproduced in *Information Services on Latin America*, June 1979, p. 85.)
63. James Nelson Goodsell, "Nicaragua Threat to Neighbors?," *Christian Science Monitor*, June 6, 1979. (Reproduced in *Information Services on Latin America*, June 1979, p. 85.)
64. Alan Riding, "Sandinistas, Patriots First—Marxists Maybe Second," *The New York Times*, June 10, 1979, p. 2E.
65. Paris AFP 1736 GMT July 14, 1985. Translated in FBISS, *Daily Report Latin America*, July 22, 1985, p. P1.
66. San Jose *La Nacion*, July 21, 1985, p. 8A. Translated in FBIS, *Daily Report Latin America*, July 30, 1985, p. P2.
67. San Jose Radio Reloj 0100 GMT, August 6, 1985. Translated in FBIS, *Daily Report Latin America*, August 6, 1985.
68. San Jose Radio Reloj 0100 GMT, July 19, 1985. Translated in FBIS, *Daily Report Latin America*, July 19, 1985, p. P3.

69. Alan Riding, "Latins Pressing Nicaraguan Left for Concessions," *The New York Times*, July 9, 1979, pp. 1, A3.

70. Ibid.

71. See *NICA*, the newsletter of the Nicaraguan Interfaith Committee for Action, November 21, 1983.

72. For an example of the Soviet tour, see David Dunn, "A Good Fabian Fallen Among the Stalinists," *Survey*, Winter 1984, pp. 15–37.

73. I want to thank Kerry Ptacek of the Institute on Religion and Democracy for allowing me to use his files of articles on Nicaragua from religious newsletters.

74. *The Presbyterian Outlook*, p. 4, date not given.

75. *The Presbyterian Journal*, April 27, 1983, p. 6.

76. Ibid.

77. Bishop James Armstrong and Reverend Russell Dilley, "A Report from Cuba," United Methodist Church, Dakotas Area, June 1977. Quoted in Institute on Religion and Democracy, *op. cit.*, p. 81.

78. *Human Rights in Nicaragua*, an Americas Watch Report, April 1984, pp. 5, 11.

79. News release, December 22, 1982, p. 6.

80. Dale Lindsey, "Delegation Investigates Nicaragua-Honduras Border Conflict," *East Ohio Today: An Edition of the United Methodist Reporter*, date not given.

81. Charles Rhoads, "Things Seen and Heard in Nicaragua," *The Texas Methodist*, date not given.

82. Raymond K. DeHainault, "U.S. Christians Should Seek to Understand Nicaragua," *United Methodist Reporter*, January 26, 1984.

83. *ABC News: This Week with David Brinkley*, July 1, 1984, pp. 15–16.

84. Sister Helena Sause, O.P., "Nicaragua Today," *Contact*, Vol XVI, no. 5, December 8, 1983, p. 7.

19
Anticipating the Next Arab-Israeli Round: Soviet Deception in Syria

Avigdor Haselkorn

Regional Deceptions in Soviet Strategy

Unlike the Western concept of the *strategic balance*, the Soviet term *correlation of world forces*, indicates relationships that are more broad in scope and dynamically interacting. In this view, the U.S.-Soviet "balance" is not only a derivative of the military forces amassed by antagonists but also a reflection of their worldwide geopolitical position. Regional standings of the superpowers thus have dual significance: on one hand they reflect local perceptions of the superpower balance, while on the other, they tend to influence the correlation of forces itself. The advancement of Soviet regional goals is therefore integral to the overall U.S.-Soviet competition in the eyes of Kremlin leaders.

Although Western observers have long recognized the linkage between the Soviet regional moves and Moscow's quest to tilt the superpower balance in its favor, only scant attention has been given to the role of deception in the Soviet Union's regional effort. Manifestly, there has been a tendency in the West to assess Soviet successes or failures in the Third World as outcomes of the skillful or wanton use of traditional instruments of Soviet foreign policy—for example, economic and military aid, technical assistance, trade, diplomacy, propaganda, and in a few rare instances, the use of military force.

The cases analyzed in Part V, however, demonstrate that deception is an integral part of a strategically motivated Soviet regional effort. Several techniques have frequently been applied by the USSR to further its objectives in the Middle East, Latin America, and Western Europe that include penetration (*proniknovenniye*), provocation (*provokatisiya*), diversion (*diverzia*), and disinformation (*dezinformatsiya*). In order to undermine the U.S. position in these areas, the Soviets have also resorted to fabrication (*fabrikatsiya*) designed to mislead U.S. allies and thus alarm them as to Washington's true motivations.

In recent months, in fact, Moscow has increasingly sought to penetrate the countries of the Persian Gulf, employing a mix of these techniques. At the same time, they endeavored to divert U.S. resources from areas in the vicinity of the USSR by opening up an anti-American counterfront in Central America. In the Middle East, via its ally Syria, the Soviet Union made extensive use of deceptional measures to position itself so as to, at the minimum, exploit to its advantage the U.S.-Israeli fears of a major provocation. Finally, Moscow has launched a massive disinformation campaign to convince the West Europeans of the dangers of U.S. nuclear modernization plans, on one hand, and their utter superfluousness in the face of a "friendly" and "defensive" USSR, on the other.

Equally important, given the link of the regional effort to the overall U.S.-Soviet correlation of world forces, Moscow has sought to camouflage setbacks it suffered in other areas. Soviet regional optimism in the face of mounting difficulties in the Third World is not unrelated to their desire to influence American thinking about its progress there. For example, the confidence recently expressed in Soviet circles about the anti-imperialist nature of liberated states, which "naturally" requires continued Soviet aid and commitment.

Deception in Syria

Quoting "Western intelligence sources," the Israeli daily *Jerusalem Post*, on 9 May 1985, reported that the Soviet Union handed over to the Syrian armed forces the SA-5 missile batteries it had deployed there in early 1983. The transfer reportedly began in December 1984 and was accompanied by the withdrawal of an "estimated 2,000 military advisers and other personnel from Syria in recent weeks."[1] The paper went on to quote its sources as suggesting that the Soviet move came about either as a consequence of a demand made by Syrian President Hafez al-Asad, who apparently was unhappy with an autonomous military presence on his soil, or because the new Soviet regime intended to lessen its active involvement in countries in potentially volatile areas.

The apparent lessening of Soviet military commitment to Syria caused by Moscow's presumed interest in disengagement (or Asad's nationalistic sentiments) could mean at least a temporary decline in Syria's ability to wage war against Israel. It might be surmised that the net outcome would favor greater stability in the Middle Eastern subsystem insofar as its Arab-Israeli aspect is concerned.

Therefore, it is surprising to learn that, in terms of Israeli perceptions, nothing would seem further from the truth. In mid-July 1985, a senior Israeli Defense Force (IDF) source was quoted as saying that "there is no doubt that Israel will have to go to war again soon, almost certainly against Syria."[2] Defense Minister Itzhak Rabin found it necessary to warn Syria against "overestimating its strength."[3] In light of repeated Soviet utterances seeking to portray the Kremlin-directed Syrian military buildup (as well as its own military presence in the country) in purely defensive terms, the Israeli concern seems puzzling. Responding to pronounced U.S.-Israeli anxiety over the introduction (under Soviet control) of SA-5 missiles into Syria, the Soviet media stated:

> Think about it: Syria is concerned for the air defense of its own territory, its cities and villages, which have already been subjected to Israeli bombings more than once. Is not that the right of a sovereign country? It has no intention of attacking anyone, where is the danger to anyone?[4]

Similarly, the Soviet Ambassador to Beirut, Aleksander Soldatov, asserted that the SA-5s were "measures which will deter aggressive ambitions including ambitions on Lebanese territory."[5] Also, Igor Belayev, foreign affairs editor of the Soviet *Literaturnya Gazeta*, said: "Syria has set up new anti-aircraft defense systems. I want especially to stress the word 'defense.' Our experts help the Syrian military in mastering them. That is all."[6]

An even stronger position was taken by Vadim Zagladin, Deputy Chief of the CPSU's International Section, who maintained that the entire Soviet-directed Syrian military buildup need not concern its neighbors nor the United States:

> As far as our aid to Syria is concerned, it is defensive aid. We have never done anything to provide Syria with an attacking force. . . . In providing this aid, we always stress, in all our conversations with the Syrian leaders, that we are in favor of a peaceful solution. [This in contrast to the] . . . United States which wants to establish itself in the region and does not conceal this intention.[7]

On the basis of these Soviet declarations, and especially in light of the reported limited disengagement referred to above, Israeli fears seem excessive, if not obsessive. The question is thus raised as to whether a plausible, rational explanation could be uncovered for this sort of "odd" Israeli conduct.

In this chapter, the argument is introduced that the divisions within Israel, and the differences between Washington and Jerusalem as to how to handle the Soviet buildup inside Syria (especially its installation of a modern integrated air defense system) reflect conflicting assumptions, often tacitly held, about the relative weight of deception in Soviet foreign and defense policies. The impact of the perception that deceptional motivations and objectives are common (if not prevalent) in Soviet politico-strategic calculations has been to sow uncertainty, discord, and confusion among Western defense decision makers who widely share this view. In turn, the proliferation of this implied assumption in the West represents a major achievement for Soviet *maskirovka*, and, in the process, vindicates Moscow's long-standing adherence to this strategic principle.

No attempt is made to argue that Soviet deception has exclusively accounted for the IDF's tolerance of the buildup inside Syria—a surprising development in light of Israel's proven commitment to a preemptive doctrine. However, this analysis explores the use of Soviet *maskirovka* and mutely held Western assumptions about the role it plays in Soviet strategy in promoting the Israeli-U.S. passivity in the face of a gradual erosion of their military advantage in the Eastern Mediterranean area. Of specific interest is why some of those in the respective defense communities of the two countries have professed alarm over the new Soviet-Syrian activities, predicting another war, while others anticipate continued stability on the basis of the same Soviet phase-out in Syria.

Scheme I: Projecting Strength as Weakness

In the wake of reports, in December 1982 and January 1983, of the introduction of SA-5 batteries into Syria by the Soviets, two schools of thought have emerged. The first has seen the move as tied to one or more of the following regional considerations:

> The stationing of SA-5s was "mainly the result of the severe blow dealt by the Israeli Air Force (IAF) to the Syrian missile deployment and Air Force."[8] In fact, some sources were quoted as saying the missiles were sent because in the wake of the June 1982 IAF strikes, "Syria was left without any real aerial defenses."[9]

> The Soviets have made a "near desperate" attempt to retrieve the influence they had in the Middle East. Accordingly, the deployment of SA-5s in Syria "signalled Soviet accommodation of Syrian pressures. Moscow was fearful that rejection of demands made by President Asad [to install advanced SAMs in Syria] would lead to the downgrading of bilateral relations, possibly undermining Soviet influence in the entire Middle East area."[10]

> The SA-5s represent a "trip-wire" aimed at drawing the line against the IAF. By dispatching missile crews and other forces into Syria, Moscow sought to warn both Israel and the United States that in the future, they might use direct power to prevent Israel from crushing the Syrian Air Force and would defend the territorial integrity of its main Middle Eastern ally.[11]

> The Soviet decision was influenced by Moscow's perception that "its credibility as a reliable supplier of advanced weapons was unmistakably damaged by widespread reports about the relative ease with which the Israeli forces, armed in part by the U.S., were able to destroy Soviet equipment."[12]

> The move was also interpreted as possibly indicating Soviet-Syrian interest

in waging a war of nerves against Israel. "In the past, the stationing of surface-to-air missiles served as the beginning of political pressures on Israel."[13]

Another school of thought saw the deployment mainly in superpower terms. Advocates of this line of thinking argued that the Soviet move was prompted by the 6 July 1982 announcement of the U.S. agreement to dispatch troops to Lebanon as part of a Multinational Peacekeeping Force (MNF). "To a large extent, the Russian entrenchment in Syria is a reaction to the large U.S. involvement in Lebanon."[14]

It was pointed out that the choice of the SA-5 as the centerpiece of the new Syrian air defense system lent further credence to this interpretation. The SA-5 Gammon (a weapon system with a slant range of 250 kilometers and a ceiling of 95,000 feet) is designed to provide long-range, high-altitude defense. An incredibly cumbersome missile (weighing around 10 tons, and 16.5 meters long), it was described by one analyst as "extremely vulnerable to many of the suppression techniques Israel used in 1982."[15] Considering that the missile has a minimum range of 60 to 80 kilometers, and is only useful once its first-stage booster has burned out, this conclusion reveals the limited value of the SA-5 in countering the IAF.

Some analysts suggested that the Gammons were stationed in Syria: to provide air cover over the U.S. Sixth Fleet's areas of operations;[16] to inhibit American high-altitude reconnaissance flights;[17] or to interfere with U.S. plans of inserting the Rapid Deployment Force (RDF) into Iran—plans that in all likelihood would make use of Turkish facilities and air space.[18]

There are numerous problems with the arguments of both schools. The regional approach disregards considerable information suggesting the decision to augment Syrian air defenses was made before the outbreak of the 1982 war. For instance, following the visit of Marshal Pavel S. Kutakhov (at the time Commander in Chief of Soviet Air Forces) to Damascus in March 1982, sources indicated that a new arms deal had been concluded with the Syrians. The Soviets reportedly agreed to provide Syria with an advanced missile network and to enhance the combat capabilities of its Air Force.[19] By all indications, the issue of modernizing Syria's air defenses has been under negotiation since the conclusion of the Soviet-Syrian Friendship Treaty of 8 October 1980. Therefore, there should be little surprise over revelations that the IDF had captured "Syrian documents about the SA-5" *during* the June 1982 fighting in Lebanon's Al-Biqa Valley.[20]

Second, some analysts claimed that, even against Israeli E-2C AWACS and other ELINT aircraft (not to mention F-15s operating in a mini-AWACS capacity) the SA-5 poses only a limited threat. According to one observer, the missile's aerodynamic controls are marginal for long-range strikes against any IAF aircraft other than the Boeing 707-ECMs, and its radio command mid-course guided with radar-homing is well within Israeli jamming capability.[21] It may be argued that such a system might cause temporary excitement among Third World publics, but military leaders preoccupied with handling specific threats could not be fooled for long. Therefore, one cannot take seriously the regional school's claim that prestige considerations, and an interest in proving its reliability as a supplier of advanced arms, motivated Moscow's decision to deploy SA-5s in Syria.

Also fraught with difficulty is the argument that the Soviet decision was motivated primarily by global considerations rather than those pertaining to the Soviet-Syrian-Isareli triangle. This ignores the dire Syrian military circumstances, and the strong pressures exerted by Damascus, which had to be addressed to preserve Soviet presence in the area. To the extent that Moscow persists in according such presence to be of strategic significance, regional demands will continue to play an important role in its policy calculations.

Further, certain globalists predicted that additional SA-5 sites would be erected in northeastern Syria to provide coverage against air routes and facilities in eastern Turkey (potentially available to transport the RDF into the Middle East). No such expansion has been recorded.[22] Generally, the usefulness of Syria as a spearhead for global (or even regional) Soviet purposes seems doubtful in light of the relative isolation of Damascus in the Arab world and the staunchly nationalistic leadership of President Asad.

Finally, both the global and regional schools find it difficult to explain satisfactorily the Soviet handover of the SA-5s to Syria and the withdrawal of Soviet missile crews from the country. This recent development seemingly undermines the regionalists' argument about the SA-5 as a signal of Soviet commitment to Syria and of Moscow's quest to deter the IDF. Similarly, none of the objectives listed by globalists as having propelled the deployment of the Gammons has been served by Moscow's recent about-face.

By both regional and global criteria, the Soviet Union's introduction of SA-5s into Syria remains a puzzle. It certainly did not demonstrate Soviet technological prowess, allegedly aimed at regaining Moscow's lost prestige; and its anti-IAF potential remains severely limited. Although, in principle, the system would have been useful for countering certain American military options in the area (since the missiles were first deployed in early 1983), there is no record of a deliberate Soviet attempt to explore this potential. Indeed, the transfer of the Gammons to Syrian hands may have effectively served to efface this line of globalist argument altogether.

It is precisely those elements directly responsible for raising questions about Soviet motives for deploying the SA-5s in Syria that offer a heretofore largely ignored alternative interpretation. The current hypothesis regards those factors most damaging to the regional and global cases (the Gammons' operational shortcomings, vulnerability, lack of quantitative or qualitative upgrading, and recent "abandonment") as crucial to the correct understanding of Soviet motivations. In addition, of major importance in the present explanation is the sequence of the Soviet introduction of the various components, into Syria, that eventually turned into a vastly improved integrated air defense system. What the Soviets actually performed in Syria, as opposed to what they refrained from doing, needs sorting out—the argument being that *both* aspects are integral to determine Soviet objectives accurately.

It seems that the SA-5s had a centerstage role in a Soviet-conceived deception scheme aimed at assuring uninterrupted installation of an advanced air defense system in Syria. Evidence supporting this contention could be marshalled in part from the study of the sequence used by the Soviets to introduce their system into the country. (See table 19–1.)[23]

According to table 19–1, a distinction should be drawn between two phases of the military buildup in Syria. Shortly after the 1982 hostilities ended, numerous sources indicated that the Soviets had embarked on a resupply effort aimed at replacing Syria's heavy losses in the conflict. In addition, they evidently had accelerated delivery of arms contracted for prior to the war.[24] In December of that year, however, Israeli intelligence detected site-preparation work underway in Syria indicating the start of a new phase. In retrospect, the subsequent appearance of the SA-5s signalled the launching (at long last) of a comprehensive Soviet effort to counter improved SAM suppression capabilities whose disturbing potential was convincingly displayed by the IAF in Al-Biqa. The manifestations of this second stage are the focus of this study.

More important, table 19–1 indicates that with the January 1983 installation of the SA-5s in Syria, the Soviets had elected to deploy the most vulnerable SAM system first, exposing the missiles to possible IAF attack for at least several weeks. Such conduct is difficult to comprehend; especially since the Soviets first could have opted to deploy less vulnerable, more sophisticated SAMs (such as the SA-6, SA-8, SA-13), thus securing an adequate umbrella under which the installation of the Gammons could have commenced. The reversed sequence highlights the fact, that in determining the order of introduction of the system's components into Syria, Moscow paid particular attention to the question of likely Israeli responses. Undoubtedly, the goal was to avoid provoking the IAF into action, thus insuring that Moscow's plans proceeded smoothly.

The Soviets had a good reason to believe that a "direct route" approach (that is, massive introduction of highly sophisticated, mobile, smaller SAMs into Syria) would trigger a strong Israeli reaction. The Israelis were on record as warning that the IAF would not tolerate deployment of a mobile SAM-belt near Israeli borders. This stance was adopted as a result of bitter lessons learned by the IAF in the 1973 October War. It may be recalled that twenty-four hours after the 8 August 1970 Egyptian-Israeli ceasefire had gone into effect (ending what Nasser called the War of Attrition), massive forward movement of Egyptian air defenses along the Suez Canal was officially disclosed. Although the ceasefire agreement specifically called on both sides to observe a standstill, the Soviets blatantly planned and directly supervised the Egyptian redeployment effort. The result of this Soviet exercise in deception was to extend the coverage

Table 19–1
Introduction Sequence of Major Components of Advanced Air Defense System into Syria

Approximate Introduction Date	Type of System	Location	Knowns	Unknowns
December 1982			Work on preparing new missile sites first observed	No definite information on type of missiles to be installed
January 1983	SA-5 *Gammon*	2 sites: Dumayer (20 miles NE of Damascus) and Shinshar (SE of Homs)	Operational since mid-February 1983. Batteries: 2 per site Launchers: 12 per site Missile stock estimated at 50. Soviet crewed and controlled (about 500 per site) No Syrian presence allowed in sites	Extent of system's hardening against ECM and suppression presumed limited
	Advanced jammers and equipment to reduce radar and C^3 vulnerability		Soviet crewed. Mission is to counter AWACS links and RPVs	Syrian absorptive capacity of advanced C^3I assets—unknown
	20 MiG-25 *Foxbat* As	Reportedly assembled by Soviets at Abu adh-Dhuhur airbase		Unclear if planes are Soviet-piloted[a]
	Advanced AA missiles			Type: unknown (AA-62?) Range: allegedly 100 kms
February 1983	Satellite communication link	Believed linked to Soviet ships in Mediterranean	Communication with Soviet PVO HQ in Moscow and Soviet Ships in E. Mediterranean—important part of May 1983 exercises	Degree of C^3I capabilities provided by link, remains uncertain
	2 Tu-126 *Moss* AWACS planes	Al-Mazzah military airfield	Soviet crewed. Last known external deployment—India, 1971	
	SA-10 BIG BIRD radars	Part of new radar chain stretching from Latakia to Mt. Hermon	Stress is on Long Track radars to establish ground control intercept/battle management system, previously lacking	Though U.S. intelligence terms deployment of the missile itself "plausible," indications are the system was recalled in November 1983

Table 19-1 (continued)

Approximate Introduction Date	Type of System	Location	Knowns	Unknowns
March 1983	SA-6 (additional batteries)	S. of Damascus paralleling Israel's border, turning northward (from Lebanese border) along Syrian coast up to Latakia	Defense of SA-5 sites by 9 SA-6 sites and 3 SA-3 sites	Possible upgrading of SA-6—unconfirmed
	SA-8, SA-9 (additional batteries)	At least some SA-8's deployed to defend SA-5 sites	First SA-8's in Syria in April 1982 SA-9 in Syria and Libyan-crewed SA-9's in Lebanon—prior to 1986 war	Reported upgrading of SA-8's apparently true, especially if allegations of Jordanian discontent with similar missiles prove accurate
March/April 1983	MiG 23 *Flogger* E&F (new deliveries)		At least some with better avionics and munitions than earlier stripped down versions in Syrian hands	Reports of introduction of MiG-27's remain unconfirmed. Reports of Soviet pledge to provide MiG-29 *Fulcrum* soon, seem reliable in light of its recent provision to India
	SA-11 (?) SA-13	Some deployed in defense of SA-5 sites	Defense of SA-5 sites in Warsaw Pact area by SA-11's. Advantage: SA-11's radar ties into net with SA-6, SA-9 and possibly ZSU-23-4 units	Though Syrian sources alleged introduction of SA-11 under exclusive Soviet control in April, confirmation for such a move has yet to be made**
April 1983	An integrated air defense system becomes operational in Syria	Stretches over 360 kms, from Latakia via Damascus to Dara'a on the Jordanian border	SA-5 fire direction radars turned toward IAF plane that month, causing latter to change flight procedures over Lebanon, intended to signal new status. Same applies to Syrian aerial ambush of IAF planes over Al-Biqa, in May	

* In early May 1982, a Soviet pilot flying a MiG-25A participated in a Syrian-laid ambush of IAF planes over Lebanon. Syrian-flown MiG-23's were acting as a bait at the time, drawing the Israeli fighters in, while the Foxbat, taking advantage of its speed and higher altitude, came in for the kill.

** But note Abu Dhabi's *Al-Ittihad* claim 24 August 1986 that SA-11s were indeed supplied to Syria.

provided by Egypt's air defense system 30 kilometers inside the (then) Israeli-held Sinai. Although at the time some IDF leaders called for the IAF to attack the forwardly deployed SAMs, under United States pressure, Israel agreed to acquiesce in exchange for the U.S. provision of additional F-4 Phantoms, anti-radiation missiles, and ECMs. The price of Israel's accommodation was fully paid three years later, when Egyptian SAMs inflicted heavy losses on the IAF in the opening phases of the Yom Kippur War.[25]

Second, many accounts indicated that the Soviets had recently eyewitnessed the IAF demonstration of the existence of such a "red line." Thus, in the wake of the June 1982 air strikes against Syrian SAM defenses in the Al-Biqa Valley on 24 July 1982, the Soviets supervised the dispatch of SA-8 batteries into the area. Within hours, the IAF attacked and destroyed these sites, reaffirming that any limitation on the fulfillment of its operational mission of providing air cover for IDF troops (stationed in Lebanon at the time) would not be tolerated.[26]

As a first stage in restructuring Syria's air defenses, a dense belt of advanced mobile SAMs created in close proximity to the Israeli border would have been viewed not only as a threat to the IAF's air superiority, but also as a prerequisite for increased Syrian military pressure on the ground—perhaps in the Golan Heights. This, given the specific role of "flying artillery" assigned the IDF, aimed at redressing Arab numerical advantages on land and to minimize Israeli casualties, that such a deployment would have severely eroded. In terms of the risk of provoking an IDF preemptive strike, the direct introduction sequence—hardly a defensive move in Israeli eyes—was, therefore, extremely undesirable, insofar as Moscow was concerned.

Instead the Soviets opted for an indirect approach; that is, they resorted to a basic deception ploy of projecting strength as weakness, by deploying the most vulnerable air defense element first. Selecting the SA-5 as an "opening card" assured that:

> Introduction of Soviet combat units (that is, SAM crews) into Syria became a legitimate defensive move because of the Gammons' installation in fixed sites deep inside Syrian territory, and their relative vulnerability to the IAF's SAM suppression capabilities.[27] In fact, some Israelis went so far as to term the growing Soviet military presence in Syria as "definitely a moderating element."[28]
>
> Smaller, mobile SAMS (for example, SA-6, SA-8, SA-9, SA-13) could be subsequently introduced under the pretext of providing the necessary defense to the vulnerable SA-5s.
>
> A diversion was created. By selecting a highly visible system, never before deployed outside Soviet borders, Moscow contributed to the West's disproportionate preoccupation with a relatively benign element of the air defense system (the Gammons). In contrast, relatively scant attention was accorded

to the less obtrusive, yet potentially more destabilizing, introduction of smaller, mobile SAMs.

Deterrence existed. Once the first-stage deployment was accomplished and the Soviet-crewed SA-5s had been installed without interruption (due at least in part, to the other three factors listed), political realities and the system's integration assured that the Soviets would be directly involved if the IAF struck.[29] In the absence of a major provocation, the risks of such an action escalating quickly were simply too high for Israeli leaders to contemplate. In turn, this first guaranteed that the subsequent flow of advanced mobile SAMs into Syria would continue uninterrupted. Second, it insured that the Soviet interest in "moderation" would persist as long as its military buildup was in progress.

Air cover was available. The installation of the Gammons provided the Soviets with some (admittedly uncertain) measure of coverage against Israeli airborne AWACS and ECM platforms. To the extent that these assets would have played a role in the IAF subsequently attacking the air defense system, it would appear that the introduction had further contributed to deterring the Israelis.

Moscow correctly assessed that the U.S. and Israeli responses to its activities in Syria would be determined by their perceptions of Soviet intentions there, *as indicated by these actions*. Consequently, the Soviets actively endeavored to project the image of defensiveness and vulnerability, realizing that their planned buildup in Syria was initially dependent on not alarming Washington or Jerusalem. *Maskirovka*, it turns out, played a key role in Soviet plans in Syria. By first demonstrating that their activities posed no danger to Israel, partly due to the centerstage role of the SA-5s, the Soviets were able to proceed unhindered with building up Syria's air defenses. As a result, however, the notion of an IAF attack was soon fraught with grave political risks, given the presence of Soviet SAM crews on the scene, not to mention an increasingly costly option from the military point of view.

Utilizing the SA-5s as a deception ploy, the Soviets succeeded in minimizing the risks that forced them to drop the more direct alternative deployment route as too dangerous. However, by effectively handling the latent IAF threat first, the Soviets were then able to accomplish their objective of erecting an advanced multilayered integrated air defense system in Syria without further delay, despite the system's offensive potential. (See figure 19–1.) Although certain Israeli civilian and military leaders reportedly pressed for attacking the Gammons once their introduction had been detected, precisely fearing this sequence, U.S.-Israeli deliberations led again to passivity and compliance.[30] It was agreed that the SA-5 was a "political bargaining chip" rather than a military threat.[31]

The introduction of eighteen SS-21s (under Soviet control) into Syria in

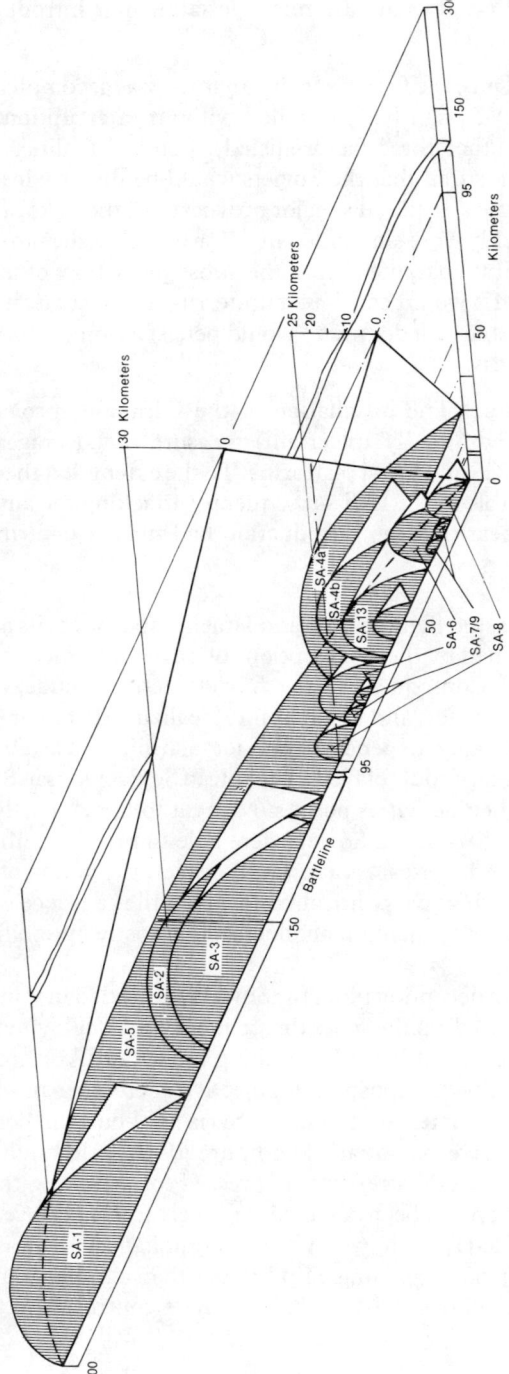

Figure 19-1. Coverage Profile of Soviet Integrated Air Defense System Deployed in Syria

Source: The data for this figure were taken from *Soviet Military Power 1986*, U.S. Department of Defense. Recent information indicates deployment of SS-11s as well.

September 1983 could be viewed as additional corroboration of the arguments expressed earlier.[32] With a 120 kilometer range and a circular error probability (CEP) variously estimated as between 200 and 500 meters, this mobile missile could not be viewed as a defensive weapon system.[33] Depending on its location, it could effectively cover many of Israel's airfields and key C^3I installations, thus allowing (theoretically at least) the launching of a conventional preemptive counterforce strike against IAF bases. Alternatively, it could provide a deterrent against Israel striking strategic targets deep in Syria, if the latter launched a new offensive under its new mobile SAM umbrella.

While there is no suggestion that such uses are likely so long as the missiles remain under Soviet command, it seems that Moscow was fully cognizant of the destabilizing effects that their introduction into the area might spur. In fact, it was reliably reported that the SS-21s were part of the same package put together by the Soviets, around August 1982, that brought the SA-5s into Syria. Their delivery was postponed, however, until the air defense umbrella inside Syria was in place and fully operational defending the missiles against a possible IAF preemption.[34] This reinforces the previous assertion that, in determining the SAM introduction sequence, a prime Soviet consideration was Israel's likely reaction. In turn, this concern led Soviet planners to conceive of deception Scheme I.

Scheme II: Escalation through Withdrawal

On 27 January 1984, the Tel Aviv daily *Davar* quoted "sufficiently senior" Soviet diplomats in the Soviet Embassy in Washington (allegedly substituting for Ambassador Dobrynin) as stating:

> . . . the SAM-5s were brought into Syria but, they are to be left for the Soviets to operate and not handed over to the Syrians, at least not in the next three years, at which time they will already be outdated.

However, less than twelve months later, the SA-5s were under Syrian control. The question of Soviet motivation has thus resurfaced.

The Gammons' transfer could be seen as consistent with the logic of the previously sketched deception ploy—a sort of a second scene in Scheme I. It may be said that, with their air defense system in place, Moscow could now afford to escalate the simmering Syrian-Israeli tensions. By this logic, on one hand, the handover of the SAMs and the withdrawal of Soviet crews from manning frontline weapon systems indicated lesser Soviet control over Syrian military decisions. On the other hand, it diminished Soviet involvement (risk) if a conflagration ensued. The net outcome is to grant Damascus greater latitude, while weakening Soviet reservations about the consequences of this extended freedom of action.

While such an analysis seems plausible, it raises the question of why Moscow would be interested in instigating Syrian-Israeli tensions in the first place. The answer lies in the impact of the 1982 war on Soviet strategic thinking, especially in regard to their air defense doctrine. It is important to recognize that unlike the situation in the United States, air defense plays a cardinal role in Soviet strategic and operational planning.[35]

The destruction by the IAF of the Syrian SAM batteries deployed in Lebanon's Al-Biqa Valley entailed significantly more than regional consequences insofar as the Soviet military was concerned. In seeking to unveil the true implications of the 1982 Syrian-Israeli air war on Soviet defense thought, three aspects deserve acknowledgment.

An American Aspect: The conflict pitted advanced U.S. SAM suppression technologies against Soviet air defense systems and concepts. In the wake of the war, in a rare Kremlin conference, the late Leonid Brezhnev told the commanders of the Soviet Army and Navy:

> Competition in military technology has sharply intensified, often acquiring a fundamentally different character. Lag in this competition is inadmissible. We expect our scientists, designers, engineers, and technicians to do everything possible to resolve successfully all tasks connected with this. [We will spare] . . . nothing to keep the armed forces up to mark [and provide them] with advanced weapons and military hardware.[36]

Many Western observers commented that Brezhnev's statement was, in part at least, aimed at allaying apprehensions among Soviet military leaders "concerned about the poor performance of advanced Soviet weaponry in the [1982] Lebanon conflict."[37] In fact, Brezhnev's declaration came within days after the Commander in Chief of Soviet Air Forces, the late Air Marshal Kutakhov, sought to reassure Soviet audiences that "no matter what weapons, or in what quantities, appear from the United States, Leonid Illich Brezhnev has said that the Soviet Armed Forces will have the requisite counter to such weapons."[38]

In addition, the Soviets had to assume that the lessons of the war would be passed by the IAF to the Americans. Thus Karen Brutents, Deputy Chief of the CPSU Central Committee, International Section, alleged that:

> . . . during the summer of 1982, Israel used 100 weapon systems developed by the Americans which had not been used before in full-scale combat operations. . . . The information obtained was passed by Israel to U.S. military and intelligence organs.[39]

A Syrian-Soviet Aspect: Since the 1973 Yom Kippur War, a persistent process of narrowing the gap between the Syrian and Soviet armed forces could have been discerned, both in terms of the weapons systems at hand, and in terms of operational doctrine. Application of Soviet military doctrine was also noticeable in Syrian land and air battles against the IDF. Consequently, in 1982, the Syrians performed in a more Soviet "style" than ever before, which enhanced the up-to-date applicability of the war's lessons for the Red Army.[40]

A Chinese Aspect: In the wake of the 1982 conflict, many reports suggested that the People's Republic of China (PRC) made overtures to Israel to obtain information about the IDF's SAM suppression techniques and antitank warfare.[41] Pentagon officials were quoted as indicating that Moscow was even interested in reaching an accord with Jerusalem to prevent transfer of Israeli military equipment and know-how to Beijing.[42]

Combined, these considerations suggest that the Soviet military should be well-disposed toward operationally testing its reconfigured air defense system in Syria. While one of the objectives of such a test is undoubtedly to vindicate Soviet arms technology, a more important aim pertains to the lessons that the PVO could draw from the engagement. These lessons would be crucial for fashioning Soviet air defense concepts in both the European and Far Eastern theaters. There are several elements that suggest that the recent Soviet disengagement from Syria is motivated by similar calculations.

First, the Soviets consistently maintained that in reality the IAF was the United States Air Force "in small." For instance, the Chief of Soviet Air Defense Forces for Combat Training, Colonel General A. Smirnov, recently drew attention to the similar role air power plays in Israeli and American military doctrines:

> The history of recent decades shows clearly that local wars have been unleashed by the imperialists, as a rule, by means of massive strikes from the air. That is how the barbarous American air raids unleashed the war in Vietnam in 1965. The same method was used by the Israeli aggressors against neighboring Arab States in 1967 and 1982.[43]

Western sources indicated that in the aftermath of the 1982 Syrian-Israeli conflict, the Soviets modified their SAM deployment in the Warsaw Pact area. The stationing of SA-5s in those Eastern European countries that border NATO member-states was noticed soon after the war.[44] Additionally, reports suggest that Moscow had taken steps to improve coordination of the Pact's air defenses.[45] In short, pitting Syria's integrated air defense system against the IAF could be the closest Soviet planners can hope to come to a realistic evaluation of PVO concepts in a superpower contest without actually becoming embroiled in a U.S.-Soviet confrontation.

Although it must be admitted that Syrian SAM crews probably are not as proficient as their Soviet counterparts, Moscow's predilection for the "remote-testing" approach may be explained by the following:

Withdrawal of Soviet SAM personnel assures that Moscow will not be *automatically* involved in the fighting.

The uncertainties facing Soviet PVO commanders are such as to prefer a somewhat distorted testing over an untested concept that could result in new technological and strategic surprises.

Soviet withdrawal militates against the United States inserting troops into the region. Were autonomous Soviet PVO units to take part in the fighting, the likelihood is high that the United States would respond in kind and establish SAM suppression assets in the area—perhaps in the eastern Mediterranean or even in Israel. As far as Soviet strategic interests in the Middle East are concerned, such a development would be tantamount to a real disaster: it would legitimize the positioning of U.S. troops "in direct proximity to Soviet southern borders," expressly contradicting the stated goal of Soviet Middle Eastern policy as a consequence.[46]

While a failed test could further humiliate the USSR and possibly even cause it to be ousted from Syria, it is a relatively cheap price to pay for shoring up Soviet confidence that such a catastrophe will not occur during a future NATO-Warsaw Pact conflict. From a Soviet perspective, a Syrian victory in another round with Israel remains illusive, dangerous, and most important, superfluous. In contrast, an IAF severely attrited by Syrian SAMs could herald a remarkable turn-around for Soviet fortunes in the Middle East and, more important, convince PVO leaders of the viability of their war doctrine. When it is defined in such terms, Soviet military commanders may indeed believe that a successful test in Syria of their integrated air defense system is already within reach.

In addition, the timing is ripe for reactivating the semidormant Syrian-Israeli conflict. A combination of three elements seem to be at work in this regard: (1) Operationally, the timing of the SAM's transfer and partial Soviet pullout was clearly determined by the relatively prolonged period required to train Syrian missile crews. (2) Strategically, the heavy price paid by the IDF in Lebanon, and the resurgence of severe socioeconomic problems at home gave rise to a commonly held notion of a weakened Israel.[47] In contrast to the perceived weariness of Israel, Syria's Army has been credited by IDF sources with regaining its "operational maturity," and President Asad's prestige appears to have reached an all-time high.[48] (3) Politically, Moscow and Damascus expressed their opposition to ongoing U.S. diplomatic efforts in the area.[49] In all likelihood, reigniting the Syrian-Israeli conflict could severely complicate Washington's Middle Eastern policy.

Rather than being a step toward enhancing regional stability, the handover of the SA-5s and limited recall of Soviet crews from Syria seem to have been motivated by the compelling need to resolve certain critical uncertainties imposed on the Soviet military by the 1982 war. To overcome this predicament, a relatively low-risk test of Soviet PVO concepts could be in the offing in Syria. To facilitate such testing, however, a Soviet disengagement ploy was conceived. Its aim is to provoke conflict without, at the same time, being accused of unleashing one. Also, the scheme could generate Israeli laxity (now that "inferior" Syrian SAM crews have moved in, and the menacing Soviet presence is out), thus enhancing the prospect for Syria to administer another strategic surprise.

In devising its deception ploy of disengagement from Syria, Moscow may be banking on triggering one of the following alternative mechanisms. Further, interaction between these two triggers will also yield an explosive scenario.

The Syrian "Trigger"

With the Soviets gone and the Gammons in Syrian hands, Damascus has extended its area of maneuverability. Consequently, the launching, at some future point, of SA-5s against Israeli planes operating in Lebanese skies has become more likely. For example, on 29 July 1985, Damascus Radio carried the following announcement by a Syrian military spokesman:

> Two Israeli enemy planes tried to strafe some civilian targets in the Barr Ilyas area [in Lebanon's Al-Biqa Valley where a PFLP-GC base has been operating] at 0650 today. . . . Our air defenses in the area intercepted them and forced them to withdraw.

A similar statement was carried by the radio a week later, when IAF planes again attacked the terrorists' headquarters.[50] It would appear that these Syrian pronouncements were made in direct response to remarks made on 14 July 1985 by IAF Commander General Lapidot on Israel Radio in Arabic:

> . . . The Air Force continues its activity in the north [i.e., Lebanon] and has not stopped flying in areas within range of these [SA-5] missiles in view of its assessment that Syria will not use these missiles in the existing situation.

Assuming that Damascus is fully aware that, if fired upon, Israeli planes would attack the SA-5 sites,[51] the launching of the Gammons could, in fact, be tailored to provoke the very response Israel has been threatening in order to: (1) settle the score with the IAF (now that an improved air defense system is under Syrian control) by inflicting heavy air losses on Israel, and (2) stall any progress toward U.S.-sponsored Arab-Israeli peace talks, which could result in isolating Syria further.

Damascus may even count on the superpowers' fear of escalation to freeze the conflict, thus leaving it with the fruits of its aggression. In 1973, Washington collaborated in such an exercise, maintaining that for Middle Eastern peace negotiations to be possible, the Arabs first needed to regain their self-esteem previously crushed by an uncooperative IDF.

The Israeli "Trigger"

The Soviets may also count on Israeli perceptions of Syrian intentions as a possible catalyst for war. In the wake of the SAMs' handover and partial Soviet pullback, Israeli fears of a Syrian military initiative have grown appreciably. For example, under the headline "To the Attention of the General Staff," on 23 June 1985 the Tel Aviv daily *Yedi'ot Aharonot* editorialized:

> Why did Al-Asad take off for Moscow [all of a] sudden? . . . This is unknown at the moment, but it is greatly to be suspected that Al-Asad may have decided this is the best moment for him to launch a war against us and he is rushing to obtain a Soviet agreement to this. . . . It is just enough to take a look at what is happening: Israel finds itself in an economic crisis from which it cannot extricate itself; the Israeli Government is engaged in internal conflicts, the likes of which have not plagued it to date; and a serious government crisis is around the corner. In addition, the government is currently facing enormous trouble in Lebanon from which Israel had withdrawn, as it were, but whose shadow still haunts Israel to this day. . . . How about the United States? The United States, which could have helped Israel, is preoccupied with problems of its own in Beirut, on the one hand, and in Latin America on the other. So we are a little isolated and why not try, then, to attack us now? The removal of the Soviet military experts from Syria indicates that the USSR has no reservations about this idea now. The Soviet Union did the same on the eve of the Yom Kippur War, and this situation strikes us as serious.

Other observers in Israel voiced their concern that war might indeed break out because the situation as detailed above might invite a Syrian miscalculation.[52] However, even in the absence of a clearcut Israeli conviction that the above calculations currently dominate Syrian thinking, a consensus seems to be shaping up among IDF commanders that another Syrian-Israeli round is a question of timing. Under these circumstances, Israel may choose to preempt, rather than conduct a campaign on the enemy's terms. In turn, Syrian suspicions that within Israel such a perspective is fast gaining respectability may already have made Damascus more nervous and, thus, "trigger-happy."[53]

Either way, the stage seems to be set for the Soviets to test their air defense system operationally. Further, this appears to be a case whether Syria's role is basically that of a co-conspirator or has evolved due to an independent miscalculation by Damascus of its chances vis-à-vis the IDF.

Scheme III: Projecting Weakness as Strength

Alternative assumptions, tacitly held, about basic Soviet practices and motives allow for a different interpretation of the recent handover of SAMs and the departure of Russian crews from Syria. At issue is a disagreement over which of the recently observed Soviet steps represent a means, and which delineate ends. While earlier it was argued that the Soviet recall was a deceptional means actually aimed at inciting and escalating Syrian-Israeli tensions, the present approach takes the opposite view; that instigation of U.S.-Israeli fears of imminent escalation provides a coverup for Moscow's basic desire to extricate itself from a highly volatile area.[54] In this view, Soviet withdrawal is an end in itself, rather than a means of attaining superior military objectives.

Proponents of this approach argue that:

The Soviet air defense system in Syria, with the Gammons at its center, is worth more as a political symbol than is any conceivable test that could end in failure.

In the event of such a test backfiring, the Soviets would face the difficult dilemma of intervening in force to defend Syria, or be ousted from that country. Intervention would put Moscow in the exact position that its pretest withdrawal allegedly attempted to avoid at all costs—namely, increased risks of a superpower confrontation while providing Washington with a ready-made excuse for inserting combat forces into the area. Moreover, the possibility of Soviet expeditional forces being engaged by the IDF, for whom the Soviets have a healthy measure of respect, cannot be overlooked.[55] On the other hand, an ouster would vindicate commonly held doubts about the value of the Soviet defense commitment, at least with regard to Third World allies.

While Moscow may be interested in a limited testing of its air defense system, it is fully aware of the marginal control it has in this regard. Numerous Israeli political and military figures have unequivocally stated that the IDF will dictate the terms of the next war, specifically rejecting a reenactment of the 1969 to 1970 War of Attrition along the Suez Canal, which pitted the IAF against Egyptian SAMs.[56]

These negative Soviet calculations combine with Moscow's presumed goals in the area to produce an argument that could be described as follows:

While a triumph of Soviet arms would be welcomed by the Soviet military, Moscow's political aim is to regain movement toward a comprehensive settlement that would endorse a permanent Russian role in the region. For this, there need not be a new round of war right away; a threat of war—which is what Soviet withdrawal from Syria amounts to—might suffice.[57]

Accordingly, the timing of the Soviet departure may be viewed as having been motivated by Moscow's search for maximum political leverage vis-à-vis both Israel and the United States: (1) The withdrawal openly signals Soviet confidence that the Syrians finally have mastered their new military hardware. (2) Perceived Israeli weakness apparently led Moscow to estimate that Jerusalem was currently more prone to politico-military pressures. (3) The forthcoming U.S.-Soviet summit indirectly invited the sides to augment their relative bargaining positions.

By seizing on these timing elements, Moscow has been able to utilize a reversed deception ploy of projecting its basic weakness in Syria as strength, not only to extricate itself from a potentially dangerous situation, but amazingly enough, to enhance its leverage in the process.

The Soviets may have hoped for an Israeli outcry that would cause the United States to rush to its side. Thus, Moscow could openly demonstrate the validity of its oft-repeated message to the Arabs that Washington was an unreliable ally and a partial mediator, with whom no cooperation should be contemplated, and that Arab leaders should not heed U.S. appeals to evince flexibility because its only aim is to help Israel.

As plausible as this argument may seem, it would be deficient without a further elaboration of the subjective factors facilitating strategic deception. It may be asked that if the Soviet position in Syria was as risky as the one described, why would Israel or the United States believe Moscow's pullout was motivated by anything other than a desire to extricate itself? If Soviet disincentives for war are as strong as those alleged, why should its "weakness-as-strength" exercise not be dismissed as simply another Soviet bluff? Why would *Syria's* militancy enhance *Soviet* leverage if the latter had in effect "bailed out" because of it?

The answer to these questions lies in recognizing the endemic uncertainties prevalent in any strategic analysis and particularly in estimating the intentions and capabilities of an actor as secretive as the USSR. Although, in reality, the Soviet withdrawal from Syria may have been motivated by considerations similar to those enumerated earlier, Moscow could have banked on Israeli sensitivities to provide it with extra leverage. In the aftermath of the 1973 Yom Kippur War, Israelis have become profoundly weary of projections indicating overwhelming enemy disincentives for launching an attack.

The speedy withdrawal of two (out of three) Syrian divisions from Lebanon closely following the exit of Israeli forces may signal Damascus's interest in disengagement. As Defense Minister Rabin indicated on Israel Radio, on 16 August 1985, the pace of the evacuation "surprised even the optimistic among our ranks." Without question, however, redeployed on Syrian soil, these divisions enhance Syria's ability to wage the type of combat it does best—a protracted warfare fought from defense positions. Consequently, the redeployment bolstered the Syrian capacity to deter or ward off a potential IDF ground attack, which Damascus apparently feared would have been launched in conjunction with any IAF response to its SAM warfare. Coming as it did on top of the SAMs' handover, the interception of Israeli planes may thus have become a more credible option in the wake of the Syrian Army's regrouping.

Given the persistence of Syrian-inspired terrorist attacks on the remaining Israeli outposts in southern Lebanon (which, according to Rabin, Damascus was certain to escalate to "torpedo" the peace process), intensification of IAF operations over Al-Biqa could be expected. Under these circumstances, the potential jointly created by the SAM transfer, the Soviet pullout, and the Syrian redeployment for the launching of an armed provocation by President Asad would not be regarded with equanimity in Jerusalem. Although the IDF may feel confident of its ability to handle this threat (should it materialize) Moscow has reinforced its bargaining position vis-à-vis Israel and, indirectly, with the United States. This is due to the fundamental Israeli interest in avoiding a clash rather than winning one and the suspicion in Jerusalem that the fewer inhibitions traditionally displayed by the Arabs in this respect were further eroded by the three developments mentioned above.

In turn, the more Israel is concerned over the possible existence of Scheme II (escalation through withdrawal), the stronger would be the rationale for the Soviets to launch Scheme III (projecting weakness as strength), not the least of which is because it simultaneously marks substantially reduced risks. This provided that the reasons for the Soviet recall were kept ambiguous, and the pullout process was prolonged enough to eliminate speculation about it being, in effect, another Soviet expulsion.

In contrast to an abrupt removal of Soviet military personnel, which could indicate a flareup was imminent (thus possibly touching off a chain reaction), a phased withdrawal also allows better regulation of the temperature under the Syrian-Israeli "pot." Strict Soviet-Syrian adherence to these principles has made it difficult for outside observers to conclude that the departure of the Russians was anything but a coordinated move, increasing suspicions that Scheme II was unfolding and enhancing Soviet leverage as a consequence.

Therefore, the possibility emerges that the sudden Soviet interest in talking with Israel (exemplified by a recent ambassadorial meeting in Paris and Soviet pronouncements that such contacts will continue) is indeed an expression of the new Soviet leverage vis-à-vis Israel and, by implication, the United States.[58] Rather than being a unilateral Soviet move, potentially harmful to Soviet-Syrian relationships, the recent Soviet overtures may be viewed as the beginning of a coordinated "cashing in" phase. Moreover, it is entirely possible that the Israeli conduct (that is, its inclination to believe that Scheme II was in the making) has played into Soviet hands. Thus, in May 1983, Moscow had its first confirmation that Israeli perceptions could be manipulated in a way beneficial to Soviet interests when an evacuation of Soviet dependents from Beirut and Damascus, timed to coincide with Soviet-directed major Syrian military exercises, caused a stir in Jerusalem and Washington.[59] In November 1983, a Soviet "rotation" of its SAM crews in Syria inspired a similar consternation, with Israeli Deputy Prime Minister David Levi declaring: "The Israeli Government is not indifferent to these reports [of Soviet withdrawal]. Past experience generally indicates that something happens after the Soviets leave a place."[60]

While some in Israel countered that the Soviet investment in Syria was simply too large to be jeopardized in a local war, claiming Moscow was apprehensive lest its advanced weaponry be compromised in the process, the recent handover of SAMs and the partial pullout have served to quash such misplaced hopes.[61] The chance of an imminent engagement by Syria against the IDF is currently viewed as being increased now that a Soviet-Syrian collusion threatens to terminate the "moderating" Soviet presence in that country. In turn, the latent pressures have intensified for Washington and Jerusalem to prevent an explosion providing Moscow with a paradoxically greater leverage the closer it gets to fulfilling its presumed goal of disengagement.

At this point, it would be a relief to find that the Scheme II versus Scheme III dilemma had been resolved and that the truth about the Soviet "game" in Syria was finally revealed. The real world deception, however, is rarely as simplistic. Besides, it is doubtful that Moscow opted for one ploy and rescinded the other; although the Soviets may be primarily interested in the potential gains promised by Scheme III, their recent moves in Syria stood the chance of being misinterpreted by the Israelis as signalling an impending Scheme II. In turn, this would have brought mounting pressures within Israel to preempt. It is therefore logical to assume that the Soviets had to make certain Syria was actually poised to engage the IDF (that is, to carry out Moscow's test plans), even if in reality they were after a pressure-generating political "brinkmanship" exercise. Moreover, even if recent Soviet contacts have sought to reassure the Israelis, such communications are unlikely to clear the air. The high state of Syria's military readiness, reaffirmed anew by a hedging rationale, would tend to perpetuate Israeli suspicions of another Soviet deception ploy. Besides, Moscow has never been viewed by Israel as exercising firm controls over Damascus.[62] Assuaging the Israelis would thus require considerably more than Soviet verbal assurances.

Conversely, for Moscow to relay pacifying messages could amount to relinquishing Scheme III (originally based on seeking leverage via unnerving Jerusalem) without necessarily modifying the preemptive advocacy of at least some in Israel. Here again, the conclusion is reached that the Soviets had to prepare for the possible unfolding of *either* scheme as a precondition for their withdrawal from Syria. With its troops physically removed from the scene, and an advanced air defense system in place, it would seem that Moscow concluded that little would be lost *either way*. The true nature of Schemes II and III as complementary ploys rather than substitutes, is thus exposed.

From this perspective, determination of the exact kill-ratio of Syria's SAMs may be considered secondary. The fact remains that, via Scheme I, Moscow assured uninterrupted introduction of an advanced air defense system into Syria, which proved instrumental in seizing the strategic initiative without a single shot being fired and without the Russians necessarily being present in massive numbers on the scene.

Summary and Conclusions

Since 1983, Soviet activities in Syria have produced three surprises: (1) The selection of the SA-5 as the centerpiece of Soviet post-1982 war air defense effort in Syria; (2) the deployment of the Gammons ahead of other more sophisticated, less vulnerable SAMs; and (3) the recent transfer of the SA-5s to Syrian hands.

In light of the SA-5s operational shortcomings, vulnerability, and limited challenge to IAF planes, their deployment in Syria could be viewed as a surprise. It would appear that the missiles were stationed in the area because of their (debatable) capability versus high-flying, relatively slow AWACS and ECM platforms—assessed by the Soviets to have played a key role in the IAF's antiair and anti-SAM campaigns of June 1982. No less important were the political saliency of the system and the advantages their introduction promised in terms of Moscow's deception plans.

The reversed introduction sequence adopted by the Soviets in Syria, initially exposing the SA-5s to a possible IAF preemptive strike, had a clearcut deceptional motivation: it helped assure an uninterrupted subsequent flow of sophisticated arms into the country. By projecting their buildup of SAMs as purely defensive and highly vulnerable, the Soviets were eventually able to build strength from weakness; that is, to erect an advanced, potentially offensive, multilayered, integrated air defense system in Syria without hindrance. Moreover, once installation of the new air defense system was completed, the Soviets could then proceed to introduce weapon systems whose offensive potential is unquestionable—such as the SS-21s.

The third surprise seems to be linked to Soviet deceptional practices as well. It might actually be part of a Soviet scheme to seek to incite Syrian-Israeli hostilities, thus allowing, at long last, the testing of Soviet PVO concepts against an American air force, "in small." The potential applicability of the engagement's lessons, especially to the Soviet Union's Western and Eastern theaters of military operations (TVDs), may have overruled what otherwise were thought to be staunch Soviet reservations. Alternatively, it could be argued that the tension-prone handover of SA-5s to the Syrians and the removal of crews from the country were a coverup for Moscow's paramount interest in extricating itself from the Syrian-Israeli quagmire. The claim could be made that, to extract concessions, Moscow was interested in stirring U.S.-Israeli fears of an imminent escalation while simultaneously covering its tracks. However, the preceding analysis has argued that it would be wrong to view these interpretations of Soviet deceptional practices as substitutes; Moscow may, in fact, have readied itself and its Syrian ally for the unfolding of either scenario.

Consequently, conclusions may be drawn with regard to three issue-areas. In terms of Soviet practices, it seems that (at least in the military field) deception is an ongoing activity. Rather than thinking about Soviet deception as individual ploys, the Russians are apparently engaged in nonstop deceptional politico-military activity aimed at continuously masquerading and camouflaging true Soviet intentions and capabilities. The idea is to never divulge Moscow's actual motivations and objectives, thus creating a permanent state of uncertainty in the minds of Western policy makers. In addition to covering up potential weaknesses, the proliferation of Soviet deception schemes promoted a Western *weltanschauung*, which increasingly holds this practice to be at the center of Soviet foreign conduct, rendering each and every Soviet move open to a multitude of alternative interpretations. In principle, the prevalence of such a Western approach may ease Moscow's administration of an actual surprise. More often, however, it will result in stimulating controversy, confusion, and indecision.

This leads into a second area of theoretical insights. It appears that deception is, in large part, a state of mind. The success or failure of a deception ploy often hinges on preconceived assumptions (some tacitly held) about the general nature of one's enemy. Since strategic analysis is invariably plagued by various types and degrees of uncertainty, such underlying conceptions are intuitively used by decision makers to fill the voids left by incomplete and nonexistent information. This intuitive process seems to have played a role in generating the hypotheses about the Soviet handover of missiles and the subsequent withdrawal from Syria.

As for projecting the future of Syrian-Israeli relations, the question must be raised as to why the Soviet pullout from Syria would trigger persistent speculation about an imminent Syrian-Israeli round if the Soviet military buildup in that country was (as Moscow pledged) purely defensive? It would seem that the answer is that depending on their estimate of the coverage provided by the air defense system, Moscow and/or Damascus might become sufficiently confident to seek, at a fortuitous moment, a *revanche* of sorts. Besides testing the viability of Soviet PVO concepts, the timing of such a move would be decided by the urgency Moscow and Damascus ascribe to impeding the progress of U.S. diplomacy in the Middle East. Also, it may well create the illusion of Syria as having reached a "strategic balance" with Israel.[63] In sharp contrast to the strategic circumstances produced by the 1982 conflict, the growing popularity of conjectures about the next Syrian-Israeli round provides an unfortunate indication that *maskirovka* has once again helped Moscow wrest the strategic initiative in the region.

Notes

1. The handover was also confirmed by the commander of the Israeli Air Force, Major General Amos Lapidot on Jerusalem Radio, in Arabic, on 14 July 1985. In *Foreign Broadcast Information Service (FBIS) Middle East and Africa (MEA)*, 15 July 1985, p. 16.
2. Cited in *Ha'aretz* (Tel Aviv), 16 July 1985.
3. *Jerusalem Domestic Service*, 3 April 1985. In *FBIS (MEA)*, 4 April 1985, p. 15.
4. *Pravda*, 2 February 1985; also *Izvestiia*, 19 January 1985.
5. Interview in *Voice of Lebanon* (Beirut), 16 March 1983. In *FBIS (MEA)*, 17 March 1983, p. G-1.
6. Interview in *Monday Morning* (Beirut), 18 July 1983, p. 50; also "Central Committee Member, Leonid Zamyatin," *Newsweek*, 2 May 1983, p. 44.
7. Interview in *Le Monde*, 25 October 1983.
8. Former Israeli Defense Minister Ariel Sharon in *Ma'ariv*, 28 January 1983.
9. "Third World Diplomats," cited in *Jerusalem Domestic Service*, 21 March 1983, in *FBIS (MEA)*, 22 March 1983, p. I-12.
10. Interview of then Israeli Defense Minister, Moshe Arens, *Los Angeles Times*, cited in *Ma'ariv*, 23 February 1983; Arens, in *Bita'on Khe'il Ha'avir (Journal of the Israeli Air Force)* (July 1983): p. 8. For a similar argument, see Admiral William J. Crowe (then CINCSOUTH), "Allied Defense of the Southern Region," *NATO's Sixteen Nations* (June-July 1983): p. 20. For reports of strong Syrian pressures on Moscow, see *Ash-Sharq* (Beirut), 5 January 1983, citing "well informed sources in Damascus"; *Boston Globe*, 28 January 1983, quoting "Western intelligence" sources.
11. *Boston Globe*, 29 January 1983, citing U.S. officials; *Atlanta Journal and Constitution*, 9 October 1983, citing "military sources" in Israel.
12. Cynthia A. Roberts, "Soviet Arms Transfer Policy and the Decision to Upgrade Syrian Air Defences," *Survival* (July/August 1983): p. 157; also *Ha'aretz*, 3 April 1983, citing U.S. officials.
13. *Jerusalem Domestic Service*, 4 January 1983, in *FBIS (MEA)*, 5 January 1983, p. I-1; IDF Radio in *FBIS (MEA)*, p. I-1, citing "political circles in Jerusalem."
14. Israeli Foreign Minister Itzhak Shamir, in *Al Hamishmar* (Tel Aviv), 25 March 1983; (then Chief of Staff, IDF) Lieutenant General Rafa'el Eytan in *Ma'ariv*, 3 April 1983, "There are U.S. soldiers in Lebanon. The presence of SA-5s in Syria may be the Soviet answer to their presence." Leonid Brezhnev (Soviet President at that time) promptly warned that if U.S. troops were sent to Lebanon, "the Soviet Union would build its policy with due consideration of this fact," *New York Times*, 9 July 1982, citing Brezhnev's letter to President Reagan as issued by TASS; *Pravda*, 26 August 1982; Alvin Z. Rubinstein, "The Soviet Union and the Peace Process since Camp David," *Washington Quarterly* (Winter 1985)" pp. 49–50.
15. Anthony H. Cordesman, "Syrian-Israeli C^{3}I: The West's Third Front," 7 January 1984, mimeographed, p. 51.
16. Lieutenant General (retired) Eytan, in *Ha'aretz*, 7 January 1983.
17. Yossef Bodansky, "A New Soviet Middle Eastern Strategy," *Bita'on Khe'il Ha'avir*, (in Hebrew), (November 1983): p. 52.
18. "Foreign Report," *Economist* (10 March 1983): pp. 4–5; Martin Sicker, "SAM-5s in Syria: What is Moscow Really Up To?" *Perspective*, (August 1983): p. 1.

19. Voice of Lebanon (Beirut), 10 March 1983, in *FBIS (MEA)* 11 March 1982, p. H–1; *Ha'aretz*, 11 March 1982; *Al-Mustaqbal* (Paris), 20 Mar. 1982, p. 14. In April 1982, reports indicated arrival of the MiG-25 Foxbat B (reconnaissance version) in Syria. *Ha'aretz*, 29 April 1982. One of the Foxbat Bs was shot down by the IAF while on a reconnaissance mission over Lebanon a few months later, *Ha'aretz*, 1 September 1982.

20. Then Israel's Knesset Speaker, Menachem Savidor, cited by *Jerusalem Domestic Service*, 1 March 1983, in *FBIS (MEA)*, 2 March 1983, p. I–5.

21. Cordesman, "Syrian-Israeli C^{3}I," p. 51.

22. Instead, it was reported by the Istanbul daily, *Gunaydin*, 11 January 1985, that Syria and the USSR were jointly constructing a military air base some "40 kms. off Turkish borders." Citing information allegedly obtained from U.S. reconnaissance satellites, the paper went on to identify the location of the base as "very close to the Kamisli District of Mardin." In *FBIS (MEA)*, 22 January 1985, p. H–2.

23. In addition to numerous sources cited earlier, the system's introduction sequence reconstructed in table 19–1 draws on *Jerusalem Domestic Service*, in *FBIS (MEA)*, 5 January 1983, p. I–3; 18 January 1983, p. I–7; 14 February 1983, p. I–4; *Ha'aretz*, 19 January 1983 (citing Commander of the IAF at the time, Major General David Ivri), 23 January 1983, 13 February 1983, 13 and 16 May 1983, 13 June 1983, 13 January 1984; *Jerusalem Post*, 27 February 1983; interview of Major General Amos Lapidot, Commander of IAF, in *Ma'ariv*, 29 July 1983; *New York Times*, 1 and 21 March 1983, 29 April 1983, 14 and 16 May 1983, 26 June 1983, 14 December 1983; *Washington Post*, 8 February 1983, 14 May 1983; *Boston Globe*, 18 January 1983, 4 March 1983; *Los Angeles Times*, 18 February 1983; *Christian Science Monitor*, 24 February 1983; *Baltimore Sun*, 28 February 1983; *Chicago Tribune*, 23 March 1983; *Times*, 8 March 1983; 13 May 1983; *Le Monde*, 26 May 1983; "Voice of Lebanon," in *FBIS (MEA)*, 1 March 1983, p. G–4; 16 May 1983, p. G–4. Also see the following periodicals: *Defense Electronics* (December 1982): p. 24, (April 1983): p. 19; *Al Mustaqbal*, 22 January 1983, pp. 10–13; *International Defense Review* 4(1983): p. 402; *Newsweek* (20 June 1983): p. 35; *Al-Majallah* (London), (25–31 August 1984): pp. 12–14. Also see Cordesman, "Syrian-Israeli C^{3}I," pp. 44–57; William H. Lewis and Stephen C. Moss, "The Soviet Arms Transfer Program," *Journal of Northeast Asian Studies*, (Fall 1984): pp. 12–13.

24. For reports of Soviet resupplies arriving in Syria by air and sea as early as 10 June 1982, see: Jerusalem Domestic Television, 15 June 1982, in *FBIS (MEA)*, 16 June 1982, p. I–13; *Ha'aretz*, 16 Jun. 1982; *New York Times*, 16 September 1982; *Washington Post*, 9 October 1982; *Washington Times*, 25 October 1982. On 8 July 1982, TASS said the Soviet Union was helping Syria to "bolster its defense capability." The statement was seen as an "admission that [Moscow] was shipping arms to Damascus," *Baltimore Sun*, 9 July 1982.

25. See, for instance, Chaim Herzog, *The Arab-Israeli Wars: War and Peace in the Middle East* (New York: Random House, 1982), pp. 214–223, 307–311. On the debate within the IAF, see Areyh Avneri, *Ha'mahaluma (The Strike)*, (in Hebrew) (Givataim, Revivim, 1983) pp. 18–37ff.

26. *Aviation Week & Space Technology*, cited in *Ha'aretz*, 10 August 1982; Philip J. Millis, "RPVs over the Bekka Valley," *Army* (June 1983): pp. 49–50.

27. On Soviet site selection calculations, see *Newsweek* (7 March 1983): pp. 49–50.

28. An IDF "military source" reportedly in a briefing to the Knesset Foreign

Affairs and Defense Committee, on IDF Radio, 14 December 1983, in *FBIS (MEA)*, 15 December 1983, p. I–1. Also, Lieutenant General Rafa'el Eytan, then Chief of Staff of the IDF in *Ma'ariv*, 3 April 1983; *Yedi'ot Aharonot* (Tel Aviv), 13 May 1983.

29. For reports of Soviet warnings, passed to Israel via the United States, not to attack the SA-5s indicating "the Soviet Union has a reaction plan," see *Jerusalem Domestic Service*, 18 March 1983, in *FBIS (MEA)*, 21 March 1983, p. I–15; *New York Times*, 30 March 1983.

30. For reports of Israeli officials pressing for a preemptive strike, see *Wall Street Journal*, 2 May 1983; *New York Times*, 14 May 1983. On U.S.-Israeli consultations see *Ha'aretz*, 6 and 7 March 1983, 1 April 1983.

31. Lieutenant General Eytan in IDF Radio, 14 March 1983, in *FBIS (MEA)*, 15 March 1983, p. I–3; Defense Minister Itzhak Rabin, in *Ma'ariv*, 20 March 1983; also *Christian Science Monitor*, 2 March 1983.

32. *Los Angeles Times*, 14 October 1983. Subsequent reports alleged, however, that the Syrians possessed one brigade each of Scud-B and Frog-7 SSMs, each with thirty-six launchers. "A full brigade of SS-21 missiles, also with thirty-six launchers has been added," *Chicago Tribune*, 28 February 1984. See also Voice of Lebanon, 13 December 1983 in *FBIS (MEA)*, 14 December 1983, p. G–2.

33. See comments made by Chief of IDF Intelligence Branch, Lieutenant General Ehud Barak in *Al Hamishmar*, 5 October 1984; *New York Times*, 7 January 1984; Cordesman, "Syrian-Israeli C^{3}I," pp. 56–57.

34. *Boston Globe*, 18 October 1983.

35. David R. Jones, "National Air Defense Force," David R. Jones, ed., *Soviet Armed Forces Review Annual*, vol. 3, (Gulf Breeze, Fla.: Academic International Press, 1979), pp. 22–24; Robert Elliot, "Soviet Air Defense—The Third Force," *NATO's Fifteen Nations*, (October-November 1982): pp. 104–106; Harriet Fast Scott, "Deadly Guardians of Soviet Airspace," *Air Force Magazine* (March 1984): pp. 13–19.

36. *Krasnaya Zvezda* (Moscow), 27 October 1982; TASS in *FBIS (SU)* (Soviet Union), 17 October 1982, p. V–3.

37. *Financial Times* (London), 29 October 1982.

38. In *Moscow Domestic Service*, 23 October 1982, in *FBIS (SU)*, 26 October 1982, p. V–2.

39. *Pravda*, 3 February 1984.

40. On active Soviet participation in Syria's "post-mortem" of the war, including "in the realm of retrospective analysis, expert advice, and debriefings about what took place—including a reenaction of the events that led to [Syria's] defeat," see Major General Amos Lapidot, Commander of the IAF in *FBIS (MEA)*, 19 July 1984, p. I–1. Further, it was reported that Moscow, enraged by Syrian foot-dragging, categorically demanded the return to the USSR of tanks and other armored vehicles knocked out by the IDF during the war. Eventually, such a shipment was reported to have arrived in the Soviet Union in late September 1982 amid indications of Soviet concern over the penetrability of its armor to IDF anti-tank munitions. *New Breed*, cited in *Ha'aretz*, 6 October 1982.

41. *Ha'aretz*, 13 July 1984, quoting U.S. intelligence sources. For continuous reports about alleged PRC-Israeli military ties in the wake of the 1982 war, see *Chicago Tribune*, 10 September 1982, *Foreign Report*, 14 July 1983, p. 4; *Die Welt*, 17 October 1984; *Jane's Defense Weekly*, cited in *Christian Science Monitor*, 21 November 1984;

Washington Times, 24 January 1985. For Soviet reaction see Radio Moscow (in Arabic), 3 August 1982, in *FBIS (SU)*, 4 August 1982, p. B–1; TASS, 19 January 1985, in *FBIS (SU)*, 4 February 1985, p. H–3; TASS, 13 February 1985, in *FBIS (MEA)*, 13 February 1985, p. B–2. For Chinese denials see *New York Times*, 3 August 1985.

42. *New York Post*, 14 February 1983.

43. In *Sotsialistcheskaya Industriya* (Moscow), 10 April 1983. Also, the Commander in Chief of Soviet Air Defense Forces, Marshal of Aviation, Aleksander Koldunov in *Vestnik Protivovozdushnoy Oborony*, April 1982, trans., in "The Soviet Strategic View," *Strategic Review* (Fall 1982): p. 114; *Krasnaya Zvezda*, 18 November 1983.

44. *Die Welt*, 19 February 1983; 4 March 1983; *Ha'aretz*, 20 February 1983, 13 July 1983. Some accounts have suggested the SA-5s deployed in Eastern Europe were an upgraded version of those stationed in Syria. See also, *Economist* (8 January 1983): p. 31.

45. *Sunday Times* (London), 5 December 1982.

46. A "senior official in the Bonn Foreign Ministry" was thus quoted in *Ha'aretz*, 24 May 1983, as indicating the Soviets were apprehensive over "a new kind of U.S. involvement in Lebanon" and were pressing Damascus to withdraw its forces from that country in order to "get the [U.S.] forces out of there [Lebanon] as soon as possible." For recent Soviet expressions of concern over the "growing U.S. threat" in the USSR's "southern strategic zone," see Admiral Nikolai Amelko, Deputy Chief of the USSR Armed Forces General Staff, in *Narodna Armiya* (Sofia), 14 June 1983; interview of Lieutenant General Dimitriy Volkogonov, of the Main Political Directorate of the Soviet Army and Navy, in *Tishrin* (Damascus), 13 November 1983; Joint communique summarizing Soviet-Syrian Foreign Ministers' talks in *Pravda*, 13 November 1983; Karen Brutents, Deputy Chief of the CPSU Central Committee, International Section, writing in *Tishrin*, 2 April 1984.

47. A recent study by the respected military correspondent of the influential *Ha'aretz* has thus concluded that the IDF was in the midst of both a quantitative and qualitative decline. See Ze'ev Schiff, *Israel's Eroding Edge in the Middle East Military Balance*, Policy Paper No. 2, (Washington, D.C.: The Washington Institute for Near East Policy, 1985). For Israeli officials' reaction to such characterizations, see Foreign Minister Itzhak Shamir, interview in *Jerusalem Domestic Service*, 19 March 1985, in *FBIS (MEA)*, 2 April 1985, pp. I–2 and I–3; Defense Minister Itzhak Rabin, interview in *La Repubblica* (Rome) 4 April 1985, in *FBIS (MEA)*, 11 April 1985, p. I–2.

48. Indications of the new Syrian assertiveness can be found in recent statements made by its leaders. For instance, General Mustafa Tlass, Syria's Defense Minister said: "The next war, if it breaks out, will be completely different from the war that took place [in the] summer [of 1982]. The Syrian Army has not been as well-equipped and prepared as it is now. In addition to this, we have become the largest army in the region, comprising 750,000 men, including the reserve forces." Interview in *Stern*, cited in *FBIS (MEA)*, 13 June 1985, p. H–2.

49. For example, on 16 April 1985, TASS quoted President Asad as pledging that "Syria will continue firm struggle against U.S. and Israel aggressive plans, their attempts to subordinate the Middle East area to their domination [through the] broadening of the number of participants in the anti-Arab Camp David collusion." In *FBIS (SU)*, 17 April 1985, p. H–4. A joint Soviet-Syrian communique summarizing President Asad's June 1985 visit to Moscow states:

During their talks on the Middle East situation, the two sides agreed that the U.S. plan to achieve a new stage in the Camp David method is aimed at imposing capitulation on the Arabs, liquidating the Palestinian question, spreading U.S. and Israeli hegemony over the region, and promoting the results of the Israeli aggression against the Arabs. The views were in agreement regarding the need to resist and confront these plans. *Damascus Domestic Service*, in *FBIS (SU)*, 11 June 1985, p. H–2. See also, Asad's address at a banquet welcoming visiting Bulgarian leader, Todor Zhivkov, in *Damascus Domestic Service*, 18 April 1985, in *FBIS (MEA)*, 29 April 1985, pp. H–2 and H–3.

50. In *FBIS (MEA)*, 29 July 1985, p. H–1; 8 August 1983, p. I–1.

51. See comments made by IAF Commander, General Lapidot in Jerusalem Domestic Service, 17 July 1983, in *FBIS (MEA)*, 19 July 1983, p. I–1.

52. For example, *Ma'ariv*, 12 July 1985.

53. Syrian nervousness may be extrapolated from its recent launching of RPVs over the Israeli-Lebanese border area. See *Jerusalem Domestic Service*, 13 June 1985, reporting the downing of a Syrian RPV, in *FBIS (MEA)*, 14 June 1985, p. I–1.

54. Moshe Arens, at the time Israel's Defense Minister, has openly advocated this view. See *Jerusalem Post*, 21 June 1983; *Jerusalem Domestic Service*, 23 June 1983, in *FBIS (MEA)*, 24 June 1983, p. I–1.

55. The Commander of the IAF, General Lapidot, has indicated, for instance, that "if the Soviets choose to fight us over Syrian territory, it will not be a unilateral engagement." Interview in *Ma'ariv*, 29 Jul. 1983. Also, *Boston Globe*, 30 April 1983. On 23 May 1985, *Davar* cited "Eastern European sources," as indicating Moscow would like Israel to "clarify" its nuclear policy. Commenting on a recent meeting in Washington between Soviet Ambassador Anatoliy Dobrynin and his Israeli counterpart, Me'ir Rosenne, the sources reportedly said "the Soviet leadership fears an Israeli mood in which the political echelon will view the use of nuclear weapons against Soviet targets, such as Soviet ships in the Mediterranean, as a possible scenario." Interestingly enough, Soviet military commentators had even praised the IDF performance in the 1973 Yom Kippur War. See Major General A.P. Maryshev, "Ground Forces in Local Wars in the post-World War II Era," in Army General I. Ye. Shavrov, ed., *Local'nye Voiny: Istoriya i Sovermennost* (Moscow: Voinzdat, 1981), pp. 239–240.

56. Israeli Defense Minister at the time, Moshe Arens, addressing the Knesset, in *Ha'aretz*, 16 Mar. 1983. Interview in *Le Figaro*, 4–5 June 1983; *Ha'aretz*, 4 April 1984. Also, Chief of Staff Lieutenant General Eytan, interviewed in Jerusalem Domestic Television, 17 April 1983, in *FBIS (MEA)*, 18 April 1983, p. I–6.

57. Dorit Landes, "The Soviet Union and the Crisis in Lebanon," *Monthly Review*, (in Hebrew) (June-July 1983), pp. 11–18; Stephens Broening in *Baltimore Sun*, 6 August 1983.

58. On recent Soviet-Israeli ambassadorial talks in Paris, see *Le Matin* (Paris), 20–21 July 1985; Israeli Prime Minister, Shimon Peres, in *Jerusalem Post*, 25 Jul. 1985, and *Ha'aretz*, 29 July 1985; *Ma'ariv*, 26 July 1985. Consequently, an increase in Soviet broadcasts promising to "consider" renewal of diplomatic ties with Israel if the latter "withdrew from the territories and recognized the rights of the Palestinians," has been noticed. Simultaneously, a spokesman for the Soviet Foreign Ministry reiterated accusations that "Israel [was] creating instability in the Middle East." See *Jerusalem International Service*, 25 July 1985, in *FBIS (MEA)*, 25 July 1985, p. I–3.

59. For accounts of the May 1983 Syrian-Israeli tensions, see *Jerusalem Domestic*

Service, 10 May 1983, in *FBIS (MEA)*, 9 May 1983, p. I–4; *Ha'aretz*, 12 May 1983; *Ar-Ra'i al Amm* (Kuwait), 25 May 1983. Israel's Deputy Prime Minister, David Levi, had accused the Soviet Union of "attempting to create a war atmosphere with statements, threats, and the evacuation of diplomats from the capital of Lebanon." *Ma'ariv*, 13 May 1983. For the Soviet role in the Syrian war exercises, see MK (member of Knesset) Shimon Peres in *Yedi'ot Aharonot*, 30 May 1983. Peres has subsequently stated that "the exercise itself was conducted apparently with Soviet planning, under Soviet supervision, and with the participation of many, various level Soviet military men who could be noticed in the area," in *Jerusalem Domestic Service*, 1 June 1983, in *FBIS (MEA)*, 3 June 1983, p. I–13. For other Soviet tension-producing measures, see also Moscow Domestic Television, in *FBIS (SU)*, 3 May 1983, p. H–3; *Washington Post*, 3 May 1983; *Observer* (London), 8 May 1983.

60. In *Ma'ariv*, 13 November 1983. Also *Ma'ariv*, 7 November 1983, reporting of UN observers stationed on the Golan Heights as predicting that war between Israel and Syria was imminent. "The U.N. soldiers said that along dozens of kilometers along the border they spotted Russian soldiers in uniform who were supervising tanks going into underground bunkers, or were driving them themselves. According to this eyewitness report, many Russian soldiers 'walking around with maps' can be seen on the Syrian side." Former IDF Chief of the Intelligence Branch, Major General Y. Sagi, was wondering why "Syria opted for a public callup [of reserves] at a time when it could have chosen another path," interview in *Ha'aretz*, 8 November 1983. See also *Yedi'ot Aharonot*, 15 November 1983; *Boston Globe*, 25 November 1983, on the Soviet "rotation" of SAM crews.

61. At the time, Israel's Defense Minister, Moshe Arens in *Ha'aretz*, 17 June 1983.

62. See Interview of IDF's Chief of the Intelligence Branch, Major General Ehud Barak, in *Bamakhane (At the Barracks)*, (in Hebrew), 8 June 1983, p. 15. On numerous occasions, Israeli leaders have expressed their concern over a reversed syndrome whereby Damascus "was liable to think [it] can drag the Soviets into a flare-up in the area," see Defense Minister Arens, in IDF Radio, 15 March 1983, in *FBIS (MEA)*, 16 March 1983, p. I–3; Interview on Jerusalem Domestic Television, 13 April 1983; in *FBIS (MEA)*, 14 April 1983, p. I–9; Briefing to the Knesset Foreign Affairs and Defense Committee, in Jerusalem Domestic Service, 20 April 1983, in *FBIS (MEA)*, 21 April 1983, p. I–4. See also, Syrian Defense Minister, General Mustafa Tlass, interview, in *Al-Safir* (Beirut), 16 May 1983.

63. For this concept as a driving principle in Syria's military program, see General Mustafa Tlass, Syria's Defense Minister, interview in *Al-Safir*, 18 June 1980; Syrian President Hafez Al-Asad, interview in *An Nahar Al-Arabi Wa Ad-Duali* (Paris), 30 October 1982; General Tlass interview in *Al-Kifah Al-Arabi*, cited in *New York Times*, 20 November 1983. Also *Ha'aretz*, 10 June 1982; 7 and 10 January 1983. For a general discussion, Dina Kehat, "Syria," in Colin Legum, Haim Shaked, and Daniel Dishon, eds., *Middle East Contemporary Survey* 4 (New York: Holmes & Meier, 1979–80), pp. 770–775.

Part VI
Deception and Strategic Planning

20
Impact of Deception on U.S. Nuclear Strategy

Leon Sloss

Introduction

As this volume seeks to demonstrate, a major objective of Soviet policy is to attack U.S. and Western strategy in peacetime in order to erode the effectiveness of that strategy, sap confidence in it, and weaken the ties between the United States and its allies. The Soviets strive to achieve their objectives without war, but at the same time to prepare for war. Should war occur, they would attempt to deny military objectives to the United States while continuing to achieve their own. They employ a variety of means to accomplish this, among which deception is one of the most important.

Soviet military deception (*maskirovka*) encompasses concealment, camouflage, feints, secrecy, disinformation, diversion, and simulation.[1] It is designed to disorient and mislead the enemy. However, deception is not strictly a defensive or passive endeavor. Rather, it is often linked in Soviet military writings with the notion of achieving surprise (*vnezapnost'*) to defeat the enemy—a central tenet in Soviet military thought.[2]

This chapter examines the impact of Soviet military deception practices on U.S. nuclear strategy and nuclear employment policy. First, trends and developments in U.S. strategy and nuclear employment policy are highlighted to illustrate objectives and capabilities required to implement the strategy. Next, a review is made of intelligence collection and evaluation efforts used to support employment policy, war planning, and targeting. The literature on strategic military deception stresses the key role that intelligence capabilities and decision making procedures play in either increasing or reducing the chance that one nation may succeed in employing deception against another.[3]

Against this background, Soviet efforts are considered that deny military objectives and complicate U.S. strategic planning and intelligence gathering and analysis. These efforts include more than just deception practices, although deception remains the primary focus. Next, an historical note is presented regarding earlier Soviet practices (that is, those of World War II). Previous Soviet deception efforts offer useful insights into current practices. Finally, some theories from a U.S. planner's perspective are offered on how to approach the problem of deception, and how knowledge of Soviet practices may bolster U.S. strategy.

Trends in U.S. Nuclear Strategy and Employment Policy

Goals and Requirements of Strategy

U.S. strategy has been evolving for over two decades.[4] Throughout this period, the fundamental objective of U.S. strategy was, and remains, deterrence—the prevention of conflict. Implementing a strategy based on nuclear deterrence requires a balanced mix of political resolve and military capabilities. Together, these elements are seen as providing the capacity to protect and defend interests vital to the United States and its allies.

U.S. strategy has not been formulated in a vacuum; it has had to be responsive to the changing Soviet threat, a factor that in turn shapes the goals of U.S. policy makers. As is well-known, since the mid-1960's, the Soviet Union markedly improved and augmented its strategic nuclear arsenal. Coupled with this development were Soviet statements on nuclear war, which (after extensive review in the United States in the late 1970's) increasingly suggested that if war were forced on them by the West, they were preparing (perhaps already prepared) to prevail. The United States took these Soviet views into account when structuring its nuclear weapons employment policy (PD-59) in 1979–80. This policy, and later versions (NSDD-13), made *denying* the Soviets *their* objectives and the possibility for achieving victory a central objective of U.S. strategic policy. Thus, as the threat has changed, so have the requirements, in both capabilities and plans, to make nuclear deterrence a credible policy.

Successive administrations have endorsed the notion that the United States must have the ability to fight a nuclear war and to control escalation. The capacity to use forces in a discriminate and flexible manner has long been viewed by U.S. leaders as vital to establishing a credible deterrent. This ability gives policy makers choices besides inaction or automatic escalation to general war. Flexibility also contributes to the war objectives of limiting damage and terminating a conflict in the most expeditious manner, on terms favorable to the United States and its allies. While this goal is desirable and appropriate as a matter of strategic theory, how it is to be accomplished, particularly through the course of a nuclear war, has never been adequately defined. Nor has the United

States acquired the necessary capabilities (forces and C³I) to achieve such an objective.

Official U.S. policy pronouncements also indicate the necessity for capabilities to support prolonged nuclear operations. As Secretary of Defense Caspar Weinberger points out in the fiscal year 1986 Department of Defense Report, the United States cannot only prepare for a short war, which would merely tempt an adversary to believe it could outlast the United States in combat. Rather, to bolster deterrence, the United States must maintain sufficient capabilities to pose to the Soviet Union the unpleasant prospect of a prolonged conflict.

The components that have been identified as necessary to meet the objectives of this strategy include:

A range of targeting options, with enemy military forces and command and control centers as the principal targets, and with collateral damage minimized (industry remains a target, but is thought of as a target of last resort);

A durable command, control, communications, and intelligence (C³I) apparatus that has the capacity not only to survive an initial assault but also to endure in a conflict in order to allow policy makers (among other things) to ascertain the extent of conflict and issue response orders deliberately. Such a system contributes to the goals of controlling escalation and presenting the Soviets with the prospect of a long war, which, it is hoped, will dissuade an initial attack;

Survivable counterforce capabilities sufficiently accurate to destroy Soviet military forces and reduce unwanted collateral damage; and

A secure reserve force that would endure beyond the initial attack to prevent postattack blackmail, and enable the U.S. to be in a position to coerce adversaries into quickly terminating the conflict on favorable terms.

To allow for more flexible and discriminate use of force, the United States developed highly accurate warheads that permit the use of smaller yields to destroy a given target, thus making limited options more feasible. They also limit unwanted damage to facilities and personnel adjoining the intended target. Another acquisition—satellite reconnaissance capabilities—permits a more comprehensive mapping of, and accounting for, Soviet strategic forces and key related facilities. These capabilities also aid the United States in meeting the goals of strategy.

As a result of the assessment of Soviet objectives, counterforce and counterleadership targets are highlighted in U.S. targeting plans. Targeting objectives fall into four categories:[5]

1. Soviet nuclear forces.

2. Military and political leadership.
3. Conventional military forces.
4. Economic and industrial targets.

Plans permit the United States to attack portions of this target set while witholding attack on other portions.

Reconciling Capabilities and Objectives

With the emphasis on greater flexibility and limited responses in U.S. strategic policy, the demands on forces to achieve these objectives inevitably increased. Of particular concern have been the requirements to assure flexibility, survivability, and endurance.

To meet these requirements, U.S. strategic systems should have an ability to attack targets other than those whose location is known and permanently fixed, for example, mobile missiles or dispersed aircraft. Similarly, even when damaged, the U.S. C^3I system must be able to:

> Determine quickly and reliably the nature and objective of an attack;
>
> Promptly select an initial response from among a range of options;
>
> Transmit execution orders for the options chosen;
>
> Execute a coordinated attack; and
>
> Assess the effects of a nuclear exchange on U.S. and enemy targets.

Once the C^3I system is attacked, its capabilities would be severely degraded. Present and programmed capabilities, both forces and C^3I, fall short of meeting this and the other principal requirements of strategy.[6]

Due to Soviet force improvements, the survivability of U.S. forces (particularly ICBMs) and C^3I is also a serious source of concern to many analysts and policy makers. Improvements in warhead design and accuracy are giving the Soviets a growing counterforce capability. Such a capability, along with an indicated doctrine of preemption, raises some troubling prospects about the ability of our forces to launch an attack under any condition of war initiation.

Finally, there is a requirement for an enduring force—meaning a force that could prosecute a war for an extended period of time should that prove necessary, but U.S. policy remains rather vague in this area. Creating a truly enduring force is naturally more costly, not to mention controversial. It is controversial because: (a) not all strategists are persuaded that a nuclear war will be protracted; (b) it is not completely clear how to acquire the capability to endure; and (c) due to budget restrictions, this mission could take resources away from other defense programs. For these reasons, policy has never precisely established how much and what kind of endurance is necessary. Without dissecting this entire issue, suffice it to say that the uncertainties associated with endurance are likely to remain even if the concept is defined more clearly and programs are identified that could carry out the function within the strictures of budget realities.

Intelligence and Decision Making

Intelligence support for nuclear strategy and war planning is a primary task of the U.S. intelligence community. The intelligence process begins with the collection of data, which is then analyzed, evaluated, and finally used to inform policy makers. In the strategic field, much effort is devoted to assessing Soviet intentions and capabilities, as well as to identifying targets for war planning purposes. The United States relies heavily on satellite reconnaissance and other sophisticated technological capabilities to monitor and obtain important information on the Soviet Union, but less elaborate sources, such as human intelligence, are also valuable.

Aside from collection, this information must be evaluated and integrated into strategy, employment policy, and war planning. Because the evaluation process involves making judgmental interpretations about what meaning to attach to key information, the process is potentially susceptible to manipulation and deception. This affects intelligence estimates, the decision making process, and as a result, U.S. strategy and plans.

This can be illustrated with a hypothetical example relating to the targeting of missile silos. Raw intelligence must be evaluated to ascertain the contents and hardness of the silo (measured in pounds per square inch [psi] of blast overpressure) and, in turn, prescribe the type and number of weapons required to destroy or disable it. The Soviets might construct the silo to make it appear harder or softer than it is in reality. If the silo is judged to be harder, extra warheads may be allocated to ensure its destruction, thus expending unnecessary resources. On the other hand, if the silo appears softer, the number of warheads placed on it may be insufficient to accomplish the targeting objective.[7]

The literature on intelligence and decision making stresses that this estimative and interpretive process is an important step in determining whether deception succeeds or fails. As was the case with German mistakes vis-a-vis the Soviets in World War II, this process often hinges on failing to overcome human constraints (for example, preconceptions) to make rational decisions, and/or organizational constraints (for example, standard bureaucratic operating procedures, decision making structure).[8]

Not only are U.S. analysts capable of self-deception, or misperception, these faulty views may be projected onto the opponent, thus engaging in ethnocentrism.[9] One relevant example of this occurred in the 1960's when U.S.

national leaders became convinced that the Soviet Union would halt their ICBM program when they reached parity with the United States.[10]

Another example relates to defenses. Following the signing of the ABM treaty in 1972, many prominent U.S. strategists assumed that the Soviet Union (like the United States) would abandon active defenses. They did not. Such projections cause the United States to misinterpret Soviet behavior and underestimate progress in their strategic programs. Thus another consequence of deception is that it can potentially create a false confidence in the ability to meet the objectives of strategy.

Failures of this kind occur frequently when pervasive uncertainty interferes—as almost always happens in international politics (and even more in wartime military operations). Decision makers and analysts must have some organizational structure, intellectual as well as governmental, simply to function and be capable of responding to great quantities of information. When that information is discordant, decision makers often rely on beliefs or past experiences for interpretation. Those who seek to deceive play on these preconceptions, providing information or signals that reinforce certain views held by decision makers, or that leads them to draw an (incorrect) analogy from a previous episode. Bureaucracies require standard procedures to operate smoothly and avoid paralysis, but they are also potentially vulnerable to deception efforts aimed at reinforcing the need to view and react to information in a predictable manner.

In the case of U.S.–Soviet competition, Soviet deception efforts contain a certain probability of success because of the boundaries formed by open and closed societies. As one Soviet diplomat somewhat caustically remarked at a negotiating forum:

> We [the USSR] know so much about how you [the U.S.] make decisions . . . [and] you know little of how we make decisions, and we are not going to tell you. Because we do know, we have some chance of influencing your decisions. Because you don't know, your chances of influencing ours are limited.[11]

Strategists and intelligence analysts are forced to grapple with the evidence of Soviet intentions and capabilities. They must be continually critical, challenging prevailing assumptions, engaging in competitive analysis, and examining an issue from a variety of perspectives—not just conventional wisdom. The military's proclivity for worst-case analysis might be cited as an example of how a governmental organization (1) socializes its members into a group viewpoint that could be manipulated by a deceiver, (thus serving as a means of distortion causing policy makers to be misled), (2) provides a source for misuse or waste of budgetary resources, or (3) unnecessarily raises public concern.[12] These are among the consequences of successful deception. Because human cognitive processes are being dealt with, there is always a chance for deception to succeed, particularly if what is seen in the data is what is wanted to be seen (for example, with regard to the target base or characteristics of weapons or arms control strategy). This was the mistake of the Germans in World War II, as well as of many others.

Deception and Other Soviet Efforts to Deny U.S. Strategic Objectives

An Historical Note

Contemporary Soviet military literature reveals that deception was extensively and effectively employed in World War II. Given the nature of this type of activity and the frequent inaccessibility to historical documents, it is necessary to be critical and cautious in the U.S. approach to Soviet deception practices. Yet the Soviet record in World War II has been fairly well analyzed and thus offers some useful generalizations and insights. Several themes stand out.

First, there was a pervasive simulation (*imitatsiya*) effort, referring to the tactical use of decoys or dummy installations and forces that drew the enemy away from real targets and, equally important, enticed the enemy to expend resources to destroy false targets. Dummy airbases were frequently constructed and supplied with wooden airplanes. They were often placed in positions that were readily detectable by the Germans, but that concealed the location of real bases nearby and diverted attacks upon them. One Soviet author contends that, as a result of simulation, "from July 1942 to May 1945, about 1,500 attacks were made, and up to 500 tons of bombs dropped on dummy airfields."[13]

In another example from a 1942 campaign, the army planned an attack on its left flank. According to one account, it

> . . . built a concentration of dummy tanks and artillery on its right flank, and added touches of realism by setting off small explosions to simulate firing and by broadcasting the sounds of tank motors.[14]

It is reported that mock tanks, vehicles, guns, aircraft, and dummies of people were also used.

In addition to this type of simulation, there is the description of a Soviet writer of a related effort to conceal air assets:

> The most widespread method involved a total system of operations to conceal the runways, taxi-ways, various structures, parking areas, and aircraft. Dummy bomb craters, ditches, and ravines were made by cutting swaths through the grass. . . . Airfields were often disguised as swampy areas using moss, slag, and grass. At airfields located near forests, aircraft were arranged so

that the tree tops concealed them. Frequently small areas in the shrubs were cleared for aircraft parking sites, and the aircraft themselves were covered with branches. . . . A rarely used airfield was disguised as an abandoned one. Damaged and burned-out vehicles were set-up there; haycocks and haystacks were put up on the landing strip, craters were dug; and buildings made to look half- demolished.[15]

A second related theme that emerges from the history of Soviet deception in World War II is that, in a number of instances, battle plans were devised to present the enemy with plausible alternatives that were identical, except in purpose. This entailed massive deception efforts. Notable examples are the Stalingrad and Belorussian offensives of 1942 and 1944.[16] Both resulted in significant German losses. In operation *Uranus*, for example, the Germans were forced to choose between two real deployments; it was the same for the later operation, *Bagration*. Concealment and simulation were employed in both cases. Troops moved at night, radio silence was maintained, and false deployments were made in open view of the Germans. Secrecy was a key concern at all times. Allegedly only four persons knew of operation *Bagration*.[17]

Historians point out that in these operations, and others, there were concommitant mistakes made by the Germans in assessing which Soviet option would likely materialize, suggesting that the Soviets successfully (wittingly or unwittingly) manipulated German perceptions. One student of this activity, Earl Ziemke, summarizes the German mistakes:

1. The Germans misjudged the extent to which the Soviet regime was capable of mobilizing the nation's human resources and the scale on which it was prepared to expend them. Consequently, the German estimates of Soviet strength were persistently low.
2. The Germans assumed the enemy would act consistently and within the bounds of his presumed limitations.
3. The German command was prone to assume that the best estimate of the enemy's intentions was the one that seemed to promise him the most favorable result in a given set of circumstances. It was arrived at by looking at the situation from the enemy's point of view, and determining what he ought to do next—what his best option was.
4. There was extreme centralization of German evaluative and decision making processes.[18]

The fundamental theme that emerges from these World War II examples is simple: in the end, properly utilized, deception saves men and equipment and contributes to the surprise of the enemy. To be sure, the Soviets suffered extreme losses in World War II, and deception my not have always worked, but catching the enemy offguard can (more often than not) conserve resources due to enemy ill-preparedness, and confusion can contribute to ultimate victory. Perhaps more important, these examples illustrate that the Russians became committed to deception as an integral part of their strategy.

Current Practices: Deception and Other Means to Deny U.S. Objectives

Military Deception. Soviet deception efforts, tested and refined in World War II, were carried forward to the postwar era. The particular concern of this chapter is how deception can be, and is, used to deny the United States strategic objectives and how it can complicate nuclear strategy, employment policy, and targeting plans. Naturally, concealment and simulation of targets are of utmost importance. Not only does it hold, as one Soviet article states

> . . . that the more powerful the means of attack are that the enemy intends to use, the more important it is to force him to expend them on dummy objectives.[19]

Such efforts also increase the survivability of Soviet forces. More broadly, there must be an awareness of other techinques (for example, the military maneuvers conducted on the eve of the invasion of Czechoslovakia) that constitute efforts to deceive and conceal intentions and create surprise to achieve their objectives. With respect to nuclear conflict, these are critical concerns. A review of Soviet nuclear strategy provides a basis for understanding their current deception practices. Specific examples will highlight Soviet military deception techniques.

Western analyses of Soviet military writings suggest that chief among the aims of the USSR in a future war would be the defense of the homeland, occupying key adjacent territory, and neutralizing enemy military forces.[20] The Soviets would seek to end a conflict on their terms. If a conflict were centered in Europe, nuclear strikes would likely be discriminate and focused on military targets, to allow for occupation of the territory and the seizure of functioning industrial assets.

In a war with the United States, Soviet doctrine stresses the value of a large strike against a diverse target set (primarily comprising U.S. nuclear forces and the C^3I apparatus) with the intention of limiting damage to themselves, and causing psychological shock, which perhaps would negate the United States's will to retaliate. Thus, key U.S. political and economic centers could also be targets. At the same time, the Soviets would utilize a variety of means to attempt to ensure the survival and continuity of their government.

Soviet writings imply that escalation is unlikely to be controlled, but some restraint will be observed, if only to conserve forces. The enormous Soviet reservoir of capabilities suggests the retention of large nuclear reserve forces.

More important, their emphasis on the element of surprise in conducting military operations with decisive results obviates or minimizes the enemy potential to respond, let alone substantially escalate.

The interrelation of surprise and deception recur; surprise removes an enemy's capacity to strike back. Nathan Leites summarizes Soviet views of the value of fast-paced offensive operations commencing with surprise: "The greater the enemy's error in target location, . . . the lower his chance of hitting us."[21] One Soviet military authority corroborates this characterization: " . . . the higher the speed of the offensive, the less exposure of the personnel to nuclear flash"[22] (in other words, the smaller the prospect of effective retaliation).

The ability to achieve the goal of surprise requires not only a doctrinal foundation but also the presence of forces capable of executing preemptive counterforce attacks and minimizing the effects of the inevitable (albeit ragged) retaliation. By almost all accounts, the Soviets have come a long way toward possessing such offensive and defensive capabilities; they continue to push ahead in strategic force acquisition and modernization. Aside from the well-publicized trend in the growth of their offensive forces, the Soviets also have taken a number of defensive steps to deny the U.S. confidence in destroying critical targets and the ability to achieve U.S. strategic objectives. This includes increased hardening of missile silos, a move toward mobile ICBMs, active defenses, and deception.

Hardening, or possible superhardening, involves a number of different ICBMs in silos estimated to be capable of withstanding over 4,000 psi in blast overpressure.[23] Certainly such silo hardness could be offset by improved accuracy (for example, the MX and D-5 missiles). For the present, U.S. forces lack such a hard-target capability. This is a result not only of accuracy problems and uncertainty over the degree of Soviet hardening but of numbers. There is a limit to the number of hard targets the United States could place under attack today. Also of concern is the Soviet reload capability for missile silos. Uncertainty exists regarding the numbers, production rate, and location of reload missiles and the Soviet doctrine for their use. Experts disagree as to how quickly reloading could be accomplished; estimates range from one to several days.

Regardless of silo hardness, the Soviets are now making a major investment in mobile ICBMs.[24] This represents an important resource expenditure. Mobile basing is much more costly, both in money and manpower, than deployment at fixed silos. Mobility can greatly reduce vulnerability, primarily because movement and camouflage of such systems can conceal their locations. Tracking and targeting such forces on a near real-time basis is difficult in peacetime, let alone in the period following the outbreak of war. If found, mobile missiles may be relocated before attacking forces can be retargeted.

Soviet defenses are another measure geared to reducing U.S. ability to achieve its objectives. The role of passive defense is a controversial subject for many Western analysts. Some question the extent of Soviet civil defense preparations, the feasibility of such defense, and the implications for the U.S. view of deterrence. The Soviets add to the controversy by denying information about civil defenses and even by deprecation of their own efforts.[25] Nevertheless, passive defense can reduce damage and provide protection of political and military leadership. Clearly it is a requirement of a strategy emphasizing preemption.

Active defense is perhaps even more controversial in the West, for it raises the possibilities of reducing the effects of the enemy's retaliatory attack and supports management of a protracted nuclear battle. The Soviets have deployed the world's most extensive air defense, creating substantial complexities and added costs for the United States to achieve penetration of its strategic bombers, which still carry a large percentage of the total U.S. payload.

They have also continued an active research effort in ballistic missile defense and have deployed ABM systems that press the boundaries permitted by the ABM treaty, using deception at times to conceal their efforts (for example, the Krasnoyarsk radar). According to the CIA, Soviet

> . . . phased-array radars provide improved ballistic missile early-warning, attack assessment, and target tracking. The SA-X-12 system can counter conventional aircraft, cruise missiles and tactical ballistic missiles. It could have the ability to intercept some types of U.S. strategic ballistic missile RVs.[26]

This nascent potential for defending wide areas or key targets complicates U.S. planning by undermining chances of destroying targets, and adding uncertainty to calculations of the effectiveness of plans.

Finally, there is deception, concealment, and simulation. As an additive to Soviet strategy, these efforts further hinder the U.S. capacity to acquire knowledge of Soviet capabilities and war preparations and to discern targets. Certainly the United States is not completely unable to locate targets or gather information on Soviet military plans. Rather, the Soviets are taking a number of measures to misinform and mislead U.S. intelligence, as the following examples show.

In strategic forces, the Soviet move toward mobile ICBMs has already been mentioned. Mobility lends itself to concealment. Launchers can be moved at night or in inclement weather, when reconnaissance capabilities would have some difficulty tracking them. Furthermore, road and rail mobile launchers (such as the SS-20, SS-X-24, and SS-X-25) do not require elaborate prepared facilities and, in fact, can be placed in facilities that are not readily characterized as parts of the nuclear target set. As a result of concealment, in a crisis the United States may not be fully confident of the location of these key targets, especially in light of the inadequacies of the C^3I system. Following a preemptive Soviet attack on the U.S. C^3I, that confidence would decline still further and might affect the willingness to retaliate. There is also a strong likelihood that, due to such efforts, the Soviets will have reserves that the United States will be unable to locate or have plans that permit them to launch reserve missiles without placing them in silos.

Similar activity occurs with regard to submarines. For example, the United States recently uncovered tunnels capable of hiding the largest Soviet SSBNs[27] and there is evidence to suggest the USSR has the capacity to reload SSBNs in protected waters.[28] This type of concealment could put the United States in an unfavorable postattack bargaining situation. ICBMs or SLBMs unaccounted for would leave the United States uncertain as to the size and composition of Soviet reserve forces, thus providing the Soviets with more options and greater flexibility. This added capability could be used to coerce or blackmail the United States or its allies, effectively undermining U.S. strategy.

Along with efforts to conceal or simulate targets, the Soviets use deception to mask the characteristics of weapons systems. Encryption of test data is an important impediment to a reliable assessment of Soviet capabilities, causing the United States to misconstrue weapons characteristics. Encryption is also an obstacle to verifiable arms control agreements. One analyst, William Harris, contends that the Soviets have introduced systematic error into their flight test program as a means of deceiving the United States about missile accuracy.[29] Although certain encryption of telemetry was prohibited in the (unratified) SALT II Treaty, the practice is still used by the Soviets.

One well-known case of deception in arms control negotiations is the SALT I SSBN deception.[30] The Soviets constructed decoy submarines and placed them in normal berthing areas. U.S. intelligence uncovered and counted six SSBNs as operational, allowing the USSR to have a higher level of submarines in the SALT existing level count. The Soviets did not account for disparities. Again, this type of deception contributes to distortions in U.S. estimates of Soviet capabilities and reduces confidence in the ability to conduct and abide by negotiated agreements.

Deception involving general purpose forces (GPF) is also widespread and easier (and usually less costly) to accomplish. Concealment and simulation are favored techniques. This includes creation of dummy targets; covering real targets; underground facilities; and sound, heat, and radio/radar camouflage. The Soviet military lexicon indicates the concern for these forces in a nuclear environment (for example, *zashchita voysk otoruzhiya massovogo porazyhenia* [protection of troops from weapons of mass destruction] and *protivoatomnya zaschita* [anti-atomic defense]).[31] The Soviets also have plans for rapidly dispersing general purpose forces on warning, thus removing many targets from under the U.S. threat and causing the waste of resources on false targets. These plans are known of in general, but well-concealed in detail.

One recent example of deception relating to GPF is the 1983 shoot-down of a Korean civilian airliner that violated Soviet airspace. During this incident, the Soviets mobilized fighters based over 1,000 kilometers away from the intrusion.

According to one analyst, this was done to protect secret air defense assets in the instrusion area from exposure to a U.S. reconnaissance satellite said to be overhead when the incident occurred. By utilizing known assets, the Soviets kept other capabilities hidden.[32]

Electronic warfare and radio deception are additional methods of protecting assets and denying the adversary the use of electronic control systems. Their use is widespread and well-integrated into Soviet operational planning.[33] For example, electronic jamming interferes with U.S. target acquisition or is conducted in a manner (for instance, issuing false instructions [*radiodezinformatsiya*] to mislead the United States on Soviet intentions). Radar reflectors are also used to create interference on enemy radar display screens, while terrain-masking techniques could be used to conceal troops and equipment from enemy reconnaissance and electronic detection. Other radio masking efforts include creation of decoy radio nets, changing of operating frequencies and call signs, or entering into communications without using standard call signs.

A third area of current Soviet deception practices concerns leadership facilities. This deception furthers the Soviet objectives of being able to prosecute a war, maintain governmental continuity, and, possibly, provide for reconstitution. Leadership facilities are dispersed, some constructed underground, some mobile. There are multiple command posts at all echelons. The CIA estimates that

> . . . with as little as a few hours' warning a large percentage of the wartime management structure would survive the initial effects of a large-scale U.S. attack. . . . There are at least 800, perhaps as many as 1,500, relocation facilities for leaders at the national and regional levels.[34]

The range of this estimate reflects some of the uncertainty that the U.S. faces due to secrecy.

The CIA further judges that as a result of having hardened many key facilities, and provided for redundant means of communication,

> it seems highly likely that the Soviets could maintain overall continuity of command and control, although it would probably be degraded and they could experience difficulty in maintaining endurance.[35]

With this Soviet C^3I capability, war-fighting and bargaining potential improve as this capacity detracts from U.S. ability to disable or threaten the Soviet command structure effectively.

A last category in which deception is employed is key industrial targets. The Soviets may have an ability to convert factories for wartime use rapidly, or an ability to harden critical elements of such facilities quickly (for example, turbines or machine tools). They also have plans to protect key industrial personnel through sheltering and evacuation. Again, the details of these plans are concealed. This capability could extend Soviet war-making potential during a prolonged conflict. Underground, or unlocatable, production centers are also of concern.[36]

Perceptions Management. The preceding methods of military deception can be complemented by other techniques, broadly referred to in this volume as perceptions management tactics, which seek to influence official or public opinion in an adversary state, either to confuse that opinion, mislead it, or (it is hoped) pursue a course of action inimical to that state's interest. Several case studies in this book show how the Soviets use propaganda, disinformation, and active measures to achieve these goals. Of particular concern to strategists is Soviet thinking (intentions and preparations) for nuclear conflict. Although limited in public discussion, Soviet professional writings are often at variance with public statements. The Soviets, to be sure, are mindful of the dangers of nuclear war, yet there are strong indications that they seek rather systematically to mislead the West concerning motives, thereby contributing to the possibility of surprise.

During the SALT negotiations in the 1970's, the Soviets encouraged the United States to believe they had accepted the theory of mutual assured destruction and a minimal role for defenses in strategy, while the Soviets were, in fact, building up defenses. They have often encouraged the West to believe they were interested in equitable arms control limits when they appear to be seeking unilateral advantage. Most recently, through an anti-SDI campaign, they have sought to convince the West that they were not pursuing strategic defense technologies comparable to the U.S. SDI, although for many years their capabilities revealed otherwise.[37] If the U.S. analysis of Soviet strategy and doctrine is accurate, these ploys are characteristic and in harmony with their writings on deception and surprise. Perceptions management is significant, for it has a tendency to confuse Western debate and could result in the shaping of decisions to conform to Soviet strategy.[38]

Conclusions

From this chapter and others in this book, it is evident that the Soviets practice deception as an integral part of their strategy. By all accounts, it appears to be widespread and married to other measures to challenge U.S. or Western strategy in peace and in war. The United States needs to be constantly aware of the possibility that deception is being widely used. Continuing efforts will be required to take account of deception in formulating U.S. nuclear strategy and employment policies.

However, the deception challenge needs to be placed in perspective. To assert that the best deception may be unknown is tautological. This discussion has shown how strategic plans and assessments can be misled. For example, by minimizing the threat, the United States may underestimate the capabilities needed to accomplish objective of strategy. By contrast, overestimating the threat may unnecessarily raise international tensions or lead to resource misallocation. Too great a concern for deception could well lead to excessive paranoia or uncalled-for alarmism if Soviet behavior is perceived to be more organized and coordinated than that of the United States—which, of course, is not always the case.[39]

Soviet deception practices are a serious matter, but they are an inevitable product of Soviet society and an integral part of their strategy. Western society and strategy are based on different precepts.

It is the job of intelligence analysts and decision makers to uncover these ploys and reduce their susceptibility to manipulation. Counterintelligence is one method of identifying the pieces of the deception puzzle. In the analytical and decision making area, a judicious use of such tools as competing analysis (or a devil's advocate) can work to overcome preconceptions, biases, bad judgment, or organizational pitfalls. Another effort might involve an institutionalized program or process to provide a check on information critical to the development of nuclear employment policy and war planning.[40]

Such measures are by no means a guarantee for success. In fact, they might have an opposite effect by lending certainty to what may remain an inherently ambiguous situation. But careful use of these and other steps may reduce the chance of successful deception and aid U.S. efforts to implement an effective strategy.

Notes

1. *Maskirovka*, and over 260 related terms, are defined in James T. Reitz, "Lexicon of Selected Soviet Terms Relating to *Maskirovka* Deception", DDB–2460–3–83 (Defense Intelligence Agency, October 1983). Richards Heuer distinguishes military deception from active measures and counterintelligence, two additional elements that can be broadly considered part of Soviet deception practices. With regard to military deception (*maskirovka*), Heuer (like Reitz and other analysts who have examined Soviet writings) identifies three components: strategic, operational, and tactical *maskirovka*. See the discussion in Richards J. Heuer, "Soviet Organization and Doctrine for Strategic Deception," in this volume, and Edgar Ulsamer, "The Fog of War," *Air Force Magazine* 68 (October 1985) p. 76.

2. Nathan Leites, *Soviet Style in War* (New York: Crane Russak, 1982), passim.; and Jennie A. Stevens and Henry S. Marsh, "Surprise and Deception in Soviet Military Thought: Part I," *Military Review* 62 (June 1982) pp. 2–11.

3. For an introduction to this literature, see the contributions in Donald C. Daniel

and Katherine L. Herbig, eds., *Strategic Military Deception* (New York: Pergamon Press, 1982).

4. See Leon Sloss and Marc Dean Millot, "U.S. Nuclear Strategy in Evolution," *Strategic Review* 12 (Winter 1984), pp. 19–28; Colin S. Gray, *Nuclear Strategy and Strategic Planning* (Philadelphia: Foreign Policy Research Institute, 1984); and Henry S. Rowen, "The Evolution of Strategic Doctrine," in Laurence Martin, ed.,*Strategic Thought in the Nuclear Age*, (Baltimore, Md: Johns Hopkins University Press, 1979), pp. 131–156.

5. Harold Brown, *Department of Defense Annual Report Fiscal Year 1982* (Washington, DC: US Government Printing Office, 1981), pp. 41–42.

6. Caspar Weinberger, *Department of Defense Annual Report, Fiscal Year 1986* (Washington, D.C.: U.S. Government Printing Office, 1985), pp. 16, 216–219. Analyses of the strategy/capabilities gap are contained in Gray, *Nuclear Strategy and Strategic Planning*; Jeffrey Richelson, "PD-59, NSDD-13 and the Reagan Strategic Modernization Program," *Journal of Strategic Studies* 6(June 1983), pp. 125–146; Samuel T. Cohen and Joseph D. Douglass, Jr., "Selective Targeting and Soviet Deception," *Armed Forces Journal International* 121 (September 1983), pp. 95–101; Alan J. Vick, "Post-Attack Strategic Command and Control Survival: Options for the Future," *Orbis* (Spring 1985), pp. 95–117; and Bruce G. Blair, *Strategic Command and Control: Redefining the Nuclear Threat* (Washington, D.C.: Brookings Institution, 1985).

7. For a brief examination of how silo hardness (and other variables) would affect damage expectancy, see U.S. Congressional Budget Office, *Modernizing U.S. Strategic Offensive Forces: The Administration's Program and Alternatives* (Washington, D.C.: U.S. Government Printing Office, May 1983), pp. 46–47.

8. On intelligence and the decision making process, see Richards J. Heuer, Jr., "Cognitive Factors in Deception and Counterdeception," and Ronald G. Sherwin, "The Organizational Approach to Strategic Deception: Implications for Theory and Policy," both in Daniel and Herbig, *Strategic Military Deception*, chapters 2 and 3; Raymond L. Garthoff, "On Estimating and Imputing Intentions," *International Security* 2(Winter 1978), pp. 22–32; Richard K. Betts, "Analysis, War, and Decisions: Why Intelligence Failures Are Inevitable," *World Politics* 32(October 1979), pp. 90–110; Shlomo Gazit, "Estimating and Fortune-Telling in Intelligence Work," *International Security* 4(Spring 1980), pp. 36–56; and Robert Jervis, *Perception and Misperception in International Politics* (Princeton, N.J.: Princeton University Press, 1976).

9. Ken Booth, *Strategy and Ethnocentrism* (New York: Holmes and Meier, 1979).

10. Ibid., pp. 46–47.

11. As told to former State Department official, now *New York Times* reporter, Leslie H. Gelb. See "What We Really Know About Russia," *New York Times Magazine*, 28 October 1984, p. 67.

12. Katherine L. Herbig and Donald C. Daniel, "Battle of Wits: Synthesizing and Extrapolating from NPS Research on Strategic Military Deception," Naval Postgraduate School (NPS) January 1981, mimeographed, [used with permission], January 1981), p. 32. Aside from such socialization, bureaucratization, excessive secrecy or politicization can also cause errors. See, Janice Gross Stein, "Military Deception, Strategic Surprise, and Conventional Deterrence: A Political Analysis of Egypt and Israel, 1971–73," *Journal of Strategic Studies* 5 (March 1982), especially pp. 96–97; and Michael I. Handel,

"Intelligence and the Problem of Strategic Surprise," *Journal of Strategic Studies* 7(September 1984), pp. 229–281.

13. Colonel Ye. Simakov, "Air Force Concealment and Deception During Offensive Operations," *Voenno-Istoricheskii Zhurnal* 12(1977), pp. 12–26.

14. Cited in Earl F. Ziemke, "Stalingrad and Belorussia: Soviet Deception in World War II," in Daniel and Herbig, *Strategic Military Deception*, pp. 246–247.

15. Colonel E. Simakov, "Operational Camouflage of Air Assets," *Soviet Military Review* 4(April 1982), pp. 26–27.

16. Ziemke, "Stalingrad," pp. 243–276.

17. Ibid., p. 260.

18. Ibid., pp. 269–271.

19. Major General Engineering Troops A. Limno and Colonel A. Gorkin, "The Effectiveness of *Maskirovka*," *Voennyi Vestnik* 5(1980), pp. 83–85.

20. On Soviet nuclear doctrine, see the analyses in inter alia, Robert P. Berman and John C. Baker, *Soviet Strategic Forces: Requirements and Responses* (Washington, D.C.: Brookings Institution, 1982), pp. 27–37; Donald W. Hanson, "Is Soviet Doctrine Superior?" *International Security* 7(Winter 1982/1983), pp. 61–83; Notra Trulock, III, "Weapons of Mass Destruction in Soviet Strategy," paper presented at Conference on Soviet Military Strategy in Europe, sponsored by Boston Foreign Affairs Group and Royal United Services Institute, Oxfordshire, England, 23–24 September 1984, mimeographed, (used with permission); and U.S. Department of Defense, *Soviet Military Power* (Washington, D.C.: U.S. Government Printing Office, 1985).

21. Leites, *Soviet Style*, p. 131.

22. Colonel V. Savkin, *Voennyi Vestnik* 4(1971), pp. 226–227, cited in Leites, *Soviet Style*.

23. See, for example, Berman and Baker, *Soviet Strategic Forces*, p. 92.

24. Robert M. Gates and Lawrence K. Gershwin, "Soviet Strategic Force Developments," testimony before a joint session of the U.S. Senate Armed Services Committee, Strategic and Theater Nuclear Forces Subcommittee, and the Senate Appropriations Committee Defense Subcommittee, 26 June 1985, p. 1, mimeographed.

25. Harriet Fast Scott and William F. Scott, *The Soviet Control Structure: Capabilities for Wartime Survival*, NSIC Paper No. 39 (New York: Crane Russak, 1983), pp. 98–99.

26. Gates and Gershwin, "Soviet Strategic Force Development," p. 5.

27. Rick Atkinson, "Soviet Tunnels Could Hide Submarines," *Washington Post*, 7 April 1984, p. A–14.

28. U.S. Department of Defense, *Soviet Military Power*, p. 28. Also the U.S. reportedly has evidence that the USSR is placing canvas covers over ballistic missile launch tubes on Typhoon-Class submarines and may be loading SSN-20 SLBMs in clips of two on the submarines. See *Aviation Week and Space Technology* (28 November 1983), p. 17.

29. William R. Harris, "Counterintelligence Jurisdiction and the Double-Cross System by National Technical Means," in *Intelligence Requirements for the 1980's: Counterintelligence*, Roy Godson, ed. (New Brunswick, N.J.: National Strategy Information Center, 1980), pp. 53–82; and Michael Mihalka, "Soviet Strategic Deception, 1955–1981," *Journal of Strategic Studies* 5(March 1982), pp. 63–64.

30. Mihalka, "Soviet Strategic Deception," pp. 73–79; and Thomas E. Dixon and Donald E. Smith, "Deception as a Tactic in Soviet Military Thought," National War College Strategic Studies Report, March 1984, pp. 32–33.

31. Reitz, *Lexicon*, pp. 19 and 38.

32. Yossef Bodansky, "Death by the Book," *Air Force Magazine* 66(December 1983), pp. 36–41. 12 August 1985.

33. Discussions of Soviet electronic warfare practices are contained in Lieutenant Colonel D.B. Lawrence, "Soviet Radio Electronic Combat," *Air Force Magazine* 65(March 1982), pp. 88–91; Jennie A. Stevens and Henry S. March, "Surprise and Deception in Soviet Military Thought: Part II," *Military Review* 62(July 1982), pp. 24–35; and Gerald Green, "Soviet Electronic Warfare," *National Defense* 69(April 1985), pp. 34–42.

34. Gates and Gershwin, "Soviet Strategic Force Development," p. 7.

35. Ibid.

36. Open-source information on underground facilities is slim. See the reference to an underground defense industry plant that suffered a major accident in late 1984 in "Disaster in Russia— Hundreds Killed," *San Francisco Chronicle*, 9 January 1985, p. 12.

37. This view pervades the Soviet publication *Star Wars: Delusions and Dangers* (Moscow: Military Publishing House, 1985).

38. Heuer writes in "Soviet Organization and Doctrine for Strategic Deception" that

. . . a good case can be made that the Soviets modified their public position [on nuclear strategy] but not their actual doctrine in response to Western policy debates, in order to strengthen the hand of those who oppose a strong Western defense posture.

39. See the discussion in Jervis, *Perception and Misperception*, chapters 8 and 9.

40. See the prescriptions contained in the literature cited in note 8. Also see William R. Harris, "A SALT Safeguards Detection Program—Coping with Soviet Deception Under Strategic Arms Agreements," P-6388 (Santa Monica, Calif: Rand Corporation, 1979).

21
Surprise Nuclear Attack

William R. Van Cleave

Introduction

The purpose of this chapter is to address the issue of a Soviet surprise nuclear attack and the possible link between deception and the achievement of surprise. This obviously involves the questions of the advantages to the Soviet Union of surprise, as compared to warning, and of the prudence of the United States planning on receiving effective warning of a Soviet attack.

Warning, surprise, and deception can be fruitfully studied in five categories of Soviet threat. The first three (with which the United States has had ample experience) are discussed in other chapters:

1. Cold war political and economic activities. Nonviolent warfare involving political influence, maneuvering, and subversion (not excluding leadership assassination, either physical or character); propaganda, disinformation, and communications warfare; economic and financial dealings and technology pilfering.[1] These are day-to-day activities designed to strengthen the Soviet side, and to weaken the United States and its alliances.
2. Low-intensity conflict. This category does not exclude activities of the first, but extends as well to state-sponsored terrorism, insurgency and "wars of national liberation," arms flows, and indirect or proxy use of military forces. Seen as a pattern, it involves a strategic action, a struggle for geostrategic position and advantage, and competition over bases.
3. Higher intensity military conflict involving the use of large military units either supported by the Soviets (and in Korea and Vietnam, the Chinese) or actually involving Soviet and Warsaw Pact military forces against Soviet satellites on the periphery of the Soviet Union, and elsewhere. These are openly imperialistic activities involving armed force.

Since World War II, there have been several examples of Category 2 threats (Africa, Iran, Central America, and the Philippines) and Category 3 threats (Korea, Hungary, Czechoslovakia, Afghanistan, and the Yom Kippur War). In each case, both strategic and operational surprise has been an important element, despite strategic warning. In each case there was warning, but nevertheless there was surprise. There was also deliberate deception, including military activities prior to the attack, which were designed to weaken resistance and to condition or desensitize the target state and their allies to warning of a threat.

There are two additional categories of threats with which the United States fortunately has had no post-World War II experience, but that are of deep concern. Even though their probability is undoubtedly lower than the preceding threats, the stakes are higher and the effects would be potentially more immediate and disastrous. These are also categories in which the questions of warning, surprise, and deception are central:

4. A Soviet/Warsaw Pact military attack on Western Europe.
5. A Soviet strategic nuclear attack on the United States.

These are the two categories that will be addressed in this chapter, with emphasis on the latter.

Surprise and Strategic Warning

For most of the period since the late 1950's, the possibility and problem of surprise attack on U.S. strategic nuclear deterrent forces (SNF) have been taken very seriously by planners and policy makers, even though the politico-military likelihood of such an attack was generally judged to be very low. Since the Rand Corporation bomber-vulnerability study of the 1950's, the Gaither Committee Report of 1957, and the development and deployment of long-range ballistic missiles, it has seemed prudent to U.S. decision makers to plan deterrent forces on the basis of their survivability against surprise attack. Force sufficiency was assessed in terms of forces surviving a "well-executed surprise attack," given existing and projected Soviet capabilities.

Unfortunately, a combination of Soviet force improvements, and relative neglect on the part of the United States, has dramatically increased the military feasibility and attractiveness of a surprise Soviet attack on U.S. deterrent forces. As Zbigniew Brzezinski observed:

> The advent of increasingly numerous and accurate systems is making it possible for planners of a strategic attack to envisage a first strike that leaves the opponent strategically crippled, capable of only a spasmodic, disorganized, and strategically aimless response—or none at all.[2]

Dr. Brzezinski went on to point out the asymmetrical vulnerability of the United States to such an attack, and the advantages of a sudden surprise attack over a presumably preemptive strike resulting from a crisis:

> From an offensive point of view, a sudden attack by highly precise and very numerous nuclear weapons is more profitable than an exchange resulting from a political crisis prompting both sides to gear their forces to a maximum alert.[3]

Dr. Brzezinski is correct, and there can hardly be any more dangerous threat to the United States, or any more important national security issue. In an understatement he warned that "it would be escapist to assume that Soviet planners would choose to ignore such an option altogether."[4]

It seems a matter of sublime irony that, as the threat of a surprise nuclear disarming attack has objectively increased, the U.S. national security apparatus has subjectively reduced its importance as a planning factor and, instead, has increasingly rejected its plausibility. The pronounced tendency today is to base force planning on the assumption that the United States has received, identified, and reacted effectively to strategic warning. This assumption leads to a conclusion that any Soviet nuclear attack (believed *highly* unlikely in *any* case) would emerge from a crisis during which our forces would have been placed on generated alert. Consequently, strategic warning, coupled with ample tactical warning from an unevenly spaced attack, would allow most of the bombers and virtually all of the ICBM force to be launched safely (viz the Scowcroft Commission Report).

As used here, *strategic warning* is that advanced warning of a future, or even imminent, attack that provides the basis for advanced politico-military alert, force dispersal and readiness, and other war preparations. Tactical warning is the warning that an attack has in fact commenced. The Joint Chiefs of Staff (JCS) definitions of these terms are consistent with this usage:

> *Strategic Warning*: Notification that enemy initiated hostilities may be imminent. This notification may be received from minutes, to hours, to days, or longer, prior to the initiation of hostilities.
>
> *Tactical Warning*: A notification that the enemy has initiated hostilities. Such warning may be received any time from the launching of the attack until it reaches target.[5]

It should be noted that for strategic warning the phrase "provides the basis for" was used. Frequently, when the term *strategic warning* is used it is merely assumed that it is correctly perceived and effectively acted upon. Neither may be the case. Indeed, historically the converse more generally has been true.

Nonetheless, the assumption of effective strategic and tactical warning has edged its way into most U.S. assessments of the adequacy of nuclear forces surviving an attack. This leads to the dangerous proposition that we need not structure all of the major force components to cope with a well-executed surprise attack. A Soviet nuclear attack, it is assumed, would find U.S. C³I sufficiently intact for reliable attack assessment, and for coordination, control, and operation of U.S. forces. C³I would be at peak anticipatory preparedness at the time of attack. Additionally, the highest force alert rates would have been generated; the decisions and steps necessary for a possible successful ICBM launch on tactical warning would have been taken; three-quarters (as against one-quarter) of the bomber force would be loaded, alerted, and dispersed; and three-quarters of the SSBN force would be at sea and alerted.

The analysis in this chapter indicates that *if* strategic warning were unambiguously received and acted upon as effectively as possible, U.S. nuclear deterrent forces would be significantly more robust than if the nation were caught by surprise. The problem with this is at least fourfold:

The assumption of effective strategic warning flies in the face of historical experience, especially for democracies;

The Soviets manifestly attach great importance to surprise and should be expected to use every means, including deception, to achieve it;

A force that relies upon strategic warning becomes very vulnerable to surprise; and

The difference between the capabilities of an alerted force and those of a surprised force is an important measure of the enemy's incentive to achieve surprise.

For both intercontinental and theater attacks, the Soviets have methodically developed a counterforce surprise attack capability, which they have supplemented by other important measures that would further reduce the likelihood and effectiveness of any retaliatory strike. Soviet efforts have not been equally matched by U.S. measures to reduce the vulnerability and maintain the effectiveness of its forces. The combination has made surprise attack more feasible than at any time in the nuclear era. The U.S. disbelief in surprise attack actually contributes to its feasibility, not only by retarding force preparedness for surprise attack, but also by reinforcing the inherent tendency to disbelieve signals warning of such an attack. Consider the following propositions:

Surprise attack could be successfully accomplished even if there is warning.

There is no such thing as unequivocal strategic warning, and possibly no such thing as unequivocal tactical warning until it is too late.

Psychologically and politically, U.S. leaders would be most unlikely to respond effectively to ambiguous warning.

Soviet deception would reinforce the ambiguities.

The literature substantiating these propositions is rich; much of it is cited elsewhere in this book and in the bibliography. Roberta Wohlstetter's classic study of Pearl Harbor concluded succinctly: "We cannot count on strategic warning;"[6] as did another study on the phenomenon of surprise despite warning: "There is always some warning . . . yet surprise seldom fails."[7] This referred to effective *military* surprise despite *strategic* warning. Harvey DeWeerd's study of the Korean War pointed out how the United States was surprised, despite warning:

> We were surprised twice in Korea in spite of multiple indications of coming events and an abundance of intelligence data. . . . It was not the absence of intelligence which led us into trouble, but our unwillingness to draw unpleasant conclusions from it. We refused to believe what our intelligence told us was in fact happening, because it was at variance with the prevailing climate of opinion in Washington and Tokyo. We also refused to believe our intelligence because it would have been very inconvenient if we had; we would have had to do something about it.[8]

Strategic warning is too often found "to have been" rather than "to be"; that is, it has been recognized after the fact rather than at the time it occurred, prior to the attack. Intelligence constituting strategic or tactical warning would have to be interpreted accurately with very high confidence in its accuracy and reliability—all the more so for warning of a nuclear attack. In the United States, the procedures that would be involved in evaluation, confirmation, and transmission of such intelligence, and in making decisions from this basis, are likely to be complicated, conservative, and time-consuming. All stages would involve judgment, subjectivism, and sheer doubt. They would involve difficult decisions ranging from whether (and of what) to inform higher authority; to whether to take the steps to place forces on generated alert (with a risk that this very action might escalate a crisis or precipitate the attack we wished to avoid); to the final decision to launch forces. (Given accident probabilities, even the decision to launch bombers with nuclear payloads is a difficult one and one that has not been made for a considerable period of time.)

When timely decisions would have to be made on whether forces are to be launched, the information available—both for strategic warning, and the early stages of tactical warning—would probably be partial and questionable. It could well be obscured in a fog of Soviet disinformation and deception; it could come after a period of Soviet conditioning and political deception, and during acts of Soviet operational and technical deception.

On the other hand, successfully conducting a surprise nuclear attack might require no strenuous conditioning or deceptive activities by the Soviets. Warning is apt to be inherently ambiguous until too late. Signals indicating the possibility (perhaps even the fact) of a surprise nuclear attack would be those most resisted by U.S. leadership. The realization that an attack is imminent, or underway, would come slowly and reluctantly. The strong disbelief in a surprise nuclear attack makes it likely that warning signals of such an attack would also be disbelieved as long as possible. For NATO, all of these encumbrances would be multiplied.

Surprise and the Soviet View

Throughout history, the great military commanders and strategists have emphasized the importance of surprise: strategic, operational, and tactical. They have written of the utility of deception, concealment of intent, disinformation, and the masking of military preparations in achieving surprise, and victory. When contemporary Soviet writers emphasize the value—virtually the necessity—of surprise, they have a rich, historical tradition to draw upon. They also have an ageless Slavic and Russian tradition. As John Dziak explains in his chapter on Soviet deception, "strategic deception, whether military or political, has been an integral feature of the Slavic tradition." It was absorbed by the tsars and has been systematically developed and modernized by the Soviets. Secrecy, deception, and disinformation are intrinsic and deeply ingrained characteristics of the Soviet system and its approach to the world. They are also cardinal elements of Soviet strategy.

The United States could well be surprised by a Soviet attack without sophisticated Soviet deception. However, deception to achieve surprise is standard Soviet theory and practice, and skillful use of it would certainly enhance the effectiveness of surprise.

Contemporary Soviet military thought and strategy emphasize the overriding importance of surprising the enemy, both strategically and tactically. They also emphasize the importance of *maskirovka* (deception) in achieving surprise. Surprise and *maskirovka*, in fact, are virtually inseparable. This strongly held view extends to nuclear attack.[9]

It is well-established that Soviet nuclear policy and doctrine stress preparedness for nuclear war and victory in nuclear war—the disruption of the enemy's strategy, the destruction of the enemy's weapons systems and defeat of his military forces, the minimization of damage to the sources of Soviet power, and the assurance of a postwar military balance favoring the USSR as heavily as possible. This policy has dictated the development of nuclear war-fighting capabilities based upon counterforce, defense, and strong nuclear reserves. The policy is also at the basis of Soviet emphasis on nuclear surprise and the deployment of systems increasingly capable of surprise attack.

Soviet military literature indicates that the Soviets believe that surprise attack could be the determinative event of a nuclear war; that a surprise attack could strategically disrupt and even forestall the enemy's use of nuclear weapons; and that surprise attack is feasible. It must be expected that the Soviets would resort to all feasible measures to achieve surprise, particularly considering how vulnerable the U.S. and NATO military deployments are to surprise. The Soviets probably would forego attack preparations that might improve their military strength if those preparations would also deny them the element of surprise. At the very least, the Soviets should be expected to conceal or obscure such preparations by a combination of political and military deception. Soviet military literature discusses the active supply of political disinformation and the concealment of preparatory measures as important means of successful surprise.

In the 1960s, the Soviets apparently examined the question whether modern surveillance technology reduced the prospects of surprise nuclear attack, or whether advanced missile systems coupled with countermeasures against surveillance systems enhanced the prospects, and concluded that the latter is the case. Soviet military literature is consistent in emphasizing the role of surprise under contemporary conditions, and it frequently couples the "unexpected use of nuclear weapons" with both strategic and tactical surprise. The Soviet *Dictionary of Basic Military Terms* proclaims that the unexpected use of nuclear weapons is among the ways to achieve decisive surprise.

Surprise and NATO

NATO planning for the contingency of a Soviet Pact attack has always assumed at least several days of effective strategic warning, with ample time not only to disperse forces and man designated defense positions, but also to reinforce from the United States:

> The standard planning assumption is that NATO would acquire clear warning of Warsaw Pact intentions to attack, would begin its mobilization and deployment within a few days after the Warsaw Pact, and would have time to build up its defenses. General Alexander Haig, former Supreme Allied Commander, Europe, stated that NATO would count on eight to fourteen days warning time.[10]

NATO nuclear weapons are customarily kept in a very few locations, or aim points, relative to U.S. SNF aim points and relative to the numbers of SS-20/22 war heads available to the USSR; and these few critical targets—kasernes, air bases, and storage sites—are all undoubtedly well-known to the Soviets. Thus, NATO's nuclear deterrent is highly vulnerable to surprise attack, especially by theater ballistic missiles. The nuclear deterrent posture of NATO in Europe historically has been based far less on the threat of surprise attack than have the U.S. SNF, which until recently were based upon the threat of a well-executed surprise attack. That test has never been applied to theater nuclear forces in Europe. Largely this has been due to the pressure of necessity: politically, economically, and militarily it has not been deemed possible to posture or defend against a surprise nuclear attack. On the other hand, it was believed possible to make the U.S. SNF adequately survivable against surprise attack *without* depending upon missile launch-on-warning.

NATO's accommodation to "reality," however, has taken a hypocritical, imprudent, and possibly self-deluding turn. NATO now merely assumes and plans on having precisely the strategic warning time needed for transition from peacetime to reinforced mobilization. Because the nuclear posture is so highly vulnerable to surprise nuclear attack by relatively few Soviet weapons, and because NATO allies for various reasons are unable to cope with that, it is assumed that such an attack will not happen.

Yet, in recent years, Soviet theater surprise attack capability has improved dramatically, and it must be assumed, deliberately. As Secretary of Defense Weinberger has pointed out, the SS-20 is well-designed for surprise attack, and for launching without lengthy or ostensible preparations, but so are the shorter range SS-22 and SS-23. The Supreme Allied Commander, Europe, General Bernard Rogers, has openly acknowledged that the Soviets have greatly improved their ability to attack across the board without warning. Yet he denies the likelihood of such an attack (indeed, he denies the likelihood of *any* attack) as a matter of faith—a plerophory. General Rogers has emphasized the need to improve NATO's ability to respond effectively to *ambiguous* warning, but that is as far as it has gone.

By the very nature of the alliance, NATO is almost certainly going to require *days* to react to warning of even slight ambiguity. If the United States is acting alone, it is conceivable that it might react promptly to warning of an attack; but in an alliance such as NATO, this is virtually impossible. Moreover, NATO has been conditioned by the Soviets not to expect an attack, not to be alarmed by massive Warsaw Pact military exercises (from which an attack might be launched), and not to respond to crises and Soviet military moves within Eastern Europe with advanced stages of alert, much less mobilization. Soviet disinformation and deception could surely mask attack preparations; and Western European leaders would likely relax with alacrity to any apparent damping of a crisis that threatened to escalate. Thus, the assumption that NATO would have effective and useable warning of several days is not only highly questionable, it is politically and logically ridiculous.

The more capable of a surprise counterforce attack Soviet forces become, the more NATO leaders and commanders deny that possibility and rely on strategic warning. This is a highly dangerous situation. However, it is one that is also emerging in the United States in regard to a surprise Soviet counterforce attack on the U.S. SNF.

U.S. Strategic Nuclear Forces and Surprise Attack

One of the major issues in strategic force planning today is whether the United States should change (or accept the change apparently underway) from an SNF posture that does not critically depend upon the assumption of strategic warning and generated alert, to a posture that does. It may be argued that a well-coordinated surprise attack on all elements of the U.S. strategic force TRIAD is so improbable that the United States does not need to resort to the expense of a force based upon that contingency. Increasingly, assessments of force adequacy produced by the Pentagon assume that U.S. forces are on generated alert when attacked, and that our systems and procedures for controlling, launching, and coordinating these forces work effectively. With such assumptions, U.S. strategic deterrent forces look fairly impressive,[11] and will become more so as the B-1 and cruise missiles enter the force, and improvements are made in C^3I. Table 21–1 reasonably depicts the force inventory, the generated alert force, and the day-to-day force. (The numbers have intentionally been rounded off and approximated to avoid any question of classification.)

But is it prudent to plan on the assumption of strategic warning, or even early tactical warning? Would the United States be justified in basing its posture critically on such expectations? Even if it took a severe crisis to raise the possibility of a Soviet attack, does it follow that U.S. forces would still not be caught by surprise? In the past, U.S. policy has been not to risk unfavorable answers to these questions, but to base force sufficiency on the contingency of being caught by surprise, and of riding out an attack (except for bomber forces).

In the past, the principles of strategic and crisis stability have dictated that the United States not allow *any* of the major strategic force components to become vulnerable to either strategic or tactical surprise. However, the Soviets have developed forces to produce that vulnerability—at least to the land-based forces and to key C^3 elements. The U.S. reaction has principally been to increase dependence on launch-on-warning, despite the many uncertainties and risks inherent in that dependence. The Scowcroft Commission Report on strategic nuclear force modernization essentially argued that a coordinated surprise attack on bombers and ICBMs would be too difficult due to timing problems; that the United States would be able to launch the ICBM force not on warning of an imminent attack, but on tactical warning provided by necessarily earlier attacks on bomber bases. This is not the place to address that proposition analytically. Suffice it to say that it has been addressed and debated for many years (back to the 1969 Safeguard ABM debate at least) and that the general conclusion has always been that while difficult, a coordinated attack on the two forces is feasible. Or, as one of the authors of the Scowcroft Commission Report put it when he was Secretary of Defense:

> It is equally important to acknowledge, however, that the coordination of a successful attack is not impossible, and that the "rubbish heap of history" is filled with authorities who said something reckless could not or would not be done.[12]

Launch-on-warning is not a satisfactory solution to the problem of ICBM vulnerability. It is an approach that carries both low confidence and high danger. It carries the dual risk that the force could or would not be launched when required (very probable for a variety of reasons), or that it might be launched by mistake (less probable despite the fallibility of warning systems). Launching a significant fraction of the force may be feasible under conditions of strategic warning (generated alert) when a possible Soviet attack is anticipated rather than disbelieved, when C^3I systems are finely tuned to their peak performance, and if political decision makers and military commanders have made difficult contingent decisions and are assembled to make immediate final decisions on receipt of tactical warning. Even then, there most likely would be initial disbelief, confusion, and delay, all of which could be reinforced by Soviet deception and disinformation. These problems would be compounded by the danger, approaching certainty, that even counterforce launch-on-warning strikes would trigger more massive Soviet attacks against U.S. military, industrial, and administrative targets.

All of this indicates the risks of relying upon our forces being in a warned, generated alert posture and being successfully launched on warning. The strategic differences involved in this risk constitute the Soviet incentive for surprise, as well. The strategic difference between the generated alert and launched on warning force, and the day-to-day (surprised) force, would be greater than the numbers alone indicate when the particular forces likely to survive in each case are taken into account along with U.S. strategic doctrine and objectives. Moreover, the day-to-day force intuitively seems more vulnerable to tactical surprise; that is, less sensitive to early tactical warning than the alerted force. More survivors, along with somewhat more flexible and significantly more counterforce weapons, would be expected from an alerted force than from the day-to-day force. Certainly more bombers would escape, and there would be the possibility of launching some portion of the ICBM force on tactical warning. The judgment contained here is that a successful launch of the ICBM force, when not on generated alert, is highly unlikely (virtually impossible in my own view) for a variety of technical, timing, and political considerations. It is possible that some portion of the force could be launched on tactical warning if it were expected, and certain crucial decisions had been made.

That situation also exists for the bomber force. Not only would a much larger percentage of the bomber force be loaded with nuclear munitions, alerted, and dispersed if there were effective strategic warning, but a larger percentage probably would escape their bases if tactical warning were anticipated. Certainly crews would be more alert, but it is more than that. The Commander in Chief of the Strategic Air Command is most reluctant to launch nuclear-loaded bombers on ambiguous tactical warning, particularly in apparent peacetime. He is accustomed to receiving occasional false alarms and experiencing occasional breakdowns of his warning and communications system. These occurrences reinforce the ambiguity of warning signals, and they increase the reluctance to launch bombers.

It might be argued that U.S. intelligence and warning systems are highly sophisticated and greatly diminish the probability that our forces would be surprised. This is not an unquestionable argument. Many of the systems and processes we depend upon, not only for seeking and receiving information, but also for analyzing, sorting, confirming, routing, and communicating the information, are fragile and vulnerable to attack and to a variety of countermeasures, including deception. Many are frankly undependable. It is most questionable whether they have kept up with available countermeasures; it is even questionable whether they can perform adequately in emergencies free of active countermeasures. Moreover, they are susceptible to conditioning. The enemy "may create a normal pattern by a sequence of exercises or penetrations of the warning system before the attack."[13]

Perhaps the major problem with relying on strategic warning is that it becomes a rationalization for not taking the necessary measures for improved force survivability against surprise attack. This then produces a situation in which there is an important strategic difference between the survivors of an alerted force, and those of a surprised force. This difference might be an important measure of the Soviet surprise attack incentive.

Tables 21–2 and 21–3, and figures 21–1 and 21–2, depict this illustratively. Table 21–2 suggests survivors in three generated alert attack scenarios: one where there is successful ICBM launch on tactical warning, one where there is partial ICBM launch-on-warning, and one where there is none. Table 21–3 hypothesizes surprise attack, post-attack forces.

The incentive for surprise attack might be measured either by comparison of the surprised surviving forces with the initial inventory, or with the generated alert survivors. In the first comparison, an impressive peacetime inventory of 10,000 warheads and 3,600 equivalent megatons (EMT) is cut to 2,500 warheads

Table 21-1
Assumed January 1986 Force

System	Warheads	EMT
Inventory		
1,000 ICBM	2,000	1,200
625 SLBM	5,000	900
250 Bombers	3,000	1,500
Total	10,000	3,600
Generated Alert		
95% ICBM	1,900	1,140
75% SLBM (27 boats)	3,700	660
75% Bombers	2,250	1,100
Total	7,850	2,900
Day-to-Day		
95% ICBM	1,900	1,140
55% SLBM (20 boats)	3,000	500
25% Bombers	750	360
Total	5,650	2,000

Table 21-2
Post-Attack Forces—Generated Alert

	Warheads	EMT
Survivors: Scenario 1		
75% ICBM[a] (Fully successful LOW)	1,500	900
60% SLBM[a]	3,000	550
50% Bombers[a]	1,800	900
Total	6,300	2,350
Survivors: Scenario 2		
37-1/2% ICBM (50% successful LOW)	750	450
60% SLBM[a]	3,000	550
60% Bombers[a]	1,800	900
Total	5,550	1,900
Survivors: Scenario 3		
5% ICBM	100	60
60% SLBM[a]	3,000	540
60% Bombers[a]	1,800	900
Total	4,900	1,500

[a] Alert weapons X .8 systems reliability

Table 21-3
Post-Attack Forces—Surprise Attack

Survivors	Warheads	EMT
5% ICBM	100	60
45% SLBM[a]	2,400	400
Zero Bomber	-0-	-0-
(5% Bomber)[b]	(150)	(75)
Total	2,500	460

[a] At-sea weapons times 0.8 systems reliability.
[b] Some bombers escape on tactical warning. Situation improves as B-1 is deployed.

and 460 EMT. In the second comparison, there is also a substantial difference for each of the three scenarios, the situation improving or worsening depending upon ICBM launch-on-warning variations.

The generated alert scenarios should also be viewed with the understanding that U.S. forces cannot be maintained on generated alert for very lengthy periods; and U.S. forces coming off of relatively protracted periods of generated alert would be *even less robust and ready* than forces in the normal day-to-day posture. Crew fatigue would be high for all forces, as would systems fatigue. More bombers would be down for maintenance. More SSBNs would be in port for resupply and crew rotation. C^3I would probably be degraded. And, the energy and alertness of key political and military personnel might be decreased.

A U.S. posture that relied on generated alert, then, could be more vulnerable to Soviet deception than one that did not. The Soviets could gain even more from a surprise attack immediately following a crisis and stand-down of U.S. forces than one during normal day-to-day alert. This, of course, increases the problem of Soviet political and strategic deception. The Soviets might seek to defuse a crisis prior to a surprise attack by any number of political overtures, indications of reasonableness and a desire to negotiate, and apparent moderation of objectives. Simultaneous expressions of anxiety and warnings about the crisis getting out of hand would increase inclinations of Western leaders to reduce military alerts. With skillful deception, Western leaders could be led to believe that the risk of war had passed.

It might be noted that the forces surviving a hypothetical surprise attack as shown by table 21-3 are very close to the 400 EMT on-target assumed for "assured destruction" toward the end of the McNamara secretaryship. This may be viewed with alarm; that willy-nilly, despite all of our efforts to escape that view of deterrence, U.S. residual force capabilities will be much closer to assured destruction criteria than to those now established. Alternatively, the position may be taken that a surviving 400 EMT assured destruction capability is adequate.

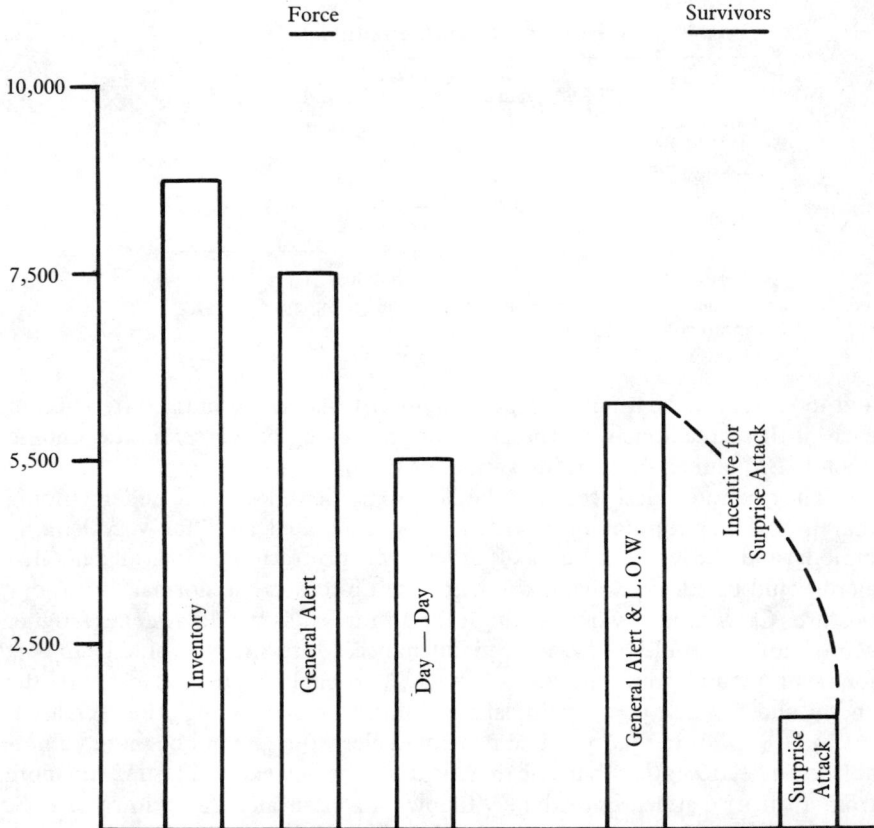

Figure 21-1. Warheads

In judging the adequacy of the U.S. forces that would survive a Soviet first strike, the doctrine, missions, and objectives that have been set for these forces must be considered. These have evolved over time, but their central features have been well-established and reaffirmed by successive administrations for at least a dozen years. The chapter in this book by Leon Sloss sets them forth clearly. As he says:

> Successive administrations have endorsed the notion that the U.S. must have the ability to fight a nuclear war and to control escalation. The capacity to use forces in a discriminate and flexible manner has long been viewed by U.S. leaders as vital to establishing a credible deterrent.

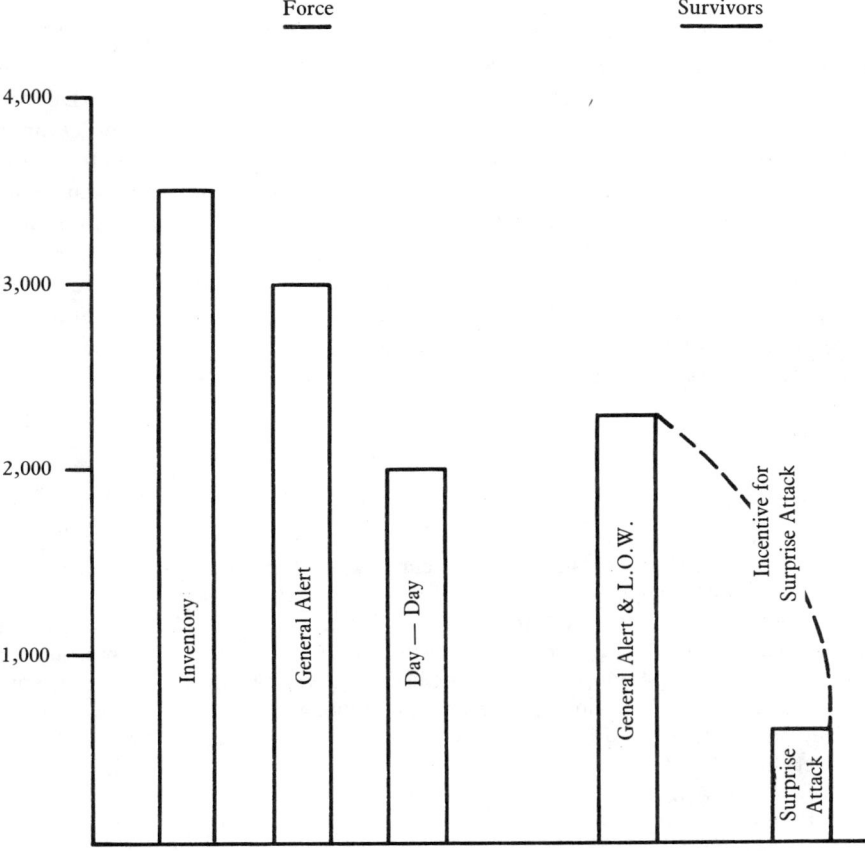

Figure 21–2. EMT

This includes the selective ability to destroy soft and hard military targets, while still retaining a secure reserve force. The 400 EMT (essentially in SLBM forces) surviving the hypothetical surprise attack hardly meets such requirements.

Conclusions

Surprise nuclear attack is feasible and in the interests of the Soviet Union in the event that nuclear war seems to them to be imminent, unavoidable, or desireable. Soviet deception, including concealment of intent, could reinforce the existing U.S. disbelief in surprise nuclear attack, and increase the probability of surprise.

Surprise attack should be the continuing standard for evaluating the adequacy of our strategic nuclear forces; it should be taken more seriously for the planning of the NATO defense posture. Yet, the assumption of effective strategic warning dominates both. That assumption makes U.S. and NATO forces appear more healthy than they actually are. It is a risky and imprudent assumption for planning purposes. This is not to suggest that measures to enhance our ability to detect and evaluate warning, and to respond effectively to ambiguous warning, should not be pursued. Nor is it suggested that in the event of strategic warning, measures to improve force survivability and capability should not be sought; but only that the adequacy of our forces should not rest upon the assumption of having effective strategic or even tactical warning. The self-deception that this introduces would only make Soviet deception more effective, and surprise more feasible.

Notes

1. Soviet efforts to obtain Western technology by legal or illegal means are well-established, documented, and chronicled. Less well-known is Soviet economic or financial penetration. For example, the media only recently reported the Soviet attempt a decade ago to gain secret control of four northern California banks. The operation was discovered in time and stopped by U.S. intelligence. Soviet benefits could have included inside access to the U.S. financial, credit, and banking system; leverage over Silicon Valley high-technology firms; additional access to U.S. technology. "Soviet Aims a Mystery in Bid for U.S. Banks," *Los Angeles Times*, 17 February 1986, p. 1.

2. "From Arms Control to Controlled Security," *Wall Street Journal*, 10 July 1984, editorial page.

3. Ibid.

4. Ibid.

5. *Dictionary of Military and Associated Terms*, U.S. Joint Chiefs of Staff, pub. 1 (Washington, D.C.: U.S. Government Printing Office, 1972).

6. Roberta Wohlstetter, *Pearl Harbor: Warning and Decision* (Stanford, Calif.: Stanford University Press, 1962).

7. Richard K. Betts, "Surprise Despite Warning: Why Sudden Attacks Succeed," *Political Science Quarterly* (Winter 1980–81): p. 553.

8. H.A. DeWeerd, "Strategic Surprise in the Korean War," *Orbis* 6(Fall 1962): pp. 451–452.

9. For Soviet policies and views pertaining to nuclear war and surprise, see inter alia, the U.S. Air Force series of translated Soviet military publications, *Soviet Military Thought*; Joseph Douglass and Amoretta Hoeber, *Selected Readings from Military Thought (Voyennaya Mysl')* (U.S. Governement Printing Office, Washington, D.C.: 1982); William T. Lee and Richard F. Staar, *Soviet Military Policy Since World War II* (Stanford, Calif.: Hoover Institution Press, 1986); and other citations in this book. For readings on deception and surprise, see the references in Donald Daniel and Katherine Herbig, *Strategic Military Deception* (New York: Pergamon Press, 1982), and Zell Stanley, *An*

Annotated Bibliography of the Open Literature on Deception, N–2332–NA (Santa Monica, Calif.: The Rand Corp., December, 1985).

10. Major Don Mercer, USA, "The Warsaw Pact Short-Warning Nuclear Attack," *Military Review* (October 1980), p. 27.

11. Even so, it must be pointed out that even with those assumptions, the U.S. SNF fall well short of the requirements of officially established doctrine and objectives—a situation that extends into the foreseeable future. See W.R. Van Cleave, "U.S. Strategic and Arms Control Policy," in Dennis Bark, ed., *To Promote Peace: U.S. Foreign Policy in the Mid-1980s* (Stanford, Calif.: Hoover Institution Press, 1984); and "Committee on the Present Danger, Can America Catch Up?" *The U.S.-Soviet Military Balance* (Washington, D.C.: 30 November 1984).

12. Harold Brown, U.S., Department of Defense, *Annual Report to Congress, FY-1980* (Washington, D.C.: United States Government Printing Office, 1979), p. 81.

13. Roberta Wohlstetter, "The Pleasures of Self-Deception," *Washington Quarterly* (Autumn 1979): p. 54.

22
Space, Intelligence, and Deception

Angelo M. Codevilla

The widely held belief that the function and location of all objects in space are readily apparent and that no significant fact on earth can long be hidden from optical and electronic devices operating from the vantage point of space is wrong. In fact, the function, location, and even the existence of objects in space are subject to concealment and deception to an extent that is arguably greater than for objects on the earth's surface. Moreover, when operating from space, optical and electronic intelligence devices are as inherently susceptible to several kinds of deception as they would be if they were operating from any other location—possibly more. Hence, intelligence about and from the high ground of space must be undertaken only with full consciousness of the likelihood of deception.

This has important implications for military planning as well as for intelligence. For example, through deception, one may dramatically improve the survivability of space-based military assets, including communications and intelligence, as well as of possible antimissile platforms. Through deception, one may enhance the performance of such assets. Also, to the extent that one understands the other side's space-based intelligence collectors, exposure to them can be managed so as to lead the other side's analysts to deceptive conclusions about one's own strategic plans. In tactical situations, space-based collectors may be fooled by more straightforward measures.

Conversely, because the United States depends on space far more than does the Soviet Union for knowledge of its principal adversary, the Soviet Union's ability to take advantage of the opportunities for deception that are inherent in space intelligence should be of interest to all Americans involved in intelligence and strategic planning.

This chapter explains how the peculiar characteristics of intelligence about, and from, space lend themselves to deception. Specifically, it examines how the United States may take advantage of the opportunities that these characteristics offer to guard against Soviet deception while itself making use of deception.

The study necessarily has two distinct foci: intelligence gathered from, or with the aid of, platforms in space and intelligence gathered about objects in space. Both kinds of collection make use of the same physical principles and of technical devices that are related to one another. Hence, we begin by examining how these physical principles define the role of space in modern intelligence. The kinds of deception practicable on these two distinct kinds of intelligence are very different. Hence, each kind must be examined separately, along with its corresponding forms of deception. Concurrently we must note whither leads the direction of technical trends. Finally, we offer some observations about how planners of U.S. intelligence and U.S. military operations can take into account the several possibilities for deception that we have described.

Given the sensitive nature of the subject, this unclassified treatment must stick close to first principles. We will not discuss the performance of specific U.S. systems or Soviet systems. Our discussion will be confined to how, given modern technology, such systems (whether or not they exist) might perform, and how either side might practice deception on systems of a given kind.

The Role and Importance of Space-Based Systems in Modern Intelligence

We begin by describing the principles of space intelligence and its targets. Next, we examine the key role that intellectual models and assumptions play in the interpretation of space intelligence. This leads to the reasons why analysts of space intelligence are reluctant to think in terms of deception.

Any object in orbit can be placed in line of sight of any number of points on the earth, either revisiting those points periodically or, if in geosynchronous orbit, hovering over them at some angle. Anyone wishing to collect images of or signals emanating from any point on the earth need only place the appropriate device in the appropriate orbit to amplify and analyze the minute amounts of light or electromagnetic signals that reach the device from that point on earth.

Light, either in the visible spectrum or in the infrared spectrum, can be collected and amplified by conventional telescopes and focused onto a plane. That plane can be occupied either by photographic film or by electro-optical devices, each of whose cells substitute (but more efficiently) for the granules on film. Electro-optical focal planes then produce computer generated images. Imaging satellites, whether photographic or electro-optical, are cameras with huge telephoto lenses. The quality of the images they produce depends on the size of the telescope and on the quality of the film or focal plane/computer. Of course, a space-based imaging system of a given quality will produce finer or coarser images, depending on its distance from the object being observed. Thus, an imaging system stationed 22,300 miles above the earth at geosynchronous orbit could "stare" at one rather large part of the earth, but could barely distinguish mountains, while the very same system orbiting at an altitude of 100 miles might be able to see a duck in a pond, but would circle the earth in little more than an hour and would be over any given objective with only time for a snapshot.

This means that to get the very best pictures, imaging satellites must fly low enough so that each image or frame of film can cover only tens of square kilometers. Closeups of high quality can be less than one square kilometer. In turn, this means that if such a satellite were able to image without interruption as it orbited the earth, (which is many orders of magnitude beyond the capability of the best satellites), it would only produce images of areas under a very thin line drawn across the earth's huge expanses. Clearly, thousands of such satellites in orbit would be required to try to do what some erroneously believe the United States and the Soviet Union already do routinely: that is, see what is happening everywhere on earth at all times. With a handful (or less) of satellites available at any given time to cover a multitude of known points of interest, it may be possible, at most, to take at least one low-quality image per year of every part of vast countries such as the United States and the Soviet Union.

Of course at night the operation of cameras that register light is impossible. But other cameras register heat—that is, infrared light. This is radiated by objects on earth that have absorbed heat from the sun or that produce heat themselves. Since objects produce and reflect heat unevenly, infrared cameras (such as those on LANDSAT) produce images that tell not just the shape of objects, but whether a field of wheat is healthy, whether an airplane is fueled, or whether a truck has been running lately.

Even as airliners carry radars that give them images of the terrain ahead and as AWACs aircraft easily distinguish faraway fighter planes against ground clutter, satellites might carry radars to produce images of objects on earth beneath them. A major U.S. company advertises a radar imaging device for analyzing earth resources and points out that such images can be obtained anytime of the day or night, and also through clouds that render cameras useless, whether visual or infrared.

Imaging devices are expensive. Therefore, no country can afford to have many in orbit. Moreover, their narrow field of view makes them best suited for taking a look at interesting objects already known to exist or at areas where there is reason to believe such objects are likely to be found. They are less suited for random searches and totally unsuited for continuous surveillance even of points of interest. The targets of imagery are all things of military, political, and economic interest. By looking at tanks, missiles, factories, movements of people, planting of crops, and so forth, it is conceivable that much could be learned about what things are available to a government and about what that government is doing with them, as well as receiving hints about what it intends to do. Yet, many of the things that make for military or economic capability normally take place under roof or are brought outdoors only when imaging satellites are not overhead. Production (even of things as large as ICBMs) takes place where eyes from space cannot see. Development of new weapons also takes place under roof. Most activities, even if they take place outdoors, also may be observed only partially, or with great difficulty. The best example is the Soviet radar at Krasnoyarsk, a huge, unmistakable structure whose existence and approximate location were known by the U.S. intelligence community as it fruitlessly searched frame after photographic frame for months, impeded by all kinds of weather. Yet finding the radar at Krasnoyarsk proved to be only the beginning of a controversy about what the Soviets intend by building it. Of course pictures tell little about intentions and their tales are inherently ambiguous.

In signals intelligence, antennae serve the function of telescopes. The bigger the antenna, the more energy it can accept. Given that a signal striking the antenna may measure only microwatts per unit area, the bigger the antenna the less work the electronic signal amplifier has to do. Clearly, the farther the antenna is from the signal, the larger it must be to perceive a signal of a given strength. It is much easier to build and to place in orbit very large antennae than it is to build optical telescopes of the same size, if only because wires weigh less than mirrors.

Hence, unlike imagery collectors, SIGINT (Signal Intelligence) collectors theoretically can work well while far enough away to receive signals from areas comprising thousands of square miles; that is, if the signals are broadcast. If the signals are beamed, regardless of the size of the antenna, the signals must be within the beam. That requires knowing the location and direction of the beam and making sure that the satellites stay in the beams as long as possible. One technique for doing this involves highly elliptical orbits that minimize the satellite's time over zones without interesting beams and, while the satellite is on the long legs of the ellipses, maximize time spent over signal-rich zones.

Interesting electronic devices may emit beams from unexpected locations. That is why it makes sense to have many signal collectors orbiting the earth to detect, identify, and report the location of the emitters whose beams they literally run across. This is feasible because, on the whole, signal collectors are cheaper than telescopic cameras.

Unlike the situation in World War II, when almost every electronic emission was interesting from the standpoint of intelligence, the electronic environment of the 1980's is tremendously dense and requires sophisticated judgment to choose which of hundreds of thousands of signals is worth recording, as well as to divide signals into kinds and to process each kind appropriately. Moreover, modern signals are seldom simple, even if not encoded. Hence, once a signal is chosen and recorded, it must be disentangled from the electronic stream of which it is a part. All of this requires much electronic processing, as do attempts to break codes. The results of signals intelligence, including that from space, depend much less on the sensitivity of antennae than on the way in which the processing and analysis of signals interact with the signals themselves.

The targets of signals intelligence include all kinds of militarily or politically significant communications: telemetry from weapons tests that bear on the quality of the weapons; actual operating characteristics of electronic equipment (especially radars); or the identification and location, at any given time, of various pieces of equipment that emit significant amounts of electromagnetic energy.

Communications are either broadcast or transmitted along more or less narrow beams. Aircraft in tactical situations have no choice other than to broadcast. Long-distance telephone traffic is relayed by wide beams from station to station or through satellites. The intelligence collector must simply contrive to place antennae within those wide beams, either on the ground or in space.

Two examples of ground-based communications interception are the antennae at Soviet embassies and consulates in the United States, which sit in the streams of microwave telephone traffic between relay towers, and the huge Soviet antenna near Lourdes, Cuba, which is within the downlink beams through which communications satellites service the east-central United States. For the collector the principle is simple: identify the target, figure out what kind of signal it emits, and place the appropriate antenna there. For the target, the principle is equally simple: check to see if an antenna is positioned to pick up a certain emission, and then either shift that communication to a safe channel, or transmit knowing that someone is listening—that means encryption and/or deception.

Fire-control radars are no longer the simple machines of yesteryear. Their ability to shift frequencies (developed to counter electronic countermeasures) also renders problematic their accurate identification. The ability to shift wavelength and waveform is characteristic of most modern radars.

The task of modern electronic intelligence is to understand any piece of equipment through its emissions and then to be able to tell wherever and whenever such equipment is operating. Space simply offers more and better physical points from which this mission can be performed.

Much more than the Soviet Union, the United States must rely on pictures and electronic emissions to be aware of, and to understand, the military equipment of its principal opponent. In the Soviet Union, there are no outlets of information about such matters equivalent to Congressional hearings, *The New York Times*, *Aviation Week*, and even such specialized journals as *Electronic Countermeasures*. However, in wartime the Soviet Union (no less than the United States) must rely on imagery and signals to find and target enemy military units. As the United States seeks to understand the intentions and plans of Soviet leaders, there is virtually no alternative to searching through Soviet communications. The Soviet Union is also very interested in American communications, but its space-based COMINT could not possibly yield the volume, the detailed accuracy, and the breadth of coverage of U.S. leadership intentions that can be gained by reading the American press.

The immediate products of space-based intelligence are not nearly so self-explanatory as a newspaper. U. S. analysts ask for pictures of tank units in North Korea to estimate the size of that country's armored forces. But it is physically impossible to see all of North Korea at once from space on a scale allowing identification of more than mountains and rivers, even if there were not a single cloud in the sky, and even if all of the tanks were outdoors on that day. So we must be content to take various snapshots of tanks in different parts of the country on the sometimes widely separated occasions on which satellites can visit them in clear weather. Therefore, if one wishes to count all the tanks in North Korea, one must devise a system that permits dividing the North Korean tank force into units, identifying the units, counting each tank photographed (more or less once), and also accounting for those that may be under roof. This is a highly uncertain business at best. Note that the CIA estimate of the North Korean army in 1977 was off by about one-third. Yet, this kind of mosaic-building is by far the most simple instance in which raw images may be translated into intelligence.

Consider a minor, routine complication. We know what tanks and trucks look like, but if asked about the size of the civil defense program of the Soviet Union, one must admit that no one knows what all Soviet civil defense installations look like from space. Through human and other technical sources, we might have been able to identify installation "X" as pertaining to civil defense. Hence, it might be reasonable to count all other similar installations as being dedicated to that end. There is no reason at all to believe that we have identified all kinds of installations primarily devoted to civil defense or that we have photographed every conceivable place where identified installations might be present. Much less do we have reason to believe that we might know of civil defense installations of whatever kind, constructed under roof or under the cover of other installations that are normally associated with other purposes.

Other complications are far more difficult. How many SS-18s does the Soviet Union have? We have pictures of 308 silos, which have been associated with the SS-18, but no American has seen each silo loaded with an 18, nor certainly has the U.S. kept a watch to make sure that none of those loaded have been taken out. Most important, no American has the least idea of how many SS-18s have come off production lines. Paramount for our purposes is the fact that space-based imagery such as we have described could not conceivably answer such questions.

There are simple exceptions. An aircraft carrier observed without catapults will not be able to launch high-performance aircraft. A field artillery piece observed to be sixteen feet long can be presumed to have a certain weight. A radar antenna of a certain shape will be able to emit certain waveforms. *But, in most cases, the products of space-based imagery do not speak for themselves.* Each picture becomes meaningful only in the context of a set of assumptions manufactured by the analyst. Those assumptions define the object photographed by comparing it to something that the analyst has decided is in a certain category. A launcher for a particular missile, for example, will be something that is capable of launching that missile, and that is regularly associated with it. An analyst will judge something to be "deployed" if he sees it associated with troops. When working with subjects whose meaning is unclear, it is natural to draw meaning from routine observations.

In signals intelligence, meaning is more elusive than in imagery. The exceptions lie in the field of terminal guidance for missiles, and fire-control for guns. When one of these "threat signals" is intercepted, it is known that a weapon is, or may be, on the way. Similarly, search radars have distinct signatures. After an analyst has associated a signal with an emitter, especially if the emitter has been seen, it is reasonable to so identify it—reasonable, but possibly erroneous. For instance, the presence of the complex communications and fire-control signals normally associated with an armored division gives much less assurance of the presence of a division than would a picture of several hundred tanks. That is because such signals can be generated without the actual presence of the division.

The meaning of most signals is not readily apparent. The telemetry from a weapon being tested may include up to a hundred channels, each reporting the readings of individual gauges throughout the weapon. The matter becomes more interesting when *two* or more gauges report on each instrument, and the readings differ. Each channel contains a modulated signal that results in a squiggle across a piece of paper. Before the analyst can make use of the information, he has to postulate both the instrument to which each channel refers and the scale on which each gauge is based. Without these postulates, which contain substantial arbitrariness, the telemetry would be nonsense.

The "vacuum cleaner" approach to communications intelligence involves an analogous problem. Since even modern equipment can record only an infinitesimal percentage of the number of channels that are theoretically available, the analyst and the collector, working together, must first devise priorities in terms of who is using the channels and what subjects are discussed. Second, analysts must postulate the extent to which the intercepted communications represent the much larger mass that is not intercepted.

As they work, analysts (and even more, collectors) of space-based intelligence do not normally think of the possibility that the subjects whose images and signals they examine might have managed their own exposure in a deceptive way. Collectors and analysts are acutely aware that the targets of space-based intelligence try to *minimize* their exposure. U.S. analysts have known since the early days of space-based cameras that the Soviet Union had figured out that certain U.S. satellites in sun-synchronous orbit took pictures, and that they therefore placed sensitive things under roof when the satellite was scheduled to pass overhead. U.S. analysts were not surprised that, after espionage and leaks told the Soviets about U.S. interception of telemetry, the Soviets began to encrypt that telemetry to unprecedented degrees. Nevertheless, U.S. analysts (and even more, collectors) have been very cool indeed to all suggestions that Soviets might not just be denying information, but biasing that which they choose not to deny.

That is because engineers who design space-based collection systems are accustomed to working against nature, picking up ever-weaker signals from ever-farther away; distinguishing signals from noise; making optical instruments for better resolution, longer life, more flexibility, and so on. These tasks are demanding enough in themselves, and those performing them are seldom concerned with the larger framework in which they work. The analysts, for their part, have the difficult task of making sense out of things whose meaning is not obvious. They hazard their postulates to come up with reasonable explanations. For analysts to consider that the evidence on which they work is not just slim, but may also be bogus, is for them to condemn themselves to hedge conclusions that were not firm in the first place.

Moreover, decision makers often regard pictures and intercepts (and all too often, anything that accompanies them) as "hard," eminently believable data. To expect those who provide such data to disagree, is to expect too much. Finally, we must also take into account the presumption (which has survived from the earliest days of space-based intelligence) that anything from the high ground of space is necessarily gathered without the other party being aware of it, or that for the sake of peace, there is a kind of tacit agreement to be as vulnerable to the means for monitoring nuclear armament as we must remain to that armament itself.

A Note on Deception

Nations have always regarded intelligence systems of other nations as excellent channels for deception. Deception involves convincing someone that a false proposition is true, or vice versa. It may also involve leading someone to draw false conclusions from true facts. In any case, the standard antidote to deception is to check how well the proposition or interpretation in question fits with a broad swath of reality. Intelligence, however, looks at very small and exceptionally important pieces of reality through narrow, special sources and methods. The narrower the keyhole, the less chance of checking the image with the broader world.

Technical means of collection open fissures through which one may gaze at tiny snatches of otherwise denied areas and intercept signals from equipment whose quality is unknown. Moreover, those very signals, however insufficient, may be the only tangible indications of what the people who own the equipment are doing in the short run and intend to do in the long run. Any nation, then, whose enemies are looking at its vital parts through technical fissures must naturally be curious about the shape and size of those fissures. It would be unnatural if a nation did not use such knowledge as it had about these technical keyholes to alter its exposure to the eyes and ears of the other side.

A fundamental requirement for deception of technical means is knowledge about what those means are and what they are observing. For a variety of reasons, perhaps first among them a kind of scientific hubris ("they couldn't imagine we would be able to do *this*") the first generation of military satellites, including intelligence devices, were launched with little thought about how much information the hostile intelligence services would gain about them, and about what would be done with the information.

How Objects in Space Can Be Militarily Useful, and How Deception May Enhance That Usefulness

During the first months of space-based imagery, we not only resolved long-standing controversies about the Soviet order of battle, especially in missiles and bombers we also gained valuable insights into Soviet standard operating procedure. Ironically, our views of what to expect from the Soviet Union were formed under conditions that changed as soon as the Soviets instituted their satellite warning program. In the few subsequent periods between the introduction of new systems and the Soviets' learning about them, we have gathered some hints of how incomplete a picture of Soviet activities we receive from our well-recognized systems. The most notable of these periods occurred before the KH-11 was betrayed by William Kampiles.

The situation in signals intelligence has been analogous. When our collection systems became known, some of the premium that unexpectedness had added to their performance was lost. Boyce and Lee's revelation of the Rhyolite telemetry collector resulted *at least* in the Soviets switching bands, lowering the strength of transmissions, and increasing encryption. Geoffrey Prime's revelation that certain long-distance telephone links were being intercepted resulted *at least* in the Soviet Union shifting a larger proportion of those links to land lines. However, the difference between the worth of expected and unexpected SIGINT becomes obvious on the few occasions in which we obtain the latter.

This leads to the obvious point: why not increase the opportunities for truly unexpected collection by deceiving the Soviets about the true location and objectives of our current space-based collectors? Since these are reasonably well known, deception would not be easy. Surely removing imaging satellites from sun-synchronous orbits and putting them into random-access orbit would make them quantitatively less efficient collectors, but it would be a first step in improving the quality of their product. Of course, the Soviets would try to find the old satellites in their new orbits. That is why another essential step would be to simultaneously place into new random-access orbits a sizeable number of decoy imaging satellites. Perhaps some of the decoys could emit some housekeeping signals while the real ones communicated strictly through relays.

New satellites could be more easily protected by constructing classified cover stories for them, and perhaps leaking or allowing that "information" to be stolen. Such deception would provide the Soviets with false explanations for the new satellites and would work to discredit any true data that the Soviets might happen to gather about them. Of course, any time the Soviets appeared to be learning the truth, reshuffling our satellites and redecoying them could restart the contest.

Making a satellite difficult to identify also contributes to its physical safety, especially in wartime. No other protective measure can be as effective. If an enemy knows the precise location of a satellite, the passive defense of that satellite is very difficult. It is true that satellites do not have to be flimsy. The use of exterior armor, hardening of electronic components, shielding of optical components, antijam programming of transmitters and receivers can radically increase the resistance of a satellite to laser radiation, electromagnetic pulse, and other nuclear effects. Bigger engines for maneuver and generous supplies of fuel for those engines can help a satellite evade simple coorbital interceptors, or help it get out of the way of preprogrammed "dumb" mines—if there is enough warning. But no satellite can be expected to survive a direct hit from a kinetic kill vehicle, a guided nuclear weapon, or a space-based laser or particle beam. Active defense of satellites against such threats, though certainly feasible, is costly. To survive against many interceptors or against a space-based laser the satellite would have to be escorted by a space-based laser dedicated to its protection.

The greatest protection for a satellite is ignorance (or doubt on the part of the enemy) as to where the satellite is located. When Sputnik was launched twenty-eight years ago, the whole world could follow it precisely because it broadcast its location and because it was the only thing orbiting the earth other than the moon. When larger U.S. satellites were launched they were unmistakable. Even untrained radar operators could not miss them. They were the only objects of their kinds. By the late 1960's, however, enough satellites and junk were in orbit that identification of any given object in space had become a problem. Each new set of objects in space, their various radar and electronic signatures, as well as their orbits, had to be entered into a central computer registry at the time of launch, and the registry had to be updated. In the early 1960's, it became impossible to make an intelligent guess about what each satellite might be doing. The satellites at geosynchronous orbit are rigorously tracked because of the relative scarcity of slots at that orbit; but even they are not necessarily identified by function.

This precarious record-keeping can be fouled up by clandestine launches. The space shuttle would be excellent for this purpose, since it could dispense any number of satellites unannounced while out of sight of Soviet radar. If it launched its clandestine satellites into an orbit occupied by spent satellites or pieces of debris while recovering such junk, the deception would be very difficult to detect. If the shuttle did not deceive by substituting a live satellite for recovered junk, it could cover its clandestine launch by releasing large numbers of cheap decoys. Clandestine satellites can also come from deep space. They could be launched and stored too far for earth-based radar to see and brought back quietly to the southern side of near-earth orbit. Perhaps several decoys could be released to test Soviet reactions. At any rate, the introduction of uncertainty about the location of satellites would be most valuable during periods in which the Soviets might be considering shooting at them. Eventually the Soviets might solve the puzzles that decoys, substitutions, and clandestine launches presented. However, if the puzzles were set before them in a crisis, they surely could not solve them in time to carry out their original plans.

Let us now briefly discuss camouflage in space, in relation to the three kinds of means by which objects in space can be detected: radar, optical, and passive electronic instruments. Anyone who has ever worked with radar knows how the shape of the object being looked at can drastically effect the return (even from short wavelength radars) depending on the viewing angle of the object. If the object has sharp corners, a slight variation in angle can give a return that is either larger or smaller, but that will certainly be different from what it would be otherwise. At any rate, aircraft designers have largely developed the art of enhancing and reducing radar signatures. Small things can be made to look large, and large things can be made to look small. The implication for decoys is obvious. Instead of being built as simple foil balloons in the precise shape of the satellite they are to simulate, they could be built in ways that would enhance the features peculiar to the target satellite. At the same time, the target satellite can be modified to mute those very features. Thus, even if radar can see a satellite, it can be misled about its identification.

The best way to see a satellite is through fine, space-based, electro-optical instruments operating in the infrared spectrum, especially after the satellite has been identified as an object of interest. Since satellites are relatively "cold" bodies, radiating very little energy other than that reflected from the sun, any optical instrument that seeks to identify them from a distance must have a focal plane supersensitized by cooling to near absolute zero. The products of such instruments are not fine images, but infrared signatures. These can be quite distinctive, but they can be easily altered, duplicated, or masked.

Masking satellites, especially against the infrared guidance systems of interceptor rockets, can be accomplished easily by hot objects that simply overload sensors calibrated for much less energy. It is also easy to alter the infrared characteristics of the satellites one may wish to protect by adding insulation in some places or perhaps some sources of heat in others. It is conceivable that infrared signatures may simply be reduced to very low levels. The prerequisite for any sort of masking or alteration of the characteristics of any satellite is a detailed analysis of those characteristics. Such analysis would also allow the design of cheaper objects that would yield signatures close to those of the real satellites.

Passive electronic means of detection can be bypassed simply by routing downlinks through relay satellites. They can be spoofed either by placing downlinks on decoys or by appearing to beam commands to decoys. Again, the deception cannot be successful from every angle, but whoever would discover it is forced to surveil every possible target from a variety of angles. Thus, for practical purposes, live satellites can appear dead and dead ones appear alive. In other words, with some initiative, anyone wishing to identify or to target a satellite can be faced, at a minimum, with tremendous uncertainty.

The implications of this transcend intelligence and communications. A serious defense against ballistic missiles must begin while those missiles are in the boost phase—that is to say, in space. Therefore, boost-phase antimissile devices must be in space. Contemplating this fact, many observers (some of whom should know better) have asserted that the inherent vulnerability of all space-based objects renders boost-phase defense almost impossible. From this assertion, there have followed technologically weird scenarios in which boost-phase defensive devices "pop up" just a few seconds after the first offensive missiles lift off, get into firing position in time to take advantage of the last few seconds of boost-phase, and fire without having their pointer-trackers stabilized, or their internal working checked out. Equally weird objections to these scenarios have featured space mines waiting in the corridors of space and time that these "pop-up" devices would have to traverse in order to rush into firing position. Yet these discussions make little sense because the premise of inherent vulnerability on which they are based is thoroughly false.

How laser or kinetic kill battle stations could protect themselves by attacking their attackers will not be discussed here, but the various means for hiding and dissimulating objects in space already outlined suggest that deception could provide substantial protection for boost-phase defensive devices. Moreover, the effect of decoying, as well as of altering, radar and infrared signatures could be enhanced by the use of orbiting screens that battle stations might sometimes hide behind while passing over the Eurasian landmass. These screens would protect the battle stations against ground-based lasers and would increase the number of possible aim points for other kinds of weapons. If attack were imminent, either the stations themselves or especially equipped decoys could dispense many more cheap decoys and flares to throughly confuse the situation. The attacker simply would not have time to sort it out.

How Knowledge of an Adversary's Space-Based Intelligence Can Be Used to Deceive Him

The narrowness of U.S. sources of information about key Soviet strategic programs, combined with substantial Soviet knowledge of U.S. collection systems provides the Soviets with significant opportunities for deception. As previously stated, the Soviet's obvious response after learning of U.S. imagery and SIGINT systems was to narrow even further what could be seen. Let us see how they might also have used their opportunity for deception.

As discussed above, the narrowness inherent in space-based sources obliges the analysts to impose artificial postulates on the data they receive. The necessity for postulates gives analysts an opportunity to indulge their own prejudices. With continued indulgence, these prejudices may harden into axioms. The proximate objective of Soviet deception operations may well be to keep U.S. analysts in the mental ruts they find so comfortable.

Consider imagery of missiles. The very beginning of space-based cameras coincided with the rise of arms control to paramountcy in American strategic thought. The fundamental assumption of American arms control has always been that both sides would have at least a minimum number of invulnerable silo-based missiles, unable to kill one another but able to inflict tremendous civilian casualties in a single spasm, and therefore able to deter war.

At the very outset of the arms control process, American negotiators tried to negotiate controls on both sides' production of ICBMs (since the Soviets flatly refused inspection of missile factories). American negotiators knew perfectly well that space-based cameras could give no clear idea of the number of ICBMs the Soviets had produced, but since they strongly wanted the arms control process to continue, they agreed to frame arrangements with the Soviet Union in terms of the things that space-based cameras could keep track of very well: silos and missile-firing submarines. Thus, in the world of arms control, launchers were to stand for missiles, and certain kinds of launchers were to stand for all launchers. To help American analysts deceive themselves that this artificial world was real, the Soviet Union merely had to minimize the exposure of its use of other kinds of launchers for its missiles and, of course, to hide from American intelligence its practice of reloading launchers. This denial of data succeeded in posturing self-deception.

By the mid-1970's, American analysts treated evidence of nonstandard launchers for Soviet silo-launched missiles as a red herring, even though the evidence was gathered by rare, unexpected collection. At this point, American analysts knew that to have accepted the proposition that there are operational missiles in the Soviet arsenal other than the ones in standard launchers would be to knock down a pillar on which the whole edifice of American political-military planning was built. For the same reason, American analysts in the mid-1970's were cool to evidence that several Soviet ICBMs are cold-launched. If the Soviets plan to reload their silos, the equation between one silo and one missile is invalid. By 1980, when evidence from Soviet military exercises showed unambiguously that reloading silos is standard Soviet procedure, U.S. analysts reported the evidence, but drew precisely none of the consequences from it. So, buttressed by many pictures of silos and submarine tubes, American diplomatic and military plans are still made according to the totally unwarranted assumption that the Soviet Union has only these ICBM launchers and that each of these launchers has only one missile.

The growth of the Soviet Union's force of mobile ICBMs has been covered by American misinterpretations that the Soviets have helped to foster. During the SALT II negotiations, the Soviets announced that the missile that the United States had observed being tested with either one or three warheads, the SS-20, was intended for Europe. American analysts have always recognized that with a single warhead, the SS-20 could hit the United States. But they routinely describe this circumstance as "offloading two warheads." It was never clear why they did not describe the SS-20 as a single-warhead ICBM intended to strike the U.S. but whose range would be limited to Europe with the *addition* of two warheads. U.S. analysts may have been helped to make this judgment by glimpses that the Soviets gave to American intelligence of a closely related missile program that never got very far: the SS-16.

The SS-16 is an intercontinental missile identical to the SS-20, but with an additional stage, and tested with a single warhead. It is fully compatible with the mobile launcher of the SS-20. Nevertheless, the Soviets built a little longer version of that launcher uniquely for the SS-16. Unusually, the SS-16 is the only Soviet missile about whose production U.S. officials believe they have knowledge. But this knowledge comes from a source that the Soviets were aware the U.S. was monitoring. On the surface, none of this makes sense. Why would the Soviets build an extra stage for the SS-20 when the basic missile would go to intercontinental range as long as it carried only one R.V.? Why would they build a distinct launcher for the SS-20—turned SS-16—when the basic SS-20 launcher would suffice? In 1980 to 1981, newer facts deepened the mystery. According to a story in the *Washington Post* attributed to high intelligence officials, routine reconnaissance photos of the Soviet missile test center at Plesetsk (where other technical sources had indicated that some SS-16s were being kept) showed tracks peculiar to the SS-16's launchers, as well as firing points meticulously cleared of snow. Hawks within the intelligence community pointed to a violation of SALT II, which bans the SS-16. The doves argued that, although there were indeed SS-16s at Plesetsk, and these were probably ready to shoot, they could not be considered a violation because they were not deployed in a normal way and thus could not be considered "deployed" in violation of SALT II.

The concentration on the few SS-16s at Plesetsk by both hawks and doves obscured more important facts concerning Soviet mobile missilery. Foremost is the existence of over 400 mobile missile launchers popularly known as SS-20 IRBM launchers, but also able to fire the SS-16 ICBM. The existence of a few launchers for the SS-16 ICBM seems to have caused many American analysts to forget that every SS-20 can be an ICBM whenever the Soviets desire and that every SS-20 launcher can launch both SS-20 ICBMs and SS-16 ICBMs. Second is the Soviet development of the SS-25 (a very accurate, reliable, small ICBM), which can also be fired from SS-20 launchers.

It is interesting that, despite the availability of these 400 launchers, we have seen no instance in which an SS-25 missile has been fired by an SS-20 launcher. Of course, this does not mean that event never happened. But for practical purposes of U.S. policy making, it does. Instead, the Soviets have built a new launcher just for the SS-25 and have allowed U.S. intelligence to glimpse it. Thus, American analysts, accustomed to thinking of the Soviet mobile missile problem in terms of a few SS-16s, may easily switch to thinking of it in terms of a small number of launchers peculiar to the SS-25. Meanwhile, of course, they do not know how many SS-16s or SS-25s are being produced, or whether the missiles in warehouses at SS-20 bases are SS-20s (with one instead of three warheads), SSs-16s, or SS-25s, or where they are targeted. In sum, *if* all of this is a deception, it is not based on substitution of fake reality by brute force, but rather on gentle reinforcement of the well-known and well-established mental categories of American analysts.

Let us now consider how the Soviet Union can use its knowledge of U.S. space-based signals intelligence for deception, beginning with the subfield of telemetry. Even before the compromise of Rhyolite, the Soviets knew that intercepts of telemetry from their missile tests were the principal source of U.S. judgments about the quality of their missiles. Their own reconnaissance of Turkey and Iran had led them to calculate that certain large American antennae in those countries, oriented toward their missile test sites, could pick up their telemetry signals. Mere geometric calculations show precisely at what point in the trajectories of the missiles their telemetry transmissions would come in line of sight with the antennae. When they learned about Rhyolite, they realized that at least one American antenna was *always* in line of sight of their missile test stations, and that more than likely at every moment the United States could geolocate the transmission precisely. Naturally this would give analysts an important clue for interpreting the telemetry.

As the Soviets considered how to manage their exposure to telemetry intercepts, they realized that the United States could not be kept from roughly estimating the size of missiles being tested because the United States could determine how fast the missile accelerated and when the several stages burned out. They also knew that U.S. radars were looking at the warheads these missiles delivered to the Pacific Ocean or the Kamchatka Peninsula. But anyone reading the U.S. press from the late 1960's to the late 1970's knew that the strategic debate in the United States was not so much over the throw-weight of Soviet missiles, but over their accuracy. Americans who wanted larger forces, who opposed MAD (Mutual Assured Destruction), and who wanted to enable American forces to strike Soviet hard targets, were arguing that Soviet missiles were accurate, and therefore designed for war fighting and war winning. Those who argued against larger forces, supported MAD, and were against American counterforce weapons said that Soviet missiles posed no threat to U.S. forces, and therefore the strategic policy of the Soviet Union was one of mere deterrence. The Soviets knew that information they were broadcasting in their telemetry about missile accuracy was perhaps *the* major piece of evidence in this argument.

As the Soviets were deciding what part of their telemetry to encrypt and how to calibrate the instruments whose reports they would allow the Americans to read, they knew they could influence the very crux of American planning. They also knew that analysis of telemetry requires judgments about the *scale* to be used in reading out each instrument. The common sense approach to making this judgment is to figure out which events occur simultaneously, which follow, and how quickly. The easiest way to influence American judgments about the accuracy of their missiles was to leave open instrument transmissions that could induce misjudgments about the scale. Using more than one gauge to report on each instrument (and perhaps calibrating each differently) gave American analysts even more leeway to indulge their prejudices. Encryption of other telemetry channels would not occur principally because they carried especially valuable facts about missiles, but rather because their denial could deprive American analysts of bases on which to test alternate hypotheses about the scale to be used on the open channels.

In fact, U.S. analysts initially misjudged the accuracy of the SS-9, possibly of the SS-11, and certainly of the SS-17 through SS-19. Those misjudgments were fully supported by telemetry. In other words, U.S. analysts applied a wrong scale to those channels. This does not prove beyond doubt that the Soviets intentionally biased the telemetry and led U.S. analysts to apply the wrong scale, but the result was as if this had happened. U.S. analysts did deceive themselves, and the Soviets helped at least by providing an excess of information about some things, and a dearth of information about others. Given the possibility of helping U.S. analysts make such errors, any Soviet official who ruled against trying would be derelict in his duty.

Turning to intelligence about radar signals, we can see even more strongly the effect of preconceived categories and the relative ease with which analysts' judgments can be kept in comfortable ruts. In a sense, radars are the easiest intelligence targets. To do their work they have to radiate so much energy that intercepting it and analyzing it is easy. In addition, large radars can be photographed. In the case of dish-type radars, the combination of the intercepted signal and the picture of the antenna that generated it gives an accurate and internally cross-checking account of what the radar can do. A dish-type may be run at different levels of power and at different rates of scan, but determining the outer limits of its performance is uncomplicated.

Phased-array radars are a different matter. Photographs can reveal the aperture and density of transmission elements. But this does not define the capability of the radar nearly so much as the shape of a dish does. Intercepts of signals from a phased-array will reveal only the waveforms and the type of scan that is produced by the software package currently being run. Any given intercept cannot prove the amount of power the radar can radiate. Moreover, intercepts do not give any indication of how the returns are being processed (for example, how much pulse compression is being performed), and of how the returns are being used.

Perhaps the biggest intelligence question of the 1980's concerns the preparations by the Soviet Union for defense against ballistic missiles. This in turn depends on judgments about the extent to which the six Soviet large, phased-array radars of the Pechora-class can be used for battle management, and the extent to which radar associated with surface-to-air missiles (for instance, the SA-12, SA-10, and even the SA-5) can be used to direct those missiles to intercept incoming warheads. The Soviets are as well aware of this as they are about which platforms intercept their radar signals.

What the Soviets have done to modify the kinds of signals these radars emit is beyond the scope of this paper. But the reaction of the intelligence community to what it has seen has consisted of doubting whether these radars should be associated with ballistic missile defense, because either the signals or the radars do not fit certain ideal notions of what ballistic missile defense should be. For example, while acknowledging that what they have seen of the SA-12 radar would permit it to defend against the most numerous U.S. strategic warhead, Army experts are reluctant to call it a BMD (Ballistic Missile Defense) device because they have only seen it emit one-fourth the power that their own design for a terminal intercept radar would emit. Officials from another agency have made analogous remarks about the Pechora-class radars. Yes, they admit, the Pechora-class radars would appear to have the ratio of power to aperture that would allow them to see warheads far enough away to do battle management for a large-scale attack; but, no, they have not seen precisely the signal that *they* would use for such a purpose. The radars could emit them but they have not, at least while the U.S. was looking.

In this regard, American arms controllers have taken this line of reasoning to its logical conclusion. In the spring of 1985, the *Washington Post* reported that Mr. Paul Nitze suggested within the administration that it settle the internal quarrel over the function of the radar at Krasnoyarsk by agreeing with the Soviet Union that it would turn on the radar to coincide with the availability of a U.S. SIGINT satellite. The intelligence community would make public the details of the intercept, showing why the intercepted signal could not be used for battle management. Although such explicit coordination between U.S. intelligence and its Soviet target would have furthered the cause of arms control, it raised too many questions about the integrity of the intelligence process. Mr. Nitze never pursued the suggestion.

Communications intelligence can be the best way of learning the intentions of a foreign power. For that very reason, it is also the most efficient means through which one power may deceive another about its intentions. COMINT is especially valuable—and liable to deception—when other avenues of access to a foreign power's decision making are lacking. Consider the opposite. If the United States were to allow the Soviet Union to intercept a deceptive set of top secret minutes from a meeting of the NSC (National Security Council) on arms control or on the number of MX missiles to be produced, the Soviets could compare these false deliberations with the thousands of open, authoritative reports about how various NSC members stand on these matters. The deceptive intercept might well cause the Soviets confusion, but the weight of evidence would be against the deception. On the other hand, because an intercepted (deceptive) conversation between two Soviet officials on an important topic (such as the production of an ICBM) would be sui generis, it would likely be effective. The United States has a small data base on how top Soviet officials talk to one another and, more than likely, no firsthand data at all regarding Soviet internal debates on that topic. U.S. analysts would have little reason to discount the conversation, especially if it fit with their prejudices on the subject.

In communications intelligence, knowledge that a channel is being intercepted is a prerequisite for deception. The various vacuum cleaner systems are reasonably well known, but these systems, as stated above, have theoretical access to many thousands of channels. How can a deception planner ensure that his message will be received if he does not even know which set of channels the vacuum cleaner will scan? If he inserts the message into too many channels, he risks misleading too many of his own countrymen and alerting enemy analysts. The competent deception planner must begin by making sure that there is a low number of channels that the enemy will find productive or promising. In other words, good deception begins with good security.

Competent deception then moves to training collectors to look to certain channels at certain times for certain types of information. Deception planners know that the vacuum cleaner's managers must begin by analyzing the entire volume of traffic to identify which channels are likely to produce what and when. The computer programs from which they select channels to scan at any given time must be based on the traffic patterns that enemy security officers have produced. What the collector regards as intelligent choices dictated by his discovery of random patterns in the traffic may well be predictable responses to a situation that enemy counterintelligence has structured. If, then, the actual intercepted channels relevant to an individual subject are relatively few, the deception planner can inject his message into a large enough fraction of these to give a reasonable probability that it will be picked up.

The wise COMINT deception planner can increase the acceptability of a message's content. Refraining from heavy-handedness can decrease the chances that intercept of similar messages on different channels will cause suspicion. The message need not be "We are going to produce X copies of A." It is enough to mention a total production of a key component of item A. The message need not say "We have decided not to defend ourselves against ballistic missiles." The same conclusion is conveyed more credibly by "We are trying to decide this question and have scheduled a decision in the not-too-distant future." If the deception planner does his work well, when events prove analysts wrong they will believe that, at worst, they made a mistake. They will not feel the need to question the reliability of sources. Perhaps the easiest and most effective deception is to make sure that the traffic the enemy intercepts confirms the impression that one shares the basic objective of the enemy, because it is framed in terms that the enemy also uses. In this manner, a good deception planner can simply reinforce the prejudices of the target. In tactical situations, or if it does not matter if subsequent events discredit a good deception channel, messages could be more heavy-handed.

Living with Deception in and from Space

Factoring the Soviet Union's knowledge of U.S. space-based collection systems into intelligence planning would be a humbling, but useful experience. U.S. intelligence officials would have to admit that the portion of our data base gathered without the knowledge of the other side is small. The bulk of the data we have collected over the past twenty years would have to be reanalyzed, asking what are the impressions the other side might have intended to give? Coming up with hypotheses would be all too easy. Much more laborious and rewarding would be attempts to *test* those hypotheses by using preexisting, noncontaminated data or by designing wholly new multidisciplinary collection operations. It would be of secondary importance if after several years, this exercise resulted in more or fewer hard facts. Most important, we would know the difference. We would still have to make suppositions in order to make sense of much of our data. We could still allow our prejudices to lead us astray. But our choices might well be more responsible.

Expanding the proportion of our data obtained through unexpected means should be a high priority, both for its own sake and because unexpected collection is a powerful check on Soviet deception. As has been shown, deceiving the Soviets about the location and/or existence of U.S. space-based collectors can result in unexpected collection. Wholly new methods of collection (for instance, accurate delivery from space of small SIGINT packages to key locations) are made conceivable by the existence of techniques for deceiving various means of surveillance. *Deceptions-in-space-can-help-guard-against-deceptions-from-space.*

The deception of Soviet space sensors can make a major difference in military operations. Without good deception about the location of boost-phase antimissile devices, such devices may not be worthwhile. However, with the protection that good deception can provide, it may be possible to count not only on the benefits of future antimissile satellites but also on retaining the benefits of current navigational and communications satellites. Prudent military planners today wistfully concede that they would have to do without these useful tools just when they would need them most. If deception is employed to protect them, commanders may well be able to count on them.

One reason why U.S. officials have paid so little attention to the many opportunities for deceiving Soviet intelligence in, from, and about space is the widespread prejudice that it is improper for a democratic society to practice deception. That prejudice, however, is well founded only as regards deception done through media open to the public. When deceptive messages consist of classified information, specifically intended to stay out of public circulation and to be "mainlined" to the Soviet leadership, the question of lying to the public does not arise. Indeed, technical intelligence is the one set of channels through which a democracy can utilize deception without polluting itself. Moreover, the United States does not lack the technical means for altering its exposure to Soviet imagery and SIGINT in interesting ways, but the United States does lack an essential element: strategic plans in the service of which deception might be accomplished.

23
Deception and the Formulation of National Intelligence Estimates

Thomas P. Rona

Introduction

The concept of strategic deception needs to be redefined if it is to be applied to the formulation of national intelligence estimates (NIE). *Strategic* in this context means any Soviet activity that is aimed at influencing our strategic decisions, that is, those that have to do with the effective marshalling of "resources" in view of reaching a favorable outcome in the "engagement" at hand.[1]

"Engagements" must be seen as occurring at several hierarchial levels, intertwined, in general, both in time and in locales (figure 23–1). There are, for instance, "strategic" decisions that affect directly the outcome of an air or land *battle*, or again that of a specific naval engagement. At the next higher level, we may conceive of strategic decisions that affect the type and size of forces present in any particular region of a given *theater*; their organization, assignment of objectives, rules of engagement, and so forth. Still at a higher level, we find strategic decisions that affect the conduct of *war at the global level*, having to do with priorities among the respective theaters, with the strengthening or modification of alliance structures. Finally, each nation or group of nations with kindred ideology, goals, and objectives underwrites some broad *national strategies* with the view of effectively applying their resources (cultural, economic, and military) to propagating further and achieving these goals.

For our purposes, we can define, as an ad hoc terminology, the following:

Engagement Strategy: Related to land, air, and naval battles

Theater or Campaign Strategy: Related to the engagements that, in the aggregate, determine the outcome of military confrontation within a given theater

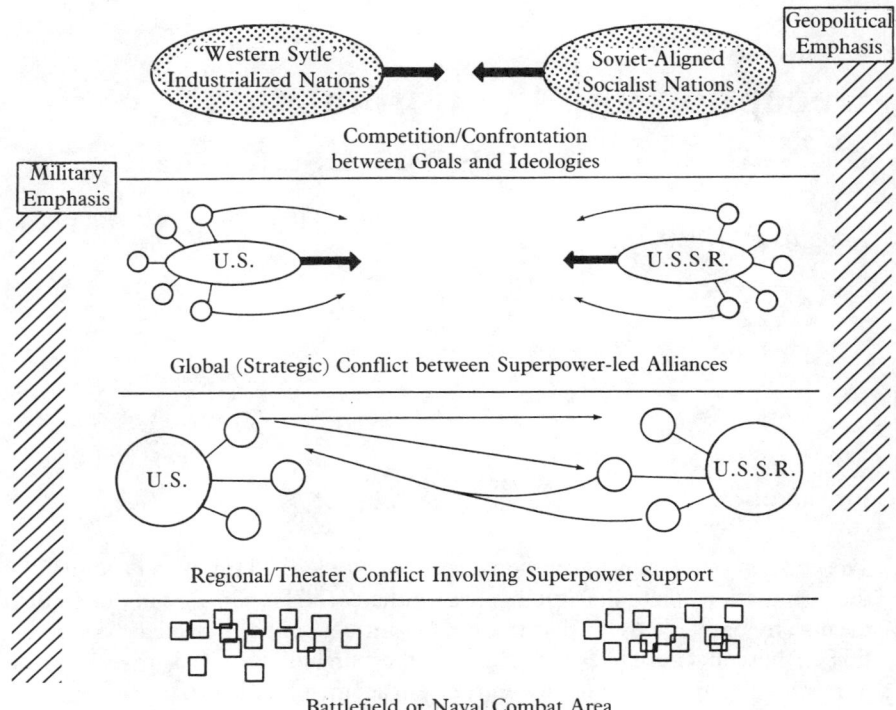

Figure 23-1. Engagement Hierarchy

Intertheater or global war strategy: Related to decisions affecting several theater or campaign strategies in view of securing termination of the armed conflict on favorable terms

National Level Strategies: Basically aimed at furthering national goals, propagating national ideologies, and achieving national objectives with the minimum risk to survival and stability of the nation.

The first three are clearly, although far from exclusively, related to military operations. The fourth category, the national level strategies, affect both military and civilian activities in the preconflict or interconflict periods usually (and erroneously) referred to as "peacetime."

In order to discuss Soviet strategic deception in the context of the national intelligence estimates, we must view the latter as contributing to the whole spectrum of U.S. and Allied strategic decisions, but, most important, to the *national level strategies*. This statement is not made to deny the role of NIEs in the formulation of strategies with strong revelance to military *operations*; it is simply to remind us that perhaps the most important effect of Soviet strategic deception is to be anticipated in the areas in which the longer-term national-level strategies are being evolved, covering several decades of cold war or crisis-punctuated "peacetime."

The Role of the NIEs

The NIEs are principally intended to influence the decisions pertaining to the evolution of our *strategic posture*. Quite obviously, the specific details entering into such estimates should, and indeed do, influence planning for wartime strategies at the global war and at the theater war level; in some specific instances the influence may be perceived down to the battlefield level. The main role is, nonetheless, to influence the posture-related decisions. To the extent that Soviet deceptive activity is aimed at modifying these decisions, it must address the domains of concern in the definition of the U.S. strategic posture.

A few illustrations would help in understanding this point.

1. The U.S. could be, at some point, concerned with defining the broad long-term goals, the general thrusts, and the distribution of resources of its space program. The major issues have to do with military versus civil orientation; "benefit of mankind" versus enhancement of military force effectiveness; potential for arms control in regard to weapons based in space or at space-deployed targets. The NIE process should project the Soviet policy goals, industrial technical potential, plans and resources related to their space activity; the *Soviet deceptive efforts could be aimed at denying us an accurate assessment of these.*

2. The United States could be faced, at some point, with the decision of committing to a major aggressive effort in biological warfare preparation, both offensive and defensive, based on recent advances and ominous predictions in biosciences. The NIE should accurately portray, both in substance and timing, the Soviet potential, plans, and resources in this area. Again, the *Soviet deceptive efforts could be aimed at denying us an accurate assessment of these.*

3. The Western strategic posture versus that of the Soviet Union and of its ideological associates is largely based on the differences in economic and technological potential. The Soviet Union is acutely aware of this fact and pursues many avenues to eliminate the causes and to attenuate the consequences of these differences. Our NIEs should inform us of the techniques used by the Soviets for this purpose, so that appropriate and timely

measures can be taken to protect the interest of the United States. Again, the *the value for the Soviets of deceiving the NIE process in this regard is evident.*

Let us agree once and for all that the nation's strategic posture comprises far more than the military forces-in-being. If our own posture is to remain competitive and (one would hope) superior to all possible adversary combinations, then we must be concerned about all of the following, pertinent to all potential adversaries, but more particularly to the Soviet Union (see figure 23–2):

National goals, possible drivers that would cause changes;

Cultural-educational, technical-industrial, demographic and sociopolitical factors;

Existing military capabilities, including budgets, force structure, and organization; the nature and characteristics of weapon systems and their deployment and support; the related employment policies and combat doctrines. (The possible deceptive efforts associated with testing and exercises should be given special consideration.)

Ideally, the sum total of up-to-date NIEs should provide competent and reliable information on all the above. Any individual NIE will illuminate a specific subset of this ensemble, selected because of its urgency and potentially decisive impact on our own posture evolution. Unfortunately, the problem of *agglomeration* (how to combine a number of individual estimates in order to reach higher level conclusions) is not trivial and is far from being understood to a degree acceptable in relation to its potential importance. Perhaps because of this, but more probably because of the understandable proclivity of analysts to select areas of endeavor that are approachable through technical judgments, NIEs dealing with top level national goals of the Soviet Union are difficult to produce with the requisite depth, insight, and authority to modify the course of our own posture development. *This is the area where Soviet deceptive efforts were quite successful in the past and are likely to pay equally ample dividends in the future.* As an example, the so-called de-Stalinization campaign of Khrushchev, starting in 1956, inaugurated a period of détente in the Cold War that managed to overcome minor incidents, such as the U-2 episode in 1960, the Cuban missile crisis of 1962, the repression of Czechoslovakia in 1968, and the Arab-Israeli war of 1973. No less than the events in Afghanistan (1979) and in Poland (1980) were required for the United States to realize the dangers of basing its policies on the assumption that the Soviets will abide by the implicit consequences of détente. The arms control negotiations leading up to SALT I and the subsequent nuclear weapon buildup differential favoring the Soviet Union are just conspicuous manifestations of the respective posture evolutions based on our erroneous perception of Soviet national goals.

	Objectives and Strategy	Capabilities-in-Being	Development Programs	Intent, Plans, Timing	Events
National Goals	X			X	
Cultural and Educational Base	X	X	X		
Industrial/Technical Base	X	X	X	X	
Demographic Factors	X	X	X		
Budgets			X		X
Force Structure	X	X	X		
Military Systems		X	X	X	
Combat Doctrines	X	X	X		
Deployment/Exercises	X	X	X	X	X

Figure 23–2. NIE's Domains of Interest

X Essential   X Important   X Moderate

492 • Deception and Strategic Planning

There is another important point to be mentioned in connection with the NIE development process. In the pre-World War II period, the NIE equivalents or predecessors could be evolved over a period of years—the corresponding U.S. courses of action could remain valid for years and perhaps for decades. Even large-scale errors or surprises could be compensated for by timely and appropriate reaction. In today's environment, and that of the predictable future, misjudgments may well result in irreversible consequences within a matter of days, or even hours. Figure 23–3 attempts to illustrate the problem of *time congruence* between the development of intelligence estimates and the tempo of events that determines the outcome of generalized engagements, as previously defined. At the lowest level, single engagement, the essential factors are tactical and technical. Capability developments (development, acquisition, testing of equipment, training and exercising military personnel) can take place in a matter of years for industrialized nations; they are thus compatible with the generation of intelligence estimates. Engagements are decided in a matter of hours and

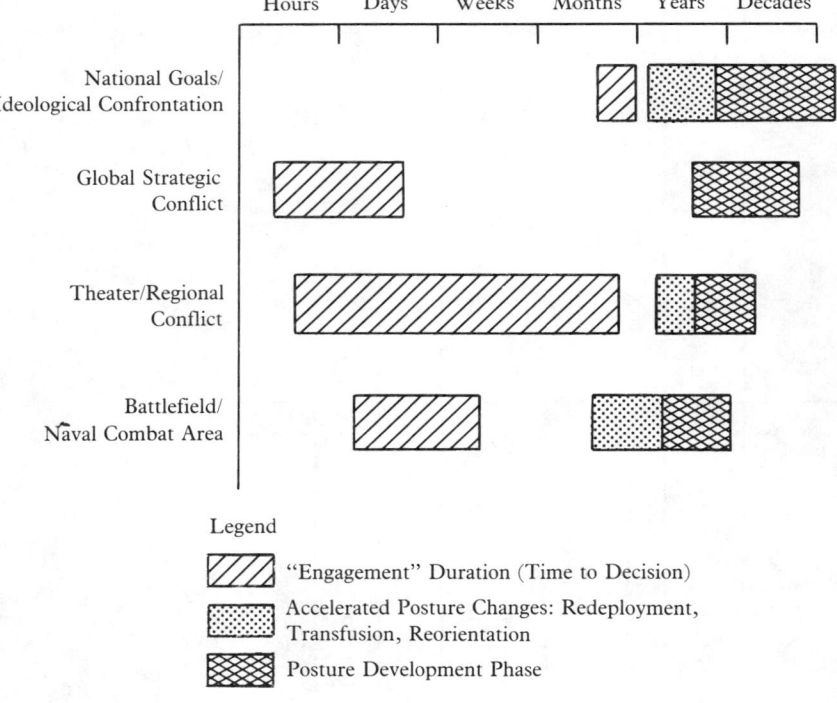

Figure 23–3. Time Congruence

days, but are rarely irretrievable in the broader theater or global engagement contexts.

By way of contrast, military capability can be *transfused to relatively small nations, or even non sovereign groups of combatants, in periods of substantially less than a year*. The buildup of air defense in Egypt (1971) by the Soviet Union, the somewhat less than successful air defense of Syria (1982), the transfer of combatant helicopters by the Soviet Union to Nicaragua (1985) are representative examples in which intelligence estimates (as contrasted to strategic and tactical intelligence) tended to underestimate the impact of the impending sequence of events. The same situation obtains with respect to broader land and air combat areas, although, by the very nature of the equipment, the transfusion times and the associated logistics burden may be considerably in excess of what would be required for isolated engagements. Naval power is a specialized case, requiring considerable investment in capital facilities, but even these can be acquired through the shift to political alignments. The acquisition by the Soviets of the U.S. facilities in Cam Ranh Bay (1975–78) is a relatively unique, but important example.[2]

Continuing in the direction of higher-level engagements (still in reference to figure 23–3), we notice that, for theater-strategic conflicts, even though development of specific military capabilities may take the usual time span of several years, local or regional supremacy can be achieved (or lost) in a matter of *months* by redeployment of forces-in-being. Recent examples include the basing of Soviet long-range bombers and the possible shift of intermediate-range Soviet missiles from Europe to Siberia (and back, of course). On the Western side, the evolution of political pressures to modify the deployment of the U.S. or NATO intermediate-range nuclear forces could have similar significance. In addition to noting the relatively rapid pace of such changes, we must also observe that, when they involve nuclear forces, the possible impact, in terms of actual outcome or escalation potential, may well be irreversible. There is no real controversy about the need for our strategic intelligence to give us warning about such moves being initiated by the potential adversary, although some would question the reliability and timeliness of such warning with the currently existing or foreseen capabilities. The essential point is that the possible goals of, the intent attributed and the options or capabilities available to, the potential adversary *must be assessed by competent intelligence estimates well before the actual event*, so that adequate reactions can be planned and implemented by the friendly side. By the same token, the adversary's interest in precluding by any and all means, including deception, the formulation of such intelligence estimates is again evident.

The same remark is applicable, *mutatis mutandis*, to global-level strategic confrontations. As remarked earlier, some theater-related military capabilities have definite revelance to global conflicts. Basic capability developments still take upward to a decade to mature into operational readiness, but relatively rapid posture changes are conceivable and even likely. Among these, the so-called strategic defense breakout (sudden unveiling of capability-in-being) is often described as potentially decisive in a global-level engagement. It may be unnecessary, but perhaps not superfluous, to add the major adverse surprises in this domain may have catastrophic, and probably irreversible, consequences for at least one of the antagonists.

Finally, at the national goals and strategies level (top row in figure 23-3), ideologies, systems of government, and corresponding political alignments may well take several years, and possibly decades, to evolve; these elements are important and, in many instances, decisive in the strategic posture evolution of the superpowers and of their alliance structure. Relatively recent events remind us, nonetheless, that relatively rapid changes are possible and must be anticipated. In 1958, France elected to withdraw from certain commitments associated with the NATO alliance. In the early 1960's, the People's Republic of China ended its ideological and political association with the Soviet Union. By the early 1970's, even during the last years of the late Mao Tse Tung, intensive economic exchanges with the West became possible and appeared increasingly desirable. In the realm of the future, let us contemplate post-World War II Japan—grown since 1956 into an economic superpower; its role and its (currently latent) military potential are decisive elements in the future U.S. strategic posture. At this point, Japan is firmly aligned with the West, but we must anticipate strenuous efforts by the Soviets to destabilize this relationship by using a combination of military threats, economic allurements, and intensive propaganda.

Other examples could be readily conjured for the future of NATO, ANZUS, and of certain Third World population foci, such as India and Brazil. The Soviet Union has its own list of potential areas of swift and adverse event sequences. Among these, the possible scenarios involving Warsaw Pact instabilities are probably being subjected to searching and sustained scrutiny. Even higher on the list of Soviet priorities should stand, according to Western rationale, the possibility or redirecting of the future course of the People's Republic of China into channels more in conformance with Soviet policy objectives.

In summary, the NIE's role is to influence the U.S. decisions in regard to its strategic posture development. This includes, but is not limited to, the military dimensions of this posture. The merits of a strategic posture at any given time are measured in the way it would respond to engagements, ranging from the conventional military battlefield through regional and global military conflicts, all the way to long-term ideological confrontation with nations that do not share our ideas on systems of government, the relationships between the state and the individual, and the manner in which the rewards of economic activity are being allocated. The difficulty in defining and developing the appropriate NIEs resides in the *tendency to focus on elements of military capability*, as contrasted to other, perhaps just as important, elements of the potential adversaries' strategic posture: the problems of *agglomerating lower level components of the estimate into meaningful top level conclusions* and in resolving the dilemma of *time congruence*, that is, how to generate estimates relevant to trends that evolve over several years or even decades (let alone the delay in perceiving the observables and deriving the estimates)—and that can be decisively modified or even reversed in a much shorter time. Given the importance of the NIEs and the difficulties involved in their production, we should expect the Soviets to target them for major deceptive efforts.

Rationale for Soviet Emphasis on Deception

Deception, to an extent not easily realized by those reared in the Western culture, is part of the Soviet political mentality. This is not a condition conceived by, or unique to, the Soviet system of government or ideology, it is rooted in centuries of Russian history going back all the way to their Byzantine cultural inheritance. In addition, the Soviet regime emphasizes, in all of its political and doctrinal publications, the importance of and the imperative need for deception in military matters. Because of the fundamental Soviet belief in the continuity of the conflict spectrum between the political, social, and military aspects of the "class struggle," the need for deception is also strongly engrained in the conduct of their foreign policies as well. It would be illogical to believe that, given the potential effects of large-scale deception on the U.S. national intelligence estimates, the Soviets would willingly forego the related deception opportunities. It is commonly asserted that the prevalence of (mutual) deception between social strata and among ethnic groups or political subdivisions also contributes to the general acceptability of deceptive practices in foreign affairs by the Soviet leadership. Within the Soviet Union, as under the Russian Empire of the tsars, the several societal groups failed to evolve the basic tenets of cooperation based on trust. They view each other with mutual suspicion and base their relations on the principle of constraint. Deception by the authorities is taken for granted; it is condoned as a matter of course in carrying out domestic policies, and in the conduct of foreign affairs, it is expected.

This is not to say that other nations, including the United States, do not practice deception as part of their military doctrine, strategy, and tactics. The important distinction is that, as we shall see later, in pluralistic political systems freedom of inquiry and of expression are taken for granted. Thus, deception attempted in the formulation of foreign or domestic policies, or in the government's actions related to carrying out these policies, is bound to become public. When this happens, the public reaction is apt to be prompt, hostile, and often devastating.

When tolerated by the political system, the practice of deception is further encouraged by its own success. Whenever the Soviet Union engaged in overt military action, either through direct participation or through the explicit support of a "client" or "satellite" nation, the results were negative and, in some cases, bordered on the catastrophic. The conflict in Greece (1947) failed to achieve the Soviet objectives; it, furthermore, led directly to the promulgation of the Truman Doctrine, essentially hostile to the Soviet Union. The support of North Korea, and later the intervention by the PRC (then allied to the Soviet Union) resulted in the quasi-permanent presence of U.S. military forces in South Korea and in the massive buildup of U.S. defenses, including the ICBM forces. The Cuban venture in 1962, an example of unsuccessful deception, was a major setback to the Soviets and was one of the reasons for Khrushchev's downfall in 1964. The interventions in Hungary (1956), in Czechoslovakia (1968), and in Afghanistan (1979) may have accomplished the immediate military objectives, but resulted in clear and lasting political setbacks for the Soviet Union. By way of contrast, Vietnam (1965-75), where the Soviet role was limited to propaganda and logistics support, the colonial "wars of national liberation" of the 1960's, and the suppression of dissidence in Poland (1980) without the direct combat use of Soviet military forces could be considered as examples of successful strategic deception in the sense that neither the United States nor its allies had any clear basis for meaningful diplomatic or military counteraction.

More specifically pertinent to deception applied to the U.S. NIEs, the potential benefits of *successful* undertakings are apt to outweigh, by far, the corresponding costs. While no accurate cost-benefit calculations are practical in such matters, the benefits derived from misdirected strategic posture decisions are thought to be potentially large in comparison to the direct costs of deception. At the same time, the latter is usually much smaller than the cost of Soviet investments that could compensate for timely and appropriate U.S. posture development decisions.

Last, there is the underlying assumption, all too widespread in both Soviet and Western thinking, that the U.S. strategic decision processes are eminently vulnerable to deception because of their relatively open and protracted nature. The U.S. political system, so the reasoning goes, is based on a quasi-adversary relationship between the two principal parties; except for the most sensitive security matters, elements of weakness and controversy are bound to reach the public domain. Thus, while the United States and its allies attempt to evolve, in concert, coherent and lasting thrusts at the policy formulation level, a large number of "input terminals" become available to inject into the strategic debate Soviet originated messages or to stimulated elements favorable to Soviet interests.

Let us now recapitulate the rationale for Soviet emphasis on deception, more particularly in the context of the U.S. NIEs. First, deception in both political and military matters is part of the Soviet cultural background and doctrinal principles. Second, the post-World War II experience brought home to the Soviets the advantages of indirect involvement, including large components of deception, as contrasted to direct, visible, military participation. Third, cost-benefit considerations favor deceptive moves (when successful), compared to direct competition against the United States in terms of resource commitments. Last, the U.S. strategic decision processes that include the developments of the NIEs are widely believed to be relatively vulnerable to deceptive or manipulative inputs.

We now propose to examine the detailed NIE generation process in order to establish whether or not the last point is valid; and, if it is, to explore the protective measures that could reduce this vulnerability.

The NIE Generation Mechanism

Information Flow Logic

In figure 23–4 (Information Flow Logic), the generalized logic of the information flow between the top decision processes of two opponents is portrayed. The decision makers for both sides, A and B, determine the actions in regard to policy goals and the corresponding evolution of strategic posture elements. (In keeping with the preceding paragraphs, let us be reminded that such posture elements are not restricted to "strategic" nuclear forces alone.) Both sides transmit

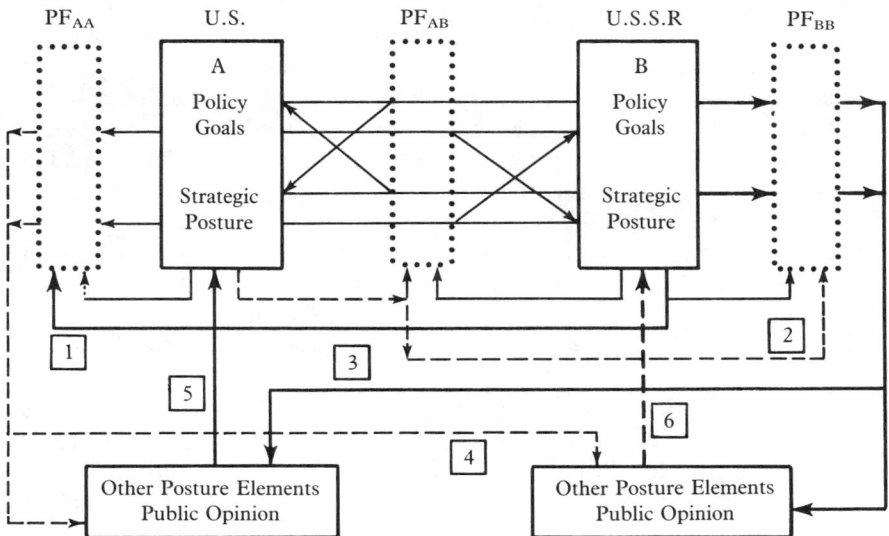

Figure 23–4. Two-Sided Information Flow Logic

information pertaining to their respective policies and postures to the opposite side. Some of these messages are provided openly and intentionally; others are intentionally but covertly "leaked" to the opponent's intelligence channels; still others are acquired by hostile intelligence, contrary to the intent, and against the interests, of the opposite side. The perception of the goals and posture elements of the potential adversary is one of the key inputs to the formulation of strategic decisions. Both sides attempt to influence (destroy, manipulate, manage—the exact term hardly matters in this context) these perceptions so that the information reaching the opponent through any of these channels does not fully or necessarily reflect the truth. Logically, this process is symbolized by a *two-directional perception filter*, PF_{AB}, subject to some degree of manipulation by both sides.

Policy goals and posture elements are also conveyed to whatever other groups or entities participate in the definition of national goals and in the implementation steps designed to further these goals.

Here again, the message reaching the intended recipients does not fully or necessarily reflect the truth, *irrespective of the intent or motivation of the originators*. Logically, this corresponds to the presence of *domestic perception filter* PF_{AA} for side A, and PF_{BB} for side B. At this point, we are not yet concerned with the nature or effectiveness of these filters. Suffice to observe that, in general, both can be subjected to manipulative attempts *by both sides*.

In the United States, policy goals and posture decisions, to the extent that they are explicitly formulated, are brought directly to the attention of Congress. Through its appropriation and authorization hearings as well as its oversight activities, Congress explicitly endorses the policies, postures, and implementation activities of the executive branch down to the minute details. The deliberate "filtering" through the PF_{AA} is minimal in practice, since in addition to formal communications, a myriad of leaks, press reports, and independent analyses by nongovernment participants convey their own elaborations and interpretations to both the Congress and the public. The strong link (1) shown between the Soviet policy makers and the U.S domestic perception filter PF_{AA} is to remind us that precisely because of the relatively open and unstructured nature of this message flow, the latter is also clearly accessible to the Soviet leadership and thus has the potential or actual capability to influence directly our "other posture elements" (including public opinion) in directions judged favorable to Soviet interests.

Conceptually, the same type of entities are present, even though the official designations and the practical means for interacting with the national-level decision processes may be essentially different. For all practical purposes, the Soviet top government officials control the substance, the timing, and the interpretations of information on their policy goals and posture development thrusts through their domestic perception filter, FP_{BB}. The U.S. ability to access this channel (shown conceptually as link "2") is minimal and has, practically, little impact on the Soviet "other posture elements," including public opinion. The same differences exist in regard to the respective abilities to present the U.S. policy goals and posture directly to the Soviet public, or the corresponding Soviet information to the U.S. public. Links "3" and "4", even though equivalent conceptually, differ quite substantially in practice. To complete the picture, we must also understand that the effective control of the "other posture elements" (again including public opinion) is in sharp contrast between the two nations. The feedback link "5" is strong and decisive in important instances for the makers of U.S. policy; the feedback link "6" is purely symbolic for the Soviet decision makers.

NIE Information Sources

Intelligence estimates are the result of cumulative information acquisition, complemented by analysis for pertinency (relevance), accuracy, and reliability. Three types of information enter into the intelligence estimate generation process:

> Primary channels, carrying newly acquired information;
>
> Secondary (reference) channels, containing information accumulated and stored, ready for retrieval in formats compatible with those of the primary channels; and
>
> Processing ground rules that serve to guide the analysis and interpretation, eventually leading to the output (the "estimate").

Primary Channels

A number of primary input channels can be made available for the purpose of generating NIEs. These can be related without difficulty to logic flow discussed earlier. Among the most significant are

1. Information resulting from direct contact with, or public statements by, Soviet officials.
2. Intelligence acquired unbeknownst to, or against the opposition of, Soviet authorities:
   a. Intelligence gathered by national assets;
   b. Intelligence gathered by assets dedicated to the objectives of individual Departments or Agencies (DOD, DOS, and so forth);
   c. Information derived from observation of tests, exercises, and operational deployment;

500 • *Deception and Strategic Planning*

   d. Information extracted from reports by defector-experts with direct past exposure to the area(s) of inquiry.
3. Manuals and publications addressed to the scientific, professional, and military communities, sponsored or authorized by the Soviet government.

On the whole and *in the opinion of the writer*, the picture offered by the ensemble of primary channels is reasonably complete in regard to *mature* weapon systems, that is, those that have been in production for some time or that are in a stage of advanced research and development. We also have, in general, a reasonably good understanding of procurement schedules, deployments, and employment concepts envisioned by the Soviet military. Missing are the corresponding information elements, in the appropriate depth or level of detail, pertinent to new systems, using advanced state-of-the-art technology, together with the related employment concepts and combat doctrines. In the broader context, we are also missing timely and reliable information about messages carried by internal Soviet Party and military command media, as well as the issues addressed, and the conclusions reached, by Soviet top government-level policy analysis task forces. (In this latter case, the originators or the recipients are in almost absolute control of the "leaks" that, in analogous situations, seem to have become a permanent way of life in the United States.)

Secondary (Reference) Channels

These are extracted from storage organized along topical and hierarchical lines to correspond, insofar as possible, to the information acquired through the primary channels. Reference channels are used to validate and assess the significance of primary-channel information. Typical questions to be answered by the assessment process are as follows:

   Is the incoming (primary) message pertaining to an object (phenomenon, construct, model, and so on) currently present in the data base?

   If in the affirmative, are there differences with respect to previously acquired information that would warrant the assignment of a new category or class within the data base or attribution to a different object within a known class?

   If in the negative, how should the data base be modified (if at all) in terms of structure and content, in order to accomodate the new information?

   In what way does the *validated* new primary information impact the currently accepted intelligence estimates?

Processing Ground Rules

Whether or not they are formally documented, these are essential to the intelligence estimate generation process. Validation, involving comparisons between primary and secondary channels is simple at relatively low levels of aggregation, where the technical characteristics are the principal discriminants. Source authentication, format, date, and context are relatively easy to establish; the message can thus be accepted, modified or rejected accordingly. Several messages, coincident in time and concurrent in substance, can be used for mutual correlation (reinforcement), especially when *deceptive correlation* can be ruled out. When aggregations at higher levels are attempted, such as those involved in capability or potential assessments, or again in predictions related to future intent on the opponent, then the "analysis" becomes increasingly judgmental. Stated in other words, when interpretation, assessment, or prediction are attempted at *higher levels of aggregation*, or when *predictions address relatively distant time frames*, or when the primary input channels have *no legitimate counterpart in our data bases*, then the role of judgmental elements could well be preponderant.

It is, therefore, necessary to have the judgments of those responsible for national-level policy formulation injected in the assessment-interpretation process as essential elements of the processing ground rules. In the ultimate analysis, these top-level policy judgments determine the interpretation and translation of the incoming primary message patterns in terms of intelligence estimates. These judgments are colored by the perceptions of the nation's policy makers.[3]

The reason for emphasis on this point is that deceptive efforts by the potential enemy can be concentrated on the processing ground rules, *including policy judgments*, as well as on the substance of primary and secondary input channels. This point has been introduced as links "1" and "3" in figure 23-4, and is made more specific in this section.

The Decision Process

Continuing the examination of mechanisms involved in the NIE generation, we are in the presence of a number of primary inputs from external sources, a number of secondary (reference) inputs extracted from the data base, and the processing ground rules, including the judgmental elements. The problem that faces us now is the *transformation* of all this into elements of the NIE end product.

Figure 23-5 shows one step in this process. It assumes the existence of a *multiple-level decision model*, in which decisions taken at level (N–1) contribute, as *primary inputs*, to the formulation of decisions at the next higher level (N); these in turn become part of the primary inputs at the next higher level (N + 1), and so on. Other ("external") primary inputs, originating directly from sources extraneous to the decision model, may enter decision elements at any level. Note

502 • *Deception and Strategic Planning*

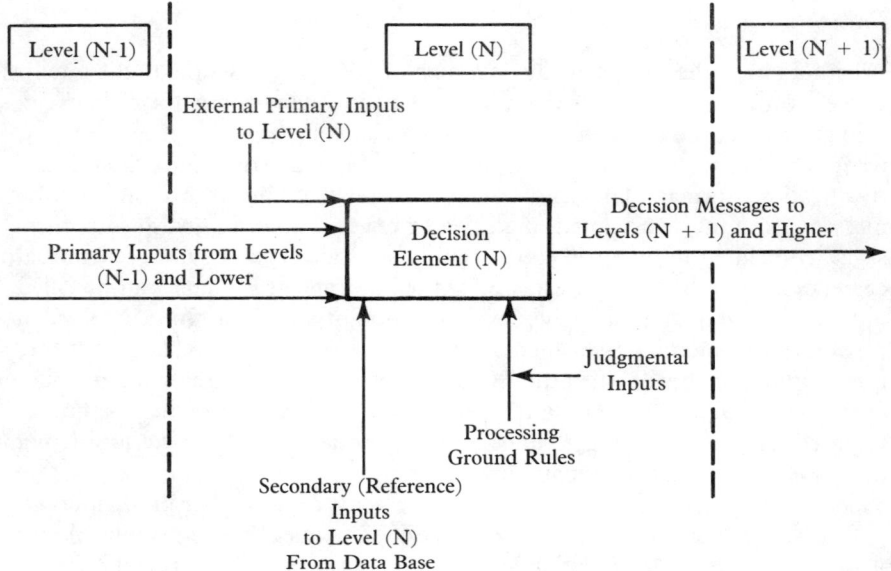

Figure 23–5. One Element of the Decision Model

that the multiple-level decision concept does not imply a tree-like structure; one output of level (N) may enter at any higher level (N + 1), (N + 2), (N + 3), and so forth; it is also possible for an output at level (N) to serve as part of the primary inputs to decision elements at more than one level.

Such a decision model exists, more or less explicitly, in any intelligence generation process as an essential part of the secondary inputs. It underlies the organization of the data base and must be obtained through (what is usually) a protracted period of empirical accumulation of information associated with the same primary input set *assumed to remain stationary during the accumulation period*. This condition is hardly ever satisfied in the real world; it constitutes one of the essential weak points of most intelligence estimates and may conceivably offer opportunities for hostile attempts at deception.

The component decision at level (N) is shown schematically on figure 23–5. Several primary inputs are seen to originate from levels (N–1) or lower; one external primary input channel is also shown. In addition, the decision element (N) also receives the pertinent subset of the data base as part of the secondary inputs. Processing ground rules and judgmental factors are made available, as applicable, at this decision level. The output of level (N) called the *decision messages*, are shown to contribute as primary inputs to higher decision levels.

The decision messages may comprise any combination of the following:

Validated changes with respect to the corresponding current information in the data base (substance, probability, and time of occurrence).

Assessment of the significance of the change; how should other, not directly connected, elements of the data base *and/or the decision model* itself be modified in order to accomodate the effects of the change(s) (in connection with other recent changes) on the opponent's posture.

Extrapolation to future trends, plans, and possible intent of the opponent, as revealed, corroborated, or modified by the change.

Validation is conceptually a simple logical step, but even this may prove to be most difficult in practice. When there is a single primary input, highly reliable and known from prior experience to be relevant, the validation step can indeed be trivial. This, in general, is not the case when several mutually contradictory input channels are present with various degrees of reliability, and relevance; correlation with the data base, therefore, may not be possible. In such situations, no firm theoretical basis exists whereupon rational validation can be performed. The subsequent assessment and extrapolation steps leading to the decision message are then based on "experience," "trained intuitions," which are nothing but quasi-synonyms for subliminal correlation without explicitly acknowledged data bases. Both experience and intuition are apt to be misleading if applied to inputs relevant to objects not previously observed, or to those subjected to deliberate attempts at deception.

We must end this section with a cautionary observation. The difficulties and weaknesses of the NIE generation process have been emphasized to suggest that theoretically rigorous "processing" is hardly possible and that, therefore, the application of deceptive practices may appear attractive to the opponent. In previous sections, the points were made that the NIEs contribute essentially to the evolution of the U.S. strategic posture, and that the Soviets are most likely to follow their traditional proclivities for deception. Here we want to point out that *overconservative assessments, interpretations, and extrapolations* do not offer adequate protection against the inherent weaknesses and vulnerabilities of the NIE generation mechanism. Over-conservatism in such matters would credit the Soviets with maximum capability and potential, while attributing to them the worst possible intentions as judged from the U.S. standpoint. This could lead to over-investment by the United States in countervailing capability, which in turn would be seen by the Soviets as additional and growing threats. Such a scenario contains elements of positive feedback, leading to the prospect of dangerous instability.

Vulnerabilities of the NIE Generation to Deception

With the preceding description of the main features of the NIE generation process, it is now possible to summarize the parts of the process that exhibit vulnerability to the Soviets' deceptive attempts:

> The primary input channels can be subjected to false messages. These must be logically consistent with the U.S. secondary channels and made available in a format acceptable to the validation process immediately following the input channel affected. The message carries information that serves the interests of the Soviet Union, as contrasted to those of the United States.
>
> Deceptive messages within several input channels can be injected with false mutual correlation characteristics. In this manner, even though correlation through the secondary channels (reference extracted from the data base) is not forthcoming, the deceptive content of these "correlated" channels would be validated and accepted.
>
> The assessment and extrapolation steps can be distorted by long sequences of logically consistent, but actually misleading, messages. This technique is called "conditioning" since it results in developing and accepting for future use data base elements and/or processing ground rules that consistently lead to erroneous decisions. Conditioning can also affect the structure of the *decision models* (explained earlier) since these are empirically constructed on the basis of prior experience.
>
> By the injection over a relatively long period of time, of deceptive messages into channels that reach directly the senior individuals responsible for national-level policy formulation, the *judgmental elements* of the processing rules acting at the highest decision levels can be modified in a direction favorable to the Soviets. This form of deception, probably the most dangerous of all, is called "misimprinting," to convey the idea that the thought processes of the nation, as given expression by the judgment of its policy makers, are being impaired.

Examples

The short list of examples following is intended to be representative, rather than exhaustive. Some of the examples are drawn from the era preceding the institution of formal NIEs, but the points illustrated remain nonetheless valid. On the other hand, some of the interesting but controversial current examples have been omitted because of security restrictions.

1. The Bomber Gap. Using primary inputs derived from industrial production and technical intelligence, the United States reached the erroneous conclusion that the Soviets would emphasize heavy bomber production during the 1950s decade. The Soviets encouraged this belief, and the U.S. Air Force contributed its own reinforcement. The countervailing U.S. investment in air defense interceptors and SAGE was probably unjustified at the time.

2. The Missile Gap and Sequels. In the late 1950s, in part because of the shock created by the Soviet Sputnik, the ICBM gap became a political issue. The intelligence estimates on Soviet ICBM development and production potential were too high. By 1963, at the peak of our own Minuteman production, the missile gap disappeared from the intelligence estimates. We essentially missed the major Soviet commitment to the buildup of their nuclear strategic forces, as well as to the creation of "blue water" surface and submarine naval forces. The U.S. intelligence underestimated well into the 1970s the growing Soviet technical sophistication in rocketry, inertial guidance, and nuclear submarine propulsion. This is believed by many to have contributed to our belief that the Soviets are not in fact seeking strategic nuclear supremacy. Secretary McNamara's personal beliefs in the willingness of the Soviets to acquiesce in a stable strategic balance may have colored, in the mid-1960s, the U.S. intelligence estimates regarding future Soviet strategic nuclear potential.

3. The 1972 Grain Sale. The U.S. economic intelligence failed to warn about the magnitude of the 1971–72 Soviet wheat crop failure. We apparently were not in possession of a monitoring system for significant Soviet commodity transactions. The Soviet negotiators managed to conclude massive purchases (perhaps with the active connivance of U.S. commodity firms) by subdividing the total into many smaller transactions not directly traceable to Soviet buyers. The result was dislocation of the U.S. grain futures market and a sizeable jump in the U.S. inflation rate.

4. Grey Area Weapons. The Soviet Union has developed and deployed the SS-20 mobile multiple-warhead nuclear ballistic missile. It is described and advertised as a theater-nuclear weapon, not to be counted under the ceilings imposed by strategic arms control or arms reduction treaties. Soviet negotiators insist that the combination of current deployment sites and payload configurations precludes use against the CONUS. The United States has primary channel inputs to the effect that other deployment modes and payload configurations are part of Soviet plans and capabilities that would make "strategic" use possible. Soviet propaganda denies this information and attempts to modify the U.S. interpretation of the related intelligence inputs.

5. Strategic Arms Reduction. The Soviet objective is to continue the quest for nuclear supremacy without provoking a major conflict with the United States. Contributory objectives are to build advanced strategic offensive and defensive systems, while constraining, insofar as possible, the strategic system developments and deployments of the United States. With this end in view, the Soviets wish to avoid detection and attendant publicity of any treaty violation on their side, while taking advantage of any possible wording or interpretation ambiguities. They also would like to constrain weapon testing by the United States while continuing their own test activities.

With these multiple and interacting objectives, the Soviets resort to a number of deceptive actions. Some of these have direct impact upon the U.S. national intelligence estimates. Among these are the following:

Encrypt, or spoof, telemetry signals originating from weapons systems under test. This denies or modifies primary input channels for decisions related to future system capabilities.

Develop strategic missile defenses under the guise of improved air defenses. This is first aimed at multiple deception objectives, in that it denies primary input information related to ABM defense; second, it conditions the U.S. assessment of the Soviet air defense capability and deployment; and, third, it weakens the U.S. negotiating position in regard to strategic defense research and development.

Press for Comprehensive Test Ban (CTB) agreements, while retaining the "peaceful nuclear explosion" (PNE) clause. At the same time, retain the expert weapon design teams as PNE observers, or under some other guise, so as to continue nuclear warhead development programs unimpeded by test restrictions. If successful, this set of confluent deceptive actions would condition the U.S. assessments of the Soviet nuclear warhead technology and production potential. It may also misimprint the higher level U.S. judgments in regard to the Soviet readiness to negotiate and the willingness to adhere to the terms of a treaty once it is completed and ratified.

Create or reinforce Western public opinion trends to the effect that the U.S. attitudes and initiatives are the basic causes of the nuclear arms race that is bound to become lethal to the whole world.

Typical thrusts are:

1. Superficially attractive, but in fact impractical, offers for reduction in offensive armaments
2. Accusations to the effect that the SDI is a sinister U.S. ploy to acquire a first strike posture vis-à-vis the Soviet Union
3. Publicity in regard to the horrors of large-scale nuclear wars (prompt espousal of "nuclear winter" and "fate of the earth" type prognostications)
4. Participation in the moral outrage of Western religious groups and authorities against nuclear war.

Such propaganda thrusts, if allowed to penetrate Western public opinions, could eventually create additional political pressures for arms control. More to the point of this discussion, they could bring forth a generation of leaders genuinely, albeit erroneously, convinced about the absolute evils of the nuclear components of the U.S. and Western strategic postures. This would logically result in a more optimistic and confident view of the future prospects of arms control or arms reduction. It would also prompt a more benign interpretation of Soviet noncompliance actions. In other words, it would misimprint the Western leadership with judgment criteria clearly favorable to the Soviet Union and potentially catastrophic for the Western democracies.

Summary

The national intelligence estimates are inputs made by the intelligence community to the future evolution of U.S. strategic posture elements. These elements comprise far more than just a panoply of nuclear weapon systems. The definition and articulation of national goals, the cultural and industrial base of the nation and its economic potential and resilience are all part of strategic posture—if this term is defined as the capability of the nation to prevail in the long-term competition against its major ideological opponent, the Soviet Union. This competition may take the form of "engagements" ranging from local military conflicts, all the way through regional and global military conflicts, to confrontation of national goals and strategies. Because of the importance of NIEs in the formulation of strategic posture evolution steps, and because of Soviet cultural and institutional proclivities, the Soviets are likely to continue and probably expand their past efforts aimed at deceiving Western intelligence and, more specifically, the U.S. NIEs.

Examination of the information flow logic between two opponents reveals a number of links that could serve as entry terminals for messages aimed at deception. While conceptually similar, these links are grossly asymmetrical when it comes to practical application of deceptive techniques. This asymmetry is believed to favor the Soviet Union at this time.

The NIE generation process itself has several areas of potential vulnerability to deception. The primary input channels (those that carry newly acquired information) can be spoofed or manipulated. The secondary input channels (those that serve as reference for validating and assessing the primary channel inputs) can be misled by false correlations, or by rapid changes in the statistical characteristics of the primary inputs. The processing ground rules, which are essential to the assessment and interpretation steps, can be conditioned so as to draw unwarranted conclusions from a given set of primary inputs. The judgmental components of interpretation, reflecting the views of the nation's top policy makers, can also be subjected to deceptive inputs leading, if successful in this case, to *misimprinting*. These higher forms of deception (conditioning and misimprinting) are less well understood, but potentially more dangerous than the relatively simple forms of deception affecting the primary input channels.

Proceeding beyond the purview of description, we may want to raise the question of possible protection of the NIEs against the deceptive attempts by the Soviet Union. This is an area of current interest, as of yet, inadequately explored. A few general recommendations should be considered for more detailed examination:

1. Gain a better understanding of the NIE generation process. This could be furthered by making the decision models explicit and by improving the analytical basis of the validation, assessment, and interpretation steps. The problem of combining messages from several channels should receive increased attention.

2. Create multiple parallel paths for validation, assessment, and interpretation. Several groups, working with the same primary input sets and the same references (data bases), should be given the opportunity to reach decision messages independently from each other, *using different set of processing ground rules*. It is possible (and in this writer's view, probable) that the benefits of cross-checks at the decision formulation level would, by far, outweigh the possible security risks resulting from the multiple-path approach.

3. Use *active countermeasures*: Although it is much further beyond our horizon, there is the realm of active countermeasures, which consists of generating and injecting into the Soviet intelligence channels messages that would tend to mislead the recipients about the effects of their deceptive attempts. Here we are touching upon esoteric concepts, not easily implemented under the conditions foreseeable for the U.S. intelligence community.

Notes

1. *Tactical* decisions, by way of contrast, have to do with the effective use of these resources once made available for the purposes of military operations.

2. A most interesting area of speculation would attempt to define, with the full benefit of hindsight, what competent, long-range intelligence estimates of the Soviet strategic goals in Southeast Asia and beyond could have prompted the U.S. to do in this regard between October 1972 (the "peace at hand" announcement by Dr. Kissinger) and June 1975 (the fall of Saigon and the end of U.S. presence). Conceivably, all the technology refinements and equipment resources could have been marshalled in order to deny, or at least to delay, the use of these naval facilities by the Soviet Union.

3. The converse should not be overlooked. In turn, the policy makers perceptions can be strongly affected by the primary intelligence inputs conveyed directly and in a timely manner.

Part VII
Conclusion

24
Soviet Strategic Deception and U.S. Vulnerability: A Net Assessment

Patrick J. Parker

In the 1840's two remarkable Frenchmen travelled abroad, one to America and the other to Russia. Both carefully recorded their observations. Alexis de Tocqueville's *Democracy in America* is well known in the West today, and no reader can fail to wonder at the currency and relevance of most of his observations. Despite the passing of almost one hundred and fifty years, during which social upheaval, civil war, and profound economic change took place and large populations with rich and diverse cultures were incorporated, his distinctive portrayal of American culture and the personality of Americans could almost have been written today. Much the same thing has been said of the Marquis de Custine's *Russia in 1839*, a journal now forbidden in Russia and little known in the West, which chronicles a journey to Russia at about the same time.[1]

While the contrasts between the two societies that emerge from these and subsequent works, and even casual observation, are varied, de Tocqueville's Americans are an open, honest lot, while de Custine's Russians are secretive, deceptive and careless with the truth, both individually and as representatives of the state. If you scratch most Americans, you find a general respect for honesty and a deep-rooted belief in the old adage that "honesty is the best policy." If you probe this belief you find it to be based, at least in part, on a practical sense that honesty and a reputation for honesty are necessary for the efficient conduct of normal day-to-day transactions among people. This does not necessarily imply that all Americans are honest, or that considerations other than practical ones are unimportant in American views of honesty. Ethical values are taken very seriously as well: saying that a man is honest is a compliment; calling him a liar or a cheat are fighting words; and if a man is generally known to be either, it is hard for him to function effectively in society. Free institutions, and especially the market for ideas, place a natural premium on the truth. Indeed so deeply rooted in American culture are these simple ideas that it is very hard for most Americans to imagine a complex modern society that does not share them, and, when dealing with foreigners, most Americans attribute to them their own basic values, views, and practices. Yet, as this book helps to make clear, our principal competitor, the Soviet Union, is very different in this regard, and failing to recognize this in dealings with the Soviets is foolish and dangerous and has been the cause of much mischief.[2] Today, as in de Custine's time, concealment, deception and lying are fundamental to the style of interpersonal relations among the Russians. One reason for this is the despotic nature of the Russian government, both then and now, which demands the appearance of total loyalty to the state (and today the Party) and enforces that loyalty through a massive system of secret police and internal spying and reporting of deviant behavior by one citizen on another or even by a member of one's own family. Even the slightest criticism of the State is regarded as evidence of disloyalty, yet no thinking person can be truly loyal: the State is visibly both cruel and clumsy, yet all must profess to believe that it is kind and efficient. Virtually the only way to even a modest amelioration of the dreary poverty that is the lot of most Russians is through Party membership and movement upward in the Party, and this requires continually preserving the appearance of loyalty to an orthodoxy whose rhetoric is increasingly in conflict with day-to-day reality. Thus deception and lying are conditions of membership and survival in Russia's elite; without them one cannot succeed. They are a fundamental part of the style of success and of the national style both internally and in dealing with the outside world. Effective lying and deception are essential for admission to the *nomenklatura* and, as such, are highly prized and respected.

While little systematic work exists on this subject, Vladimir Lefebvre has developed both theory and data that support the proposition that the two cultures not only evince very different behavior in experimental situations related to honesty and truthfulness, but also demonstrate profoundly different ethical values.[3] The persistence of these differences between the Americans and the Russians over a very long period of time suggests that they will continue, and that Americans must understand them and deal with them in order to compete effectively with the Soviets. The deeply rooted belief that all civilized people (including the Russians) value honesty makes the Americans particularly susceptible to a well-orchestrated and carried out Russian program of lying and deception, especially in peacetime.

This general credulity of Americans is exacerbated in matters relating to the national defense by another characteristic of democracies noted by de Tocqueville and still clearly true today—namely a general reluctance to maintain strong military forces in time of peace and a sense that peaceful solutions can be found to international problems through negotiations amongst men of good will. Nuclear weapons have added an additional urgency to this belief: it must be so, for the alternative is too grim to contemplate. Thus Americans are most susceptible to Russian deception than ever; the tendency to attribute to others their own basic honesty and desire for peace is reinforced by the urgent wish that it were so with the Russians as well.

This book addresses a range of considerations that, taken together, should improve our understanding of these issues as they relate to national security and help us deal more effectively with the Soviet Union. First, and perhaps most important, the picture that emerges from these pages is of a society that not only uses deception extensively, but also uses it effectively. Effective deception must be based on a keen understanding of the object of deception, and the Soviet Union clearly works hard to achieve that understanding. The Institute for the Study of the USA and Canada and the Institution of World Economy and International Relations (IMEMO) are just the tip of a very large iceberg. The Soviets study Western culture and political institutions, identify those influential individuals and groups with views especially helpful to them, and seek to strengthen such groups and reinforce their ideas. The issue of Mutual Assured Destruction (MAD) is an illuminating case in point and a useful example. There is virtually no evidence that supports the proposition that Soviet civilian or military leaders think of nuclear forces in these terms at all, and there is much evidence that indicates a very different Soviet view, which includes a nuclear war fighting doctrine and a theory of victory. However there is a substantial community of influential U.S. and European MAD adherents, and the Soviet Union finds the positions advocated by them very useful. They are in general against improved ICBM accuracy, civil defense and ballistic missile defenses, all prominent features of the Soviet defense program, all contributors to the Soviet metric of world power, the "correlation of forces," and all viewed as improving the position of the possessor. Therefore the Soviets have come to understand the tortured logic of MAD and how to exploit it in dealing with the West. In personal encounters, meetings of professional societies, and Western journal articles, they encourage MAD ideas and suggest that right-minded people, influential at the highest levels, exist in the Soviet Union and pursue the same goals and that the prospects for world peace can be improved by vigorous lobbying by these groups, each in its own country. While it is clear that no such group in fact exists in Russia, Western MAD activists want to believe that it does and are therefore easily deceived and led to redouble their efforts. No one can examine the U.S. national security debates over the past twenty-five years and not conclude that they have been very considerably influenced by the advocates of MAD.

There are some underlying beliefs that appear to be held in common by most of the authors in the book. First, there is a fundamental Soviet antagonism toward the United States and our democratic allies that will continue as long as Russia is ruled by a Marxist-Leninist oligarchy, and the United States seeks to preserve free political and economic institutions at home and encourage them abroad. Second, the Soviet leadership cannot accept the international status quo and will continue to support worldwide Marxist revolutionary change and expand Soviet hegemony into areas contiguous to the Soviet Union. Third, peaceful coexistence means to the Soviets precisely what Lenin said it means, that is, carrying on the struggle against capitalism using all means short of war, and lying and deception are tools useful and probably essential to success in that struggle. Fourth, if the Soviets assess the correlation of forces to be clearly in their favor in a region or globally, they may use violent means to exploit the opportunity, and in that case, cover and deception will be essential elements in achieving surprise and pursuing victory. In short, competition between the Western democracies and the Soviet Union will continue to be the dominant reality in international affairs, both now and for the foreseeable future. The competition also requires of the Soviet leaders massive deception at home in order to deny the obvious—namely the existence in the West of a form of social organization much preferable to virtually all who see it. This, in turn, has a profound influence on the attitudes and practices of the entire Soviet society; domestic lying and deception are a necessary and deeply ingrained consequence of the despotic and inefficient Soviet social contract. And these practices manifest themselves in vigorous programs of lying, deception, and propaganda toward the West; they find a particularly fertile ground in America for the reasons discussed earlier.

What does this suggest for the future? The backdrop will remain the living lie, largely unchanged: the Soviet Union, where the mass of the people work long, hard hours for very low wages that can be spent only in stores with inferior quality merchandise specifically designated for them, will continue to be touted as the "workers' paradise"; rule by a small, ruthless, highly privileged and increasingly hereditary minority will remain "the dictatorship of the proletariat;" and a cruel, repressive, and expansionist foreign policy, which has enslaved the people of Eastern Europe and now Afghanistan and aspires to worldwide hegemony, will continue to be presented as championing peace and freedom. These grand Orwellian lies are necessary at home, successful in much of the Third World, and remarkably effective in the Western democracies, particularly among what Beichman calls "the American high culture." The Soviets will continue to try to affect Western strategy, military forces, and resolve by influencing public opinion and opinion makers. They will use direct recruitment, active measures and propaganda. Portrayal of the Soviet leaders as temperate, humane, and deeply committed to the avoidance of war will be a major theme worldwide, while in Europe the horrors of war (especially nuclear war) and the destabilizing effect of the American military presence will be an added theme.

But there will be a new element. The Soviet military buildup is maturing into a war machine of unprecedented size and power, far in excess of what is needed for the defense of Russia, and dominant over the opposing allied forces in many parts of the globe, and Soviet nuclear forces may have achieved many of the elements needed for dominating the escalation process against a wide-range of possible circumstances. Soviet foreign policy over the next decade or so will almost certainly reflect these new realities, while deep Soviet domestic problems, exacerbated by the recent large drop in the price of oil, provide further incentives for a somewhat more adventurous strategy than in the past. It will be aimed at the following objectives, and deception will play a part in the Soviet strategy for achieving all of them:

1. Increase the spread of communism and sap Western resolve to resist it.
2. Separate the United States from its allies, especially Germany in Europe, and Japan, Korea, and the Philippines in the Pacific.
3. Prevent further rapprochement between the United States and China.
4. Reduce popular and political support for the overall U.S. defense program.
5. Conclude arms control agreements advantageous to the Soviet Union and disadvantageous to the West.
6. Stop or cripple the SDI.
7. Ensure continued Western apathy toward civil defense.
8. Encourage the West to reduce or abandon restrictions on Soviet imports of high technology.
9. Grant favorable terms of trade for Soviet agricultural imports.
10. Bring about major reductions in non-Soviet oil production.
11. Conceal and deny any Soviet involvement in international terrorism, assassination or other Soviet sponsored violence.
12. Achieve surprise, especially in any preparations for war or initiation of war.

In each of these cases there is a perception that the Soviets will seek to establish or reinforce, and a reality that they will seek to hide. At the most fundamental level, they must deal with the failure of Marxism and the success of capitalism. The prosperity and growth that large masses of ordinary people have come to enjoy under systems of private property, economic competition and the rule of law must be denied by the Soviet Union, as must the wide-ranging personal liberty and increasing equality of income that almost always go hand-in-hand with capitalism. Capitalism's wide popular appeal is attested to by large immigrant populations and long immigration waiting lines. Since the success of capitalism is based in significant measure on harnessing man's greed through competition for the common good, it is founded on a somewhat pessimistic view of human nature, a view denied in Marxism but confirmed by our experience with it. In contrast to the success of capitalism, Marxism is a failure. Wherever it has been established economic performance has been poor, political freedom and dissent have been repressed, and the distribution of income and wealth has become progressively more unequal. Communist states have no voluntary immigration; instead they must have laws and fences to keep people in, and flight is a crime often punished by death. Once a Marxist regime is established, peaceful political change is impossible. Obviously the truth makes few converts to the Soviet way. Its appeal must be based on concealment of reality and deceptive propaganda; it is especially strong among the ignorant and poor. Marxism promised economic betterment through equal sharing and central planning and spiritual elevation through service to the State instead of ones self. It portrays capitalism as perpetuating poverty and degrading the spirit by encouraging greed and self-interest. Promoting these myths is necessary for successful Marxist revolution. Where the Soviet reality cannot be hidden, as is the case for cadres sent to be trained in Russia, it is either described as harsh but necessary transition or, more cynically, as a chance to become a member of a priviledged class, the Party elite in a new "workers paradise." Thus, propaganda and deception will continue to characterize Soviet efforts, especially in the Third World.

Marxist revolution is probably not a realistic Soviet goal among America's major allies, but driving wedges between them and the United States almost certainly is. Fear of war, especially nuclear war, is natural. While there can be little doubt that, without serious countervailing power, the Soviets would expand rapidly in Europe and the Far East, this will be stoutly denied, and the safety and security of Western Europe from Soviet imperialism will be constantly asserted. The American presence will be portrayed as unnecessary, destablizing, and dangerous and as increasing the likelihood of nuclear war. All these themes were prominent during the recent debates surrounding the INF deployment, and while they failed to stop it, attitudes were changed, particularly in Germany and particularly among the increasingly powerful younger voters. More and more one hears that *nothing* would be worth the price of nuclear war. For example, today the platform of the SPD for the first time calls for the removal of all nuclear weapons and foreign forces from German soil. Over the next decade the combined themes of intimidation and reassurance will be prominent.

The Soviets view international relations largely in the context of the struggle between capitalism and communism, a struggle in which there will eventually be a winner and a loser and that they are preordained to win. While they do not view the situation precisely as a zero-sum game, they clearly tend to see most events that effect both the Americans and the Russians as also having a winner and a loser and thereby affecting the long run competition. While they clearly recognize events that can leave both nations better or worse off (for example, excellent crop weather or global nuclear war), they always calculate which side will emerge from any specific situation *relatively* better off and by how much, and they are very reluctant to enter into any arrangement with the West, no matter how great the absolute benefits to them, if it does not enhance their relative position.

Americans do not see the world in the same way. We live daily with the benefits of exchange and trade and are usually pleased to see both sides to a transaction benefit. We are generally more interested in our gains than in whether we get the best of the other person, unless we are engaged in a fight. To the Soviets, the fight model is the normal paradigm; to the Americans it is voluntary exchange for mutual benefit.

This difference is crucial in understanding Soviet-American relations. When Americans are generous and forthcoming, it indicates to the Russians weakness and a lack of seriousness. Those communities in the United States that advocate generosity, restraint, and a genuine long-term peaceful coexistence are seen as contributing to the weakness of their own society and as such, are to be used to advantage in the struggle. They will be told by their Russian acquaintances what they want to hear and encouraged to make their voices heard. In private, they are despised as bourgeois intellectuals. By contrast, efforts are made to discredit those who are effective in dealing with the Russians.

Aspects of all these ideas are developed and documented in this book. The underlying reality of Soviet long-term strategic aims, the public denial by the Soviets of those aims in the West, and the continued encouragement by the Soviets of those in the West who advocate policies that they believe benefit them. One area was not covered—there was no speculation about future Soviet initiatives. American intelligence has a poor record in anticipating new Soviet actions. Readers of this book should not be surprised by that; the Soviets are good at cover, deception, and surprise, and U.S. intelligence does not report or warn until it has tangible evidence. Yet we have come to understand much about the Soviet style of international competition, and we should be able to use our knowledge to make informed guesses about the future. I believe that today the Soviets face a unique opportunity to change the correlation of forces in their favor, an opportunity that their style may well lead them to exploit. The Soviets are the world's largest oil producers and oil and gas exports have been their major source of hard currency. The breakdown of OPEC and the resultant drop in the price of oil has given them a serious economic setback, and they would benefit greatly from a return to the status quo ante, which would require a large reduction in non-Soviet oil production. Such a reduction would not be very hard to accomplish. For example, a competent attack on the Saudi oil fields could reduce Saudi production to very low levels for several years, and such an attack could be accomplished without overt Soviet involvement. The consequences would be very favorable to the Soviets, both politically and economically, and the risks would be small. The Soviets would become the principal supplier of oil to West Germany and also a major supplier to the rest of Western Europe at much higher prices reflecting the reduced world supply. They could demonstrate their reliability and good will in the short run and later use their newly won economic leverage to exact major political and military concessions. Eventually, they might offer the prospect of an unarmed, reunified Germany free of Russian or American "occupation forces" and relieved of the threat of nuclear war. A new, more youthful and naive West German electorate might be beguiled by the prospect and surprised in the aftermath, but by then it would be too late. It is not my purpose to suggest this as the only scenario we should worry about, or even that it is the most likely one. But it is my purpose to suggest that if we wait for intelligence to warn us, artful use of cover and deception may well insure that the warning comes too late. Despite Soviet propaganda to the contrary, Russians view the long-term competition differently from the West, and we must understand how they think in order to anticipate them, recognizing that they will be trying to lead us off the scent. Thus, we must expect Soviet cover and deception to cause intelligence to be lacking or ambiguous, especially in situations that require warning and call for prompt decisive action. Being gulled is an ignominious reason to lose. This vicious, deceitful, and repressive dictatorship must not be allowed to use its guile on American credulity to bring about a new dark age.

Notes

1. de Custine, the Marquis, *Journey For Our Time*, journals Phillis Penn Kohler, ed. and trans. (London: Arthur Barker, Ltd., 1951).

2. Perhaps the most notable case in point occurred at Yalta in February 1945. For an incisive analysis of the Yalta deception, see Crozier, Middleton and Murray-Brown *This War Called Peace*, especially ch. 1. "Yalta: Image and Reality".

3. Vladimir A. Lefebvre, *Algebra of Conscience: A Comparative Analysis of Western and Soviet Ethical Systems* (Boston: D. Reidel Publishing, 1982).

Glossary

ABM	Antiballistic missile
Abwehr	Defense (intelligence/counterintelligence)
ACDA	Arms Control and Disarmament Agency
AIDS	Acquired immune deficiency syndrome
AM	Active measures
ANZUS	Trilateral Defense Pact between Australia, New Zealand, and the United States
ASAT	Antisatellite
AWAC	Airborne Warning and Control (System)
BMD	Ballistic missile defense
BND	West German Federal Intelligence Service (*Bundesnachrichtendienst*)
BW	Biological warfare
CAP	Combat Air Patrol
CBW	Chemical/biological warfare
CDU	Christian Democratic Union, West Germany (*Christlich-Demokratische Union*)
CEP	Circular error probable
CEPAD	Evangelical Committee for Development Assistance (*Comitie Evangelico para Asistencia y Desarrolo*) (Worked closely with the Sandinista government)
CHEKA	Extraordinary Commission, from *VECHEKA*, the All-Russian Extraordinary Commission for Combating Counterrevolution, Speculation, Sabotage, and Misconduct in Office, formed 20 December 1917 by the Central Executive Committee (*Chrezvychainaya Komissiya*) Successive names: GPU, OGPU, KGB
CIA	Central Intelligence Agency
C^3I	Command, control, communications, and intelligence
COCOM	Council Coordinating Committee (Responsible for Western technology export control against the Soviet Union)
COMINT	Communications intelligence
CONUS	Continental United States

COSEP	Superior Council of Private Enterprises (*Superior Consejo de Empresas Privados*)
CPSU	Communist Party of the Soviet Union (*Kommunisticheskaya Partiya Sovetskovo Soyuza-KPSS*)
CSCE	Conference on Security and Cooperation in Europe
CSU	Christian Social Union, West Germany (*Christlich-Soziale Union*)
CTB	Comprehensive test ban
Darzhavna Sigurnost	Bulgarian Intelligence Service
DGI	General Directorate of Intelligence (*Direccion General de Inteligencia*)
DIA	Defense Intelligence Agency
DKP	West German Communist Party (*Deutsche Kommunistische Partei*)
ECM	Electronic countermeasures
ELINT	Electronic intelligence
EMT	Equivalent megatrons
EURATOM	European Atomic Energy Community
FBIS	Foreign Broadcast Information Service
FDP	Free Democratic Party, Federal Republic of Germany (*Freie Deutsche Partei*)
FMLN	Farabundo Marti National Liberation Front
FRG	Federal Republic of Germany (*Bundesrepublik Deutschland—BRD*)
FSLN	Sandinista National Liberation Front (*Frente Sandinista Liberacion Nacionale*)
GAC	The President's General Advisory Committee on Arms Control
GDR	German Democratic Republic (*Deutsche Demokratische Republik—DDR*)
GKO	Soviet State Committee of Defense (*Gosudarstvenny Komitet Oborony*)
GLCM	Ground-launched cruise missile
GNP	Gross national product
GPF	General Purpose Forces (*Sily Obshchevo Znacheniya*)
GPU	State Political Administration (*Gosudarstzvennoye Politicheskoye Upravleniye*)
GRU	Main Intelligence Directorate of the Soviet General Staff (*Glavnoye Razvedivatelnoye Upravleniye*)
GUSM	Principal Directorate of Strategic Deception (*Glavnoe Upravlenie Stratigicheskoy Maskirovka*)
IAF	Israeli Air Force
ICBM	Intercontinental ballistic missile

ID	International Department of the CPSU
IDF	Israeli Defense Force
IID	International Information Department of the CPSU
INF	Intermediate-range nuclear force
I&O Table	Input and output table
KINTEX	Bulgarian "business" firm controlled by *Darzhavna Sigurnost*
Knesset	Israeli Parliament (or House of Representatives)
KGB	Committee for State Security (*Komitet Gosudarstvennoy Bezopasnosti*)
LANDSAT	Land satellite
LOW	Launch-on-warning
MAP	Multiple aim point
MBFR	Mutual Balanced Force Reduction
MBMW	Machine building/metalworking
MEA	Middle East and Africa
MNF	Multinational Force (Peacekeeping)
MOTsR	Monarchist Association of Central Russia (*Monarkhicheskaya Organizatisiya Tsentral'noi Rossii*)
MRBM	Medium-range ballistic missile
MX	Missile, experimental
NATO	North Atlantic Treaty Organization
NEP	New Economic Policy (*Novaya Ekonomicheskaya Politika*)
NIE	National intelligence estimate
NKVD	People's Commissariat of the Interior (*Narodnaya Kommisiya Vautrennysch Dei*)
Nomenklatura	Positions over which the Central Party authorities have complete control, and the people who fill these positions
NPS	Naval Postgraduate School
NSA	National Security Agency
NSC	National Security Council
NTM	National Technical Means
NTS	People's Labor Alliance (*Narodnyi Trudovoi Soyuz*)
OGPU	Unified State Political Administration (*Ob'edinyonnoye Gosudarstzvennoye Politicheskoye Upravleniye*)
OKH	Army High Command (*Oberkommando des Heeres*)
Okhrana	or *Okharanka*, or *Okharana*: Secret political police department in tsarist Russia
OKW	High Command of the Armed Forces (*Oberkommando der Wehrmacht*)

Ostpolitik	West German policy of rapprochement with Eastern Europe
PFLP-GC	Popular Front for the Liberation of Palestine-General Command
PNE	Peaceful nuclear explosion (or PW)
POW	Prisoner of war
psi	Pounds per square inch
PRC	People's Republic of China
PVO	Air defense (*Protivovozdushnaya Obrona*)
R&D	Research and development
RDF	Rapid deployment force
RDT&E	Research, development, testing, and evaluation
RKP(b)	Russian Communist Party of the Bolsheviks (*Russkaya Kommunist-icheskaya Partiya (Bolsheviki)*)
RPV	Remotely piloted vehicle
RV	Reentry vehicle
SAGE	Semi-automatic ground environment
SALT	Strategic Arms Limitation Talks
SAM	Surface-to-air missile
SCC	Standing Consultative Commission (Article XIII, ABM treaty)
SD	Security Service (*Sicherheitsdienst*)
SDI	Strategic defense initiative
SED	Socialist Unity Party, East Germany (*Sozialistische Einheitspartei Deutschlands*)
SHAPE	Supreme Headquarters, Allied Powers Europe
SIGINT	Signals intelligence
SLBM	Submarine-launched ballistic missile
SNF	Strategic Nuclear Force
SPD	Social Democratic Party, West Germany (*Sozialdemokratische Partei Deutschlands*)
Spetsnaz	Special Purpose Forces (*spetsalnaya Nazncheniya*)
SS	Black Shirts/National Socialists (*Schutzstaffe*)
SSBN	Ballistic missile submarine, nuclear powered
START	Strategic Arms Reduction Talks
STAVKA	General Headquarters of the Soviet Supreme High Command
SU	Soviet Union
TASS	Telegraph Agency of the Soviet Union: The official Soviet press agency (*Telegrafnoye Agenstvo Sovyetskovo Soyuza*)

TRIAD	The tripartite U.S. strategic retaliatory force, which comprises manned bombers, intercontinental ballistic missiles, and submarine-launched ballistic missiles
TTBT	Threshold Test Ban Treaty
tu quoque	You also (a retort charging an adversary with being or doing what he criticizes in others)
TVD	Soviet Theater of Military Operations (*Teatra Voyennykh Deystvi*)
UB	Polish Intelligence Service (*Sluzba Bezpieczenstwa—SB*)
UN	United Nations
UNEF	United Nations Emergency Force
VGK	Soviet Supreme High Command (*Verkhovnovo Glavnokomandovaniye*)
Vozhd	Leader
Weltanschauung	Philosophy of life, outlook, view
WiN	Freedom and Independence (Army) (*Wolnosc i Niepodleglosc*)
WPA	World Psychiatric Association
WTO	Warsaw Treaty Organization

Index

ABM systems, 180, 240–241, 255n.35
ABM treaty (1972), 210, 225–259; radar violation issues, 237; SDI and, 250; Soviet military strategy and, 228–229; Soviet motives behind, 226; U.S. ballistic missile modernization and, 316–318; U.S. self-deception and, 227–228, 229–244
Abwehr, 10
Academy of Sciences, U.S.S.R., 237–238
Active measures (*aktivnyye meropriyatiya*), 23–35, 46; acquiring knowledge about, 87; anti-American sentiment and, 78–79; covert action vs., 23–24; definition of, 21; democratic culture and, 77–91; doctrine of moral equivalence and, 78–79; effectiveness of, 78–80; essence of, 84–86; evaluation of, 32–35; on INF in West Germany, 349; International Department (ID) and, 26, 27; International Information Department (IID) and, 26, 28; Marxism and, 85–86; objectives of, 25; Politburo and, 25–27; Second Chief Directorate of KGB and, 26, 31–32, 35; Service A of KGB and, 26, 28–31, 41–42; U.S. intelligence analysis and, 33–34. *See also* Disinformation (*dezinformatsiya*)
Adelman, Kenneth, 247
Adomeit, Hannes, 359
Afghanistan, chemical agents used in, 331
AFL-CIO, 83
Agayants, Colonel, 12–13
Agent of influence (*agentz po vliyaniyu/agent vliyaniye*), 4
Agranov, Yakov S., 4
AirLand Battle concept, 289
Akhmatova, Anna, 108
Alexiev, Alexander R., 84
Allies, Soviet attempts at splitting, 269, 516
Andropov, Yuri, 355–356, 357

Anglo-German Naval Agreements (1935–1937), 134, 192–193
Anglo-Soviet Trade Agreement (1921), 162
Antennae for communications interception, 471
Antiballistic missiles. *See* ABM systems
Antisatellite (ASAT) programs, 180, 242
Antisubmarine warfare, 180
"Apologentsia," 189
Appeasement policy, 57
Arbatov, Georgi, 78, 238–244, 347–348
Arms control, 173–184; deception opportunities and hazards in, 177–180; disinformation on, 65–66; intelligence and assumptions about, 206; intelligence and Soviet violations of, 217–221; *maskirovka* preceding negotiations on, 200–202; without safe shelter, 185–188; sanctions against violations of, 219; Soviet compliance with, 214; Soviet noncompliance with, 179, 208, 210–215; in strategic defensive area, 180; in strategic offensive area, 179–180; treaty commitments, 174–175; U.S. assumptions about, 177–178; U.S. compliance initiatives and, 208–209; *See also* Mutual and Balanced Force Reduction (MBFR) talks
Arms control verification, 178–179; countermeasures to, 199–200; by data exchange, 192–193, 198–199; evolving regimes for, 190–200; functions of, 188–190; by inspection, 190–194; *maskirovka* and, 185–224; by national technical means, 194–200; success of, 186; under Treaty of Versailles (1919), 190–192
Arms reduction, strategic, 505–506
Arrow in the Blue (Koestler), 128
Artuzov, Artur K., 4
Aspaturian, Vernon V., 149

Assassinations, 334

Bagration operation, 47, 438
Ballistic missiles. *See* Missile(s)
Baltic States, Soviet seizure of, 129
Barnet, Richard J., 78
Baskakov, V.M., 266–267
Bateson, Gregory, 102, 111
Belayev, Igor, 401
Berezkin, A., 308–309
Berlin tunnel operation, 41
Bessedovskiy, Gregoriy, 12, 158–160
Biological Warfare and Toxin Weapons Convention (1972), 201
Biological weapons and warfare. *See* Chemical and biological warfare
Bittman, Ladislav, 14, 45
Blake, George, 41
Blunt, Anthony, 10
Bolsheviks, 119–120, 147–151
Bomber gap, 504
Bombers, U.S., surprise nuclear attack and, 459
Boost-phase defensive devices, 478
Borchgrave, Arnaud de, 327
Borge, Tomás, 378
Bowdler, William, 385
Bravo, Obando y, 382–383
Brest-Litovsk, Soviet-German agreement at (1917–1918), 153–154
Brezhnev, Leonid, 94, 352, 412
Browder, Robert Paul, 165
Brutents, Karen, 412
Brzezinski, Zbigniew, 385, 450–451
Budget, Soviet defense, 313–316
Bulgaria, drug-running by, 336
Bullitt, William C., 165
Byzantium, 174

Cabinet, Sandinista, 382
Cameras, infrared, 469
Campaign strategy, 487
Capitalism, success of, 515–516
Cardenal, Ernesto, 378
Carr, E.H., 157
Carter administration, 205, 385
Castro, Fidel, 376, 377
Chamorro, Violeta, 379–380
"Change of landmarks" (*smenovekhovtsvo*) movement, 7
CHEKA, 4–6, 17
Chemical and biological warfare, 181, 197, 219, 325–339
China, Syrian-Israeli war (1982) and, 413–414
Christian Democratic Union/Christian Social Union (CDU/CSU), 356, 361

Christian, Shirley, 383–384
Church, Catholic, Nicaraguan revolution and, 382–383
CIA, 38, 314–316
Civil defense, U.S. and Soviet, 243
Cohn, Norman, 120
Cold Dawn: The Story of SALT (Newhouse), 248
Cold war political and economic activities, 449
Combat engagement, control of, 280–281
Combination (*kombinatsiya*), 4
Comintern, 5, 155–156, 162–163
Command, control, communications, and intelligence (C^3I) system, U.S., 433, 434
Committee for State Security. *See* KGB
Communications intelligence, 471, 473, 484–485
Communism, international, disinformation on, 67–68
Communist Party factions in, 61–63, 136–137; ideology and, 123 importance of individual over, 63–64
Comprehensive Test Ban (CTB) agreements, 506
Concealment of weapons, 441–442
Conditioning, 504
Congress, Soviet overtures to, 257n.47
Constitution, Soviet, 71, 105
Control, reflexive. *See* Reflexive control
Conventional Weapons Convention (1981), 213
Correlation of world forces, 399
Costa Rica, 387
Counterintelligence, defined, 21–22
Counterintelligence, Soviet, 35–42; evaluation of, 40–42; limited access Soviet double agents, 36–38; non-Soviet double agents, 36; purpose of, 35; well-placed officials and, 38–42
Counterrevolution, export of, 140
Covert action, active measures vs., 23–24
Covert propaganda, 29
Cruz, Arturo, 380
Cuba, 213, 336
Cuban Missile Crisis, 144, 198
Cuban revolution, 375–376
Custine, Marquis de, 173–174, 511
Czechoslovak Politburo, 122

Dashevskiy, General, 284
Data encryption, 442, 482, 506
Data exchange, arms control verification by, 192–193, 198–199
Deane, Michael, 246
Deception: contemporary Soviet views on,

279–289; defined, 175–176; development of theory of, 277–279; rationale for emphasis on, 495–497; surprise and, 439–440; taxonomy for analysis of, xvii–xix use of term, xvi–xvii
Decision making: elements of, 295–296; *maskirovka* and, 281–282; U.S. nuclear strategy and, 435–437. *See also* Reflexive control
Decoys, 297
Defense Authorization Act (1987), 217
Defenses, Soviet active and passive, 440–441; budget, 313–316. *See also* Military, Soviet
Democracy in America (de Tocqueville), 511
Democracy, Soviet sense of, 94
Democratic culture, active measures and, 77–91
Denial, defined, xvi–xvii
Department D (KGB), 12–13
Department 11, 26, 31
Department 12, 26, 30–31
De-Stalinization campaign, 490
Détente, 490; economic, 318–319; INF in West Germany and, 362–364, 367–369; Soviet behavior during, 366–367
Deterrence, nuclear, 228–229, 432
DeWeerd, Harvey, 453
Diplomatic deception, 147–169, 269–270; Bolshevik, 147–151; calculated ideological moderation and, 154–155; by concealing military cooperation with Germany, 156–157; by denying links to Comintern, 155–156; diplomatic posts and, 158–160; dissimulation, 158–160; embassies and, 158–160; funding of subversion and, 160; lack of scholarly treatment of, 166n.6; Marxist-Leninist ideology and, 148–149; by professing Western political ideal, 157–158; shift toward traditional diplomacy as, 152–153; simulation, 151–158; Soviet-German agreement at Brest-Litovsk (1917–1918) and, 153–154; types and varieties of, 150–151; U.S. recognition of Soviet Union and, 163–165; Western self-deception and, 160–164
Diplomats, drugging of, 335
Directorate K (KGB), 35, 41–42
Disarmament, 176, 185–186
Disinformation (*dezinformatsiya*), 4, 24, 29–31, 55–75; on change in Soviet Union, 64; on defense orientation of Soviet military, 64–65; on existence of international communism, 67–68; on factions in Kremlin, 61–63; on ideology, 59–61; on importance of individual over Communist Party, 63–64; to keep U.S. on defensive, 70; military planning and, 283; on mutual arms control, 65–66; organizational structure for, 4–9; on Soviet insecurity, 68–70; Soviet perceptions management and, xvi; on threat to U.S., 66–67; on U.S. military threat, 68–70
Dismantling Procedures (1974), 210
Dissidents, CIA contact with, 38
Dissimulation, diplomacy as, 158–160
Diversion (*diversiya*), 4
"Dizzy With Success" (Stalin), 110
Djilas, Milovan, 121–122
Dobrynin, Anatoly, 258n.59
Doce, Los, 380–381
Double agents, Soviet, 35–42
Drug running, 335–337
Druggings, 334–335
Druzhinin, V.V., 301–302, 309
Dzerzhinskiy, Felix, 4, 6
Dziak, John, 454

Economic deception, 313–323; ballistic missile modernization and, 316–318; economic détente and, 318–319; in next quinquennium, 319–320; Soviet defense budget and, 313–316
Economic penetration by Soviets, 464n.1
Economic statistics, Soviet, 33
Economy, Soviet, disinformation on arms control and, 65–66
Ecuador, 387
Egypt, Soviet deception of (1967), 145–146
Elections, Soviet, 71–72
Electronic warfare, 443
Embassies, diplomatic deception and, 158–159
Embassy and journalistic reporting, 33–34
"Emergency Confinement of Mentally Ill Persons Who Represent a Social Danger, On," 109
Emigration, the Trust and, 8
Encryption of data, 442, 482, 506
Encyclopedias, Soviet rewriting of, 125–127
Engagement strategy, 487
Esalen Experiments in Soviet-American Understanding, 112
Escalation control, 359, 432
Escalation dominance, concept of, 359
Espionage, 158–160
Evtushenko, Evgeniy, 110

Fabrication (*fabrikatsiya*), 4
Felfe, Heinz, 41

Fiction-to-truth ratio in deception, 176–177
Financial penetration by Soviets, 464n.1
Fischer, Louis, 154, 161
Foreign affairs, ideology and, 128–129
Foreign Affairs, Ministry of (Soviet), 72–73
Forgeries, 29

Galaktionov, M.P., 278
Game theory, reflexive control over opponent who is using, 307–308
Garthoff, Raymond L., 79
Gehlen, General Major Reinhard, 9–10
General purpose forces, deception involving, 442
Geneva Protocol (1925), 213
Genoa Conference (1922), 157
Genscher, Hans-Dietrich, 356
George, David Lloyd, 161–162
Germany: arms control under Versailles Treaty and, 190–192; *maskirovka* against, 437–438; Soviet military cooperation with, 156–157
Ginzberg, Eugenia, 115
Glavit, 127
Glavnoye Razvedyvatelnoye Upravleniye. See GRU
Glossary, 519–523
Goldhamer, Herbert, 358
Golitsyn, Anatoliy, 152–153
Gorbachev, Mikhail, 6, 93
Gorshkov, S.G., 139, 141
Graham, Billy, 106–107
Grain sale to U.S.S.R. (1972), 505, 323n.26
Grand Strategy of the Roman Empire, The (Luttwak), 230
Graybeal, Sidney, 216
Green, William, 235
Greenfield, Meg, 82
Greens (West German party), 357
Grey area weapons, 505
Grey, Viscount, 162
Gromyko, Andrei A., 266
Ground-launched cruise missiles (GLCMs) *See also* Intermediate nuclear forces (INF) in West Germany
GRU, 22, 36, 42, 327–328
GUSM (*Glavnoe Upravleniye Stratigicheskoy Maskirovki*), 15–16

Handel, Michael, 46
Harbin, German Consulate in, 9
Hardening of missile silos, 440
Harris, William, 442
Hassner, Pierre, 363
Hayter, William, 261
Helsinki Final Act (1975), 213
Heuer, Friedrich, 350

History, Soviet manipulation of, 95–96, 125–127
Hitler, Adolf, 219
House of Representatives, U.S., acquiring knowledge of active measures and, 87
Hungarian Revolution (1956), 143–144
Hunt, George N., III, 390

ICBMs, Soviet, American self-deception about, 479–480
ICBMs, U.S., launch-on-warning and vulnerability of, 457–459
Identity of Soviet laborer, 99–100
Ideology, Soviet, 119–131; attitude to truth and, 125–127; calculated moderation in, 154–155; Communist Party teaching and, 123; disinformation theme in, 59–61; foreign affairs and, 128–129; language and, 120–121; morality and, 124–125; October Revolution and, 119–120; policy and, 122–123. *See also* Marxist-Leninist ideology
Imaging devices, 468–469, 472–473, 475
Industrial targets, 443–444
Influence operations, 28–29
Influence, agent of, 4
Information for national intelligence estimates, 499–501; role of thresholds in limiting, 102–103; Soviet filtering of, 235–237. *See also* Intelligence, U.S.
Infrared cameras, 469
Inspection, arms control verification by, 190–194
Intelligence, U.S., xviii–xix, 231–232; active measures and, 33–34; arms control assumptions and, 206; communications, 471, 473, 484–485; external influences on, 177; about radar signals, 482–484; on Soviet subversion, 333–334; Soviet violations of arms control and, 217–221; time congruence between tempo of events and, 492; U.S. nuclear strategy and, 435–437. *See also* National intelligence estimates; Space-based intelligence systems
Intermediate nuclear forces (INF) in West Germany, 84, 343–374; active measures on, 349; delegitimization of, 346; détente and, 362–364, 367–369; local Communist parties and front organizations and, 349; negotiations on, 352–354; peace movement and, 349–350; perceptions management and, 364; political polarization from, 345–346, 359–362; socialization of West Germans and, 346; Soviet efforts to influence West German perceptions of, 347–357; Soviet military

buildup and, 362–363; themes for West German audiences regarding, 354–357; themes for Western audiences regarding, 350–354
International Atomic Energy Agency, 194
International Department (ID) of Communist Party, 14, 26, 27, 68
International Information Department (IID) of Communist Party, 26, 28
Ionov, M., 299, 300, 308–309
Ira, Longin F., 10
Iraqi-Turkish plot to invade Syria, 144–145
Israeli-Syrian war (1982), Soviet defense thought and, 412–415. *See also* Syria
Ivankiad, The (Voinovich), 127–128

Jones, Reginald B., 177
Journalistic reporting, 33–34
Journals, Soviet military, as channels for deception, 45–46
Junta, Nicaraguan, 381

Kampiles, William, 475
Katz, Amrom, 207
Kauders, Fritz, 10
Kautsky, Karl, 105
Kecskemeti, Paul, 86–87
Kennedy, Edward M., 233
KGB, 22 Department D of, 12–13; Directorate K of, 35, 41–42; First Chief Directorate, 26, 28–31; sabotage department of, 327–328; Second Chief Directorate, 26, 31–32, 35; Service A, 26, 28–31, 41–42
Khalkin-Gol River, battle of, 278
Khrushchev, Nikita, 12
Kidnapping, 334–335
Kissinger, Henry, 361, 258n.59
Klatt case. *See* Max-Moritz case
Koestler, Arthur, 128
Kohl, Helmut, 356, 357, 366
Kolkhoz, 72
Komitet Gosudarstvennoy Bezopasnosti. See KGB
Kontorov, D.S., 301–302, 309
Koppel, Ted, 245
Korean airliner, downing of, 442–443
Krasnoyarsk radar, 247, 470
Krepon, Michael, 216
Kulaks, 98
Kulikov, Marshal, 282
Kutakhov, Marshal, 412
Kvitsinskii, Iu. A., 262

Laborer, Soviet, identity of, 99–100
Labour Party, British, 345
Language, Soviet, 93–118; Bolsheviks and, 97–104; form and content in, 94–95; ideology and, 120–121; myth and, 103–104; structuring of, 104; voices of, 94. *See also* Sovietspeak
Latin America, 328, 387–388. *See also* Nicaraguan revolution
Launchers, SS-20 IRMS, 481
Law of the Sea Convention (1982), 213
Leadership facilities, deception concerning, 443
Lefebvre, Vladimir A., 293–294, 295, 300, 512
Leites, Nathan, 148, 149, 440
Lenczowski, John, 151–152
Lenin, V.I., 6, 94–95, 99–104, 124, 154–156
Levchenko, Stanislav, 23, 29–30, 238
Limitation of Anti-Ballistic Missiles, Treaty on. *See* ABM treaty (1972)
Limited Test Ban Treaty (1963), 198
Lipavsky, Sanya, 38
Lippmann, Walter, 176
Litvinov, 156
Lockhart Plot, 6
London Naval Treaty (1930), 192
Low-intensity conflict, 449
Luttwak, Edward, 230

Main Intelligence Directorate of the General Staff. *See* GRU
Marshall, Charles Burton, 232
Marx, Karl, 107
Marxism: abandonment of, 107–108; active measures and, 85–86; failure of, 515–516; propaganda and, 86–87
Marxist-Leninist ideology, 119; diplomatic deception and, 148–149; transfer of power and, 135
Maskirovka, 15, 42–47; against Germans in World War II, 437–438; during arms control negotiations, 202; arms control verification and, 185–224; categories of, 42–43; as combat support activity, 280; components of, 431; defined, 22, 42, 279; enemy decision-making cycle and, 281–282; evaluation of, 46–47; international peace and, 204–205; nuclear arms and, 43–44; operational, 280, 284–285; pace of warfare and, 287–288; preceding arms control negotiations, 200–202; reconnaissance systems and, 286; Standing Consultative Commission (SCC) and, 214–217; strategic, 280–284; surprise and, 454; tactical, 280, 285; U.S. failure to deter, 205–207; U.S. nuclear strategy and, 439–444. *See also* Military planning, Soviet
Matsuylenko, General, 279

Max-Moritz case, 10, 46–47
Mayorov, General, 282–283
McCallum, R.B., 220
McNamara, Robert S., 228–229, 505
Media, acquiring knowledge of active measures and, 87
Mel'nikov, General, 288
Mensheviks, 105
Menshikov, Stanislav, 245–246
Mexico, 387
Military deception. *See Maskirovka*
Military parades, deception during, 45
Military planning, Soviet, 275–292; ABM treaty and, 228–229; disinformation and, 283; objectives of, 280–281; reflexive control in, 293–311, 253n.22; sources on, 276–277
Military science, Soviet, 113–114
Military, Soviet buildup of, 362–363; disinformation on defense orientation of, 64–65; SALT and, 248–251
Military-political deception, 133–146; Communist Party factions and, 136–137; export of counterrevolution and, 140; Soviet war doctrine and, 139–142; transfer of power and, 135. *See also* Diplomatic deception; *Maskirovka*
Mills, C. Wright, 388
Mind control drugs, 336–337
Mirror-imaging, American, 232–234. *See also* Self-deception, Western
Miskito Indians, 390–391
Missile gap deception, 25–26, 504–505
Missile(s), 179–180; antiballistic, 180, 240–241, 255n.35; ballistic, protocol limiting launchers of, 210; ballistic, Soviet defense against, 483; defenses against, 506. *See also* ABM treaty (1972); specific types of missiles
Moch, Jules, 189
Molotov-Ribbentrop Pact, 96
Monarchist Association of Central Russia (MOTsR). *See* Trust (*Trest*) legend
Montreny Convention (1936), 213
Moral equivalence, doctrine of, 78–79
Morality Bolshevik, 148; ideology and, 124–125
Morgan, J.H., 191, 220
Moscow Municipal Credit Association. *See* Trust (*Trest*) legend
Moskvin, M.A. *See* Trilliser, Mikhail Abramovich
Mowbray, Stephen de, 34–35
Muskie, Edmund, 386
Mutual and Balanced Force Reduction (MBFR) talks, 261–272; attempts to split NATO unity during, 269; deceptions in, 265–267; framework for, 262–265; inversions of truth during, 267–269
Mutual Assured Destruction (MAD), 229, 233, 513; myth of Soviet adherence to, 244–247
MX/MPS system, 317–318
Myth, Soviet language and, 103–104

Nakanune (newspaper), 7
Narcotics running, 335–337
National intelligence estimates, 487–508; decision process in, 501–503; examples of, 504–507; generation mechanism for, 497–504; information flow logic and, 496, 497–499; information sources for, 499–501; role of, 489–495; strategic deception and, 487–489; vulnerabilities to deception of, 503–504
National level strategies, 488
National technical means (NTM), 194–200
NATO, 288–289 main roles of, 372n.44; surprise nuclear attack and, 455–457. *See also* Intermediate nuclear forces (INF) in West Germany; Mutual and Balanced Force Reduction (MBFR) talks
Negotiations on INF, 352–354
New Economic Policy (NEP), 154–155, 162, 164
Newhouse, John, 229, 248
Newspapers, Soviet, 72
Nicaraguan revolution, 375–397; broad front formation of, 375–377; Catholic Church and, 382–383; Communist deception strategy in, 375–377; Cuban and Soviet presence and, 392; Los Doce and, 380–381; economic aid and, 386–387; elections and, 391; front organizations during, 380–382; the junta and, 381; Latin American reaction to, 387–388; Miskito Indians and, 390–391; Pastora and, 383–384; press freedom and, 391; promises of pluralism and, 378–380; Sandinista cabinet and, 382; Terceristas and, 381–382; U.S. apologists for Sandinistas and, 388–392; U.S. attempt to create moderate government and, 384–385; U.S. policy and, 392–393
Niemeyer, Gerhart, 104
Nitze, Paul, 483–484
Nosenko, Yuri, 38–40
Nouns in Sovietspeak, 98
Novosti (news service), 30
Nuclear arms: *maskirovka* and, 43–44; Soviet doctrine on, 32–33. *See also* Arms control; Arms control verification; Missile(s); specific weapons
Nuclear attack, surprise. *See* Surprise

nuclear attack
Nuclear strategy, U.S., 431–448; decision making structure for, 435–437; goals and requirements of, 432–433; historical perspective on Soviet deception and, 437–439; intelligence support for, 435–437; perceptions management and, 444; reconciling capabilities and objectives in, 434–435; Soviet military deception and, 439–444; trends in, 432–435
Nuclear Test Moratorium (1958–61), 212

October Revolution, Soviet ideology and, 119–120
Odio, Rodrigo Carazo, 388
Ogarkov, Nikolai V., 199–200, 248, 262, 258n.59
Oil production, 517–518
Okhrana, 17
OPEC, 517
Organization for deception: bureaucratization of, 4–6; tradition of, 3–20; the Trust, 6–8. *See also* Active measures (*aktivnyye meropriyatiya*); Counterintelligence, Soviet; *Maskirovka*
Ortega, Humberto, 376–377
Oudenaren, John Van, 368–369
Outer Space Treaty (1967), 198

Panama, 387
Parades, military, 45
Paranoia, Soviet, 69
Parity, Soviet interpretation of, 114
Partiinost, 122
Passive deception, 46
Pasternak, Boris, 124
Pastora, Edén (Commander Zero), 383–384
Peace movements, 67, 349–350
Peace, international *maskirovka* and, 204–205
Peaceful coexistence, Soviet definition of, 332
"Peaceful nuclear explosion" (PNE) clause, 506
Penetration (*proniknovenniye*), 3
People's Commissariat of Foreign Affairs, 5
Perception, thresholds of, 102–103, 112
Perceptions management, 230; components of, 358–359; defined, xviii; disinformation and, xvi; examples of, 244–251; impact of, xviii–xix; during INF affair, 364; peacetime politico-military objectives and, 230; Soviet military's authority in SALT and, 248–251; U.S. nuclear strategy and, 444; war-readiness and, 230; Western self-deception and, xvi, 231

Perez, Carlos Andres, 388
Pershing II ballistic missiles. *See* Intermediate nuclear forces (INF) in West Germany
Pezzulo, Lawrence, 386
Photographs, manipulation of, 126
Pilsudski, Marshal, 8
Policy, Soviet ideology and, 122–123
Politburo, 25–27, 122
Political-military deception, 133–146; Communist Party factions and, 136–137; export of counterrevolution and, 140; Soviet war doctrine and, 139–142; transfer of power and, 135. *See also* Diplomatic deception; *Maskirovka*
Ponschab, August, 9
Posner, Vladimir, 78
Poveda, Leonel, 384
Power, transfer of, 135
Propaganda, 90n.17 covert, 29; Marxism and, 86–87; Western self-deception and, 142–143
Provocateurs, 35
Provocation (*provokatisiya*), 3
Psychotoxins, 329–330
Public policy debates, Western, exploitation of, 238–244
Public statements, Soviet, 33

Radar(s), 239; ABM treaty and, 237; fire-control, 471; intelligence about, 482–484; Krasnoyarsk, 247, 470; phased-array, 483; SA-5, 231; SAM, 234, 235
Radio deception, 9–11, 443
Ramirez, Sergio, 378–379, 384, 386
Rapallo Treaty (1922), 157
Reagan administration, 205, 206–207, 261, 361
Reality management, 358–359, 366
Reconnaissance systems; *maskirovka* and, 286; satellites (Western), 44–45. *See also* Intelligence, U.S.
"Reconnaissance-strike complexes," 289
Reflexive control, 293–311, 253n.22; of bilateral engagement by third party, 306; concept of, 294–296; by creating a goal for opponent, 298–300, 301–302; over opponent using game theory, 307–308; over opponent using reflexive control, 306–307; Soviet research on, 308–309; by transfer of image of own doctrine, 305; by transfer of image of own goal, 303–305; by transfer of image of own perception of situation, 302–303; by transfer of image of situation, 296–298, 301–302; by transfer of own image of

532 • *Soviet Strategic Deception*

situation to make opponent deduce his own goal, 305–306; by transferring a decision, 301
Regional deception, 399–400. *See also* Intermediate nuclear forces (INF) in West Germany; Nicaraguan revolution; Syria
Reilly, Sidney, 6, 7
"Returnism" (*vozvrashchentsvo*) movement, 7
Rezanov, A., 4–5
Rhinelander, John B., 233
Roetter, Charles, 174
Rogers, Bernard, 456
Rostow, Eugene, 220
Ruhle, Hans, 359
Russia in 1839 (Custine), 511
Russian Orthodox Church, 73

SA-5 interceptor and radar, 231
SA-5 missiles in Syria, 400–411
Sabotage, chemical and biological warfare and, 327–332
SALT I (1972), 198, 210, 229; Kissinger-Dobrynin "back channel" and, 258n.59; Soviet military and, 248–251; SSBN deception in, 442; U.S. ballistic missile modernization and, 316–318; U.S. domestic constraints and Soviet behavior during, 244
SALT II (1979), 198–199, 206, 211
SAM interceptors and radars, testing of, 234
SAM missiles, 236
Sanctions against arms control violations, 219
Sandinistas. *See* Nicaraguan revolution
Satellites. *See* Space-based intelligence systems
Savinkov, Boris, 7
Scherhorn, Heinrich, 10–11
Schmid, Gunther, 349, 360
Schmidt, Helmut, 355
Scowcroft Commission Report, 457–458
Secrecy, Russian tradition of, 69–70, 174
Secret diplomacy, 148
Seitz, Konrad, 344, 361
Sejna, Jan, 14, 327
Self-deception, Western, 102–103; ABM treaty and, 227–228, 229–244; about Soviet ICBMs, 479–480; diplomatic deception and, 160–164; propaganda and, 142–143; Soviet perceptions management and, xvi; strategic deception and, 56–59. *See also* Disinformation (*dezinformatsiya*); Mirror-imaging, American
Semenov, Vladimir S., 248
Senate, U.S., acquiring knowledge of active measures and, 87

Service A (KGB), 26, 28–31, 41–42
Shelepin, Alexander, 12–13
Shulgin, V.V., 7
Shultz, George P., 93, 266
SIGINT (Signal Intelligence) collectors, 470–471, 473, 475
Silos, hardening of, 440
Simulation (*imitatsiya*), 437–438; diplomacy as, 151–158
Skorzeny, Otto, 11
Slogans, implied threat in, 97–98
Sloss, Leon, 463
Smirnov, A., 413
Smith, Gerard, 233
Smolyan, G.L., 300
Social Democratic Party (SPD), 345–346, 356, 361, 364
Sofaer, Judge, 250
Soldatov, Aleksander, 401
Solzhenitsyn, Alexander, 123–124
Somoza. *See* Nicaraguan revolution
"Soviet Deception and the Onset of the Cold War" (de Mowbray), 34–35
Soviet Viewpoint, The (Arbatov), 347–348
Sovietologists, reduction in number of, 138
Soviets in World Affairs, The (Fischer), 154
Sovietspeak, 93; grammar of, 95–97; standard enemies used in, 110; strategy of, 112–115. *See also* Language, Soviet
Space-based intelligence systems, 467–486; camouflaging and protecting, 475–478; imaging devices, 468–469, 472–473, 475; infrared cameras, 469; role and importance of, 468–474; signal intelligence collectors, 470–471, 473, 475; Soviet deception and, 479–485
SS-16 missile, 480–481
SS-20 ballistic missile, 480, 505
SS-20 IRMS launchers, 481
SS-20 Mobile IRBM Deployment Moratorium (1982–1983), 213
SS-21 missiles in Syria, 409–411
Stalin, Joseph, 8, 43, 105, 108, 110, 156
Standing Consultative Commission (SCC), 214–217
State Security, Committee for. *See* KGB
STAVKA VGK, 282
Strategic deception, 56; national intelligence estimates and, 487–489; during peacetime, 358; tactical deception vs., 133; use of term, xvi–xvii; in war, 358; Western self-deception and, 56–59. *See also* Disinformation (*dezinformatsiya*)
Strategic defense breakout, 493–494
Strategic Defense Initiative (SDI), 31, 226; ABM treaty and, 250
Strategic nuclear forces, U.S., surprise

nuclear attack and, 457–463
Structural/institutional deceptions, 71–74
Submarines, 180, 442
Subversion, funding of, 160
Surprise: deception and, 439–440; *maskirovka*, 454
Surprise nuclear attack, 449–465; NATO and, 455–457; Soviet view and, 454–455; strategic warning and, 450–454; survivability after, 459–463; U.S. strategic nuclear forces and, 457–463
Suvorov, Viktor (pseudonym), 15–16, 44–45
Syria, 399–428 installation of Soviet advanced air defense system in, 405–408; projection of strength as weakness in, 402–411; projection of weakness as strength in, 417–421; SA-5 missiles in, 400–411; Soviet promotion of tension between Israel and, 414–416; SS-21; missiles in, 409–411; Turkish-Iraqi plot to invade, 144–145
Syrian Communist Party, 122
Syrian-Israeli war (1982), Soviet defense thought and, 412–415

Tactical deception, 56; strategic deception vs., 133 See also *Maskirovka*
Tactical decisions, 508n.1
Tarakanov, K.V., 294, 299, 306, 309
Taubman, William, 79
Telemetry signals, 473, 481–482, 506
Terceristas, 381–382
Theater strategy, 487, 493
Three Capitals (Shulgin), 7
Threshold Test Ban Treaty (1974), 198, 212
Tocqueville, Alexis de, 511
"Tourlandia," Soviet, 73–74
Trade unions, Soviet, 73, 83–84
Treaty commitments, arms control, 174–175
Trilliser, Mikhail Abramovich, 5
Trotsky, Leon, 153–154
Trusov, K., 258n.59
Trust (*Trest*) legend, 6–8, 37
Truth-to-fiction ratio in deception, 176–177
Tukhachevskiy affair (1937), 8–9
Tunnerman, Carlos, 380
Turkish-Iraqi plot to invade Syria, 144–145
Turkul, Anton V., 10

Uldricks, Teddy J., 159–160
Unions, trade, Soviet, 73, 83–84
United States: disinformation for, 66–67, 70; failure to deter expansion of illegal *maskirovka* programs, 205–207; government of, acquiring knowledge of active measures and, 87; recognition of Soviet Union, 163–165; source of

tensions in relations with Soviets, 57–59
Uranus operation, 438

Vaky, Viron, 385
Venezuela, 387
Verbs in Sovietspeak, 96–97
Verification, arms control. See Arms control verification
Versailles, Treaty of (1919), arms control verification under, 190–192
Vishnevskaya, Galina, 127
Vogel, Hans-Jochen, 356
Voinovich, Vladimir, 127–128

Warfare, Soviet doctrine on, 139–142
Warning strategic, 450–454; tactical, 451. See also Surprise nuclear attack
Warsaw Treaty Organization (WTO). See also Mutual and Balanced Force Reduction (MBFR) talks
Weinberger, Caspar, 433, 456
West German Communists (DKP), peace movement and, 349–350
West Germany, INF in. See Intermediate nuclear forces (INF) in West Germany
Wettig, Gerhard, 349
Whalen, William, 26
Whaley, Barton, 47
Whelan, Joseph, 152
Wohlstetter, Roberta, 134, 453
Wolnosc i Niepodleglosc (WiN) operation, 11–12, 38
Woods Hole Summer Study, 194–198
World Federation of Trade Unions, 83–84
World Psychiatric Association (WPA), 336
World War II, Soviet deception during, 9–11, 437–438

Yalta Conference, 96

Zagladin, Vadim, 352, 401
Zamyatin, Leonard, 28
Zhukov, Marshal, 278
Ziemke, Earl, 438

About the Contributors

Robert Bathurst is a former assistant naval attaché at the U.S. Embassy in Moscow, professor of operations at the Naval War College, and presently a professor in national security affairs at the Naval Postgraduate School. He has written widely about Soviet naval affairs and U.S.-Soviet relations and has acted as an interpreter during negotiations.

Arnold Beichman, a Visiting Scholar at the Hoover Institution, is the author of four books, the most recent of which is *Yuri Andropov: New Challenges to the West*. Besides serving as professor of political science, he has also been a foreign correspondent for several major newspapers.

David Blair, a senior economist at PAN Hueristics, is a specialist in Soviet economics, Latin America, and military strategy. He has a Ph.D. in economics from UCLA; he has also been an editorial writer for the summer at the *Wall Street Journal*.

Angelo M. Codevilla is a Senior Research Fellow at the Hoover Institution, Stanford University, and was a member of the staff of the Senate Select Committee on Intelligence. He is also distinguished adjunct professor at the Naval Postgraduate School, a former Foreign Service officer, Naval Intelligence officer, and consultant to industry and academic institutions.

Robert Conquest is a Senior Research Fellow at the Hoover Institution on War, Revolution, and Peace. He has written extensively on the domestic and foreign affairs of the Soviet Union and on Soviet intelligence. He has served in diplomatic posts and been a professor of economics and political science in both the United States and England.

Joseph D. Douglass, Jr., currently a senior analyst for Falcon Associates, previously served as deputy director of the tactical technology office in the DoD Advanced Research Projects Agency. He is the author of *Soviet Military Strategy* in *Europe* and co-author of *Soviet Strategy for Nuclear War*. He has recently co-authored *Decision Making in Communist Countries: An Inside View*, and *America the Vulnerable: The Threat of Biological and Chemical Terrorism*.

John J. Dziak is presently the director of the International Applications Office of the Defense Intelligence Agency, where he has served since 1965. In addition to serving as an adjunct professor of history and international affairs at George Washington University and a visiting lecturer at senior service colleges and universities, he was co-editor of the *Bibliography of Intelligence Literature*. His latest book is *Soviet Perceptions of Military Power: The Interaction of Theory and Practice*.

William R. Graham is the White House Science Advisor to the President of the United States and director of the Office of Science Technology Policy. He was formerly the deputy administrator at NASA and has also served as acting administrator (1986). He was chairman of the President's General Advisory Committee on Arms Control, which wrote a report on Soviet Treaty Compliance.

William R. Harris has served as senior staff member of the behavioral and social sciences departments at Rand Corporation for the past thirteen years. He is also a consultant to the President's General Advisory Committee on Arms Control, the U.S. Arms Control and Disarmament Agency, and the U.S. Senate Select Committee on Intelligence. He has written on international law, arms control and verification, energy policy, and intelligence policy.

Avigdor Haselkorn serves as senior analyst at Analytical Assessments Corporation as well as outside scholar at the Center for Advanced Research of the Naval War College. He presently works as a consultant to the Office of the Secretary of Defense, the Stanford Research Institute, and the Hudson Institute. He has prepared testimony on strategic problems in the Middle East for the U.S. Senate Foreign Relations Committee.

Richards J. Heuer, Jr., was a CIA officer for 28 years. He is now retired from government service and employed as a consultant on ways to improve judgment and decision making. He has previously written on the psychology of deception, cognitive processes in intelligence analysis, and the methodology of intelligence analysis.

Kerry M. Kartchner is an assistant professor of national security affairs at the Naval Postgraduate School, Monterey, California. He has taught military strategy at the University of Southern California, and was formerly a visiting research scholar at the Hoover Institution, and a consultant for nuclear policy to the Computer Sciences Corporation.

John Lenczowski is presently serving as the Director of European and Soviet Affairs at the National Security Council in Washington, D.C. and adjunct professor at Georgetown University. He has formerly served in the Department of State, U.S. Congress staff, and lectured at the University of Maryland. He is the author of *Soviet Perceptions of U.S. Foreign Policy*.

Uri Ra'anan is professor of international politics at the Fletcher School of Law and Diplomacy. He also serves as director of the International Security Studies Program and is a fellow of the Russian Research Center at Harvard. He has authored numerous works on the U.S.-Soviet strategic balance, the Sino-Soviet conflict, Soviet foreign policy, Soviet arms transfers to the Third World, and related subjects.

Clifford Reid is a senior analyst for U.S. intelligence and an expert in Soviet military strategy and intelligence. He holds Ph.D.s in engineering and mathematics. He has been involved in intelligence for over thirty years. This article represents his first public writing on soviet military issues.

Thomas P. Rona, presently serving as special assistant for space policy in the Office of Assistant Secretary of Defense for Command, Control, and Communications (C^3I), is the author of *Our Changing Geopolitical Premises*. For the past twenty-five years, he has engaged in extensive lecturing and consulting activities for government and industry on subjects such as military command and control.

Steven Rosefielde is an associate professor of economics at the University of North Carolina and an adjunct professor at the Naval Postgraduate School. He is the author or editor of four books and numerous articles, and, with colleagues at the Central Economics and Mathematics Institute (Moscow), he is researching the technical efficiency of the Soviet economic system.

Leon Sloss, President of Leon Sloss Associates, previously directed the study of nuclear targeting policy for Secretary of Defense Harold Brown, which led to Presidential Directive 59 in 1980. He has served as director of international security policy and assistant director in the Bureau of Politico-Military Affairs, Department of State. In 1976–77 he was assistant director (and later acting director) at the U.S. Arms Control and Disarmament Agency.

Richard F. Staar is coordinator of the International Studies Program and a Senior Fellow of the Hoover Institution on War, Revolution, and Peace at Stanford University. He formerly served as U.S. Ambassador to the Mutual Balanced Force Reduction Negotiations from 1981 to 1983.

Notra Trulock III, currently Senior Analyst at Pacific-Sierra Research on Soviet military issues, was formerly the manager of Threat Assessment Programs at

SAI's Foreign Systems Research Center and formerly was manager of the Surveillance and Reconnaissance Exploitation department of the BDM Corporation.

William R. Van Cleave, University Professor and Director of the Center for Defense and Strategic Studies at Southwest Missouri State University, he is also a Senior Research Fellow for National Security at the Hoover Institution, Stanford University; Chairman of the Strategic Alternatives Team; member of the Executive Committee of the Committee on the Present Danger; and Trustee for the American Committee for the International Institute for Strategic Studies.

David S. Yost is coordinator of European security studies and associate professor of national security affairs at the Naval Postgraduate School. Dr. Yost worked in the Department of Defense, primarily in the Office of Net Assessment, in 1984–86 under the auspices of fellowships from NATO and the Council on Foreign Relations.

About the Editors

Brian D. Dailey is adjunct professor of national security affairs at the Naval Postgraduate School, Monterey, California, and a Hubert H. Humphrey Arms Control Fellow of the U.S. Arms Control and Disarmament Agency. He is a former Visiting Research Scholar at the Hoover Institution and consultant to the Computer Sciences Corporation on historical issues regarding strategic nuclear system survivability.

Patrick J. Parker, formerly Chairman of the Department of National Security Affairs of the Naval Postgraduate School, Monterey, California, is currently a professor in that department. He has served as Chairman of the Chief of Naval Operations Executive Panel, as the Deputy Assistant Secretary of Defense (Intelligence Assessment), as Associate Dean of the Graduate School of Business, University of Rochester, and as President and Chief Executive Officer of the Hickok Manufacturing Company.